Leo Laporte's
2005
Technology Almanac

Leo Laporte
Michael Miller

CONTENTS
AT A
GLANCE

INTRODUCTION

January 2005 1

February 2005 37

March 2005 71

April 2005 107

May 2005 143

June 2005 179

July 2005 213

August 2005 249

September 2005 285

October 2005 319

November 2005 355

December 2005 389

A   Facts and Figures 425

B   Leo's Black Book 445

C   Glossary 459

Index 493

A Division of Pearson Technology Group, USA
800 East 96th Street
Indianapolis, Indiana 46240

LEO LAPORTE'S 2005 TECHNOLOGY ALMANAC

International Standard Book Number: 0-7897-3319-6

Library of Congress Catalog Card Number: 2004096205

Printed in the United States of America

First Printing: October 2004

07   06   05   04   4   3

Trademarks

Warning and Disclaimer

Bulk Sales

Que Publishing offers excellent discounts on this book when ordered in quantity for bulk purchases or special sales. For more information, please contact

U.S. Corporate and Government Sales
1-800-382-3419
corpsales@pearsontechgroup.com

For sales outside the United States, please contact

International Sales
international@pearsoned.com

PUBLISHER
Paul Boger

ASSOCIATE PUBLISHER
Greg Wiegand

EXECUTIVE EDITOR
Rick Kughen

DEVELOPMENT EDITOR
Rick Kughen

MANAGING EDITOR
Charlotte Clapp

PROJECT EDITOR
Tonya Simpson

INDEXER
Ginny Bess

PROOFREADER
Juli Cook

PUBLISHING COORDINATOR
Sharry Lee Gregory

PHOTOGRAPHY
Mark Compton

STYLIST
Jan Rhodes

MAKEUP
Robin Graham

PHOTOGRAPHY ACQUISITIONS
Judi Wade
Kate Hollcraft

INTERIOR DESIGNER
Anne Jones

COVER DESIGNERS
Anne Jones
Commercial Artisan

PAGE LAYOUT
Susan Geiselman

TABLE OF CONTENTS

INTRODUCTION ....**XXVII**

JANUARY 2005 1

On This Day: AT&T Divests Bell System
Companies (1984) 3

Breaking in Your New Computer 3

Fact of the Week 3

On This Day: Isaac Asimov Born (1920) 4

Connect by Color 4

Software of the Week 4

On This Day: Spirit Rover Lands
on Mars (2004) 5

Favorite Firewall Software 5

PC Gadget of the Week 5

On This Day: First Pocket Scientific
Calculator (1972) 6

Hardware Firewalls 6

Download of the Week 6

On This Day: FM Radio
Demonstrated (1940) 7

Spy on Your Spouse and Kids 7

Mac Gadget of the Week 7

On This Day: *Schoolhouse Rock*
Debuts (1973) 8

Phishing Schemes 8

Web Site of the Week 8

On This Day: Transatlantic Phone Service
Begins (1927) 9

Evaluating Your Risk 9

Portable Gadget of the Week 9

On This Day: Hollerith Tabulating Machine
Patented (1889) 10

Detecting a Computer Attack 10

Fact of the Week 10

On This Day: Accelerating Galaxies
Announced (1998) 11

Protecting Against an Attack 11

Software of the Week 11

On This Day: RCA Introduces
45 RPM Record (1949) 12

Covering Your Tracks 12

PC Gadget of the Week 12

On This Day: ALGOL Language
Developed (1960) 13

Email Encryption 13

Download of the Week 13

On This Day: Fictional HAL
Computer "Born" (1997) 14

Encrypting PC Files 14

Mac Gadget of the Week 14

On This Day: Wham-O Introduces
the Frisbee (1957) 15

Everything You Post Exists Forever 15

Web Site of the Week 15

On This Day: *The Simpsons*
Premieres (1990) 16

Protecting Your Children's Privacy 16

Portable Gadget of the Week 16

On This Day: National Center for
Supercomputer Applications
Opens (1986) 17

Creating Stronger Passwords 17

Fact of the Week 17

On This Day: SAGE Announced (1956) 18

Preventing Identity Theft 18

Software of the Week 18

On This Day: First Nuclear Submarine
Launched (1955) 19

The Three C's 19

PC Gadget of the Week 19

On This Day: Bryce Outlines the Harvard
Mark I (1938) 20

Turn Your iPod Into an
Emergency Rescue Disk 20

Download of the Week 20

On This Day: Howard Hughes Sets
Transcontinental Air Record (1937) 21

Save Time with the Services Menu 21

Mac Gadget of the Week 21

On This Day: First Live Televised Inauguration
Address (1953) 22

Troubleshooting Your Mac 22

Web Site of the Week 22

On This Day: First Commercial Supersonic
Flight (1976) 23

Replace the OS X Finder 23

Portable Gadget of the Week 23

On This Day: Apple Computer
Launches the Macintosh (1984) 24

Copying iTunes Music
to a New Mac 24

Fact of the Week 24

On This Day: Integrated Circuit
Conceived (1959) 25

Favorite Free Mac OS X Utilities 25

Software of the Week 25

On This Day: IBM Dedicates
the SSEC (1948) 26

Digital SLR Cameras 26

PC Gadget of the Week 26

On This Day: Transcontinental
Telephone Service Inaugurated (1915) 27

Organizing Your Photos 27

Download of the Week 27

On This Day: Lotus 1-2-3
Released (1983) 28

Digital Photos Without a Computer 28

Mac Gadget of the Week 28

On This Day: Apollo 1 Disaster (1967) 29

Offloading Digital Picture Files 29

Web Site of the Week 29

On This Day: Challenger Space
Shuttle Explosion (1986) 30

Shooting RAW 30

Portable Gadget of the Week 30

On This Day: "The Raven"
Published (1845) 31

Digital Camera Accessories 31

Fact of the Week 31

On This Day: Beatles Perform
Last Public Concert (1969) 32

Underwater Cameras 32

Software of the Week 32

On This Day: First U.S. Satellite
Launched (1958) 33

Digital Camcorder Formats 33

PC Gadget of the Week 33

FEBRUARY 2005 37

On This Day: Space Shuttle Columbia
Disaster (2003) 39

Configuring Your System for
Video Editing 39

Download of the Week 39

On This Day: *Star Trek*'s Data
Born (2338) 40

Preparing Your Hard Disk for
Digital Video 40

Mac Gadget of the Week 40

On This Day: The Music Died (1959) 41

Using Windows Movie Maker 41

Web Site of the Week 41

On This Day: Bill Gates Gets a
Pie in the Face (1998) 42

Choosing a Semi-Pro Camcorder 42

Portable Gadget of the Week: Archos
AV300 Portable Video Player 42

On This Day: Indiana Redefines the
Value of Pi (1897) 43

Converting Film and Tape to
Digital Video 43

Fact of the Week 43

On This Day: Monopoly
Goes on Sale (1935) 44

Moviemaking Accessories 44

Software of the Week 44

On This Day: Bubble Boy Leaves
Bubble (1984) 45

Using Third-Party
Applications with Your TiVo 45

PC Gadget of the Week 45

On This Day: Patent Received for Envelope
Folding Machine (1898) 46

TiVo Backdoor Codes 46

Download of the Week 46

On This Day: First Flight of
Boeing 747 (1969) 47

Leo's Favorite Backdoor Secrets 47

Mac Gadget of the Week 47

On This Day: Fire Extinguisher
Invented (1863) 48

Troubleshooting TiVo Problems 48

Web Site of the Week 48

On This Day: Thomas Edison
Born (1847) 49

Upgrading TiVo's Hard Drive 49

Portable Gadget of the Week:
Casio TV Remote Control Watch 49

On This Day: Boston Computer
Society Founded (1977) 50

Networking TiVos 50

Fact of the Week 50

On This Day: Dresden
Firebombed (1945) 51

Build Your Own DVR 51

Software of the Week 51

On This Day: ENIAC Unveiled (1946) 52

Instant Messaging Clients 52

PC Gadget of the Week 52

On This Day: Galileo Born (1564) 53

Instant Messaging Incompatibility 53

Download of the Week 53

On This Day: King Tut's
Tomb Unsealed (1923) 54

Chatting Online 54

Mac Gadget of the Week 54

On This Day: Thomas J. Watson,
Sr. Born (1874) 55

Internet Relay Chat 55

Web Site of the Week 55

On This Day: Pluto Discovered (1930) 56

Learn the Lingo! 56

Portable Gadget of the Week 56

On This Day: Copernicus Born (1473) 57

Chat Tips 57

Fact of the Week 57

On This Day: First U.S.
Astronaut Orbits Earth (1962) 58

Sex Chat 58

Software of the Week: IMSecure 58

On This Day: DNA Structure
Discovered (1953) 59

Three Types of Broadband 59

PC Gadget of the Week 59

On This Day: Popcorn
Introduced (1630) 60

How DSL Works 60

Download of the Week 60

On This Day: First Mass Inoculation
For Polio (1954) 61

How Broadband Cable Works 61

Mac Gadget of the Week 61

On This Day: Steve Jobs Born (1955) 62

Installing a Cable Modem 62

Web Site of the Week 62

On This Day: Colt Patents the
Revolver (1836) 63

How Satellite Broadband Works 63

Portable Gadget of the Week 63

On This Day: Bomb Explodes Under
World Trade Center (1993) 64

Tweaking Your Broadband Connection ...64

Fact of the Week 64

On This Day: Reichstag Fire (1933) 65

Troubleshooting Broadband Problems 65

Software of the Week 65

On This Day: Linus Pauling Born (1901) 66

How Google Works 66

PC Gadget of the Week 66

MARCH 2005 71

On This Day: LISP Programmer's
Manual Released (1960) 73

Put the Google Toolbar in Your
Browser 73

Download of the Week 73

On This Day: Dr. Seuss Born (1904) 74

Fine-Tune Your Google Search 74

Mac Gadget of the Week 74

On This Day: First Meeting of the
Homebrew Computer Club (1975) 75

Narrow Your Results with Google's
Advanced Search Operators 75

Web Site of the Week 75

On This Day: An Wang Sells Core
Memory Patent to IBM (1956) 76

Wildcards and Automatic Stemming 76

Portable Gadget of the Week 76

On This Day: Nuclear Non-Proliferation
Treaty Goes Into Effect (1970) 77

Search for Specific Types of
Information 77

Fact of the Week 77

On This Day: Michelangelo
Virus Strikes (1992) 78

Google Does More Than Just
Search the Web 78

Software of the Week 78

On This Day: Telephone
Patented (1876) 79

Use the Direct Address 79

PC Gadget of the Week 79

On This Day: PC DOS 2.0
Announced (1983) 80

It's a Search Engine—and a Directory 80

Download of the Week 80

On This Day: Mailbox Patented (1858) 81

Get Free Email—and Listen
to It By Phone 81

Mac Gadget of the Week 81

On This Day: First Telephone
Call (1876) 82

Use My Yahoo! As Your Start Page 82

Web Site of the Week 82

On This Day: Luddite Riots
Begin (1811) 83

Hang Out in Yahoo!
Message Boards and Groups 83

Portable Gadget of the Week 83

On This Day F.D.R. Delivers
First Fireside Chat (1933) 84

Use Yahoo! to Manage Your
Schedule and Contacts 84

Fact of the Week 84

On This Day: Uranus Discovered (1781) 85

Store and Share Files and Photos 85

Software of the Week 85

On This Day: Albert Einstein
Born (1879) 86

Searching, Pre-Google 86

PC Gadget of the Week 86

On This Day: Escalator Patented (1892) ...87

Favorite Search Sites 87

Download of the Week 87

On This Day: First Liquid-Fueled Rocket
Launched (1926) 88

Metasearch Engines 88

Mac Gadget of the Week 88

On This Day: New Element, Californium,
Announced (1950) 89

Power Up Your Search with
Boolean Operators 89

Web Site of the Week 89

On This Day: Schick Markets First
Electric Razor (1931) 90

Tips for More Effective Searching 90

Portable Gadget of the Week 90

On This Day: IBM Pulls the
Plug on the PC Jr. (1985) 91

Searching for People 91

Fact of the Week 91

On This Day: Terrorists Attack
Japan Subway (1995) 92

Tips for People Searching 92

Software of the Week 92

On This Day: Tennessee Passes
Anti-Evolution Law (1925) 93

What Is an Easter Egg? 93

PC Gadget of the Week 93

On This Day: Apple Sues
Microsoft (1988) 94

Windows Easter Eggs 94

Download of the Week 94

On This Day: America's First Two-Person
Space Flight (1965) 95

Macintosh Easter Eggs 95

Mac Gadget of the Week 95

On This Day: Jules Verne Dies (1905) 96

Software Easter Eggs 96

Web Site of the Week 96

On This Day: RCA Ships First
Color TV (1954) 97

Game Easter Eggs 97

Portable Gadget of the Week 97

On This Day: Heaven's Gate Mass
Suicide (1997) 98

DVD Easter Eggs 98

Fact of the Week 98

On This Day: FDA Approves
Viagra (1998) 99

Instant Messaging Easter Eggs 99

Software of the Week 99

On This Day: Three Mile Island
Nuclear Accident (1979) 100

Make a Link Disappear 100

PC Gadget of the Week 100

On This Day: Mariner 10 Flies
Past Mercury (1974) 101

Make Text Fade In and Out 101

Download of the Week 101

On This Day: Pencil with
Eraser Patented (1858) 102

Cycle Your Page's
Background Colors 102

Mac Gadget of the Week 102

On This Day: Descartes Born (1596) 103

Display a Mouseover Alert Box 103

Web Site of the Week 103

APRIL 2005 ....**107**

On This Day: Big Bang Theory
Proposed—No Foolin' (1948) 109

Make a Picture Fade In and Out 109

Portable Gadget of the Week 109

On This Day: Radar Patented (1935) 110

Shake a Window 110

Fact of the Week 110

On This Day: First Cell
Phone Call (1973) 111

Nag Users to Make Your Page
Their Start Page 111

Software of the Week 111

On This Day: Martin Luther King
Assassinated (1968) 112

The History of Computer Viruses 112

PC Gadget of the Week 112

On This Day: Hostess Twinkies
Invented (1930) 113

Reduce Your Chances of Infection 113

Download of the Week 113

On This Day: Post-It Notes
Introduced (1980) 114

Removing the Sasser Virus 114

Mac Gadget of the Week 114

On This Day: IBM Ships First Mainframe
Computer (S/360, 1964) 115

Cleaning a Virus from an Infected PC 115

Web Site of the Week 115

On This Day: Largest Sunspot
Observed (1947) 116

Restoring Your Windows XP
Machine After a Virus Attack 116

Portable Gadget of the Week 116

On This Day: NASA Announces Seven
Mercury Astronauts (1959) 117

Don't Open Email Attachments 117

Fact of the Week 117

On This Day: Titanic Sets Sail (1912) 118

Virus Hoaxes 118

Software of the Week 118

On This Day: First Jet to Take Off
and Land Vertically (1957) 119

How Spam Works 119

PC Gadget of the Week 119

On This Day: First Man in
Space (1961) 120

How Your Name Gets on a
Spam List 120

Download of the Week 120

On This Day: Air Brake
Patented (1869) 121

How to Keep Your Email
Address Private 121

Mac Gadget of the Week 121

On This Day: Apollo 13
Accident (1970) 122

Spoofing Addresses and
Spamouflage 122

Web Site of the Week 122

On This Day: Leonardo da
Vinci Born (1452) 123

Software Giants Join
to Can Spam 123

Portable Gadget of the Week 123

On This Day: Cronkite First Anchors
the CBS Evening News (1962) 124

How to Block Spam 124

Fact of the Week 124

On This Day: Ford Unveils the
Mustang (1964) 125

Anti-Spam Software 125

Software of the Week 125

On This Day: San Francisco
Earthquake (1906) 126

Upgrading to Service Pack 2 126

PC Gadget of the Week 126

On This Day: Oklahoma City
Federal Building Bombed 127

Favorite Free Windows Utilities 127

Download of the Week 127

On This Day: Electron Microscope
Demonstrated (1940) 128

Setting Up Windows for
Two Monitors 128

Mac Gadget of the Week 128

On This Day: First Extra-Solar Planets
Discovered (1994) 129

Use a Web Page As a Desktop
Background 129

Web Site of the Week 129

On This Day: Robert Oppenheimer
Born (1904) 130

Activating XP Special Effects 130

Portable Gadget of the Week 130

On This Day: New Coke
Introduced (1985) 131

Adding Programs to the XP
Start Menu 131

Fact of the Week 131

On This Day: Hubble Telescope
Launches into Space (1990) 132

Closing Stuck Programs in XP 132

Software of the Week 132

On This Day: First Solar Battery
Announced (1954) 133

What Is Linux? 133

PC Gadget of the Week 133

On This Day: Chernobyl Nuclear
Disaster 134

Different Versions of Linux 134

Download of the Week 134

On This Day: First Weather
Bureau Kite (1898) 135

Downloading Linux—for Free 135

Mac Gadget of the Week 135

On This Day: Apple Opens iTunes Music
Store (2003) 136

Linux Software 136

Web Site of the Week 136

On This Day: Google Files for
IPO (2004) 137

Installing Linux Software 137

Portable Gadget of the Week 137

On This Day: Existence of the
Electron Announced (1897) 138

Linux Links 138

Fact of the Week 138

MAY 2005 ....**143**

On This Day: BASIC
Introduced (1964) 145

Uninstalling Linux 145

Software of the Week 145

On This Day: First Science Fiction Film
Premieres (1902) 146

Understanding Digital Audio Formats 146

PC Gadget of the Week 146

On This Day: First U.S. Heart
Transplant (1968) 147

Music Download Stores 147

Download of the Week 147

On This Day: Magellan Venus
Probe Launched (1989) 148

Peer-to-Peer File Trading 148

Mac Gadget of the Week 148

On This Day: Screw-On Bottle
Cap Patented (1936) 149

Ripping Music from CD 149

Web Site of the Week 149

On This Day: Hindenburg
Disaster (1937) 150

Choosing a Digital Music Player 150

Portable Gadget of the Week 150

On This Day: Lusitania Torpedoed
by German U-Boat (1915) 151

Internet Radio 151

Fact of the Week 151

On This Day: Coca-Cola
Invented (1886) 152

Converting Records
and Tapes to MP3 152

Software of the Week 152

On This Day: Laser Beam Bounced
Off of Moon (1962) 153

PC-Based Gaming Consoles 153

PC Gadget of the Week 153

On This Day: Valence Theory
Announced (1852) 154

Playing Games Online 154

Download of the Week 154

On This Day: Spam Trademarked
by Hormel (1937) 155

Choosing a Game Controller 155

Mac Gadget of the Week 155

On This Day: First U.S. Planetarium
Opened (1930) 156

Game Cheats and News 156

Web Site of the Week 156

On This Day: VELCRO
Trademarked (1958) 157

Play Classic Console Games on
Your PC 157

Portable Gadget of the Week 157

On This Day: U.S. Unveils New
Tinted $20 Bill (2003) 158

Specialized Game Controllers 158

Fact of the Week 158

On This Day: First British Jet (1941) 159

Building a State-of-the-Art Gaming
System 159

Software of the Week 159

On This Day: *Pet Sounds* and *Blonde on
Blonde* Released (1966) 160

Upgrading Versus Buying a New PC 160

PC Gadget of the Week: i-Duck 160

On This Day: Nuclear Reactor
Patented (1955) 161

Common Upgrades 161

Download of the Week 161

On This Day: Mount St. Helens
Erupts (1980) 162

Before You Upgrade 162

Mac Gadget of the Week 162

On This Day: FDA Approves First
Genetically Engineered
Tomato (1994) 163

Upgrading from the Outside 163

Web Site of the Week 163

On This Day: Spirit of St. Louis
Takes Off (1927) 164

Upgrading from the Inside 164

Portable Gadget of the Week 164

On This Day: Removable Tire
Rims (1906) 165

Changing System Settings 165

Fact of the Week 165

On This Day: Windows 3.0
Released 166

Upgrading from an Old PC
to a New One 166

Software of the Week 166

On This Day: Robert Moog
Born (1934) 167

What Is Modding? 167

PC Gadget of the Week 167

On This Day: *Star Wars*
Premieres (1977) 168

Building Your Own PC 168

Download of the Week 168

On This Day: First Atomic
Cannon Fired (1953) 169

Creating a Quieter PC 169

Mac Gadget of the Week 169

On This Day: Microfilm Camera
Patented (1931) 170

Modding Web Sites 170

Web Site of the Week 170

On This Day: Masking Tape
Invented (1930) 171

Case Mod Painting 171

Portable Gadget of the Week 171

On This Day: Golden Gate Bridge
Opens (1937) 172

Overclocking Your Video Card 172

Fact of the Week 172

On This Day: Mount Everest
Conquered (1953) 173

Extreme PCs 173

Software of the Week 173

On This Day: First Running of the
Indianapolis 500 (1911) 174

Troubleshooting Connection
Problems 174

PC Gadget of the Week 174

On This Day: Petri Born (1852) 175

How the Web *Really* Works 175

Download of the Week 175

JUNE 2005 179

On This Day: *Sgt. Pepper's Lonely
Hearts Club Band* Released (1967) 181

Create Your Own Personal Start
Page 181

Mac Gadget of the Week 181

On This Day: Velveeta Cheese
Invented (1928) 182

Accessing Problem Web Pages 182

Web Site of the Week 182

On This Day: First American
Walks in Space (1965) 183

Use Proper Netiquette 183

Portable Gadget of the Week 183

On This Day: VisiCalc Debuts (1979) 184

Webcams 184

Fact of the Week 184

On This Day: Robert Kennedy
Assassinated (1968) 185

Downloading Files 185

Software of the Week 185

On This Day: *1984* Published (1949) 186

Your Favorite Sites in Internet
Explorer 186

PC Gadget of the Week 186

On This Day: Typesetting Machine
Patented (1887) 187

Browsing Offline 187

Download of the Week 187

On This Day: Missile Mail
Launched... Literally (1959) 188

Revisiting Your Browsing History 188

Mac Gadget of the Week 188

On This Day: Les Paul Born (1915) 189

Searching from Within Internet
Explorer 189

Web Site of the Week 189

On This Day: Apple Ships First
Apple II Computer (1977) 190

Use Internet Explorer—Safely 190

Portable Gadget of the Week 190

On This Day: *E.T.: The Extra-Terrestrial*
Released (1982) 191

Browsing Faster 191

Fact of the Week 191

On This Day: *Rock Around the
Clock* Released (1954) 192

Switch to Mozilla Firefox 192

Software of the Week 192

On This Day: Pioneer 10 Leaves
the Solar System (1983) 193

How Email Works 193

PC Gadget of the Week 193

On This Day: Univac Dedicated (1951) 194

Avoiding Email Viruses 194

Download of the Week 194

On This Day: Ben Franklin
Flies a Kite (1752) 195

Email Protocols 195

Mac Gadget of the Week 195

On This Day: First Helicopter
Demonstrated (1922) 196

Adding a Signature to Your Emails 196

Web Site of the Week 196

On This Day: Rubber Processing
Patented (1837) 197

Working with File Attachments 197

Portable Gadget of the Week 197

On This Day: Ride, Sally Ride (1983) 198

Troubleshooting Email Problems 198

Fact of the Week 198

On This Day: George "Superman"
Reeves Commits Suicide (1959) 199

Sending a Mass Mailing 199

Software of the Week 199

On This Day: Cotton Gin Patent
Application (1793) 200

How Wi-Fi Works 200

PC Gadget of the Week 200

On This Day: First Private Space
Flight (2004) 201

Searching for Hotspots 201

Download of the Week 201

On This Day: Doughnut
Invented (1847) 202

Connecting to a Wi-Fi Hotspot 202

Mac Gadget of the Week 202

On This Day: Alan Turing Born (1912) 203

Wi-Fi vs. Bluetooth 203

Web Site of the Week 203

On This Day: First Flying
Saucers Sighted (1947) 204

Let Sleeping Macs Lie 204

Portable Gadget of the Week 204

On This Day: First Color TV
Broadcast (1951) 205

Setting Up a Home Wi-Fi Network 205

Fact of the Week 205

On This Day: First Bar Code
Scanned (1974) 206

Connecting Without Wi-Fi 206

Software of the Week 206

On This Day: First Pen with
Erasable Ink (1978) 207

Setting Up a Wired Network 207

PC Gadget of the Week 207

On This Day: First U.S. Aerial
Tramway (1938) 208

Cabling Your House 208

Download of the Week 208

On This Day: Soyuz 11 Tragedy (1971) 209

Buying a Router 209

Mac Gadget of the Week 209

On This Day: Tunguska Meteorite
Explosion (1908) 210

Sharing an Internet Connection 210

Web Site of the Week 210

JULY 2005 ....**213**

On This Day: Leibniz Born (1646) 215

Troubleshooting Network Problems 215

Portable Gadget of the Week 215

On This Day: IBM Announces
Model 650 Computer (1953) 216

Configuring a File Server 216

Fact of the Week 216

On This Day: Foam Rubber
Developed (1929) 217

Sharing Files and Folders Across Your
Network 217

Software of the Week 217

On This Day: Adams and
Jefferson Die (1826) 218

Shopping for a Portable Music Player 218

PC Gadget of the Week 218

On This Day: The Bikini Debuts (1946) 219

Loving My iPod 219

Download of the Week 219

On This Day: First Mobile
Exploration of Mars (1997) 220

iPod Alternatives 220

Mac Gadget of the Week 220

On This Day: Joseph Marie
Jacquard Born (1752) 221

Microdrive Players 221

Web Site of the Week 221

On This Day: The Roswell
Incident (1947) 222

Flash Memory Players 222

Portable Gadget of the Week 222

On This Day: Tron Premieres (1982) 223

iPod Accessories 223

Fact of the Week 223

On This Day: Scopes
"Monkey Trial" Begins (1925) 224

iPod Cases 224

Software of the Week 224

On This Day: Alfred Binet Born (1857) 225

How CD Burning Works 225

PC Gadget of the Week 225

On This Day: George
Eastman Born 226

Burning CDs with
Musicmatch Jukebox 226

Download of the Week 226

On This Day: Live Aid Concert (1985) 227

Copying CDs 227

Mac Gadget of the Week 227

On This Day: Tape Measure
Patented (1868) 228

Burning a Data CD 228

Web Site of the Week 228

On This Day: Margarine
Patented (1869) 229

Labeling Your CDs 229

Portable Gadget of the Week 229

On This Day: Shoemaker-Levy
Comet Hits Jupiter (1994) 230

Troubleshooting CD/DVD
Drive Problems 230

Fact of the Week 230

On This Day: First Recorded
Solar Eclipse (709 BC) 231

How to Fix a Scratched CD 231

Software of the Week 231

On This Day: Intel Incorporated (1968) ...232

A Short History of Computing 232

PC Gadget of the Week 232

On This Day: Charles Mayo
Born (1865) 233

The Mechanical Era of
Computing: 1623–1900 233

Download of the Week 233

On This Day: Neil Armstrong
Walks on the Moon (1969) 234

Early 20th Century Computers 234

Mac Gadget of the Week 234

On This Day: Jean Picard
Born (1620) 235

First-Generation
Computers: 1940–1956 235

Web Site of the Week 235

On This Day: First Around-the-
World Solo Flight (1933) 236

Second-Generation
Computers: 1956–1963 236

Portable Gadget of the Week 236

On This Day: Cloned Mice
Announced (1998) 237

Third-Generation Computers:
1964–1971 237

Fact of the Week 237

On This Day: First Launch
from Cape Canaveral (1950) 238

Fourth-Generation Computers:
1972–Present 238

Software of the Week 238

On This Day: First Test
Tube Baby Born (1978) 239

Movies and Music 239

PC Gadget of the Week 239

On This Day: Stanley Kubrick
Born (1928) 240

News on the Web 240

Download of the Week 240

On This Day: Bugs Bunny
Debuts (1940) 241

Sports on the Web 241

Mac Gadget of the Week 241

On This Day: Earl Silas Tupper,
founder of Tupperware, Born (1907) 242

Really Stupid Web Sites 242

Web Site of the Week 242

On This Day: First Iron Lung
Installed (1927) 243

Health and Medicine Online 243

Portable Gadget of the Week 243

On This Day: Henry Ford
Born (1863) 244

Surfing for Seniors 244

Fact of the Week 244

On This Day: First Close-Up
Pictures of Moon's Surface (1964) 245

Online Greeting Cards 245

Software of the Week 245

AUGUST 2005 .... **249**

On This Day: Oxygen Identified (1774) 251

Home Page Communities 251

PC Gadget of the Week 251

On This Day: Greenwich Mean
Time Adopted (1880) 252

Home Page Community Complaints 252

Download of the Week 252

On This Day: TRS-80
Announced (1977) 253

Understanding HTML 253

Mac Gadget of the Week 253

On This Day: Fairness Doctrine
Rescinded (1987) 254

Changing Text and Background
Colors 254

Web Site of the Week 254

On This Day: Completion of First
Transatlantic Cable (1858) 255

Troubleshooting Bad HTML 255

Portable Gadget of the Week 255

On This Day: Atomic Bomb
Dropped on Hiroshima 256

Adding Mailto: Links 256

Fact of the Week 256

On This Day: Mata Hari Born (1876) 257

Putting Ads on Your Site 257

Software of the Week 257

On This Day: Refrigerator
Patented (1899) 258

Basic Troubleshooting Tips 258

PC Gadget of the Week 258

On This Day: Netscape Goes
  Public (1995) 259

Using Windows Troubleshooters 259

Download of the Week 259

On This Day: Leo Fender Born (1909) 260

Undoing Windows Problems with
  System Restore 260

Mac Gadget of the Week 260

On This Day: Steve Wozniak
  Born (1950) 261

Managing Windows Drivers 261

Web Site of the Week 261

On This Day: IBM Personal Computer
  Introduced (1981) 262

Fixing Big Problems with System
  Information 262

Portable Gadget of the Week 262

On This Day: Felix Wankel
  Born (1902) 263

Editing the Windows Registry 263

Fact of the Week 263

On This Day: Wiffle Ball
  Invented (1953) 264

Starting Windows in Safe Mode 264

Software of the Week 264

On This Day: Dental Chair
  Patented (1848) 265

Making Learning Fun 265

On This Day: Vertical Loop Roller
  Coaster Patented (1898) 266

Homework Help Online 266

Download of the Week 266

On This Day: Pierre de Fermat
  Born (1601) 267

Online Libraries 267

Mac Gadget of the Week 267

On This Day: Hewlett-Packard
  Incorporated (1947) 268

Laptops for College 268

Web Site of the Week 268

On This Day: Gordon Bell
  Born (1934) 269

Choosing a College 269

Portable Gadget of the Week 269

On This Day: Television System
  Patented (1930) 270

Surviving on Campus 270

Fact of the Week 270

On This Day: Voyager 2 Approaches
  Neptune's Moon (1989) 271

After School 271

Software of the Week 271

On This Day: Aerosol Spray
  Patented (1939) 272

Reviving Windows Explorer—and the
  DOS Prompt—in Windows XP 272

PC Gadget of the Week 272

On This Day: First Ship-to-Shore
  Wireless Message (1889) 273

Changing the Way Files Are
  Displayed in Windows XP 273

Download of the Week 273

On This Day: Windows 95
  Released (1995) 274

Personalizing the Send To Menu 274

Mac Gadget of the Week 274

On This Day: First Parachute
  Wedding Ceremony (1940) 275

Start Up Windows Faster 275

Web Site of the Week 275

On This Day: Cannon First Used
  in Battle (1346) 276

View Detailed System Information 276

Portable Gadget of the Week 276

On This Day: Mariner 2
Launched (1962) 277

Manage Your User Settings—
and Picture 277

Fact of the Week 277

On This Day: Locomotive
Races Horse (1830) 278

Waiting for Longhorn 278

Software of the Week 278

On This Day: Astronaut Speaks to
Aquanaut (1965) 279

Filtering Inappropriate Content 279

PC Gadget of the Week 279

On This Day: John Mauchly
Born (1907) 280

Kid-Safe Browsers 280

Download of the Week 280

On This Day: Jack the Ripper
Strikes (1888) 281

Kid-Safe Searching 281

Mac Gadget of the Week 281

SEPTEMBER 2005 ....**285**

On This Day: World War II
Begins (1939) 287

Educational Software 287

Web Site of the Week 287

On This Day: Andrew Grove
Born (1936) 288

Encouraging Safe Behavior Online 288

Portable Gadget of the Week 288

On This Day: Viking 2 Lands on
Mars (1976) 289

Fun Sites for Kids 289

Fact of the Week 289

On This Day: John McCarthy
Born (1927) 290

Pets and Animals Online 290

Software of the Week 290

On This Day: A.C. Nielsen Born (1897) 291

Editing Text in Microsoft Word 291

PC Gadget of the Week 291

On This Day: First Gasoline Tractor
Sold (1892) 292

Checking Spelling and Grammar
in Word 292

Download of the Week 292

On This Day: David Packard
Born (1912) 293

Fixing Word's Annoying
Overtype Mode 293

Mac Gadget of the Week 293

On This Day: *Star Trek*
Premieres (1966) 294

Create a PowerPoint Presentation from
a Word Outline—and Vice Versa 294

Web Site of the Week 294

On This Day: First Computer
Bug (1945) 295

Emboss a PowerPoint Template 295

Portable Gadget of the Week 295

On This Day: Stephen Jay Gould
Born (1941) 296

Adjusting Column Width in Excel—
Automatically 296

Fact of the Week 296

On This Day: World Trade Center
and Pentagon Attacked (2001) 297

Including Other Cells in an
Excel Formula 297

Software of the Week 297

On This Day: H.L. Mencken
Born (1880) 298

Understanding Spyware 298

PC Gadget of the Week 298

On This Day: Osborne Computer
Declares Bankruptcy (1983) 299

Avoiding and Removing Spyware 299

Download of the Week 299

On This Day: Soviet Luna 2
Reaches Moon (1959) 300

Browser Hijackers 300

Mac Gadget of the Week 300

On This Day: Association for Computing
Machinery Is Founded (1947) 301

Stopping Pop-Ups 301

Web Site of the Week 301

On This Day: *The Outer Limits*
Premieres (1963) 302

The Evil Code to Make Your Own
Pop-Ups 302

Portable Gadget of the Week 302

On This Day: First 33 1/3 Record
Demonstrated (1931) 303

Other Web Annoyances 303

Fact of the Week 303

On This Day: *New York Times*
Launches (1851) 304

Managing Cookies 304

Software of the Week 304

On This Day: Carpet Sweeper
Patented (1876) 305

Choosing an HDTV Display 305

PC Gadget of the Week 305

On This Day: First FORTRAN Program
Executed (1954) 306

How Letterboxing Works 306

Download of the Week 306

On This Day: Yes, Virginia, There *Is*
a Santa Claus (1897) 307

Analog vs. Digital Television 307

Mac Gadget of the Week 307

On This Day: *Man from U.N.C.L.E.*
Premieres (1964) 308

Going High-Def 308

Web Site of the Week 308

On This Day: Neptune Discovered
(1846) 309

Connect Your Computer to Your
Home Theater with a Digital
Media Hub 309

Portable Gadget of the Week 309

On This Day: CompuServe
Launches (1979) 310

Building a Great-Sounding
Home Theater 310

Fact of the Week 310

On This Day: Aerosols and
Ozone Depletion (1974) 311

Understanding Surround Sound
Formats 311

Software of the Week 311

On This Day: First Televised
Presidential Debate (1960) 312

Palm OS or PocketPC? 312

PC Gadget of the Week 312

On This Day: Cosmic
Near Miss (2003) 313

PDA Software 313

Download of the Week 313

On This Day: Seymour Cray
Born (1925) 314

Graffiti Tips 314

Mac Gadget of the Week 314

On This Day: Enrico Fermi
Born (1901) 315

Emulating Game Platforms on Your Pocket
PC 315

Web Site of the Week 315

On This Day: Hoover Dam
Dedicated (1935) 316

Accessorizing Your PDA 316
Portable Gadget of the Week 316

OCTOBER 2005 319

On This Day: Model T
Introduced (1908) 321
PDA or Smart Phone? 321
Fact of the Week 321
On This Day: First Atomic
Clock (1956) 322
PDA Cases 322
Software of the Week 322
On This Day: First Fax Sent (1922) 323
Understanding CPUs 323
PC Gadget of the Week 323
On This Day: Space Race
Begins (1957) 324
Upgrading Memory 324
Download of the Week 324
On This Day: Robert Goddard
Born (1882) 325
Shopping for Hard Drives 325
Mac Gadget of the Week 325
On This Day: Thor Heyerdahl
Born (1914) 326
Adding a Second Hard Drive—the
Easy Way 326
Web Site of the Week 326
On This Day: Dark Side of the Moon
Photographed (1959) 327
Better Computer Graphics 327
Portable Gadget of the Week 327
On This Day: First Pacemaker
Implanted 328
Working with Ports 328
Fact of the Week 328
On This Day: Electric Blanket
Introduced (1946) 329

Shopping for Printers 329
Software of the Week 329
On This Day: Ed Wood Born (1924) 330
Notebook Accessories 330
PC Gadget of the Week 330
On This Day: First Apollo Mission
Launched (1967) 331
Different Types of Notebooks 331
Download of the Week 331
On This Day: Search for
Extraterrestrial Life Begins (1992) 332
Macintosh Notebooks 332
Mac Gadget of the Week 332
On This Day: U.S. Navy Uses
Dolphins for Surveillance (1987) 333
Shopping for the Perfect Notebook 333
Web Site of the Week 333
On This Day: Chuck Yeager
Breaks the Sound Barrier (1947) 334
Portable Memory Devices 334
Portable Gadget of the Week 334
On This Day: Killer Bees Invade
Texas (1990) 335
Upgrading Notebook Memory 335
Fact of the Week 335
On This Day: First Use of
Anesthetic (1846) 336
How to Get the Most Out of Your
Notebook 336
Software of the Week 336
On This Day: Albert Einstein Arrives in
America (1933) 337
Basic System Maintenance 337
PC Gadget of the Week 337
On This Day: RCA Founded (1919) 338
Cleaning Keyboards and Mice 338
Download of the Week 338

On This Day: Amdahl Corp.
Founded (1970) 339

Defrag Your Hard Disk 339

Mac Gadget of the Week 339

On This Day: Louisiana Purchase
Ratified (1803) 340

Delete Unnecessary Files 340

Web Site of the Week 340

On This Day: Edison Demonstrates
Electric Light (1879) 341

Perform a Hard Disk Checkup 341

Portable Gadget of the Week 341

On This Day: Kennedy Announces
Cuban Missile Crisis (1962) 342

Backing Up Important Data 342

Fact of the Week 342

On This Day: Oldest Fossils
Discovered (1977) 343

Prepare a PC Survival Kit 343

Software of the Week 343

On This Day: Antony van
Leeuwenhoek Born (1632) 344

Understanding Blogs 344

PC Gadget of the Week 344

On This Day: First Electronic
Wristwatch (1960) 345

Why Blog? 345

Download of the Week 345

On This Day: Killer Smog in
Pennsylvania (1948) 346

Best Sites for Blogging 346

Mac Gadget of the Week 346

On This Day: NYC Subway
Opens (1904) 347

Leo's Favorite Blogs 347

Web Site of the Week 347

On This Day: Bill Gates Born (1955) 348

Creating Your Own Blog 348

Portable Gadget of the Week 348

On This Day: John Glenn Returns
to Space (1998) 349

Working with RSS Feeds 349

Fact of the Week 349

On This Day: *War of the Worlds*
Radio Broadcast (1938) 350

Photoblogs and Moblogs 350

Software of the Week 350

On This Day: Vatican Admits
Galileo Was Right (1992) 351

Copying DVDs 351

PC Gadget of the Week 351

NOVEMBER 2005 ....**355**

On This Day: U.S. Explodes
First Hydrogen Bomb 357

DVD Region Codes 357

Download of the Week 357

On This Day: George Boole
Born (1815) 358

Playing DVDs with Windows
Media Player 358

Mac Gadget of the Week 358

On This Day: Soviets Send First
Dog into Space (1957) 359

Using My DVD to Burn Movies
on DVD 359

Web Site of the Week 359

On This Day: B.F. Goodrich
Born (1841) 360

Creating a DVD Photo Album 360

Portable Gadget of the Week 360

On This Day: Vikings Discovered
in Canada (1963) 361

Understanding DVD Formats 361

Fact of the Week 361

On This Day: Microsoft Signs
DOS Contract with IBM (1980) 362

Troubleshooting DVD Problems 362

Software of the Week 362

On This Day: Marie Curie Born (1867) 363

How an Online Auction Works 363

PC Gadget of the Week 363

On This Day: Jack Kilby Born (1923) 364

Track All Your Auctions with
My eBay 364

Download of the Week 364

On This Day: Carl Sagan Born (1934) 365

Sniping to Win 365

Mac Gadget of the Week 365

On This Day: First Documented
Computer Virus (1983) 366

Secrets of Successful Bidders 366

Web Site of the Week 366

On This Day: Kurt Vonnegut, Jr. Born 367

Secrets of Successful Sellers 367

Portable Gadget of the Week 367

On This Day: Alan Turing Defines the
Universal Machine (1937) 368

Use an Auction Management Service 368

Fact of the Week 368

On This Day: Holland Tunnel
Opens (1927) 369

Running an eBay Business 369

Software of the Week 369

On This Day: Buckyball
Discovered (1985) 370

Finding Bargains on Amazon.com 370

PC Gadget of the Week 370

On This Day: Dry Cell Battery
Patented (1887) 371

Read and Write Amazon Product
Reviews 371

Download of the Week 371

On This Day: Gene Amdahl
Born (1922) 372

Become an Amazon Associate 372

Mac Gadget of the Week 372

On This Day: Computer Mouse
Patented (1970) 373

Jump Directly to Any Amazon
Product Listing 373

Web Site of the Week 373

On This Day: Mickey Mouse Debuts in
Steamboat Willie (1928) 374

Save on Amazon Shipping Costs 374

Portable Gadget of the Week 374

On This Day: Ford Halts Production
of the Edsel (1959) 375

Power Search for Books 375

Fact of the Week 375

On This Day: Windows 1.0
Released (1985) 376

Create Your Own Amazon Lists
and Guides 376

Software of the Week 376

On This Day: First Manned Balloon Flight
(1783) 377

The Best Way to Pay 377

PC Gadget of the Week 377

On This Day: President Kennedy
Assassinated (1963) 378

Shopping Safely 378

Download of the Week 378

On This Day: First Jukebox
Installed (1889) 379

Look for Manufacturer Rebates 379

Mac Gadget of the Week 379

On This Day: Darwin's *Origin of Species*
Published (1859) 380

Research Your Purchase Before You Buy 380

Web Site of the Week 380

On This Day: Dynamite
Patented (1867) 381

Using a Price Comparison Site 381

Portable Gadget of the Week 381

On This Day: First Polaroid Camera Sold
(1948) 382

Saving with Online Coupons 382

Fact of the Week 382

On This Day: Konosuke Matsushita
Born (1894) 383

Shopping for Liquidation Bargains 383

Software of the Week 383

On This Day: Mariner 4
Launched (1964) 384

Creating a Glamour Glow 384

PC Gadget of the Week 384

On This Day: Atari Releases
PONG Arcade Game (1972) 385

Monitor Wars: LCD or CRT? 385

Download of the Week 385

On This Day: Mark Twain Born (1835) ...386

Replacing Ugly Backgrounds 386

Mac Gadget of the Week 386

DECEMBER 2005 389

On This Day: First Drive-Up
Service Station Opened (1913) 391

Downloading Clipart 391

Web Site of the Week 391

On This Day: First Controlled
Nuclear Chain Reaction (1942) 392

Creating a Transparent GIF in
Photoshop Elements 392

Portable Gadget of the Week 392

On This Day: John Backus Born (1924) ...393

Graphics for Web Pages 393

Fact of the Week 393

On This Day: Thomas Edison
Invents the Phonograph (1877) 394

Understanding Graphics File Formats 394

Software of the Week 394

On This Day: Werner Heisenberg
Born (1901) 395

Tweak Windows with the Group
Policy Editor 395

PC Gadget of the Week 395

On This Day: Microwave Oven
Patented (1945) 396

Change the Location of
System Folders 396

Download of the Week 396

On This Day: Last Moon
Mission Launches (1972) 397

Optimize Your Display with
ClearType 397

Mac Gadget of the Week 397

On This Day: John Lennon
Killed (1980) 398

Windows File Tricks 398

Web Site of the Week 398

On This Day: Grace Murray
Hopper Born (1906) 399

Put a CPU Meter in the Taskbar 399

Portable Gadget of the Week 399

On This Day: Ada Byron Born (1815) 400

Change Your Computer's
Identification 400

Fact of the Week 400

On This Day: J.L. Kraft Born (1874) 401

Change the Size and Quality of
Thumbnail Images 401

Software of the Week 401

On This Day: Apple Computer
IPO (1980) 402

Shopping for the Geek on Your List 402

PC Gadget of the Week 402

On This Day: First Functioning
Communications Satellite
Launched (1962) 403

Shopping for the Hardcore Gamer 403

Download of the Week 403

On This Day: First Non-Refueled
Flight Around the World (1986) 404

Shopping for the Home Video
Enthusiast 404

Mac Gadget of the Week 404

On This Day: Ice Cream Cone
Patented (1903) 405

Shopping for the Digital Photography
Enthusiast 405

Web Site of the Week 405

On This Day: Arthur C. Clarke
Born (1917) 406

Shopping for the Home Theater
Enthusiast 406

Portable Gadget of the Week 406

On This Day: Wright Brothers Make First
Manned Flight (1903) 407

Shopping for the Road Warrior 407

Fact of the Week 407

On This Day: Inventor of FM
Radio Born (1890) 408

Books for Geeks 408

Software of the Week 408

On This Day: Altair 8800
Goes on Sale (1974) 409

Create Your Own Menus 409

PC Gadget of the Week 409

On This Day: Van de Graaff
Born (1901) 410

Enter Foreign Characters from
the Keyboard 410

Download of the Week 410

On This Day: First Full-Length
Animated Film (1937) 411

Use Word As a Spreadsheet 411

Mac Gadget of the Week 411

On This Day: Christmas Tree Lights
Invented (1822) 412

Add a Watermark to a Word
Document 412

Web Site of the Week 412

On This Day: First Men Orbit the
Moon (1968) 413

Type "Shortcuts" to Long Words 413

Portable Gadget of the Week 413

On This Day: First Solar Heated
House (1948) 414

Make Your PowerPoint Text POP! 414

Fact of the Week 414

On This Day: Sir Isaac Newton
Born (1642) 415

Animate Your PowerPoint Slide
Backgrounds 415

Software of the Week 415

On This Day: Charles Babbage
Born (1791) 416

Getting Rid of Your Old PC 416

PC Gadget of the Week 416

On This Day: Johannes Kepler
Born (1571) 417

Powering Up—for the Very First
Time 417

Download of the Week 417

On This Day: Chewing Gum
Patented (1869) 418

Learning Important Windows
Operations 418

Mac Gadget of the Week 418

On This Day: Charles Goodyear
Born (1800) 419

Understanding Files and Folders 419

Web Site of the Week 419

On This Day: New Galaxy
Discovered (1924) 420

Installing New Software 420

Portable Gadget of the Week 420

On This Day: Smallpox Virus
  Scheduled to Be Destroyed—
  Not (1993) 421
Shutting Down Your Computer 421
Fact of the Week 421

A FACTS AND FIGURES 425

Computer Hardware and Software 426
The Internet 427
Spam, Viruses, and Attacks 434
Searching 435
Online Advertising 436
Online Shopping 437
Playing Games 439
Consumer Electronics 441

B LEO'S LITTLE BLACK BOOK 445

Antivirus and Security 446
Audio/Video Systems and
  Components 446
Batteries 448
Cables and Networking 448
Cellular Phones 449
Cellular Phone Services 449
Computer Accessories 449
Computer Hardware 450
Computer Monitors 450
Computer and Consumer
  Electronics Retailers 451
Computer Software 451
Digital Cameras 452
Digital Satellite Systems 452
ISPs and Online Services 453
Keyboards and Mice 453
Media Player Software 453
Memory 454
PDAs 454

PDA Cases and Accessories 455
Personal Video Recorders 455
Portable MP3 Players 456
Printers 456
Remote Controls 457
Removable Storage Media and
  Memory Cards 457
Scanners 458
Sound Cards 458
Video Games 458

C GLOSSARY 459

INDEX 493

ABOUT THE AUTHORS

Leo Laporte is the former host of two shows on TechTV: *The Screen Savers* and *Call for Help*. Leo is a weekend radio host on Los Angeles radio KFI AM 640. He also appears regularly on many other television and radio programs, including ABC's *World News Now* and *Live with Regis and Kelly* as "The Gadget Guy." He is the author of *Leo Laporte's 2003 Computer Almanac* and *Leo Laporte's 2004 Screensavers Technology Almanac*, both of which have been bestsellers. Leo also is the author of three newly published books on consumer technology in his Leoville Press series: *Leo Laporte's Guide to TiVo*, *Leo Laporte's Mac Gadget Guide*, and *Leo Laporte's 2005 Gadget Guide*, all published by Que.

Michael Miller has written more than 50 nonfiction books over the past 15 years. His books for Que include *Bargain Hunter's Guide to Online Shopping*, *Absolute Beginner's Guide to Computer Basics*, and *Absolute Beginner's Guide to eBay*. He was also a contributor to *Leo Laporte's 2003 Technology Almanac*.

ACKNOWLEDGMENTS

Thanks to the usual suspects at Que, including but not limited to Greg Wiegand, Rick Kughen, Tonya Simpson, Judi Wade, Kate Hollcraft, and Sharry Lee Gregory.

WE WANT TO HEAR FROM YOU!

As the reader of this book, *you* are our most important critic and commentator. We value your opinion and want to know what we're doing right, what we could do better, what areas you'd like to see us publish in, and any other words of wisdom you're willing to pass our way.

As an associate publisher for Que, I welcome your comments. You can email or write me directly to let me know what you did or didn't like about this book—as well as what we can do to make our books better.

Please note that I cannot help you with technical problems related to the topic of this book. We do have a User Services group, however, where I will forward specific technical questions related to the book.

When you write, please be sure to include this book's title and author as well as your name, email address, and phone number. I will carefully review your comments and share them with the author and editors who worked on the book.

Email: feedback@quepublishing.com

Mail: Greg Wiegand
          Associate Publisher
          Que Publishing
          800 East 96th Street
          Indianapolis, IN 46240 USA

For more information about this book or another Que title, visit our Web site at www.quepublishing.com. Type the ISBN (excluding hyphens) or the title of a book in the Search field to find the page you're looking for.

INTRODUCTION

This is a book for people who love computers and technology but hate computer books. I'm not all that fond of them, myself, although I have to read a lot of them for my job.

Allow me to introduce myself. My name is Leo and you might have seen me on TV or heard me on the radio talking about computers and technology. I read all those computer books and magazines so you don't have to. Every week on my radio show, and every night on television, I try to distill gallons of information into a fun, fast-paced, and informative brew. It's my goal to keep you up to date on what's happening with technology while showing you a darn good time.

This book is all those shows put on paper. Inside these pages is a year's worth of information—stuff you can really use, surrounded by stuff that's not so useful but fascinating and fun to know nevertheless. Mary Poppins had it right: Just a spoonful of sugar helps the medicine go down. There's lots of sugar mixed in with the medicine in this book.

This is the 2005 edition of the Almanac, brand new for the brand new year. There's a page for every day of the year—but there's no need to read them in order, or to wait for the calendar to read that day's entry. We designed this book so you could jump around in it, read a little bit whenever you have the time or inclination, or devour it all at once, if you have a mind to. Each page stands alone, with a feature article, plus a look at this date in technology history, downloads, favorite Web sites, fun gadgets, and more. Each week focuses on a single area in technology: online auctions, hardware, Windows, digital audio, digital photography, and so on. But it's an almanac, not an encyclopedia. You won't find an exhaustive (or exhausting) discussion of any topic inside. You will come away from each week knowing a lot more about the subject than you did before. I've included plenty of links to Web pages where you can learn more if you want to.

A note about those links: To save space (and to save you typing) I've eliminated the redundant http:// from the Web addresses in the Almanac. Type the address as printed into your browser, and unless the page has moved or disappeared, it will work. Don't type any punctuation after the address. Many URLs in the book are followed by commas or periods—they're not part of the address, they're to keep Mrs. Kandel, my sixth-grade English teacher, happy. I checked every single Web address just before publication, and they were all working, but the Web being what it is, it's possible that some of them will not be working by the time you get around to trying them. I apologize if that happens, but don't forget that you can always find a similar page by going to Google or some similar search engine. Just leave the period off the end.

Before I wrap this up, I want to thank you—not just for buying this book, but for wanting to learn more about how this stuff works. Technology is a wonderful thing, and computers are remarkable tools. They're probably the most complex machines humankind has ever invented, and yet a six-year-old can use one with seeming ease. For those of us over the age of six, it takes a little more effort, but that effort pays off handsomely. The computer is an amplifier for the mind, giving any individual the power to change the world. It's my mission in life to show people just what buttons to push and dials to twist so they can begin to use technology to make a difference in their own lives. Thanks for your willingness to try. Now, let's get going—I can't wait to see what you're going to do with the stuff you learn in here!

IS THIS BOOK FOR YOU?

If you're just picking this book up in the store, you might wonder whether it's for you. I'll save you the trouble of reading the next paragraph. Yes, this book is for you. In fact, it's for everyone you know. I suggest you buy copies for all your friends. Buy a copy for that guy standing next to you looking at that *Microsoft Excel for Nudniks* book. Buy a copy for the nice bookstore clerk. In fact, buy every copy on the shelf and hand them out to people on the street as you walk by. Spread the Almanac goodness! Hallelujah!

Well, okay, no book is for everyone, not even this fine volume. The *Leo Laporte 2005 Technology Almanac* is for people who spent a lot of money on a computer and are now wondering what to do with that expensive piece of plastic on their desks. Every page contains something fun or useful you can do right now.

It's not just for super geeks, but even computer experts will learn something in here. It's not just for novices, but even a beginner will be able to understand and use the tips inside. It's really for anyone who wants to bring the fun back into tech. We live in an age when the best toys are being designed for grown-ups. This book will help you rediscover how to play with them.

This book is designed for users of all mainstream computer platforms: Windows, Mac OS, and Linux. In fact, most of the tips and info are applicable cross-platform—especially the Internet-related information.

HOW THIS BOOK IS ORGANIZED

Inside, you'll find a page for every day of the year. Each week has a primary focus: online shopping, digital photography, Microsoft Office, and so on. On each page, you'll find a short article related to the week's subject. There's also a short feature for each day, detailing my favorite Web sites, downloads, gadgets, and so on. It's my evil plan to have you shouting "A-ha!" and "Wow, I never knew that!" on every page.

On each page, you'll also find an historic event in technology—everything from Pascal's birthday to the day that the Whiffle ball was invented. Be sure to visit the related links, which point to a Web site with lots more interesting material about the event. There are many fun surprises, too. Each month also ends with a page of fun technology, historical, and pop culture anniversaries from that month. These tidbits will help you amaze your friends, be a hit at cocktail parties and flaunt your pure geeky goodness.

At the end of the book we've provided one of the best technology glossaries ever. There's also a statistics chapter that's fascinating to comb through, and I've included a little black book of important addresses and phone numbers you should know.

Leo Laporte's 2005 *Technology Almanac* is the computer book I've always wanted to read. I know you'll enjoy reading it as much as I've enjoyed writing it.

Leo

Leo Laporte

September 30, 2004

WHAT'S THIS LEOVILLE PRESS THING?

Books branded with the "A Leoville Book" moniker represent the next revolution in consumer technology books written for real people who depend on technology at work and at home. Gone are the days when being a geek meant that you wore a pocket protector, high-water pants and stayed in the computer lab. Today's geeks are school teachers, construction workers, lawyers, doctors, athletes, performers, and corporate professionals. Today, being a geek is cool, stylish, and sexy. Leoville Books celebrate mainstream technology, tackle technical topics, and deliver what you need to know, when you need to know—all in Leo Laporte's engaging, humorous and indelible style that has given him national attention on major news and entertainment programs.

Leoville Press books are published exclusively by Que Publishing. Look for more Leoville Press books at your favorite book store or online retailer.

Be sure to visit Leo's Leoville Web site (www.leoville.com) for the latest on Leo's books, radio and television appearances, as well as an active blog where you can keep up with Leo (see Figure 1.1).

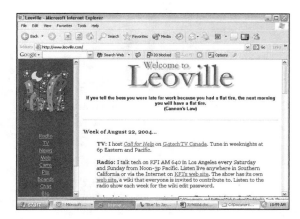

FIGURE 1.1

Leo updates his blog (see Figure 1.2) daily with tech tips, news, updates on his public appearances and photos from his travels.

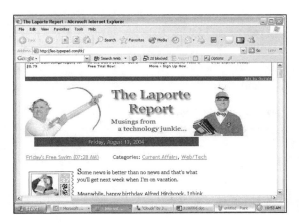

FIGURE 1.2

Other Books in the Leoville Press Series

Leo Laporte's 2005 Gadget Guide

Dedicated to the leagues of mainstream geeks who integrate technology into every facet of their lives, *Leo Laporte's 2005 Gadget Guide* is the definitive source for your gadget-buying needs in 2004-05. Leo boils down the reams and reams of product specs, slices through the marketing hype and delivers his best of breed picks for everything from digital cameras to MP3 players, from GPS units to cell phones, and from home theater equipment to computer gadgetry. If you're a bona fide gadget connoisseur, then this is the one book you need to ensure that your hard-earned bucks are put to good use. If you're buying for the geek you love, then this book is your indispensable guide for buying just the right gadget to make your geek purr.

ISBN 0-7897-3208-4, 320 pages; full-color, Cover Price $24.99

Leo Laporte's Mac Gadget Guide

Right out of the box, today's Macs are absolutely stylish, surprisingly elegant and defiantly cool. Once chided as not playing well with the PC world, Macs have come a LONG way in recent years, offering more compatibility, innovation and more moxie than most PC users care to admit. Enter *Leo Laporte's Living the iLife: A Guide to Mac Gadgets*—a book that takes the first honest look at the plethora of gadgets and add-ons available to today's Mac user. No longer are Mac users the red-headed stepchildren of the computing universe. Today, Mac users not only enjoy the spoils that were once reserved for PC users, but are now blessed with technologies designed specifically for the Macintosh (and rapidly copied by PC makers). In this one-of-a-kind book, Leo shows users how to setup and use a variety of gadgets with their Macs, including the explosively popular iPod, wireless technologies and PocketPCs, PDAs and more!

ISBN 0-7897-3174-6, 300 pages; full-color, Cover Price $24.99

Leo Laporte's Guide to TiVo

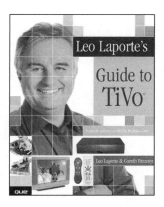

Leo Laporte's Guide to TiVo is a fun, light-hearted, easy-to-follow guide to all things TiVo, from the simplest remote control trickery, to upgrading hardware, to even building your own Personal Video Recorder. Besides not reading like the Federal Tax Code, this book is different from the competition in that we don't cover every single software and hardware hack available. We only focus on (and clearly describe) the hacks, upgrades, and improvements that most TiVo users are likely to perform. Let's face it, trying to use your TiVo to play your MP3s might sound cool, but given the TiVo's lack of sound processing hardware, the results are hardly worth it (though the competition wastes precious space on this ridiculous hack). We focus on the things that will make life with your TiVo worth living—things such as adding a CallerID display to your television, adding a new hard drive, remote control hacks that anyone can perform and adding Web capabilities.

ISBN 0-7897-3195-9, 400 pages, 2-color, Cover Price $29.99

January 2005

January 2005

SUNDAY	MONDAY	TUESDAY	WEDNESDAY	THURSDAY	FRIDAY	SATURDAY
						1 New Year's Day
2 1920 Isaac Asimov born	**3** 1892 J.R.R. Tolkien is born	**4** 1642 Isaac Newton is born	**5** 1896 X-rays first discovered	2001 **6** Congress certifies George W. Bush winner of 2000 elections over Democrat Al Gore	**7** 1927 Transatlantic phone service begins	**8** 1942 Stephen Hawking is born
9 894 First motion picture is copyrighted	1901 **10** Oil is discovered in Beaumont, TX – the first major oil discovery in U.S. history	**11** 1935 Amelia Earhart flies from Hawaii to California	**12** 1896 First X-ray photo taken	1910 **13** Lee De Forest makes the first radio broadcast from the Metropolitan Opera	**14** 1784 Continental Congress ratifies the Treaty of Paris	1861 **15** Safety elevator is first used, replacing dangerous steam-driven elevators
16 1953 Chevrolet introduces the Corvette	**17** 1706 Benjamin Franklin is born	**18** 1974 *Six Million Dollar Man* debuts	1955 **19** Dwight D. Eisenhower becomes first president to host TV news conferences	**20** Martin Luther King Day 1930 Buzz Aldrin is born	**21** 1954 First nuclear-powered submarine is launched	**22** 1984 Apple Macintosh computer commercial airs
23 1960 Using a reinforced vessel, scientists descend 35,810 ft in Pacific	**24** 1986 Voyager II makes the closest approach to Uranus in history	1955 **25** Atomic clock accurate to within one second in 300 years is developed	1962 **26** U.S. launches Ranger 3 to the moon, but missing its target by about 22,000 miles	**27** 1967 Apollo 1 fire kills three U.S. astronauts	**28** 1986 Challenger Space Shuttle explosion	**29** 1924 First ice cream cone rolling machine patent is issued
30 1948 Mohandas Gandhi is assassinated in New Delhi	1971 **31** Apollo 14 departs for the moon, eventually landing there on February 5					

THIS WEEK'S FOCUS: YOUR NEW PC

ON THIS DAY: AT&T DIVESTS BELL SYSTEM COMPANIES (1984)

In 1974, changes in the telecommunications industry led to an antitrust suit by the U.S. government against AT&T. The suit was settled in January 1982, when AT&T agreed to divest itself of the wholly owned Bell companies that provided local phone service. The divestiture took place on January 1, 1984; in the place of the old Bell System was a new AT&T (over $100 billion smaller) and seven regional "baby Bell" operating companies.

Related Web site: www.att.com/history/

BREAKING IN YOUR NEW COMPUTER

It's important to prepare the space where you'll be putting your new PC. Obviously, the space must be big enough to hold all the components—though you don't have to keep all the components together. You can, for example, spread out your left and right speakers, place your subwoofer on the floor, and separate the printer from the system unit. Just don't put anything so far away that the cables don't reach! (And make sure you have a spare power outlet—or even better, a multi-outlet power strip—nearby.)

You also should consider the ergonomics of your setup. You want your keyboard at or slightly below normal desktop height, and you want your monitor at or slightly below eye level. Be sure your chair is adjusted for a straight and firm sitting position with your feet flat on the floor, and then place all the pieces of your system in relation to that.

Wherever you put your system, you should make sure that it's in a well-ventilated location free of excess dust and smoke. (The moving parts in your computer don't like dust and dirt, or any other such contaminants that can muck up the way they work.) Because your computer generates heat when it operates, you must leave enough room around the system unit for the heat to dissipate. *Never* place your computer in a confined, poorly ventilated space; your PC can overheat and shut down if it isn't sufficiently ventilated.

For extra protection to your computer, connect the power cable on your system unit to a surge suppressor rather than directly into an electrical outlet. A *surge suppressor*—which looks like a power strip, but with an on/off switch—protects your PC from power-line surges that could damage its delicate internal parts. When a power surge temporarily spikes your line voltage (causes the voltage to momentarily increase above normal levels), a surge suppressor shuts down power to your system, acting like a circuit breaker or fuse.

FACT OF THE WEEK

The National Safety Council (NSC) estimates that 315 million computers will be junked in 2004, up from 20 million in 1998. In 1998 (the last year this was monitored), only 11% of the PCs that were thrown out were recycled. Unfortunately, old PCs tossed into landfills contain dangerous chemicals and metals that can leak toxins into the environment—a good reason to recycle your machine when you buy a new one.

January 2, 2005

SUNDAY

THIS WEEK'S FOCUS: YOUR NEW PC

ON THIS DAY: ISAAC ASIMOV BORN (1920)

Writer Isaac Asimov was born in Petrovichi, Russia, on January 2, 1920; he died on April 6, 1992. Asimov was one of the most prolific authors of our time, with more than 500 books to his name. His most popular titles include *I, Robot*; *The Gods Themselves*; *Fantastic Voyage*; *The Foundation* series; and several collections of Black Widower stories.

Related Web site: www.asimovonline.com

CONNECT BY COLOR

Most PC manufacturers color-code the cables and connectors to make the connection even easier—just plug the blue cable into the blue connector, and so on. If you're not sure what color cable goes to what device, take a look at the standard cable color coding below, as specified in the PC 99 System Design Guide.

Connector	Color
VGA (analog) monitor	Blue
Digital monitor	White
Video out	Yellow
Mouse	Green
Keyboard	Purple
Serial	Teal or turquoise
Parallel (printer)	Burgundy
USB	Black
FireWire (IEEE 1394)	Grey
Audio line out (left)	Red
Audio line out (right)	White
Audio line out (headphones)	Lime
Speaker out/subwoofer	Orange
Right-to-left speaker	Brown
Audio line in	Light blue
Microphone	Pink
Gameport/MIDI	Gold

SOFTWARE OF THE WEEK

Norton Ghost is a backup program that does more than simple backups. Use Ghost to create a mirror image of your entire hard drive, and store the backup data on removable media, a backup hard disk, or another computer on your network. Get it at www.symantec.com for $69.95.

4

January 3, 2005

MONDAY

THIS WEEK'S FOCUS: COMPUTER SECURITY

ON THIS DAY: SPIRIT ROVER LANDS ON MARS (2004)

In June and July of 2003, NASA launched two Mars exploration rovers toward the red planet. The first rover, Spirit, landed on Mars on January 3, 2004. Within hours of touchdown, Spirit beamed back stunning black-and-white images from its new home, heralding a new era of Mars exploration.

Related Web site: marsrovers.jpl.nasa.gov/home/index.html

FAVORITE FIREWALL SOFTWARE

If you have only a single machine, you should use a firewall of some sort to protect yourself from hackers. Windows XP has a built-in firewall (which I'll discuss tomorrow) that works okay; turn it on by right-clicking My Computer, selecting Properties, and then clicking the Advanced tab. Check the Firewall box to turn it on.

If you want a more powerful—and free—firewall, ZoneAlarm is available from ZoneLabs (www.zonelabs.com). More expert users might prefer the additional control of the Sygate Personal Firewall (www.sygate.com), also free.

Mac users are protected by the built-in firewall that comes with BSD, ipfw. You can get very fancy with ipfw, but for most users turning it on using the Sharing System Preference pane is enough. Click the Firewall tab and click the Start button. The default settings are fine for most people. If you want to get really fancy, you can use the shareware application Brickhouse (www.securemac.com/brickhouse.php) to write rules for you.

A little warning is in order here for people who plan to install one of these third-party firewalls: Software firewalls are complicated programs that modify system files, so some people experience problems after installing them. I've tested and used ZoneAlarm and Sygate and have found them to be reliable, but it's a good idea to back up your data and set System Restore points before you install. The firewalls built into Windows XP and Mac OS X are safer to use, if not as sophisticated.

By the way, if you're running behind a broadband router you're off to a good start. Even if they don't claim to be firewalls, routers hide your network from the outside world, providing considerable protection against hackers. Some routers, like the SMC Barricade, have built-in firewalls for additional protection.

PC GADGET OF THE WEEK

If you have a notebook computer, you have to worry about another kind of security—security from theft. The simplest way to secure your notebook PC is to chain it down, using a device such as Targus's DEFCON CL Notebook Computer Cable Lock ($34.99). If you want even more security, check out Targus's DEFCON 1 Ultra Notebook Computer Security System ($49.99), which combines a 3' steel cable with a four-digit combination lock and high-decibel alarm unit, complete with motion sensor. Find them both at www.targus.com.

5

January 4, 2005

TUESDAY,

THIS WEEK'S FOCUS: **COMPUTER SECURITY**

ON THIS DAY: **FIRST POCKET SCIENTIFIC CALCULATOR (1972)**

On January 4, 1972, Hewlett-Packard introduced the HP-35, the world's first pocket electronic scientific calculator. Known as "the electronic slide rule," the HP-35 was priced at $395, and H-P sold more than 100,000 of them the first year. By the time the HP-35 was discontinued in 1975, just three and a half years after its introduction, more than 300,000 units had been sold.

Related Web site: www.hp.com/hpinfo/abouthp/histnfacts/museum/personal systems/0023/

HARDWARE FIREWALLS

Here's an unfortunate fact: Firewall programs are very invasive. They have to be, to get the job done. The programs I recommended yesterday are good and reliable, but as with any system-level software they can cause problems on your machine. And, because they're free, you can't expect any support from the vendor. I've had good results with these programs, but your mileage may vary.

That's why for most people I don't recommend a software firewall. A better solution is to go the hardware route. A hardware firewall is more effective and less likely to cause problems—although it's not free.

An Internet router provides most of the protection of a software firewall without the reliability issues. If you're using DSL, a broadband router has the added advantage of replacing the software PPPoE dialer, which is convenient and can also improve reliability. Broadband routers are relatively cheap, as little as $50.

Two of my favorite routers are the Linksys Etherfast (www.linksys.com) and Netgear 318 (www.netgear.com). Configure them properly (which includes replacing the default password) and you'll have a fairly safe system.

DOWNLOAD OF THE WEEK

Want to remove the vocals from your favorite recordings—all the better to sing along with? Then check out AnalogX's Vocal Remover, which works with Winamp. It works by swapping the phase of the left and right channels, canceling out anything recorded equally in both channels—which is usually the vocals. Results can be quite good—and quite awful—depending on how the song was mixed. Get it for free at www.analogx.com.

THIS WEEK'S FOCUS: COMPUTER SECURITY

ON THIS DAY: FM RADIO DEMONSTRATED (1940)

Edwin H. Armstrong gave the first formal demonstration of FM radio to the Federal Communications Commission on January 5, 1940. Armstrong had completed his first field test of the technology on June 9, 1934; on May 20, 1940, the FCC officially took Channel 1 off the television band and allotted it to FM. The FCC assigned FM the frequencies between 42 and 50 MHz, enough for 40 FM channels, and authorized commercial service beginning January 1, 1941.

Related Web site: www.wsone.com/fecha/armstrong.htm

SPY ON YOUR SPOUSE AND KIDS

If you want to find out what Web sites your kids—or your spouse—have been visiting, it's actually fairly easy to do a little inside-the-PC spying.

First, you need to know that the obvious approach isn't very accurate. Sites that show up in Internet Explorer's History list—or even files in the temporary Internet files folder—aren't conclusive proof. That's because every page visited, even those displayed as pop-up ads, show up there.

That said, the best thing to do is check the address history by clicking the drop-down icon in Internet Explorer's address window. This will list any address typed into the Address bar—proof positive that the visit was intentional.

Another approach is to install a program that automatically emails keystrokes to a specific address; this way you'll have a record of all activity, including instant messages and chat room conversations. Two good keystroke-logging programs are eBlaster

(www.eblaster.com) and Perfect Keylogger (www.blazingtools.com).

If you want evidence that can stand up in court, you'll need to hire a pro to do the tracking for you. A search for "computer forensics" on Google will turn up some companies that do this kind of thing—for a price.

MAC GADGET OF THE WEEK

M-Audio's Keystation 49e is a MIDI controller that makes it possible for your Mac to play songs in Apple's GarageBand or any other MIDI-compatible software. When you use the Keystation to play notes, you either cause your Mac to sound an instrument "voice" that you've selected in the software application, or you can "write" music by playing notes on the keyboard that are translated by the software application. It connects to your Mac via USB; buy it for $129 at www.m-audio.com.

January 6, 2005

THURSDAY,

THIS WEEK'S FOCUS: **COMPUTER SECURITY**

ON THIS DAY: *SCHOOLHOUSE ROCK* **DEBUTS (1973)**

The very first *Schoolhouse Rock* cartoon debuted on the ABC network on this Saturday morning in 1973. Millions of kids sang along with—and learned a little from—*Schoolhouse Rock* from 1973 to 1985. There were 41 segments in all; the first broadcast was "Three Is a Magic Number."

Related Web site: www.school-house-rock.com

PHISHING SCHEMES

Think very carefully before you click on any links in those official-looking emails you get that say you need to verify some bit of personal information. Chances are that email is a fraud—part of a scam called a *phishing* scheme. Clicking on the link in the email—which appears to be a legitimate secure link—takes you to a hacker's server, gussied up to look just like the official site. Enter any information there, and it'll get stolen.

According to Webopedia, phishing is the act of sending a fraudulent email claiming to be from a major company, directing you to an imitation Web site that then collects your personal and financial information with the aim of ripping you off. Emails posing as "official" communications from Citibank, AOL, eBay, and Paypal are particularly popular. No reputable company or Web site will send out this sort of message, ask you to send personal information via email, or include a direct link to an input form.

If you get such an email, do *not* click the link in the message. Instead, go to the *real* site by typing in the URL on your own—do not duplicate the URL in the email. Go to the company's main page and navigate from there. If you really do need to update your personal information, you can do it manually, without navigational aid from the email message.

If you fall for a phishing scheme, assume your identity is being stolen. Put a fraud alert on your credit reports, and notify the Web site or company about what's happened. You might even want to close your checking account, if you gave up that information.

WEB SITE OF THE WEEK

Read more about phishing at the Anti-Phishing Working Group site (www.antiphishing.org). You can even use links on this site to report phishing emails to the proper authorities.

THIS WEEK'S FOCUS: COMPUTER SECURITY

ON THIS DAY: TRANSATLANTIC PHONE SERVICE BEGINS (1927)

It took 50 years from the invention of the telephone to make transatlantic phone calls. On this date in 1927, Bell Laboratories and the British Post Office engineered the first two-way conversation (using radio) between New York and London. Over the next few years the service spread throughout North America and Europe.

Related Web site: www.att.com/attlabs/reputation/timeline/

EVALUATING YOUR RISK

If you're a typical home computer user, your risk of being the victim of an Internet-based computer attack is relatively low. That risk is lower if you connect to the Internet via a dial-up connection, and even lower if you're the sole user. Your risk increases if you have an always-on broadband Internet connection, and if your spouse and kids (and household visitors) also use your computer.

Your risk also increases if you run your own Web site. Any public exposure creates a more visible and attractive target for crackers. Let's face it, putting a site on the Web is like flashing a business card in a busy coffeehouse; you announce your presence, and—for crackers—your vulnerability.

This is true even if your public presence is just a personal Web page. While experienced crackers will pass up personal pages (too small a challenge), beginning crackers might appreciate the practice they can get, at your expense. Besides, most personal Web sites have very little security; they're an easy target.

For a more accurate evaluation of your risk of attack, there are several Web sites that offer free security tests. These tests typically involve sending different types of messages to your PC to see how well your system is insulated from each different type of attack. Test your site at HackerWhacker (www.hackerwhacker.com), Secure-Me (www.broadbandreports.com/secureme/), Shields UP! (www.grc.com), or Symantec Security Check (security.norton.com).

PORTABLE GADGET OF THE WEEK

The Olympus DM-1 is a high-capacity, extremely versatile digital voice recorder. It records directly to SmartMedia cards; you can get up to 22 hours of recording on a 64MB card or 44 hours on a 128MB card. It's USB-compatible, which makes it easy to download your audio recordings to your PC—or transfer digital audio files to the DM-1. That's right, you can also use the DM-1 as a digital music player, which is a nice case of double duty. Buy it for $24.9.99 at www.olympusamerica.com.

January 8, 2005

SATURDAY

THIS WEEK'S FOCUS: COMPUTER SECURITY

ON THIS DAY: HOLLERITH TABULATING MACHINE PATENTED (1889)

In 1886, Herman Hollerith constructed the first electromechanical adding and sorting machine. This machine, which he dubbed a "tabulator," received a patent on January 8, 1889, and was put to its first commercial use in 1890 for the U.S. Census Bureau. Hollerith's tabulator could read census data that had been punched into rectangular cardboard cards, later known as punch cards; the use of these punch cards significantly reduced the incidence of data entry errors, increased the speed of data entry, and served as a crude form of data storage.

Related Web site: www.columbia.edu/acis/history/hollerith.html

DETECTING A COMPUTER ATTACK

How do you know if your computer is under attack? One surefire sign is the presence of a large number of port scans to your system. A port scan occurs when a potential intruder searches your computer for unprotected ports in which to enter your system; a successful port scan is often followed by the insertion of a backdoor file or other malicious code.

Fortunately, most firewall programs monitor port scans, and alert you of unusual activity in this area. You can also install a separate port scan monitor, such as Nuke Nabber (files.electrocities.com). This type of program monitors all the port activity on your system, looking for port scans from the outside. While a certain number of port scans is to be expected anytime you're connected to the Internet, an undue number of scans, as well as scans of certain types, are indicative of a current or upcoming attack.

Another sign of attack is the unauthorized use of so-called sniffer (or packet sniffer) programs. Sniffers are network monitoring programs commonly used to steal account and password information. Some intruders surreptitiously install sniffer software on your system, where it works in the background recording your user activity. The intruder can then reenter your system, retrieve the sniffer's log file, and have all your keystrokes and other activity right there, in black in white.

By themselves, sniffer programs are relatively invisible—until they start to send their results to the attacker. The best way to sniff out a sniffer is to use an anti-sniffer utility, such as PromiscDetect (ntsecurity.nu/toolbox/promiscdetect/).

FACT OF THE WEEK

The Gartner Group reports that nearly 2 million Americans have had their checking accounts raided by criminals in the past twelve months. The trend neatly follows a sharp rise in phishing emails; Gartner reports that at least 1.8 million consumers have been tricked into divulging personal information in phishing attacks.

THIS WEEK'S FOCUS: **COMPUTER SECURITY**

ON THIS DAY: ACCELERATING GALAXIES ANNOUNCED (1998)

On this date in 1998, two teams of scientists announced the discovery that galaxies are accelerating, flying apart at ever faster speeds. This discovery implied the existence of a mysterious, self-repelling property of space called the cosmological constant, first proposed by Albert Einstein.

Related Web site: www-supernova.lbl.gov

PROTECTING AGAINST AN ATTACK

The first step to protect against an Internet-based attack is to use passwords—everywhere. Enable password-protection in Windows, and in all your applications. Password-protect all your key documents, and make sure you've changed the default password on your network—especially if you're running a Wi-Fi network.

Next, turn off file sharing in Windows. Even if someone breaks into your network, if you've disabled file sharing, they won't be able to access your key files and folders.

You should also make sure that all your software—especially Windows itself—is constantly updated. Those monthly Windows updates are a pain in the butt, but they're necessary to keep all the security holes plugged.

Naturally, you should have firewall software installed on your system. And use the firewall protection provided by your network router.

Finally, you can fend off a lot of attacks by using a generous amount of common sense. Don't let anyone talk you into divulging your passwords or credit card numbers. Don't reply to instant messages and emails asking you to supply private information, no matter how official-sounding the request. Don't accept files from anyone over IRC or instant messaging networks—or open files you receive via email. And, if you work in an office, don't leave your password taped to your computer monitor or sitting out in the open on your desk. In other words, keep your private information private, and be properly aware of all the dangers that exist online.

SOFTWARE OF THE WEEK

Norton Internet Security is an all-in-one solution to the problem of protecting your PC. The package isn't without its problems (it can interfere with a number of other programs, unfortunately), but it offers fairly strong protection against all manner of computer attacks, viruses, and privacy threats. Buy it for $69.95 at www.symantec.com.

January 10, 2005

MONDAY

THIS WEEK'S FOCUS: PRIVACY

ON THIS DAY: RCA INTRODUCES 45 RPM RECORD (1949)

Back in 1948, the Columbia company had perfected the 12-inch, 33 1/3 rpm, long-playing vinyl disc known as the LP. A year later, on January 10, 1949, Columbia's rival, RCA Victor, introduced a competing format, a 7-inch disc that played at 45 revolutions per minute. The 45's greatest success came with the onset of rock and roll, reaching its sales peak in the mid-1960s.

Related Web site: www.recording-history.org

COVERING YOUR TRACKS

Want to keep others from finding out what Web sites you've visited? Here's what you need to do.

First, you want to clear your Internet Explorer history. From the Tools menu, select Internet Options. When the Internet Options dialog box appears, select the General tab, and then click the Clear History button.

While you're on this tab, you should also delete all your Internet temporary files, which are essentially copies of pages and images from the sites you've visited. Click the Delete Files button to do this.

Next, you want to clear all the AutoComplete information you've entered for sites you've visited. From the Internet Options dialog box, select the Content tab, and then click the AutoComplete button. When the AutoComplete Settings dialog box appears, click the Clear Forms button. If you also want to clear any passwords you've entered, click the Clear Passwords button as well.

There are also several software programs you can use to clear your history information. Microsoft's TweakUI has several "paranoia" features you can configure to clear your AutoComplete and history entries every time you log in or log out. Also worth checking out are Free History Eraser (smartprotector.com/eraser/free-history-eraser.htm) and Tracks Eraser (www.acesoft.net).

PC GADGET OF THE WEEK

Keep unauthorized users from accessing your PC, programs, or documents with the Sony Puppy Fingerprint Identity Token. The Sony Puppy looks like a keychain USB device and attaches to any PC's USB port. You program the Puppy with your fingerprint and the appropriate PC and program passwords. Then, instead of entering a password, all you have to do is press your finger to the Puppy's touchpad. Buy it for $169.99 from www.sony.com/puppy/.

January 11, 2005

TUESDAY

THIS WEEK'S FOCUS: PRIVACY

ON THIS DAY: ALGOL LANGUAGE DEVELOPED (1960)

In 1959, John Backus presented a paper on "the proposed international algebraic language." This language evolved into ALGOL (for ALGOrithmic Language), as specified by the ACM-GAMM Committee that convened in Zurich on this day in 1960. ALGOL is one of several high-level languages designed specifically for programming scientific computations; although it never achieved the popularity of FORTRAN or COBOL, it is considered the most important language of its era in terms of its influence on later language development.

Related Web site: www.engin.umd.umich.edu/CIS/course.des/cis400/algol/algol.html

EMAIL ENCRYPTION

Your private email is anything but private. Believe it or not, your email can legally be read by your ISP, the receiving ISP, and any server in the middle. For this reason, encrypting email is even more important than ever before.

Securing your email can take two forms. An email signature can ensure that the message was sent by you and has not been tampered with—although the message can still be read. You can send a signed email to anyone, but they'll need some software to verify it. You can use a program like PGP to sign mail (that's what I do), or get a certificate from somewhere like Thawte.

Encrypting your email scrambles it completely, so only the recipient can read it. To send an encrypted email you'll first need the recipient's public key. Many folks, including me, put our public keys on the various keyservers like keyserver.pgp.com and keys.pgp.net. Your PGP software should be able to search the servers for an appropriate key.

For free PGP software, visit PGP International (www.pgpi.org). You can also get a free version for non-commercial use from PGP Corporation (www.pgp.com). Thawte (www.thawte.com) offers free email certificates suitable for signing or encrypting.

An even easier way to send secure email is through Hushmail (www.hushmail.com), a Web-based email service. Hushmail offers both free and paid encryption services.

DOWNLOAD OF THE WEEK

Anonymyzer Total System Sweeper is a neat little utility that erases cookies and other temporary files from your PC. It uses military-grade removal methods, for total peace of mind. Download it from www.getprivatenow.com—use my name (Leo) to get it for free.

January 12, 2005
WEDNESDAY

THIS WEEK'S FOCUS: PRIVACY

ON THIS DAY: FICTIONAL HAL COMPUTER "BORN" (1997)

On this fictional day in a fictional 1997, the world's most famous fictional computer became operational. As written in Arthur C. Clarke's book 2001: A Space Odyssey, the HAL 9000 supercomputer was "born" on January 12, 1997, at Urbana, Illinois. (Interestingly, the film 2001: A Space Odyssey gives HAL an alternate "birth" date of January 12, 1992.)

Related Web site: www.palantir.net/2001/

ENCRYPTING PC FILES

If you're worried about your company spying on the files stored on your company PC, you're in good company. Not to be paranoid about it, but it's always a good idea to presume that the company is spying on you. They have a legal right—and in many cases an obligation—to do so.

To keep your private files private, I recommend encrypting any data you want to keep others from reading. Know, however, that your bosses can demand the password if it's on a work PC.

If you're using Windows XP and your disk is formatted with NTFS, you can use the system's built-in encryption to keep others—even the system administrator—from reading your files. From within My Computer, right-click the folder you want to encrypt and select Properties from the pop-up menu. When the Properties dialog box appears, click the Advanced button. When the Advanced

Attributes dialog box appears, check the Encrypt Contents to Secure Data option. Click OK to apply the encryption.

If you're not using XP, I recommend MaxCrypt, available free from KinoCode (www.kinocode. com/maxcrypt.htm). It offers easy-to-use encryption that works on any Windows platform.

MAC GADGET OF THE WEEK

When Apple removed the microphone/line-in port from Mac models in the early 2000s, it left a lot of people scratching their heads. The ports are back now, but you still might find use for Griffin Technology's iMic, regardless of whether or not your Mac has a line-in port. That's because the iMic not only connects to your Mac (via USB), it also enables you to connect a standard mini-plug style microphone, for speech or recording. Buy it for $24.95 from www.griffintechnology.com.

THIS WEEK'S FOCUS: PRIVACY

ON THIS DAY: WHAM-O INTRODUCES THE FRISBEE (1957)

The first plastic flying disc was actually manufactured back in 1948, by Fred Morrison, a California carpenter and building inspector. In 1955 Morrison joined the Wham-O company, and on this date in 1957 Wham-O introduced the toy as the Pluto Platter. The name was changed to Frisbee the following year, and over the next 50 years Wham-O sold more than 200 million of them.

Related Web site: www.wham-o.com

EVERYTHING YOU POST EXISTS FOREVER

You might not realize it, but every public posting you make online becomes part of the undying fabric of the Internet. It doesn't matter whether you post to a Usenet newsgroups, Web-based message board, chat room, blog, or whatever. Once you put a message out there, it stays out there—*forever*.

Consider the Usenet archive available at Google Groups (groups.google.com). This archive stores every single newsgroup posting from the start of Usenet to today. If you posted something nasty about your boss five years ago, that posting still exists. If you mentioned a fling you had with a neighbor back in the early '90s, that posting still exists. If you asked a question about a particular illness, or proffered an opinion about a particular make of car, or let slip where you live, that information is still available to a dedicated searcher.

Which means, of course, that the biggest threat to your privacy is *you*.

It also reinforces the general warning that all veteran Internet users should know: Don't post anything in a newsgroup, message board, or chat room that you wouldn't want your future boss or spouse to read. Not to be overly paranoid about it, but you need to watch what you write. Big Brother—and anybody else with access to Google—could be watching.

WEB SITE OF THE WEEK

The Electronic Frontier Foundation (www.eff.org) is a nonprofit group that works to protect everyone's electronic rights. The EFF was particularly vocal in alerting users to the threats posed by the USA PATRIOT act, and continues to speak out in favor of civil liberty and online privacy. They're good folks.

January 14, 2005

FRIDAY

THIS WEEK'S FOCUS: PRIVACY

ON THIS DAY: *THE SIMPSONS* PREMIERES (1990)

Originally conceived as a short segment on the *Tracey Ullman Show*, the cartoon *The Simpsons* premiered with its own prime-time show on this date in 1990, on the Fox network. The brainchild of cartoonist Matt Groening, *The Simpsons* has since become the longest-running comedy in television history. D'oh!

Related Web site: www.thesimpsons.com

PROTECTING YOUR CHILDREN'S PRIVACY

Web sites want information—even from your kids. In fact, children are a great source of information; they're not as guarded as adults are, making them more prone to divulge personal details to unscrupulous Web marketers.

As a parent, you can protect against this sort of child-oriented privacy abuse by closely monitoring your children's online activities. You should also be aware of the various laws in place to protect you and your children from this type of privacy abuse.

For example, the Children's Online Privacy Protection Act (COPPA) requires that parental permission be obtained before a Web site gathers information on children younger than 13. You can read more about COPPA at the Center for Media Education's (CME) KidsPrivacy.org Web site (www.kidsprivacy.org)—which also offers some fine practical advice for protecting children online.

More important, you need to caution your children about providing personal information to any Web site without your explicit permission. You also might want to install blocking software that prevents your children from giving out their name, address, and phone number online, or install content filtering software that restricts the Web sites that your children can visit.

Bottom line: It's likely that if your children are online, they *will* be targeted by people and companies who want them to divulge personal information. It's up to you to train your kids to resist these queries, and preserve their anonymity online.

PORTABLE GADGET OF THE WEEK

The Magellan SporTrak Color is one full-featured handheld GPS device. It features a big color display and includes a base map of North America; you can also upload other maps from your PC. The SporTrak Color is accurate to within three meters, which is pretty darned close, and includes a built-in barometer and three-axis compass. Buy it for $349.99 from www.magellangps.com.

ON THIS DAY: NATIONAL CENTER FOR SUPERCOMPUTER APPLICATIONS OPENS (1986)

On this date in 1986, the National Science Foundation (NSF) established the National Center for Supercomputing Applications (NCSA), at the University of Illinois at Urbana-Champaign (UIUC). (Enough acronyms for you?) The NCSA works with research centers nationwide to build cyberinfrastructure, tools, and applications for grid computing.

Related Web site: www.ncsa.uiuc.edu

CREATING STRONGER PASSWORDS

One of the most popular ways for an unscrupulous person to steal your personal information is to enter your account through the front door—by using your own password. Many identity thieves use special password cracker programs to suss out passwords. These cracker programs operate at computer speed to enter thousands of possible passwords every second. If your password is short and simple, one of these programs can crack it in a matter of seconds.

On the other hand, if your password is long and complex, it might take days to crack—if it can be cracked at all. Which leads to the blatantly obvious observation that the longer and more complex your password is, the harder it will be to crack.

To keep your password private, you need to increase the password's length (8 characters is better than 6—and way better than 4), and use a combination of letters, numbers, and special characters (!@#$%). You should also use a combination of uppercase and lowercase letters, if a particular account lets you use case-sensitive passwords.

Equally important, when creating your password, you should avoid using real words you might find in a typical dictionary. That's because most cracker programs use words from existing dictionaries as possible passwords. Also, don't use easily guessed words, like your middle name or your wife's maiden name or the name of your dog or cat. Better to use nonsense words, or random combinations or letters and numbers—anything that won't be found in a dictionary.

You should also make sure you don't use the same password on multiple sites. (You don't want a cracker to obtain one password and be able to break into multiple accounts.) It also helps if you change your passwords with some regularity, so that any cracked password has a short shelf life.

FACT OF THE WEEK

According to a City & Guilds survey, only one in seven IT specialists rate themselves as "very happy" in their work. That compares with one in three happy hairdressers, plumbers, and chefs, and one in four ecstatic florists. Overall, IT workers came in at number nine in the happiness index; topping the poll of contented occupations are care assistants, while real estate agents rank as the unhappiest professionals of them all.

January 16, 2005

SUNDAY

THIS WEEK'S FOCUS: PRIVACY

ON THIS DAY: SAGE ANNOUNCED (1956)

The Semi-Automatic Ground Environment computer, or SAGE, was an automated control system for collecting, tracking, and intercepting enemy bomber aircraft. SAGE was announced on this day in 1956, went operational in 1958, and was used by NORAD into the 1980s. SAGE was, for all intents and purposes, an air-traffic control system, which explains why the FAA used SAGE systems in its own automated control systems until quite recently.

Related Web site: www.fact-index.com/s/sa/sage_1.html

PREVENTING IDENTITY THEFT

While you can't totally prevent your personal information from being stolen, you can minimize the risk—both online and in the real world. You have to be careful about what you disclose, and to whom.

Here are some tips:

- Never provide personal information to anyone or any organization via email or instant messaging.
- Only enter personal information over the Internet directly at an official Web site, and only if that site is secure.
- Pay close attention to your credit card billing cycles; if you haven't received an expected account statement, immediately contact your credit card company.
- Deposit all your outgoing bill payments in public post office boxes, *not* in your personal mail box.
- Promptly remove mail as soon as it's delivered to your postal mail box—or consider obtaining a drop box at your local U.S. Post Office.

- If you plan on being away from home for an extended period of time, have your mail put on "vacation hold" until you return.
- Shred all charge card receipts, account statements, and voided checks before you take out your trash.
- Don't give out your Social Security number to anyone, unless absolutely necessary.
- Once a year, order a copy of your credit report from one of the major credit reporting agencies; check this report for any unexpected, unauthorized, or incorrect activities.

SOFTWARE OF THE WEEK

Fast-Eraser performs a number of privacy-related tasks. It shreds deleted files, erases your browser's cache and cookie files, blocks unwanted additions to the Favorites folder, and erases Windows' Recent Documents list. It even comes with a "panic button" to instantly clear all traces of your activities and close all open browser windows. Buy it for $49.95 from www.fast-eraser.com.

THIS WEEK'S FOCUS: MACINTOSH

ON THIS DAY: FIRST NUCLEAR SUBMARINE LAUNCHED (1955)

In July 1951, Congress authorized construction of the world's first nuclear-powered submarine. Four years later, on the morning of July 17, 1955, the Nautilus's first commanding officer, Commander Eugene P. Wilkinson, ordered all lines cast off and signaled the memorable and historic message, "Underway on nuclear power"—and the age of the nuclear Navy had begun.

Related Web site: www.ussnautilus.org

THE THREE C'S

You know about the three R's. Now learn about the three C's—the three different kinds of programs that can run under OS X.

Classic applications are older apps designed for OS 9. They can run only under the Classic environment—essentially, a protected OS 9 mode. When a Classic app is running, you'll see the OS 9 menu bar. If a Classic application crashes, it can bring down the entire environment, although OS X will usually continue undamaged. (Microsoft Office 2001 is an example of an OS 9 Classic app.)

Carbon applications are typically OS 9 apps that have been modified to run under OS X. They're not true OS X apps, in that they weren't designed from the ground up to run with OS X. That said, these apps run in OS X native mode and can take advantage of OS X features, such as the Aqua user interface and protected memory. But Carbon is not intended for use in new OS X apps. It's primarily a bridge between the old OS 9 API and OS X.

Cocoa applications are fully native OS X apps. They take advantage of all of OS X's features. Naturally, OS X works best with Cocoa apps.

PC GADGET OF THE WEEK

If you give a lot of PowerPoint presentations, you'll love the Logitech Cordless Presenter. As the name implies, it's a cordless controller with two buttons (back and forward) you can use to switch from slide to slide. It also doubles as a simple two-button optical mouse—and it features a built-in laser pointer. Buy it for $199.95 at www.logitech.com.

January 18, 2005

TUESDAY

THIS WEEK'S FOCUS: MACINTOSH

ON THIS DAY: BRYCE OUTLINES THE HARVARD MARK I (1938)

The modern era of computing commenced with the Harvard Mark I, the first large-scale automatic digital computer. Formerly known as the Automatic Sequence Controlled Calculator (ASCC), the Mark I was an electromechanical machine that executed commands in a step-by-step fashion; instructions were fed into the machine via paper tape or punch cards, or by setting switches. It was on this date in 1938 that co-creator James W. Bryce first outlined the design of the Mark I, based on a concept proposed by Howard Aiken. The computer was finally completed in 1944, and it was kept in operation for more than 15 years.

Related Web site: www-1.ibm.com/ibm/history/exhibits/markI/markI_intro.html

TURN YOUR IPOD INTO AN EMERGENCY RESCUE DISK

If you have a Macintosh and an iPod (a popular combination, to be sure), you can use your iPod as an emergency rescue disk for your Mac—quite useful if you run into major system problems.

You see, in addition to being a first-rate digital music player, your iPod is also a standard FireWire hard drive. You can boot from it just as you can any hard drive, assuming you have the appropriate system software installed.

First, turn on FireWire mounting for the iPod by opening iTunes with the iPod connected to your Mac. Select the iPod in the source window, and then click the little iPod icon in the lower-right corner of the window. Check the Enable Disk Use icon.

Now you can install OS X onto the iPod, as you would on any hard drive. You also might want to copy any file utilities you use to the drive. This makes the iPod a useful recovery disk.

DOWNLOAD OF THE WEEK

NewsMac is an RSS news aggregator that lets you view news headlines and story descriptions from more than 120 different news sites, all in one place. You can even specify keywords to have NewsMac highlight the stories you're most interested in. NewsMac is freeware, available at www.thinkmac.co.uk/newsmac/.

January 19, 2005

WEDNESDAY

THIS WEEK'S FOCUS: MACINTOSH

ON THIS DAY: HOWARD HUGHES SETS TRANSCONTINENTAL AIR RECORD (1937)

On January 18, 1937, aviator/inventor/future bizillionaire Howard Hughes took off from Burbank, California, in his H-1 Winged Bullet. Despite the fact that his oxygen mask failed and he almost blacked out, Hughes arrived in Newark, New Jersey, setting a new cross-country record of just 7 hours, 28 minutes, 25 seconds. The achievement secured him the year's Harmon International Trophy, for the world's most outstanding aviator.

Related Web site: www.howardhughes.com

SAVE TIME WITH THE SERVICES MENU

One of the most powerful—and most overlooked—features of Mac OS X is the Services menu. Not many people use this menu, but I love it.

You see, many programs install items into the Services menu. For example, I downloaded the free OmniDictionary application on my Mac, and the installation added a Look up in OmniDictionary command to the Services menu. All Services-aware applications have these built-in shortcuts—and, luckily, most applications are Services-aware. Here are some of my favorite programs that tap into this menu:

- OmniDictionary (www.omnigroup.com/applications/omnidictionary/) provides definitions on the fly. If you highlight a word in a Service-aware application, then press the Command button and the equals sign simultaneously (Command-=), it will automatically look up a word.
- The free Nisus Thesaurus (www.nisus.com/Thesaurus/) does the same thing for synonyms.

- PGP email encryption (www.pgp.com) installs itself in Services, too, making it easy to sign, encrypt, and decrypt text.
- Highlighting some text and pressing Command-Shift-L searches Google (www.google.com) for the selected word(s).
- The Devon-Technologies (www.devon-technologies.com/products/freeware/freeware.php) Web site is a great source for free Services. Their Easy Find is a search tool for your hard drive; Calc Service will calculate formulas in applications; and Word Service adds text to speech and other handy text-processing commands.

MAC GADGET OF THE WEEK

Apple offers its first-class Cinema Displays in three sizes: 20-inch ($1,299), 22-inch ($1,999), and 30-inch ($3,299). All have a wide-aspect ratio, which makes it easier not only to watch or edit widescreen movies, but also to have multiple applications open and working at the same time. Learn more at www.apple.com.

January 20, 2005

THURSDAY

THIS WEEK'S FOCUS: MACINTOSH

ON THIS DAY: FIRST LIVE TELEVISED INAUGURATION ADDRESS (1953)

President Eisenhower ushered in the age of live media coverage when his initial inauguration address was carried live on coast-to-coast television. The oath of office was administered by Chief Justice Frederick Vinson on two Bibles—the one used by George Washington at the first inauguration, and the one General Eisenhower received from his mother upon his graduation from the Military Academy at West Point.

Related Web site: www.bartleby.com/124/pres54.html

TROUBLESHOOTING YOUR MAC

Whenever you're having a problem with your Macintosh, here are three troubleshooting steps you can follow to track down the cause of the problem. (And if they don't work, a system re-install may be indicated—sorry.)

1. Repair permissions. Open Applications > Utilities > Disk Utility, click on your startup drive, and then click on Verify Disk Permissions.
2. Delete the preferences for the malfunctioning program. Check both the Home > Library > Preferences and the Library > Preferences folders.
3. Finally, test whether the problem is local to the current user or is systemwide, by creating a new user. (This is a good idea to do, anyway.) If things work as the new user, you know the problem is not specific to the program, but is a problem with your particular setup.

WEB SITE OF THE WEEK

MacFixit (www.macfixit.com) is an incredibly well-informed and well-connected Mac troubleshooting blog. The site also includes a large archive of reports and tutorials and is one of my first stops for getting the latest poop on Mac-related issues.

January 21, 2005

FRIDAY

THIS WEEK'S FOCUS: MACINTOSH

ON THIS DAY: FIRST COMMERCIAL SUPERSONIC FLIGHT (1976)

On January 21, 1976, British Airways ushered in the era of supersonic air travel with the first commercial flight of the Concorde, from London to Bahrain. Unfortunately for jet-setters everywhere, the age of supersonic flight came to an end just 27 years later, on October 24, 2003, when the Concorde made its last commercial flight, from New York to London.

Related Web site: www.concordesst.com

REPLACE THE OS X FINDER

The OS X Finder is a work of art, balancing power with ease of use. But if you're an advanced user, you might be willing to sacrifice some of the Finder's elegance for more power.

A versatile alternative to the Finder is Cocoatech's Path Finder (www.cocoatech.com). This Finder replacement upgrades several key features, including

- Faster results for file searches
- A built-in FTP client (this feature alone justifies the price for me)
- The ability to burn discs and create disc images
- Screen-capture capabilities
- Integrated command-line terminal
- Advanced file info and previews
- An innovative Drop Stack feature that simplifies drag-and-drop operations

- A utility that lists all running processes and applications

Path Finder is not free. You get a free 21-day trial period, but if you want to keep it you'll need to pay $34. I did.

PORTABLE GADGET OF THE WEEK

The iSun Solar Charger is a personal solar panel that can supply power to any small electronic device—PDAs, portable audio players, cell phones, you name it. It's a great accessory when you run out of juice too far away from the nearest power outlet. The only drawback, of course, is that the sun needs to be out; the iSun won't work at night and delivers considerably less power than normal on cloudy days. Buy it for $79.95 at www.icpsolar.com.

January 22, 2005

SATURDAY

THIS WEEK'S FOCUS: MACINTOSH

ON THIS DAY: APPLE COMPUTER LAUNCHES THE MACINTOSH (1984)

Twenty-one years ago today Apple announced what would be one of the world's most popular personal computers, the Macintosh. The Mac received widespread exposure thanks to Apple's legendary commercial dlf-tiuring hame of the 1984 Super Bowl; that commercial, directed by Ridley Scott and designed as a tongue-in-cheek reference to George Orwell's novel, *1984*, cost $1.6 million to produce, and ran only once—although you can view it today on the Web, at www.apple.com/hardware/ads/1984/.

Related Web site: library.stanford.edu/mac/

COPYING ITUNES MUSIC TO A NEW MAC

What do you do with all your accumulated (and paid for) digital music files when you buy a new Mac? If you're using iTunes, you can use FireWire to transfer your digital files from one Mac to another.

Start by connecting the two machines with a FireWire cable. Now reboot the old machine, while holding down the T key. This Mac will now boot into Target Disk Mode, and its hard drive will show up on the new machine as an external FireWire drive.

Now you can open iTunes on the new Mac and open the preferences. Click the Advanced tab and make sure the Copy Files to iTunes Music Folder option is checked. Close preferences, select Add

to Library from the File menu, and then navigate to the old machine's iTunes library folder. Click OK, and let the copying begin.

It's a little complicated, but it's better than losing all your old tunes—or paying for them again from the iTunes Music Store!

FACT OF THE WEEK

The Gartner Group confirms what many of us already suspected: The Macintosh is a more efficient business machine. According to Gartner, a business Mac user gets $24,000 more work done per year, and his computer is down 14% less. Bottom line? The Mac costs less to support than any other platform.

24

THIS WEEK'S FOCUS: **MACINTOSH**

ON THIS DAY: INTEGRATED CIRCUIT CONCEIVED (1959)

In January 1959, Robert Noyce was working at Fairchild Semiconductor, then a small startup company, when he realized that an entire circuit could be placed on a single chip. That spring, Fairchild began a push to build what they called "unitary circuits;" in 1961, Noyce received the first patent for what was finally called the integrated circuit.

Related Web site: www.ideafinder.com/history/inventors/noyce.htm

FAVORITE FREE MAC OS X UTILITIES

Here are five of my favorite free Macintosh utilities. Leo commands you to download them now!

- Launchbar (www.obdev.at/products/launchbar/)— Run, do not walk, to download this must-have launcher for the Mac. Access any file within a couple of keystrokes. This is a shareware program, but you can use it free for up to seven different items, which is enough for most people.

- Konfabulator (www.konfabulator.com)—This is a very cool widget factory that makes it possible for anyone to write their own useful little desktop utilities. It's shareware, but it works fine even if you don't pay the measley $25.

- Locator (www.sebastian-krauss.de/software/)— Find files fast with Locator. It offers regular expression searches, is able to index removable media like CDs, and a lot more. Did I mention it's free?

- Weatherpop (glu.com)—Put the weather in your toolbar (where it belongs). It's free, but you'll end up paying $8 for the advanced features.

- Fink (fink.sourceforge.net)—A whole world of free UNIX software awaits you with Fink. Download and install the command-line version, or use the free GUI Fink Commander. It's the easiest way to find and install UNIX programs on OS X.

SOFTWARE OF THE WEEK

LemkeSoft's   Mac-only GraphicConverter is most capable at something that seems implicit in its name—converting image files between various computer file formats (175 in all). Beyond importing and exporting, GraphicConverter also lets you change the color depth, resolution, size, cropping, rotation and many filter settings for your images. Buy it for $30 at www.lemkesoft.com.

THIS WEEK'S FOCUS: DIGITAL **PHOTOGRAPHY**

ON THIS DAY: IBM DEDICATES THE SSEC (1948)

One of the most visible early computers, IBM's Selective Sequence Electronic Calculator (SSEC), was installed on this date at the IBM Headquarters building in Manhattan, where it occupied the periphery of a room 60 feet long and 30 feet wide. The SSEC was visible to pedestrians on the sidewalk, and inspired a generation of cartoonists to portray the computer as a series of wall-sized panels covered with lights, meters, dials, switches, and spinning rolls of tape.

Related Web site: www.columbia.edu/acis/history/ssec.html

DIGITAL SLR CAMERAS

A digital single-lens reflex (SLR) camera is a step or two above your typical digital camera. D-SLRs look, feel, and work like good 35mm film cameras, thanks to a reflex mirror apparatus that lets you view through the lens itself. You also get the ability to use interchangeable lenses and larger image sensors, often as big as 35mm film, which provide better results in low-light conditions. In addition, these cameras are usually designed by the companies' 35mm camera divisions (instead of their consumer electronics divisions) and provide all the operating flexibility you need to make great photos, fast.

My favorite D-SLR is my favorite digital camera, period—the Nikon D70. With the D70, you get high-end D-SLR performance at a relatively affordable price, all things considered. This camera is fast (operation is instant-on, and you can shoot up to three frames per second), rugged (black metal case), and versatile. You can shoot in a variety of preprogrammed modes, as well as aperture priority, shutter priority, or manual mode; you can also override the auto focus just by touching the manual focus ring on the lens.

Speaking of versatility, this camera gives you three types of auto focus: single area AF, dynamic area AF, and closest subject priority dynamic area AF. It shoots in either JPEG or RAW (NEF) format, with ISO settings of 200–1600. Buy a big CompactFlash card (I or II) to hold all those big images!

Image-wise, the D70's performance is exemplary. Images are sharp and clean, with a remarkable depth of field. (Resolution is 6.1 megapixels.) Of course, some of that depends on which lens you use, and the D70 works with any Nikkor lens—even those you use with your 35mm camera. You can buy the D70 body-only or in a package with an 18–70mm zoom lens; I recommend the package, which is surprisingly affordable.

PC GADGET OF THE WEEK

Logitech's io Personal Digital Pen combines a normal ballpoint pen with an optical sensor and a small amount of computer memory. Anything you write is automatically stored digitally inside the pen; when you place the pen back in its cradle, it gets transferred to your PC. Included software helps you organize your notes and integrate with Microsoft Outlook and Lotus Notes. Buy it for $199.95 at www.logitech.com.

January 25, 2005

TUESDAY

THIS WEEK'S FOCUS: Digital Photography

ON THIS DAY: TRANSCONTINENTAL TELEPHONE SERVICE INAUGURATED (1915)

The first New York to San Francisco telephone call was made on this date in 1915. Four locations participated in that first call, including Alexander Graham Bell in New York and his one-time assistant Thomas Watson in San Francisco. At one point during the call, someone asked Professor Bell if he would repeat the first words he ever said over the telephone. Bell obliged, picking up the phone and repeating "Mr. Watson, come here, I want you"—to which Watson, in San Francisco, replied, "It would take me a week now."

Related Web site: www.att.com/history/

ORGANIZING YOUR PHOTOS

Get a digital camera and before long you have hundreds—if not thousands—of digital photos on you hands. How do you keep track of what's what, and what's where?

To organize the photos on your hard drive, you can just stick everything into Windows' My Pictures folder, or you can use a separate photo organizer program. These programs let you file your photos by a variety of criteria, rename and resize your files, and sometimes do a little bit of basic editing, besides. I recommend Adobe Photoshop Album (www.adobe.com)—try the free starter edition—or Lifescape's Picasa (www.picasa.com), which is freeware, period.

Of course, if you have a Mac, you have a built-in photo organizer, in the form of iPhoto. It's hard to beat!

However you decide to store your photos, you'll need lots of space to do so. I recommend investing in a second external hard disk, 100GB or larger, just for digital media storage. At today's prices, this won't cost more than a couple hundred bucks, and it's worth that much to have all your digital photos stored in one place. Plus, with an external drive, you can move your photos from one computer to another with relative ease.

To share photos with your friends, you can upload your photos to an online photo service. I like Ofoto (www.ofoto.com) and Shutterfly (www.shutterfly.com), both of which offer free software, too.

DOWNLOAD OF THE WEEK

I mentioned it above, and I'll recommend it again here. Picasa is essentially iPhoto for Windows, and one of my all-time favorite apps. It used to cost real money, but Google recently bought Picasa and is giving the application away for free now. Get it at www.picasa.com.

January 26, 2005

WEDNESDAY

THIS WEEK'S FOCUS: DIGITAL PHOTOGRAPHY

ON THIS DAY: LOTUS 1-2-3 RELEASED (1983)

Twenty-two years ago today, Lotus Development Corporation (now part of IBM) launched its first product, the 1-2-3 spreadsheet package. Lotus sold 60,000 copies in the first month of the release, and 1-2-3 went on to sell tens of millions of copies, driving the early success of the IBM PC platform and paving the way for several other spreadsheet applications, including its eventual successor and reigning spreadsheet champ, Microsoft Excel.

Related Web site: www.ibm.com/software/lotus/

DIGITAL PHOTOS WITHOUT A COMPUTER

I've had numerous listeners of my radio call-in show ask me to recommend simple digital cameras and photo printers for their computer-phobic friends and family. What they want, specifically, is a camera/printer combination that you don't need a computer to use. Fortunately, there are several good products that fit the bill.

For ease-of-use, I happen to like Kodak cameras (www.kodak.com). Their EasyShare cameras offer point-and-click convenience, and fit into the accompanying EasyShare Printer Dock that lets you create 4" × 6" borderless prints at the press of a button. Nothing could be easier.

Also good is the Canon Powershot S400 and matching Canon i560 printer (www.canonusa.com). Like the Kodak EasyShare camera, the camera and printer work together so you don't need a computer to create prints.

Of course, you don't have to limit yourself to matching products like these. There are numerous photo printers that will print directly from your camera's memory card. You can also look for a camera with built-in Direct Print capability. This is a new industry standard that lets you connect a compatible camera directly to a photo printer, typically via USB. There is no need at all for a computer. Most major camera companies are releasing Direct Print cameras.

MAC GADGET OF THE WEEK

The Apple Wireless Keyboard is very sexy. It uses Bluetooth technology to connect to your Mac, which lets you do your typing up to 30 feet away from your Mac. It takes up a minimum of space for a keyboard that includes function keys across the top, as well as keys for controlling volume and ejecting CDs and other removable media. Buy it for $69 at www.apple.com.

THURSDAY

THIS WEEK'S FOCUS: DIGITAL PHOTOGRAPHY

ON THIS DAY: APOLLO 1 DISASTER (1967)

On January 27, 1967, on launch pad 34, astronauts Edward White, Virgil (Gus) Grissom, and Roger Chaffee died in a fire during a preflight test of the Apollo 1 space capsule. Five and a half hours after they had entered the command module, after a series of tests and drills (and numerous problems), Chaffee said into the intercom, "Fire, I smell fire." Rescue efforts were unsuccessful, and just moments after that first communication, all three astronauts were dead from smoke inhalation. It was the space program's first fatal accident.

Related Web site: spaceflight.nasa.gov/history/apollo/

OFFLOADING DIGITAL PICTURE FILES

You're traveling with your digital camera, and after a busy day of shooting you've completely filled up your camera's memory card. You didn't bring your PC with you, so there's no way to free up your card's memory to shoot more pictures. Or is there?

When you fill up your flash card—and don't have a PC handy—you have a few options. First option, of course, is to buy a second memory card. It's always good to have a spare, in any case, and the bigger the better.

Another option is to invest in a photo wallet—essentially a portable hard drive with a Compact Flash interface. Insert your memory card, offload the photos to the portable hard disk, and you're ready to shoot some more. A good choice for this purpose is Archos' Gmini (www.archos.com), which offers 20GB of storage. The Gmini also functions as

an audio recorder and MP3 player, and costs about $300.

Of course, if you already have a hard-drive–based digital music player you might be able to use it as a photo wallet. For example, Belkin (www.belkin.com) offers a $100 media reader that works with the newer iPods. Connect the media reader to your iPod, insert your camera's memory card, and transfer your photos. (Belkin also offers a slightly lower-priced Digital Camera Link that lets you transfer photos from your camera to your iPod via USB.)

WEB SITE OF THE WEEK

Can't decide which digital camera to buy? Then check out the comprehensive reviews and user forums at Digital Photography Review (www.dpreview.com). This is *the* site for serious digital photographers on the Web.

January 28, 2005

FRIDAY

THIS WEEK'S FOCUS: DIGITAL PHOTOGRAPHY

ON THIS DAY: CHALLENGER SPACE SHUTTLE EXPLOSION (1986)

Historically, this is not a good week for the space program. On this date in 1986, almost 20 years to the date after the Apollo 1 disaster, the space shuttle Challenger exploded, just 73 seconds after launch. The explosion killed the entire crew, including the first teacher to fly into space, Christa McAuliffe. The cause of the explosion was found to be the failure of an "O-ring" seal in one of the shuttle's solid-fuel rockets; the faulty design of the seal, coupled with unusually cold weather, resulted in a leak of hot gases, which then burned through the external fuel tank.

Related Web site: www.life.com/Life/space/challenger.html

SHOOTING RAW

To get the sharpest pictures of fine details, take your digital photos in RAW format, if your camera supports it. A RAW file is comparable to the raw image contained on a piece of undeveloped film; it holds exactly what the camera's imaging chip recorded. The benefit to using a RAW file is that you can extract the maximum possible image quality from your picture, either now or when you edit it in the future.

RAW files truly are "raw." Unlike a JPG- or TIFF-format, which the camera essentially "finishes" before saving, a RAW-format picture is left unfinished: The camera saves the image with no compression, manipulation, or other artifacts. There's no contrast adjustment, no color adjustment, no white balance—no nothing. That means you have the untouched original file to work with in your photo editing program—you don't have to compensate for any previous changes.

Even better, the RAW file is a 12-bit image. This means that the file has 2,048 brightness levels to work with, compared to the 256 brightness levels in an 8-bit JPG image. This is important when editing an image, particularly if you're trying to open up shadows or alter brightness in any significant way.

Of course, 12-bit files take up a lot of memory space, and some users complain that RAW files are just too large. That may be true, especially if you're shooting low-resolution pictures for Web use. But for large, high-quality prints, dealing with large RAW files is a necessary evil. Besides, with memory card, hard disk and DVD-R disks at all-time low prices, the cost for storage is relatively small. Splurge on a bigger memory card, and shoot all your important photos in RAW format.

You should be able to import RAW-format images into your photo editing program, do the editing or manipulation you need, and then save to a format with wider compatibility, such as JPG or TIFF. Both Photoshop CS and Photoshop Elements have built-in RAW processors, so importing is relatively easy.

PORTABLE GADGET OF THE WEEK

The JB1 007 Digital Spy Camera is the kind of gadget you'd expect Agent 007 to carry. With the JB1, you get a digital camera built in to a cigarette lighter case—small enough to fit in any pocket and inconspicuous enough not to draw attention if Blofeld's around. Just flip and click, as if you were playing with the lighter. No one will know you just took a picture. Buy it for $99.99 from www.jbcamera.com.

THIS WEEK'S FOCUS: DIGITAL PHOTOGRAPHY

ON THIS DAY: "THE RAVEN" PUBLISHED (1845)

On this date in 1845, Edgar Allen Poe's poem "The Raven" was published in the *New York Evening Mirror*, of which Poe is assistant editor. In November of the same year, this and other poems were collected in book format, in *The Raven and Other Poems*.

Related Web site: www.poemuseum.org

DIGITAL CAMERA ACCESSORIES

To get the most use out of your digital camera, it pays to fill up your camera bag with a variety of useful accessories. This is maybe less true if you have a low-price point-and-shoot camera, but accessorizing is definitely a good idea if you've spent north of five bills for a more fully featured model.

How will camera accessories help you take better pictures? Here are some examples:

- *Lens filters* reduce glare and improve color rendition in all your photos; see www.tiffen.com for a good variety.

- An *external flash kit* provides better fill lighting for both indoor and outdoor shots; I like the kits offered by Metz (www.metz.de).

- A *lighting kit* helps you shoot more detailed portraits and indoor still-life photos; Smith Victor's KT500 (www.smithvictor.com) is my personal favorite.

- A solid *tripod* holds your camera steady and helps eliminate blurry shots, especially when you're shooting in low light; VidPro (www.vidprousa.com) makes some really good models.

- An *LCD hood* makes it easier to view your camera's monitor, especially in bright sunlight; check out the selection at www.hoodmanusa.com.

- A *cleaning kit* helps you keep your camera free of dust and dirt and extend its working life; Norezza (www.norazza.com) makes kits for most popular digital cameras.

FACT OF THE WEEK

Statistics analyzed by the Swedish business magazine *Veckans Affarer* suggest that the founder of Ikea is now richer than Microsoft's Bill Gates, long recognized as the world's richest man. The most recent *Forbes* magazine put Gates' worth at $46.6 billion, while Ingvar Kamprad's wealth is estimated at $52.5 billion. Kamprad, a reclusive 77-year-old known for his frugal habits, lives in Switzerland and no longer takes part in the daily running of the privately owned company.

January 30, 2005

SUNDAY

THIS WEEK'S FOCUS: DIGITAL PHOTOGRAPHY

ON THIS DAY: BEATLES PERFORM LAST PUBLIC CONCERT (1969)

As documented in the film *Let It Be*, the Beatles performed together in public for the last time today in 1969, on the roof the Apple Building in London. Along with guest musician Billy Preston, the lads performed 11 songs: three versions of "Get Back"; two each of "Don't Let Me Down" and "I've Got A Feeling"; single renditions of "The One After 909," "Dig A Pony," and "God Save the Queen"; and a few seconds of "Danny Boy." By the beginning of the third performance of "Get Back," the police had arrived and the performance was over.

Related Web site: www.beatles.com

UNDERWATER CAMERAS

If you like to snorkel or scuba dive, you know you can't take your standard-issue digital camera underwater with you; it'll fritz out at the first good dunk. But some cameras are designed especially for underwater use and hold up under all sorts of wet conditions. These are the cameras you need when you want to shoot in the water.

For basic snorkeling, I recommend Sony's DSC-U60 ($249.95). This rugged, waterproof camera is designed for what Sony calls the "sports utility lifestyle." It can take pictures up to 5 feet underwater, and the unique vertical design is perfect for one-handed operation. It features 2-megapixel resolution and has a 1" LCD monitor. There's even an MPEG video mode (no audio) for taking short movies while you're underwater. Learn more at www.sonystyle.com.

For more serious underwater photography, you need something a little more substantial. Designed for scuba-diving photographers, SeaLife's ReefMaster ($399.95) is depth-tested up to 200 feet—it'll withstand the pressure of the ocean depths. The ReefMaster has a rubber-armored body with soft grips and pop-up manual viewfinder, as well as a 1.6" LCD color monitor. The one-button operation makes it easy to use when you're diving, and you'll appreciate the high-quality 3.3-megapixel pictures. Learn more at www.sealife-cameras.com.

You can also buy waterproof housings for your existing digital camera. There's a good selection at UnderwaterPhotography.com—along with tons of other information, tutorials, and underwater pictures from other users.

SOFTWARE OF THE WEEK

Adobe makes the best and most popular photo editing software out there. For serious digital photographers, the standard is Photoshop CS, a full-featured program that sells for a hefty $649. If you're on a budget—or want something a little simpler to use—the $99 Photoshop Elements will probably do everything you need. Get them both from www.adobe.com.

THIS WEEK'S FOCUS: DIGITAL VIDEO

ON THIS DAY: FIRST U.S. SATELLITE LAUNCHED (1958)

The first U.S. satellite, Explorer I, was launched on this day in 1958. The spacecraft was built within the fourth stage section of a Jupiter C rocket, and was designed to provide preliminary information on the environment and conditions in space outside the Earth's atmosphere. It circled the Earth more than 58,000 times before reentering the Earth's atmosphere over the South Pacific March 31, 1970, and resulted in the discovery of the Van Allen radiation belts.

Related Web site: msl.jpl.nasa.gov/Programs/explorer.html

DIGITAL CAMCORDER FORMATS

The key to successful digital moviemaking—whether you're making independent films or movies of your kids' birthday parties—is to start with a digital camcorder. Fortunately, now that analog VHS camcorders have been relegated to the garbage bin (or to eBay—kind of the same thing), virtually every camcorder sold today records in a digital format. But which format is the right one for you? Here's a brief comparison of the currently available formats:

- **MiniDV**—This is the most popular and most common digital camcorder format. It records broadcast-quality video (500+ lines of resolution) on small, low-priced cassettes, about 1/12 the size of a standard VHS tape.

- **MicroMV**—This is a newer and smaller digital format, somewhat proprietary to Sony camcorders. MicroMV tapes are 70% smaller than MiniDV tapes and record in the MPEG-2 format rather than in the more universal DV format. As a result, MicroMV tapes are incompatible with most video editing software.

- **DVD**—DVD camcorders don't use tape at all; they record directly to DVDs, in either DVD-RAM or DVD-R/RW format. You can get up to 120 minutes on a blank DVD.

- **Digital8**—This is an older, and generally lower-priced, digital format. For compatibility with older analog recorders, Digital8 camcorders can view 8mm or Hi-8 tapes.

Most digital camcorders today are in the MiniDV format, although some low-priced Digital8 models are still floating around. Look for a model that feels good in your hand, offers a wide zoom range, and delivers a good picture under all lighting conditions.

PC GADGET OF THE WEEK

The Canopus ADVC300 is a high-end, high-quality video capture/conversion unit. Its bidirectional operation easily converts analog videotapes to DV and back in one simple step. What's neat about the ADVC300 is how it filters and stabilizes poor analog source video prior to digital conversion. You can connect it to your computer via FireWire, or use it sans-PC in standalone mode. Buy it for $599 from www.canopus.us.

MORE JANUARY FACTS

January 1

1735 Paul Revere is born

1962 The Beatles auditioned for Decca records, only to be rejected because the company felt "groups of guitars are on the way out"

1942 United Nations is created

1919 Edsel Ford succeeds his father, Henry Ford, as president of the Ford Motor Company

January 3

1952 Dragnet debuts

January 4

1974 President Nixon refuses to hand over Watergate tapes

1954 Elvis Presley records his first demos: "Casual Love Affair" and "I'll Never Stand in Your Way"

January 5

1959 Buddy Holly's last record, "It Doesn't Matter Anymore," is released

January 6

2001 Congress certifies George W. Bush winner of 2000 elections over Democrat Al Gore

January 7

1927 Transatlantic phone service begins

1999 President Bill Clinton impeachment trial begins

1985 General Motors creates Saturn

January 8

1642 Astronomer Galileo dies in Italy

1935 Elvis Presley is born

January 10

1946 First meeting of the United Nations takes place

January 12

1876 Jack London, author of *Call of the Wild*, is born

January 13

1807 Napoleon Bonaparte Buford is born

1910 Lee De Forest makes the first radio broadcast from the Metropolitan Opera

1929 Wyatt Earp dies in Los Angeles

January 14

1955 First rock-and-roll dance concert at St. Nicholas Arena in New York (featuring the Drifters, Fats Domino, and Joe Turner) is held

1952 *The Today Show* debuts

January 15

1929 Martin Luther King Jr. is born

1974 *Happy Days* premieres

1981 *Hill Street Blues* debuts

January 17

1949 TV's first sitcom, *The Goldbergs*, debuts

January 20

1961 John F. Kennedy is inaugurated

1945 Franklin D. Roosevelt is inaugurated to fourth term

1981 Iran hostage crisis ends after 444 days

January 21

1959 Carl Switzer, better known as Alfalfa from *Our Gang*, is shot and killed in barroom brawl

1976 First Concorde flights leave simultaneously from London and Paris

January 22

1968 Rowan and Martin's *Laugh-In* premieres

1973 U.S. Supreme Court decriminalizes abortion in its Roe v. Wade decision, one of the most hotly debated decisions in U.S. court history

January 23

Roots miniseries premieres on ABC, becoming the most watched program in American history

January 24

1965 Winston Churchill dies

1927 First Alfred Hitchcock film, *The Pleasure Garden,* opens

January 25

1971 Cult leader Charles Manson and others are convicted on "Helter Skelter" murders

January 26

1962 U.S. launches Ranger 3 to the moon, but the probe missed its target by about 22,000 miles.

1976 *Dukes of Hazzard* debuts

1942 United Nations is created

January 27

1967 Apollo 1 fire kills three U.S. astronauts

1976 *Laverne and Shirley* premieres

January 28

1956 Elvis Presley makes first TV performance on Stage Show, singing "Heartbreak Hotel"

1978 *Fantasy Island* premieres

January 31

1958 First U.S. satellite is launched

1971 Apollo 14 departs for the moon, eventually landing there on February 5

1950 President Harry S. Truman announces the development of the H-bomb

February 2005

February 2005

SUNDAY	MONDAY	TUESDAY	WEDNESDAY	THURSDAY	FRIDAY	SATURDAY
		1 1923 First leaded gasoline goes on sale in Dayton, OH	**2** Groundhog Day 1947 First Polaroid camera is demonstrated	**3** 1966 Soviet Union's Lunik 9 is first manmade object to land safely on Moon	**4** 1941 Teflon is patented by Roy Plunkett	**5** 1952 First Don't Walk signs are installed in New York City
6 Super Bowl Sunday— Alltel Stadium, Jacksonville, FL	**7** 1804 John Deere is born	**8** 1924 First coast-to-coast radio broad-cast is made	**9** 1965 U.S. sends first combat troops to South Vietnam	**10** 1961 The Styrofoam cooler is invented	**11** 1847 Thomas Edison is born	**12** 1809 Charles Darwin is born
13 1923 Chuck Yeager, first pilot to break the sound barrier, is born	**14** Valentine's Day 1978 The first microprocessor is patented by Texas Instruments	**15** 1903 The first teddy bear is intro-duced to shoppers in Brooklyn, NY	**16** 1937 Nylon is patented	**17** President's Day 1817 The first street is lighted with gas lights in Boston, MA	**18** 1930 Pluto is discovered	**19** 1473 Nicholas Copernicus is born
20 1962 The first U.S. astronaut (John Glenn) orbits Earth	**21** 1953 DNA structure is discovered	**22** 1732 George Washington is born	**23** 1965 Michael Dell is born	**24** 1955 Steve Jobs is born	**25** 1928 The first television license is issued	**26** 1993 World Trade Center is bombed
27 1900 Aspirin is patented in the U.S. by Felix Hoffman	**28** 1993 The ATF raids the Branch Davidian com-pound in Waco, TX					

February 1, 2005

TUESDAY

THIS WEEK'S FOCUS: DIGITAL VIDEO

ON THIS DAY: SPACE SHUTTLE COLUMBIA DISASTER (2003)

The entire seven-member crew of the shuttle Columbia was killed on February 1, 2003, when the craft disintegrated during reentry into the Earth's atmosphere. Contact was lost while the shuttle was flying at about 38 miles above north-central Texas, at more than 12,500 miles per hour. A seal on the shuttle's left wing was struck by foam during liftoff and fell off the next day, creating a gap that let hot gas enter the ship during reentry, causing the fatal accident.

Related Web site: www.nasa.gov/columbia/home/

CONFIGURING YOUR SYSTEM FOR VIDEO EDITING

Preparing your PC for video editing is fairly simple. All you have to do is connect your camcorder or VCR to your PC system unit. How you do this depends on what type of camcorder or VCR you have.

If you have an older VHS, VHS-C, SVHS, 8mm, or Hi8 recorder, you'll need to buy and install an analog-to-digital video capture card in your PC. You'll plug your recorder in to the jacks in this card (typically using standard RCA connectors), and it will convert the analog signals from your recorder into the digital audio and video your computer understands.

If you have one of the latest digital video (DV) recorders in the Digital8 or MiniDV formats, you don't need a video capture card. What you do need is an IE1394 FireWire interface, which is included with most new PCs and all new Macs. This type of connection is fast enough to handle the huge stream of digital data pouring from your DV recorder into your PC. (Using any other type of connection, including USB 2.0, is not only slower but might result in some degree of frame loss.)

Of course, for the best results you should strive for a completely digital chain. Start with digital video shot on Digital8 or MiniDV, edit the video digitally with Windows Movie Maker or a similar software program, and then output the completed movie to a DVD or video CD in WMV format.

DOWNLOAD OF THE WEEK

DivX is an increasingly popular digital video format that offers high-quality picture and sound with extremely efficient compression. Download the DivX codec (for playback) for free; download the Dr. DivX application ($49.99) to create your own DivX-format videos. Find them both at www.divx.com.

February 2, 2005

WEDNESDAY

THIS WEEK'S FOCUS: DIGITAL VIDEO

ON THIS DAY: *STAR TREK'S* DATA BORN (2338)

Well, actually, that was the date he was supposedly activated. (Androids aren't really born.) According to *Star Trek* lore, Data was created by Dr. Noonien Soong and Dr. Juliana O'Donnell Soong Tainer on this date in 2338. Data was the fifth and next-to-last model created; he was later discovered by members of a U.S.S. Tripoli away team, became the first android to attend Star Fleet Academy, and served as operations officer on the U.S.S. Enterprise.

Related Web site: www.startrek.com

PREPARING YOUR HARD DISK FOR DIGITAL VIDEO

Digital video files take up a lot of hard disk space. If you plan on doing a lot of video editing, you'll want to have a large—100GB or bigger—hard drive in your computer. Even better, install an external drive dedicated exclusively to storing your video files, ideally connected via FireWire. The bigger and faster, the better.

If you use the same drive for digital videos and your other files, you probably want to create a separate partition on that disk for your video files. The reason this is a good idea is because disk fragmentation can cause frame dropping when you're capturing video. Keeping the video on a separate partition reduces fragmentation.

To perform the partitioning, you need a non-destructive partitioning program. I recommend Norton PartitionMagic, from Symantec. You can order or download it for $69.95 from www.symantec.com.

It's also a good idea to run Windows Disk Defragmenter utility before trying to capture any video. Select Start > All Programs > Accessories > System Tools > Disk Defragmenter, and then click the Disk Defragment button. And don't be in a hurry—if you have a big hard disk, this can take a few hours.

MAC GADGET OF THE WEEK

The point of the Lacie Big Disk Extreme is pretty straightforward—it's designed to be big and it's designed to be fast, which makes it great for storing digital video files. For the latest Macs, the drive supports FireWire 800, the newer FireWire standard that can move data from your Mac to the drive at twice the old throughput. The 320GB model costs $369, the 400GB model costs $449, and the humongous 500GB model runs $549. Buy them at www.lacie.com.

THIS WEEK'S FOCUS: DIGITAL VIDEO

ON THIS DAY: THE MUSIC DIED (1959)

On a cold winter's night in 1959 a small private plane took off from Clear Lake, Iowa bound for Fargo, N.D—but it never made its destination. When that plane crashed, it claimed the lives of Buddy Holly, Ritchie Valens, and J.P. "Big Bopper" Richardson—three of the rock and roll era's most popular and influential musicians. As Don McLean wrote in his song "American Pie," it was "the day the music died."

Related Web site: www.fiftiesweb.com/crash.htm

USING WINDOWS MOVIE MAKER

If you want to do basic video editing and don't want to invest a bundle in software, you're in luck. Microsoft bundles the Windows Movie Maker (WMM) program for free with Windows XP, and it does a decent job at most editing tasks.

First, make sure you have the latest version (2.0) of WMM installed; earlier versions weren't nearly as full-featured. You can upgrade for free at www.microsoft.com/windowsxp/moviemaker/.

Launch the program by selecting Start > All Programs > Windows Movie Maker. For most WMM projects, your main source material will be your original videotape(s). You use WMM to record the tape in real time to your hard disk as you play it back on your VCR or camcorder. You can also import existing video files or digital photographs.

The program works by dividing your home movie into scene segments it calls *clips*. You can then rearrange and delete specific clips to edit the flow of your movie. You assemble all your clips in the Storyboard area at the bottom of the Movie Maker window; just drag the clips you want down into the Storyboard. You can insert clips in any order, and more than once if you want to. After the clips are in the Storyboard, you can drag them around in a different order to edit the flow of your movie.

WMM also lets you add some neat bells and whistles to your video movies. You can add titles and credits, transitions between clips, special effects (sepia tone, slow motion, and so on), background music, and narration. Just select the option you want from the Tools menu, then drag and drop the element onto the Storyboard. When you're done, select File > Save Movie to save your project as a WMV-format file.

WEB SITE OF THE WEEK

If you're in the market for a new digital camcorder, check out the reviews, news, and forums at Camcorderinfo.com (www.camcorderinfo.com). This is a site for digital video buffs, quite informative.

February 4, 2005

FRIDAY

THIS WEEK'S FOCUS: DIGITAL VIDEO

ON THIS DAY: BILL GATES GETS A PIE IN THE FACE (1998)

On this date in 1998, Bill Gates was visiting European Union officials in Brussels—and got hit in the face with a cream pie. The man behind the pie, Noël Godin, has made it a sport to throw cream cakes in celebrities' faces. His exploits have become so renowned that a French word has been coined to describe the act of being creamed: *entarter*.

Related Web site: www.bitstorm.org/gates/

CHOOSING A SEMI-PRO CAMCORDER

The very best consumer camcorders deliver digital pictures good enough for television or film use. These pro-level camcorders look, feel, and perform just like the type of camcorder you see TV news crews or independent filmmakers lugging around. More important, they come with a bevy of automatic recording modes and manual adjustments that let you custom-tailor your movies to a variety of shooting styles and situations. Picture quality is second to none, of course, especially under difficult lighting conditions.

I particularly like Sony's DCR-VX2100, which looks like a professional video camcorder—and performs like one, too. This MiniDV model uses HAD progressive-scan CCD technology that delivers superior low-light performance and a sharper picture under any lighting conditions. It's a 3-CCD imaging system, of course; each 1/3" CCD has 380,000 pixels for brilliant digital picture quality. Expect 530 lines of horizontal resolution.

Lens-wise, this Sony has a 58mm aspherical lens that minimizes distortion and compensates for varying lighting situations. The lens has a 12X optical zoom. Recording is in the 16:9 widescreen format, with sound in 16-bit digital PCM stereo. And Sony's Super SteadyShot optical stabilization system uses motion sensors and an optical active prism stabilization system to deliver super-steady pictures under a variety of conditions.

You'll pay about $3,000 for this puppy, but you get what you pay for. Get more information at www.sonystyle.com.

PORTABLE GADGET OF THE WEEK: ARCHOS AV300 PORTABLE VIDEO PLAYER

The Archos AV300 series was the first portable video player to hit the market. You view programming on the 3.8" color LCD screen, which takes up most of the faceplate. Archos manufactures 20GB ($499.95), 40GB ($599.95), and 80GB ($799.95) versions; the big one can store up to 320 hours of video in MPEG-4 format. You can also use the AV300 to store and view digital photos and play digital music. Buy it at www.archos.com.

February 5, 2005

SATURDAY

THIS WEEK'S FOCUS: DIGITAL VIDEO

ON THIS DAY: INDIANA REDEFINES THE VALUE OF PI (1897)

Edwin J. Goodwin was a physician in the community of Solitude, Indiana, who thought he had discovered a way to square the circle. He wrote a bill incorporating his new ideas, and had it was introduced to the Indiana House of Representatives on this date in 1897. His "new mathematical truth" redefined the value of pi as the ratio of 5/4 to 4, or 3.2—a nice round number, but wrong. Fortunately for all circular objects in the Hoosier state, the bill didn't pass.

Related Web site: www.agecon.purdue.edu/crd/Localgov/Second%20Level%20pages/Indiana_Pi_Story.htm

CONVERTING FILM AND TAPE TO DIGITAL VIDEO

If you want to convert your old VHS movies to DVD, the trick is to get the analog VHS video onto your PC's hard drive. To do this, I recommend Pinnacle's MovieBox DV—an external box with FireWire connection to your computer. (FireWire is far superior to USB—even USB 2.0—for importing video.) The MovieBox comes with the software you need to edit and burn the video.

Another option is to go the consumer electronics route and buy a combo VCR/DVD recorder that you can hook up to your home theater system. Just pop the videotape into the VCR side, press the right button combination, and record the tape onto a blank DVD.

If your movie collection goes all the way back to the 8mm or 16mm film era, you face additional challenges. For 8mm film, your best bet is to use a film-to-disc conversion service, like that offered by many local photo labs, unless your film is really old. If you're dealing with old 16mm film, search for "film conservators" on Google; they'll be able to handle your fragile film with the proper care.

It gets worse if your 16mm film is on nitrate stock. If the film has a vinegary smell, that's good—it means it's acetate based, and not particularly flammable. Nitrate film stock, on the other hand, is highly flammable, and should be transferred by an expert immediately. It won't be cheap.

By the way, the Library of Congress has a good article on conserving old film stock. Read it here: www.loc.gov/preserv/care/film.html.

FACT OF THE WEEK

The Motion Picture Association of America claims that one-in-four Internet users has downloaded a pirated movie. Of those illegal downloaders, 17% are spending less time at the theater.

February 6, 2005

SUNDAY

THIS WEEK'S FOCUS: DIGITAL VIDEO

ON THIS DAY: MONOPOLY GOES ON SALE (1935)

Monopoly was first published commercially by Parker Brothers on this date in 1935. Charles B. Darrow had invented the game a year earlier, but Parker Brothers initially rejected the game because it contained "52 design errors." Darrow then self-published the game, selling 5,000 homemade sets at a Philadelphia department store. Parker Brothers subsequently came to their senses, and—65 years later—have sold more than 200 million copies of the game worldwide.

Related Web site: www.hasbro.com/monopoly/

MOVIEMAKING ACCESSORIES

The well-equipped filmmaker has a variety of accessories at his disposal to help make better home movies. Spend a few bucks on the right accessories, and you end up with better-looking pictures and a better-sounding soundtrack.

What kinds of accessories are we talking about? Here's a short list:

- *Camera stabilizers* keep your camera steady no matter how much you move around—sort of like the Steadycam units that Hollywood camera-men use. Check out the FlowCam stabilizers offered by VariZoom (www.varizoom.com).

- *Robotic tabletop mounts* provide remote operation of your camcorder, or let you use it as a high-end Web cam. Eagletron (www.trackercam.com) makes some good models.

- *Video lights* brighten the room and provide more light when you shoot—absolutely necessary for getting great-looking pictures. I like the Sunpak models offered by ToCAD (www.tocad.com).

- *External microphones* pick up what everyone is saying in a scene. Take your pick from camera-top mics (some in stereo) or wireless mics that clip onto the subject's shirt. Sony (www.sonystyle.com) has a nice selection of models.

SOFTWARE OF THE WEEK

Perhaps the easiest to use and most widely distributed DVD creation program is Sonic MyDVD. This program makes it easy to burn DVDs of your own home movies, as well as create DVD slideshows of your digital photographs. Buy it for $49.99 at www.sonic.com.

February 7, 2005

MONDAY

THIS WEEK'S FOCUS: TIVO

ON THIS DAY: BUBBLE BOY LEAVES BUBBLE (1984)

On this date in 1984, 12-year-old David Vetter, born without immunity to disease, touched his mother for the first time after he was removed from a plastic "bubble." Born with a rare disorder called severe combined immune deficiency, or SCID, he had lived since birth in a protective, germ-free environment at Texas Children's Hospital in Houston. Unfortunately, he died two weeks later, on February 22.

Related Web site: www.scid.net

USING THIRD-PARTY APPLICATIONS WITH YOUR TIVO

Many third-party applications have been written to extend the functionality of your TiVo unit. The bad news for Series 2 users is that most of these apps are for Series 1 TiVos only; the good news is that much of their functionality can be found in the official Home Media Option software. Here's a sampling:

- **elseed**—This small program displays Caller ID information on your TV screen through your TiVo unit. Just connect your TiVo to your Caller ID-enabled home phone line. Download the program here: www.bah.org/~greg/tivo/.

- **JPEGWriter**—This little app allows you to display JPEG images on your TV through TiVo. This application is especially useful as a support app in programs such as TiVo Control Station, for displaying things such as weather maps. Download it here:
www.allaboutjake.com/tivo/jpegwriter.html.

- **TiVo Control Station**—This is a sort of uber-application that can control a number of TiVo

software hacks that bring Web-based content to your TiVo. Currently, TCS offers stock quotes, sports scores, and weather forecasts/maps; the information is laid over the TV signal in colored text. Download the program here: www.zirakzigil.net/tivo/TCS.html.

- **JavaHMO**—This is a Series 2 app that can be used to replace the TiVo Desktop program. You get a lot of added functionality, including local movie listings, Internet streaming radio, and Internet Webcam. Download it at
javahmo.sourceforge.net.

PC GADGET OF THE WEEK

Pinnacle's PCTV Deluxe turns your computer into a full-fledged television and DVR, without the need to open your PC and install a new video card. It functions as a state-of-the-art television tuner, controlled by software you install on your PC, and also incorporates high-quality DVR technology to record TV programming to your computer's hard disk. It offers TiVo-like performance, but without the monthly subscription fees. Buy it for $199.99 at www.pinnaclesys.com.

February 8, 2005
TUESDAY

THIS WEEK'S FOCUS: TIVO

ON THIS DAY: PATENT RECEIVED FOR ENVELOPE FOLDING MACHINE (1898)

In 1898, James Ames Sherman of Worcester, Massachusetts, received a patent for his envelope folding and gumming machine. Sherman had designed a "mechanism for folding and sealing envelopes," which reduced the manufacturing cost per thousand from 60 cents to 8 cents.

Related Web site: www.royalenvelope.com/history/

TIVO BACKDOOR CODES

TiVo offers a handful of hidden features, accessible by entering special backdoor codes via your remote control. Before you can use any of the secret codes, you first have to activate the backdoor codes on your TiVo. You do this by entering a specific sequence of numbers and letters via TiVo's text-entry screen (TiVo Central > Pick Programs to Record > Search by Title > All Programs).

The following table lists the known backdoor activation codes for all Series 1 machines. To find out which software version you have, go to TiVo Central > Messages & Setup > System Information. (With the introduction of Series 2 machines, TiVo has been tightening up its security and making it harder for diligent snoops to unearth the software's secrets; as such, Series 2 backdoor access codes are, as of this writing, still unknown.)

Software Version	Backdoor Activation Code	Notes
OS 1.3	0V1T	Also OS 1.50 and OS 1.51 in the U.K.
OS 1.5.2	10JoM	U.K. only
OS 2.0	2 0 TCD	
OS 2.5	B D 2 5	Also OS 2.5.5 in the U.K.

Software Version	Backdoor Activation Code	Notes
OS 2.5.2	B M U S 1	For DirecTiVo
OS 3.0	3 0 BC	Latest Series 1 backdoor code

After you've entered the code, press the Thumbs Up button. You should hear five of the system dings, letting you know the code worked. The words "Backdoors enabled!" will also display in the text entry window.

When the backdoors are opened, you can enter any number of special codes to perform a variety of secret operations. I talk about two of my favorite backdoor operations tomorrow; you can find a listing of these codes on the TiVo Community Forum site (www.tivocommunity.com). Just search for **almost complete codes list** in the forums.

DOWNLOAD OF THE WEEK

TiVoTime is a freeware Windows program that calculates the remaining capacity of your TiVo unit. Just input the list of shows you've recorded, and TiVoTime computes how much space/time is left, at each level of recording quality. Download it at www.9thtee.com/tivotime.htm.

February 9, 2005

WEDNESDAY

THIS WEEK'S FOCUS: TIVO

ON THIS DAY: FIRST FLIGHT OF BOEING 747 (1969)

Boeing's first 747, the 747-100, rolled out of the Seattle works on September 30, 1968, and made its first flight on February 9, 1969. Far bigger than anything before it, the 747 slashed operating costs per seat and thus cut the cost of long-haul international airline travel.

Related Web site: www.boeing.com/history/boeing/747.html

LEO'S FAVORITE BACKDOOR SECRETS

Here's the good stuff—my two favorite TiVo backdoor secrets. Both require you to first activate your unit's backdoor codes, as I showed you yesterday.

My first secret is the undocumented 30-second skip. Here's how to do it:

1. Start playing back a program that you've recorded.
2. Press the follow sequence on your TiVo remote: Select-Play-Select-3-0-Select.
3. Listen for the three system chimes (a.k.a. "dings") that tell you this feature has been enabled.
4. Try out the skip by pressing the Advance button on your remote. It should skip through the recording by 30-second jumps.

By enabling this feature, you will no longer be able to use the Advance button to skip to the end of a program, but that's not a feature too many people will miss.

My second secret is the Sort command for the Now Playing List:

1. Enter Now Playing.
2. Press Slow-0-Record-ThumbsUp.
3. You can now enter 1 to sort normally, 2 to sort by expiration date, and 3 to sort alphabetically.

Also, be sure to check out a copy of my recently published *Leo Laporte's Guide to TiVo* with Gareth Branwyn.

MAC GADGET OF THE WEEK

Want to use your Mac as a TiVo-like DVR? Then check out Elgato's EyeTV, an outboard video tuner and controller for your Mac. The EyeTV 200 is a FireWire version that includes a built-in cable tuner; the EyeTV 300 is designed for digital satellite television. Both let you record television programming on your Mac's hard disk. Buy either one for $349 at www.elgato.com.

February 10, 2005

THURSDAY

THIS WEEK'S FOCUS: TIVO

ON THIS DAY: FIRE EXTINGUISHER INVENTED (1863)

On February 10, 1863, Alanson Crane of Fortress Monroe, Virginia, was granted a patent on a fire extinguishing system for buildings. This was a built-in system, using a series of perforated water pipes to flood the floors and quickly extinguish a fire.

Related Web site: www.hanford.gov/fire/safety/extingrs.htm

TROUBLESHOOTING TIVO PROBLEMS

Just in case you run into difficulties with your TiVo, here's a short list of the most common problems—and how to address them:

- **TiVo stops recording**—Try turning Suggestions off, restarting TiVo, turning Suggestions back on, and then restarting TiVo. When you've done this, force TiVo to make a manual daily call; this should do the trick.

- **Blue screen instead of TiVo screen**—First, check to make sure your cable box (if you have one) is turned on. If that isn't it, unplug TiVo for 10 seconds or so, and then plug it back in.

- **Audio and video are out of sync**—This happens periodically during normal operation. It's easily fixed by simply pausing whatever you're watching, and then starting it up again.

- **Stuttering audio/video**—This is what TiVo-types call the "stopples." One common cause is power spikes or fluctuations; you can deal with these by getting an uninterrupted power supply. Also, check TiVo's internal temperature at TiVo Central > TiVo Messages & Setup > Settings > System Information. If your TiVo is running hot, make sure there's plenty of airspace around the unit. If TiVo continues to run hot, you might have a blown cooling fan, which can easily be replaced. If none of this fixes the stoppies, you could have a hard drive on death's doorstep.

WEB SITE OF THE WEEK

Share tips and tricks with other TiVo users at the TiVo Community Forum (www.tivo-community.com). It's a great place to find out what's new and happening—or just shoot the breeze.

February 11, 2005

FRIDAY

THIS WEEK'S FOCUS: TIVO

ON THIS DAY: THOMAS EDISON BORN (1847)

Thomas Alva Edison, born this day in 1847, was more responsible than any other single person for creating the modern world. Hailed as the "wizard of Menlo Park" and the "father of the electrical age," he was considered one of the most prolific inventors of his time, holding a record 1,093 patents in his name. His list of inventions include the phonograph, the electric light, and motion pictures.

Related Web site: www.thomasedison.com

UPGRADING TIVO'S HARD DRIVE

If you find yourself filling up your TiVo on a consistent basis, you can replace your unit's built-in hard drive with a larger-capacity version. The easiest way to upgrade your TiVo's hard drive is with a prepared upgrade kit. This is a kit with a new TiVo drive already prepped with the TiVo OS for your specific model. Installing the kit involves little more than opening your TiVo, unscrewing and unplugging the old drive, and plugging and screwing in the new one.

You can replace your current drive with 165 hours of storage capacity (via a 160GB drive) for less than $200. Good sources are WeaKnees (www.weaknees.com) and PTVUpgrade (www.ptvupgrade.com).

Another option is to format a blank hard drive with the TiVo OS, using your PC. PTVUpgrade sells "InstantCake" CDs ($20), tailored to your particular TiVo model. You still have to buy a hard drive and do the installation, but this method can save you a few bucks over a prepared upgrade kit.

You can also increase your TiVo's capacity by adding a second hard drive to your unit. Again, WeaKnees and PTVUpgrade sell hard drive add-on kits, for about the same price as the prepared upgrade kits. The steps involved in using an add-on kit are basically the same as installing a replacement drive; the big difference is that you have to mount the new drive in a second drive bracket inside your TiVo, and then plug the second drive into the second connector on the internal IDE cable. The add-on kit should come with the appropriate instructions.

PORTABLE GADGET OF THE WEEK: CASIO TV REMOTE CONTROL WATCH

Here's a high-tech watch for extreme couch potatoes. Casio's CMD30B-1T Technowear watch functions as a remote control for your television, cable box, or VCR. Several very small buttons let you control power on/off, volume up/down, and channel up/down for the TV, and play, stop, rewind, and fast forward for your VCR. Buy it for $79.95 at www.casio.com.

February 12, 2005

SATURDAY

THIS WEEK'S FOCUS: TIVO

ON THIS DAY: BOSTON COMPUTER SOCIETY FOUNDED (1977)

The Boston Computing Society, founded on this date in 1977, was for years the largest computer user group in the world. It closed its doors in 1996, having split into multiple factions and locations, essentially collapsing under its own weight—a shame, given the great community it hosted during its heyday.

Related Web site: None (sigh)

NETWORKING TIVOS

Next to adding more hard drive space on your TiVo, the upgrade most users are interested in is networking. Since, at this point, more people likely have Series 2 machines than Series 1, that's the one I'll cover here.

To connect TiVo to an Ethernet network, you need to buy (for each series 2 TiVo you want to connect) a device called a USB-to-Ethernet adapter. All you have to do is plug the USB-to-Ethernet adapter into one of the two USB ports on your TiVo, plug your Ethernet cable into the other end, and then plug the Ethernet cable into a free RJ-45 Ethernet jack on your home network router/gateway.

Setting up a Series 2 TiVo to talk to a wireless home network is done much the same way as a wired network—minus the wire. In this situation, you also need a special network adapter that connects to one of TiVo's available USB ports. For this, you'll need a USB-to-Wireless adapter. This gizmo sends the signal through the USB port to a small radio transceiver and then over the 2.5GHz Wi-Fi radio spectrum, to the antenna on your router/gateway.

Once you have your Series 2 TiVo networked, either via wire or wireless, you'll need to sign up for TiVo's Home Media Option, which you do from the Manage My Account page. You'll pay a one-time fee of $99 for the first TiVo you connect, and $49 for each additional unit you register. Once you sign up, it will take up to three days for the HMO software to be automatically downloaded to your TiVo. You'll know it's arrived when you see the Music & Photos choice added to TiVo Central's menu.

When you register for the HMO service, you'll also be given a link to the TiVo Desktop application. This is the software that you'll need on your host computer to be able to serve music and photos over the network to your TiVo. Download it at your convenience.

FACT OF THE WEEK

TiVo reports that Janet Jackson's breast exposure during the 2004 Super Bowl was the most replayed moment ever measured on its service. TiVo said it used its technology to measure audience behavior among 20,000 users during the game, and discovered a 180% spike in viewership at the time of the "wardrobe malfunction."

THIS WEEK'S FOCUS: TIVO

ON THIS DAY: DRESDEN FIREBOMBED (1945)

On the evening of February 13, 1945, Allied bombers attacked the defenseless city of Dresden, Germany, one of the great cultural centers of northern Europe—a target with little or no military value. As recorded by Kurt Vonnegut, Jr., in his book *Slaughterhouse-Five*, the planes dropped more than 700,000 phosphorous bombs, creating a firestorm that destroyed the city and killed more than a half million women, children, and elderly. It was one of the many senseless tragedies of the war.

Related Web site: www.rense.com/general19/flame.htm

BUILD YOUR OWN DVR

Don't want to pay TiVo bills every month? Then turn your PC into a TiVo-free digital video recorder, using your computer's hard disk to store your favorite programs.

To turn your PC into a DVR, you first have to turn it into a TV. That means adding a television tuner to your computer, either with an external device (typically connected via USB) or with an internal video/TV card. I like both the Hauppauge WinTV-PVR-350 (www.hauppauge.com) and All-in-Wonder 9800 Pro (www.ati.com) internal cards; the Hauppage runs about $200, the All-in-Wonder about twice that amount.

Then, you need special software to save that television signal to hard disk and to display the necessary television program guide (to make recording specific shows easy). I like the Sage TV (www.sage.tv) software; also good is Snapstream's Beyond TV (www.snapstream.com) and the open source Freevo (freevo.sourceforge.net). Freevo is freeware, of course; you'll pay $70 or so for one of the other programs—but no monthly subscription fees.

The other thing you need to turn your PC into a DVR is a big hard disk. Using the standard MPEG2 compression, a 1-hour program takes up 2GB of disk space. So, for example, if you have 20GB free, you can record only 10 hours of programming. I'd recommend a 200GB model, just to have a little headroom.

Put it all together, connect your PC to your antenna, cable, or satellite box, and you're ready to go. Which is about the time you'll start thinking about getting a bigger monitor, maybe one of those widescreen models...

SOFTWARE OF THE WEEK

As I discussed above, Sage TV is a great little DVR program for your PC. It offers an onscreen guide with 14 days of programming in advance, the ability to search for upcoming shows, and all the normal DVR features—including the ability to pause and rewind "live" television. It even offers Music Jukebox and Picture Library features, for playback and viewing anywhere on your home network. Buy it for $79.95 at www.sage.tv.

February 14, 2005

MONDAY

THIS WEEK'S FOCUS: CHAT AND INSTANT MESSAGING

ON THIS DAY: ENIAC UNVEILED (1946)

The most famous first-generation computer was arguably the Electronic Numerical Integrator and Computer, or ENIAC, developed as a result of a wartime commission by the U.S. Army Ordinance Corps. It was completed on this date in 1946, and immediately put into service for calculations involved in the design of the hydrogen bomb. ENIAC served as the nation's main computational workhouse through 1952, and was finally dismantled in 1955.

Related Web site: www.seas.upenn.edu/~museum/

INSTANT MESSAGING CLIENTS

Instant messaging lets you communicate one on one, in real-time, with your friends, family, and colleagues. It's faster than email and less chaotic than chat rooms (which I'll talk about on Wednesday). There are several big players in the instant messaging market today, including

- **AOL Instant Messenger (**www.aim.com**)**—AIM is the most-used instant messaging program, available in a free Web-based version and in a version built into the proprietary America Online interface. Users of the Web version of AIM can communicate directly with users of the AOL-specific version; in fact, a single user ID will suffice if moved from the Web version to the AOL version of the program.

- **ICQ (**web.icq.com**)**—ICQ is the granddaddy of all instant messaging programs. (Say it out loud—it stands for "I seek you.") ICQ was birthed by a company named Mirabilis back in 1996, but was purchased by America Online in 1998. Today, AOL maintains ICQ and AIM as separate programs—so separate that ICQ users can't talk to AIM users, or vice versa.

- **Windows Messenger (**messenger.msn.com**)**— Windows Messenger does all the main things AIM and ICQ do, including voice chat and the ability to page a contact's mobile phone. By the way, Windows Messenger is the version of the program that comes bundled with Microsoft Windows; MSN Messenger is the almost-identical variant that connects to Microsoft's MSN online service.

- **Yahoo! Messenger (**messenger.yahoo.com**)**—Not to be left behind, Yahoo! has its own instant messaging service for its tens of millions of worldwide users. Yahoo! Messenger not only offers instant messaging services, it also lets you receive up-to-the-minute stock prices, news headlines, sports scores, weather forecasts, and notification of any waiting Yahoo! Mail.

PC GADGET OF THE WEEK

Whether you want to back up the contents of your hard drive or just need more storage for all your digital media files, you can't go wrong with Western Digital's Media Center external hard drives. The Media Center connects to your PC via either USB 2.0 or FireWire and includes a front-mounted power switch; it's available in 160GB ($299.99), 200GB ($349.99), and 250GB ($399.99) versions. Check them out at www.wdc.com.

THIS WEEK'S FOCUS: CHAT AND INSTANT MESSAGING

ON THIS DAY: GALILEO BORN (1564)

Galileo Galilei was born on February 15, 1564 in Pisa, Italy. Galileo pioneered the "experimental scientific method," and was the first to use a refracting telescope to make important astronomical discoveries—including the moons of Jupiter and the phases of Venus. He died in 1642, the same year Isaac Newton was born.

Related Web site: es.rice.edu/ES/humsoc/Galileo/

INSTANT MESSAGING INCOMPATIBILITY

The biggest complaint among instant messaging users is that users from one system can't talk to users on another system. The issue here is interoperability—or, rather, the lack of it.

Unfortunately, all the various instant messaging clients we talked about yesterday don't work well (or at all) with each other. If you're using Windows Messenger, for example, you won't be able to communicate with someone running AOL Instant Messenger. That means you'll have to limit your messaging to other users of the same program you're using—or download and install multiple messaging clients.

America Online appears to be the villain in the quest for universal interoperability among all instant messaging systems. While other companies have tried to build links into the AIM system, America Online has resisted these efforts, claiming (in essence) that the proprietary America Online system could be compromised if all those "outsiders" got in the front door.

So, for now, if you use Windows/MSN Messenger or Yahoo! Messenger, you simply can't talk to your friends who use AIM or ICQ. There's hope on the horizon, however—especially for corporate users. Microsoft has announced that its upcoming Live Communications Server 2005 will be able to communicate with multiple IM providers, including Yahoo!, AOL, and MSN. It's a milestone in instant messaging interoperability; let's hope these three companies extend their cooperation to include home users sometime soon.

DOWNLOAD OF THE WEEK

Easy Message is a cross-platform instant messaging client that works with AOL, ICQ, MSN, and Yahoo!. It's small, it's fast, and it gives you the same interface no matter which instant messaging network you connect to. Easy Message is freeware; download it at www.easymessage.net.

February 16, 2005

WEDNESDAY

THIS WEEK'S FOCUS: CHAT AND INSTANT MESSAGING

ON THIS DAY: KING TUT'S TOMB UNSEALED (1923)

Young King Tutankhamen was only 19 when he died, perhaps murdered by his enemies. His tomb, hidden by his successors, laid undiscovered for more than 3,000 years—until an Englishman named Howard Carter discovered it in 1922. Several months later, on February 16, 1923, Carter unsealed the tomb—and revealed the secret of King Tut.

Related Web site: www.kingtutone.com/tutankhamun/

CHATTING ONLINE

An online chat is different from an instant message. Whereas instant messaging describes a one-to-one conversation between two users, online chat involves real-time discussions between large groups of users. These chats take place in public *chat rooms* (sometimes called *chat channels*).

If you're serious about online chat, you might want to check out some of the other major chat communities on the Web. These sites include

- Excite Super Chat (`chat.excite.com`)
- Internet TeleCafe (`www.telecafe.com`
- Talk City (`www.talkcity.com`
- Yahoo! Chat (`chat.yahoo.com`)

If you're a subscriber to America Online or MSN, you can also access those services' proprietary chat rooms. These are some of the busiest chat rooms on the Internet, but they're reserved exclusively for AOL or MSN subscribers.

Most of these Web-based chats operate by creating a Java-based chat window on your desktop. (You'll need to have Java enabled in your browser for this to work, of course.) Even though you navigate to the site with your Web browser, you'll do all your chatting from within this new window—although you'll probably have to keep the original Web page open in your browser, as well.

MAC GADGET OF THE WEEK

Plantronic's DSP-300 is a must-have USB headset if you're spending any time audio chatting using iChat. The DSP-300 is nice in that it offers its audio in stereo, meaning it also works well for gaming audio or music, along with voice solutions such as iChat. Buy it for $89 at `www.plantronic.com`.

THIS WEEK'S FOCUS: CHAT AND INSTANT MESSAGING

ON THIS DAY: THOMAS J. WATSON, SR. BORN (1874)

On this day in 1874, Thomas J. Watson, Sr., was born. Watson rose within the ranks of the National Cash Register Co., and then in 1914 became president of the foundering Computing-Tabulating-Recording Company. In 1924 Watson renamed the company International Business Machines (IBM), and the rest is history. At the time of Watson's death in 1956, IBM had assets of more than $600 million and a world market of 82 countries.

Related Web site: www.watson.ibm.com

INTERNET RELAY CHAT

The granddaddy of live online chat is Internet Relay Chat (IRC), which was around and thriving long before instant messaging came into existence. IRC runs on more than two dozen separate networks (nets), all connected to the main Internet backbone. Each net has its own group of servers, based at various locations around the world.

Each IRC net has its own group of channels, organized by topic—some of the larger nets have more than 10,000 channels active at any given time. To participate in IRC, you have to connect to an IRC server dedicated to a specific IRC network; you can connect to only one network at a time. When you run your IRC client, you first choose which net you want to use. Then, connect to a server on that net and join one or more chat channels.

To connect to IRC, you need a software program called an *IRC client*. The most popular IRC client is mIRC, a shareware program you can download from www.mirc.com. mIRC enables you to connect to any IRC server and then chat in one or more channels, simultaneously.

When it comes to picking a chat channel, you should keep a few things in mind. First, all chat channels start with a # and contain no spaces, like this: **#channelname**. Second, each IRC net contains thousands of different channels, so it's almost impossible to find the one you want by scrolling through an alphabetical list. This means that you probably want to use the search function within your IRC software to find channels that contain specific words or parts of words.

You can find a complete list of available IRC networks and their associated servers at www.mirc.com/servers.html. More important, most IRC programs include lists of networks and servers for easy one-click connections. And if you're not sure which IRC net contains the channel you want, you can search for channels across multiple networks at www.irchelp.org/irchelp/chanlist/.

WEB SITE OF THE WEEK

Talk City (www.talkcity.com) is the Web's premiere chat portal. The site features thousands of chat rooms and message boards, as well as IRC access (for subscribers only). There's even easy access for WebTV/MSN TV users, something not all chat sites provide. Chat rooms are organized by location, age, and interest.

February 18, 2005

FRIDAY

THIS WEEK'S FOCUS: CHAT AND INSTANT MESSAGING

ON THIS DAY: PLUTO DISCOVERED (1930)

Pluto, the ninth planet from the Sun as well as the smallest and most remote planet known in the solar system, was discovered on this day in 1930. The astronomer Percival Lowell, at his private observatory in Flagstaff, Arizona, had funded three separate searches for a "trans-Neptunian" planet; the third search, conducted by Clyde W. Tombaugh, was successful. Interestingly, Pluto is the only of the nine planets discovered by an American astronomer.

Related Web site: www.nineplanets.org

LEARN THE LINGO!

When you're chatting or instant messaging online, quickness takes precedence over accuracy. A lot of online chatters talk in their own unique shorthand, which is easier and faster to type than spelling out complete words and sentences.

Part of this shorthand is the use of acronyms in place of common phrases. Here's a list of the TLAs and FLAs (three-letter and four-letter acronyms) you're most likely to encounter:

Acronym	Means
AKA	Also known as
ASAP	As soon as possible
BRB	Be right back
BTW	By the way
FWIW	For what it's worth
FYI	For your information
GDR	Grinning, ducking, and running
IMHO	In my humble opinion
IOW	In other words
LOL	Laughing out loud
NP	No problem
OTOH	On the other hand

Acronym	Means
PITA	Pain in the, er, ankle
PMJI	Pardon me for jumping in
ROFL	Rolling on the floor laughing
RT	Real time (as in, arrange a real-time meeting)
TTFN	Ta ta for now!

It's also okay to abbreviate longer words and to use so-called *emoticons* and *smileys*—such as <g> and :) —to help you get your point across. Keep it short and to the point, and you'll fit right in!

PORTABLE GADGET OF THE WEEK

With so many portable devices using rechargeable batteries, you need a decent battery charger to keep everything recharged. The Powerex Charger/Conditioner isn't like other "dumb" chargers; it features a built-in microprocessor controller with trickle charge for intelligent battery cycling. It even rejuvenates old batteries by subjecting them to an automatic discharge/charge cycle. Buy it for $39.99 at www.meritline.com.

SATURDAY

THIS WEEK'S FOCUS: CHAT AND INSTANT MESSAGING

ON THIS DAY: COPERNICUS BORN (1473)

Nicolaus Copernicus, born on this date in 1473, was the founder of modern astronomy—and he made all his discoveries "bare eyeball," 100 years before the invention of the telescope. In 1530, Copernicus completed and gave to the world his great work *De Revolutionibus*, which asserted sthat the earth rotated on its axis once daily and traveled around the sun once yearly, which was a fantastic concept for the time.

Related Web site: www-gap.dcs.st-and.ac.uk/~history/Mathematicians/ Copernicus.html

CHAT TIPS

To ensure a safe and enjoyable chat experience, here are some tips to keep in mind:

- Don't feel like you have to jump right in and participate in every single discussion. It's okay to sit back, take your time, and watch the conversations flow before you decide to add your two cents' worth. (This is called *lurking*.)

- Don't assume you're really talking to the person you *think* you're talking to. It's pretty easy to hide behind a nickname and create a totally different persona online.

- For that matter, it's okay to create an online persona for yourself that bears no relation to the real you. It's actually kind of fun to pretend to be someone else when you're chatting online—and see how others respond to the "new" you.

- If you want to get personal with someone you meet in a chat channel, send a private message. Don't subject everyone in a room to your private conversations.

- Don't give out your real name, address, or phone number in any chat session—public or private.

- Beware of law enforcement personnel posing as potential chat room victims. If you're thinking of discussing anything remotely illegal, just remember that the person you're chatting with could be a member of your local police force!

- Be very careful about accepting files sent to you during a chat session. Online chat and instant messaging are the "hot" new methods for spreading viruses over the Internet. Examine carefully any file sent to you in a chat session, and reject anything that is the least bit suspicious. Better safe than sorry!

FACT OF THE WEEK

High-tech job losses continued in 2003, although at a slower pace than in recent years, according a report by AeA, an electronics industry trade group. Employers in the high-tech industry cut 234,000 positions nationwide in 2003, down from 539,000 in 2002. Overall, about 13% of the country's tech jobs have vanished since 2001.

February 20, 2005

SUNDAY

THIS WEEK'S FOCUS: CHAT AND INSTANT MESSAGING

ON THIS DAY: FIRST U.S. ASTRONAUT ORBITS EARTH (1962)

On February 20, 1962, John Glenn piloted the Mercury-Atlas 6 Friendship 7 spacecraft on the United States' first manned orbital mission. Glenn completed a successful three-orbit mission around the earth, reaching a maximum altitude of 162 miles and an orbital velocity of approximately 17,500 miles per hour. Mission duration from launch to impact was 4 hours, 55 minutes, and 23 seconds.

Related Web site: www.johnglennhome.org

SEX CHAT

Many online chat rooms and channels exist solely to facilitate conversations of an adult nature. Yes, we're talking sex here—and there's a lot of it going on online.

At the least, there's a lot of *talking* about sex going on. Whether you're talking on Yahoo! Chat, America Online, or IRC, it's not hard to find a chat room designed to either talk about sexual matters or facilitate real-time liaisons. Many of these rooms are explicit in their intent (and are named accordingly); other times adult conversations just spring up in more general-interest chat rooms.

The very real fact is that a lot of people get their kicks from engaging in sexy conversations in online chat rooms. If nothing else, online sex is safe sex, and is very popular among users of both sexes and all sexual persuasions.

Online sex can turn harmful, however, if you take it offline. No matter how familiar that person might seem to you, hooking up with someone from a chat room is only a small step away from hooking up with a stranger. You don't *really* know what that person is like, or where they've been, or what they do when they're not chatting online. Not to say that

offline hookups should always be avoided; it's just that you should exercise the proper degree of caution, just as you would when meeting anyone for the very first time.

Sex chat can also be harmful to any real-world relationships you may currently be engaged in. You may *think* that anonymous online chat is your little secret, but know that anything you do online can be tracked—and the conversations you have in chat rooms can (with the right tools) be recovered from their temporary storage places on your hard disk. As with anything in life, you should be prepared to pay the consequences for what you do online—even if it's just some seemingly innocuous dirty talk.

Finally, it should be noted that we are not advocating online sex. We're merely pointing out the facts.

SOFTWARE OF THE WEEK: IMSECURE

Zone Labs' IMSecure keeps your instant messaging sessions private, blocks IM spam, and prevents identity thieves from stealing your personal information. Download the basic version for free, or purchase the more powerful IMSecure Pro for $19.95. Try it and buy it at www.zonelabs.com.

February 21, 2005

MONDAY

THIS WEEK'S FOCUS: BROADBAND INTERNET

ON THIS DAY: DNA STRUCTURE DISCOVERED (1953)

On this day in 1953, scientists Francis Crick and James Watson discovered the basic structure of DNA. They showed that each strand of the DNA molecule was a template for the other; during cell division, the two strands separate and on each strand a new "other half" is built, just like the one before. This discovery has been called the most important biological work of the last 100 years, and won Watson and Crick the Nobel Prize in 1962.

Related Web site: www.dna50.org.uk

THREE TYPES OF BROADBAND

Unlike your old analog phone line, a broadband connection is an end-to-end digital connection. When you don't have to modulate and demodulate the data from digital to analog (and back again), the all-digital data can travel much faster from your computer to other points on the Web.

Three types of digital broadband connections are available today. When you want to speed up your connection, you can choose from

- **DSL (Digital Subscriber Line)**—DSL piggybacks on your existing telephone lines and provides speeds of at least 384Kbps—and more typically in the 500Kbps-1Mbps range.
- **Digital cable**—Cable modems are the most popular form of broadband connection today. They connect to the digital cable lines that are working their way into homes across the country, which makes for a very easy—and a very fast—connection. Minimum speeds are around 500Kbps, with typical speeds between 1Mbps-2Mbps.

- **Digital satellite**—If you can't get broadband by wire at your location, get it via satellite. The DIRECWAY service provides broadband Internet access via the same type of small satellite dish that DirecTV uses for satellite TV. Connection speeds average 500Kbps.

Which type of broadband you choose depends on what's available in your area (not all phone or cable companies offer broadband at this point in time), and who offers the best deal. Expect to pay anywhere from $30-$60 per month for your broadband service.

PC GADGET OF THE WEEK

Scanners don't have to take up an entire desktop; here's one that looks just like a ballpoint pen. The Planon DocuPen is battery-operated and contains 2MB of flash memory. Drag it across the document you want to scan, then connect the DocuPen to your PC via USB to download the scanned images. Buy it for $199.99 at www.planon.com.

February 22, 2005

TUESDAY

THIS WEEK'S FOCUS: BROADBAND INTERNET

ON THIS DAY: POPCORN INTRODUCED (1630)

In 1630, popcorn was introduced to the English colonists by a Native American named Quadequina. Turns out Native Americans had been growing it for more than 1,000 years before the arrival of European explorers; in 1964, scientists in southern Mexico found a small cob of popcorn discovered to be 7,000 years old.

Related Web site: www.jollytime.com

HOW DSL WORKS

DSL is a phone line–based broadband connection. It works by splitting your existing phone line into two or three frequency bands. Those types of DSL that use two bands use one for upstream data flow and the other for downstream data flow. DSL variations that use three bands reserve the third band for standard voice communications—which don't demand much bandwidth.

The DSL signal, then, goes into the standard phone line, using a device called a *DSL access multiplexer (DSLAM)*. At your end of the connection the phone line connects to a DSL modem, which extracts the DSL signal and feeds it to your computer.

There are actually several different types of DSL, each using a variation of the basic DSL technology.

Name	Description
ADSL	Asymmetric DSL is a high-priced variation, targeted at large businesses. Provides different upstream and downstream rates—as fast as 8.5Mbps downstream.
ADSL Lite	Also known as DSL-Lite, Consumer DSL (CDSL), or Universal ADSL (UADSL). Maximum downstream speed is 1.5Mbps, with upstream

Name	Description
	speed of 384Kbps or so. This is the type of DSL typically offered to home and small business users.
HDSL	High-bit-rate DSL is the original DSL technology offering 1.5Mbps speed.
RADSL	Rate adaptive DSL varies connection speed dynamically according to line conditions.
SDSL	Symmetric DSL, also known as HDSL-2, works with only one pair of wires, providing 1.1Mbps connections.
VDSL	Very-high-bit-rate DSL is targeted at large companies, and typically is delivered over fiber-optic networks. Access speeds reach 34Mbps in both directions.

And then there's xDSL—so-called "generic" DSL that encompasses all the possible DSL acronyms.

DOWNLOAD OF THE WEEK

Dan Elwell's Broadband Speed Test is a nifty little utility that lets you test the speed of your broadband connection, identify any areas of concern, monitor performance, and generate diagnostics. Try it for free, register it for $15, at www.broadbandspeedtest.net.

February 23, 2005

WEDNESDAY

THIS WEEK'S FOCUS: BROADBAND INTERNET

ON THIS DAY: FIRST MASS INOCULATION FOR POLIO (1954)

On February 23, 1954, the first mass inoculation of children against polio with the Salk vaccine began in Pittsburgh. Jonas Salk had developed a trial vaccine in 1952; the vaccine was composed of a "killed" polio virus, which retained the ability to immunize without the risk of infecting the patient. In 1954 he published his findings in the *Journal of the American Medical Association,* and began nationwide testing on nearly two million schoolchildren. The results proved Salk's polio vaccine to be safe and effective.

Related Web site: www.accessexcellence.org/AE/AEC/CC/polio.html

HOW BROADBAND CABLE WORKS

Where DSL piggybacks over your telephone lines, cable broadband piggybacks on your cable signal. Or, more accurately, it piggybacks *inside* your cable signal.

You see, the cable Internet signal occupies a defined space (called a *tunnel*) within the signal that travels through the cable company's coaxial or fiber-optic cable. Most cable companies assign Internet signals to a 6MHz slot within the cable signal, which enables downstream speeds as high as 5Mbps. (This theoretical maximum is seldom achieved; speeds in the 500Kbps to 2Mbps range are more common.) Upstream signals are assigned to a subset of the total data tunnel, which produces slower upstream rates—typically in the 128Kbps to 384Kbps range.

The data signals are extracted from the cable line via a cable modem, which feeds directly into your computer. The modem also serves to pack your computer's data signals back in to the cable signal for upstream transmission.

To distribute this broadband Internet signal, your cable company creates a large network to service its Internet customers. Each neighborhood in the coverage area is served by a separate network node. Most cable companies provide 27Mbps or so worth of bandwidth for each node on the network. This available bandwidth on a network node is shared by all the users connected to that node—which makes cable broadband a shared-bandwidth technology. It also means that the more users connected, the slower each connection—which explains why your cable broadband connection sometimes slows down right after dinner, when all your neighbors are online.

MAC GADGET OF THE WEEK

Say you've got an Ethernet network in your home or office and you need plenty of storage that everyone can access, but you don't want to install Mac OS X Server or dedicate one of the Macs to that function. All you have to do is purchase and install LaCie's Ethernet Disk, configure it using any Web browser, and then share the disk via AppleShare. Buy it at www.lacie.com; prices range from $599 to $1,199, depending on capacity.

February 24, 2005

THURSDAY

THIS WEEK'S FOCUS: BROADBAND INTERNET

ON THIS DAY: STEVE JOBS BORN (1955)

Steven Paul Jobs, the co-founder and CEO of Apple Computer, was born on this day in 1955. He's responsible for just about every major development in the Apple world, from the Macintosh to the iPod. Happy birthday, Steve!

Related Web site: `www.apple.com/pr/bios/jobs.html`

INSTALLING A CABLE MODEM

To establish a cable broadband connection, you might have to schedule a professional installation from your local cable guy, or you might be able to do it yourself. Many cable companies offer self-installation kits that include installation software, a cable modem with USB connection, and easy-to-follow instructions.

The basic installation is relatively simple, which is why you don't really need to spend $50–$100 for the cable guy to do it. You start by connecting a coaxial cable from the cable outlet on the wall to your cable modem. You then connect the cable modem to your PC's USB port, make sure the power cord is plugged in, and then run the cable company's installation software. In a perfect world, the installation software configures the necessary network settings within Windows to recognize the new connection, and you're up and ready to surf—typically in less than half an hour.

It's a fairly simple procedure. In some instances, though, you might need to install a low-cost coaxial splitter so that a single cable outlet can feed both your TV and your PC. No big deal.

Note, however, that since your broadband cable connection is part of a neighborhood-wide network, your computer could be visible to—and possibly accessible by—other neighbors on your node of the network. Smart cable operators know how to hide each connection from the larger network, but not all cable operators are smart. That's why you probably want to disable Windows' file- and print-sharing features for the network, and definitely want to install some type of firewall software.

WEB SITE OF THE WEEK

BroadbandReports (www. broadbandreports.com) is *the* Web site for anything and everything broadband related. Here you can find broadband speed tests, reviews of all major broadband providers, and tons of other information. I find it essential.

THIS WEEK'S FOCUS: BROADBAND INTERNET

ON THIS DAY: COLT PATENTS THE REVOLVER (1836)

During the Civil War, a popular slogan went like this: "Abe Lincoln may have freed all men, but Sam Colt made them equal." Sam did this by inventing a handgun with a revolving chamber. After patenting his revolver in 1836, he became the biggest supplier of handguns for the Civil War—and the Colt Peacemaker became the most popular handgun in the West.

Related Web site: www.colt.com

HOW SATELLITE BROADBAND WORKS

If neither DSL nor cable broadband is available in your area, you have another option—connecting to the Internet via satellite. Any household or business with a clear line of sight to the southern sky can receive digital data signals from a geosynchronous satellite, at a connect speed of 500Kbps or so. Although this is slower than many cable or DSL connections, it's a whole lot faster than dial-up.

The largest provider of satellite Internet access is Hughes Network Systems. (Hughes also developed and markets the popular DIRECTV digital satellite system.) Hughes' DIRECWAY system (www.direcway.com) enables you to send and receive Internet signals via a 24-inch oval dish that you mount outside your house or on your roof. Monthly subscription fees are in the $60–$100 range, depending on which plan you pick.

Internet service via satellite works by beaming Internet data off an orbiting satellite down to a satellite dish that is connected to your PC. When you access a Web page, the request to view that page is sent (via satellite) to DIRECWAY's Network Operations Center (NOC) in Maryland. The NOC sends a request to the Web page's server, and the data that makes up that page is then sent from that server back to DIRECWAY's NOC. The NOC then beams the data for the Web page up to the DIRECWAY satellite (22,000 miles up); the signal bounces off the satellite back down to your DirecPC dish (22,000 miles down), at 400Kbps. The signal then travels from your dish to a broadband modem in your PC.

Because of the huge distances involved in transmitting data via satellite, there is typically some delay (called *latency*) in the receipt of the requested page. Typical latency is close to a full second. While this latency is virtually unnoticeable when dealing with typical Web viewing or email communications, it could be a problem when playing real-time multiple-player online games.

PORTABLE GADGET OF THE WEEK

I can't help it; I think this geeky little gizmo is super cool. The Eyetop Centra is a wearable video screen, ensconced in a pair of wraparound shaded glasses. The video is projected onto the shades, delivering the virtual equivalent of a 14" screen; attached earphones provide stereo sound. Buy it for $499 at www.eyetop.net.

February 26, 2005

SATURDAY

THIS WEEK'S FOCUS: BROADBAND INTERNET

ON THIS DAY: BOMB EXPLODES UNDER WORLD TRADE CENTER (1993)

On February 26, 1993, a car bomb was planted by Islamic terrorists in the underground garage below Tower One of the World Trade Center. When the bomb exploded, it opened a 30 meter wide hole through four sublevels of concrete. Six people were killed, and at least 1,040 others were injured. Eight years later, the twin towers would be felled and thousands killed by an even greater terrorist attack.

Related Web site: www.fas.org/irp/world/iraq/956-tni.htm

TWEAKING YOUR BROADBAND CONNECTION

Broadband Internet connections pump a lot of data into and out of your computer. Unfortunately, Windows doesn't come optimized for this level of throughput—which means that you're probably not getting the maximum performance from your broadband connection. You can get around this problem by tweaking a handful of important Windows system settings in the Windows Registry.

One of the first tweaks to try is the MTU (Maximum Transmittable Unit), which controls the size of the data packets sent from your system. Go to the `HKEY_LOCAL_MACHINE\System\CurrentControlSet\Services\Class\NetTrans\0000` key, and then enter a higher value for the MaxMTU setting; I recommend something in the 1500 range. (For your manual MTU setting to be recognized, you'll also need to turn off Windows' Path MTU Discovery feature, which you do by setting the EnablePMTUDiscovery key to 0.)

Another good tweak is the RWIN (Receive Window) setting, which determines how many data packets are transmitted before your system determines the integrity of the data transfer; the higher, the better. You can find the RWIN setting (labeled DefaultRcvWindow) under the `HKEY_LOCAL_MACHINE\System\CurrentControlSet\Services\VXD\MSTCP` key. The setting you use depends on your connection speed, as detailed in the following table:

Line Speed	Typical RWIN Setting
512Kbps	9600
784Kbps	14700
1.0Mbps	18750
1.5Mbps	28125
2.0Mbps	37500

Another good source of tweak information and tools is the Tweaks section of the BroadbandReports Web site (www.broadbandreports.com/tweaks/).

FACT OF THE WEEK

According to the Pew Internet and American Life Project, 48 million Americans, or 25% of all adults, have broadband Internet at home. Of these users, 54% connect via cable modem, 42% use DSL, and the remaining few connect via satellite.

February 27, 2005

SUNDAY

ON THIS DAY: REICHSTAG FIRE (1933)

On February 27, 1933, the German Parliament (Reichstag) burned down. The next day, President Hindenburg and Chancellor Hitler used this incident to invoke Article 48 of the Weimar Constitution, which permitted the suspension of civil liberties in time of national emergency. The Nazi government took advantage of an unfortunate situation in order to solidify their control over the country, at the expense of civil rights.

Related Web site: worldatwar.net/event/reichstagsbrand/

TROUBLESHOOTING BROADBAND PROBLEMS

Problems with broadband connections are similar to the types of problems you encounter with dial-up connections. There could be a problem at your end of the connection (in your PC, in the broadband modem, or in the connection between the two), in the connection between your location and the broadband ISP, or with your ISP's connection to the Internet. If you're having problems with your broadband connection dropping out, here are some things to try:

- Check the connection to your broadband modem, and from your modem to your PC. Make sure all connections are firmly tightened and that your modem's power cable is firmly plugged in.

- Some broadband modems can get out of synch and behave as if they're not actually connected. Try turning off or unplugging your modem for about 30 seconds, and then turning it back on. This should reset the modem, and resynch your connection.

- If you're using DSL, you could have a dirty phone line. (And I don't mean the kinds of calls you receive!) Try installing a filter to drop the line's noise level, or call your telco to do a line cleaning.

- Many types of broadband connect to your computer through an Ethernet network card—which means your system needs to be configured for network use. Check the instructions for your network card (and router, if you're using one) to make sure your system is configured properly.

- If you're using Norton Internet Security, uninstall it. I've found that this program is the single largest source of Internet problems.

- Renew your IP address. In Windows, click Start > Run, enter `ipconfig /release`, and press Return. Then do the same thing to run `ipconfig /renew`.

SOFTWARE OF THE WEEK

Broadband Wizard lets you test, tweak, and hopefully speed up your cable or DSL broadband connection. It walks you step-by-step through a variety of system tweaks and lets you undo any change that has negative results. Try it at `www.broadbandwizard.net`, or buy it for $19.95.

THIS WEEK'S FOCUS: **GOOGLE**

ON THIS DAY: **LINUS PAULING BORN (1901)**

The late Linus Pauling was the only man in the world to win two unshared Nobel Prizes, for Chemistry (1954) and Peace (1962). He discovered that sickle cell anemia is caused by a genetic defect, and helped to decipher the makeup of the human genes. Dr. Pauling was born on this date in 1901, and died in 1994.

Related Web site: www.paulingexhibit.org

HOW GOOGLE WORKS

Like most online search engines, Google doesn't actually let you search the Web. Instead, it pre-searches the Web for you and stores its results in a large database, called a search index. When you search Google, you're actually searching this database of sites, not the Web itself.

Google assembles the pages in its search index by using special "searchbot" or crawler software to scour the Web. Found pages are automatically added to Google's ever-expanding database—more than six billion individual pages, at last count.

But how does Google determine which pages rank at the top of the search results? Google uses proprietary PageRank technology to measure how many other pages link to a particular page; the more links to a page, the higher that page ranks. In addition, PageRank assigns a higher weight to links that come from higher-ranked pages. So if a page is linked to from a number of high-ranked pages, that page will itself achieve a higher ranking.

The theory is that the more popular a page is, the higher that page's ultimate value. While this sounds a little like a popularity contest (and it is, to be frank), it's surprising how often this approach delivers high-quality results.

The number of Web pages indexed by Google is among the largest of all search engines (Google and AllTheWeb are continually jockeying for "biggest" bragging rights), which means you stand a fairly good chance of actually finding what you were searching for—and why most users, me included, like Google so much.

PC GADGET OF THE WEEK

Don't feel like positioning your Webcam manually? Then check out Logitech's QuickCam Orbit, the Webcam that follows you as you move around the room. That's right, this camera features automatic face tracking software and a mechanical pan-and-tilt mechanism with digital zoom to keep the camera focused on your face. Buy it for $129.99 at www.logitech.com.

MORE FEBRUARY FACTS

February 1

1790 First session of the U.S. Supreme Court is held

1893 Construction of world's first movie studio begins in New Jersey

1950 Texas Instruments is issued a patent for an integrated circuit

1951 The first nuclear blast is televised from Frenchman Flats, Nevada

1972 The first scientific hand-held calculator (the HP-35) is introduced for $395

February 2

1795 The first food is canned by Nicholas Appert, a French chef who was paid by the French government to invent a method for preserving food for its armies

1852 First modern public restrooms open in London

1935 First polygraph test is administered to suspects in a crime in Portage, WI

1949 First around-the-world, non-stop flight is completed; the plane was a B-50 bomber, which flew 23,452 miles in 94 hours

1962 Eight of the nine planets lined up—the first such occurrence in 400 years

1978 Sid Vicious of "The Sex Pistols" dies

1982 *Late Night with David Letterman* debuts

February 3

1938 Bud Abbott and Lou Costello first appear as regulars on the Kate Smith Hour radio program

1959 Rock stars Buddy Holly, Richie Valens, and J.P. "The Big Bopper" Richardson are killed in Iowa plane crash

1966 U.S. launches its first operational weather satellite, ESSA-1

February 4

1789 George Washington is elected first president of U.S.

1868 Charles Darwin begins writing one of his two defining works, "The Descent of Man and Selection in Relation to Sex"

1902 Charles Lindbergh is born

February 5

1850 First adding machine with keys is patented by Du Bois Parmelle of New Paltz, NY

1870 First animated photographic picture projection is exhibited to the public in Philadelphia, PA

1974 U.S. space probe Mariner 10 returns first close-up photos of the cloud structure surrounding Venus

February 6

1937 John Steinbeck's *Of Mice and Men* is published

1944 First successful fertilization of a human egg in a test tube is performed

1959 The U.S. test-fires the first ICBM from Cape Canaveral

February 7

1938 Harvey Firestone, founder of Firestone Tire and Rubber Company, dies

1964 Beatles arrive in U.S. for the first time, signaling the beginning of "The British Invasion"

February 8

1928 First trans-Atlantic transmission of a televised image is made between Purley, England and Hartsdale, NY

1969 The Boeing 747 makes its maiden flight

February 9

1964 Beatles make their first appearance on the Ed Sullivan Show and are watched by about 40% of the U.S. population

1981 Bill Haley, who recorded the classic "Rock Around the Clock," dies

February 10

1992 Alex Haley, author of *Roots*, dies

February 11

1650 Rene Descartes, known as the "father of modern philosophy" and famous for his quote, "I think, therefore I am," dies

1752 First U.S. hospital opens in Philadelphia

1809 The steamboat is patented by Robert Fulton

1847 Thomas Edison is born

1928 The La-Z-Boy recliner is invented, eventually being offered to the public in 1929

1939 First paper on nuclear fission is published, paving the way for the development of nuclear chain reaction

1963 The Beatles record their first album, "Please Please Me"

February 12

1878 Baseball catcher's mask is patented at Harvard University

1941 First test-injection of penicillin on a human is performed

1999 President Bill Clinton is acquitted in impeachment hearing

February 13

1923 Chuck Yeager, first pilot to break the sound barrier, is born

February 14

1876 Alexander Graham Bell is issued a patent for the telephone

1946 ENIAC, the world's first electronic digital computer, first demonstrated at the University of Pennsylvania; built from 17,468 electronic vacuum tubes, this behemoth occupied a 30'×50' room, was the single largest electronic device in the world at the time, and paved the way for modern PCs

1962 First televised tour of the White House airs, hosted by Jackie Kennedy

1984 First combined heart-liver transplant is performed

1990 U.S. space probe Voyager I takes the first photograph of the entire solar system

February 15

1758 Mustard is first advertised for sale in U.S.

1954 Scientists achieve an ocean exploration depth record of 13,287 feet (more 2,000 fathoms, or 2 1/2 miles) by reaching the Atlantic Ocean floor, near Dakar, Senegal

February 16

1923 King Tutankhamen's tomb in Thebes, Egypt is opened

1946 First commercial helicopter—the four-seat Sikorsky S51—is flown

1968 First 911 emergency telephone system introduced in Haleyville, AL

February 17

1869 Periodic Table of Elements is created by Dmitri Mendeleev

1911 First automobile self-starter was installed in a Cadillac, replacing the dangerous crank starter used on earlier automobiles

February 18

1564 Michelangelo dies

1898 Enzo Anselmo Ferrari is born

1901 First vacuum cleaner is patented

1977 First space shuttle orbiter, the Enterprise, is flight tested atop a 747 jet

February 19

1831 The first coal-burning locomotive makes its first run in Pennsylvania

1878 Phonograph is patented by Thomas Edison

February 20

1986 Soviet Union launches space station Mir

February 21

1512 Amerigo Vespucci, for whom America was named, dies

1902 First U.S. brain surgeon, Harvey Cushing, performs brain surgery

1931 Alka Seltzer is introduced, much to the joy of over-indulgers everywhere

1965 Malcom X is assassinated

February 22

1785 Jean-Charles-Athanase Peltier, founder of the Peltier effect used in extreme PC cooling systems today, is born

1857 Radio innovator Heinrich Hertz is born

February 23

1893 The first diesel engine is patented

1896 The Tootsie Roll is introduced

1997 First sheep is cloned in Scotland—the first mammal ever successfully cloned from a cell from an adult animal

February 24

1871 Charles Darwin's *Descent of Man* is published in London

1991 Gulf War U.S. ground attack begins in Kuwait and Iraq

February 25

1616 Under threat of imprisonment by the church, Galileo renounces his claims that the Earth revolves around the sun

1837 The first practical electronic motor is patented by Thomas Davenport

1913 The 16th Amendment is ratified, paving the way for income tax collection

February 26

1829 Levi Strauss is born

1895 The first glass blowing machine is patented

1935 Radar is first demonstrated in England

1949 First nonstop, around-the-world flight is completed

1984 Last U.S. Marines leave Beirut after an 18-month peace-keeping mission

February 27

1879 Artificial sweetener, Saccharin, is discovered at Johns Hopkins University

1900 Aspirin is patented in the U.S. by Felix Hoffman

1922 19th Amendment is passed, protecting the voting rights of U.S. women

1936 Ivan Petrovich Pavlov dies

February 28

1983 Last episode of *M*A*S*H* airs

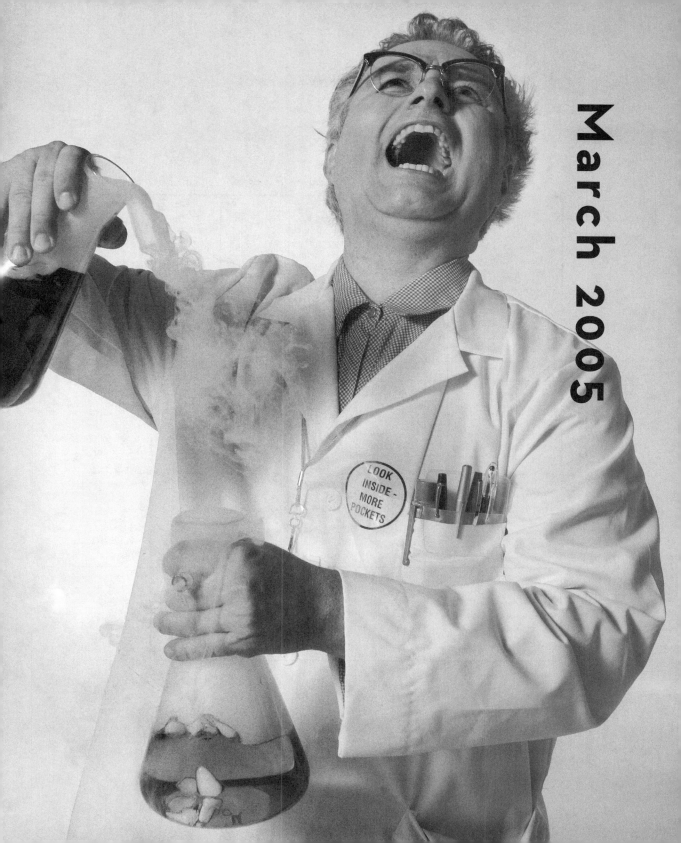

March 2005

March 2005

SUNDAY	MONDAY	TUESDAY	WEDNESDAY	THURSDAY	FRIDAY	SATURDAY
		1 1941 The first commercially licensed FM station begins transmitting from Nashville, TN	**2** 1949 First automatic streetlight is installed in New Milford, CT	**3** 1847 Alexander Graham Bell is born	**4** 1997 Human cloning research funding is banned in U.S. by President Bill Clinton	**5** 1868 Stapler is patented in Birmingham, England
6 1950 Silly Putty is invented	**7** 1876 Telephone is patented	**8** 1983 PC-DOS is released by IBM	**9** 1822 Artificial teeth are patented in Graham, NY	**10** 1876 Alexander Graham Bell makes first telephone call	**11** 1927 First rear-projection screen is installed	**12** 1923 First movie with sound is recorded on film
13 1877 Earmuffs are patented in Farmington, Maine	**14** 1879 Albert Einstein is born	**15** 1892 Escalator is patented	**16** 1926 First liquid-fueled rocket is launched in Auburn, MA	**17** St. Patrick's Day 1845 The rubber band is patented in London	**18** 1931 First commercial electric razor is introduced by Colonel Jacob Schick	**19** 1831 First recorded bank robbery in U.S. history occurs in New York
20 1916 Albert Einstein's "Theory of General Relativity" is published	**21** First day of Spring 1963 Alcatraz closes, never again to house prisoners	**22** 1960 Laser (Light Amplification by Stimulated Emission) is patented	**23** 1812 The Dixie Cup is invented	**24** 1989 The Exxon Valdez wrecks in Prince William Sound in southern Alaska	**25** Good Friday 1954 RCA announces production of the first color television sets	**26** 1872 Fire extinguisher is patented
27 Easter Sunday 1860 Corkscrews with 'T'-shaped handles are patented	**28** 1899 Guglielmo Marconi sends the first wireless telegraph message	**29** 1886 First batch of Coca-Cola is brewed over a fire in a backyard in Atlanta, Georgia	**30** 1842 Anesthesia (sulfuric ether) is first used for surgery	**31** 1880 Wabash, IN becomes the first U.S. town to use electric lighting		

March 1, 2005

TUESDAY

THIS WEEK'S FOCUS: GOOGLE

ON THIS DAY: LISP PROGRAMMER'S MANUAL RELEASED (1960)

The LISP programming language was developed by John McCarthy and other researchers at MIT in late 1958. It's a symbolic functional recursive language based on lambda calculus, used especially for artificial intelligence and symbolic math. The language's official programmer's manual was released on March 1, 1960.

Related Web site: www.lisp.org

PUT THE GOOGLE TOOLBAR IN YOUR BROWSER

You don't have to go to the Google site to use Google search. When you install the Google Toolbar in Internet Explorer, you can perform all types of Google searches from within your browser.

The search box in the Google Toolbar is where you do all your searching. Enter your query here and click the Search Web button; your query is sent to the Google Web site, and results are displayed in your browser window. Pull down the Search Web list to display a list of other available Google searches (Google Images, Google Groups, and so on).

To view a cached snapshot of the current page, list similar pages, or display other information, click the Page Info button. To highlight (in yellow) the words you searched for, on the current page, click the Highlight button.

My favorite part of the Google Toolbar, however, is the Pop-Up Blocker. With Google's Pop-Up Blocker activated, you'll no longer be pestered by those annoying pop-up ads as you surf the Web. This feature alone makes the Google Toolbar worth installing.

And here's the best part about the Google Toolbar—it's free! Download your copy from toolbar.google.com.

DOWNLOAD OF THE WEEK

GGSearch is a freeware program that consolidates a variety of Google searches—newsgroups, images, news, and so on—into a single application. If you do a lot of Google searching, GGSearch lets you do it all from a separate toolbar that can either float freely on your desktop or dock to any Web browser. Download it at www.frysianfools.com/ggsearch/.

March 2, 2005
WEDNESDAY

THIS WEEK'S FOCUS: GOOGLE

ON THIS DAY: DR. SEUSS BORN (1904)

Theodor Seuss Geisel, AKA Dr. Seuss, was born March, 1904, in Springfield, Massachusetts. His first book, *I Saw It on Mulberry Street*, was published in 1937; he went on to become one of the most famous children's authors in history with such classics as *The Cat in the Hat* and *Green Eggs and Ham*. Geisel passed away in 1991.

Related Web site: www.seussville.com

FINE-TUNE YOUR GOOGLE SEARCH

One of the best ways to fine-tune your Google search is to go to the Advanced Search page; just click the Advanced Search link on the main page. You can also perform many of the same advanced functions from the main-page search box—as long as you know which search parameters to use!

Here are some tips for using Google's advanced search parameters to perform more accurate searches:

- Search for synonyms of a given word by adding a tilde (~) before the keyword, like this: ~red.
- Search for one word or another (an either/or search) by adding an OR between the keywords, like this: red OR green.
- Exclude specific words from your results by adding a minus sign (–) before the undesired keyword, like this red - green.

- Search for an exact phrase by including the phrase within quotation marks, like this: "red green".
- Google automatically ignores certain commons words, such as "the" and "a." If you want to include these words—called *stop words*—in your search, enter a plus sign (+) before the word, like this: +the saint.
- Search for items that fall within a specific numeric range by entering the lowest and highest number, separated by two periods, like this: 100..200.

MAC GADGET OF THE WEEK

The Wacom Cintiq is not only a touch-sensitive graphics pad, it's also—wait for it—either a 15-inch or 18-inch LCD display. The 18-inch is particularly nice (as you knew it would be) with a decent response time, support for DVI and, of course, the ability to draw on the freakin' screen. Price is $1,499 for the 15-inch or $2,499 for the 18-inch; buy 'em at www.wacom.com.

March 3, 2005

THURSDAY

THIS WEEK'S FOCUS: GOOGLE

ON THIS DAY: FIRST MEETING OF THE HOMEBREW COMPUTER CLUB (1975)

The legendary Homebrew Computer Club was the first of its kind, the place where the roots of many Silicon Valley companies were located. From its ranks came the founders of many famous tech companies—Bob Marsh, Adam Osborne, Steve Jobs, and Steven Wozniak among them. The club's first meeting was held on this date in 1975, in a member's garage in Menlo Park.

Related Web site: www.bambi.net/bob/homebrew.html

NARROW YOUR RESULTS WITH GOOGLE'S ADVANCED SEARCH OPERATORS

Google lets you use a variety of search operators to narrow your results by specific criteria. For example, you can choose to search for specific file types, within a specific Web domain, within a specified date range, and so forth.

The following table presents the most useful search operators and what they do. Just insert the operator at the beginning of your query, in Google's main search box.

Operator	Example	Description
filetype:	filetype:pdf	Limits your search to a specific type of file
site:	site:.biz or site: leoville.com	Limits your search to a specific domain or Web site
intitle:	intitle:leo	Searches only within page titles
inurl:	inurl:leo	Searches only within page URLs
intext:	intext:leo	Searches only within page text

Operator	Example	Description
inanchor:	inanchor:leo	Searches only within the link text on a page
cache:	cache:www. leoville.com	Displays the version of a specific page stored in Google's historic cache
link:	link:www. leoville.com	Displays all pages that link to the specified page
related:	related:www. leoville.com	Displays pages that are similar to the specified page
info:	info:www. leoville.com	Displays key information about the specified page

WEB SITE OF THE WEEK

Two Google-related sites for you today. Catch up on the latest news about Google at the unofficial Google Weblog (google.blogspace.com). It's a great resource to find out what's happening at your favorite search site. Or, for a more official view of things, read the internal Google Blog, located at www.google.com/googleblog/.

March 4, 2005

FRIDAY

THIS WEEK'S FOCUS: GOOGLE

ON THIS DAY: AN WANG SELLS CORE MEMORY PATENT TO IBM (1956)

The earliest work on core computer memory was carried out by the Shanghai-born American physicist, An Wang. Dr. Wang received a patent for his work in 1955, by which time core memory was already widely in use. This started a long series of lawsuits, which eventually ended on this date in 1956, when IBM paid Wang several million dollars to buy the patent outright.

Related Web site: www.invent.org/hall_of_fame/149.html

WILDCARDS AND AUTOMATIC STEMMING

Unlike most other search sites, Google doesn't let you use wildcards to complete a word. That means you can't enter book* to search for all forms of the word "book."

Instead, Google employs a technology called *automatic stemming*, where all forms of a word are automatically searched when you enter a query. So if you search for book, Google will automatically search for *book, books, booking*, and so on.

In a way, this is a better approach than using wildcards, because the additional searching is done for you automatically. Just enter the simple form of a word and let Google figure out all the plurals and tenses that might be available.

You can, however, use a whole-word wildcard within a phrase to indicate a missing word. For example, if you enter "i * a dream", Google will return results for "i have a dream," "i want a dream," "i am a dream," and so forth.

PORTABLE GADGET OF THE WEEK

This might be the smallest consumer camcorder on the market today. Philips's key019 is half the size of a typical mobile phone, weighs less than a pound, and contains 128MB of memory—enough to hold 25 minutes of continuous video recording in MPEG-4 format. The camcorder's small size lets you take pictures from just about anywhere—even hidden inside your shirt pocket or tucked away in a corner of your purse. Buy it for $299.99 at www.philips.com.

March 5, 2005

SATURDAY

THIS WEEK'S FOCUS: GOOGLE

ON THIS DAY: NUCLEAR NON-PROLIFERATION TREATY GOES INTO EFFECT (1970)

The Treaty on the Non-Proliferation of Nuclear Weapons (NPT) is one of the great success stories of arms control. With nearly 190 signatory countries, it established a political and legal barrier to the spread of nuclear weapons. Work on the treaty began in 1965, negotiations were completed in 1968, and on March 5, 1970, the treaty went into effect.

Related Web site: www.un.org/Depts/dda/WMD/treaty/

SEARCH FOR SPECIFIC TYPES OF INFORMATION

Most users don't know that Google can let you search for all types of specific information from the main search box. Google is a virtual storehouse of information, if you know how to ask for it—and here are some of my favorites:

- Look up stock quotes by entering the stock ticker in the query box; display more detailed information by using the `stocks:` operator, like this: `stocks:msft`

- Look up word definitions by adding the keyword `define` to your query, like this: `define defenestrate`

- Look up an address by including the person or business' name, address, and city in the search box

- Display a street map by entering a specific address (including city, state, and ZIP code) in the search box

- Perform a reverse phone number lookup by using the `phonebook:` operator, like this: `phonebook:555-555-1212`

- Search by USPS, UPS, and FedEx tracking number, just by entering the number in the search box; you can similarly look up vehicle ID (VIN) numbers, UPC codes, and telephone area codes

- Display flight information by entering the airline and flight number in the search box, like this: `united 2348`

And here's my very favorite Google secret. You can use Google as a calculator, simply by entering an equation into the search box. If you enter `5 * 2`, Google displays `10`; enter `(54/3) + 7 * 5/4` and Google displays `26.75`. You can also use Google to display units of measure and conversions; enter `5 feet in meters` and Google displays `1.524 meters`.

FACT OF THE WEEK

Google is more than a Web site—it's a brand. The 4,000 branding professionals at Brandchannel.com voted Google the Global Brand of the Year for 2003. Runners-up included Apple, Mini, Coke, and Samsung.

March 6, 2005

SUNDAY

THIS WEEK'S FOCUS: GOOGLE

ON THIS DAY: MICHELANGELO VIRUS STRIKES (1992)

The Michelangelo computer virus was first launched in 1991. But it wasn't until the following year that the virus struck big, threatening to erase users' hard disks on March 6th. Upwards of five million computers were expected to be hit, but the virus ended up affecting fewer than 20,000 PCs—the bark being much worse than the bite.

Related Web site: www.vmyths.com/fas/fas_inc/inc1.cfm

GOOGLE DOES MORE THAN JUST SEARCH THE WEB

Google offers more than simple Web searching. Explore the entire Google site, and you'll find a raft of useful information and features, including:

- **Froogle (`froogle.google.com`)**—Search online shopping sites for the lowest prices
- **Gmail (`gmail.google.com`)**—Web-based email
- **Google Answers (`answers.google.com`)**—Query professional researchers, for a fee
- **Google Catalog Search (`catalogs.google.com`)**—Search and browse mail order catalogs online
- **Google Directory (`directory.google.com`)**—Google's version of the human-edited Open Directory
- **Google Groups (`groups.google.com`)**—Search Usenet newsgroups
- **Google Groups 2 (`groups-beta.google.com`)**—A beta version of Yahoo! Groups-like discussion groups
- **Google Image Search (`images.google.com`)**—Search for pictures on the Web

- **Google Local (`local.google.com`)**—Search for local businesses
- **Google News (`news.google.com`)**—Display news headlines from across the Web, as well as search thousands of news sites
- **Google U.S. Government Search (`www.google.com/unclesam/`)**—Search government Web sites
- **Google University Search (`www.google.com/options/universities.html`)**—Search university Web sites

All these different sites make Google something like a portal—but without a messy portal-like home page!

SOFTWARE OF THE WEEK

Advanced Page Rank Analyzer is a third-party tool that retrieves the Google PageRank values for any Web site. It also finds the number of inbound links for each URL and checks each site for availability in the Google/Open Directory and Yahoo! Directory. It's great for optimizing your site's Google ranking. Buy it for $39.95 at www.pagerankanalyzer.com.

March 7, 2005

MONDAY

THIS WEEK'S FOCUS: YAHOO!

ON THIS DAY: TELEPHONE PATENTED (1876)

On this date in 1876, Alexander Graham Bell patented an "Improvement in Telegraphy," which established the principle of the telephone. The telephone model submitted for the patent, called simply "The Patent Model," was a modified version of Bell's previous Gallows Model, and employed a relatively inefficient hinged armature.

Related Web site: atcaonline.com/phone/

USE THE DIRECT ADDRESS

Yahoo! is more than just a search site; it's a huge portal that encompasses dozens of different sub-sites. In fact, there's so much there it's hard to find exactly what you want. Better to bypass the portal and go right to a specific site with the direct URL.

Without listing all the URLs available (which are too numerous to fit on this single page), I can show you how to figure out each address. All you have to do is take the name of the Yahoo! site or service, put a dot after it, and follow it with yahoo.com. So, for example, if you want to go to Yahoo! Chat, put the chat in front of the yahoo.com, and you have the direct URL: chat.yahoo.com. Want to go to Yahoo! Mail? Put the mail in front of the yahoo.com, and go directly to mail.yahoo.com. The URL for Yahoo! Maps is maps.yahoo.com, the URL for Yahoo! News is news.yahoo.com, and the URL for Yahoo! Yellow Pages is (a little tricky, but not too much so) yp.yahoo.com. Easy, eh?

It gets even better. If entering an entire URL is too much work, Yahoo! lets you use special shortcuts in its search box to go directly to a particular Yahoo! site. All you have to do is enter the site or service name, followed by an exclamation mark, and you'll be transferred directly to that site. For example, to go to Yahoo! Travel, enter travel! into the search box, and then click the Search button. To go to Yahoo! Mail, enter mail!. To go to Yahoo! Weather, enter weather!. Just don't forget the exclamation mark!

And if you're not sure just what exactly Yahoo! offers, scroll down to the bottom of the home page and click the Even More Yahoo! link. This displays the More Yahoo! page, which lists all the available sites and services, by category. There's a lot there, believe me.

PC GADGET OF THE WEEK

The D-Link SecuriCam DCS-5300W is a wireless camera designed for surveillance use that also makes a darned good PC-based Webcam. Thanks to the Wi-Fi operation, you can put the camera anywhere in your house and not bother with running a cable to your PC. It also features built-in motion detection and motorized operation; you can pan and tilt the unit from any PC connected to the Internet. Buy it for $399.95 at www.dlink.com.

March 8, 2005

TUESDAY

THIS WEEK'S FOCUS: YAHOO!

ON THIS DAY: PC DOS 2.0 ANNOUNCED (1983)

The initial version of PC DOS was developed in 1980, to power the first IBM PC. The second release of PC DOS was announced on this date in 1983, to supplement the release of the IBM XT. PC DOS 2.0 contained more than twice the number of commands found in 1.0, and included support for hard disk drives.

Related Web site: www.skrause.org/computers/dos_history.shtml

IT'S A SEARCH ENGINE— AND A DIRECTORY

Yahoo! was created in 1994 as a hand-picked directory of Web sites. Stanford University Ph.D. students David Filo and Jerry Yang started keeping track of their favorite sites on the Web, collecting and classifying hundreds and then thousands of different Web pages, ultimately creating a custom database to house all those Web links. They named the database Yahoo!—an acronym for Yet Another Hierarchical Officious Oracle.

Because of its somewhat exclusive nature—along with its easy-to-use categories—the Yahoo! Directory became the most popular search site on the Web. The advent of the automated search engine, however, took away a lot of Yahoo!'s cachet. Let's face it: Google's six billion index pages is a lot more appealing than the Yahoo! Directory's two million pages. (That's *billion* versus *million*—a really big difference.) That's why, several years ago, Yahoo! began to supplement its directory results with results from third-party search engines. Yahoo! first partnered with HotBot, and later with Google, and today offers results from its own proprietary search engine. (Actually, it uses technology from Inktomi, which Yahoo! acquired in 2003.)

Today, when you do a basic Yahoo! search, you get results from the Yahoo! search engine—*not* from the Yahoo! Directory. (Well, sometimes directory results are folded into the search engine results, but still...) If you want higher-quality results, you need to manually limit your search to the Yahoo! Directory only. You can, of course, *browse* the directory (the categories are on the left side of the Yahoo! home page), but it's easier to search.

To search the directory, you have to go to the Yahoo! Search page, located at search.yahoo.com. Select the Directory tab, then enter your query. Your results will be pulled from the Yahoo! Directory only, and should be a bit more targeted than the results you get from the search engine.

DOWNLOAD OF THE WEEK

WebMail Assistant provides additional functionality to both Yahoo! Mail and Hotmail. It offers a more versatile address book, better spam control, the ability to save messages to your local hard disk, templates and stationary, and personalized mail merge. Download it for $19.99 at www.oneseek.com.

March 9, 2005

WEDNESDAY

THIS WEEK'S FOCUS: YAHOO!

ON THIS DAY: MAILBOX PATENTED (1858)

On this date in 1858, the first street mailbox was patented by Albert Potts of Philadelphia. Potts' mailbox comprised a simple metal box designed to attach to a lamppost, and by August these boxes were found along the streets of Boston and New York City.

Related Web site: sblom.com/mailbox/

GET FREE EMAIL—AND LISTEN TO IT BY PHONE

Chances are you already have one or more email accounts through your Internet service provider or place of employment. Why in the world would you want yet another email account?

Well, it's always good to have another email account—especially if it's free, which Yahoo! Mail is. You can use a new account to hide from spammers, or to use for specific purposes. In addition, having a Web-based email account is great when you're traveling; you can access your e-mail from any Web browser on any computer anywhere there's an Internet connection.

If you've already signed up for a Yahoo! service, you already have a Yahoo! ID and password. Your Yahoo! ID becomes your Yahoo! Mail address; just add @yahoo.com to your ID, and you're ready to go. (And if you haven't yet signed up for Yahoo!, do so now—it doesn't cost anything.)

You access Yahoo! Mail at mail.yahoo.com. Yahoo! also offers a paid email service, called Yahoo! Mail

Plus (mailplus.yahoo.com). For $19.99 a year, you get more storage capacity (2GB as of this writing), as well as advanced spam filtering and message management. And no ads, which you get plenty of with the regular Yahoo! Mail service.

Whether you subscribe to Yahoo! Mail or Mail Plus, there's a way to access your messages when you don't have access to a PC. The Yahoo! by Phone service lets you listen to your email messages over any telephone. You access your account by voice recognition; just dial 1-800-MY-YAHOO to retrieve all waiting messages. (Know, however, that Yahoo! by Phone costs $4.95 per month; sign up at phone.yahoo.com.)

MAC GADGET OF THE WEEK

Dr. Bott's DVIator lets you connect older ADC-only displays to newer DVI-based Macs. This neat little device does the same job as Apple's official ADC-to-DVI adapter, but for a few bucks less. Good deal! Buy it for $94.95 at www.drbott.com.

March 10, 2005

THURSDAY

THIS WEEK'S FOCUS: YAHOO!

ON THIS DAY: FIRST TELEPHONE CALL (1876)

On March 10, 1876, Alexander Graham Bell made what was, in effect, the first telephone call. His assistant, Thomas Watson, located in an adjoining room in Boston, heard Bell's voice over the experimental device say those famous words: "Mr. Watson, come here. I want you." Later that year, Bell succeeded in making a phone call over outdoor lines.

Related Web site: inventors.about.com/library/inventors/bltelephone.htm

USE MY YAHOO! AS YOUR START PAGE

With everything Yahoo! has to offer, it's not surprising that many users use Yahoo! as their start page for all their Web travels. While the normal Yahoo! home page is an okay start page, it's rather generic. Wouldn't it be better to create your own personal version of Yahoo!, comprised of those services that you use most every day?

Well, Yahoo! makes it easy to create your own personal Yahoo! It's called My Yahoo!, where you can pick and choose what you see—and what you *don't* see—every time you log on. Access it at my.yahoo.com. (Easy to remember, eh?)

My Yahoo! can display a variety of different types of content, each in its own module. It's up to you to choose which content modules you want to display. To select which modules are displayed on your My Yahoo! page, click the Choose Content button. When the Personalize Page Content page appears, put a check mark next to each module you want to display and uncheck those topics you don't want to display.

In addition, most modules let you customize the content that is displayed within; for example, you can create your own list of stocks to display in the Portfolios module and choose what types of news are displayed in the My Front Page Headlines module.

After you've decided on all your content, you need to arrange that content on your page. By default, My Yahoo! uses a two-column layout, with the left column narrower than the right. You can also choose a three-column layout, with a big center column; just click the Choose Layout button to make your selection. You can then assign different content modules to different areas of the page.

In addition, if you don't like the default colors of the My Yahoo! page, you can change that, too. Just click the Change Colors button, and then choose from one of the predefined color themes—or click the Customize Theme link to choose your own colors for each page element.

WEB SITE OF THE WEEK

Check out the latest news and rumors about Yahoo! at the Unofficial Yahoo! Weblog (yahoo.weblogsinc.com). It's run by Nino Marchetti, a former Yahoo! employee, and part of the large Webslog, Inc. family of blogs.

March 11, 2005
FRIDAY

THIS WEEK'S FOCUS: YAHOO!

ON THIS DAY: LUDDITE RIOTS BEGIN (1811)

On March 11, 1811, the Luddite riots began in Nottingham, England. A group of laborers blamed the low wages and poor living conditions on new machinery they feared would replace them, and took their frustrations out on the factory itself. The word Luddite has since come to stand for anyone opposed to technological change.

Related Web site: www.spartacus.schoolnet.co.uk/PRluddites.htm

HANG OUT IN YAHOO! MESSAGE BOARDS AND GROUPS

Yahoo! makes it easy for you to hang out with people who share your special interests via Yahoo! Message Boards and Yahoo! Groups. These are two similar—yet different—ways to communicate with your fellow users.

Yahoo! Message Boards (messages.yahoo.com) are the electronic equivalent of old-fashioned bulletin boards. Each message board is devoted to a specific topic; users can read the messages posted on the board and then reply or post their own new messages. Naturally, all messages are visible to the entire public.

By the way, some of the liveliest and most informative Yahoo! Message Boards are those created for specific stocks and securities. If you want inside information about a specific stock, go to that stock's message board and read to your heart's content. (To find a stock's message board, search for the specific stock symbol on the Yahoo! Message Boards home page.)

A Yahoo! Group is similar to a message board, but with added features. A group is more akin to an online "club" where you can gather with others who share your particular interests. The literally millions of different Yahoo! Groups are each devoted to a specific topic or interest; each group includes message boards, photo and file archives, related links, and so on.

You can search for groups of interest from the Yahoo! Groups home page (groups.yahoo.com). Once you find a group you like, you have to apply for membership; some groups have open membership, others need to manually approve new members, still others have invitation-only policies. You can find out more on the home page for each individual group.

PORTABLE GADGET OF THE WEEK

The Grundig Emergency Radio is the perfect radio to have on hand for emergencies, big and small. It receives AM, FM, and shortwave signals, and runs on AC, DC, or battery power. Or, in case of a major emergency, you can power it with the hand crank; two turns per second for 90 seconds provides 40–60 minutes of operation. Buy it for $39.95 at www.grundig.com.

March 12, 2005

SATURDAY

THIS WEEK'S FOCUS: YAHOO!

ON THIS DAY F.D.R. DELIVERS FIRST FIRESIDE CHAT (1933)

On this Saturday morning in 1933, President Franklin Delano Roosevelt gave his first radio talk to the country. Informal and relaxed, these "fireside chats" made Americans feel as if President Roosevelt was talking directly to them. (The first chat, by the way, was on the current bank crisis.)

Related Web site: www.fdrlibrary.marist.edu/firesi90.html

USE YAHOO! TO MANAGE YOUR SCHEDULE AND CONTACTS

Most computer users have an electronic calendar of some sort, as well as an electronic address book. The only problem is, you probably have your calendar on your work PC, so you can't access it from home. Or you have your address book on your home PC, and you can't access it from work, or when you're on the road. The solution to this machine-centric problem is to use a Web-based calendar and scheduler—which Yahoo! happens to offer.

Yahoo! Calendar (calendar.yahoo.com) is a scheduling and calendar utility that houses your information on Yahoo!'s Web servers. Because the information is stored on Yahoo!'s computers, not yours, you can access your schedule from any PC with an Internet connection and a Web browser. All you have to do is enter your Yahoo! ID and password and you have universal access to your appointments and events.

Even better, Yahoo! Calendar lets you do more than just track simple appointments and events. You can also use Yahoo! Calendar to manage a to-do list, track public events and holidays, share your calendar publicly (with family, co-workers, and so

on), and synchronize with another calendar program or PDA.

If you want universal access to your contacts, no matter where you are (or what PC you're using), use Yahoo! Address Book (address.yahoo.com). Like Yahoo! Calendar, Yahoo! Address Book stores your contact information on Yahoo!'s Web servers so that you can access the information from any PC with an Internet connection and a Web browser.

And, if you already have an address book in another application—such as Microsoft Outlook—you can have Yahoo! Address Book import that data so that you don't have to re-enter it manually. Just click the Import/Export link on the Yahoo! Address Book page and follow the onscreen instructions. To synchronize the data in your Yahoo! Address Book with a contact management program or Palm Pilot organizer, click the Sync link and follow those instructions.

FACT OF THE WEEK

Yahoo! is one of the busiest sites on the Web. As of March 2004, traffic across the entire Yahoo! network averaged 2.4 billion page views per day. That traffic came from more than 274 million unique users.

84

March 13, 2005

SUNDAY

THIS WEEK'S FOCUS: **YAHOO!**

ON THIS DAY: URANUS DISCOVERED (1781)

Uranus, the seventh planet from the Sun (and the third largest in the solar system) was discovered by William Herschel on March 13, 1781. Herschel also discovered Uranus' two largest moons, Titania and Oberon, six years later.

Related Web site: www.solarviews.com/eng/uranus.htm

STORE AND SHARE FILES AND PHOTOS

If you want to access your files and photos from multiple PCs—or share them with friends and family—then you need a Web-based storage solution. Yahoo! offers two.

Yahoo! Briefcase (briefcase.yahoo.com) is a way to store files online—on Yahoo!'s Web servers—and then access them from any PC with an Internet connection and a Web browser. You can even set selective access to your Briefcase files so that your friends, family, and co-workers can view, access, and download designated files.

You share the files or photos in your Briefcase by setting access levels for your Briefcase folders. If you want others to access your Yahoo! Briefcase page, they access a Web address that looks like this: briefcase.yahoo.com/*yahooID*/. Replace *yahooID* with your own Yahoo! ID to complete the URL. Anyone accessing a folder in your Yahoo! Briefcase can download any of the files in the folder.

Yahoo! Photos (photos.yahoo.com) is a separate service designed specifically for the management of digital photographs. Not only can you use Yahoo! Photos to print your photos, you can use Yahoo! Photos to store your photos online and then share them with friends and family.

To share your photos online, you first have to create a photo album. You do this by clicking the Create a New Album link. You can then upload your digital photo files to this (or another) album; once you're done uploading, others can access your album and view your photos in their own Web browsers. To share your photos, use this address: photos.yahoo.com/*yahooID*/. Replace *yahooID* with your own Yahoo! ID to complete the URL.

SOFTWARE OF THE WEEK

SpyMail for Hotmail and Yahoo! lets you track all your kids' Web-based email. It captures all messages sent or received, and sends them to your separate email address. Also available for Outlook Express and for capturing instant messages. Buy it for $29.95 at www.internetsafetysoftware.com.

MONDAY

THIS WEEK'S FOCUS: **WEB SEARCHING**

ON THIS DAY: ALBERT EINSTEIN BORN (1879)

The twentieth century's greatest mind was born on March 14, 1879, in Ulm, Württemberg, Germany. His researches include the special and general theories of relativity, quantum theory, relativistic cosmology, and much, much more. He migrated to the United States before the outbreak of WWII, and died in 1955 in Princeton, New Jersey.

Related Web site: www.alberteinstein.info

SEARCHING, PRE-GOOGLE

Today I'll present a bit of a history lesson. Youngsters might not realize this, but the Internet itself existed long before the World Wide Web came along in 1994. Even in those pre-Web days, lots of information was stored on Internet servers around the globe, and lots of users needed to find specific bits of that information. How did they do it?

In those days, information on the text-based Web was stored in various file formats on various computers. Four main tools were available for getting at those text files, all of which are essentially obsolete today:

- **Gopher** was a tool for organizing files on dedicated servers, and it was extremely popular in universities across the U.S. Gopher used a hierarchical file tree; you clicked folder links to see their contents and navigated up and down through various folders and subfolders.

- **Veronica** was a server-based tool used to search multiple Gopher sites for information. You used Veronica somewhat like you use one of today's Web search engines—you entered a query and clicked a Search button, which generated a list of matching documents.

- **WAIS**, which stands for *wide area information server*, let you use the old text-based Telnet protocol to perform full-text document searches of Internet servers.

- **Archie** was a tool for searching FTP sites— Internet servers that store files for downloading. You used Archie to hunt for specific files to download.

Of course, after the Web came along, these old tools went the way of the horse carriage and buggy whip. Although you might still find a few old Gopher servers up and running on one college campus or another, very little new information has been added to these servers since 1994.

PC GADGET OF THE WEEK

This gadget might seem comically odd at first, but I guarantee it'll win you over—especially if you're a pet lover. It's a "remotely controlled pet communication system" that you connect to the Internet, via your PC, and fill with food and water. Then you can use any Internet-connected computer to call your pet, release some food, and watch Fido or Fluffy via the built-in Webcam. Buy it for $500 at www.iseepet.com.

March 15, 2005

TUESDAY

THIS WEEK'S FOCUS: WEB SEARCHING

ON THIS DAY: ESCALATOR PATENTED (1892)

On March 15, 1892, Jesse Reno patented his moving stairs—or what he called the "inclined eleva-tor." He later created a new novelty ride at Coney Island from his patented design, a moving stairway that elevated passengers on a conveyor belt at a 25 degree angle. It took until 1899 for the Otis Elevator Company to produce the first commercial escalator.

Related Web site: www.ic.sunysb.edu/Stu/sthomas/history.htm

FAVORITE SEARCH SITES

When it comes to searching today, you have two main alternatives—Google, and everybody else.

Google (www.google.com), as you already know, is far and away the most popular search engine on the Web. But it's not the only search site out there. Let's look at some of today's search alternatives.

- **AllTheWeb** (www.alltheweb.com)—AllTheWeb is host to the FAST search engine. It's almost as big as Google, and it provides the driving tech-nology behind Yahoo!'s search engine. I like it as a solid number-two behind Google.

- **AltaVista** (www.altavista.com)—Not near as big or as fast as it used to be, AltaVista is still a reasonable alternative to Googling. I particu-larly like its extremely versatile search tools, including full Boolean search.

- **AOL Search** (search.aol.com)—Worth mention-ing only because so many AOL users use it. Results are provided by Google.

- **Ask Jeeves!** (www.askjeeves.com)—This site first gained notice as a natural language search engine, meaning you could ask questions in plain English. When that natural language stuff

didn't work all that well, they turned Ask Jeeves into a more traditional search engine.

- **HotBot** (www.hotbot.com)—Used to be a big shot, now it's in the second tier, behind Google and AllTheWeb. One nice feature is that it lets you send your query to other search engines, right from the main page.

- **MSN Search** (search.msn.com)—Isn't much yet, but Microsoft is developing its own proprietary search technology, so look for big things in the future from this site.

- **Teoma** (www.teoma.com)—An up and coming search engine, poised to give AllTheWeb a run for the money.

As good as some of these sites are, I still do most of my searching at Google. If I can't find it there, then I turn to AllTheWeb or one of the other sites. Google is hard to beat!

DOWNLOAD OF THE WEEK

WebFerret is a freeware metasearch utility for Windows. Enter a query, and it automati-cally searches a dozen different search sites in par-allel. Download your copy at www.ferretsoft.com.

March 16, 2005
WEDNESDAY

THIS WEEK'S FOCUS: WEB SEARCHING

ON THIS DAY: FIRST LIQUID-FUELED ROCKET LAUNCHED (1926)

Dr. Robert H. Goddard, a New England physics professor, was America's foremost rocket pioneer. After 17 years of theoretical and experimental work, Dr. Goddard finally achieved flight of a liquid fueled rocket on March 16, 1926. The flight took place at his Aunt Effie's farm, in Auburn, Massachusetts.

Related Web site: pao.gsfc.nasa.gov/gsfc/service/gallery/fact_sheets/general/frocket/frocket.htm

METASEARCH ENGINES

Different search engines spider the Web according to different criteria, and thus generate different results to your queries. While you could jump from site to site to capture all the possible results, there's a better solution—use a metasearch engine.

A metasearch engine is a site that searches multiple search sites. That is, you enter your query once, and the metasearch engine sends your query to a variety of other sites. The results are then presented on a single page, for your convenience.

The top metasearch sites today include

- Dogpile (www.dogpile.com)
- GoGettem (www.gogettem.com)
- Mamma (www.mamma.com)
- MetaCrawler (www.metacrawler.com)
- Search.com (www.search.com)
- Vivisimo (www.vivisimo.com)

Not all metasearch sites are created equal. Check each site to see which search engines are searched; not all metasearchers search the same search engines. In addition, see how they display results. Some metasearchers display results from different engines in separate sections, while others fold all the results together into a big list—and some even filter out duplicate pages!

MAC GADGET OF THE WEEK

Last week I talked about Dr. Bott's DVIator ADC-to-DVI adapter. Now let's go the other direction with Dr. Bott's DVI Extractor, which lets you connect a DVI display to a Mac with an ADC connector. It's what you need if you want to use a new display with an older Mac. Buy it for $37.95 at www.drbott.com.

THURSDAY

THIS WEEK'S FOCUS: WEB SEARCHING

ON THIS DAY: NEW ELEMENT, CALIFORNIUM, ANNOUNCED (1950)

Fifty-five years ago today, in 1950, scientists at the University of California at Berkeley announced they had created a new radioactive element. They named it Californium, and it was the sixth transuranium element to be discovered.

Related Web site: `pearl1.lanl.gov/periodic/elements/98.html`

POWER UP YOUR SEARCH WITH BOOLEAN OPERATORS

Most search sites—Google being the unfortunate exception—let you fine-tune your search with Boolean operators. These operators come from a form of algebra called Boolean logic, in which all values are reduced to either TRUE or FALSE. For example, if a page matches all conditions of a query, the result is TRUE.

You get to the TRUE or FALSE points by employing Boolean operators, the most common of which are the following:

- AND—A match must contain *both* words to be TRUE. For example, searching for monty AND python will return Monty Python pages or pages about pythons owned by guys named Monty, but not pages that include only one of the two words.

- OR—A match must contain *either* of the words to be TRUE. For example, searching for monty OR python will return pages about guys named Monty, or pythons, or Monty Python.

- NOT—A match must *exclude* the next word to be TRUE. For example, searching for monty NOT python will return pages about guys named Monty but will not return pages about Monty Python—because you're *excluding* "python" pages from your results.

In addition, Boolean searching lets you use parentheses, much as you would in a mathematical equation, to group portions of queries together to create more complicated searches. For example, suppose you wanted to search for all pages about balls that were red or blue but not large. The search would look like this:

```
balls AND (red OR blue) NOT large
```

Use Boolean operators—when you can—to produce a narrower, more focused list of matching sites.

WEB SITE OF THE WEEK

Find out everything that's happening in the world of search at Danny Sullivan's SearchEngineWatch (`www.searchenginewatch.com`). Here you'll find search tips, search engine reviews, search-related news, and a link to the excellent *Search Engine Report* newsletter.

THIS WEEK'S FOCUS: WEB SEARCHING

ON THIS DAY: SCHICK MARKETS FIRST ELECTRIC RAZOR (1931)

The electric razor was invented by a Canadian, Jacob Schick, in the 1920s. Schick was obsessed by shaving and believed that a man could extend his years to 120 by correct, everyday shaving. He was wrong, of course, but he still came up with the first electric razor, which went on sale this day in 1931. It sold for $25.

Related Web site: `www.xs4all.nl/~pedewei/index.htm`

TIPS FOR MORE EFFECTIVE SEARCHING

Here are a half-dozen really good tips you can use to produce the most effective results from your online searches:

- **Use descriptive words to narrow your search**— Using multiple words helps the search engine get a handle on the concept you're looking for— the more words the better. So instead of searching for a `ford`, search for a `1964 ford mustang`.

- **Put the important stuff first**—You get different results with `sport car` than you do with `car sport`; the first word typically gets greater weighting.

- **Search for synonyms**—Is it big or is it large? Use `big OR large OR huge` to catch all possible variations.

- **Search for specific phrases**—Use quotes to search for exact phrases. If you want to search for the movie *Heavy Metal*, search for `"heavy metal"` not `heavy metal`—which will return a lot of sites about heavy filing cabinets made of metal!

- **Group like items**—Think of your query as an algebraic expression. Group related items in parentheses, and think left-to-right. For example, if you want to search for heavy metal or music sites that don't include Def Leppard, write it like this: `("heavy metal" OR music) NOT "def leppard"`.

- **Truncate words or use wildcards**—If you want to pick up both singular and plural versions of your keywords, don't search for the plural! Many search engines use automatic stemming, so searching for `truck` will return both truck and trucks (and trucking, for that matter). For those engines that don't automatically stem, stick a "*" wildcard after the keyword (`truck*`, using the current example).

PORTABLE GADGET OF THE WEEK

The Skymaster Weathermaster is a portable weather station in the body of a small pocket knife. It provides all sorts of weather info, including temperature, wind chill, heat index, wind speed, relatively humidity, dew point, barometric pressure, and altitude. Buy it for $175 at `www.speedtech.com`.

THIS WEEK'S FOCUS: **WEB SEARCHING**

ON THIS DAY: IBM PULLS THE PLUG ON THE PC JR. (1985)

Designed as a low-cost computer that anyone could afford, the PC Jr. was also very small in size and weight compared to the IBM PC and XT of the day. It cost between $1000–$2000 but was less functional and upgradeable than its older siblings, and featured a fairly unuseable wireless keyboard. Unfortunately for IBM, it was not taken seriously; introduced in 1983, the PC Jr. was officially killed on this day in 1985.

Related Web site: www.obsoletecomputermuseum.org/ibmpcjr/

SEARCHING FOR PEOPLE

As good as Google and other general search sites are for finding specific Web pages, they're not that great for finding people. When there's a person (or an address or a phone number) you want to find, you need to use a site that specializes in people searches.

People listings on the Web go by the common name of *white pages directories*, the same as traditional white pages phone books. These directories typically enable you to enter all or part of a person's name and then search for his address and phone number. Many of these sites also let you search for personal email addresses and business addresses and phone numbers.

The best of these directories include

- AnyWho (www.anywho.com)
- InfoSpace (www.infospace.com)
- Switchboard (www.switchboard.com)
- WhitePages.com (www.whitepages.com)
- WhoWhere (www.whowhere.lycos.com)

There's also a metasearch site for people searchers—The Ultimates (www.theultimates.com). I really like The Ultimates, especially its capability to perform reverse phone number lookups from its main search page. (Another good site for reverse phone number lookups is the Reverse Phone Directory, at (www.reversephonedirectory.com.)

FACT OF THE WEEK

When it comes to searching, Google knows what you want. Here are Google's top 10 queries for 2003: 1. britney spears; 2. harry potter; 3. matrix; 4. shakira; 5. david beckham; 6. 50 cent; 7. iraq; 8. lord of the rings; 9. kobe bryant; and 10. tour de france.

SUNDAY

THIS WEEK'S FOCUS: WEB SEARCHING

ON THIS DAY: TERRORISTS ATTACK JAPAN SUBWAY (1995)

On March 20, 1995, during morning rush hour, the terrorist group AUM Shinrikyo released deadly sarin gas on several lines of the Tokyo subway system. Twelve people were killed and 6,000 more were injured, making this the most serious terrorist attack in Japan's modern history.

Related Web site: www.wordiq.com/definition/Sarin_gas_attack_on_the_Tokyo_subway

TIPS FOR PEOPLE SEARCHING

Whichever white pages directory you use, here are some general tips that will help you find the people you're looking for:

- The more information you enter, the better the results. At the very least, enter a last name and a state. Follow this strategy if you know exactly who you're looking for and have a good idea where they live.

- Conversely, the less information you enter, the broader your results. Follow this strategy if you don't have a clue who you're really looking for.

- If you know only part of an item, enter that part. For example, if you're not sure whether someone goes by Sherry or Sheryl, enter sher. If you're not sure of her first name—but you know it begins with an "s"—enter s. If you don't remember her first name at all, leave the First Name field blank. And if the site uses wildcards, add a wildcard after the last part of the name you know (sher* or s*, using the above example).

- Remember, many women don't list their phone numbers using their full first name—try searching by their first initial, instead.

- Many married women don't list their phone numbers with their own name, preferring either to list their husband's name only or to list *both* their names, husband first. If you're looking for a married woman, try looking for her husband, or for lastname, husband and wife.

- If you're not sure precisely where someone lives, enlarge your search area. Many of these sites let you select an option to search surrounding towns and regions within a larger metropolitan area.

SOFTWARE OF THE WEEK

Copernic Agent lets you filter, group, and summarize search results from a number of different search sites. Copernic Agent Basic is free; the more fully featured Copernic Agent Personal costs $29.95. Buy it at www.copernic.com.

THIS WEEK'S FOCUS: EASTER EGGS

ON THIS DAY: TENNESSEE PASSES ANTI-EVOLUTION LAW (1925)

On March 21, 1925, the state of Tennessee passed the Butler Act, which outlawed the teaching of evolution as the descent of man from lower animals. This was the statute under which John T. Scopes was charged, leading to the famous Scopes Monkey Trial. Believe it or not, the Butler Act remained the law in Tennessee until 1968.

Related Web site: www.law.umkc.edu/faculty/projects/ftrials/conlaw/evolution.htm

WHAT IS AN EASTER EGG?

An Easter Egg is a hidden feature in a software program, game, or DVD. Easter Eggs are created—and hidden—by the software developers or DVD creators, for their amusement and yours. They're inside jokes, or a way for creators to "sign" their work without their bosses knowing about it.

Easter Eggs can be anything, really. Some Easter Eggs list the names of the program's developers. Others offer hidden commands or levels. Still others offer up jokes, animations, or additional games. You'd be surprised what an Easter Egg can contain!

The one common feature of all Easter Eggs is that they're hidden. That is, they're undocumented, and not terribly obvious. You have to hunt for them, like you do real eggs on Easter morning. They're also entertaining, not malicious. (A hidden "feature" that does any sort of harm is actually a bug!)

How do you find Easter Eggs? Most Easter Eggs are discovered by other users, and spread via word of mouth or on Web sites and newsgroups devoted to the hobby. These users sometimes get information leaked to them by the product's creators; sometimes they stumble over the hidden features; and sometimes they just click around until something comes up. It's easier to find Easter Eggs on DVDs, where they often pop up when you cursor around the menu screens. Discovering software Easter Eggs is a bit more difficult, where you often have to enter a complex series of keystrokes to make the Egg appear.

However you uncover them, Easter Eggs are fun to find. And once you know they're there, finding new ones can become an obsession!

PC GADGET OF THE WEEK

My PC gadget pick this week is simple to describe: It's a big freakin' knob. So, why do you need a big freakin' knob? Well, you can program the Griffin PowerMate to control just about anything you want on you computer. The most obvious use is as a volume knob, but you can also use it as a video editing jog/shuttle wheel, to scroll through Word or Excel documents, to scrub through songs in music sequencing applications, to browse through email messages, and more. Buy it for $45 at www.griffintechnology.com.

TUESDAY

THIS WEEK'S FOCUS: EASTER EGGS

ON THIS DAY: APPLE SUES MICROSOFT (1988)

To the untrained eye—and even to the trained one—the Windows graphical user interface looks suspiciously similar to the Macintosh interface. That explains why, on March 22, 1988, Apple filed an 11-page lawsuit against Microsoft. (And against Hewlett-Packard, whose NewWave software ran on Windows.) The ensuing court battle raged on for five years, until it was ultimately dismissed for lack of cause.

Related Web site: applemuseum.bott.org/sections/gui.html

WINDOWS EASTER EGGS

What easier place to look for Easter Eggs than within your operating system? Here are some tried-and-true Easter Eggs for various versions of Microsoft Windows.

Windows Me

Select Start > Run, enter `edit   c:\WINDOWS\SYSTEM\hid.dll`, and press Enter. On the seventh line of the resulting file, it will say "I Hate Jello."

Windows 98/ME

Right-click anywhere on the desktop and select Properties from the pop-up menu. When the Properties dialog box appears, select the Screen Saver tab and choose 3D Pipes. Click Settings and choose Multiple Pipes, Traditional with Mixed Joints, Solid Texture, and maximum resolution. Click OK and watch the resulting screensaver; every so often, the pipe joint will be a teacup!

Windows 98/ME

Select Start > Run, enter `welcome.exe` (in Windows 98) or `regwiz-r` (in Windows ME), and press Enter. When prompted, click Register Now. When the first screen of the Registration Wizard appears, hold down Ctrl+Shift and right-click on the image to the left. This should display a hidden credits screen.

Windows 95

Right-click anywhere on the desktop and select New > Folder from the pop-up menu. Name the new folder `and now, the moment you've all been waiting for`. Now right-click the new folder on the desktop and rename it to `we proudly present for your viewing pleasure`. Right-click the new folder again and rename again to `The Microsoft Windows 95 Product Team!` Open the folder to display the product team credits.

Windows NT

From the Control Panel, open the 3-D text screensaver, and enter `I love NT` as the screensaver text. When the screensaver starts, watch what text it actually displays.

DOWNLOAD OF THE WEEK

This week's download has an Easter egg theme. The 3D Flying Easter Eggs Screensaver is a fun and free screensaver for your desktop, one of many holiday-themed screensavers available at www.acez.com/eastereggs.htm.

WEDNESDAY

THIS WEEK'S FOCUS: EASTER EGGS

ON THIS DAY: AMERICA'S FIRST TWO-PERSON SPACE FLIGHT (1965)

On this day in 1965, Gemini 3—America's first two-person space flight—blasted off from Cape Kennedy. Astronauts Virgil I. Grissom and John W. Young manned the capsule for a total flight time of 4 hours and 54 minutes.

Related Web site: www.nytimes.com/learning/general/onthisday/big/0323.html

MACINTOSH EASTER EGGS

Easter Eggs aren't just for Windows users. Here are some cool Easter Eggs for Mac users everywhere.

OS X

Go to the Applications folder and launch the pCalc2 app. Notice the icon for 6x7=?, go up to the Constants menu, and select Ultimate Answer. Fans of *Hitchhiker's Guide to the Galaxy* should appreciate the solution.

OS X

Open the Finder, then open any window and click the minimize button while holding down Cmd+Shift. This will minimize the window in slow motion, using the new "genie effect."

OS X

Go to the Applications folder and look for the Mail icon. Ctrl+Click the icon, and then select Show Package. Open the Contents-Resources folder, and then open senders.tiff with Preview. Watch for the new layers to the right of the window—and the eight people who are "somehow close to the app."

OS 9

Hold down Ctrl+Option+Cmd, then go to the Apple menu and choose About the Mac OS 9 Team. These are the guys! (This also works for some older versions; choose the appropriate option on the Apple menu.)

OS 7.5

Restart computer, and as soon as the screen goes black, hold down the Option+Cmd+Q+T keys. Keep holding them down while your Mac boots up; after about halfway through the process, a movie and song should start playing.

MAC GADGET OF THE WEEK

For the past two weeks, I've recommend Mac gadgets that help you cope with Apple's abandonment of the ADC connector. Well, here's another one, Gefen's VGA to ADC adapter. This gadget is particularly useful for connecting an older ADC display to a Mac PowerBook with a VGA connector. Buy it for $299 at www.gefen.com.

March 24, 2005

THURSDAY

THIS WEEK'S FOCUS: EASTER EGGS
ON THIS DAY: JULES VERNE DIES (1905)

Jules Verne, the enormously popular founding father of the science fiction genre, died on this date in 1905. His influential works included *A Journey to the Center of the Earth* (1864), *From the Earth to the Moon* (1865), and *Around the World in Eighty Days* (1873).

Related Web site: www.kirjasto.sci.fi/verne.htm

SOFTWARE EASTER EGGS

For your viewing pleasure—some cool Easter Eggs for popular software programs!

Microsoft Word

Open a new Word document, type =rand(200,99), and press Enter. Wait a few seconds and you'll see a typing demonstration.

Excel 2000

Select File > Save as Web Page. Select Publish Sheet and Add Interactivity, and then save the HTM page in a convenient folder. Launch Internet Explorer and open the HTM page you just saved; you should have an Excel worksheet in the middle of the browser. Select row 2000, and tab so that WC is the active column. Hold down Shift+Crtl+Alt and click the Office logo in the upper-left of the page. Excel now launches a spy hunter-like game. Use the arrow keys to drive, space to fire, O to drop oil slicks, and H to use your headlights.

Excel 97

Open a blank worksheet. Press F5, go to r97c12:r97c24, and press Enter. Press the Tab key, then hold down Ctrl+Shift and click the Chart Wizard button in the toolbar. This launches a hidden version of Flight Simulator. Have fun!

Microsoft Works 7 or WorkSuite 2003

From the home page of the Works Task Launcher, click Start a Blank Project. In the Project Title section, type weiVtcejorP. (That's "Project View" backwards, without the space.) Click in any empty space below the title and press Ctrl+F6—and start playing whack-a-mole! (Those Microsoft developers really like the games...)

Winamp Version 5

Make sure you're using the default Winamp Modern skin. Select the main window and type nullsoft. (The Open File dialog box will open every time you type an "l," so press Esc each time to close it.) This causes the main window to flash bright and dark along with the beat of the song you're listening to.

WEB SITE OF THE WEEK

The Easter Egg Archive (www.eeggs.com) is one of the best sites on the Web to find all manner of software and DVD Easter Eggs. Search for Eggs by software/movie title, or submit any Eggs you find yourself.

March 25, 2005

FRIDAY

THIS WEEK'S FOCUS: EASTER EGGS

ON THIS DAY: RCA SHIPS FIRST COLOR TV (1954)

Production of RCA's first commercial color TV sets began on this date in 1954 at RCA's Bloomington, Indiana, plant. The CT-100 ("The Merrill") came with a 15-inch picture tube and retailed for $1,000—quite a high price for the day.

Related Web site: www.novia.net/~ereitan/

GAME EASTER EGGS

Next up—Easter Eggs for some popular PC games.

Unreal Tournament 2004

Install the Community Bonus Pack 2. Start a regular deathmatch in the map Killbillybarn (DM-CBP2-KillbillyBarn). In the map, near the wooden fence, there is a small shed. Pick up the lightning gun that is leaning there, and walk to the fence immediately behind the shed. You will see a small rock formation ahead of you, with a red mark on the rocks. Aim at it, and fire. The truth is out there!

The Sims

Start the game and make a new family. Lock the family in a room of a house, with no appliances, until they die. Take their urns and put them in a corner, then make a new family and put them in the same house. Now press Ctrl+Shift+C and type Dig_Up_Her_Bones. Watch Mom rise from the dead!

Zoo Tycoon

Lots of Eggs in this one. Here are a few:

- During October 31st on the in-game calendar, pause the game. Under Scenery, you will be able to buy a Jack-o-Lantern.

- During December 25th on the in-game calendar, pause the game. Under Scenery you can buy a snowman (that won't ever melt!), and under Foliage you can now grow a Christmas tree.

- Rename any guest Mr. White to change all of your guests' clothing white. (This also changes the buildings' roofs white.) This also works with Mr. Orange, Mr. Pink, Mr. Brown, and Mr. Blue.

- Rename an exhibit to Cretaceous Corral to be able to adopt Triceratops.

- Rename an exhibit to Xanadu to be able to adopt unicorns.

- Rename a guest to Alfred H to have a flock of birds chase all your guests out of the zoo.

- Place a lion, tiger, and bear in the same exhibit to be able to purchase "Yellow Brick Road" pathways.

PORTABLE GADGET OF THE WEEK

This is the gadget you need before you host your next party. The Bar Master Deluxe is a handheld drinks guide—like a PDA for bartenders, with recipes for more than 1,000 different mixed drinks. It lets you call up drink recipes by name, type of drink, kind of alcohol, occasion, or type of glass used. Buy it for $24.95 at www.thebarmaster.com.

March 26, 2005

THIS WEEK'S FOCUS: EASTER EGGS

ON THIS DAY: HEAVEN'S GATE MASS SUICIDE (1997)

On March 26, 1997, the bodies of 39 members of the Heaven's Gate techno-religious cult were found inside a mansion in Rancho Santa Fe, California. The cult, comprised of professional Web page designers who used the Internet to win converts, committed suicide over a several-day period in late March. They died in shifts, with some members helping others take a lethal cocktail of phenobarbital and vodka before downing their own doses of the fatal mixture.

Related Web site: www.rickross.com/groups/heavensgate.html

DVD EASTER EGGS

And now for something completely different—DVD Easter Eggs!

Reservoir Dogs (10th Anniversary Edition)

On the Special Features menu of the second disc, enter the K-BILLY Radio section and select the button closest to the right side of the screen. This plays a recreation of the ear-cutting scene, using action figures!

Hellboy (2 Disc Special Edition)

On the main menu of the second disc, select Kroenen's Lair. On the next menu, select Animatics. Highlight "Back," and then press the down key once. You should now be highlighting three bullet holes; select these and press Enter. A hidden animatic!

X-Men

Go to the Special Features section. Select Theatrical Trailers and TV Spots, and then press the left arrow on your remote. A symbol of a rose should be highlighted; press Enter. Special guest hero: Spider-Man!

Spider-Man (Special Edition)

On disc one, go to the Commentaries section. Click the picture of Harry Osborne on the left side of the screen, and you'll see lotsa CGI bloopers—including Spidey and the Green Goblin doing aerobics!

South Park—The Second Season

On disc one, go to the main menu and select Languages. On the Languages screen, move the cursor up and to the right to select Mr. Hanky's tie, and then press Enter. Mr. Hanky is a drug addict!

FACT OF THE WEEK

Here's more proof that sex sells. According to Web monitoring firm Hitwise, online porn sites get three times the traffic of Google and other Internet search engines. Their survey says that adult sites receive 18.8% of all Web visits, entertainment sites get 8%, business and finance 7.4%, shopping and classifieds 7%, and search engines and directories a mere 5.5%. As *USA Today* put it, ogle definitely beats Google.

THIS WEEK'S FOCUS: **EASTER EGGS**

ON THIS DAY: FDA APPROVES VIAGRA (1998)

The phrase "staying up all night" gained new meaning on this date in 1998, when the Food and Drug Administration approved the sale of Viagra. The little blue pill, made by Pfizer, was designed to fight male impotence—and became the subject of millions of spam emails.

Related Web site: www.viagra.com

INSTANT MESSAGING EASTER EGGS

Finally, some cool instant messaging Easter Eggs.

MSN Messenger with Messenger Plus Add-In

Start a conversation with another person who also has the Messenger Plus add-in running, and then type the command **/insult**. A random insult will appear, and the Word Dueler box will launch. Your opponent can then pick a comeback—or be a coward.

The Messenger Plus add-in also offers some hidden sound effects. All you have to do is enter the appropriate command:

- /sbrb—"Be right back," Ah-nold style.
- /sdoh—Homer Simpson says "D'oh!"
- /sevillaugh—"Muahahahha!"
- /skiss—Smack!
- /shello—*South Park*'s Mr. Hanky says "Howdy how!"

Yahoo! Messenger

The big Easter Egg in Yahoo! Messenger is a ton of hidden smileys. Just enter the appropriate characters to see the smiley icons, as noted in the following table:

Enter This	Smiley
b-(	Winking face being punched
@-)	Dazed eyes
$-)	Money eyes
:^o	Pinocchio nose growing
[-x	Shaking finger, no-no style
>:D<	Wants a hug
~o)	Coffee cup
**==	American flag
*-:)	Light bulb
8-X	Skull
=:)	Alien
<@:)	Clown
@};-	Rose
3:O	Cow

SOFTWARE OF THE WEEK

This being Easter Sunday, our recommend software title of the week has a religious theme. QuickVerse Deluxe is the ultimate Bible study guide, offering everything from daily reading plans to Greek/Hebrew Word study. It includes the texts of 16 different Bibles, along with more than 1,000 full-color pictures, illustrations, and maps. Buy it for $299.95 at www.quickverse.com.

March 28, 2005

MONDAY

THIS WEEK'S FOCUS: WEB PAGE TRICKS

ON THIS DAY: THREE MILE ISLAND NUCLEAR ACCIDENT (1979)

The very scary 1979 accident at the Three Mile Island nuclear power plant near Middletown, Pennsylvania, was the most serious in U.S. commercial nuclear power plant operating history. Even though the TMI-2 suffered a partial meltdown of the reactor core, there was only a small release of radioactivity, and no deaths or injuries.

Related Web site: www.nrc.gov/reading-rm/doc-collections/fact-sheets/3mile-isle.html

MAKE A LINK DISAPPEAR

With April Fool's Day coming up, I thought I'd pass on some tricks you can play on visitors to your Web site. Most of these tricks work via JavaScript. Fortunately, you don't have to learn JavaScript programming to take advantage of these tricks. All you need to do is insert the JavaScript code into your page's HTML, using whichever Web page editor you like.

We'll start with a simple little trick that makes a text link disappear when the user clicks it. Actually, it turns the normal link text white, so that it's "invisible" against a white page background. If your background is a different color, change the color in the code accordingly.

Here's the code that does the trick. It's pretty simple; just insert this code into the head of your document.

```
<style>
a:hover {color:#ffffff;}
</style>
```

What a cruel trick to play on visitors to your Web site. They'll think they've really done something wrong when the link they click disappears!

PC GADGET OF THE WEEK

Kensington's FlyLight is a small LED flashlight on a flexible gooseneck, powered by your notebook's USB port. All you have to do is plug it in and you have personal lighting no matter where you might happen to be—on an airplane, in a dark conference room, or in your home office with the lights turned off. Buy it for $19.99 at www.kensington.com.

THIS WEEK'S FOCUS: **WEB PAGE TRICKS**

ON THIS DAY: MARINER 10 FLIES PAST MERCURY (1974)

Mariner 10 was the seventh successful launch in the Mariner series, the first spacecraft to use the gravitational pull of one planet (Venus) to reach another (Mercury), and the first spacecraft mission to visit two planets. Mariner's flyby of Mercury happened on this date in 1974, returning the first-ever close-up images of the planet.

Related Web site: nssdc.gsfc.nasa.gov/nmc/tmp/1973-085A.html

MAKE TEXT FADE IN AND OUT

Here's a cool trick that makes selected text on your page fade in and out. Watching a piece of text vanish before your eyes is kind of neat—unless you're trying to read it, of course.

To fade a piece of text in and out (from white to black and back again), you use a two-part script. The first part of the script goes in the head of your HTML document; the second part goes in the body where you want the fading text to appear. (This effect works only with Internet Explorer, by the way.)

Start by typing the following code into the head of your document:

```
<script language="JavaScript1.2">
<!--
ie4 = ((navigator.appVersion.indexOf("MSIE")>0)
&& (parseInt(navigator.appVersion) >= 4));
var count = 0, count2 = 0, add1 = 3, add2 = 10,
timerID;
function textFade()
{if (ie4)
{count += add1;
count2 += add2;
delay = 30;
if(count2 > 100) count2 = 100;
if(count > 100)
{count = 100;
add1 = -10;
add2 = -3;
delay = 350;}
```

```
if(count < 0) count = 0;
if(count2 < 0)
{count2 = 0;
add1 = 3;
add2 = 10;
delay = 200;}
fader.style.filter =
"Alpha(Opacity="+count2+",FinishOpacity="+count+"
,style=2)";
timerID = setTimeout("textFade()", delay);}}
window.onload = textFade;
//-->
</script>
```

Now insert the following code in the body of your document; replace *text* with the text you want to fade.

```
<div id="fader" style="width:480;
Filter:Alpha(Opacity=0,FinishOpacity=0,style=2)">
text</div>
```

You can apply any normal HTML formatting to the fading text, by inserting `<font>` or formatting or heading tags around the `<div>` tag.

DOWNLOAD OF THE WEEK

1st JavaScript Library, AKA Coocool Stupid Web Tricks Tools, is a shareware program that lets you add advanced JavaScript and DHTML code to your web pages. You can create fun and annoying effects, without any knowledge of Java or JavaScript programming. Try it for free or buy it for $29.95 at www.1stss.com/javascript/.

March 30, 2005

WEDNESDAY

THIS WEEK'S FOCUS: **WEB PAGE TRICKS**

ON THIS DAY: **PENCIL WITH ERASER PATENTED (1858)**

In 1839, Charles Goodyear discovered a way to cure rubber and make it a lasting and useable material. Philadelphian Hyman Lipman took advantage of this better rubber and came up with a way to attach a rubber eraser to a pencil. He received a patent for his invention on this day in 1858, although the patent was later held to be invalid—it was merely the combination of two existing things, without a new use.

Related Web site: www.pencils.com

CYCLE YOUR PAGE'S BACKGROUND COLORS

This trick makes your Web page's background cycle through a variety of colors. All you have to do is copy the following script and insert it after the `<body>` tag in your HTML document:

```
<script language="JavaScript">
<!--
function ChangeColor()
{color = "#";
for (i = 0; i < 6; i++)
{hex = Math.round(Math.random() * 15);
if (hex == 10) hex = "a";
if (hex == 11) hex = "b";
if (hex == 12) hex = "c";
if (hex == 13) hex = "d";
if (hex == 14) hex = "e";
if (hex == 15) hex = "f";
color += hex;}
document.bgColor = color;
setTimeout("ChangeColor();",2000);}
ChangeColor();
//-->
</script>
```

You can change the cycling time between colors by changing the `setTimeout` value. The default value (2000) is about two seconds.

MAC GADGET OF THE WEEK

Elgato's EyeHome acts as an interface between your Mac and a television set or home theater system. Once connected, the EyeHome can be used to play multimedia items on your Mac—it specifically ties into your iLife applications and plays back movies (from iMovie), songs (from iTunes), and photos (from iPhoto) that you have stored in your home folder on your Mac. Buy it for $249 at www.elgato.com.

THIS WEEK'S FOCUS: **WEB PAGE TRICKS**

ON THIS DAY: DESCARTES BORN (1596)

René Descartes was born on March 31, 1596. During his lifetime, Descartes gained fame as a physicist, physiologist, and mathematician, but it is as a highly original philosopher that he is most frequently read today. He is famous for the phrase, "I think, therefore I am." As a mathematician, his work *La géométrie* applied algebra to geometry to create what we now call Cartesian geometry.

Related Web site: `www-gap.dcs.st-and.ac.uk/~history/Mathematicians/Descartes.html`

DISPLAY A MOUSEOVER ALERT BOX

This trick displays an alert box (with text of your choosing) whenever a user hovers over a link on your page. Users have to click OK to close the alert—a really annoying trick!

Begin by inserting the following code into the head of your HTML document:

```
<script language="JavaScript">
<!--
function linkAlert(messageText)
{newMessage = messageText
alert (newMessage);}
//-->
</script>
```

Now use the following code within the body of your document to associate an alert box with a specific link; replace *message* with the desired text for your dialog box.

```
<a href="url" onMouseOver="linkAlert
('message')">linktext</a>
```

When a user hovers over the link, the dialog box will appear and stay visible until the user clicks the OK button. What's *really* annoying is that the user can't ever click the link—the dialog box keeps popping up and getting in the way!

WEB SITE OF THE WEEK

The JavaScript Source (javascript.internet.com) is an excellent resource for all manner of JavaScript tricks. It offers tons of "cut and paste" JavaScript examples you can use to spice up your Web pages. And its all free!

MORE MARCH FACTS

March 1

1692 Salem Witch Hunt begins

1896 Radioactivity is discovered

1950 *Ripley's Believe It or Not* debuts

1966 Soviet probe crashes into Venus

March 2

1969 Concorde SST Supersonic jet makes maiden flight

1972 Pioneer 10 launched to Jupiter, traveling 620 million miles and reaching the planet in December 1973; currently, the probe is more than 75 billion miles from Earth

March 3

1820 *Star-Spangled Banner* is made the official U.S. national anthem

1885 AT&T is incorporated

1991 Rodney King police beating is caught on video

March 4

1789 First session of U.S. Congress is held

1933 *The Lone Ranger* movie is released

March 5

1558 Smoking tobacco is introduced in Europe by Francisco Fernandes

1616 Copernican Theory is ruled "false and erroneous" by the Catholic Church; Galileo subsequently violated this decree and was placed under house arrest for eight years

1770 The Boston Massacre—a clash between American colonists and British soldiers—touches off the American Revolutionary War

1875 Wisconsin state legislature offers $10,000 to anyone inventing a cheap and practical substitute for horses as a means of personal transportation, thus starting the race to invent and patent the first automobile

March 6

1475 Michelangelo Buonarroti is born in Caprese, Italy

1886 First AC power plant begins operation in Great Barrington, MA

1930 First individually packaged frozen foods on sale in Springfield, MA

March 7

1897 World's first cornflakes served to patients at a mental hospital in Battle Creek, MI

1996 First photographs of Pluto are taken by the Hubble Space Telescope

1999 Stanley Kubrick dies

March 8

1972 The Goodyear blimp is flown for the first time

March 9

1858 Mailboxes are patented in Philadelphia, PA

1955 James Dean makes film debut in *East of Eden*

March 10

1964 First Ford Mustangs are produced

March 11

1989 *Cops*—the first reality-based television show—premieres on FOX

March 12

1755 First steam engine is used in New Jersey

1894 First bottles of Coca-Cola are sold

1922 Jack Kerouac is born

1933 First U.S. presidential radio address is given by Franklin D. Roosevelt and dubbed the first "Fireside Chat"

March 13

1781 Uranus is discovered

1969 *The Love Bug* is released by Walt Disney Studios

March 14

1990 Mikhail Gorbachev is elected president of the Soviet Union; though his presidency was short-lived, he is credited with an amazing number of reforms, thus loosening the grip of communism on the people of the Soviet Union

March 15

44 B.C. Julius Caesar is murdered

March 16

1966 First U.S. manned docking of two spacecraft; the Gemini VIII and Gemini Agena successfully docked

March 17

1958 U.S. launches its first manmade object into space—the Vanguard I satellite

March 18

1834 First U.S. railroad tunnel is completed, connecting Johnstown and Hollidaysburg, Pennsylvania

1850 American Express is founded

March 19

1831 First recorded bank robbery in U.S. history occurs in New York; the suspect is caught almost immediately

March 20

1727 Sir Isaac Newton dies

March 21

1980 U.S. boycotts the Olympics being held in Moscow after Soviet Union does not withdraw troops from Afghanistan

March 22

1895 First motion picture is shown on a screen in Paris, France; the film, *La Sortie des ouvriers de l'usine Lumière* was viewed by 44 people

1907 First cabs in London with taximeters begin operating, giving the cab its modern name, "taxi"

March 23

1983 President Ronald Reagan calls for the U.S. to develop antimissile technology that would make the country nearly impervious to attack by nuclear missiles, marking the beginning of what came to be known as the controversial Strategic Defense Initiative (SDI)—and more commonly known a "Star Wars" program. Some 10 years and $30 billion later, the project was abandoned with little hoopla.

March 24

1874 Harry Houdini is born

1955 First seagoing oil drill rig (for drilling in over 100 feet of water) is placed into service

1989 The worst oil spill in U.S. territory begins when the Exxon Valdez runs aground on a reef in Prince William Sound in southern Alaska, spilling about 11 million gallons of oil into the Pacific Ocean

March 25

1970 The Concorde airplane makes its first sound barrier-breaking flight

March 26

1941 Italy attacks the British fleet at Suda Bay, Crete, using the first manned torpedoes in existence

1997 Thirty-nine victims of a mass suicide are found in San Diego, CA. The dead were members of Heaven's Gate, a religious cult, whose leaders preached that suicide would allow them to leave their bodily "containers" and enter an alien spacecraft hidden behind the Hale-Bopp comet, which passed near earth that same year; it is not known whether these wayward souls managed to catch their flight.

1998 Intel CEO Andy Grove steps down; Grove is credited with driving Intel to becoming the world leader in CPU, chipset and motherboard innovator and manufacturer

March 27

1855 Process for obtaining oil from shale and cannel coal is patented; the result: kerosene

1961 First mobile computer—essentially a UNIVAC Solid-State 90 computer filling an entire van—is used

March 28

1866 First hospital ambulances are used

1979 Three Mile Island nuclear accident

March 29

1886 First batch of Coca-Cola is brewed over a fire in a backyard in Atlanta, Georgia, by Dr. John Pemberton; advertised as a "brain tonic and intellectual beverage," Coke originally contained cocaine until 1904, when the drug was banned by Congress

1903 Regular news service begins between New York and London using Guglielmo Marconi's wireless telegraphing system

1974 U.S. satellite Mariner 10 takes the first close-up pictures of Mercury after being launched in November 1973; on its way to Mercury, Mariner 10 flew by Venus on February 5, 1974 and discovered evidence of the planet's rotating clouds

March 30

239 B.C. First recorded passage of what we now know as Halley's Comet by Chinese astronomers

1858 The first pencil with an attached eraser is patented

1870 The 15th Amendment, granting African-American men the right to vote, is formally adopted into the U.S. Constitution

1950 The invention of the phototransistor is announced

1981 President Ronald Reagan is wounded in an assassination attempt; he recovered fully and served two full terms as President of the United States; three others were seriously wounded in the attack

March 31

1932 Ford Motor Company unveils its "V-8" engine, the first of its kind

April 2005

April 2005

SUNDAY	MONDAY	TUESDAY	WEDNESDAY	THURSDAY	FRIDAY	SATURDAY
				1 April Fool's Day 1976 Apple Computer is founded	**2** 1978 Velcro is first offered for sale
3 1973 First cellular phone call is made	**4** 1983 Space Shuttle Challenger makes its maiden voyage	**5** 1994 Nirvana vocalist, Kurt Cobain, commits suicide in Seattle, WA	**6** 1954 TV dinners are first made available by Swanson & Sons	**7** 1827 First matches go sale in England	**8** 1862 First aerosol dispenser is patented	**9** 1959 NASA names first seven astronauts in history
10 1972 U.S. joins 70 other nations in an agreement banning biological warfare	**11** 1986 Halley's Comet makes its last approach to Earth until 2061	**12** 1994 First Internet spamming program is used in Arizona	**13** 1970 Apollo 13 disaster	**14** 1912 Titanic strikes iceberg in the North Atlantic and sinks the next morning	**15** 1878 Ivory soap is first made available	**16** 1947 First television camera zoom lens is demonstrated
17 1790 Benjamin Franklin dies	**18** 1955 Albert Einstein dies	**19** 1995 Oklahoma City, OK Federal Building is bombed, killing 168 people	**20** 1940 First electron microscope is demonstrated	**21** 1910 Mark Twain dies	**22** Earth Day	**23** Administrative Professionals' Day (Secretaries Day)
24 1962 First satellite television signals are sent	**25** 1953 DNA structure is published	**26** 1986 Chernobyl nuclear accident occurs	**27** 1981 First computer to use a mouse—Xerox STAR 8010— is introduced	**28** 1930 Eclipse of the sun is first filmed	**29** 1923 Zipper is patented in Hoboken, NJ	**30** 1939 Commercial TV debuts

April 1, 2005

FRIDAY

THIS WEEK'S FOCUS: **WEB PAGE TRICKS**

ON THIS DAY: **BIG BANG THEORY PROPOSED—NO FOOLIN' (1948)**

On this date in 1948, *Physical Review* published the paper "The Origin of Chemical Elements," by physicists Ralph Alpher, Hans Bethe, and George Gamow. That paper proposed that the universe was created in a "big bang," which helped to explain the relative abundances of light elements in the universe.

Related Web site: ssscott.tripod.com/BigBang.html

MAKE A PICTURE FADE IN AND OUT

Our April Fool's Day trick starts out by displaying a blank spot on your Web page. When users hover the cursor over the blank spot, the underlying picture slowly fades into view—and fades back out again when they remove the cursor. Just type the following code into the body of your document:

```
<script language="JavaScript1.2">
<!--
var startOpacity = 0;
var endOpacity =100;
var currentOpacity = startOpacity;
var fadeSpeed = 2;
var si;
var cleared = true;
function fadeImage(what,doshow)
{if (document.all)
{cleared = false;
(doshow) ? currentOpacity+=fadeSpeed :
currentOpacity-=fadeSpeed;
eval(what+".filters.alpha.opacity=
"+currentOpacity);
if (currentOpacity <= startOpacity ¦¦
currentOpacity >= endOpacity)
{clearInterval(si);
cleared = true;}}
if (document.layers) clearInterval(si);}
function startFade()
```

```
{if (!cleared) clearInterval(si);}
//-->
</script>
<img name="picture1" src="filename" border=0
style="filter:alpha(opacity=0)"
onMouseover="startFade();si=setInterval
('fadeImage(\'picture1\',true)',10);"
onMouseout="startFade();si=setInterval
('fadeImage(\'picture1\',false)',10);">
```

Replace *filename* with the URL and name of the picture file you want to appear. You can control how fast the image fades in by changing the value of the *fadeSpeed* variable; the higher the number, the faster the change.

PORTABLE GADGET OF THE WEEK

Okay, there's nothing really high-tech about this gadget, but it's kind of fun anyway. The AirZooka is a small gun that shoots a ball of compressed air up to 40 feet. Just pull back and release the plastic air launcher; then watch the fun begin. Buy it for $14.95 at www.airzooka.net.

April 2, 2005

SATURDAY

THIS WEEK'S FOCUS: WEB PAGE TRICKS

ON THIS DAY: RADAR PATENTED (1935)

On this date in 1935, Robert Watson-Watt was granted a patent for radio detection and ranging—otherwise known as radar. Watson-Watt's originally began work for the British military on a "death ray" that could melt metal and incapacitate pilots; when that proved infeasible, research turned to a system of radio-location using a pulse/echo technique. The resulting radar system proved instrumental in defending Britain against Germany's air raids in the later years of the second world war.

Related Web site: www.penleyradararchives.org.uk

SHAKE A WINDOW

This is a neat trick that will make your visitors think that something is wrong with their browser—or their PC. Add this code to your page and any visitor's browser window will shake (briefly), as if it had a chill.

To shake a window, type the following code into the head of your HTML document:

```
<script language="JavaScript1.2">
<!--
function windowShake(n)
{if (parent.moveBy)
{for (i = 10; i > 0; i--)
{for (j = n; j > 0; j--)
{parent.moveBy(0,i);
parent.moveBy(i,0);
parent.moveBy(0,-i);
parent.moveBy(-i,0);}}}}
//-->
</script>
```

To activate the shake when the page is loaded, add the onLoad event handler to the <body> tag, like this:

```
<body onLoad="windowShake(2)">
```

You can extend the length of the shake by increasing the windowShake variable (default=2) in the onLoad event.

FACT OF THE WEEK

Internet access is anything but universal. The United Nations' Economic Commission for Africa says there is only one Internet user for every 250 people in Africa. And most of these connected users are in South Africa. This 1-in-250 number compares with a worldwide average of one Internet user for every 35 people.

April 3, 2005

SUNDAY

THIS WEEK'S FOCUS: WEB PAGE TRICKS

ON THIS DAY: FIRST CELL PHONE CALL (1973)

On April 3, 1973, the first portable phone call was placed by inventor Martin Cooper. A tad larger than today's cell phones, Cooper's phone was 10 inches high, 3 inches deep, and an inch-and-a-half wide; it weighed a hefty 30 ounces.

Related Web site: www.cellphonecarriers.com/cell-phone-history.html

NAG USERS TO MAKE YOUR PAGE THEIR START PAGE

Our last Web page trick nags users to make your page their default start page. Read carefully; it's a bit involved.

First, you have to change the normal `<html>` tag at the top of your document to read as follows:

```
<html XMLNS:IE>
```

Next, type the following code into the head of your document:

```
<style>
@media all
{IE\:HOMEPAGE {behavior:url(#default#homepage)}}
</style>
<script language="JavaScript">
<!--
function netscapeAlert()
{if (confirm("Do you want to return and make the
previous page your home page?"))
{location.href = "url";}}
function setPage()
{if ((navigator.appName == "Microsoft Internet
Explorer") && (navigator.appVersion>="4"))
```

```
{thisPage.setHomePage("url");}
else
{netscapeAlert()}}
//-->
</script>
<IE:HOMEPAGE ID="thisPage" />
```

Finally, add the following `onUnload` event to the `<body>` tag, as follows:

```
<body onunLoad="setPage()">
```

Be sure to replace both instances of *url* with the full address of your current page.

SOFTWARE OF THE WEEK

Microsoft FrontPage is one of the most popular Web page editors in use today. It works pretty much like Microsoft's Office applications, and lets you create pages in a WYSIWYG fashion, or by editing raw HTML code. Buy it for $199 at www.microsoft.com/frontpage/.

THIS WEEK'S FOCUS: COMPUTER VIRUSES

ON THIS DAY: MARTIN LUTHER KING ASSASSINATED (1968)

Dr. Martin Luther King, Jr. was a pivotal figure in the civil rights movement. He helped organize the Montgomery bus boycott, was a founder and president of the Southern Christian Leadership Conference, and galvanized both blacks and whites in the cause of civil rights. His "I Have a Dream" speech is one of the most famous and inspiring speeches of the modern era. On the afternoon of April 4, 1968, Dr. King was standing on the balcony of the Lorraine Motel in Memphis, Tennessee, when he was shot and killed by assassin James Earl Ray. The nation still mourns the passing of this great man.

Related Web site: thekingcenter.com

THE HISTORY OF COMPUTER VIRUSES

Hard as it is to believe, the first computer virus predates the modern computer era. Technically, the first computer virus was conceived way back in 1949, when computer pioneer John von Neumann wrote a paper titled "Theory and Organization of Complicated Automata." In that paper he postulated that a computer program could be self-replicating—thus predicting today's self-replicating virus programs.

The theories of von Neumann came to life in the 1950s at Bell Labs. Programmers there developed a game called "Core Wars," where two players would unleash software "organisms" into the mainframe computer, and watch as the competing programs would vie for control of the machine—just as viruses do today

The first virus in the wild infected Apple II floppy diskettes in 1981. The virus went by the name of Elk Cloner, and didn't do any real damage; all it did was display a short rhyme onscreen. At the time, Elk Cloner wasn't identified as a virus, however, because the phrase "computer virus" had yet to be coined. That happened in 1983, when programmer Len Adleman designed and demonstrated the first experimental virus on a VAX 11/750 computer. From Adleman's lab to the real world was but a short step.

In 1986, the Brain virus became the first documented file infector virus for MS-DOS computers. That same year, the first PC-based Trojan horse was released, disguised as the then-popular shareware program, PC Write.

From there, things only went downhill, with the popularity of computer bulletin board services (BBSs)—and later, the Internet—helping to spread viruses beyond what was previously physically possible. Where early viruses tended to be spread via infected floppy disks, today's viruses are spread primarily over the Internet, particularly in bogus email attachments. And the chaos continues.

PC GADGET OF THE WEEK

The USB Air Purifier plugs in to your computer's USB slot and provides constant air freshening by removing smoke, dust, germs, and other airborne contaminants. It's small enough to not get in the way (just 3" × 2.5"); just plug it in and let it silently do its job. Buy it for $29.99 at www.thinkgeek.com.

April 5, 2005

TUESDAY

THIS WEEK'S FOCUS: COMPUTER VIRUSES

ON THIS DAY: HOSTESS TWINKIES INVENTED (1930)

Twinkies were created on this day in 1930 when Jimmy Dewar, manager of the Schiller Park, Illinois, bakery, noticed that the pans for Hostess' Little Shortbread Fingers were only used during the summer months. Dewar decided to make use of the pans throughout the year by filling them with golden sponge cake and banana filling. (Today's vanilla filling was the result of a banana shortage during World War II.) Twinkies were introduced nationwide in 1933, by the Continental Baking Company.

Related Web site: www.twinkies.com

REDUCE YOUR CHANCES OF INFECTION

If you want to make yourself less of a target for virus infection, you should take the following preventive measures:

- **Don't open any email attachments you weren't expecting**—The majority of viruses today arrive in your mailbox as attachments to email messages; resist the temptation to open or view every file attachment you receive—even those that appear to come from friends or colleagues.

- **Restrict your file downloading to known or secure sources**—The surest way to catch a virus is to download an unknown file from an unknown site; try not to put yourself at risk like this unless you absolutely have to.

- **Use an up-to-date anti-virus program or service**—Anti-virus programs work; they scan the files on your computer (as well as new files you download, and email messages you receive) and check for any previously identified viruses. They're a good first line of defense, providing you keep the programs up-to-date with information about the very latest viruses.

- **Enable macro virus protection in all your applications**—Most current Microsoft applications include special features that keep the program from running unknown macros—and thus prevent your system from being infected by macro viruses.

My friend Steve Gibson makes the additional recommendation that Internet Explorer users configure the browser's security settings to High. This will keep HTML-based viruses from breaching any IE security holes. If you need to load apps for a given site to work, you can add that site to IE's trusted sites.

DOWNLOAD OF THE WEEK

AVG Anti-Virus FREE Edition is, as the name implies, a free anti-virus utility. It's actually quite effective, every bit as reliable as Norton or McAfee. Plus, of course, it's free. (AVG also makes a more fully-featured Professional Edition of the program, which you can purchase for $33.30.) Download it at free.grisoft.com.

April 6, 2005

WEDNESDAY

THIS WEEK'S FOCUS: COMPUTER VIRUSES

ON THIS DAY: POST-IT NOTES INTRODUCED (1980)

The basic idea for Post-It Notes came to 3M researcher Spencer Silver way back in 1970, when he was trying to invent a strong adhesive; instead, he created a weak adhesive that stuck to objects, but could easily be lifted off. No one knew what to do with the stuff, however, so the idea languished until another 3M scientist got the idea of applying the weak adhesive to pieces of paper. The idea stuck (so to speak), and 3M introduced Post-It Notes nationwide on this date in 1980.

Related Web site: www.3m.com/us/office/postit/

REMOVING THE SASSER VIRUS

Sasser is a particularly nasty virus that spreads over computer networks. To prevent infection, run Windows Update and install all critical updates. A firewall should also block infection—and, of course, you should make sure that your anti-virus software is updated with the latest virus definitions.

To remove a Sasser infection, follow these steps:

1. Disconnect from the Internet.
2. Disable Sasser to keep your system from rebooting. Click Start, select Run, and enter **shutdown -a**. Press OK, and this should stop the worm.
3. Turn on your Windows XP firewall. Open Network Connections, right-click your network connection icon, and select Properties. Click the Advanced tab and turn on the firewall. This will prevent reinfection.
4. Reconnect to the Internet.
5. Update your anti-virus software and then disin-fect your computer, or download Symantec's free Sasser removal tool (www.sarc.com/avcenter/venc/data/w32.sasser.removal.tool.html).
6. Run Windows Update and install all critical updates (which you should do regularly, in any case).

MAC GADGET OF THE WEEK

Focus Enhancements' I-TVView/Mac is a scan converter, which is simply a device that can take a standard VGA-out connection and display that connection on a TV or similar video component (such as a VCR). This Mac-specific model is designed to work with typical Macintosh display resolutions; the device includes a feature that scales display of the Mac's desktop so that it appears proportional on the TV screen. Buy it for $119 at www.focusinfo.com.

THIS WEEK'S FOCUS: COMPUTER VIRUSES

ON THIS DAY: IBM SHIPS FIRST MAINFRAME COMPUTER (S/360, 1964)

The IBM System/360 (S/360), the company's first mainframe computer, was announced on April 7, 1964. The S/360 family, created by chief architect Gene Amdahl, ranged from the model 20 minicomputer (with 24KB of memory) to the model 91 supercomputer, which was built for the North American missile defense system.

Related Web site: www.thegalleryofoldiron.com

CLEANING A VIRUS FROM AN INFECTED PC

When you realize your computer has been infected with some sort of virus, the most common initial reaction is panic (yikes!), often followed by despair (why me?). While this type of reaction is understandable, it's important to know that catching a virus isn't the end of the world. Most virus attacks can be successfully recovered from, with minimal effort on your part. You don't, as a friend of mine once thought, have to throw away your PC and buy a new one; with today's anti-virus tools, you can extricate the virus from your system and recover most infected files, with relative ease.

If you think your computer has been hit by a virus attack, the first thing to do is *not panic*. Sit back, take a few deep breaths, and get your wits together. This isn't the end of the world; you can probably recover.

Once you've calmed down, you have to get your system up and running again (if it's not running, that is), and then remove the virus from your system. You should be able to reboot using your anti-virus software's emergency disk, or with your original Windows installation/startup CD. You can then run an emergency scan to remove the virus from your system, then reboot under more normal conditions.

With your system running again, the virus-cleaning procedure can be accomplished by running a full-system scan with your anti-virus software. When your system is functional and clean, you can then work on restoring any files that were damaged or deleted during the infection and removal processes.

In any case, you need to keep several items handy as part of your disaster preparation plans. You'll need the following: anti-virus software, anti-virus emergency disk, Windows installation/startup CD, backup copies of your data files, and the original installation CDs for all the programs installed on your hard disk.

WEB SITE OF THE WEEK

HouseCall (housecall.trendmicro.com) is a free Web-based virus scanner from Trend Micro. Use it to scan any Internet-connected PC for all current viruses. (And while you're online, visit the rest of the Trend Micro site to learn more about current virus threats.)

April 8, 2005

FRIDAY

THIS WEEK'S FOCUS: COMPUTER VIRUSES

ON THIS DAY: LARGEST SUNSPOT OBSERVED (1947)

On this day in 1947, the largest sunspot ever recorded was observed on the sun's southern hemisphere. The sunspot's size was estimated at an astounding 7 billion square miles.

Related Web site: www.exploratorium.edu/sunspots/

RESTORING YOUR WINDOWS XP MACHINE AFTER A VIRUS ATTACK

What do you do if your Windows XP machine gets hit hard with a particularly nasty virus—and you can't even boot the machine?

The first step is to retrieve a good copy of the data on your hard drive. I use Norton Ghost for that. You can create a Ghost boot CD and, if you have a CD burner in the machine, you can make a backup of the entire drive. I'd do that before taking any further action, just to make sure you have a good backup. You can even use the Explorer feature in Ghost to restore your data to another PC.

If you don't have Ghost or a burner, you could remove your PC's hard drive and put it in a working machine as the secondary drive, and then copy that drive's data. Either way, make sure you back up your data before trying to fix XP.

Unlike older versions of Windows, it's not easy to get XP back on its feet. I'd suggest booting to the Windows XP install disc and act as if you're going to install XP (in other words, don't choose the recovery option). Once you accept the license agreement, you'll be offered a chance to Repair the existing XP install. While this has yet to work for me (now you know why I spent so much time talking about backing up first), it's about your only option.

If this fails, you'll have to format your hard drive and install everything—including Windows—from scratch. Obviously, this is should be your last-chance option.

PORTABLE GADGET OF THE WEEK

The Roomba Pro is a robotic vacuum cleaner that scuttles around the floor like some sort of mechanical algae sucker. Just turn it on and watch it traverse your room in seemingly random patterns. It isn't really random, however; the Roomba Pro uses artificial intelligence algorithms to cover more of your floor than you can with an upright vacuum. Buy it for $229.99 at www.roombavac.com.

THIS WEEK'S FOCUS: COMPUTER VIRUSES

ON THIS DAY: NASA ANNOUNCES SEVEN MERCURY ASTRONAUTS (1959)

NASA's first manned space program was Project Mercury, and the seven Mercury astronauts represented the best and the brightest test pilots from each of the country's armed forces. On this date in 1959, NASA announced the country's first astronauts: Scott Carpenter, Gordon Cooper, John Glenn, Virgil "Gus" Grissom, Walter Schirra, Alan Shepard, and Donald "Deke" Slayton.

Related Web site: www.hq.nasa.gov/office/pao/History/SP-4201/toc.htm

DON'T OPEN EMAIL ATTACHMENTS

I say it all the time, but now more than ever I must strongly remind you: *DON'T OPEN EMAIL ATTACHMENTS!*

There have been many viruses recently that attach themselves to email messages, and install themselves on your machine when you open the attachment. One of the nastiest is called MyDoom or Novarg, depending on which anti-virus company you listen to. The email it comes in tricks people into opening the attached file with pseudo-tech speak messages like "The message cannot be represented in 7-bit ASCII encoding and has been sent as a binary attachment." and "Mail transaction failed. Partial message is available." Don't believe it!

Once you open the attachment the virus will send itself to everyone in your address book. If you have Kazaa installed it will add itself to your shared files, posing as a pirated application; it then lies in wait for a planned attack on a specific Web site. The virus also installs a backdoor and a keylogger, neither of which you really want on your machine.

And don't assume that if the email comes from someone you know that it's okay to open. Many email viruses spread themselves by spoofing names in an infected PC's address book. So it's not uncommon to get virus-infected messages that appear to come from friends and colleagues—or even from yourself!

As always, make sure you're running an up-to-date anti-virus (AVG is good and free if you don't already have one) and never open email attachments. NEVER!

FACT OF THE WEEK

InformationWeek Research estimates the yearly cost of security-related downtime to U.S. businesses at $273 billion. Worldwide, the tally is $1.39 trillion.

THIS WEEK'S FOCUS: COMPUTER VIRUSES

ON THIS DAY: TITANIC SETS SAIL (1912)

At noon on Wednesday, April 10, 1912, the luxury liner *Titanic* cast off from Southhampton, England, en route to New York City. The giant ship was on its maiden voyage, but on April 14 hit an iceberg about 400 miles south of Newfoundland, and subsequently sank. More than 1,500 lives were lost.

Related Web site: search.eb.com/titanic/

VIRUS HOAXES

A virus hoax is a phony warning, typically delivered via email, about a nonexistent computer virus. The sender of the warning—or, in most instances, the *resender*—is typically earnest in intent; he or she was sent the same warning, believed it, and wanted to warn you (and others) about the pending danger. Unfortunately, all virus hoaxes do is spread unnecessary panic—which not only leads to physical stress, it sometimes causes users to do stupid things, like delete perfectly good (and eminently useful) files from their hard disks.

For a virus hoax to propagate, it must convince you of its authenticity. To that end, most successful hoaxes have two things in common: technical-sounding language, and some sort of credibility-by-association. The more technical the language, the more a message impresses many non-technical readers. (If it's really technical-sounding, it must be true!) The same goes with the source of the message; you might not believe a hoax if it came from the janitor at your local supermarket, but if it's from someone with a big title who works at an official-sounding company or organization, the message suddenly becomes more reliable. (It doesn't matter whether the individual, title, or organization is real or not—it just needs to *sound* real.)

While it would be a mistake for you to ignore all virus warnings that hit your inbox (some might actually be legitimate), you have to guard against the huge number of prank warnings circulating across the Internet today. If you receive a virus warning in your inbox, check it out at one of the many sites that post news about the latest virus hoaxes. These sites include:

- F-Secure Hoax Warnings (www.datafellows.com/virus-info/hoax/)
- Hoaxbusters Internet Hoax Information (hoaxbusters.ciac.org/)
- Hoaxkill (www.hoaxkill.com)
- Symantec Security Response Hoaxes (www.symantec.com/avcenter/hoax.html)
- Vmyths.com (www.vmyths.com)

SOFTWARE OF THE WEEK

Norton AntiVirus is the top-selling antivirus program today, and for good reason. Norton does a great job of stopping viruses from infecting your machine, and in cleaning things up if you do get infected. Just make sure you keep the virus definitions updated! Buy it for $49.95 at www.symantec.com.

April 11, 2005

MONDAY

THIS WEEK'S FOCUS: **STOPPING SPAM**

ON THIS DAY: **FIRST JET TO TAKE OFF AND LAND VERTICALLY (1957)**

The Ryan X-13 Vertijet was designed to test the idea of vertical takeoff and landing for jet aircraft. The Vertiject made history on April 11, 1957, when it completed its first full-cycle flight at Edwards AFB, California. It took off vertically from its mobile trailer, rose into the air, nosed over into a level attitude, and flew for several minutes. It then reversed the procedure to vertical flight and slowly descended to its trailer for a safe landing.

Related Web site: www.nasm.si.edu/research/aero/aircraft/ryan_X13.htm

HOW SPAM WORKS

If you have an e-mail account, you know what spam is—it's those unsolicited, unauthorized, and unwanted marketing messages that show up on a daily basis in your email inbox. (In fact the official name for spam is unsolicited commercial email, or UCE.) These messages are sent en masse to millions of users across the Web, hawking adult Web sites, mortgage refinancing, and Viagra without a prescription.

Some of the spam you receive is fairly simple—a plan text message, perhaps with a link to a related Web site. Other spam is much more elaborate, with graphically intense HTML messages, complete with buttons and links and all sorts of things to click. Of course, when you click a link in a spam message, you're hooked—and you'll find a lot more spam in your inbox tomorrow. That's because the spammer now has your full email address, so you can be targeted for numerous future mailings.

The process of spamming is actually fairly easy to understand. The spammer creates his message, gathers a list of email addresses, and then bulk emails his message to all the names on his list. It costs very little to spam thousands of people; unlike traditional junk mail, where you have to put a stamp on every envelope, the only cost to the spammer is for his Internet connection. It doesn't matter whether he sends out a hundred, a thousand, or a million messages; the cost is the same.

The spammer's bulk mailing typically is routed through the email server on an unsuspected open mail relay (OMR). This is a separate server (*not* the email server offered by the spammer's ISP) that forwards—without restriction—email aimed at third parties. Spammers bounce their email off OMRs to mask the true origin of the spam; when you receive a bounced message, it looks like it came from the OMR server, not from the spammer.

By some accounts, there are close to 100,000 of these vulnerable servers worldwide, many located in China and other Asian countries. Lists of OMRs (called *blackhole lists*) can be used to block email coming from these servers. Anti-spam activists estimate that up to 90% of all spam could be eliminated by closing down or blocking messages from these servers.

PC GADGET OF THE WEEK

Tired of cold coffee? The USB Beverage Warmer is a low-voltage heat pad with Velcro fastener that you can wrap around cups, mugs, and even baby bottles.

April 12, 2005

TUESDAY

THIS WEEK'S FOCUS: STOPPING SPAM

ON THIS DAY: FIRST MAN IN SPACE (1961)

Russian cosmonaut Yuri Alekseyevich Gagarin made history on April 12, 1961, when he became the first human to travel into space. Yuri's spacecraft Vostok 1 was launched atop a converted missile originally designed for nuclear warheads; he made a single orbit, returning to Earth 108 minutes after liftoff.

Related Web site: www.kosmonaut.se/gagarin/

HOW YOUR NAME GETS ON A SPAM LIST

To keep your email address out of the hands of spammers, you need to know how spammers assemble their lists of potential victims. Armed with this knowledge, you can more easily avoid being captured in their nets.

The easiest way to obtain email addresses for a spam mailing is to buy them. Spammers can purchase commercial CD-ROMs containing tens of millions of names and addresses for just a few hundred dollars, and then use these names for their mailings. In addition, many legitimate Web sites sell lists of their members' names and addresses to third parties—just as real-world magazines and catalogs sell their mailing lists to other companies. This type of activity is prohibited by some sites' privacy policies, but other sites have no qualms about selling any information you provide to the highest bidder.

More sophisticated spammers use automated software—called *spambots*—to scour the Internet for publicly available email addresses. These email addresses can come from a variety of sources, including Web pages, public directories of user names and addresses (like Yahoo! Profiles), Web-based message boards, Usenet newsgroup postings, and IRC and Web-based chat rooms.

The most popular approach uses spambots to scour the major Web search sites (Google, Yahoo!, and so on) for email addresses. Just search for "@" and you'll see how easy it is to harvest addresses in this fashion. If your email address is on a Web page listed at the search site, it's available to the spambot via a quick search of the search engine.

Finally, some spammers generate email addresses via dictionary spam. This method uses special software to guess every possible name in a given domain. For example, the spammer might start sending email to aaa@thisdomain.com, and end with a message to zzz@thisdomain.com. More sophisticated dictionary spammers include all known given names (and possible first- and last-name combinations), so if you have a common name at a major ISP—mike@aol.com or jimbrown@att.com—you're likely to get hit with an inordinate amount of spam.

DOWNLOAD OF THE WEEK

iHateSpam is one of the better shareware spam filters. It works with a variety of email clients, including Outlook, Outlook Express, and Eudora. Try it for free, or buy it for $19.95 at www.sunbelt-software.com.

120

April 13, 2005
WEDNESDAY

THIS WEEK'S FOCUS: STOPPING SPAM

ON THIS DAY: AIR BRAKE PATENTED (1869)

In 1869, the first U.S. patent for an air brake was issued to George Westinghouse of Schnectady, New York. Westinghouse's steam power brake was used on an experimental train carrying officials of the Panhandle Railroad. Fifteen years later, he invented an automatic brake.

Related Web site: memory.loc.gov/ammem/papr/west/westair.html

HOW TO KEEP YOUR EMAIL ADDRESS PRIVATE

The best way to hide your email address from spammers is to not give it out—unless absolutely necessary. Don't fill out Web-based registration forms. Don't fill out online surveys. Don't include your email address when you post on Usenet newsgroups and public message boards. Don't put your email address on your Web site. And don't add your name and email address to any user directory, at your ISP or elsewhere. In short, don't post your email address in any public environment.

Another way to foil spambots is to list an email address that really isn't your email address. While you can just leave a phony email address, a more sophisticated approach is to use a *spamblock*, an email address that's been altered by the insertion of supplementary characters—such as SPAM-BLOCK or NOSPAM. For example, if your email address is myname@myisp.com, you might alter the address you leave behind to mySPAMBLOCKname@myisp.com, or myname@NOSPAM.myisp.com. The benefit of using a spamblock is not only that it foils spambots, but also that real human beings can typically figure out your real email address (by removing the spamblock), and still send you personal email if they like.

Still another solution is to use two separate email addresses: one for all your public postings and Web site registrations, and the other a private one for your personal email. All the spam will go to your public address, leaving your private inbox relatively unclogged—and easier to deal with on a day-to-day basis.

Finally, remember that many spammers get your address when you give it to them. For that reason, you don't want to reply to any spam messages—period. It's when you reply that they harvest your email address; don't reply, and they're left empty handed.

Along the same lines, don't click the "unsubscribe" link found in many email messages. This link seldom leads to a legitimate unsubscribe function, and more often just adds your email address to the spammer's email database. The best thing to do is delete any unsolicited email messages you receive—as soon as you receive them.

MAC GADGET OF THE WEEK

The "big disk" approach can be handy for a home or office machine, but the power of a RAID—Redundant Array of Independent Disks—can be handy when you've got to get professional computer work done. The Vanguard III FireWire RAID is a hardware RAID with good performance and very little setup requirement; it's basically plug-in-and-go. Price runs $699-$1049, depending on capacity,

at www.wiebetech.com.

THURSDAY

THIS WEEK'S FOCUS: STOPPING SPAM

ON THIS DAY: APOLLO 13 ACCIDENT (1970)

The Apollo 13 mission was launched on April 13, 1970. Fifty-six hours into the mission, on April 14, an explosion and rupture occurred in oxygen tank number 2 in the service module. All oxygen stores were lost, along with loss of water, electrical power, and use of the propulsion system. With the prayers of an anxious world behind them, the astronauts had to abort their moon mission, ricochet their crippled spacecraft around the moon, and perform an emergency landing in the Pacific ocean on April 17.

Related Web site: nssdc.gsfc.nasa.gov/planetary/lunar/apollo13info.html

SPOOFING ADDRESSES AND SPAMOUFLAGE

One problem with spam, from the spammer's standpoint, is that it's becoming more and more difficult to get users to click on your particular spam message. For that reason, many spam messages try to trick you into not deleting them.

One trick is to spoof the address of a trusted institution, such as the Bank of America or eBay. (Both have been victims of this type of spoofing.) When you see an email in your inbox from one of these companies, or from a friend or colleague, you're apt to at least look at it—and thus read the spammer's message.

How does a spammer spoof a specific address or domain? It's all in the software. There are spoofing programs available today that make it relatively easy to insert any address or domain name into the spam message's header. Some software even works interactively, inserting the recipient's address (that's you) into the sender's address field, so it looks as if the email you receive is actually coming from you.

The problems posed by these types of header spoofs are obvious. By spoofing a trusted address or domain, a spam message is less likely to be filtered by spam blocking software and services. In addition, you're more likely to open a message if it looks as if it's coming from some person or organization you know.

By the way, when a spammer spoofs the sender's email address, it's called *spamouflage*, and there's not much you can do about it. Just continue to filter out the offending messages and learn to deal with it. This too shall pass.

WEB SITE OF THE WEEK

The Official Spam Home Page isn't about email spam, it's about that delicious Hormel luncheon meat, the one immortalized in the Monty Python song, the one and only original Spam in a can. Go to www.spam.com to learn the history of Spam, buy Spam-related merchandise, and join the Official Spam Fan Club. Yummy!

April 15, 2005

FRIDAY

THIS WEEK'S FOCUS: STOPPING SPAM

ON THIS DAY: LEONARDO DA VINCI BORN (1452)

Leonardo da Vinci was a Florentine artist, one of the great masters of the Renaissance, a painter, sculptor, architect, engineer, and scientist. Born on this date in 1452, he influenced the worlds of art and science for centuries after his death—and somehow inspired the writing of the best-selling book, *The Da Vinci Code*.

Related Web site: www.mos.org/leonardo/

SOFTWARE GIANTS JOIN TO CAN SPAM

On June 22, 2003, software giants Microsoft, Yahoo!, America Online, and Earthlink announced that they were joining forces to find a caller ID for email systems. This would help verify that an email message was actually coming from the person who appeared to be sending it. Since about half of all spam is sent with forged return addresses, this type of user authentication is thought by experts to be the only effective way to eliminate spam.

The companies say that they're working on two different technological solutions. One method, backed by Microsoft, AOL, and Earthlink, involves checking the address of an incoming email against its numerical Internet identifier—the digital equivalent of the post office matching people's names with their registered home addresses. If there's no match, the email doesn't go through.

The other method, backed by Yahoo!, adds a unique digital signature, or key, to each outgoing message. The recipient's email provider then matches the signature against another key to make sure it is authentic.

The companies also made several recommendations for Internet service providers and consumers to help stop unwanted email. For ISPs, the recommendations include closing common security holes and limiting the amount of email a user can send. (Thousands of emails coming from a home user is a common sign that computer is being used as a zombie.) For consumers, recommendations included installing firewalls and anti-virus software, as well as using spam filters.

Good advice—although the spam problem obviously calls out for the kind of technological solution that the companies are working on.

PORTABLE GADGET OF THE WEEK

Gramin's Rino 130 is a two-way radio with built-in GPS technology. Not only can you use it as a walkie-talkie, but you can also transmit your exact location with the press of a button. The GPS function includes a base map of North America and tracks 12 GPS satellites; the unit also includes a NOAA weather radio and barometric pressure sensor. Buy it for $375 at www.garmin.com.

123

April 16, 2005

SATURDAY

THIS WEEK'S FOCUS: **STOPPING SPAM**

ON THIS DAY: CRONKITE FIRST ANCHORS THE *CBS EVENING NEWS* (1962)

On this date in April, 1962, Walter Cronkite took over the anchorman's position on the *CBS Evening News*. Unlike many of today's talking heads, Cronkite lived by the credo, adopted from his days as a wire service reporter, to get the story, "fast, accurate, and unbiased." His trademark exit line was (all together now): "And that's the way it is."

Related Web site: www.museum.tv/archives/etv/C/htmlC/cronkitewal/cronkitewal.htm

HOW TO BLOCK SPAM

To keep spam from hitting your inbox, you have to somehow identify spam messages, and then block them. To that end, there are two different types of spam blocking—content filtering and block lists. Various anti-spam software and services use some combination of these two methods.

Content filtering blocks email based on specific words and phrases in the message text. Each message is searched for a list of specific words and phrases—"incredible offer," "buy today," and so on. Any messages containing the verboten phrases are blocked.

Block lists block mail from specific addresses, domains, and servers. You can create your own block lists from the addresses of the spam you personally receive, or you can use block lists assembled from third parties. For example, the Mail Abuse Prevention System (www.mailabuse.org) and Spamhaus (www.spamhaus.org) both create block lists that list IP addresses known for sending spam.

Block lists can block individual addresses or complete domains. For example, if you think that you're getting too much spam from the spamyou.com domain, you can block all email from any address originating from spamyou.com. You can even block all messages coming from a specific country; you could block, for example, all British email by blocking the complete .uk domain.

That said, spam blockers are often overzealous, blocking good messages along with the bad. This is especially the case with block lists that block out all the messages coming from a particular domain. This blocks the spammer's email, but it also blocks any email coming from that domain that isn't spam. It's like throwing the baby out with the bathwater; to block the spam, you risk missing legitimate messages coming from the same domain.

FACT OF THE WEEK

MessageLabs says that 76% of all email is now spam. According to Nucleus, in 2004 the average employee received twice as much spam as the previous year, an average of 7,500 junk messages.

THIS WEEK'S FOCUS: STOPPING SPAM

ON THIS DAY: FORD UNVEILS THE MUSTANG (1964)

The ultimate American muscle car, the original Ford Mustang, was introduced on April 17, 1964. The Mustang racked up over 22,000 sales its first day, and one million sales in its first two years. The pony car class that the Ford Mustang helped create is the only class of muscle car that still exists today.

Related Web site: www.fordheritage.com/mustang/

ANTI-SPAM SOFTWARE

When you're really overwhelmed by spam, it's time to take drastic measures—in the form of anti-spam software. Most anti-spam software uses some combination of spam blocking or content filtering to keep spam messages from ever reaching your inbox; their effectiveness varies, but they will decrease the amount of spam you receive, to some degree.

The most popular anti-spam programs include

- **ANT 4 MailChecking (**ant4.com**)**—Combination of spam email filter and notification.
- **MailWasher (**www.mailwasher.net**)**—Lets you view, delete, and bounce unwanted email messages.
- **RoadBlock (**www.roadblock.net**)**—Program enables you to view waiting email before downloading to your email client, and delete spam before it hits your PC.
- **Spambam (**www.epage.com.au/spambam/**)**—This program sits between your email client and your email server to filter and block spam messages.

- **SpamEater Pro (**www.hms.com/spameater.asp**)**— Goes online to your ISP's email server and checks all messages found there—before you download them to your regular email program.
- **SpamKiller (**www.mcafee.com**)**—SpamKiller lets you block messages by sender's address, message subject, or message text.

You should also take advantage of any spam filters available from your ISP. These filters will help stop spam from ever reaching your inbox—thus alleviating the need for client-side anti-spam programs.

SOFTWARE OF THE WEEK

There's one more anti-spam program to consider, and it's one I heartily recommend. Norton AntiSpam works with any POP3 email program (including Outlook and Outlook Express) and filters incoming email on multiple levels. It also offers the bonus of blocking pop-up and banner advertisements in your Web browser. Buy it for $39.95 at www.symantec.com.

April 18, 2005

MONDAY

THIS WEEK'S FOCUS: MICROSOFT WINDOWS

ON THIS DAY: SAN FRANCISCO EARTHQUAKE (1906)

The California earthquake of April 18, 1906 ranks as one of the most significant earthquakes of all time. The first foreshock hit at precisely 5:12 a.m. local time; the great earthquake broke loose some 20 to 25 seconds later. The earthquake was felt from southern Oregon to south of Los Angeles, and inland as far as central Nevada. The massive quake spawned an equally massive fire in San Francisco proper; at least 700 people died as a result.

Related Web site: www.sfmuseum.org/1906/06.html

UPGRADING TO SERVICE PACK 2

If you're using Windows XP, Microsoft's Service Pack 2 is a must have. It will upgrade your system with a number of bug fixes, security patches, and new features. Download it the minute it's available, from www.microsoft.com/windowsxp/.

Here's what's new in Service Pack 2:

- Much improved firewall—eliminates the need for a third-party firewall. Now on by default, and accessible from the Control Panel.

- File sharing is now network safe.

- Instant block all button.

- Major improvements in Web browser security.

- Internet Explorer blocks pop-ups.

- MIME sniffing.

- No more Web bugs in HTML email.

- Default viewer is rich edit, not HTML.

- Improved version of Windows Update.

If you're on a dial-up connection, downloading the service pack can be a real pain. You probably want to order the CD version. You can order one (for $10) from Microsoft's Web site, or by calling (800) 360-7561. Once you do the big update by CD, though, you should still use Windows Update regularly to plug the latest holes. If you update often enough, the download sizes shouldn't get out of hand.

PC GADGET OF THE WEEK

The USB Glowing Aquarium is a miniature fake aquarium, completely powered from your computer's USB port. The USB powers the aquarium's high-intensity blue LED light, as well as the small motor used to generate the small water current. It comes with the plexiglass tank, two "fish," and a USB cable. Just add water to the tank, attach it to your computer via USB, and watch the fake fish swim around. Buy it for $22 at www.addlogix.com.

April 19, 2005

TUESDAY

THIS WEEK'S FOCUS: MICROSOFT WINDOWS

ON THIS DAY: OKLAHOMA CITY FEDERAL BUILDING BOMBED (1995)

The first major act of U.S. domestic terrorism took place on April 19, 1995, at 9:03 a.m. Twenty-seven year-old Timothy McVeigh exploded a massive bomb inside a rental truck that was parked outside the Murrah Federal Building in downtown Oklahoma City, blowing half of the nine-story building into oblivion and killing 168 people. McVeigh was later executed for his crime.

Related Web site: www.cnn.com/US/OKC/

FAVORITE FREE WINDOWS UTILITIES

Windows is pretty feature-heavy on its own, but even with this massive feature bloat one still longs for functionality that doesn't exist in the main operating system. That's why they make third-party utilities, and here are five of my favorites:

- **Windows PowerToys**—This is a collection of utilities for Windows XP, some small and simple and others more robust. My favorite PowerToy is TweakUI, a must-have utility for customizing your system. All are downloadable for free from Microsoft, at www.microsoft.com/windowsxp/downloads/powertoys/xppowertoys.mspx.

- **Stuffit Expander**—WinZip is still the best for making ZIP files, but for unpacking them you can't beat this free alternative. Get it at www.allume.com/win/.

- **XP Visual Tools**—This is a set of utilities that let you change the look and feel of Windows XP. XP Transparency makes the Start menu and taskbar transparent; XP Visual Style makes old-style programs look XP-like; XP Logon lets you manage your logon screens; and XP Wallpaper randomly changes your desktop wallpaper. Download for free at www.cronosoft.com.

- **PGP**—The best way to protect your data is to encrypt it. PGP is back, and free—although once the open-source Gnu Privacy Guard is easier to use, I might recommend that instead. Get PGP at www.pgp.com.

- **AVG Antivirus**—You have to have an antivirus program. This one is free and Grisoft keeps it up to date. Get it at www.grisoft.com.

DOWNLOAD OF THE WEEK

Win Guides Tweak Manager lets you activate hundreds of tweaks that can speed up the way Windows XP runs. Try it for free, or buy it for $29.95 at www.winguides.com/tweak/.

April 20, 2005
WEDNESDAY

THIS WEEK'S FOCUS: MICROSOFT WINDOWS

ON THIS DAY: ELECTRON MICROSCOPE DEMONSTRATED (1940)

In 1940, Dr. Vladimir Zworykin of RCA Laboratories publicly demonstrated the first electron microscope, in Philadelphia, Pennsylvania. The apparatus was 10 feet high and weighed half a ton; it was capable of producing a magnification of 100,000 times.

Related Web site: www.davidsarnoff.org/gallery-em.htm

SETTING UP WINDOWS FOR TWO MONITORS

Some computer-related activities are easier if you can see two things at once. For example, programmers might like to see their code on one monitor, and the results of that code on a second screen. If you're running a PowerPoint presentation, you could use one monitor to display your presentation and a second to display your private notes.

If you have two monitors—and two video cards—installed in your system, you can configure Windows XP to run two separate displays.

1. Be sure that when you install Windows XP, you have only one video card installed in your system. After Windows XP installation is complete, shut down your computer and add the second display card to your system, following the installation instructions from the card's manufacturer.
2. From the Control Panel, click the Display icon.
3. After you've installed your second video card, the Display Settings dialog box has a new tab, labeled Monitors, that replaces the standard Settings tab. Select the Monitors tab.
4. Your primary monitor should already be configured properly. Select the secondary display/monitor combination, and choose Use This Device as Part of the Desktop. Set the other properties as appropriate, dragging the screen images to set relative screen placement for the two monitors.
5. To change the resolution of the second monitor, click the Settings button and make the appropriate changes. Click OK to register your changes.

This dual-monitor feature works great in XP, even though it's been problematic in older versions of Windows. If you really want multi-monitor support as easily as possible, with great performance, consider a "dual-head" graphics card. Matrox (www.matrox.com) makes my favorite dual-head card these days.

MAC GADGET OF THE WEEK

The Digi 002 is a hardware sound mixer board that connects to your Mac via FireWire and works directly with Pro Tools LE software to let you mix multiple audio inputs at once. It has eight inputs that you can use for microphones or line-level instruments. Call it a studio in a box; you should be able to produce your entire band with a single Digi 002. Buy it for $2,495 at www.digidesigns.com.

April 21, 2005

THURSDAY

THIS WEEK'S FOCUS: MICROSOFT WINDOWS

ON THIS DAY: FIRST EXTRA-SOLAR PLANETS DISCOVERED (1994)

On this date in 1994, Penn State astronomer Alexander Wolszczan announced the discovery of the first planets outside of our solar system. The discovery was a cluster of three planets orbiting an unusual neutron star located 1,200 light years away, in the constellation Virgo.

Related Web site: www.astrosociety.org/education/publications/tnl/19/19.html

USE A WEB PAGE AS A DESKTOP BACKGROUND

Find a Web page that you really, really like? Windows XP lets you display any Web page as your desktop background. When you do this, your desktop background functions like a live Web page whenever you're connected to the Internet. It's a great way to put your favorite Web page or list of links at your fingertips.

Here's how to do it:

1. From the Control Panel, click the Display icon.
2. When the Display Properties utility appears, select the Desktop tab and click the Customize Desktop button.
3. When the Desktop Items dialog box appears, select the Web tab.
4. To use your current home page as the desktop background, select it from the Web pages list.
5. To use another page as the desktop background, click the New button to display the New Active Desktop Item dialog box. Enter the URL of the page into the Location box, and then click OK.
6. To automatically update the content of this Web page, click the Properties button and select the Schedule tab. Check the Using the Following Schedules option, and then click the Add button. When the New Schedule dialog box appears, set a time for updating, check the If My Computer Is Not Connected... option, and then click OK.

Your selected Web page is now displayed as your desktop background—with live links, ready to click!

WEB SITE OF THE WEEK

SuperSite for Windows is put together by Windows expert Paul Thurrott. This is *the* site for Windows-related news, rumors, reviews, and more. Check it out at www.winsupersite.com.

April 22, 2005

FRIDAY

THIS WEEK'S FOCUS: MICROSOFT WINDOWS

ON THIS DAY: ROBERT OPPENHEIMER BORN (1904)

J. Robert Oppenheimer, born this day in 1904, was the scientific director of the Manhattan Project, the World War II effort to develop nuclear weapons, at the Los Alamos National Laboratory in New Mexico. Known as "the father of the atomic bomb," Oppenheimer later lamented their killing power after they were used to destroy Hiroshima and Nagasaki. He passed away on February 18, 1967.

Related Web site: www.nap.edu/html/biomems/joppenheimer.html

ACTIVATING XP SPECIAL EFFECTS

Windows XP includes all sorts of visual special effects that affect the way certain elements look, or the way they pull down or pop up onscreen. Some of these special effects can be changed from the Display Properties utility. Others are changed from the System Properties utility.

You access the Display Properties utility by clicking the Display icon in the Control Panel. When the utility opens, select the Appearance tab and click the Effects button. Here you can choose to make menus and ToolTips scroll or fade in and out; display drop shadows under all Windows menus; display large icons on your desktop; display the contents of windows when they're being dragged; or hide those underlined letters on menu items.

The second set of special effects is available from the System Properties utility, which you get to by clicking the Systems icon in the Control Panel. When the utility opens, select the Advanced tab and click the Settings button (in the Performance section). When the Performance Options dialog box appears, click the Visual Effects tab and choose which effects you want. Here you can choose to animate windows when minimizing and maximizing; display a gradient color in window captions; enable per-folder type watermarks; fade in the taskbar; fade out menu items; fade/slide menus and ToolTips; slide taskbar buttons; smooth the edges of screen fonts; smooth-scroll list boxes; use Web view in folders; and much more.

If you experience a performance hit, experiment with turning off some of these effects. But if your system has the horsepower—especially enough RAM and a powerful enough video card—you should try turning on all these special effects.

PORTABLE GADGET OF THE WEEK

The Pretender is a fun little gizmo that generates four different sounds you can play into your telephone handset to get you off the hook when you receive an unwanted call. Press a button and generate a baby cry, a dog bark, a doorbell ring, or a call waiting sound. "Sorry, I have another call coming in." Clever! It also functions as a digital voice changer, so you can distort your voice and make yourself unrecognizable to whomever you're talking to. Buy it for $79 at www.safetytechnology.com.

April 23, 2005

SATURDAY

THIS WEEK'S FOCUS: MICROSOFT WINDOWS

ON THIS DAY: NEW COKE INTRODUCED (1985)

In 1985, Coca Cola appeared to be losing the cola wars. Consumers favored the taste of Pepsi over Coke, which inspired Coca Cola to come up with a new, sweeter formula. New Coke was launched on April 23 of that year, to the outrage of millions of Coke loyalists worldwide. Three months later, on July 11, the return of Coca Cola Classic was announced. New Coke promptly faded from the scene. Later, the "Classic" was dropped from the product name.

Related Web site: members.lycos.co.uk/thomassheils/newcoke.htm

ADDING PROGRAMS TO THE XP START MENU

The Start menu in Windows XP is a lot different from the Start menu you got used to in previous versions of Windows. It does a good job of hiding things you don't use that often, while keeping your most frequently used programs front and center.

If you don't like the way programs move on and off the Start menu, depending on when you last used them, you can choose to dock any icon to the Start menu—permanently. Just follow these steps:

1. From the Start menu, click the All Programs link to display the Programs menu.
2. Navigate to the program you want to add to the Start menu, and right-click that program.
3. From the pop-up menu, select Pin to Start Menu.

The program you selected now appears on the Start menu, just below the browser and email icons. To remove a program you've added to the Start menu, right-click its icon and select Unpin from Start Menu.

By the way, you can use this same method to add *any* program file to the Start menu, even if it doesn't appear on the Programs menu. Just use My Computer to navigate to an application file, and then right-click the file and select Pin to Start Menu from the pop-up menu.

And if you want to change the way the Start menu behaves, right-click the Start button and select Properties from the pop-up menu. When the Taskbar and Start Menu Properties dialog box appears, select the Start Menu tab and click the Customize button. Select the Advance tab, and then you can choose to animate the Start menu, make submenus open when you point at them, and highlight the newest applications on the Start menu.

FACT OF THE WEEK

To get an idea of how complex the Windows operating system really is, Microsoft reports that Windows has 50 million lines of code, and grows 20% with every release. It's put together by 7,200 people, comes in 34 languages, and has to support 190,000 devices—digital cameras, printers, handhelds, and so on.

April 24, 2005

SUNDAY

THIS WEEK'S FOCUS: MICROSOFT WINDOWS

ON THIS DAY: HUBBLE TELESCOPE LAUNCHES INTO SPACE (1990)

On this date in 1990, the space shuttle Discovery launched the Hubble telescope into space. The Hubble is the size of a large school bus, and cost $1.5 billion at launch. It completes one orbit every 97 minutes, and transmits about 120 gigabytes of science data every week.

Related Web site: hubblesite.org

CLOSING STUCK PROGRAMS IN XP

As robust as Windows XP is, especially compared to older versions, there still are occasions where a program freezes on you. This is typically a less serious situation than with older versions of Windows, when a stuck program could bring down your entire system. Now when a program freezes, it seldom affects anything else. All you have to worry about is closing the stuck program.

The first thing to do is press **Ctrl+Alt+Del** (what us old-timers call the "three-fingered salute") to display the Windows Task Manager. (You can also get to it by right-clicking the taskbar.) This is a souped-up version of the old Close Program dialog box found in previous versions of Windows, and it offers a lot more functionality.

When the Windows Task Manager opens, select the Applications tab. This tab displays a list of all programs currently running on your system. If a program is frozen, this might be indicated in the Status column. Or it might not. In any case, you want to select the frozen program, and then click the End Task button. Nine times out of ten, this should take care of your problem.

If this doesn't make the program close, go back to the Windows Task Manager and click the Processes tab. Find the file that's frozen, select it, and then click the End Process button. By the way, if you're forced to use the "end processes" method to shut down a program, you probably should restart Windows to clear up any loose ends still floating around system memory.

The worst-case scenario is that you can't close the frozen program no matter what you try, and it then starts to affect the rest of your system. If this happens to you, you need to restart Windows. If things get so bad you can't restart the operating system, you'll have to reboot your computer by pressing **Ctrl+Alt+Del** twice.

SOFTWARE OF THE WEEK

DesktopX is a utility that lets you add widgets, themes, icons, and other objects to the basic Windows XP desktop. It's kind of a Konfabulator for XP, available in both free and enhanced ($19.95) versions. Get it at www.stardock.com/products/desktopx/.

April 25, 2005

MONDAY

THIS WEEK'S FOCUS: LINUX

ON THIS DAY: FIRST SOLAR BATTERY ANNOUNCED (1954)

Gerald Pearson, Calvin Fuller, and Daryl Chapin invented the first solar battery, and announced it to the world on this date in 1954. Their research was funded by Bell Labs. The Bell Solar Battery was an array of several strips of silicon, about the size of a razorblade, that turned the free electrons in sunlight into electrical current.

Related Web site: www.bellsystemmemorial.com/belllabs_photovoltaics.html

WHAT IS LINUX?

Linux is an operating system, like Windows or the Mac OS, but derived from the older UNIX OS. It was created as a hobby by Linus Torvalds, then a student at the University of Helsinki in Finland. He began work on Linux in 1991, and released version 1.0 in 1994.

Unlike operating systems from Microsoft or Apple, the Linux source code is freely available to the public. Programmers worldwide have helped to further the development of Linux, and several companies market (or give away) their own versions of the operating system. Linux can run on a wide variety of hardware; you can install Linux on your IBM-compatible PC, or on a Mac.

Linux is a particularly robust operating system, meaning its less prone to crashes or security breaches than Windows or OS X. However, it's not quite as user-friendly as either of those two operating systems, which explains its relatively small user base. You'll find Linux most used on network and Web servers, where it's more important to be bullet proof than it is to be pretty looking.

There aren't a whole lot of enduser applications written for the operating system, and Linux hasn't yet become a household name. That doesn't mean it doesn't have its hard-core supporters, however, especially among Web masters and network administrators. They've even given Linux a mascot—a penguin named Tux. So if you see a stuffed penguin sitting in a techie's cube, now you know why—the techie is a Linux fan!

PC GADGET OF THE WEEK

Let's talk about USB drives—in particular the Sandisk Cruzer Mini USB Flash Drive. What I like about the Sandisk Cruzer Mini is that it's smaller than most other high-capacity USB drives. The Cruzer's thin design doesn't obstruct the stacked USB ports found on many computers; if space is tight, this drive will fit. It comes in 128MB ($49.99) and 256MB ($79.99) versions, at www.sandisk.com.

April 26, 2005

TUESDAY

THIS WEEK'S FOCUS: LINUX

ON THIS DAY: CHERNOBYL NUCLEAR DISASTER (1986)

The world's worst nuclear accident took place at reactor number four at the Chernobyl nuclear power plant, located 80 miles north of Kiev in the Ukraine. At 1:23 a.m., local time, the chain reaction in the reactor became out of control, creating explosions and a fireball which blew off the reactor's heavy steel and concrete lid. The accident killed more than 30 people immediately, and many more over the long term, due to the ensuing high radiation levels in the surrounding area.

Related Web site: www.chernobyl.co.uk

DIFFERENT VERSIONS OF LINUX

If you want to install Linux on your computer, you can choose from several different available versions. All utilize a similar Linux Kernel, but offer different interfaces and (to some degree) functionality.

For newbies, I recommend Knoppix. This version is the best for trying Linux out, because you don't have to install it—you can run the operating system from a bootable CD. Which means you don't have to muck about with dual-booting and other such nonsense if you want to have both Windows and Linux installed on your system. You can buy it for five bucks or less at many online stores; get more information at www.knoppix.org.

If you like what you see and you want to permanently install Linux on your system, I recommend SuSE Linux, available at www.suse.com/us/. It's definitely the nicest Linux out right now. I like its interface, and the way it works. You can buy the

Personal version for $29.95; the Professional version runs $89.95.

SuSE's not the only Linux out there, of course. Other popular versions include Debian (www.debian.org), Mandrakelinux (www.mandrakesoft.com), and Red Hat Linux (www.redhat.com). You can also find a list of companies that offer free Linux distributions at www.linux.org/dist/. (Note that the free distributions are hefty downloads, and require a bit of technical know-how to install and use; the boxed versions from SuSE, Red Hat, and others are a lot easier for casual users to work with.)

DOWNLOAD OF THE WEEK

OpenOffice is a free Microsoft Office-like productivity suite for the Linux environment. It includes a word processor, spreadsheet, presentations program, drawing program, and database. Download it at www.openoffice.org.

April 27, 2005

WEDNESDAY

THIS WEEK'S FOCUS: LINUX

ON THIS DAY: FIRST WEATHER BUREAU KITE (1898)

Before there were weather satellites, there were weather kits. On April 17, 1898, the first Weather Bureau kite was launched, from Topeka, Kansas. This was a large box kite, 8 feet long, 7 feet wide, and 3 feet high. Later launches created kite stations with up to seven kites attached to the same wire, for multiple observations.

Related Web site: www.nws.noaa.gov

DOWNLOADING LINUX—FOR FREE

If you choose to go the low-cost route, you'll be downloading a version of Linux called a *distribution*. Most Linux distributions are free for download, or you can sometimes pay a little to get it delivered on CD.

Before you download a Linux distribution, keep these points in mind:

- You'll need a high-speed Internet connection. Distributions typically run hundreds of megabytes, which make them impractical to download via dial-up.

- What you'll be downloading are the ISO images for the distribution. You then use the ISO image files to burn your own installation CD. The actual installation will be made from the CD that you burn.

- Chances are you don't want to wipe out your computer's existing operating system—which means you want to create a dual-boot system. You'll do this by repartitioning your hard disk, and then installing Linux onto the second partition.

Remember, because you're getting a free version of Linux, you get what you pay for—especially in terms of documentation and technical support. If you run into any problems, you're pretty much on your own.

If any or all of this seems daunting, then the free download route probably isn't for you. Instead, check out one of the "commercial" versions of Linux I discussed yesterday, and spend a little money for an installation CD, user manual, and tech support.

MAC GADGET OF THE WEEK

Keyspan's Digital Media Remote is an add-on wireless remote control you can use to control all your Mac's media software, including AppleCD Audio Player, Apple DVD Player, QuickTime Player, and more. Press a button, and the Digital Media Remote sends the same keystrokes you would if you were controlling the application from the keyboard. Buy it for $49 at www.keyspan.com.

April 28, 2005

THURSDAY

THIS WEEK'S FOCUS: LINUX

ON THIS DAY: APPLE OPENS ITUNES MUSIC STORE (2003)

On August 18, 2003, Apple opened its iTunes Music Store, selling song downloads for 99 cents apiece. Apple hit the 100-million download mark less than a year later, when 20-year-old Keven Britten of Hays, Kansas downloaded Zero 7's "Somersault (Dangermouse remix)" on July 11, 2004.

Related Web site: www.apple.com/itunes/

LINUX SOFTWARE

Once you have the Linux operating installed, what do you do with it? After all, any operating system is only as good as the applications that run on it.

In the case of Linux, most applications are—just like the operating system itself—distributed free of charge, or on a low-cost CD. Here's a list of the some of the most popular Linux apps:

- **AntiVir (www.hbedv.com)**—Anti-virus scanner
- **Bluefish (bluefish.openoffice.nl)**—HTML editor
- **GNUCash (www.gnucash.org)**—Personal finance manager
- **KOffice (koffice.kde.org)**—Office application suite, with word processor, spreadsheet, presenter, flowchart, and more
- **Linux Media Player (www.forensicgames.com)**—Digital audio player
- **Mozilla Firefox (www.mozilla.org/products/firefox/)**—Web browser
- **Mozilla Thunderbird (www.mozilla.org/projects/thunderbird/)**—Email client
- **OBA Accounting System (oba.sourceforge.net)**—Accounting and inventory Management
- **Opera (www.opera.com)**—Web browser
- **Plan (www.bitrot.de/plan.html)**—Desktop calendar and day planner
- **Rekall (www.thekompany.com/projects/rekall/)**—Database management
- **ShowImg (www.jalix.org/projects/showimg/)**—Image viewer
- **Webmin (www.webmin.com)**—Contact manager

WEB SITE OF THE WEEK

Find everything Linux—from distributions and applications to news and reviews—at Linux Online (www.linux.org). This site is the premiere portal to the world of Linux—an essential place to learn about and get involved with the Linux community.

April 29, 2005

FRIDAY

THIS WEEK'S FOCUS: LINUX

ON THIS DAY: GOOGLE FILES FOR IPO (2004)

Google, the world's number-one Internet search engine, filed for its initial public stock offering on April 29, 2004. The company said in its filing that it expected to raise as much as $2.7 billion from the offering, which would be conducted in a somewhat unique online auction format.

Related Web site: www.google-ipo.com

INSTALLING LINUX SOFTWARE

One of the things that makes Linux a little less than user-friendly is the way applications are installed. Unlike in Windows or on the Mac, installing a program in Linux requires knowledge of command-line instructions; it's not a point-and-click operation.

Most Linux applications come in a compressed file, typically in the GNU zip (gzip) format, with a .gz or .tgz extension. This is the Linux equivalent of a zip file, and works pretty much the same way. Of course, since you're working in the Linux environment, you have to issue a command-line instruction to extract the software from the compressed file. Here's the command; replace *filename* with the full name of the file, of course:

```
tar -zxvf filename
```

Next, you need to change to the directory to which you just extracted the file and then compile the program's source code. This is easier than it sounds, and requires just three command-line instructions, in this order:

```
./configure
make
make install
```

Naturally, wait for each command to fully execute before you enter the next command. The result should be a completely extracted, compiled, and installed program, all ready for you to use.

By the way, if your program comes in binary format, this entire procedure might be a bit easier. Read the publisher's instructions on how to best install the binaries.

PORTABLE GADGET OF THE WEEK

Want to view your digital photos on your big TV screen without messing around with your computer? Then you want SanDisk's Digital Photo Viewer, a small box you connect directly to your television set via composite video or S-Video cables. Insert a digital media card, and see your digital pictures onscreen. Just connect the device, insert a media card from your digital camera, and let the slideshow begin. Buy it for $69.99 from www.sandisk.com.

April 30, 2005

SATURDAY

THIS WEEK'S FOCUS: **LINUX**

ON THIS DAY: **EXISTENCE OF THE ELECTRON ANNOUNCED (1897)**

On this date in 1897, at the Royal Institution Friday Evening Discourse, Joseph John Thomson first announced the existence of electrons. Thomson told his audience that earlier in the year, he had discovered a particle of matter a thousand times smaller than the atom. He called it a "corpuscle," although the name "electron" was later adopted.

Related Web site: www.aip.org/history/electron/

LINUX LINKS

There's a lot to learn about Linux, and the best place to learn is on the Web. There are a ton of good Web sites devoted to the Linux community. In addition to Linux Online (www.linux.org), which I've already talked about, these sites include:

- **freshmeat.net (freshmeat.net)**—A great source for all manner of Linux software.
- **Google Search Linux (www.google.com/linux/)**—A special version of Google that searches only Linux-related Web sites.
- **JustLinux (www.justlinux.com)**—A huge online forum for Linux users.
- **Linux Forums (www.linuxforums.org)**—Message boards for and tutorials for all levels of Linux users.
- **Linux Gazette (www.linuxgazette.com)**—A Linux-related blog, with related message boards.
- **Linux.com (www.linux.com)**—News and articles about using Linux in the enterprise.
- **SourceForge (sourceforge.net)**—More open source Linux software.
- **The GNU Project—Free Software Foundation (www.gnu.org)**—Lots of free Linux (and Unix) software here.
- **The Linux Documentation Project (www.tldp.org)**—FAQs and documentation for everything Linux.
- **The Linux Journal (linuxjournal.com)**—The Web site for the popular print magazine.

And if you're looking for Linux software, don't forget Tucows (www.tucows.com) and the other standard software download sites, most of which let you search and browse by operating system—and offer a ton of Linux apps and utilities.

FACT OF THE WEEK

Linux is supposed to be all about open source and freeware, right? Well, dig this: Hewlett-Packard made $2.5 billion on its Linux business in fiscal 2003. How's that for free?

MORE APRIL FACTS

April 1

1889 First dishwashing machine is offered for sale in Chicago, IL

1890 Electric trolley car is patented

1960 First weather observation satellite, Tiros I, is launched from Cape Kennedy and transmitted the first television images from space

April 2

1827 First lead pencils are manufactured

1902 First U.S. motion picture theater opens in Los Angeles

April 3

1860 Pony Express mail service begins

1968 2001: A Space Odyssey premiers

1973 First cellular phone call is made by Martin Cooper, who invented the cellular phone

1973 Twin blade razors are patented

1996 John Kaczynski, better known as the "Unabomber," is arrested in Montana after sending 16 mail bombs that injured 23 and killed three; currently, he's serving four life terms

April 4

1828 Chocolate milk powder is patented

1949 NATO (North Atlantic Treaty Organization) is formed

1968 Rev. Martin Luther King is assassinated in Memphis, TN

1983 Space Shuttle Challenger makes its maiden voyage; in 1986, the Challenger exploded shortly after leaving the launch pad on its tenth mission, killing all on board

April 5

1806 First apple cider mill is patented in Stanfield, CT

1923 Firestone begins production of balloon tires, which are still used today on agricultural and earth-moving vehicles

April 6

1917 U.S. enters World War I

1938 Teflon is accidentally discovered during research into refrigerant gases

April 7

1947 Henry Ford dies

2000/2001 Mars Odyssey spacecraft is launched; the rocket traveled for more than a year to reach Mars

April 8

1953 First 3D movie, Man in the Dark, is released in theaters

April 9

1974 Disposable syringes are patented

April 10

1949 Safety pins are patented in New York

1970 Paul McCartney announces that the Beatles had disbanded

April 11

1970 Apollo 13, the third manned lunar landing mission, is launched from Cape Canaveral

1984 U.S. Challenger astronauts make the first in-space satellite repair; a pair of astronauts repaired the malfunctioning astronomy satellite, Solar Max

1986 Halley's Comet makes last approach to Earth until 2061; the comet travels on a 76-year orbit

April 12

1633 Galileo is convicted of heresy by the Roman Catholic Church; more than 300 years later, the Church admitted that Galileo's beliefs that the Earth revolves around the Sun were correct

1861 The U.S. Civil War begins

1945 President Franklin Delano Roosevelt dies

1961 Russian cosmonaut Yuri Gagarin becomes the first human in space, orbiting the Earth in Vostok I

1981 Space Shuttle Columbia is launched from Cape Canaveral, becoming the first reuseable manned space craft; on February 1, 2003, the Columbia exploded over Texas during its 28th mission, killing all seven aboard

1988 First patent issued on an animal life form to scientists at Harvard for a genetically engineered mouse

April 13

1743 President and well-known scientist, inventor, and mathematician Thomas Jefferson is born

1960 First U.S. navigational satellite, Transit-1B, is launched

1970 Apollo 13 disaster; all three astronauts survived, but it took a massive NASA effort to bring the astronauts home safely

April 14

1818 Webster's *American Dictionary of the English Language* is published

1865 President Abraham Lincoln is shot at Ford's Theater in Washington, D.C., while attending a play; Lincoln died early the next morning (April 15, 1865)

1912 The Titanic struck an iceberg in the North Atlantic about 11:42 p.m. and sank by 2:20 a.m. the next morning, killing about 1,500, while 700 made it safely onto life boats

1918 First American aerial dogfight with enemy German fighter planes over Toul, France

1965 173rd Airborne Brigade ordered to South Vietnam, the first major Army ground combat unit sent to fight the Vietnamese

1986 U.S. launches air strikes against Libyan forces led by Muammar al-Qaddafi

1988 Soviets withdraw from Afghanistan after years of unsuccessful attempts to quell the Afghans

April 15

1452 Leonardo da Vinci is born

1923 Insulin first becomes available for diabetic patients

April 16

1943 Hallucinogenic effects of LSD first discovered by a Swiss chemist researching drugs to treat respiratory problems

April 17

1790 Benjamin Franklin dies

April 18

1775 The famous ride of Paul Revere and William Dawes begins

1906 The Great San Francisco earthquake occurs, killing at least 700 people, destroying almost 30,000 buildings and wiping out nearly all of the central business district

1983 U.S. embassy in Beirut is destroyed by a suicide bomber

April 19

1775 First bloodshed in the American Revolutionary War

1993 Branch Davidian compound in Waco, TX burns, ending a tense 51-day standoff with the FBI and ATF; 80 members of the armed religious cult and four ATF agents were killed

1995 Oklahoma City, OK Federal Building is bombed, killing 168 people

April 20

1957 First commercial use of the computer language FORTRAN

April 21

753 B.C. Rome is founded

1956 "Heartbreak Hotel" becomes Elvis Presley's first No. 1 single

1989 Chinese students protest at Tiananmen Square

April 22

1724 Immanuel Kant, philosopher, mathematician, and physicist, is born

1915 Chemical weapons ("mustard gas") are first used in war by German troops in Ypres, Belgium, killing 5,000 French soldiers

April 23

Administrative Professionals' Day (Secretaries Day)

1896 First movie is shown to a paying audience in New York City

1962 First U.S. satellite headed for the moon, Ranger IV, is launched

1975 President Gerald Ford announces the U.S. was pulling out of Vietnam; days later the South Vietnamese army surrendered to North Vietnamese forces, thus ending the war

April 24

1833 The soda fountain is patented

1886 Oil is first discovered in the Middle East, on the Egyptian shore of the Red Sea

1980 Mission to rescue hostages held in Iran fails, leaving eight U.S. soldiers dead

April 25

1719 *Robinson Crusoe* is published

1937 Guglielmo Marconi, inventor of the radio, dies

April 26

1921 First weather radio broadcast is made from St. Louis, MO

April 27

1880 Hearing aid is patented

April 28

1992 Four Los Angeles police officers are acquitted in beating motorist Rodney King; mass rioting ensued; those same officers were later convicted of violating King's civil rights

April 29

1813 Rubber is patented in Philadelphia, PA

1923 Zipper is patented in Hoboken, NJ, though the zipper wasn't used for clothing until 1930

April 30

1945 Dachau, the first concentration camp created by Nazi Germany, is liberated by U.S. soldiers, freeing thousands of political prisoners

1992 CERN announces that the World Wide Web technology will be free to anyone

May 2005

May 2005

SUNDAY	MONDAY	TUESDAY	WEDNESDAY	THURSDAY	FRIDAY	SATURDAY
Space Day **1** 1931 The Empire State Building is dedicated to New York City	1933 **2** Infamous Loch Ness Monster is first sighted in Loch Ness, Scotland	1968 **3** First successful heart transplant is performed	2003 **4** First cloned mule is born at the University of Idaho	1961 **5** U.S. makes its first manned space flight	**6** 1856 Sigmund Freud is born	1992 **7** Space shuttle Endeavor makes its maiden voyage
8 Mother's Day 1847 Rubber tires are first patented	**9** 1960 First birth-control pill is approved by the FDA	**10** 1954 First silicon transistor is announced by Texas Instruments	**11** 1928 First regularly scheduled TV broadcasts begin	**12** 1816 First printing press is patented	**13** 1981 Pope John Paul II is shot in Rome's St. Peter's Square	**14** 1944 George Lucas, creator of the *Star Wars* saga, is born
15 1940 Nylon stockings are first offered for sale	**16** 1990 Jim Henson, creator of *The Muppets*, dies	**17** 1973 Televised Watergate hearings begin	**18** 1980 Mount St. Helen's volcano erupts	1998 **19** U.S. Department of Justice files antitrust suit against Microsoft	1990 **20** First photograph from space is sent to Earth from the Hubble Space Telescope	1980 **21** *Star Wars: Episode V: The Empire Strikes Back* is released
22 1906 Wright brothers are issued the first airplane patent	**23** 1785 Bifocal glasses are invented by Benjamin Franklin	**24** 1543 Nicolaus Copernicus dies	**25** 1983 *Star Wars: Episode VI: Return of the Jedi* is released	**26** 1977 *Star Wars* is released	**27** 1937 Golden Gate Bridge opens in San Francisco, CA	**28** 2003 First cloned horse is born in Cremona, Italy
29 1953 First explorers reach the Mount Everest summit	**30** Memorial Day 1971 Mariner 9 is launched for Mars	**31** 1990 *Seinfeld* premieres				

THIS WEEK'S FOCUS: LINUX

ON THIS DAY: BASIC INTRODUCED (1964)

The BASIC (Beginners' All-purpose Symbolic Instruction Code) programming language was created by Dartmouth math professors Thomas Kurtz and John Kemeny and introduced on this date in 1964. Designed as a relatively easy-to-use programming tool, it became widespread on personal computers in the 1980s, and remains popular today.

Related Web site: www.basicguru.com

UNINSTALLING LINUX

If you think installing Linux is tricky, just try uninstalling it—without messing up the rest of your system, in particular your main Windows partition. Here's how to do it, carefully.

The first step in removing Linux, believe it or not, is to use your Windows installation CD. Insert the Windows CD in your CD drive and reboot your system. As you boot from the CD, follow the onscreen instructions until you get to the screen that shows all the partitions on your hard drive. You'll probably see more than one partition, typically labeled `linux ext2`, `linux ext3`, and `linux swap`. Use this opportunity to delete all these Linux partitions from your drive.

Next, you'll need to fix your system's master boot record to remove all references to your Linux installation. Once again, reboot your machine using the Windows installation CD. Start the Recovery Console, and then enter the command `fixmbr`. This will rewrite the master boot record for your new non-Linux installation.

Now you can remove the Windows CD and reboot your computer again. When your computer restarts, you should have a nice, relatively clean, Windows-only machine—with no traces of Linux left.

SOFTWARE OF THE WEEK

Sun's StarOffice is probably the most professional office suite for Linux users. You get word processing, spreadsheet, presentation, graphics, and database applications, all in a relatively familiar interface. Buy it for $79.95 at wwws.sun.com/software/star/staroffice/.

May 2, 2005
MONDAY

THIS WEEK'S FOCUS: DIGITAL MUSIC

ON THIS DAY: FIRST SCIENCE FICTION FILM PREMIERES (1902)

The screen's very first science fiction story was released on this date in 1902, in France. *Le Voyage dans la Lune* (a.k.a. *A Trip to the Moon*) was a 14-minute masterpiece, created by imaginative French director and master magician Georges Melies. The film was inspired by both Jules Verne's *From the Earth to the Moon* and H. G. Wells' *First Men in the Moon*.

Related Web site: www.filmsite.org/voya.html

UNDERSTANDING DIGITAL AUDIO FORMATS

Even if you've never downloaded any music from the Internet, chances are you've still heard of MP3 files. MP3 is a particular type of digital audio format that compresses music to fit within reasonably sized computer files—while maintaining near-CD quality sound. A typical three-minute song in MP3 format takes up about 3MB of disk space, which explains why it's such a popular format among online music traders.

As popular as the MP3 format is, it's not the only digital audio format you'll encounter online. Let's take a quick look at what's out there.

- **AAC**—This is the audio format used by Apple's iTunes and iPod. AAC offers better sound quality than MP3 files, along with strong digital rights management (DMA) to prevent unauthorized use. Unfortunately, most non-Apple music players won't play AAC-format songs—but if you're an iPod user, this is the format you'll be using.

- **MP3**—The most widely used digital audio format today, with a decent compromise between small file size and sound quality. Just about every digital music player and player program can handle MP3-format music.

- **OMG**—OMG stands for Open Magic Gate, which is the digital rights management wrapper Sony uses for its proprietary ATRAC3 digital audio format. Incompatible with everything except Sony products.

- **WAV**—This format (pronounced "wave") produces an exact copy of the original recording, with zero compression. The result is perfect fidelity but with very large file sizes. It's not a good choice for portable use because it takes up too much storage space.

- **WMA**—Microsoft's Windows Media Audio format is promoted as an MP3 alternative with similar audio quality at half the file size. That might be stretching it a bit, but WMA does typically offer a slightly better compromise between compression and quality than you find with MP3 files. It also provides strong digital rights management.

PC GADGET OF THE WEEK

Logitech's Z-680 is one heck of a sound system—whether you're listening to CDs or playing your favorite shoot'em-up games. Buy the whole shebang for $399.95 at www.logitech.com.

THIS WEEK'S FOCUS: DIGITAL MUSIC

ON THIS DAY: FIRST U.S. HEART TRANSPLANT (1968)

On May 3, 1968, Dr. Denton Cooley performed the first successful heart transplant in the United States. The recipient was Everett Thomas, whose heart was damaged from rheumatic heart disease. Cooley's operation came five months after the world's first heart transplant, performed on December 3, 1967 by South African surgeon Christiaan Barnard.

Related Web site: www.donors1.org

MUSIC DOWNLOAD STORES

There are two ways to get digital music onto your hard disk. One is to rip it from a CD (which we'll discuss on Thursday), and the other is to download it from the Internet. So, where do you go to download your favorite songs? You have a lot of choices, but the easiest is to shop at an online music store. These are Web sites that offer hundreds of thousands of songs from your favorite artists, all completely legal. You pay about a buck a song and download the music files directly to your computer's hard disk.

The most popular online music store today is Apple's iTunes Music Store. The iTunes Music Store (www.apple.com/itunes/store/) offers more than 700,000 songs for just 99 cents each. All songs are in Apple's proprietary AAC file format, which means they won't play in most third-party music player programs or on most non-Apple portable music players. But you can use Apple's iTunes software to play the files, and (of course) play all downloaded songs on your Apple iPod.

If you don't have an Apple iPod, you'll want to check out some of the non-Apple online music stores that offer songs in Microsoft's WMA file format. One of the best of these stores is Napster 2.0 (www.napster.com). This is a completely new digital music service named after the pioneering (and long defunct) Napster online music site. The new Napster offers more than 500,000 songs for downloading at 99 cents apiece; entire albums can be downloaded for $9.95.

And that's not all. Companies are starting up new online music stores left and right, all offering a similar selection at similar pricing. Because there are some minor differences between stores, you should also check out BuyMusic.com (www.buymusic.com), eMusic (www.emusic.com), Musicmatch Downloads (www.musicmatch.com/download/), Rhapsody (www.rhapsody.com), Sony Connect (www.connect.com), and Wal-Mart Music Downloads (musicdownloads.walmart.com).

DOWNLOAD OF THE WEEK

SDP (Streaming Media Project) is a streaming audio recorder for your PC. I use it to record my weekly Tech Guy show on radio station KFI-AM; you can use it to record any Internet radio or other streaming audio. Download it for free at sdp.ppona.com.

May 4, 2005

WEDNESDAY

THIS WEEK'S FOCUS: DIGITAL MUSIC

ON THIS DAY: *MAGELLAN* VENUS PROBE LAUNCHED (1989)

The *Magellan* spacecraft was launched May 4, 1989, and arrived at Venus on August 10, 1990. Over the next four years *Magellan* created radar maps of 98% of the Venusian surface, with a resolution of approximately 100 meters. Its mission completed, the spacecraft made a dramatic plunge into the planet's dense atmosphere on October 11, 1994.

Related Web site: www2.jpl.nasa.gov/magellan/

PEER-TO-PEER FILE TRADING

Some of the best music on the Internet doesn't come from any Web site—it comes from other users. Over the past few years, the Web has seen a profusion of peer-to-peer file-trading networks, where you can swap music files with your fellow computer users. You connect your computer (via the Internet) to the network, which already has thousands of other users connected; when you find a song you want, you transfer it directly from the other computer to yours.

Most file-trading networks require you to download a copy of their software and then run that software whenever you want to download. You use their software to search for the songs you want; the software then generates a list of users who have that file stored on their computers. You select which computer you want to connect to, and then the software automatically downloads the file from that computer to yours.

The most popular of these file-sharing services include

- Gnutella (www.gnutelliums.com)
- Grokster (www.grokster.com)
- iMesh (www.imesh.com)
- LimeWire (www.limewire.com)
- KaZaA Media Desktop (www.kazaa.com)
- Morpheus (www.morpheus.com)

File-trading networks are great for finding even the most obscure songs—for free—but have more than a few downsides. First, if you're trading copyrighted songs (which you probably are), it's illegal—and the Recording Industry Association of America could sue you. Second, when you install some file-trading programs (KaZaA in particular), you also install spyware, which nobody likes. And third, many file-trading networks are rife with computer viruses; you might think that you're downloading an audio file, but instead find yourself loading the latest computer virus onto your hard disk.

These risks, however, are unique to file-trading networks. If you download from a reputable online music store, or even one of the free music download sites, you don't face any of these issues

MAC GADGET OF THE WEEK

The SoundSticks II is a great 2.1 speaker system that just happens to look great with your Mac. Harman Kardon created the SoundSticks to augment the design of the iMac flat panel and other Apple models, and they sound just as good as they look. Buy the system for $199 at www.harmankardon.com.

May 5, 2005
THURSDAY

THIS WEEK'S FOCUS: DIGITAL MUSIC

ON THIS DAY: SCREW-ON BOTTLE CAP PATENTED (1936)

On this date in 1936, Edward A. Ravenscroft of Glencoe, Illinois, received a patent for the first bottle with a screw cap and a pour lip. Abbott Laboratories of North Chicago manufactured the bottles.

Related Web site: www.gono.com/cc/bottle.htm

RIPPING MUSIC FROM CD

If you have a decent compact disc collection and a CD-ROM drive in your computer system, you can make your own digital music files from the songs on your CDs. You can then listen to these files on your computer, transfer the files to a portable music player for listening on the go, share them with other users via the Internet, or use these files to burn your own custom mix CDs. This process of copying files from a CD to your hard disk is called *ripping*.

Before you start ripping files from your CDs, you need to have the proper software installed on your PC. Fortunately, most of these programs are free downloads—and the ones that aren't don't cost that much. While almost all music player programs have ripping capability, I particularly like Musicmatch Jukebox (www.musicmatch.com), which is fast and easy to use. (Windows Media Player will do the job, but will only rip songs to WMA or WAV format files; it won't rip to MP3s.)

The ripping process is fairly simple. You start by inserting the CD you want to copy from into your PC's CD-ROM drive. Then you launch the ripper program and select which songs on your CD you want to rip. You'll also need to select the format for the final file (MP3, WAV, or WMA) and the bit rate you want to use for encoding; the higher the bit rate, the better the sound quality. (And the larger the file size!) After you've set everything up, click the appropriate button to start the encoding process.

If you're using Musicmatch Jukebox, you start the ripping process by clicking the Rip from CD button to open the Recorder window. When you insert the CD you want to copy, Musicmatch synchs up (over the Internet) with CDDB, an online database, to obtain track information. Then you check the boxes next to the tracks you want to copy, click the Record button, and let it rip!

One word of warning. After you've started the ripping process, do *not* use your computer to do anything else while encoding; doing so runs the risk of adding "skips" to your digital music files.

WEB SITE OF THE WEEK

In addition to the standard music and artist information, Lycos Music (music.lycos.com) offers a terrific MP3 search engine. Enter the name of an artist or song, and Lycos searches the Web for MP3s to download. And it's all free!

May 6, 2005

FRIDAY

THIS WEEK'S FOCUS: DIGITAL MUSIC

ON THIS DAY: HINDENBURG DISASTER (1937)

At 803.8 feet in length and 135.1 feet in diameter, the German passenger airship Hindenburg (LZ-129) was the largest aircraft ever to fly. On May 6, 1937, the Hindenburg was approaching Lakehurst, New Jersey, after a flight from Europe. A spark of static electricity ignited the dirigible's highly flammable hydrogen gas, creating a horrifying fireball that killed 35 people.

Related Web site: www.nlhs.com/hindenburg.htm

CHOOSING A DIGITAL MUSIC PLAYER

Just as you need a CD player to play your compact discs, you need a digital music player to play your digital audio files. Most digital audio players do more than just play back MP3 and other format files; some let you rip files from CD to hard disk, some let you burn digital files to CD, and some even let you play back video files.

Here's a short list of some of the most popular digital music player programs—most of which you can download for free:

- **MacAMP** (www.macamp.com)—Digital music player for Macintosh computers; also a great streaming audio player/broadcaster for Internet radio.

- **Musicmatch Jukebox** (www.musicmatch.com)— One of the best combination MP3 players/rippers.

- **PCDJ** (www.pcdj.com)—Digital audio player designed especially for DJ use, complete with basic audio mixing functions, such as cross-fading and pitch change; Blue and Red versions also record.

- **RealPlayer** (www.real.com/player/)—Digital music player, CD ripper, Internet radio player, and more.

- **Sonique Media Player** (sonique.lycos.com)— Customizable digital music player from Lycos.

- **UltraPlayer** (www.ultraplayer.com)—Multimedia player program; supports a wide variety of audio and video formats.

- **Winamp** (www.winamp.com)—One of the most popular digital music players today.

- **Windows Media Player** (www.microsoft.com/windows/windowsmedia/)— Microsoft's all-media player, included as part of Windows; also available for separate download.

And let's not forget the music player programs that come with the various online music stores—iTunes, Napster, and so on. These programs perform many of the same functions as the freestanding player programs.

PORTABLE GADGET OF THE WEEK

The Shure E3c sound isolating earphones—actually canal phones—provide a true audiophile listening experience. These are high-end earphones with high-end performance, made of studio-grade components that deliver an extended frequency response. Buy your own for $179.99 at www.shure.com.

150

THIS WEEK'S FOCUS: DIGITAL MUSIC

ON THIS DAY: LUSITANIA TORPEDOED BY GERMAN U-BOAT (1915)

The Lusitania was a British cargo and passenger ship that had crossed the Atlantic peacefully many times over the years, but as World War I escalated, German submarines became more of a threat. On May 7, 1915, the Lusitania was too slow in noticing both the periscope and the torpedo of a German submarine, and she took a solid hit that sealed her fate.

Related Web site: www.lusitania.net

INTERNET RADIO

Many real-world radio stations—as well as Web-only stations—broadcast over the Internet using a technology called *streaming audio*. Streaming audio is different from downloading an audio file. When you download a file, you can't start playing that file until it is completely downloaded to your PC. With streaming audio, however, playback can start before an entire file is downloaded. This also enables live broadcasts—both of traditional radio stations and made-for-the-Web stations—to be sent from the broadcast site to your PC.

Internet radio can be listened to with most music player programs. For example, Windows Media Player has a Radio Tuner tab that facilitates finding and listening to a variety of Internet radio stations. In addition, many Internet radio sites feature built-in streaming software or direct you to sites where you can download the appropriate music player software.

When you're looking for Internet radio broadcasts (of which there are thousands, daily), you need a good directory of available programming. Here's a list of sites that offer links to either traditional radio simulcasts or original Internet programming:

- LAUNCHcast (launch.yahoo.com/launchcast/)
- Live365 (www.live365.com)
- Radio-Locator (www.radio-locator.com)
- RadioMOI (www.radiomoi.com)
- SHOUTcast (yp.shoutcast.com)
- VirtualTuner.com (www.virtualtuner.com)
- Web-Radio (www.web-radio.com)

And remember, although you can listen to Internet radio over a traditional dial-up connection, you'll get much better quality sound over a broadband connection.

FACT OF THE WEEK

According to a Pew Internet and American Life Project survey, more than 17 million Americans stopped downloading music over the Internet following a recent crackdown on the practice. Almost 14% of adult Internet users said they had once downloaded music files but are no longer doing any downloading. Interestingly, the number of Americans who said they are still downloading music increased to 23 million from an estimated 18 million during the same four-month period between November 2003 and February 2004.

SUNDAY

THIS WEEK'S FOCUS: DIGITAL MUSIC

ON THIS DAY: COCA-COLA INVENTED (1886)

Coca-Cola was invented on this date in 1886 by Dr. John S. Pemberton in Atlanta, Georgia. The sugary concoction was first sold at a soda fountain in Jacob's Pharmacy in Atlanta; during its first year, sales of Coca-Cola averaged six drinks a day, for total sales of a whopping $50. Today, Coca-Cola products are consumed at the rate of more than 834 million drinks per day.

Related Web site: www.cocacola.com

CONVERTING RECORDS AND TAPES TO MP3

As you've learned, ripping songs from CD to hard disk is relatively easy. But what if you have music in other formats that you want to digitize?

If you have lots of music on old cassette or reel-to-reel tapes, or even on vinyl records, there's a way to capture that music on computer. Since the original music is in analog—not digital—format, you'll need to rerecord the music in real time onto your computer's hard disk.

You start by connecting your old hardware to your PC's sound card. You'll probably need an RCA to mini-phono cable, or a straight audio cable with an RCD to mini-phono adapter.

Then, get a program that can record from your line-in. Musicmatch Jukebox works great, and it will split your recording into individual tracks. (Otherwise, you'll end up with one big digital musicfile that contains multiple songs.) There are also some dedicated programs you can use for this task, such as RIP Vinyl (www.wieser-software.com/ripvinyl/).

Now it's time for some clean-up and editing. To get rid of the pops and crackles after you've ripped your files, use Magix Audio Cleaning Lab (www.magix.com). To normalize the sound levels between tracks and insert fade-in/fade-out effects, check out MP3trim or WAVtrim (www.logiccell.com/~mp3trim/), depending on which format you ripped to. To break up a long file into individual tracks, check out Audacity (audacity.sourceforge.net). And to perform all these tasks in a single program, consider investing in Adobe Audition (www.adobe.com), formerly known as Cool Edit Pro, a semi-pro level audio editing program.

Finally, you can use Musicmatch Jukebox or any burning software to make a CD. Skip this step if you want to store your music on your hard drive.

SOFTWARE OF THE WEEK

Adobe Audition (formerly Cool Edit Pro) is an audio editing program that offers many professional features, including advanced audio mixing, editing, and effects processing. You can use it to edit all your MP3 and other digital audio files. Buy it for $299 at www.adobe.com.

THIS WEEK'S FOCUS: GAMING

ON THIS DAY: LASER BEAM BOUNCED OFF OF MOON (1962)

On May 9, 1962, scientists in Lexington, Massachusetts, focused a beam of pulsed optical radiation—in other words, a laser—on the surface of the moon, and detected its echoes. The source was a ruby optical laser radiating pulses of approximately 50 joules energy, 0.5 msec. duration; the echoes were received on a 48-inch Cassegrain telescope.

Related Web site: www-istp.gsfc.nasa.gov/stargaze/Smoon2.htm

PC-BASED GAMING CONSOLES

You're used to playing video games on a videogame console and PC games on a PC—but what about a game console that lets you play PC games on your home TV?

That's the whole idea behind the ApeXtreme (pronounced "Apex Extreme," not "Ape Extreme," despite the spelling), which brings console functionality to PC games and connects to any TV or home theater system. The ApeXtreme (www.apexdigitalinc.com) combines a specialized PC, DVD player, and PVR hard-disk recorder in one component-sized unit. Hardware-wise, it has a 40GB hard drive and 256MB memory; it uses an AMD Athlon XP 2000+ microprocessor, with NVIDIA nForce 2 IGP video. The unit has five USB connections, as well as a broadband video connection, and it sells for just $399—cheap for all you get.

Up to four players can connect to the ApeXtreme at the same time. It incorporates Digital Interactive Systems' DISCover Drop and Play engine that lets you load a PC game and play it almost immediately. The engine also automatically installs patches and mods for more than 2,000 games.

Along the same lines, the Phantom Game Receiver (www.phantom.net) is a PC-based gaming device disguised as a game subscription service. The Phantom Network, scheduled to launch in November, 2004, offers a library of PC game titles. You can try, rent, or buy games on demand, and then have the games streamed to you on demand over the Internet.

The Phantom Game Receiver—like the ApeXtreme, pretty much a modified PC—is free when you purchase a two-year subscription to the Phantom Network, or $199 if you buy it outright. It connects to your TV and to any broadband Internet connection, and lets you play the games you buy right in your living room.

PC GADGET OF THE WEEK

Logitech's Cordless RumblePad is one of the best general gamepads on the market—and it's wireless, to boot! It connects to your PC via 2.4GHz RF signals and has a 20-foot range, so you can put some space between you and the screen. The RumblePad also incorporates realistic vibration feedback effects that let you feel every explosion as you play. Buy it for $49.95 at www.logitech.com.

May 10, 2005

TUESDAY

THIS WEEK'S FOCUS: GAMING

ON THIS DAY: VALENCE THEORY ANNOUNCED (1852)

On May 10, 1852, the theory of valence was announced by English chemist Sir Edward Frankland. The theory states that any atom can combine with a certain, limited number of other atoms, which is fundamental to the understanding of chemical structure.

Related Web site: webserver.lemoyne.edu/faculty/giunta/frankland.html

PLAYING GAMES ONLINE

Some of the most fun PC games don't have to be installed on your hard disk. Many sites on the Web offer all sorts of games to play online. Whether you're looking for a quick game of checkers or an evening-long session of Quake II, you can find dozens of sites to satisfy your craving for action and strategy.

Most of these sites offer simple single-player online games; some offer more sophisticated multi-player games. If you're interested in some quick fun, check out the following game portals:

- All Games Free (www.allgamesfree.com)
- ArcadeTown.com (www.arcadetown.com)
- Boxerjam (www.boxerjam.com)
- Games.com (play.games.com)
- Internet Chess (www.chessclub.com)
- Internet Park (www.internet-park.com)
- Lycos Gamesville (www.gamesville.lycos.com)

- MSN Games (zone.msn.com)
- Playsite (www.playsite.com)
- Pogo.com (www.pogo.com)
- Uproar (www.uproar.com)
- Yahoo! Games (games.yahoo.com)

There are also several sites that offer PC games you can download to your computer's hard disk, many for free. Check out Free Games Net (www.free-games-net.com), GameDaily (www.gamedaily.com), GameSpot (www.gamespot.com), and Tucows Games (games.tucows.com).

DOWNLOAD OF THE WEEK

3D UltraPong is an award-winning 21st-century update of the classic paddle game. It features state-of-the-art 3D graphics and improved computer artificial intelligence, but it's still just as easy to play as the original Pong was 30-odd years ago. Download it for free at dpi.hypermart. net/3dpong.htm.

May 11, 2005
WEDNESDAY

THIS WEEK'S FOCUS: GAMING

ON THIS DAY: SPAM TRADEMARKED BY HORMEL (1937)

In Austin, Minnesota, the folks at Hormel hit upon a recipe for a spicy ham packaged in a handy dandy 12-ounce can. That tasty product, trademarked on this date in 1937, was originally called Hormel Spiced Ham. The company held a contest to give the product a more distinctive name, with a top prize of $100. The winning entry combined the "sp" from "spiced" and the "am" from "ham" to create the unique word "spam." More than 65 years later, more than 6 billions cans of the stuff have been sold.

Related Web site: www.spam.com

CHOOSING A GAME CONTROLLER

Playing games is serious business, as you can tell from the plethora of different game controllers on the market today. You can find game controllers to fit just about any type of game you want to play.

When you're shopping for a controller, here are the major styles to choose from:

- **Gamepad**—The default controller for most videogame consoles, complete with a variety of buttons and the directional D-pad, versatile enough for just about any type of game.

- **Flight/combat stick**—A type of joystick with 360-degree movement and firing buttons, ideal for flight games and first-person shooters.

- **Racing wheel**—Combines a full-function steering wheel, gear shift, and gas and brake pedals for playing racing games.

- **Light gun**—Lets you shoot at on-screen objects, ideal for all types of shooting games.

What should you look for in a game controller? Many players like controllers that offer *force feedback*, which uses one or more built-in motors to vibrate the controller to correspond with onscreen action. *Programmable buttons* are also popular (the more the better), so you can dedicate one or more pushbuttons to specific game actions. If you want to cut the cord, go for a *wireless* controller that lets you play from anywhere in the room. And if you're prone to sweaty palms, check out a controller with *cooling technology* that lets you keep cool doing hot gaming sessions.

Most important, make sure you like how the controller feels and how it plays. Be sure it's sturdy enough to hold up through intense game play, and comfortable enough for long gaming sessions. Then plug it in, settle back, and start playing!

MAC GADGET OF THE WEEK

USB game controllers can work on either the PC or Mac platforms, although in most cases they tend to work a little better for PC than for Mac. The Logitech Dual-Action Gamepad is that rare controller that works great on the Mac—just plug and go. It's a comfortable and useable controller, even though it's a touch flimsy and lightweight—but, hey, whaddya expect for 20 bucks? Buy it for $19.95 at www.logitech.com.

May 12, 2005

THURSDAY

THIS WEEK'S FOCUS: GAMING

ON THIS DAY: FIRST U.S. PLANETARIUM OPENED (1930)

The Adler Planetarium in Chicago, opened on this date in 1930, was the first planetarium built in the Western hemisphere. The money for the planetarium came from Max Adler, a senior officer and early stockholder in Sears, Roebuck and Company. He decided to invest part of his fortune in a public facility that would benefit future generations of Chicagoans; the resulting facility, based on a German planetarium, bears his name.

Related Web site: www.adlerplanetarium.org

GAME CHEATS AND NEWS

As sophisticated as today's state-of-the-art video games are, it's tough to advance to the top levels without a little help. Hence, the growth of so-called "cheats" sites, which offer the tips you need to rack up high scores on the latest games.

Here are some of the most popular cheat sites on the Web:

- ChapterCheats (www.chaptercheats.com)
- Cheat Elite (www.cheat-elite.com)
- Cheat Planet (www.cheatplanet.com)
- Cheater's Guild (www.cheaters-guild.com)
- CheatStation (www.cheatstation.com)
- Freaky Cheats (www.freaky-cheats.com)
- Super Cheats (www.supercheats.com)

Also useful are sites that offer a variety of videogame news and reviews, such as

- Console Gameworld (www.consolegameworld.com)
- Future Games Network (www.fgn.com)
- IGN.com (www.ign.com)
- The Magic Box (www.the-magicbox.com)
- VideoGame.net (www.videogame.net)

Many of these news and review sites also offer a variety of game cheats—the best of both worlds!

WEB SITE OF THE WEEK

Joystiq (www.joystiq.com) is a blog devoted to all manner of gaming news. Turn here for the latest dope on PC games and video games, all platforms.

May 13, 2005

FRIDAY

THIS WEEK'S FOCUS: GAMING

ON THIS DAY: VELCRO TRADEMARKED (1958)

In 1958, the VELCRO trademark was registered for a fabric hook and loop fastener that is used today in just about every imaginable way. Velcro's Swiss inventor, George de Mestral, masterminded his invention in the early 1940s while walking his dog. During the walk, he noticed that his dog's coat and his pants were covered with burrs. His curiosity led him to examine the burrs under a microscope, where he discovered their natural hook-like shape. That discovery became the basis for a unique, two-sided fastener—one side with stiff "hooks" like the burrs and the other side with the soft "loops" like the fabric of de Mestral's pants. VELCRO.

Related Web site: www.velcro.com

PLAY CLASSIC CONSOLE GAMES ON YOUR PC

Old-school gaming is hip again. If you long to play those classic '70s, '80s, and '90s console games—but don't want to haul your old Atari 2600 or Intellivision out of the attic—there's a way to turn your PC into a classic videogame console. And it doesn't take a lot of work.

You just install special *emulator* software on your PC—it turns your PC into a virtual game console, capable of running just about any game written for that console. Emulators are available for most classic video-game consoles, and tons of those old games ready to be run.

Here are some emulators for the top classic consoles:

- **Atari 2600**—The Atari 2600 was the first wildly popular programmable videogame, with tons of great games available in the 1970s and early 1980s. The most popular Atari 2600 emulator is Stella, available at stella.sourceforge.net.

- **NES**—The Nintendo Entertainment System (NES) was the most popular video game system of all time. There are many good NES emulators available; the best are Nestopia (sourceforge.net/projects/nestopia/) and FCE Ultra (fceultra.sourceforge.net).

- **Super NES**—The Super NES was Nintendo's first 16-bit game console. The top Super NES emulator is ZSNES (www.zsnes.com).

- **PlayStation**—Sony's PlayStation dominated the console market in the mid-1990s. There are lots of PSX emulators out there; the best two are ePSXe and PSXeven, both downloadable from www.emulator-zone.com/doc.php/psx/.

After you install an emulator, you need to load the ROM for each game you want to play. You can search the Internet to find ROMs for your particular console emulator, or you download ROMs from the collections at CoolROM (www.coolrom.com) or FreeRoms (www.freeroms.com).

PORTABLE GADGET OF THE WEEK

TV Games let you experience old-school gaming on any TV—no PC or game console required. These are portable, self-contained game systems; everything is contained in the joystick controller device. Just connect the joystick to your TV and start playing; each joystick device contains six or so popular games. Buy 'em for $20 each at www.jakkstvgames.com.

May 14, 2005
SATURDAY

THIS WEEK'S FOCUS: GAMING

ON THIS DAY: U.S. UNVEILS NEW TINTED $20 BILL (2003)

The $20 bill got a facelift on May 13, 2003, complete with new colors, a new number arrangement, and a new background. The redesign was part of the government's latest effort to thwart counterfeiters, and featured subtle green, peach, and light blue hues. The picture of Andrew Jackson remained.

Related Web site: www.moneyfactory.com/newmoney/

SPECIALIZED GAME CONTROLLERS

Wednesday we talked about game controllers in general. Today, I'll discuss some specialized game controllers that you can use with specific types of games.

Racing Wheels

When it comes to racing games, you need a steering wheel and pedals that feel and function just like the real thing. Two racing wheels get my recommendation. The officially licensed Nascar Pro Digital 2 (us.thrustmaster.com) has a full-sized rubber-coated wheel that makes it feel like you're driving an actual NASCAR car. And Logitech's MOMO Racing Force Feedback Wheel (www.logitech.com) lets you feel every turn, slide, and bump on the course. Both units feature sturdy foot pedals.

Flight Sticks

For flying games, such as Microsoft Flight Simulator, you want a good flight stick. I like the Combatstick 568 USB (www.chproducts.com), which is simply the best flight stick controller available today. It has a realistic 3-axis F-16 handle, side slide throttle wheel, and 18 buttons, complete with 34 programmable functions. You even get dual rotary trim controls for precision adjustment of ailerons and elevators. But the best thing about this flight stick is its sturdy base and solid feel; this is one controller that just feels right.

Keypad Controllers

Many games don't play well with just a joystick or traditional game controller; they require some amount of keyboard input. This is where the (www.belkin.com) really shines, as it combines keyboard and gamepad functionality into one compact device. This cool little gadget includes a 14-button keypad, a mouse wheel, and a directional pad, all in one cleverly designed unit.

FACT OF THE WEEK

Market researcher NPD Group said U.S. retail sales of video games with online features rose 182% in 2003, reaching 23 million units. Sports games represented 51% of the online-capable videogame market, shooting games were 22%, racing games were 15%, and role-playing games 4%.

May 15, 2005

SUNDAY

THIS WEEK'S FOCUS: GAMING

ON THIS DAY: FIRST BRITISH JET (1941)

On May 15, 1941, Britain's first jet-propelled aircraft, the Gloster-Whittle E.28/39, flew for the first time, taking off from RAF Cranwell on a historic 17 minute flight. Its jet engines were designed by Frank Whittle, "the father of the jet engine."

Related Web site: inventors.about.com/library/inventors/bljetengine.htm

BUILDING A STATE-OF-THE-ART GAMING SYSTEM

Believe it or not, it takes more computing horsepower to play games than it does to crunch numbers or surf the Web. With all those fancy graphics, gee-whiz sound effects, and high-speed action, computer games definitely put your computer system through its paces.

What can you do to beef up your system for better game play? Here are some things to keep in mind:

- If you're using an older PC, you might think about buying a new system with a fairly powerful processor. Think Pentium 4 or AMD Athlon, running at 3GHz or more.

- Whether you have a newer or an older PC, you'll want to increase its memory to at least 1GB.

- You'll also need a lot of hard disk storage because the newer games take up a lot of disk space. Go for at least a 100GB hard disk—bigger if you can afford it.

- You should also consider upgrading to a DVD drive, because many new games come on single DVDs rather than multiple CDs.

- You'll probably need to upgrade your sound card, too. Consider going with a high-quality 3D sound card, and be sure you have a quality multi-speaker system, complete with sub-woofer.

- The capability to handle rapidly moving graphics is essential. Today's hottest games require a 512MB video card with 3D graphics accelerator and DirectX 9 compatibility.

- Big games look better on a big screen, so think about a 19" CRT or 17" LCD monitor.

- Finally, you need something other than your mouse to control your games. You'll want to invest in a good-quality joystick or similar game controller.

SOFTWARE OF THE WEEK

The GameShark is a software-based game enhancer that lets you access final levels, hidden areas, and secret characters, weapons, and vehicles in your favorite videogames. Load it up and get access to an incredible number of secret codes and game saves. There are different versions of GameShark available for PlayStation 2, Xbox, GameCube, and Game Boy Advance, priced from $24.99 to $44.99 at www.gameshark.com.

May 16, 2005

MONDAY

THIS WEEK'S FOCUS: UPGRADING YOUR PC

ON THIS DAY: *PET SOUNDS* AND *BLONDE ON BLONDE* RELEASED (1966)

Two of the seminal LPs of the 1960s were released on this day in 1966. The Beach Boys' *Pet Sounds*, almost a Brian Wilson solo record, layered track upon track of vocals and instrumentals to create a rich, symphonic sound; Bob Dylan's *Blonde on Blonde* blended blues, country, rock, and folk with Dylan's rich lyrics. Both albums inspired countless other artists (including the Beatles) and remain two of the most critically acclaimed rock albums of all time.

Related Web site: www.allmusic.com

UPGRADING VERSUS BUYING A NEW PC

Paradoxically, it's easier to upgrade a newer PC than it is an older one; that's because newer PCs have fast USB ports and are compatible with all the new peripherals available today. Of course, if you have a newer PC, you have less need to upgrade. In fact, if your computer is *too* old, you'll find upgrading both problematic and overly expensive; when you add up the costs of the new components you want to add, you'll probably find that it's cheaper to buy a new PC.

How old is too old? Some techies use the "three years and out" rule and say that if your PC is more than three years old, don't bother upgrading. There's a good reason for this, as really old PCs often don't have the oomph necessary to accept newer, higher-performing components. It's also possible that some components of your old PC might be obsolete, which would necessitate the purchase of a totally new system.

Cost is also a factor. As low-priced as new PCs are these days, you don't want to put too much money into an old machine when a few bucks more will buy you a brand-new system.

Of course, many minor upgrades are both feasible and affordable, even if your PC is more than three years old. Memory, for example, is a cheap and easy upgrade that can boost the performance of just about any PC. Adding a second hard drive—especially if your PC has a USB or FireWire connector, so you can add an external model—is also relatively cheap and easy, and a real godsend if you're running short on storage space for all your graphics and music files.

If your computer is a Pentium III or later and has at least one free USB port, you don't need to worry. Upgrading a newer system is comparatively easy, if not always cheap!

PC GADGET OF THE WEEK: I-DUCK

The i-Duck is a uniquely Japanese flash memory device that looks like a little ducky. Plug it in to your PC's USB port and the ducky lights up. Six colors are available: pink, yellow, blue, tangerine, Army (camouflage), and Heart (with little red hearts on it). The i-Duck comes in three capacities: 16MB ($49), 256MB ($149), and 512MB ($329). Buy one at www.dynamism.com/iduck/.

TUESDAY

THIS WEEK'S FOCUS: UPGRADING YOUR PC

ON THIS DAY: NUCLEAR REACTOR PATENTED (1955)

On May 17, 1955, Enrico Fermi and Leo Szilard received a patent for an atomic reactor. The patent related to the general subject of nuclear fission and particularly to "the establishment of self-sustaining neutron chain fission reactions in systems embodying uranium having a natural isotopic content." Got that?

Related Web site: www.fnal.gov

COMMON UPGRADES

When it comes to adding stuff to your PC, what are the most popular upgrades? Memory is always good, but other upgrades are driven more by the particular applications for which you use your computer. That said, here's a short list of the most popular hardware you can add to your system.

Hardware	Approximate Cost	Reason to Upgrade
Memory	$40-$60 (128MB)	To increase the speed at which your applications run and the number of programs that run at the same time
Ports	$20-$100	To let you add more or different devices to your system
Video card	$20-$400	To display higher-resolution pictures and graphics and provide smoother playback for visually demanding PC games
Monitor	$100-$2,000	For a larger viewing area or for a flatter display (LCD types)
Sound card	$20-$250	To improve the audio capabilities of your PC system

Hardware	Approximate Cost	Reason to Upgrade
Speakers	$15-$200	To upgrade the quality of your computer's sound system
Keyboard and/or mouse	$10-$100	To upgrade to a more ergonomic or wireless model
Game controller	$10-$300	To get better action with your favorite games
CD-R/RW drive	$30-$200	To add recordable/rewritable capabilities to your system
DVD drive	$50-$500	To add DVD playback or recording capability to your system
Hard drive	$70-$400	To increase the storage capacity of your system
Network interface card (NIC)	$10-$30	To connect your computer to a LAN
Wireless network adapter	$30-$80	To connect your computer to a wireless network

DOWNLOAD OF THE WEEK

When you run into problems after upgrading your system, troubleshoot what's changed with MSR Assist. Try it for free, or buy it for $39.95 at bwbox.com/msr/assist/.

THIS WEEK'S FOCUS: UPGRADING YOUR PC

ON THIS DAY: MOUNT ST. HELENS ERUPTS (1980)

At 8:32 Sunday morning, May 18, 1980, Mount St. Helens in Washington state erupted. A mushroom-shaped column of ash rose thousands of feet skyward and drifted downwind, turning day into night. The north face of the mountain collapsed in a massive rock debris avalanche, and nearly 230 square miles of forest was blown over or left dead.

Related Web site: `vulcan.wr.usgs.gov/Volcanoes/MSH/framework.html`

BEFORE YOU UPGRADE

Before you dive headfirst into the upgrading waters, it helps to know what you're getting yourself into. If nothing else, you need to know whether your system can accept the upgrade you want to make; not all PCs are compatible with all the new peripherals on the market today.

Then there is the unsettling fact that even the simplest upgrades—the ones where you plug a new peripheral into an open port—don't always go smoothly. On the off chance that your upgrade either doesn't take or somehow messes up something else in your system, you want to be able to undo the damage and return your system to its pre-upgrade (or *working*) state.

That said, here is a checklist of what you need to prepare *before* you attempt a PC upgrade:

- Determine whether the peripheral you want to add will work on your system.
- Assemble your upgrade toolkit—an assortment of flat and Phillips-head screwdrivers, a pair of tweezers or needle-nose pliers, an anti-static wrist strap, maybe a chip puller—whatever is necessary for the particular upgrade you're planning.

- Use Windows' Device Manager to print out a system hardware report, so you'll know exactly what hardware is installed on your system.
- Make a note of your system's key configuration settings.
- Gather your original Windows installation CD, just in case your system won't restart normally.
- Make a backup of your important data files.
- If you're running Windows XP or Windows Me, set a System Restore point.
- Read the instructions of the item you want to install.

Now all you have to do is make the upgrade!

MAC GADGET OF THE WEEK

The M-Audio Sonica Theater is a USB device that adds to your Mac's bag of audio tricks the capability to support 7.1 surround sound for DVD or other audio playback. The small box offers eight analog-out ports for the various speakers, as well as a digital output designed to work with surround sound speaker systems. Buy it for $119 at www. m-audio.com.

THIS WEEK'S FOCUS: **UPGRADING YOUR PC**

ON THIS DAY: FDA APPROVES FIRST GENETICALLY ENGINEERED TOMATO (1994)

The first genetically engineered product gained FDA approval on this day in 1994. The Flavr Savr tomato, marketed by Calgene, Inc. (now part of Monsanto) can be shipped vine-ripened without rotting rapidly.

Related Web site: vm.cfsan.fda.gov

UPGRADING FROM THE OUTSIDE

The easiest way to add new devices to your system is to add them via an external connector; this way, you don't have to open your PC's case to make the upgrade. Of course, the easiest way isn't always the *best* way. That's because some types of peripherals run faster if they're installed internally rather than externally. For example, an internal hard disk will probably run faster than an external one. Still, for most users, an external connection is the way to go.

The most common external connector today is the USB port. USB is a great concept (and truly "universal") in that virtually every type of new peripheral comes in a USB version. Want to add a second hard disk? Don't open the PC case; get the USB version. Want to add a new printer? Forget the parallel port; get the USB version. Want to add a wireless network adapter? Don't bother with Ethernet cards; get the USB version.

Another nice thing about USB, in addition to its universality, is that USB peripherals are *hot swappable*. That means you can just plug the new device into the USB port, and Windows will automatically recognize it in real time; you don't need to reboot your machine to finish the installation.

Currently, two flavors of USB are available. The older USB standard, version 1.1, has been around for awhile and, if your PC is more than a year or so old, is probably the type of USB you have installed. The newer USB 2.0 protocol is much faster than USB 1.1 and is now standard on most new computers.

If you're upgrading a hard drive or CD/DVD driver, you might want to upgrade via the FireWire port instead of the USB port. That's because FireWire offers faster data transfer than does USB—even USB 2.0. And, like USB, FireWire peripherals are hot-swappable, so a FireWire upgrade is pretty much a plug-and-play operation.

WEB SITE OF THE WEEK

Tom's Hardware Guide is one of the best sites on the Web for anyone thinking about upgrading their PC. Tom's features all manner of news and reviews of various peripherals and components, as well as an assortment of how-to tutorials. Check it out at www.tomshardware.com.

May 20, 2005

FRIDAY

THIS WEEK'S FOCUS: UPGRADING YOUR PC

ON THIS DAY: SPIRIT OF ST. LOUIS TAKES OFF (1927)

Early in the morning on May 20, 1927, Charles Lindbergh took off in The Spirit of St. Louis from Roosevelt Field near New York City. Thirty-four hours later he landed at Le Bourget Field in France, having become the first person to fly solo across the Atlantic Ocean. Lindbergh became an instant hero, having captured the imagination of the American—and the global—public.

Related Web site: www.charleslindbergh.com

UPGRADING FROM THE INSIDE

Adding an internal device—usually through a plug-in card—is slightly more difficult than adding an external device, primarily because you have to use your screwdriver and get "under the hood" of your system unit. Other than the extra screwing and plugging, however, the process is pretty much the same as with external devices. Here's what you need to do:

1. Turn off your computer and unplug the power cable.
2. Take the case off your system unit, per the manufacturer's instructions.
3. If your new card has switches or jumpers that need to be configured, do this before inserting the card into your system unit.
4. Find an open card slot inside the system unit. If you need to remove the slot's cover (on the back of the system unit), do so now.
5. Insert the new card according to the manufacturer's instructions. Be sure the card is firmly plugged in; if you can wiggle it, you haven't made a good connection.
6. After the card is appropriately seated and screwed in, put the case back on the system unit, plug in the unit, and restart your system.

7. After Windows starts, it should recognize the new device and automatically install the appropriate driver. If not, you might need to run the Add Hardware Wizard manually.

Because electrical discharges can damage critical electronic components, you should avoid creating static electricity when working inside your system unit. That means working on a clean wooden or tile surface—*not* a carpet—and wearing cotton or other natural-fiber clothing. You also might want to consider using an anti-static work mat or an anti-static grounding strap, both available at Radio Shack and most computer retailers.

PORTABLE GADGET OF THE WEEK

When it comes to satellite radio, I tend to like the XM system a little better than Sirius, and I really like the SKYFi portable XM receiver. This palm-sized gizmo gives you satellite radio on the go—in your car or at home. Combine the receiver with the SKYFi Audio System boombox, and you have yourself at-home and in-car satellite listening. Buy the receiver for $129.99 and the boombox for $99.99 at www.xmradio.com.

THIS WEEK'S FOCUS: UPGRADING YOUR PC

ON THIS DAY: REMOVABLE TIRE RIMS (1906)

On this day in 1906, Louis Henry Perlman of New York City applied for a patent for his invention of the demountable "tyre"-carrying rim. These were similar to those used on today's cars, but wider. The patent was finally issued on February 4, 1913.

Related Web site: www.autoshop-online.com/auto101/facttext.html

CHANGING SYSTEM SETTINGS

Some devices you add to your PC—in particular, memory and disk drives—might need to be configured at the system level, before you ever get into Windows. These settings make up your system's BIOS and are stored in a special battery-powered memory called CMOS (Complimentary Metal-Oxide Semiconductor) RAM.

To change the settings stored in your system's BIOS, you need to reboot your computer and then interrupt the startup process before Windows launches. Most systems, on startup, display an onscreen message that tells you what key to press to access your BIOS settings; it's typically one of the function keys, such as F2 or F8 or F10. (If you don't see this message, look in your computer's instruction manual for the setup key.) The following table shows the startup interrupt key for some common types of computer BIOS.

Computer BIOS	Key(s)
AMI BIOS	Del
Award BIOS	Del or Ctrl+Alt+Esc
Compaq	F10
IBM Aptivas and Thinkpads	F1
Microid Research (MR BIOS)	Esc

Computer BIOS	Key(s)
Phoenix BIOS	F2
Toshiba notebooks/laptops	Esc, then F1 at prompt

When you enter the BIOS setup utility, you can change a number of basic system settings, such as which disk drives boot first, what kind of hard disk you have, or how much memory is installed. There are typically several "pages" of settings in this utility, so make sure you page through until you find the settings you want to change. After you make any changes to your system's BIOS, follow the onscreen instructions to save your settings and exit the setup utility. Your computer will then resume the startup process, using the new settings you just entered.

One warning: Be especially careful when changing system settings with the Setup utility. If you make the wrong choices, you can make your system unbootable!

FACT OF THE WEEK

The Environmental Protection Agency says electronics now account for 220 million tons of waste in the U.S. alone, much of it containing poisonous metals.

May 22, 2005

SUNDAY

THIS WEEK'S FOCUS: UPGRADING YOUR PC

ON THIS DAY: WINDOWS 3.0 RELEASED (1990)

Microsoft released version 3.0 of the Windows operating system on this day in May 1990. Windows 3.0 was a complete overhaul of the original Windows environment, with a much more powerful user interface and the capability to address memory beyond 640K. This was the first version of Windows to meet with widespread user acceptance.

Related Web site: www.microsoft.com

UPGRADING FROM AN OLD PC TO A NEW ONE

When you're upgrading from one computer to another, you don't have to worry about installing new components or reconfiguring system settings. Instead, you have to worry about transferring your old data to your new PC—and then figuring out what to do with the old iron.

Windows XP includes a new Files and Settings Transfer Wizard that lets you pick and choose which files and configuration settings you want to keep when you move to a new machine. It then copies those files, templates, and settings to some form of removable storage (you can burn a CD or use a Zip disk, or beam the files and settings across a network), which you can take with you to your new machine. Then you run the wizard on the new machine and copy your old files and settings to the new PC. You run the wizard by selecting Start > All Programs > Accessories > System Tools > Files and Settings Transfer Wizard.

The only problem with the Files and Settings Transfer Wizard is that I've never been able to get it to work reliably. Maybe it's just me. Maybe not. In any case, you can perform pretty much the same operation (more reliably) with Aloha Bob PC Relocator. It uses a similar wizard-type presentation to walk you step-by-step through the file relocation process, and is smart enough to know what it can and cannot safely copy over to the new machine. Just connect your two machines with a USB or FireWire cable, and run the program. You can buy it for $29.95 at www.eisenworld.com.

Once you have all your data transferred to the new PC (and you're *sure* the data is all there!), you can prepare your old machine for the junk heap—or, hopefully, the recycle bin. (You might even want to think about donating it to a worthy school or charity.) But before you let the old machine out of the house, you want to thoroughly erase all the data on the hard disk, with a secure data-removal tool like Eraser (www.tolvanen.com/eraser/). Even better, physically remove the hard drive and dispose of it separately.

SOFTWARE OF THE WEEK

Norton SystemWorks is a comprehensive suite of diagnostic and repair utilities that any upgrader will find useful. The suite includes Norton AntiVirus, Norton Utilities (still one of my favorites), Norton Password Manager, Norton Goback, and Norton Cleansweep. Buy it for $69.95 at www.symantec.com.

THIS WEEK'S FOCUS: HARDWARE MODS

ON THIS DAY: ROBERT MOOG BORN (1934)

Robert Moog, born on this day in 1934, was the father of the music synthesizer. He started out building and selling Theremin kits, and in 1964 began to manufacture the first electronic music synthesizers, which were designed in collaboration with the composers Herbert A. Deutsch and Walter (later Wendy) Carlos, of *Switched on Bach* fame.

Related Web site: www.moogmusic.com

WHAT IS MODDING?

Last week we covered simple PC upgrades. This week we cover PC modding, which is kind of like upgrading—on steroids. The word *mod* comes from *modification*, and PC modding involves adding cool elements like fans, cooling systems, lights, windows, and fancy cases to make a truly custom system unit. Modding can also involve souping up your hardware's operation using high-performance video cards, sound cards, hard drives, and such.

This type of extreme upgrading is especially popular among PC gamers, who need high-performance machines to play the most demanding of today's games. It's also a hobby for a lot of computer geeks and IT professionals; it's a way to show off your creativity while at the same time creating a unique state-of-the-art computer system.

Just what can a hardware mod involve? Here's a quick list:

- Case mods comprised of custom painting or creating a new case from scratch. Look for day-glow colors, wild graphics, and lots of clear panels—the better to view inside the modded PC. And don't forget the lights; most case mods involve cool LED or neon lighting of some sort.

- High-performance components, including fast (and often overclocked) CPUs, humongous hard disks used in (or multiple disks used in a RAID array), the latest video and sound cards, and gobs of memory.

- Beefed-up power supplies, the better to handle the demands of the other high-performance components.

- Custom cooling solutions to cool off those power supplies, either with multiple fans or some sort of water-cooling system.

The best PC mods are truly artistic creations. One of the coolest mods I've ever seen involved a water-cooling system that did double-duty as a fish tank; the PC had clear side panels so you could see the fish inside. Wild!

PC GADGET OF THE WEEK

When you're putting together your hardware mod, cool cables complete the package. ThinkGeek offers some really neat illuminated USB cables, with your choice of blue, red, or white lights at the ends. Buy them for $5.99 each at www.thinkgeek.com.

May 24, 2005
TUESDAY

THIS WEEK'S FOCUS: HARDWARE MODS

ON THIS DAY: *STAR WARS* PREMIERES (1977)

The movie that changed the movies premiered on this date in 1977. With gargantuan spaceships, a bevy of eclectic aliens, and state-of-the-art special effects filling the entire screen, *Star Wars* redefined the science fiction film—and spawned a decades-long geekfest industry. The final of six *Star Wars* movies envisioned by creator George Lucas is due to hit theaters in spring 2005.

Related Web site: www.starwars.com

BUILDING YOUR OWN PC

The ultimate mod involves building a custom PC from scratch. But where do you start?

Your first choice is which microprocessor to use, which will determine where you go from there. I recommend AMD; get an Athlon XP 3000+ with the 200 mhz bus (as little as $137) or, for top-of-the-line performance, the 64 FX (for about $700!). Then choose a motherboard that supports the chip; for AMD CPUs, I like the nVidia nForce chipsets.

You start the actual building with the system case. Open up the empty case and lay it on its side, so the motherboard can be dropped into place. Be sure that all the plates and holes line up properly, and make any custom modifications you want to make.

Now you want to populate the motherboard—which is easier to do before you mount it in the case. Install the processor first, making sure to apply a thin film of thermal grease over the processor's core. Install the memory next; the RAM modules should plug right in. Once the CPU and memory are installed, you can mount the motherboard in the already prepped case. Line up all the holes, use the appropriate copper spacers, and screw it in.

Next, you need to prepare all the cabling. Most motherboards come with two IDE cables and a floppy drive connector. Attach the cables to the motherboard, making the runs as clean as possible. When the cables are ready, you can install all your internal drives—hard drive, CD/DVD drive, floppy drive, and so on. Be sure each drive is properly designated "master" or "slave," using the jumpers on the back of each drive.

After this is done, you can insert your system's graphics and sound cards. You should also connect all the switches and LEDs from the case to the motherboard. When you have everything connected, you can power up the system, configure the BIOS, and—if everything is working properly—button up the case. You're done!

DOWNLOAD OF THE WEEK

PowerStrip is a shareware utility that lets you go absolutely insane tweaking your video card and monitor performance. You can overclock just about any card, from the venerable ATI Mach 64 to the latest GeForce 6800 and ATI X800. Try it for free; buy it for $29.95 from entechtaiwan.net/util/ps.shtm.

THIS WEEK'S FOCUS: **HARDWARE MODS**

ON THIS DAY: FIRST ATOMIC CANNON FIRED (1953)

At Frenchman Flat, Nevada, on May 25, 1953, the U.S. Army successfully fired the first atomic artillery shell. The shell, fired from the Army's new 280mm artillery gun, burst with precision accuracy seven miles downrange of the Nevada test site. Twenty 280mm cannons were eventually manufactured; none were ever used in battle.

Related Web site: www.vce.com/grable.html

CREATING A QUIETER PC

Personal computers are noisy. And the more you add to your PC, the noisier it's likely to get. That's why most mods involve some type of noise reduction.

The loudest component of your PC is typically the CPU's fan and heat sink. One relatively easy mod is to replace the stock heat sink with a more efficient model that can run with a nearly silent fan. Checkout the Thermalright SLK-800 (www.thermalright.com), or one of Zalman's Flower models (www.zalman.co.kr).

Next, you can replace your existing fans with quieter models. I like Vantec's Stealth fans (www.vantecusa.com), which are among the quietest on the market. To make things even quieter, you can add a fan speed controller and adjust the speed to minimize the noise level.

Hard drives can also generate a lot of noise, due to the vibration caused by constantly spinning the discs at a high r.p.m. If you have room inside your case, use NoiseMagic's NoVibes III drive enclosure (www.noisemagic.de) to suspend the drive in rubber O-rings, which should significantly reduce the noise level.

Ultimately, a water cooled PC is the quietest way to go. Waterblocks move heat from the tiny surface of the CPU core to a larger surface (the radiator) to dissipate it—kind of like a giant heatsink. If you want to take this step, check out water cooling kits from Coolwave (www.coolwave.com.cn) and Titan (www.titan-cd.com).

For more information on building a quieter PC, check out CompuQuiet (www.directron.com/silence.html) and The Silent PC (www.silent.se).

MAC GADGET OF THE WEEK

The ProScope isn't technically a Mac-only gadget (it works with Windows, too), but it's pretty neat, in any case. It's a hand-held digital microscope, like the kind they use on *CSI*, that connects to your Mac via USB. It sends images to your Mac, where the accompanying software captures snapshots, intervals, or movies at various magnifications. Buy it for $229 at www.theproscope.com.

May 26, 2005
THURSDAY

THIS WEEK'S FOCUS: HARDWARE MODS

ON THIS DAY: MICROFILM CAMERA PATENTED (1931)

On this date in 1931, New York City banker George L. McCarthy received a patent for a microfilm camera. He had developed the first practical commercial microfilm in the 1920s, and received another patent in 1925 for his Checkograph machine, designed to make permanent copies of bank records, using movie film. In 1935 he perfected a 35mm microfilm camera, and (through Kodak's Recordak division) began filming and publishing the *New York Times* on microfilm.

Related Web site: www.heritagemicrofilm.com

MODDING WEB SITES

If you're heavy into the PC modding scene, you'll want to hang out at Web sites that cater to fellow modders. Here are some of my favorite modding Web sites, all with lots of news and reviews, and some with galleries where you can see other users' mods—and post pictures of your own.

- **AnandTech (www.anandtech.com)**—One of my favorite sites for hardware news and reviews.
- **Creative Mods (www.creativemods.com)**—Tons of equipment reviews, mod guides, and an active community of forums.
- **eXtreme-computing (www.extreme-computing.net)**—Articles, forums, and a cool gallery.
- **Furioustech (www.furioustech.com)**—Reviews, articles, and lots of forums.
- **[H]ard|OCP (www.hardocp.com)**—Gamer-oriented hardware reviews, articles, and forums.
- **HiTechMods.com (www.hitechmods.com)**—Articles, modding diagrams, and a gallery.
- **Maximum PC (www.maximumpc.com)**—The Web site of the popular hardware/modding magazine, complete with articles, reviews, and forums.
- **Modthebox.com (www.modthebox.com)**—A Canadian modding site, with articles, reviews, forums, and a gallery.

- **PC-Mod (www.pc-mode.com)**—Articles, reviews, and lots of case mod pics.
- **PimpRig (www.pimprig.com)**—Articles, reviews, guides, forums, and a gallery—plus a really great name.
- **Sharky Extreme (www.sharkyextreme.com)**—News, reviews, and forums about all manner of PC hardware—as well as a weekly CPU and memory price comparisons.
- **The Best Case Scenario (www.thebestcasescenario.com)**—Articles, news, and loads of photos from a true PC modding artist, Paul Capello. Be sure to check out Paul's book, *Maximum PC Guide to Hardware Hacking*. Available winter 2004 from Que Publishing and *Maximum PC*.

And when it comes to buying all the pieces and parts you need to make your own mod, check out Crazy PC (www.crazypc.com), PCToyland (www.pctoyland.com), Voyeurmods.com (www.voyeurmods.com), or Xoxide (www.xoxide.com).

WEB SITE OF THE WEEK

Yoshi's Forums (yoshi.us/forums/) is the online home of my old friend and colleague Yoshi DeHerrera, expert modder. Ask a question, get an answer, and hang out with some of the top hardware modders around.

170

May 27, 2005

FRIDAY

THIS WEEK'S FOCUS: HARDWARE MODS

ON THIS DAY: MASKING TAPE INVENTED (1930)

Dick Drew was one of 3M's driving innovators, and on this date in 1930 he invented something we all now take for granted—masking tape. The idea came from the need for a less-adhesive tape to mask off areas when painting the era's popular two-tone cars. Before masking tape, they used heavy adhesive tape—which peeled off a lot of paint!

Related Web site: www.3m.com/about3M/pioneers/drew.jhtml

CASE MOD PAINTING

One of the first things most modders do is create some sort of custom case. You can find a selection of cases at most PC retailers, or you can revamp an existing case with a custom paint job.

Everything you need to paint a computer case can be purchased at your local hardware store. You'll need aerosol paint (in whatever color you prefer), sandpaper, Formula 409 cleaner, and masking tape.

Start by disassembling your computer, so that you're left with an empty case. Use Formula 409 or some similar cleaner to clean the exterior of your case, and then use your sandpaper to wet sand the case until flat. Use masking tape to mask off any exposed parts you don't want painted, such as switches, LEDs, and clear panels.

Now place the case outside, in your garage, or someplace where you have good ventilation. Start spray painting the case, using thin, even coats. Spray from the bottom up, so the wet paint will absorb the overspray. It's easy to spray it on too thick, so keep your distance and move around the case at a fairly brisk pace.

If you want your case a solid color, you're done. If you want to paint some sort of graphic on your case, you need to let your base coat dry, and then use masking tape to mask off your pattern. Repeat the spray painting with a different color, taking care to stay within the masked area.

When you're all done—and the paint is completely dry—remove the masking tape and reassemble your system. You now have a custom case mod!

PORTABLE GADGET OF THE WEEK

Timex's GPS Watch is a double-duty gizmo that uses GPS technology to help you calculate speed and distance data when running or jogging. In addition to the watch itself, you get an armband- or belt-mounted GPS transceiver (supplied by Garmin) that calculates speed and distance data, triangulated from a network of GPS satellites. The transceiver unit wirelessly transmits the data to the watch, where you view it on the watch's LCD display. Buy it for $199.95 at www.timex.com.

THIS WEEK'S FOCUS: HARDWARE MODS

ON THIS DAY: GOLDEN GATE BRIDGE OPENS (1937)

The engineering marvel we know as the Golden Gate Bridge opened to vehicular traffic at noon on May 28, 1937. (It had opened for pedestrian traffic the day before.) Amazingly, the bridge was completed ahead of schedule and under budget.

Related Web site: www.goldengate.org

OVERCLOCKING YOUR VIDEO CARD

For hardcore gamers, one of the most common mods is to overclock the video card. This increases the core and/or memory clock speed, and makes the card faster. For example, a stock Voodoo2 card runs at 90MHz, while overclocking can boost the speed to 105MHz, resulting in a rather significant performance increase when game playing.

Overclocking is relatively simple to do, but note that it will void your card's warranty because you're pushing the speed higher than the manufacturer intended. Even though you can do it, you're pushing the limits.

To overclock your video card, all you need is the appropriate utility. Two of the most popular over-clocking utilities are Rivatuner (www.guru3d.com/rivatuner/) and PowerStrip (entechtaiwan.net/util/ps.shtm); there are also a number of card-specific overclocking programs available.

Once you've run the overclocking software, you need to see if your overclock is stable. The easiest way to do this is to play a quick five-minute stint of some 3D-accelerated game. If you don't encounter any system freezes or visual artifacts (such as tex-ture tearing), your overclock is fine. In fact, you might want to go back and raise the clock by another 10Mhz or so!

If your PC freezes after overclocking, your video card is running too hot. You can either lower the clock speed or add cooling to your video card. Common cooling solutions include additional heatsinks on the video card or another fan inside your case. This combination of overclocking and additional cooling is a good one. It lets you run your games faster—often at higher frames per second—without risking system shutdown.

FACT OF THE WEEK

The FTC logged 214,905 cases of identity theft in 2003, up 33% from 2002. Some law-enforce-ment authorities say identity theft is the fastest growing crime in the U.S. Identity theft is a relatively low-risk, high-reward crime because credit card issuers often don't prosecute thieves who are caught. Because credit card com-panies can write off a certain amount of fraud as a cost of doing business, crimes often aren't prose-cuted because it costs more to exact justice than it does to simply write it off. For more information, see www.identitytheft.org.

May 29, 2005

SUNDAY

THIS WEEK'S FOCUS: HARDWARE MODS

ON THIS DAY: MOUNT EVEREST CONQUERED (1953)

On May 29, 1953, Sir Edmund Hillary and his Nepalese sherpa, Tenzing Norgay, became the first human beings to conquer Mount Everest—at 29,028 feet, the highest point on the planet. Up until that year, Hillary had lived in relative obscurity as a beekeeper in Auckland, New Zealand.

Related Web site: teacher.scholastic.com/activities/hillary/

EXTREME PCS

The kissing cousin of the PC mod is the extreme PC. This is a new PC, typically sold by a specialty manufacturer, that is customized for state-of-the-art gaming. Extreme PCs are also good for video editing and other high-performance multimedia uses.

What makes an extreme PC extreme? First, you get high-end performance, with the fastest CPUs and video cards. In some cases, manufacturers ship their PCs with overclocking software, to further push the performance envelope. You'll also find hefty power supplies and unique cooling solutions, either with multiple fans or some sort of water cooling. In any case, you get a blazing-fast machine, capable of handling just about any game or application you throw at it.

Second, and perhaps most notable, most extreme PCs come in custom cases. You won't find the typical beige box here; extreme PCs are typically in wild colors with lots of clear panels and flashing lights. Some cases are even custom formed, in interesting shapes.

Where can you buy an extreme PC? While Dell and Gateway profess to offer extreme models, you really want to turn to a specialized manufacturer. My favorites include Alienware (www.alienware.com), Falcon Northwest (www.falcon-nw.com), Overdrive PC (www.overdrivepc.com), and Voodoo PC (www.voodoopc.com). There are also lots of smaller manufacturers who can custom-build you an extreme PC; shop around in the back pages of *Maximum PC* or similar magazines to find something you like.

All extreme PC manufacturers let you customize your configuration and offer a variety of high-performance components. These PCs are fun to play and even more fun to look at. I particularly like Alienware's truly "alien"-looking cases!

SOFTWARE OF THE WEEK

PassMark Performance Test is a comprehensive benchmarking tool you can use to fine-tune your hardware mod. It includes a variety of CPU, 2D graphics, 3D graphics, disk, and memory tests, as well as numerous advanced performance tests. Try it for free, or buy it for $24 at www.passmark.com/products/pt.htm.

May 30, 2005
MONDAY

THIS WEEK'S FOCUS: THE INTERNET

ON THIS DAY: FIRST RUNNING OF THE INDIANAPOLIS 500 (1911)

The Indianapolis Motor Speedway (actually located in Speedway, Indiana, not Indianapolis proper) was built to capitalize on the nation's fascination with the then-new sport of auto racing. The Speedway's first 500-mile race—200 laps of the 2.5-mile oval—was held on May 30, 1911. Ray Harroun bested the other 39 drivers in the field, winning the race with an average speed of 74.59 miles per hour. It took him six hours and 42 minutes to finish.

Related Web site: www.indy500.com

TROUBLESHOOTING CONNECTION PROBLEMS

If you're having trouble connecting to the Internet, the problem could be your phone line, the cable between your phone line and your modem, your modem, the port on your PC to which your modem is connected, the configuration settings for your modem or ISP account, your ISP, or the Internet itself. That said, let's look at how to troubleshoot a troublesome Internet connection.

- Is your phone line working? Is your modem plugged into the phone jack? Is your modem connected properly to your computer? Is your modem receiving power?

- Do you have a noisy phone line? If you can, connect your PC and modem to a different phone line; if things are better there, you have problems with your line.

- Do you have call waiting on your line? If so, you need to add a *70 to your dial-up number, to turn off call waiting while you're online.

- Is your modem configured properly? If you're not sure, run Windows' Modem Troubleshooter and follow the instructions to isolate the problem.

- Are you trying to connect during a busy time of the day? The busier your ISP is, the more likely you'll connect at a slower speed—or not at all.

- Did you get disconnected after being online for awhile? Check with your ISP to see if it automatically disconnects you if you've been idle for a specific period of time. (AOL is notorious for this.) You might need to do *something* every few minutes just to stay connected. Also, Windows itself will disconnect you if you're idle too long. Open the Properties dialog box for your modem, go to the Connection tab, and *uncheck* the Disconnect a Call If Idle box.

If you run into frequent connection problems—or are just tired of slow speeds—consider upgrading to a high-speed broadband connection. Cable and DSL connections are typically more reliable than older dial-up connections.

PC GADGET OF THE WEEK

Logitech's QuickCam Pro is the best-selling Webcam today, and for good reason—it's a solid performer in a compact package that's easy to use, is easy to connect, and delivers a host of useful features. But it for $99.95 at www.logitech.com.

May 31, 2005
TUESDAY

THIS WEEK'S FOCUS: THE INTERNET

ON THIS DAY: PETRI BORN (1852)

Robert Julius Petri, a German physician and bacteriologist, was born on this date in 1852. He is best remembered for the dish that bears his name. The Petri dish is a shallow, cylindrical dish made of plastic or glass, with a cover, that is typically used for tissue cultures.

Related Web site: www.whonamedit.com/doctor.cfm/1079.html

HOW THE WEB *REALLY* WORKS

You're used to accessing a Web site by entering an address—properly known as a uniform resource locator, or URL—into your Web browser and pressing Enter. But how does that simple act find the proper page and load it into your browser?

A URL precisely points to a single Web page through the use of addressing standards. By itself, a URL doesn't reveal the location of a specific Web page; the URL is really a virtual address that can then be linked to a physical server connected to the Internet. Each computer connected to the Internet is assigned a unique IP address. (The IP address is numeric, and looks something like this: 216.70.44.183.)

To link the virtual URL address to the physical IP address, the Internet uses a scheme called the Domain Name System (DNS). DNS is essentially a huge database that maps text-based URLS to numeric IP addresses. When you enter a URL, that request passes through a DNS lookup server that looks up the IP address linked to the URL, and then routes your page request to the proper physical server.

Entries are added to the DNS database when a Web site host registers a specific domain name. For example, if you register the domain name bob.com, you would have to tell the registration service the IP address of the server that will be holding your Web pages. This information is entered in the IP database, which is propagated to multiple DNS servers across the Internet—and is updated on a regular basis with new and changed domain names.

Interestingly, the path that your URL request (and the subsequent Web page information) travels is not predetermined. Data and requests are routed from one server to another by special computers called *routers*, and each server that a data packet passes through is called a *hop*. You can check the number of hops it takes to get from your computer to a specific site with the TRACERT utility; just open a DOS window and enter **tracert** *address*. Interesting!

DOWNLOAD OF THE WEEK

Internet Download Manager is a software program you can use to increase download speeds and resume and schedule downloads at your convenience. It's great when you have really big files to download or. Try it for free, or buy it for $29.95 at www.snapfiles.com/get/idlmanager.html.

MORE MAY FACTS

May 1

1884 Construction begins on the first skyscraper, the 10-story Home Insurance Company building in New York

1931 The Empire State Building is dedicated to New York City by President Herbert Hoover

1946 First radar for a commercial ship operates on the maiden voyage of the S.S. African Star

1947 First radar for commercial and private planes is demonstrated at Culver City, CA

1964 Computer language BASIC is first run on a computer at Dartmouth University

May 2

1519 Leonard da Vinci dies

May 4

1970 National Guardsmen fire on anti-war demonstrators at Kent State University in Kent, OH, killing four, wounding eight, and paralyzing another

1973 Construction on the Sears Building in Chicago, IL, is started; construction was completed in 1974 with the building topping at 1,707 feet, including the antennas

2003 First cloned mule is born at the University of Idaho; the mule's name is Idaho Gem

May 5

1821 Napoleon dies

1936 Bottles with screw-style caps are patented in Glencoe, IL

1961 U.S. makes its first manned space flight; Alan Bartlett Shepherd, Jr. spent 15 minutes in suborbital flight aboard the capsule Freedom 7

1963 First successful liver transplant is performed

May 6

1851 Patent issued for the first mechanical refrigerator

1862 Henry David Thoreau dies

1937 The Hindenberg bursts into flames, killing 36 passengers and crewmembers

May 7

1847 American Medical Association is founded

1963 U.S. launches the Telstar II communications satellite; Telstar II later transmitted the first transatlantic TV program in color

1992 Space shuttle Endeavor—the $2 billion replacement to the destroyed Challenger spacecraft—makes its maiden voyage

1998 Chrysler and Daimler-Benz merge

May 8

1840 First photographic patent is issued in New York City

1984 Soviets boycott Olympics held in Los Angeles, CA

May 9

1882 Stethoscope is patented

May 10

1924 J. Edgar Hoover begins his storied FBI career

1994 Nelson Mandella is sworn in as the first black president of South Africa after spending 27 years as a political prisoner of South Africa

May 11

1928 Radio station WGY in Schenectady, NY, begins the first regularly scheduled TV broadcasts

1949 Polaroid camera is first offered for sale in New York City

1997 IBM computer Deep Blue defeats world chess champion Garry Kasparov

May 12

1847 Odometer is invented in Utah

1896 The street sweeper is patented

1936 The Dvorak typewriter keyboard is patented

May 13

1637 First table knife is created; until this time daggers were used to cut meat and pick teeth

May 14

1804 Meriwether Lewis and William Clark begin their exploration of the Northwest, from the Mississippi River to the Pacific Ocean

1973 First U.S. space station, Skylab One, is launched

May 15

1963 U.S. launches Faith 7 with astronaut Gordon Cooper aboard; Cooper orbited Earth 22 times and spent 34 hours in space—the longest time any human had spent in space at that time

May 16

1866 Root beer is invented

1946 First magnetic tape recorder is demonstrated

1988 Nicotine is declared addictive in ways similar to heroin and cocaine by U.S. Surgeon General C. Everett Koop

1995 First dual-processor PC is introduced by Dell

May 17

1886 John Deere dies

May 18

1830 Manufacture of the first lawn mower begins

1969 Apollo 10 is launched, performing a "dress rehearsal" for Apollo 11, the first manned landing on the moon

May 19

1857 First patent for a city fire alarm is issued in Boston, MA

May 20

1830 Fountain pen is patented in Reading, PA

1873 Process for rivet-strengthening canvas trousers is patented; later these new trousers became known as Levi's

1892 The clothes dryer is patented

1913 Hewlett-Packard co-founder, William R. Hewlett, is born

May 21

1881 American Red Cross is founded

1932 Amelia Earhart completes the first transatlantic plane flight

May 22

1841 Patent for the first reclining chair is issued

1892 Patent for rollable toothpaste tubes is issued

1961 The first U.S. revolving restaurant—the Space Needle in Seattle, WA—is dedicated

1990 Windows 3.0 is released

May 24

1844 First telegraph line is started in Washington, D.C.

1938 Parking meters are patented in Oklahoma City, OK

1993 HDTV alliance formed between major technology makers in order to set a much needed standard for the emerging technology

May 25

1787 Constitutional Convention begins in Philadelphia, PA

1992 Jay Leno's first appearance as the regular host of *The Tonight Show*

May 26

1868 President Andrew Johnson is acquitted in impeachment trial

1897 Bram Stoker's novel, *Dracula*, goes on sale in London

1907 John Wayne is born

1930 Scotch tape is invented in St. Paul, MN

May 27

1755 First municipal water pumping plant is opened in Bethlehem, PA

1796 The piano is patented

1890 Jukebox is patented

May 28

1738 Joseph Ignace Guillotin, inventor of the guillotine, is born

1959 Computer language COBOL is developed

May 29

1919 Albert Einstein's theory of relativity is proved

1992 First digital TV is tested by Zenith and AT&T

May 30

1431 Joan of Arc is burned at the stake for heresy

1821 Fire hose is patented

1959 First experimental hovercraft makes its first trip

May 31

1819 Walt Whitman is born

June 2005

June 2005

SUNDAY	MONDAY	TUESDAY	WEDNESDAY	THURSDAY	FRIDAY	SATURDAY
			1 1880 First pay telephone service begins in New Haven, CT	**2** 1928 Velveeta Cheese is invented by Kraft	**3** 1965 First U.S. spacewalk	**4** 1896 Henry Ford test drives first automobile
5 1968 Senator Robert F. Kennedy is assassinated in Los Angeles	**6** 1944 D-Day Normandy invasion	**7** 1887 Monotype typesetting machine is patented	**8** 1957 Scott Adams, creator of "Dilbert," is born	**9** 1981 First Xerox PC—the Xerox 820—is released	**10** 1936 First cable television broadcast	**11** 1982 *E.T.: The Extra-Terrestrial* is released
12 1897 Swiss army knife is patented	**13** 1983 Space probe Pioneer 10 becomes the first manmade object to leave our solar system	**14** Flag Day 1834 Sandpaper is patented in Springfield, VT	**15** 1752 Benjamin Franklin conducts his famous kite-flying experiment	**16** 1893 Cracker Jack is invented	**17** 1946 First mobile telephones are installed in cars	**18** 1815 Napoleon is defeated at Waterloo, Belgium
19 Father's Day 1941 Cheerios cereal is invented	**20** 1977 Trans-Alaska pipeline is opened	**21** First day of summer 1788 U.S. Constitution is ratified	**22** 1946 Jet airplanes are first used to transport mail	**23** 1868 The typewriter is patented	**24** 1963 The first television video recorder is demonstrated in London	**25** 1951 First color television broadcast
26 1974 Bar codes first used in supermarkets	**27** 1978 First ink pen with erasable ink is introduced	**28** 2000 Human genome, or DNA, is mapped	**29** 1995 U.S. space shuttle Atlantis docks with Soviet space station Mir and orbits Earth	**30** 1971 Three Russian astronauts become the first humans to die in space		

June 1, 2005

WEDNESDAY

THIS WEEK'S FOCUS: THE INTERNET

ON THIS DAY: *SGT. PEPPER'S LONELY HEARTS CLUB BAND* **RELEASED (1967)**

It was 38 years ago today that the Beatles released their landmark album, *Sgt. Pepper's Lonely Hearts Club Band*. It's an incredible—and an incredibly influential—album, with terrific songs that resonate in our consciousness even today. This may be the most important album in rock history; after *Sgt. Pepper's*, everything sounded different.

Related Web site: www.iamthebeatles.com

CREATE YOUR OWN PERSONAL START PAGE

When it comes to personalizing your Internet experience, there's nothing better than creating your own personal start page, custom-tailored with the information, services, and links that are most important to you.

There are several sites on the Web that let you create your own customized information pages. Most of these sites start with the word "My," as in "My Yahoo!" and "My Excite." The most popular of these custom startup pages include

- My Excite (my.excite.com)
- My Lycos (my.lycos.com)
- My MSN (my.msn.com)
- My Netscape (my.netscape.com)
- My Yahoo! (my.yahoo.com)
- My Way (www.myway.com)

My favorite of these pages is My Yahoo!, which launches whenever I start up my Web browser. However, you can customize each of these "My"

sites in much the same fashion. In most cases, you can select to display all sorts of news and information, in your own personal page layout and colors.

For example, you might choose to display national headlines at the top of your page, stock quotes for each security in your portfolio along the left side, and local weather and sports scores along the right. You tell the page what to display—down to specific cities, companies, and teams—and where to put it. The result is your own personal start page, which you can select to be your home page whenever you start your Web browser.

MAC GADGET OF THE WEEK

One of the best—and the priciest—Mac Webcams is Apple's iSight. It's designed to attach to the top of pretty much any Mac model, including PowerBooks and iBooks. It has an auto-focusing lens (to keep you in focus even when you're moving) and incorporates a wide aperture 1/4-inch CCD that Apple says lets in more light than other Webcams—all the better for shooting in typically low room light. Buy it for $149 at www.apple.com.

THIS WEEK'S FOCUS: THE INTERNET

ON THIS DAY: VELVEETA CHEESE INVENTED (1928)

On this date in 1928, the folks at J.L. Kraft Bros. cheese factory in Stockton, Illinois, invented Velveeta cheese. It was packaged in a tinfoil lining that could house the cheese inside a wooden box; when melted, it was as smooth as velvet (hence its name), and it would never curdle when heated.

Related Web site: www.kraft.com

ACCESSING PROBLEM WEB PAGES

The biggest problem with the Web is connecting to the right Web page. URLs can be long and convoluted, and easily mistyped (either by you—in your browser's Address box—or by the person coding a hyperlink on another Web page). Chances are if you have trouble accessing a page, you have the wrong URL.

One trick to try if you can't access a specific page on a Web site is to try to access other pages on the site. You can do this by *truncating* the URL. For example, if you couldn't access www.mysite.com/mydirectory/mypage.html, then truncate the last part of the URL and try accessing www.mysite.com/mydirectory/. If that doesn't work, keep truncating until you get to the main site URL (in this case, www.mysite.com). On many sites, the home page contains a search function you can use to find specific pages on the site; it's possible you can search for the page that you couldn't access, in case the site administrator changed URLs on you.

Server and traffic issues can also temporarily block access to overloaded Web sites. (Only so many users can connect to a server at one time, no matter how large the site—and servers sometimes are taken "offline" for maintenance.) If you can't

connect to a site now, check your URL and try again a little later.

If you jump to a page and the page "hangs" or only partially loads, there can be several causes. First, the page might actually still be loading, but it's a really big page and it's not done yet; click the Stop button on your browser, and then try reloading the page. (Note that pages that contain background sounds and music can *appear* to be hung, but are actually just waiting for the music file to download.) Second, the connection to this site might have gone bad in mid-load; if you can't reload this and other pages, disconnect from your ISP, wait a few minutes, and then reconnect. Finally, the problem might be with your Web browser; try "flushing" your browser's cache and history files to clear disk space and memory.

WEB SITE OF THE WEEK

The Internet Public Library is the first and foremost public library for and of the Internet community. It was launched back in 1995 and offers a library-like front end to tons of useful information—arranged by subject collections. Check it out at www.ipl.org.

June 3, 2005

FRIDAY

THIS WEEK'S FOCUS: THE INTERNET

ON THIS DAY: FIRST AMERICAN WALKS IN SPACE (1965)

The first American to perform a space walk was Ed White, on this day in 1965. As part of the Gemini IV mission, White "walked" for 36 minutes. By the way, the term "space walk" is a bit of a misnomer, because astronauts actually float, not walk, in space; a more correct name is extravehicular activity, or EVA.

Related Web site: www.thespaceplace.com/history/gemini/gemini04.html

USE PROPER NETIQUETTE

When you're communicating online, especially in newsgroups and message forums, you need to follow a set of unstated usage rules, or netiquette. Break the rules and you risk offending other users—and possibly setting off a flame war of diatribes and personal attacks.

Here are the basic rules:

- Don't write in all capital letters—it looks like you're SHOUTING!

- Be specific when creating a message header; this helps readers determine which messages to read and which to avoid.

- Don't post off-topic messages. Postings that veer off topic just add unnecessarily to the clutter and noise level.

- Don't make your messages longer than they need to be. Brevity is a prized trait when communicating online.

- Don't *cross-post* a message in more than one section in an online forum, or in more than one newsgroup.

- Don't advertise. It isn't seemly, and it's sure to inspire a rash of vitriolic replies.

- Be polite. Don't use offensive language, don't be unnecessarily insulting, and treat other users as you would like to be treated yourself.

By the way, it's okay to read a message and not reply. You're not required to respond to every message you see online!

PORTABLE GADGET OF THE WEEK

Garmin's iQue 3600 is a Palm OS PDA with built-in GPS technology and mapping software. It features a flip-up patch antenna for best reception, and a speaker for turn-by-turn voice commands. The unit's 32MB of memory lets it incorporate base maps for North America, South America, Europe, and the Pacific Rim, making this the GPS unit of choice for international travelers. Plus, by integrating GPS and PDA functions, you only have to carry one gadget with you when you travel. Buy it for $590 at www.garmin.com.

June 4, 2005

SATURDAY

THIS WEEK'S FOCUS: **THE INTERNET**

ON THIS DAY: **VISICALC DEBUTS (1979)**

The first spreadsheet application for personal computers was VisiCalc, which launched on this date way back in 1979. The guy who thought up VisiCalc was Dan Bricklin, who needed a computer tool to complete repetitive calculations associated with case studies at the Harvard Business School. VisiCalc gained popularity as an Apple application; it was later sold to Lotus Development Corporation and led to the development of the Lotus 1-2-3 spreadsheet for the PC.

Related Web site: www.bricklin.com/visicalc.htm

WEBCAMS

A *Webcam* is nothing more than a simple digital camera, attached to your computer. The camera connects to your PC, typically via the USB or FireWire port, and feeds images into a special Webcam software program. This program is configured to periodically grab single frames from the camera, and saves the pictures as JPG graphic files. The individual JPG files are then fed to a Web server, which then embeds the pictures into a constantly refreshing Web page. (The embedding and refreshing is typically controlled via an HTML meta tag, JavaScript, or a Java applet.)

There are thousands of Webcams on the Internet. Some are outdoor cams, some are indoor cams, some are pointed at really interesting people and things, and some are pointed at potted plants and coffee machines. If you want to see what's playing on your favorite Webcam, check out one of the big Webcam directories, such as Camscape.com (www.camscape.com), Camville.com (www.camville.com), WebcamSearch (www.webcamsearch.com), or WebCamWorld (www.webcamworld.com).

To set up your own Webcam site, all you need is a Web camera, frame-grabber software (such as CoffeeCup WebCam, found at www.coffeecup.com/webcam/), and a Web server to host your Webcam. It's relatively easy to hook up the camera to your PC, and the frame-grabber software isn't tough to install or configure. The biggest challenge is finding a host server—although you can always run your own server, if you're technically adept.

If you're new to the whole Webcam business, the best solution is one of the sites that specialize in hosting and listing Webcams. Most of the sites I listed above also offer Webcam hosting services, and can serve as a one-stop-shop when you're first getting set up.

Wherever your server is, you'll need a relatively persistent connection between your home computer and the host server. The connection has to be up all the time in order for your Webcam images to be constantly updated. This means that you probably need a DSL or cable modem connection; a dial-up connection is less viable for Webcam use.

FACT OF THE WEEK

According to Nielsen/NetRatings, 75% of all U.S. households now have Internet access. Internet penetration for women aged 35–54 was 81.7%, compared with 80.2% penetration for men in the same age group. For the 25–34 age group, Internet usage was 77% for women and 75.6% percent for men.

THIS WEEK'S FOCUS: THE INTERNET

ON THIS DAY: ROBERT KENNEDY ASSASSINATED (1968)

On June 5, 1968, 15 minutes after midnight, Senator Robert F. Kennedy was making his way from the ballroom at the Ambassador Hotel, Los Angeles, to give a press conference, after winning the California Primary. As he walked through the hotel's kitchen, a Palestinian Arab named Sirhan Sirhan stepped forward and fired a .22 revolver at the Senator. Kennedy died the next day, effectively ending any chances for a Kennedy family presidential dynasty.

Related Web site: www.rfkmemorial.org

DOWNLOADING FILES

The Internet is chock full of fun and useful files to download—but where do you find them?

The best places to look for files are Web sites dedicated to file downloading, such as Download.com(download.cnet.com), Jumbo (www.jumbo.com), and my favorite, Tucows (www.tucows.com). These file archive sites store a huge variety of freeware and shareware programs and utilities.

Downloading a file from any of these archives is fairly easy. Once you locate the file you want, you're prompted to click a specific link to begin the download. Some sites will begin the download automatically; other sites will prompt Windows to display a dialog box asking if you want to save or open the file (you want to save it), and where you want to save it. Follow the onscreen instructions to begin the download.

However, you don't have to go to a software archive to find files to download. You can actually download files you find on any Web page—especially graphics files. To download a graphics file from a Web page, all you have to do is right-click the picture and select Save Picture As from the pop-up menu. When prompted, select a location for the file, and then click Save. The graphics file will now be downloaded to the location you specified.

Outside of the Web, you can also find a lot of files on FTP (File Transfer Protocol) servers. You can access FTP servers with specific FTP client software, or with any Web browser. When you access an FTP server via your browser, be sure to replace the standard http:// with ftp://. And because there aren't near as many FTP servers as there are Web servers, hunting for one is a bit of a task. You can find lists of FTP servers at LapLink FTPSearch (ftpsearch.laplink.com) or TILE.NET/FTP (tile.net/ftp-list/).

SOFTWARE OF THE WEEK

WS-FTP Professional is the commercial release of one of my long-time favorite programs. You use WS-FTP to access FTP servers, where you can upload or download files as necessary; you can also use it to upload pages to your own Web site. Try it for free, or buy it for $54.95 at www.ipswitch.com/products/ws_ftp/.

THIS WEEK'S FOCUS: WEB BROWSERS

ON THIS DAY: *1984* **PUBLISHED (1949)**

The year 1984 has come and gone, but George Orwell's prophetic vision of the totalitarian world we are in danger of becoming is timelier than ever. Orwell's book, *1984*, which introduced the concept of an all-knowing Big Brother, was published on this date in 1949.

Related Web site: www.gerenser.com/1984/

YOUR FAVORITE SITES IN INTERNET EXPLORER

When you find a Web page you like, add it to a list of Favorites within Internet Explorer. With this feature, you can access any of your favorite sites just by choosing it from the list.

To add a page to your Favorites list, navigate to the page you want to save and select Favorites > Add to Favorites. When the Add Favorite dialog box appears, confirm the page's Name, and then click the Create In button to extend the dialog box. Select the folder where you want to place this link, and then click OK.

To view a page in your Favorites list, click the Favorites button in the IE toolbar. The browser window will automatically split into two panes, with your favorites displayed in the left pane. Click any folder in the Favorites pane to display the contents of that folder; click a favorite page and that page will be displayed in the right pane.

If you add a lot of pages to your Favorites list, it can become unwieldy. To reorganize the Favorites list,

use your mouse to drag a favorite page into a new folder or position. To delete a favorite, just highlight it and press Delete.

For even better Favorites management, check out LinkStash. This program helps you store and organize all your favorites links, and works with any browser out there—including Internet Explorer, Mozilla, and Opera. Buy it for $19.95 at www.xrayz.co.uk/linkstash/.

PC GADGET OF THE WEEK

When every mouse and keyboard starts to resemble every other mouse and keyboard, Logitech's diNovo Media Desktop stands out from the crowd. This mouse and keyboard combo features hip styling and the latest Bluetooth wireless technology. The really unique part of the Media Desktop, however, is a separate piece that docks to the keyboard, called the MediaPad; it's a numeric keypad that you can also use to control all your digital media playback. Buy it for $249.95 at www.logitech.com.

THIS WEEK'S FOCUS: WEB BROWSERS

ON THIS DAY: TYPESETTING MACHINE PATENTED (1887)

On June 7, 1887, Tolbert Lanston of Washington, D.C., received a patent for a monotype typesetting machine. This machine cast individual pieces of type for each character; this patent came three years after Ottmar Mergenthaler obtained his first patent for the Linotype machine, which cast solid lines of type.

Related Web site: www.ippaper.com/gettips_pp_history.html

BROWSING OFFLINE

You don't have to be connected to the Internet to browse the Web. Internet Explorer lets you cache pages on your hard drive, and then access them at your leisure—even if you're offline.

To activate offline browsing, you first have to save a site to your hard drive. Surf to the site you want to save, and then select Favorites > Add to Favorites. When the Add Favorite dialog box appears, check the box that says Make Available Offline, and then click the Customize button.

When you're saving a site, remember that you need to save more than just the home page. In fact, you may want to save pages several layers deep. Of course, the deeper you go, the more space the files will take up on your hard drive—and the longer it will take to save the site.

Once the site is stored on your hard disk you can open it from your Favorites list. Just remember that when you're viewing a site from your hard drive, you're viewing a version of the site that you saved in the past; it won't be as up-to-date as the site you access when online.

Why would you want to save a site for offline browsing? One of the callers to my radio show noted that his two year-old son likes the Elmosworld.com site, but gets impatient with the download times of the Java- and Flash-heavy pages. Browsing the site from your hard disk is a lot faster than browsing the same pages online, and waiting for all those Java and Flash applets to download—which better suits a two-year-old's attention span!

DOWNLOAD OF THE WEEK

The 550 Access Toolbar offers some really useful browsing utilities, all on a toolbar that docks to your Web browser. You get a universal search utility (that also blocks search ads in your search results), AutoFill, a pop-up protector, and a privacy manager that automatically erases your surfing history, cookies, and temporary files. Download it for free at www.550access.com/toolbar_main.asp.

June 8, 2005

WEDNESDAY

THIS WEEK'S FOCUS: **WEB BROWSERS**

ON THIS DAY: **MISSILE MAIL LAUNCHED... LITERALLY (1959)**

On this date in 1959, the first official U.S. missile mail was launched from the submarine USS Barbero to the Mayport Auxiliary Naval Station near Jacksonville, Florida. The 36-foot Regulus 1 winged missile carried 3,000 letters, including one from President Eisenhower. Postmaster General Arthur E. Summerfield declared the experiment a success: "Before man reaches the moon, mail will be delivered within hours from New York to California, to Britain, to India or Australia." Yeah, right.

Related Web site: www.usps.com/history/

REVISITING YOUR BROWSING HISTORY

Internet Explorer has two ways of keeping track of Web pages you've visited, so that you can easily revisit them without having to reenter the URL.

To revisit one of the last half-dozen or so pages viewed in your current session, click the down-arrow on the Back button. This drops down a menu containing the last nine pages you've visited. Highlight any page on this menu to jump directly to that page.

To revisit pages you've viewed in the past several days, you use IE's History pane. Click the History button in the toolbar, and the browser window splits into two panes, with your history for the past several days displayed in the left pane.

Your history is organized into folders for each of the past several days. Click any folder in the History pane to display the sites you visited that day. Each site you visited on a particular day has its own subfolder. Click a subfolder to display the pages you visited within that particular site.

To sort the sites in the History pane by site, by most visited, or by most visited today, pull down the View menu within the pane and make a new selection. To increase or decrease the number of days' history displayed, select Tools > Internet Options, and then go to the History section of the General tab and enter a new value for Days to Keep Pages in History. (The default value is 3.)

And, to keep others from viewing the sites you've visited, you can clear IE's History. Just select Tools > Internet Options, and then select the General tab and click the Clear History button.

MAC GADGET OF THE WEEK

Add DVD burning—in both + and - formats—to your Mac with Fantom's Titanium FireWire burner. The external 8X DVD+/-RW burner connects to your Mac via FireWired and includes free DVD Studio software. Buy it for $175 at www.fantomdrives.com.

June 9, 2005
THURSDAY

THIS WEEK'S FOCUS: WEB BROWSERS

ON THIS DAY: LES PAUL BORN (1915)

Guitar legend and recording pioneer Les Paul was born Lester William Polfus on this date in 1915. Not only did he invent the solid body electric guitar—including the model that bears his name—he also created the concept of multi-track recording and the use of overdubbing, played with the Fred Waring and Bing Crosby big bands in the 1930s and 1940s, and had a string of pop hits in the 1950s.

Related Web site: smithsonianassociates.org/programs/paul/paul.asp

SEARCHING FROM WITHIN INTERNET EXPLORER

Internet Explorer has two features that make Web searching easier. In both cases, you can initiate your searches from within the browser, without having to go directly to Yahoo! or Google or any other search site.

The first feature to take note of is called Autosearch, which enables you to enter a search query directly into the Address box. Just enter a question mark followed by one or more search words (like this: `? red balloon`), and then press Enter. IE will now initiate a search and display the results in the browser window.

To select which search service is used with Autosearch, click the Search button in the toolbar to open the Search Assistant, and then click the Custom button to display the Customize Search Settings window. Now click the Autosearch Settings button, and select which search service you want to use.

The second IE search feature is the Search Assistant. When you click the Search button, IE displays the Search Assistant in the left pane. Select what kind of search you want to perform. Just check which you want to do: Find a Web Page, Find a Person's Address, Find a Business, Find a Map, Look Up a Word, Find a Picture, or view your Previous Searches.

If you choose to Find a Web Page, Search Assistant sends your query to the MSN Search engine. To use another search service, click the Customize button in the Search pane. When the Customize Search Settings window appears, select which search services you want to use—you can choose more than one.

After you've accessed a specific Web site, select Tools > Show Related Links. This displays, in the Search pane, a list of Web sites that are somehow related to the displayed page. This feature is powered by technology supplied by Alexa. (Go to www.alexa.com to learn more about Alexa's full menu of navigation services.)

WEB SITE OF THE WEEK

The World Wide Web Consortium is *the* official site of the World Wide Web—really! The WC3, as its called, was created by Tim Berners-Lee and other founders of the Web, and serves as a clearinghouse for all sorts of information, activities, and protocols. Check it out at

June 10, 2005
FRIDAY

THIS WEEK'S FOCUS: **WEB BROWSERS**

ON THIS DAY: **APPLE SHIPS FIRST APPLE II COMPUTER (1977)**

The venerable Apple II computer was released on this date in 1977. Apple's first commercially viable machine, the Apple II superceded the original hand-built Apple I, which was sold primarily to hobbyists. The Apple II sold for $1,298 and was popular with both home and business users, especially after the release of the VisiCalc spreadsheet program. It remained in Apple's product list until 1980.

Related Web site: apple2history.org

USE INTERNET EXPLORER—SAFELY

When security expert Steve Gibson of ShieldsUp fame was on my KFI-AM radio show, he told us that he still uses Microsoft's Internet Explorer in Windows, despite the browser's ongoing security and spyware issues. While I think Mozilla Firebox is a safer browser (which I'll discuss on Sunday), Steve says that there are ways to use IE safely. Here's what he recommends.

First, set a high security level. Select Tools > Internet Options to display the Internet Options dialog box, and then select the Security tab. Select the Internet zone and click the Custom Level button. When the Security Settings dialog box appears, reset the custom settings to High.

Doing this will make a large number of sites unuseable, so when you get to a site that doesn't work, you can add its URL to the list of Trusted Sites. To do this, open the Internet Options dialog box and click the Security tab again. Select the Trusted Sites icon and click the Sites button. When the Trusted Sites dialog box appears, click the Add button. (You can also uncheck the Require Server Verification option.) Naturally, you should add to your trusted list only sites that you know are safe.

To prevent browser hijacking, Steve recommends installing Spyware Blaster (www.javacoolsoftware.com/spywareblaster.html). Although this is technically unnecessary if you have IE security set to high, it's useful just in case you accidentally give access to a bad site.

And don't forget to keep up to date with Microsoft's IE security updates. Whenever Microsoft discovers a new security hole, it issues a patch; for the most protection, you want your browser to have all the latest patches. Go to www.microsoft.com/windows/ie/ to learn more.

PORTABLE GADGET OF THE WEEK

Into bird watching? Like to get up close at sporting events? Then check out the EZBinoCam LX, which builds a small digital camera into a pair of high-quality binoculars. Just zero in on what you want to shoot and snap the picture; it lets you take 2-megapixel photos at 8X magnification, with automatic exposure for focus-free shooting. Buy it for $199.99 at www.shopezonics.com.

June 11, 2005
SATURDAY

THIS WEEK'S FOCUS: WEB BROWSERS

ON THIS DAY: *E.T.: THE EXTRA-TERRESTRIAL* RELEASED (1982)

On June 11, 1982, Steven Spielberg's magical *E.T.: The Extra-Terrestrial* was released to theaters. With a budget of $10 million (big for the time) and state-of the art special effects by George Lucas' Industrial Light and Magic Company, *E.T.* was warmly accepted by film audiences worldwide. It won four Oscars and spurred a huge buying spree for Reese's Pieces, not to mention spurring the catch phrase, "E.T. phone home."

Related Web site: www.suntimes.com/ebert/ebert_reviews/1999/01/ET1001.html

BROWSING FASTER

When you're using Internet Explorer on a slow connection, there are several settings you can adjust to improve your browser performance. The most significant speed enhancement comes from resizing the amount of hard disk space that IE uses to hold previously viewed Web pages and graphics. This disk space is called a *cache*, and the bigger it is, the faster your browser will reload pages that haven't changed since they were last viewed.

To change the cache in Internet Explorer, select Tools > Internet Options, and then select the General tab. In the Temporary Internet Files section, click the Settings button; when the Settings dialog box appears, go to the Amount of Disk Space to Use section and either adjust the slider or enter the precise amount of disk space, in MB.

Of course, a cache is no good if your browser downloads every single element every time you visit a page. Faster performance can be had by forcing your browser to use the cache, and only check for new content periodically. While you can force IE to verify all pages on every visit, you'll speed up the process if you choose to verify pages no more than once per session (or every time you start your browser). You'll experience even fewer delays if you turn off page verification entirely—although then you run the risk of not always loading the latest Web page content.

To configure verification in Internet Explorer, open the Internet Options dialog box, select the General tab, and then click the Settings button. When the Settings dialog box appears, go to the Check For Newer Versions of Stored Pages, and make your desired selection.

Another, more drastic, thing you can do to speed up Web page loading is to not load graphics. You turn off IE's graphics from the Internet Options dialog box; select the Advanced tab, scroll down to the Multimedia section, and deselect the Show Pictures option.

FACT OF THE WEEK

According to research firm KN/SRI, kids want their Internet. Given a choice of six media, one-third of children aged 8–17 said that the Web would be the medium they would want to have if they couldn't have any others. Television was picked by 26% of the kids, telephone by 21%, and radio by 15%.

THIS WEEK'S FOCUS: WEB BROWSERS

ON THIS DAY: *ROCK AROUND THE CLOCK* **RELEASED (1954)**

The record that many peg as the first rock-and-roll record (it wasn't; *Rocket 98* or *The Fat Man* more properly takes that honor) was first released on this date in 1954. The initial release of *Rock Around the Clock*, by Bill Haley and the Comets, was only a modest hit, topping out at around 75,000 units sold. The song got a second lease on life in 1955 when it was included on the sound-track to the movie *The Blackboard Jungle*, and became the #1 song in America for 22 weeks.

Related Web site: www.billhaley.co.uk

SWITCH TO MOZILLA FIREFOX

After all this talk about Internet Explorer, I have to confess that my favorite browser is a new one—Mozilla Firefox. Actually, it isn't all that new; Firefox is the current version of the venerable Netscape browser. It offers a richer feature set than IE, and is also more secure.

Feature-wise, I really like Firefox's tabbed browsing. Instead of opening a separate browser window for each site you want to visit, you can open multiple sites within the same window when using tabs. You can also set a group of tabs as your home page.

Firefox also offers a fairly effective built-in pop-up blocker, which suppresses both pop-up and pop-under windows. You also get a decent cookie man-ager and a download manager that makes it easier to organize the files for download.

To download your copy of Firefox, go to www.mozilla.org/products/firefox/ and click the Download Now! link. It's free.

When you install Firefox, it runs an import wizard that imports your existing settings from Internet Explorer. The wizard imports your Favorites, Internet Options settings, cookies, stored pass-words, and so forth. This makes the migration from IE to Firefox relatively painless.

Unfortunately, once you start using Firefox, you can't delete Internet Explorer from your system. That's because you still need IE for some things, like updating Windows from the Microsoft site. So keep IE around for when you need it, and use Firefox for everything else!

SOFTWARE OF THE WEEK

Visual Communicator lets you put yourself in a live news report—or a convincing imita-tion of one, at any rate. The program includes a teleprompter-type interface and a green screen feature (called V-Screen) that replaces a green backdrop with any image or video of your choosing. Just hook up your Web cam, and you're ready to broadcast—or create a really cool presentation. Buy it for $199.95 at www.seriousmagic.com.

June 13, 2005
MONDAY

THIS WEEK'S FOCUS: EMAIL

ON THIS DAY: PIONEER 10 LEAVES THE SOLAR SYSTEM (1983)

Launched on March 2, 1972, Pioneer 10 was the first spacecraft to travel through the asteroid belt, and the first spacecraft to make direct observations and obtain close-up images of Jupiter. On June 13, 1983, it also became the first man-made object to leave the confines of our solar system. It lost contact with NASA in 2003, and continues to coast silently through deep space, a ghost ship heading for the red star Aldebaran—68 light years away.

Related Web site:

spaceprojects.arc.nasa.gov/Space_Projects/pioneer/PNhome.html

HOW EMAIL WORKS

When you send an email message to another Internet user, that message travels from your PC to your recipient's PC (via the Internet) almost instantly. Your message travels at the speed of electrons over a number of phone lines and Internet connections, automatically routed to the right place just about as fast as you can click the Send button. That's a lot different from using the U.S. Postal Service, which can take days to deliver a similar message!

However, when you send an email message, it doesn't go *directly* to the recipient. Instead, it is sent (via the Internet) to your ISP's or mail service's email servers. The message is then sent from your service's servers to the email servers of your recipient's ISP. The next time the recipient accesses his or her ISP account, your email message is downloaded to their personal computer—and stored in their email program's inbox.

The same process works in reverse for messages sent to your email address. The message starts out on the sender's PC, is uploaded to their ISP's email servers, is sent to your ISP's servers, and then is downloaded to your PC (and your email program's inbox) the next time you connect and check your mail.

The traditional way to send and receive email uses a protocol called the Post Office Protocol (POP), which requires the use of a dedicated email client program on your computer. The other form of email today is Web-based email, such as that offered by Hotmail and Yahoo! Mail.

The email you receive from your Internet service provider is POP email. Most ISPs maintain two email servers, an incoming mail server (also called a POP3 or IMAP server) and an outgoing mail server (also called an SMTP server). If your ISP has only a single server, use that address for both the incoming and outgoing settings in your email program; otherwise, you'll have to enter separate incoming and outgoing server addresses.

PC GADGET OF THE WEEK

The Dazzle 10-in-1 is a versatile, extremely fast digital media reader. The speed comes from the USB 2.0 connection, and the versatility comes from the formats it supports: CompactFlash I, CompactFlash II, IBM Microdrive, SmartMedia, Memory Stick, Magic Gate Memory Stick, Memory Stick PRO, MultiMediaCard, Secure Digital, and xD-Picture Card. Buy it for $69.95 at www.ziocorp.com.

June 14, 2005

TUESDAY

THIS WEEK'S FOCUS: EMAIL

ON THIS DAY: UNIVAC DEDICATED (1951)

The UNIVAC I (UNIVersal Automatic Computer I) was the first commercial computer made in the United States. It was designed by J. Presper Eckert and John Mauchly, the men behind the first electronic computer, the ENIAC. The first UNIVAC was delivered to the United States Census Bureau on March 30, 1951, and was dedicated on June 14 of that year.

Related Web site: ei.cs.vt.edu/~history/

AVOIDING EMAIL VIRUSES

Microsoft Outlook is a great email client, even though its Preview Pane leaves it vulnerable to viruses spread via HTML email—which are just as dangerous as similar Web pages in Internet Explorer. Fortunately, you can reduce this vulnerability.

The easiest way to get around this issue is simply to not view any HTML email. Because the Preview Pane automatically previews any selected email message, you want to turn off the Preview Pane. In Outlook 2003, you do this by selecting View Menu > Reading Pane > Off. In Outlook 2000/XP, select View Menu > Preview Pane. In Outlook Express, select View Menu > layout, then remove the checkmark beside the Show Preview Pane option.

Outlook 2003 also lets you turn off HTML mail entirely—a good idea, in my opinion. Just select Tools > Options to display the Options dialog box; then select the Preferences tab. Click the Email Options button, and when the next dialog box appears, check the Read All Standard Mail in Plain Text option. Of course, when you deactivate HTML email your messages won't be as pretty, but your email won't be as much of a security hazard, either.

Because most email viruses seem to target Outlook, an even safer solution is to move to another email client. My favorite Outlook alternative is Eudora (www.eudora.com), although Mozilla Thunderbird (www.mozilla.org/projects/thunderbird/) and Pegasus Mail (www.pmail.com) are also very safe. On the Macintosh, I use the excellent PowerMail (www.ctmdev.com)—it has the fastest full text search of any program I've ever used, and no HTML mail!

DOWNLOAD OF THE WEEK

To back up your Outlook Express email check out the Outlook Express Backup Wizard, which installs on the OE toolbar. Try it for free, or buy it for $39.95 at www.outlook-express-backup.com.

June 15, 2005

WEDNESDAY

THIS WEEK'S FOCUS: EMAIL

ON THIS DAY: BEN FRANKLIN FLIES A KITE (1752)

On this date in 1752, Benjamin Franklin flew a kite with a key attached, during a thunderstorm. This experiment, explained in a later issue of the Pennsylvania Gazette, proved that lightning and electricity were related. Old Ben was fascinated with electricity; in September of that year he equipped his house with a lightning rod, connecting it to bells that rang when the rod was electrified.

Related Web site: www.ushistory.org/franklin/

EMAIL PROTOCOLS

When you configure your email program to work with your particular ISP, you'll run into a variety of acronyms—SMTP, IMAP, POP3, and such. These acronyms describe specific protocols that define how email is stored and transmitted. Although it's not necessary to have a thorough understanding of these protocols, it is nice to know what all the acronyms mean.

SMTP (Simple Mail Transfer Protocol) is the general protocol for transmitting all email across the Internet. You send email from your PC using SMTP; email sent from one server to another also uses SMTP.

When it comes to retrieving the email stored on your ISP's server, two different protocols can be used. With *POP3* (Post Office Protocol 3), your email messages are stored on the ISP's server only until your email program retrieves them, at which time they are deleted from the server. With *IMAP* (Interactive Mail Access Protocol), you don't actually download messages to your computer; instead, you view your email messages as they're stored on the ISP's server. Both POP3 and IMAP protocols are supported by most major email programs.

To keep things straight, just remember that you use SMTP to *send* messages, but you use POP3 or IMAP to *retrieve* messages waiting for you on your ISP's mail server.

MAC GADGET OF THE WEEK

Griffin Technology's SightLight is a external light for your iSight camera. The SightLight slips right over the iSight, shares its FireWire connection, and adds a warm glow of light that improves your onscreen appearance. Buy it for $39.99 at www.griffintechnology.com.

June 16, 2005
THURSDAY

THIS WEEK'S FOCUS: EMAIL

ON THIS DAY: FIRST HELICOPTER DEMONSTRATED (1922)

On June 16, 1922, Henry A. Berliner demonstrated the first helicopter prototype for representatives of the U.S. Bureau of Aeronautics in College Park, Maryland. Berliner made this first-ever controlled horizontal helicopter flight in a war-surplus Nieuport 23 fighter outfitted with a tilting tail rotor and 14-ft helicopter blades on the tips of the wings.

Related Web site: www.helis.com

ADDING A SIGNATURE TO YOUR EMAILS

An important part of any email message is your "signature," those two or three lines at the end of your email message that include your name and some other parting message. This is how you let your recipients know who you are; it's a way to personalize otherwise-impersonal messages.

You can type a signature manually every time you send a message, or you can create a universal signature that is automatically appended to the end of all your messages. Personally, I go the automatic signature route; it's a lot less work.

To create a signature in Outlook Express, select Tools > Stationery to display the Stationery dialog box. Then, select the Mail tab and click the Signature button. To include this signature on all new messages, select the Add This Signature option. If you'd prefer not to include your signature on replies to messages, select Don't Add Signature to Replies and Forwards.

Now select Text and enter the text for your signature. Click OK when done. To see what your new signature looks like just create a new message; the signature line should appear at the bottom of the message. By the way, signatures are not HTML-dependent; they can be added to any email message, plain text or HTML.

As you're well aware, many Internet users take great pride in their creative (and often lengthy) signatures. That said, fancy signatures can get annoying over time. So if you want to avoid the ire of other users, keep your signature to no more than three lines—and avoid the use of fancy fonts.

WEB SITE OF THE WEEK

Google's Gmail is the hottest Web-based email around. If you don't mind Google's bots reading your mail and inserting topic-related advertisements, Gmail gives you a whopping 1GB of storage—and it's totally free. Sign up at gmail.google.com.

THIS WEEK'S FOCUS: EMAIL

ON THIS DAY: RUBBER PROCESSING PATENTED (1837)

On June 17, 1837, Charles Goodyear obtained his first rubber-processing patent. Goodyear devised a process that made rubber less sticky and prone to melting in the summer heat, by treating India rubber with various metallic solutions.

Related Web site: www.goodyear.com

WORKING WITH FILE ATTACHMENTS

Some email messages have additional files "attached" to the mail message. Attaching files to an email message is a way to send files from user to user over the Internet.

What kinds of files can you attach to email messages? Just about anything, really. You can send and receive graphics files, audio files, video clips, and application documents. You probably don't want to send program files (executables) via email, as they'll be blocked by most anti-virus programs. And, of course, you definitely don't want to open any executable files you receive via email; that's a sure-fire way to infect your system with a computer virus.

If a message contains an attachment, you'll see a paper clip or some similar icon in the message header. When you receive a message with an attachment, you can open it or save it to your hard disk.

To work with attachments in Outlook Express, start by double-clicking the message header that contains the attachment. This displays the message in a new window; the attached file will be displayed (as an icon) in a separate pane under the main message text. To open the attached file, right-click the file icon and select Open. To save the attached file to your hard disk, right-click the file icon and select Save As; when the Save Attachment As dialog box appears, select a location for the file and click Save.

If you want to send a file to someone over the Internet, the easiest way to do so is to attach that file to an email message. To attach a file in Outlook Express, start by creating a new email message, and then click the Attachment button. When the Insert Attachment dialog box appears, locate the file you want to send and click Attach; the attached file now appears as an icon in a new pane under the main text pane of your message. Click the Send button to send the message with the attachment to the Outbox.

PORTABLE GADGET OF THE WEEK

Kenwood's DT-7000S lets you listen to Sirius satellite radio through your home audio system. It sits alongside your other audio components and connects to your receiver via a digital optical output. The unit has a built-in four-line scrolling LCD display and comes with a wireless remote control. Buy it for $300 at www.kenwoodusa.com.

THIS WEEK'S FOCUS: EMAIL

ON THIS DAY: RIDE, SALLY RIDE (1983)

Dr. Sally Ride became the first American woman in space on this date in 1983, when she rode the space shuttle Challenger into orbit for a seven-day mission. It was the Challenger's second mission; on subsequent flights, Dr. Ride logged a total of 343 hours in space.

Related Web site: www.jsc.nasa.gov/Bios/htmlbios/ride-sk.html

TROUBLESHOOTING EMAIL PROBLEMS

The most common problem with email is an incorrect address. It's easy to mistype an address or get the wrong address from someone. If you're having trouble getting a message to another user, try to verify the email address with the recipient personally.

You can sometimes track down the cause of a bounced message by carefully deciphering the error message that accompanies the returned message. You'll often find specific reasons why the message was returned, which can help you formulate your reaction.

Of course, sometimes the Internet just sort of bogs down and things don't get to where they're supposed to go. This can be caused by problems at your ISP's mail server, at your recipient's mail server, or anywhere in between. So, if you get an email message bounced back to you and you know it was addressed correctly, try resending it.

Sometimes a message with a large attachment can take so long to retrieve that it times out your email program. (Any message more than 1MB in size could cause this sort of problem on a normal 56Kbps connection.) The really bad thing is, if you can't download this message, it clogs up your message retrieval so you can't grab any other message after this one, either. If you run into this sort of problem, call your ISP's voice support line and ask them to remove the extra-large message from the queue so you can retrieve the rest of your message. (And email the person who sent the large message and ask them to either compress it—using a Zip utility—or break it up into several smaller messages.)

It's also possible that your ISP has a message size limit. Some ISPs won't let you send or receive messages larger than 3MB or so. Check the help files at your ISP's Web site to see if you're affected by this sort of artificial constraint—and if you are, learn how to either compress or break up your attachments into smaller messages.

FACT OF THE WEEK

According to market research firm IDC, the total number of email messages sent daily will exceed 60 billion worldwide by 2006. That compares with 31 billion email messages sent daily during 2002.

THIS WEEK'S FOCUS: EMAIL

ON THIS DAY: GEORGE "SUPERMAN" REEVES COMMITS SUICIDE (1959)

George Reeves was the second actor to portray Superman on screen (the first was Kirk Allyn in a pair of late-1940s movie serials), but definitely the most recognized, thanks to his confident performance as the Man of Steel in the television series *The Adventures of Superman*. Unfortunately, Reeves felt typecast by the role, and committed suicide on this date in 1959.

Related Web site: www.jimnolt.com

SENDING A MASS MAILING

Most of your email will go to just one or a handful of recipients. However, you can use any email program to manage large lists of recipients, effectively creating your own mini-mass mailings that you can initiate with a single click of your mouse.

The key to managing a mass mailing is to create a *mailing group* in your address book or contact list. Once this group is created, you can compose a single message, address it to the group, and then send it on its way. Even though you only had to enter one "address" in the To: field (for the group), your message will automatically be sent to all the individual recipients you included when you created the group address.

To illustrate how to create a mass mailing list, I'll use Outlook Express as the sample program. Start by selecting Go > Inbox, and then click the Address Book button. When the Address Book window appears, click the New Group button; when the New Group dialog box appears, enter the name of the group in the Group Name box. To add individual names to the group, click the Select Members button, select names from the Address Book list, and then click the Select button. Click OK to proceed.

When you're ready to send your mass mailing from within Outlook Express, select Go > Inbox, and then click the New Mail button. When the New Message dialog box appears, click the Address Book button on the toolbar. When the Select Recipients dialog box appears, select the name of your mailing group, click the To: button, and then click OK. Compose your message as normal, and when your message is complete, send it to the Outbox by clicking the Send button.

Sometimes, you might want members of your mailing group not to see the addresses of other recipients of your mailing. If this is the case, enter the name of your group (or of individual recipients) into the Bcc: field, and enter your own email address into the To: field. When you do this, recipients will see only your address among the recipient list; all other recipients will be "blind," per the Bcc: designation.

SOFTWARE OF THE WEEK

If you do a lot of bulk emailing—newsletters, customer lists, and the like—check out G-Lock Easy Mail. Buy it for $39.95 at www.glocksoft.com/em/.

June 20, 2005
MONDAY

ON THIS DAY: COTTON GIN PATENT APPLICATION (1793)

Eli Whitney was the inventor of the cotton gin, a machine that automated the separation of cottonseed from the short-staple cotton fiber, making Southern cotton a profitable crop for the first time. Whitney applied for a patent on his invention on this day in 1893; the patent was granted the following year.

Related Web site: inventors.about.com/library/inventors/blcotton_gin.htm

HOW WI-FI WORKS

Wi-Fi—short for *wireless fidelity*—is a specific standard for transmitting data wirelessly. You use Wi-Fi networks to connect multiple computers over short distances, and to share an Internet connection among multiple computers.

Officially, Wi-Fi uses the 802.11 wireless networking protocol. Basic Wi-Fi uses the 802.11b protocol, which transmits at 11 megabits per second. Wi-Fi can also utilize the newer 802.11g protocol, which transmits at a much faster 54 megabits per second.

Wi-Fi components are actually miniature radios. That's because Wi-Fi utilizes the 2.4GHz radio frequency (RF) band—the same band used by many cordless phones, baby monitors, and even microwave ovens. (It's a busy band!) The typical Wi-Fi transmitter has a range of 100 feet or so.

A connection point for a Wi-Fi network is called a *hotspot*. When you set up a Wi-Fi network in your home, the wireless access point or wireless router that broadcasts the Wi-Fi signal serves as the hotpot. Outside your home, you can find lots of public hotspots that let you tap your notebook computer into the Internet—wirelessly. For example, most Starbucks locations are Wi-Fi hotspots.

To receive Wi-Fi signals, your computer must have a Wi-Fi access card of some sort. This can take the form of a PCI expansion card or external Wi-Fi adapter for a desktop machine, or a PCMCIA Wi-Fi card for a notebook PC. Many notebooks come with Wi-Fi technology built in; Intel's Centrino technology includes a built-in Wi-Fi adapter.

Bottom line is that you use your PC's Wi-Fi adapter to connect to the Wi-Fi access point or router of a Wi-Fi hotspot. Once connected, you're part of the network—which means you can share the network's Internet connection, share files, or do whatever you would do if you were connected to the network via an Ethernet cable. But it's all wireless!

PC GADGET OF THE WEEK

The Linksys Wireless Compact USB Adapter is an 802.11b Wi-Fi adapter in the form of a USB keychain device. Just plug the USB Adapter in to the USB port of your notebook or desktop PC and get instant access to all nearby Wi-Fi networks. The adapter is hot-swappable, so you can easily move it between different computers. Buy it for $69 at www.linksys.com.

June 21, 2005

TUESDAY

THIS WEEK'S FOCUS: WI-FI

ON THIS DAY: FIRST PRIVATE SPACE FLIGHT (2004)

One year ago today, SpaceShipOne became the first privately funded manned space initiative to actually go into space. The project, headed by Burt Rutan and funded by tech pioneer (and Microsoft co-founder) Paul Allen, took pilot Michael Melvill 100 km above the Earth, just outside the atmosphere.

Related Web site: www.scaled.com

SEARCHING FOR HOTSPOTS

Just two years ago there were hardly any Wi-Fi hotspots outside New York and San Francisco. Today, there are literally tens of thousands of hotspots across the country (and around the world); chances are you're only a mile or two away from a hotspot somewhere in your city.

Probably the easiest way to find a hotspot is to drive or walk to your nearest Starbucks. The coffeehouse chain has partnered with T-Mobile to offer Wi-Fi access in almost all its locations.

Outside of Starbucks, you never know where you'll find a hotspot. Lots of hotels offer Wi-Fi access, as do many local coffeehouses and restaurants. You'll find hotspots throughout most college campuses, and around many public parks and buildings. They're everywhere!

Well, not quite everywhere. If you need to find a hotspot near you, search one of the following Wi-Fi hotspot directories:

- HotSpot Haven (www.hotspothaven.com)
- Hotspot Locations (www.hotspot-locations.com)
- JiWire Wi-Fi Hotspot Locator (www.jiwire.com)
- Wi-Fi Zone Finder (www.wi-fizone.org)
- Wi-FiHotSpotList.com (www.wi-fihotspotlist.com)
- WiFi 411 (www.wifi411.com)

Unfortunately, none of these sites is fully comprehensive. Most list the obvious commercial hotspots, but you might have to hunt a little harder to find unofficial free hotspots, as well as hotspots in other countries.

DOWNLOAD OF THE WEEK

JiWire's Portable Hotspot Locator is a free utility you can carry around with you on your notebook computer. Use it to search for hotspot locations anywhere in the U.S., using the same directory found on the JiWire site. Download it at www.jiwire.com/hotspot-locator-laptop.htm.

THIS WEEK'S FOCUS: WI-FI

ON THIS DAY: DOUGHNUT INVENTED (1847)

On this date in 1847, Rockport, Maine, sea captain Hanson Crocket Gregory first poked the soggy centers out of his wife's doughy treats, so that he might slip them over the spokes of his ship's wheel and thus be able to nibble while keeping an even keel. Mmm... doughnuts!

Related Web site: www.mrbreakfast.com

CONNECTING TO A WI-FI HOTSPOT

Assuming that your notebook computer has Wi-Fi capability, how do you go about connecting to a hotspot?

The answer is: It depends. Connecting to a Wi-Fi hotspot can be very easy and automatic, or it can be a manual process that requires you to manipulate a variety of system settings. Which type of connection you encounter depends on how the hotspot is set up and configured.

The first thing to try is simply turn on your PC. Many public hotspots offer free access for anyone in the vicinity. If you're lucky, your PC will recognize the hotspot and connect to it automatically. Try launching your Web browser and see what happens. If the network is freely accessible, you should be able to surf to any Web site you enter.

Other hotspots charge for access. The best of these automatically "hijack" your browser and load their own access page. The hotspot access page will prompt you for your user ID and password—if you're a previous customer—or tell you how much you need to pay to join. Most of these pay-for-play hotspots let you sign up by the day, the month, or even the year. Just supply your credit card number, and you'll be in.

If you try to access a public hotspot and get nothing, try again. Sometimes the browser hijacker doesn't work, so you have to try to go to another page. Other hotspots require you to enter the access page's URL manually. In any case, if you're having trouble connecting, ask someone at that location for help. There might be special instructions you need to follow to sign on to the network.

Things get more complicated if you have an older PC. While Windows XP should automatically scan and recognize the local Wi-Fi network, older operating systems might require you to perform a manual scan to locate an available network. Depending on your Wi-Fi card, you might need to run the card's Wi-Fi management utility to create a new network location.

MAC GADGET OF THE WEEK

Apple's AirPort Express is a portable 802.11g router and hub. Plug a broadband connection into the bottom of the device, plug it in, and you'll be able to share the connection with any AirPort-capable Macs. Buy it for $129 (the stereo connection kit is $39 extra) from www.apple.com.

THIS WEEK'S FOCUS: WI-FI

ON THIS DAY: ALAN TURING BORN (1912)

Alan Mathison Turing, born on this date in 1912, was a British mathematician, logician, and cryptographer. Turing is considered to be one of the fathers of modern computer science, and invented the conceptual computer known as the Turing machine.

Related Web site: www.turing.org.uk/turing/

WI-FI VS. BLUETOOTH

The two hot wireless technologies today are Wi-Fi and Bluetooth. Wi-Fi is used most often for networking, whereas Bluetooth is more of a cable-replacement technology. Bluetooth is slower than Wi-Fi (1Mbps vs. 10Mbps) and has a shorter range (30 feet vs. 100 feet or more).

Wi-Fi has proven itself as a good technology for both large, high-speed networks and smaller home networks. Because of its cost and operational complexity, however, it is less suitable for the kind of ad hoc device-to-device connections that Bluetooth excels at. You see Bluetooth most often used to connect wireless headsets to cell phones, or keyboards and mice to your PC.

It's conceivable that you would use Bluetooth to connect your peripherals to your PC, and use Wi-Fi technology to connect your PC to the home or office network. The two technologies coexist relatively well, although there are some possible interference issues between Bluetooth and Wi-Fi signals because they both use the same 2.4GHz RF band. (Interestingly, this interference affects the Wi-Fi connection only, slowing it down slightly while Bluetooth transmissions are active.)

Bluetooth is particularly popular outside the U.S., where cell phone technology is more advanced. The ability to connect two phones on an ad hoc basis is a popular feature, and Bluetooth is particularly suited for these types of instant and anonymous connections. Wi-Fi doesn't function well on an ad hoc basis, as it requires a relatively complex (technologically) setup routine.

In the end, Wi-Fi and Bluetooth are both complementary and competitive. It will be interesting to see how these technologies learn to live with each other over the next few years.

WEB SITE OF THE WEEK

The Wi-Fi Alliance is the official association formed to certify and promote the Wi-Fi standard. Their Web site is a great source of information about Wi-Fi protocols and vendors; check it out at www.wi-fi.org.

June 24, 2005

FRIDAY

THIS WEEK'S FOCUS: WI-FI

ON THIS DAY: FIRST FLYING SAUCERS SIGHTED (1947)

The term *flying saucer* came into vogue when pilot Kenneth Arnold spotted nine unidentified flying objects "skipping like a saucer" on this date in 1947. Arnold, a Boise, Idaho pilot and forest service employee, spotted the objects—which actually resembled flying wings—over Mount Rainer in Washington state, flying at an incredible speed. This is generally considered the first major UFO sighting in the U.S.

Related Web site: www.ufoevidence.org

LET SLEEPING MACS LIE

Some Macs have trouble with Wi-Fi networks. In particular, you might find that your Mac loses sync with your network when it goes to sleep. It's a known problem—Macs can have problems rejoining a Wi-Fi network after sleeping.

If this happens to your Mac, there are some things you can try. First, be sure to update your Mac OS to the latest version, by running System Update. You should also update your Airport software.

You also might want to set the Mac to join a specific network when wakening. In Jaguar, set it to either Join Most Recently Used Available Network or Join a Specific Network. If you leave it on Join Network with Best Signal, it can sometimes fail to find the network.

Your best bet, if you don't use Wi-Fi on the road, is to set it to join a specific network each time. In Panther, open the Network System Preference pane and open your Airport settings. Where it says By Default, Join:, select A Specific Network.

Worse comes to worst, you'll have to manually reconnect your Mac to the network each time you wake it up.

PORTABLE GADGET OF THE WEEK

In a strange city and looking for the nearest Wi-Fi hotspot? Then you need Kensington's Wi-Fi Finder, a handheld device that detects all available Wi-Fi networks at the touch of a button. Three lights indicate signal strength; it detects Wi-Fi hotspots up to 200 feet away. Buy it for $39.95 at www.kensington.com.

SATURDAY

THIS WEEK'S FOCUS: WI-FI

ON THIS DAY: FIRST COLOR TV BROADCAST (1951)

On June 25, 1951, CBS broadcast the entertainment show *Premiere*, starring Ed Sullivan and Arthur Godfrey. It was the first color television broadcast, transmitted to fewer than two dozen CBS-Columbia TV receivers in four select cities.

Related Web site: www.tvofyourlife.com

SETTING UP A HOME WI-FI NETWORK

Wi-Fi is the way to go if you're setting up a home network and don't want to bother with running a lot of Ethernet cables. A wireless network is easy to set up, and equally easy to use.

When you're setting up a Wi-Fi network from scratch, you'll need to buy a wireless access point router. This is a single box that contains a network router, an Ethernet hub, a port to connect to your cable or DSL modem, a firewall, and a wireless access point. You can choose from either 802.11b (cheaper) or 802.11g (faster) routers; I see no reason not to go the faster route.

You can connect your main desktop PC to the wireless router either wirelessly (via Wi-Fi) or with traditional Ethernet cables. For the other PCs in your home—that is, those computers that aren't sitting right next to the router—you'll want to take advantage of the Wi-Fi connection. That means using your notebook's built-in Wi-Fi capability or, lacking that, buying and inserting a Wi-Fi access card. For your other desktop PCs, you can either install a Wi-Fi expansion card or (even easier) connect an external Wi-Fi adapter via USB.

Once everything is installed and connected, you'll want to run the network software that came with the wireless router. You also might need to run Windows' Network Connection Wizard; follow the instructions that came with your router.

If you already have an existing Ethernet home network, you can add Wi-Fi capability simply by connecting a wireless access point to the network. This is typically an external device that connects to your main computer via USB. Follow the instructions to install and configure it properly.

FACT OF THE WEEK

According to a survey commissioned by Intel, the San Francisco Bay area is the number-one U.S. metropolitan market in wireless Internet access points. Orange County, California was ranked #2; Washington, D.C. came in at #3; Austin, Texas was #4; and Portland, Oregon ranked #5.

THIS WEEK'S FOCUS: WI-FI

ON THIS DAY: FIRST BAR CODE SCANNED (1974)

On June 26, 1974, at 8:01 a.m., a package of Wrigley's chewing gum with a bar code printed on it passed over a scanner at the Marsh Supermarket in Troy, Ohio, becoming the first product ever scanned under the new Universal Product Code (UPC) computerized recognition system. The now-ubiquitous UPC, a 12-digital bar code that represents the manufacturer's identity and an assigned product number, was invented by IBM.

Related Web site: www.upcdatabase.com

CONNECTING WITHOUT WI-FI

What if you're on the road and need to go online—but there aren't any hotspots nearby? You're not completely out of luck; you might be able to use your cell phone to connect to the Internet.

Most of the new digital cell phones offer some form of Internet data connection. You'll probably need to purchase a data connection kit made specifically for your model of phone. These kits typically consist of a cable that runs from your phone to your PC's USB port, and the appropriate software. You'll need to install the connection/dialer software on your notebook, and then you can use your cell phone as a wireless modem. Connect the cable, start up the dialer software, and your notebook dials into your ISP via your cell phone.

The big problem with this type of connection is speed. Depending on your phone service provider, you could experience speeds as low as 14.4Kbps—about a quarter as fast as a normal dial-up connection. Other providers offer faster connections; I use Sprint PCS, and typically connect in the 128Kbps range, which isn't bad. And if you're shopping for a new phone, ask what kind of Internet/data service is offered, before you buy.

If you go online via your cellular phone, be sure you don't have flat-rate data service. At a per-minute rate for online access, the costs can really add up.

Another alternative, in select locations, is the Ricochet service. Ricochet is a high-speed wireless access service that delivers 176Kbps connection speed. Unfortunately, Ricochet only operates in Denver and San Diego at the moment. Check www.ricochet.com for updates.

SOFTWARE OF THE WEEK

The PCTEL Roaming Client manages access to Wi-Fi networks. It automatically detects and connects your PC to available Wi-Fi networks, and helps you manage your connection preferences. It even includes an integrated location finder and supports roaming between Wi-Fi and cellular networks. Try it for free, or buy it for $19.95 at www.pctel.com/roamingclient.html.

THIS WEEK'S FOCUS: COMPUTER NETWORKS

ON THIS DAY: FIRST PEN WITH ERASABLE INK (1978)

On this date in 1978, the first pen with truly erasable ink, the Gillette *Eraser Mate*, was invented. What makes erasable ballpoint pens work is the ink, which is made of a liquid rubber cement that is capable of being easily erased shortly after writing. After about 10 hours, the ink hardens and becomes non-erasable.

Related Web site: home.howstuffworks.com/pen.htm

SETTING UP A WIRED NETWORK

Connecting multiple computers in a wired network is actually fairly simple. The first thing you need to do is install a network interface card (NIC) in each computer you want to network. Each NIC then connects, via Ethernet cable, to the network *hub*, which is a simple device that functions like the hub of a wheel and serves as the central point in your network. Then, after you make the physical connections, each computer has to be configured to function as part of the network and to share designated files, folders, and peripherals.

Here's the specific hardware you'll need to set up your wired network:

- Network interface cards (one for each PC, and possibly a second card for your gateway PC)
- Ethernet network hub (one for the entire network)
- Router or residential gateway device (optional, for sharing an Internet connection)
- Enough Ethernet cables to run from each PC to the hub

Naturally, you should follow the instructions that come with your networking hardware to properly set up your network. In general, however, you start by powering down your main computer and installing a NIC into an open expansion slot. After you close up the case, reboot the computer and run the NIC installation software. Then, you should connect the network hub to a power source and run an Ethernet cable from your main computer to the hub. Run the network configuration utility (or the Windows XP Network Setup Wizard) to set up your network, then move on to each of the other computers on your network and repeat the whole shebang for each one.

After you've connected all the computers on your network, you can proceed to connect your broadband modem, as well as configure any devices (such as printers) you want to share over the network.

PC GADGET OF THE WEEK

Hewlett-Packard's dc4000 is an external DVD burner with built-in analog video capture. Just connect your VCR or camcorder to the dc4000, insert a blank DVD, and activate the Video Transfer Wizard for automated and unattended conversion of your home movies to DVD. Buy it for $299.99 at www.hp.com.

June 28, 2005

TUESDAY

THIS WEEK'S FOCUS: COMPUTER NETWORKS

ON THIS DAY: FIRST U.S. AERIAL TRAMWAY (1938)

On June 28, 1938, the first aerial tramway in North America was dedicated in Franconia, New Hampshire. The tramway was built to lift skiers from Franconia Notch to the 4,200-foot summit of Cannon Mountain on the north face. The tramway's wooden cabins held 28 skiers.

Related Web site: www.nhstateparks.com/franconia.html

CABLING YOUR HOUSE

If you're building a new house, you have the opportunity to put in all the cables necessary for a whole-house network. You can also use this opportunity to put in cabling for television, security, and home automation. Even though everyone is going wireless, it's nice to have wire when you need it.

One of my KFI-AM listeners works for a cable company, and he forwarded the following recommendations:

- For cable television, put a large junction box in the master bedroom. Then run RG6 Quad video cable from the main box on the outside of your house to the junction box, with feeder runs to all the other rooms.

- If you run more than 8 TVs, you might require a signal booster. Many cable companies will provide this free of charge; if not, Radio Shack sells 'em. Some cable companies can bring in more signal from the street to the house, instead of using a booster. It doesn't hurt to ask.

- Run CAT-5 cable to each room, perhaps even to multiple walls in selected rooms. A single CAT-5 cable can handle one data line and two phone lines. Run the master cable to your main junction box, and install your router and cable modem there.

- While you're at it, don't forget your security system. These systems work best when they're hard wired, which should result in fewer false alarms. Be sure to run a sensor to the box on the outside of the house, or else burglars can just cut the line there.

- Run all these wires through a flex plastic conduit. Also install a pull string, for future use. You also might want to run a piece of fiber optic cable from the outside junction box to the master panel in the bedroom; you never know what you might need in the future!

DOWNLOAD OF THE WEEK

Activity Monitor is a remote surveillance program that monitors all computers on your network, in real time. You can view screens, keystrokes, visited Web sites, and used programs. You can also start programs or execute commands remotely, turn off or restart remote computers, log off users, copy files, and send instant messages to remote users. Try it for free, or buy it for $59.95 at www.softactivity.com.

June 29, 2005

WEDNESDAY

THIS WEEK'S FOCUS: COMPUTER NETWORKS

ON THIS DAY: SOYUZ 11 TRAGEDY (1971)

Soyuz 11 launched into space on June 6, 1971, and returned from its 24-day mission on June 29. Shortly after Soyuz 11 undocked from the Salyut space station and made an initial retro fire, communication was lost with the crew. A valve had been jerked open during the undocking maneuver, causing the crew's oxygen to bleed out into space. When the hatch was opened after landing, all three cosmonauts—Georgi Dobrovolski, Vladislav Volkov, and Viktor Patsayev—were dead.

Related Web site: www.astronautix.com/flights/soyuz11.htm

BUYING A ROUTER

A router is a good addition to your network, especially if you want to share a cable or DSL broadband connection. The router can function as a firewall, which provides a very secure connection to the Internet.

As to brands, there are a lot of good ones out there. I recommend routers from D-Link (www.dlink.com), Netgear (www.netgear.com), SMC (www.smc.com), Asante (www.asante.com—especially good with Macs), and, with the following caveat, Linksys (www.linksys.com).

To test a router or firewall visit Steve Gibson's Shields Up (www.grc.com). A properly configured router will show all ports in stealth mode—that is, invisible to hackers.

Unfortunately, some Linksys routers do not stealth the IDENT port, 113. That's because, historically, IRC and FTP servers have used that port to verify your IP address. This technique is seldom used these days, however, and port 113 should be stealthed as any other. For this reason, many experts no longer recommend Linksys routers as firewalls. You can, of course, manually fix this problem, and the latest firmware updates from Linksys also seem to fix it.

MAC GADGET OF THE WEEK

Asante's FriendlyNET FR1004 is an Internet router that works especially well on Mac networks. It includes a four-port Fast Ethernet switch that moves data at 100Mbps, as well as an integrated firewall. Buy it for $117 at www.asante.com.

THIS WEEK'S FOCUS: COMPUTER NETWORKS
ON THIS DAY: TUNGUSKA METEORITE EXPLOSION (1908)

At 7:17 a.m. on June 30th, 1908, a large meteorite exploded eight kilometers above the skies of Tunguska, Russia. The meteorite, estimated to be 50 meters in diameter, was traveling at approximately 60,000 miles per hour. Because the object exploded in the atmosphere, instead of hitting the ground, it left no crater. Still, the explosion was mind-boggling; the blast released 10–50 megatons of energy, destroying 2,200 square kilometers of forest and leaving no trace of life in its wake.

Related Web site: www-th.bo.infn.it/tunguska/

SHARING AN INTERNET CONNECTION

There are several ways to share a broadband connection among multiple PCs, and they all involve setting up some sort of home network. Which configuration you choose is dependent on how much work you want to take on, what kind of connections you want for each PC, and the type of service offered by your broadband ISP.

The most common type of network configuration for sharing an Internet connection is called a *bridge*. In this configuration, the broadband connection is routed first to the broadband modem, and then to your network hub or router, to which all the other PCs are also connected. The chief advantage of the bridge configuration is that it's easy to set up and configure. It's also a popular configuration for users with wireless networks. (Most wireless-based stations also function as network hubs or routers.)

If you have a DSL connection, some DSL modems also function as network hubs. To use a DSL modem/hub to connect multiple PCs, you create a modified bridge configuration. The broadband connection is routed directly to the modem/hub, and then each PC is connected to the modem/hub. This is a nice option if offered by your DSL supplier.

It's probably the easiest configuration possible, and it eliminates the need to purchase and install a separate network hub.

The last option, the *gateway* configuration, uses a lead computer as a "gateway" to the Internet. This gateway computer is the only computer on your network that is visible to the Internet, and it manages the connections for all the other PCs. You set up a gateway configuration by routing the broadband connection first to your broadband modem, and then to the gateway PC. The gateway PC then connects to your network hub; all your other PCs are also connected to the hub.

This type of gateway network is what you create when you use the Windows XP Network Setup Wizard. It's a very secure configuration; the gateway computer can serve as a type of firewall for the other PCs on your network.

WEB SITE OF THE WEEK

Confused about wiring or configuring a home network? Then turn to HomeNetHelp, a site full of articles, reviews, and lots of step-by-step instructions and flowcharts. It's all free; check it out at www.homenethelp.com.

MORE JUNE FACTS

June 1

1880 First pay telephone service goes into service in New Haven, CT

1968 Helen Keller dies

1992 The E-Lamp, an electric, electrodeless 20-year light bulb, is announced

June 2

1873 Ground is broken on San Francisco's Clay Street, the world's first cable-powered railroad

1889 Hydroelectric power is made available for the first time to consumers in Portland, OR

June 3

1856 Machine for making pointed screws is patented; prior to this invention, screws had blunted ends

1965 Edward White makes first U.S. spacewalk, though Soviets beat the U.S. to the punch, walking in space on March 18 of the same year

June 4

1825 Natural gas is first used for illumination in Fredonia, NY

1872 Vaseline is patented

1984 Scientists in Berkeley, CA clone DNA sequences from an extinct animal, the quagga, which inhabited South Africa before being hunted into extinction in the early 19th Century

1937 First shopping carts are introduced at the Humpty Dumpty supermarket in Oklahoma City, OK

June 5

1956 Elvis Presley creates a media frenzy with his "suggestive hip gyrations" during a televised performance of "Hound Dog" on *The Milton Berle Show*

1977 Apple II is released

1981 A disease later known as AIDS is first described in a newsletter; this is the first published notice on the disease that has since become a world epidemic

June 6

1639 First gunpowder mill is granted 500 acres of land in Pecoit, MA

1949 George Orwell's *1984* is published, foretelling of "Big Brother"

June 7

1954 Alan Turing, a pioneer in the field of computer theory, dies

1954 First lab for the study of microbiology is opened at Rutgers University

June 8

1873 The first post cards are used

1874 Apache Chief Cochise dies

1983 First triplets resulting from in-vitro fertilization are born in Adelaide, Australia

June 9

1934 Donald Duck makes his first film appearance in "The Wise Little Hen"

June 10

1692 First Salem Witch hanging occurs

1935 Alcoholics Anonymous is founded

1943 The ballpoint pen is patented

1952 Mylar is patented

1936 First cable television broadcast is made from Radio City to the Empire State Building in New York City

June 11

1889 First folding chair is patented

1962 Three prisoners escape—and are never found, alive or dead—from Alcatraz

1963 University of Alabama is desegregated under military pressure from President John F. Kennedy

June 12

1849 The gas mask is patented

1913 First animated cartoon, "The Artist's Dream," is released

1994 O.J. Simpson's wife and her friend are murdered; Simpson becomes the primary suspect

June 13

323 B.C. Alexander the Great dies

1844 The Yale door lock is patented

1983 Space probe Pioneer 10 crosses the orbit of Neptune and becomes the first manmade object to leave our solar system

June 14

Flag Day

1777 Continental Congress adopts the flag of the United States with 13 alternating red-and-white stripes, with 13 stars—one for each state of the union—on a blue field

1951 Univac I computer debuts

1972 DDT is banned by the EPA

June 15

1752 Benjamin Franklin conducts his famous kite-flying experiment, confirming that lightning was a naturally occurring electronic current

1844 Vulcanized rubber is patented by Charles Goodyear

June 16

1903 Ford Motor Company is incorporated

1903 Pepsi-Cola is trademarked in New Bern, N.C.

1963 Valentina Tereshkova becomes the first woman in space aboard the Russian spacecraft Vostok 6

June 17

1972 Watergate burglars are arrested

1994 O.J. Simpson is arrested after a nationally televised attempt to flee from police in his white Ford Bronco

June 18

1923 First Checker Cab Company cab is produced

1983 Sally K. Ride becomes the first U.S. woman in space aboard the space shuttle Challenger

June 19

Father's Day

1623 Mathematician Blaise Pascal is born

1885 The Statue of Liberty, a gift from France, arrives in New York City's harbor

June 21

First day of summer

1893 The first Ferris wheel is introduced at the World Fair in Chicago

1948 First long-playing records, more commonly known as LPs, are introduced in New York City

1948 First stored-program computer—the SSEM—runs its first program

June 23

1775 First American-made book, titled Impenetrable Secret, is advertised in the Pennsylvania Mercury

1912 Alan Turing is born

1964 The Hula-hoop is patented

June 25

1867 Barbed wire is patented in Kent, OH

1876 General George Custer is killed at the Battle of Little Big Horn in Montana

1903 George Orwell is born

June 26

1498 The toothbrush is invented in China

1974 Bar codes are first used in supermarkets; the first item scanned was a pack of Wrigley's chewing gum

June 27

1978 Seasat, an ocean surveillance satellite, is launched

June 28

1958 The Mackinac Bridge—the world's longest suspension bridge—is dedicated; the bridge is 26,444 feet and joins the upper and lower peninsulas of Michigan

1965 First satellite phone call is made

June 30

1971 Three Russian astronauts become the first humans to die in space when the Soyuz II fell victim to internal cabin pressure changes upon reentry into Earth's atmosphere

July 2005

July 2005

SUNDAY	MONDAY	TUESDAY	WEDNESDAY	THURSDAY	FRIDAY	SATURDAY
					1 Canadian Independence Day 1941 NBC airs first official TV commercial	**2** 1937 Amelia Earhart's plane disappears somewhere in the South Pacific
3 1929 Foam rubber is invented	**4** Independence Day 1997 Pathfinder probe enters Mars' atmosphere	**5** 1946 The bikini is introduced to the U.S. by French designers	**6** 1957 Paul McCartney and John Lennon meet at a church picnic near Liverpool	**7** 1936 Phillips-head screwdriver is patented	**8** 1776 First public reading of the *Declaration of Independence* in Philadelphia, PA	**9** 1815 The first natural U.S. gas well is discovered accidentally in Charleston, WV
10 1933 First police radio system begins operation in Eastchester Township, NY	**11** 1985 Coca-Cola's original recipe is changed	**12** 1962 The Rolling Stones give their first public performance	**13** 1881 Billy The Kid is shot dead by Pat Garrett in Lincoln County, NM	**14** 1868 Spring tape measure is patented	**15** 1996 MSNBC is launched	**16** 1969 First U.S. manned flight, Apollo 11, is launched to the moon
17 1959 Oldest human skull on record is found in Tanzania	**18** 1968 Intel incorporates	**19** 1935 First U.S. parking meters are installed in Oklahoma City, OK	**20** 1976 Viking I lands on Mars—the first human space-craft to make a safe landing on this plane	**21** 1946 First jet is launched from a ship deck;	**22** 1998 Bill Gates turns over his position of president and CEO of Microsoft to Steve Ballmer	**23** 1996 First commercial HDTV broadcast is made by WRAL in Raleigh, NC
24/31 1975 Controversial labor leader Jimmy Hoffa disappears	**25** 1997 Stem cells are lab cultured for the first time from aborted human embryos	**26** 1908 FBI is founded	**27** 1928 Stanley Kubrick, director of *A Clockwork Orange*, is born	**28** 1868 14th Amendment to the Constitution is adopted	**29** 1954 J.R.R. Tolkien's *Lord of the Rings: The Fellowship of the Ring* is published	**30** 1928 First television station is broadcast

July 1, 2005
FRIDAY

THIS WEEK'S FOCUS: COMPUTER NETWORKS

ON THIS DAY: LEIBNIZ BORN (1646)

Gottfried Wilhelm von Leibniz, born the first of July in 1646, was a philosopher, scientist, mathematician, diplomat, librarian, and lawyer. Along with Isaac Newton, Leibniz is jointly credited for the development of modern calculus; in particular, he developed the integral and the product rule.

Related Web site: www-gap.dcs.st-and.ac.uk/~history/Mathematicians/Leibniz.html

TROUBLESHOOTING NETWORK PROBLEMS

It happens sometimes. You go to transfer files to another computer on your network, but that computer isn't there. Where did it go?

First, check the obvious. Is the other computer turned on? (Sleeping computers don't show up on the network.) Is it connected to the network? (Double-check both ends of the cable.) If you're on an Ethernet network, are both computers connected to the hub, and does the hub have power? You should also check the ends of the network cables; if the connection is working, there should be a blinking light where the cable connects to the PC.

Here's another simple thing to try: Reboot your computer. For whatever reason, "lost" computers on a network will often get found when you reboot the computer that can't see them. (I have to reboot my main computer a few times a week for this very problem.)

Now for some serious troubleshooting. In Windows XP, open the Help and Support Center, click the Fixing Problem link, click Networking Problems, and then run the Home and Small Office Networking Troubleshooter. Chances are this will fix most simple networking problems.

You might have a bad network connection on either one of the two computers. To repair a host of connection problems, open the Network Connections utility from the Control Panel. Right-click the problem connection, and then select Repair from the pop-up menu.

If worse comes to worst, delete the problematic connection from the second PC, and then rerun the Network Setup Wizard to reinstall the network. You also might have to rerun the wizard on your host PC (to recognize the now-new PC).

PORTABLE GADGET OF THE WEEK

Casio's WQV10D-2, part of the company's innovative Technowear line, is a fancy watch that doubles as a digital camera. The built-in camera has a 2X digital zoom and shoots 176×144 pixel JPG pictures; the watch face is actually a color LCD screen that lets you preview and view the pictures you shoot. Buy it for $329.95 at www.casio.com.

THIS WEEK'S FOCUS: COMPUTER NETWORKS

ON THIS DAY: IBM ANNOUNCES MODEL 650 COMPUTER (1953)

The IBM 650 Magnetic Drum Data Processing Machine was announced on July 2, 1953. IBM sometimes refers to the 650 as its first computer, which it definitely wasn't; you can more accurately call the 650 IBM's first commercial business computer, as it was IBM's first computer to make a meaningful profit.

Related Web site: www.columbia.edu/acis/history/650.html

CONFIGURING A FILE SERVER

If you have an older PC just sitting around the house, you can rejig it to function as a dedicated file server on your home network. File servers are becoming more popular everywhere, even in homes, as a central backup and storage device.

You can buy file servers, sometimes called *network addressable storage (NAS)*, fairly inexpensively these days. Try Buffalo's Linkstation Network Storage Center (www.buffalotech.com) with 120GB storage for $290, or the 160GB Ximeta NetDisk (www.ximeta.com) for $250. It's much easier to buy new, but you can build your own if you're in the mood for an interesting project.

File servers are typically nothing more than a computer with a big hard drive running the Linux or BSD operating systems. They don't need a keyboard, mouse, or monitor (that is, they're headless) because they can be maintained from any computer on the network.

Your server will also be running Samba, which is the software that makes the server's hard drive visible as a network drive to Windows machines. To learn more about Samba, and how to get it running on your file server, read the excellent Samba How-To

at Linux Orbit (www.linuxorbit.com/howto/sambahowto.php3).

As far as I know, there's no Linux distribution dedicated to creating a file server, but most distros come with Samba ready to run. I recommend SuSE, but there are many other good choices. A minimal install will do—just be sure to include Samba and basic networking functionality. Don't bother to install X Window—you'd don't need a GUI to do this! Do install SSH, so you can log in to your server securely. You'll also need PuTTY to log in from a Windows machine.

FACT OF THE WEEK

Jupiter Research predicts that 28 million U.S. households will have a home network by 2006. If you're thinking about breaking down and installing a home network to share an Internet connection, work wirelessly, share files, game with your pals or just about anything else, I recommend picking up a copy of *Absolute Beginner's Guide to Home Networking*, by Mark Edward Soper (Que). This book will have you up and running in no time—and best of all, you don't need to be a deep geek to do it.

THIS WEEK'S FOCUS: COMPUTER NETWORKS

ON THIS DAY: FOAM RUBBER DEVELOPED (1929)

On this date in 1929, foam rubber was first developed at the Dunlop Latex Development Laboratories in Birmingham, England. British scientist E.A. Murphy whipped up the first batch of the stuff, using an ordinary kitchen mixer to froth natural latex rubber.

Related Web sites: www.dunloptire.com

SHARING FILES AND FOLDERS ACROSS YOUR NETWORK

When you have your network up and running, it's time to take advantage of it—by copying or moving files from one computer to another.

To share files between the PCs on your network, you must enable file sharing on the PC that contains those files. You must do this for each folder you want to share, although it's pretty easy.

In Windows XP, you start by using My Computer to navigate to the folder that contains the file you want to share. Right-click the folder icon and select Sharing and Security from the pop-up menu; this displays the Properties dialog box. Select the Sharing tab, and then check the Share This Folder on the Network option. Click OK when done—then repeat this procedure for every folder you want to share on every computer connected to your network.

Be cautious about turning on file sharing, however. When you let a folder be shared, anyone accessing your network can access the contents of the folder. This can be particularly bad if your network is compromised—which can sometimes happen if you're not careful about your wireless configuration. If in doubt, turn off file sharing across the board—and activate it only when you actually have a file to transfer from one PC to another.

SOFTWARE OF THE WEEK

IP-Tools is an award-winning program that offers a variety of TCP/IP utilities, including a port scanner, connection monitor, UDP scanner, and more. Try it for free, or buy it for $35 from www.ks-soft.net.

July 4, 2005
MONDAY

THIS WEEK'S FOCUS: PORTABLE MUSIC PLAYERS

ON THIS DAY: ADAMS AND JEFFERSON DIE (1826)

In one of those weird but fitting strokes of fate, two of America's founding fathers died on the same day. John Adams, the country's second president, and Thomas Jefferson, our third president, died on Independence Day, 1826—exactly 50 years after the birth of our new nation. On his death bed, Adams' final words were "Thomas Jefferson survives." He didn't know that Jefferson had passed away a few hours earlier that same day.

Related Web sites: www.whitehouse.gov/history/presidents/

SHOPPING FOR A PORTABLE MUSIC PLAYER

If you want your music to go, you need a portable music player that stores and plays back digital audio files. Download music from the Web or rip songs from CDs; then transfer the files to your portable music player.

Another advantage to these digital music players is that you can program them to play back your own personalized music mix, in the form of customized playlists. Put together one mix for your drive to work, another mix for your drive home, and a third to listen to on weekends. It's normally as simple as dragging and dropping specific songs in a PC-based music player program and then transferring the songs—and the playlist—to your portable device.

When you're shopping for a portable music player, you can choose from three types of storage: flash memory (64MB–1GB capacity), microdrives (1.5GB–4GB capacity), and larger 1.8" hard drives (10GB–40GB). Flash devices are small, lightweight, inexpensive, and won't skip if you're jogging; microdrive devices offer a good compromise between size and capacity.

The other thing to think about is where you're going to get your songs. If you're ripping songs from CDs,

any of these players will do; they're all compatible with the MP3 format. But if you plan to download music from an online music store, choose your player carefully. The Apple iTunes Music Store downloads files in the not-so-ubiquitous AAC format; Apple's iPods are compatible with this format, but most players aren't. Other online stores and services, including Napster and BuyMusic, download files in Microsoft's WMA format. Almost all music players—except the iPod—are compatible with this format. So, if you want an iPod, you're stuck with the iTunes Music Store; if you want to download from another site, you'll have to pass on the iPod.

PC GADGET OF THE WEEK

Don't have space for a big speaker system? Want big sound from a notebook PC? Then check out Olympia's Soundbug. This neat little gadget turns any smooth, hard surface into a loudspeaker. Just plug the Soundbug into your PC's audio jack (or the headphone jack of any portable music player) and lay it on a flat surface. The Soundbug translates the audio signal into vibrations that create a sounding-board out of whatever it's up against. Buy it for $39.95 at www. soundbug-us.com.

July 5, 2005

TUESDAY

THIS WEEK'S FOCUS: PORTABLE MUSIC PLAYERS

ON THIS DAY: THE BIKINI DEBUTS (1946)

On this day in 1946, in Paris, designer Louis Reard showed an incredibly small two-piece swimsuit. Named after the Pacific atoll where the U.S. had just exploded an atomic bomb, the bikini took the world by storm. Reard's bikini was so small, in fact, that no Parisian models at the time would wear it on the runway; he had to hire Micheline Bernardini, a nude dancer at the Casino de Paris, to model it.

Related Web site: www.absolute-bikini.com

LOVING MY IPOD

Imitators come and imitators go, but the coolest portable music player remains Apple's trendsetting iPod. The iPod is that rare gadget that's both stylish and popular with the masses; it's the best-selling portable music player in history, with more than three million units sold to date.

Apple now makes three models of iPod; the difference is the size of the hard disk—and the price, of course. (See them all at www.apple.com/ipod/.) Opt for the 40GB model and you can store up to 10,000 songs. You can also use the iPod to store regular computer data, including digital photos and the like.

Even though the iPod is Apple's baby (and the styling definitely reminds you of the family connection), it's that rare Apple product that's compatible with both Apple and Windows computers. It stores and plays back music in the AAC, MP3, WAV, and AIFF formats.

Cool features (besides the trendy looks) include the handy click-wheel navigator, high-resolution backlist display, dual USB 2.0 and FireWire

compatibility, and the seamless interface to Apple's top-notch iTunes Music Store. And if you use the FireWire connection, you can recharge your iPod directly from your PC; FireWire doubles as a power connection for the portable device.

Weaknesses include a relatively short battery life (just 6 hours in typical use), no built-in FM radio or CompactFlash slot, and incompatibility with Microsoft's WMA file format. This last weakness is the biggest because you can't use your iPod to download songs from Napster, BuyMusic, or any non-Apple online music service.

DOWNLOAD OF THE WEEK

Music Label 2004 is a shareware program you can use to organize your entire music collection. Track info for your CDs is indexed automatically, using the Gracenote CDDB music database; images of your CD covers are retrieved from Amazon.com. The program supports traditional media such as CDs and vinyl albums, as well as all digital media. Try it for free, or buy it for $39.95 at www.codeaero.com.

July 6, 2005
WEDNESDAY

THIS WEEK'S FOCUS: PORTABLE MUSIC PLAYERS

ON THIS DAY: FIRST MOBILE EXPLORATION OF MARS (1997)

The Mars Pathfinder Sojourner Rover, a lightweight machine on wheels, accomplished a revolutionary feat on this date in 1997. For the first time, a sophisticated robot rover began a rolling exploration of the planet Mars. Sojourner moved slowly (just 1.5 feet per minute) and stopped a lot along the way to sense the terrain and process information, but it was a rousing success.

Related Web site: www.solarviews.com/eng/rover.htm

IPOD ALTERNATIVES

If you want a music player with lots of storage but don't like the iPod (maybe you don't want to be limited to using the iTunes Music store), then here are some iPod alternatives to consider.

The first alternative to consider is Archos Gmini 220, which gives you maximum storage in minimum space. The Gmini features a huge 20GB hard drive in a very compact 6-oz. package and offers long battery life (10 hours), to boot. Even better, the Gmini offers a PDA-like interface and the capability to store files in folders, which makes it particularly powerful as a file-storage device. Also cool is the CompactFlash slot, which lets you easily back up your digital photos to Gmini's hard drive, and the built-in photo viewer software. Buy it for $350 at www.archos.com.

If you prefer Napster to iTunes, check out the Samsung Napster Player. This is an iPod-like device, but designed to work smoothly with the Napster online service. You get 20GB of storage in a package that's just a tad larger and heavier than an iPod. Unlike the iPod, it works with WMA files (along with MP3s). It also has a built-in FM tuner and (even better) a built-in FM transmitter, for listening over your car radio. Buy it for $350 at www.samsung.com.

Finally, check out the Dell Digital Jukebox (DJ), available online at www.dell.com. It comes in 15GB ($199) and 20GB ($279) versions, and plays back both MP3 and WMA files. It's more affordable than the competition, offers extremely long battery life, and has a great interface, too. CNET gave it an Editor's Choice award, if that means anything.

MAC GADGET OF THE WEEK

Apple Pro Speakers are designed by Harman Kardon, so you know they sound good. They also look good sitting next to your iMac or Power Mac, with their clear eyeball-like design. Buy a pair for $59 from www.apple.com.

THIS WEEK'S FOCUS: PORTABLE MUSIC PLAYERS

ON THIS DAY: JOSEPH MARIE JACQUARD BORN (1752)

Joseph Marie Jacquard was born on this day in 1752. A silk weaver, he invented a loom—the Jacquard Loom—that automatically controlled the warp and weft threads by recording patterns of holes in a string of cards. This same concept was the inspiration behind the computer punch card.

Related Web site: inventors.about.com/library/inventors/bl_jacquard.htm

MICRODRIVE PLAYERS

When you want something smaller than an iPod but still want to store a fairly large amount of music, consider one of the many microdrive players on the market today. A microdrive is a smaller hard disk than what you find in the iPod and other large players, but still holds a lot more songs than a flash memory–based device.

The king of the microdrive players is the iPod Mini. This sweet little puppy delivers all the great features of the original iPod in a much smaller package. The Mini incorporates a fairly robust 4GB microdrive within its tough anodized-aluminum casing and is available in five cool colors. (I like blue, myself.) Like the bigger iPod, it connects to your PC via either FireWire or USB 2.0 and syncs easily with Apple's iTunes Music Store.

What's not to like about the Mini? Well, it would be nice if Apple threw in a docking cradle, and the $250 Mini would be a much better value at a $50 lower price. All in all, though, the iPod Mini is ideal for trendsetters who want a small form-factor portable music player—or just a smaller version of their beloved iPod. Check it out at www.apple.com/ipod/.

If you don't want to go the Apple route, Creative's MuVo² is a decent alternative to the iPod Mini. It's small and stylishly squarish, the controls are easy to operate, and it costs less than an iPod Mini. Best of all, it stores and plays WMA-format files (as well as MP3s), something the iPod Mini doesn't do. Inside, the MuVo² has either 1.5GB ($119.99) or 4GB ($199.99) of storage, depending on the model—enough to store either 50 or 128 hours of WMA-format music. Find out more at www.creative.com.

Also interesting is the SoniqCast Aireo, the first portable music player to incorporate Wi-Fi wireless technology, which lets you download music and data files directly from your PC, no cables necessary. The Aireo offers a 1.5GB microdrive and includes a built-in FM transmitter, so you can wirelessly transmit music directly from the Aireo to a car stereo. Buy it for $300 at www.soniqcast.com.

WEB SITE OF THE WEEK

Everything iPod can be found at the iPodlounge. By everything, I mean articles, reviews, downloads, forums, and a comprehensive gear guide. Check it out at www.ipodlounge.com.

THIS WEEK'S FOCUS: PORTABLE MUSIC PLAYERS

ON THIS DAY: THE ROSWELL INCIDENT (1947)

On or around Independence Day, 1947, during a severe thunderstorm near Roswell, New Mexico, an Air Force experiment using high altitude balloons blew apart and fell to the earth. Or so said the U.S. government 50 years later. On July 8, 1947, the *Roswell Daily Record* reported the following: "The intelligence office of the 509th Bombardment group at Roswell Army Air Field announced at noon today, that the field has come into possession of a flying saucer... the disk was recovered on a ranch in the Roswell vicinity." So who's telling the *real* truth?

Related Web site: www.abovetopsecret.com/pages/record.html

FLASH MEMORY PLAYERS

If you're willing to trade off storage capacity for a smaller and lighter player, consider a flash memory player. Depending on a device's flash RAM capacity, they may only support somewhere between 50 and 150 songs, but if that's all you need, you can get a flash memory audio player smaller than a credit card or shaped like a pen. These puppies are small enough to fit in the tightest of pockets.

And, because Flash RAM players often use the same technology as USB "key" disks and similar devices, you'll find that you can use them for storage as well as for music playback. Another plus: Because there aren't any moving parts, the music won't jump when you're jogging—a particular problem with hard drive and microdrive players.

The first flash player I'd consider is the iRiver iFP-390T, the latest upgrade to one of my all-time favorite flash memory players. It's a slick package, with a neat little joystick-based navigational system. What makes the iFP-390T especially useful is the integrated FM radio and voice recorder and its capability to record directly from the audio line-in jack. You can record up to 8 hours of MP3-format audio from the radio or line-in jack or 72 hours of mono audio from the built-in microphone. Battery life is an exceptional 24 hours. Buy it for $200 at www.iriveramerica.com.

Also cool is the MuVo TX. This is a miniature music player that incorporates a built-in USB 2.0 flash drive. Slide the player out of the battery module and plug it in to your PC's USB drive to transfer files; the USB connector is on the end of the player module. The player itself is extremely small, like a keychain USB drive, and has a built-in microphone, an LCD display, and a scroller button to select your favorite tunes and playlists. MuVo TX models are available in 128MB ($119.99), 256MB ($179.99), and 512MB ($249.99) versions. Find out more at www.creative.com.

PORTABLE GADGET OF THE WEEK

Altec Lansing's inMotion Portable Audio System is my pick for best iPod accessory on the market today. The inMotion is an audio system designed around the iPod; insert your iPod and the sound is amplified and fed through right and left speakers. The entire system is battery powered, so there aren't any power cables to bother with. An auxiliary input jack on the back lets you connect a CD player or other device. Buy it for $149.95 at www.alteclansing.com.

July 9, 2005

SATURDAY

THIS WEEK'S FOCUS: PORTABLE MUSIC PLAYERS

ON THIS DAY: *TRON* PREMIERES (1982)

On July 9, 1982, Disney Studios released the groundbreaking science-fiction film *Tron*. Starring Jeff Bridges and featuring then-state-of-the-art computer-generated special effects, *Tron* was a fantasy inspired by the world of video games. It still looks cool today—check out the double-disc DVD rerelease to see for yourself.

Related Web site: www.tron-sector.com

IPOD ACCESSORIES

With more than three million units sold, the Apple iPod is the single most popular portable music player—and one of the most popular consumer electronics devices, period. The iPod is so popular that a large market has sprung up for iPod accessories, from cases to connectors and more. Here are some of my favorites:

- **naviPod Wireless Remote Control**—The naviPod is a two-part device. The receiver unit attaches to the top of your iPod; the palm-sized infrared remote control unit is a cool-looking circular device that includes play/pause, fast forward, reverse, and volume up/down buttons. Buy it for $49.95 at www.tentechnology.com.

- **iTrip FM Transmitter**—Listen to your iPod music through any FM radio—in your car, in your home, wherever. The iTrip is a miniature FM station that transmits music from your iPod to any nearby FM radio; just tune in the radio to listen to your iPod tunes. Buy it for $35 from www.griffentechnology.com.

- **Monster iCarPlay FM Transmitter**—Here's another gadget that transmits your iPod music to any FM radio. The iCarPlay includes a Smart Digital Charger that plugs into your car's DC/lighter jack; it not only powers the iCarPlay, but also recharges your iPod. Buy it for $69.95 at www.monstercable.com.

- **Belkin Digital Camera Link**—With Belkin's Digital Camera Link, you can use your iPod to store hundreds of digital photos, transferred directly from your digital camera. All you have to do is connect your digital camera (via USB) to the Digital Camera Link, connect the Digital Camera Link to your iPod, and then transfer the pictures. Buy it for $89.99 at www.belkin.com.

- **Belkin iPod Media Reader**—Here's another way to transfer your digital photos—via a digital media card reader. Belkin's Media Reader connects directly to your iPod and reads a variety of digital media formats. Buy it for $109.99 at www.belkin.com.

FACT OF THE WEEK

According to London-based research firm Informa Media, the installed base of portable music players will reach 21.5 million units by the end of 2004. Apple's iPod is the dominant player, with a projected installed base of well over 5 million.

THIS WEEK'S FOCUS: PORTABLE MUSIC PLAYERS

ON THIS DAY: SCOPES "MONKEY TRIAL" BEGINS (1925)

It was billed as the trial of the century, pitting evolutionists against creationists in a small Dayton, Tennessee courtroom. The trial of high school biology teacher John Scopes, accused of illegally teaching the theory of evolution, began on this date in 1925. The trial pitted prosecuting attorney William Jennings Bryan, populist three-time presidential candidate, against defense attorney Clarence Darrow, one of the foremost legal minds of the day. The trial, which ended with a guilty verdict (later reversed on a technicality by the Tennessee Supreme Court), was fictionalized in the memorable movie *Inherit the Wind*.

Related Web site: www.law.umkc.edu/faculty/projects/ftrials/scopes/scopes.htm

IPOD CASES

Whether you want to keep your iPod or iPod Mini in pristine condition or make a fashion statement, you need to check out some of these cool cases:

- **iSkin eVo iPod Protector**—This is a snug-fitting molded silicone case, complete with clear screen protector and beveled button cutouts. It's *tres* cool-looking, available in a variety of trendy colors—from Arctic and Blush to glow-in-the-dark Lava and Wasabi. Buy it for $29.99 at www.iskin.com.

- **iPod Armor**—When you want hardcore protection for your iPod, check out the iPod Armor aluminum hard case with foam padding interior. Slip the iPod inside, close it, and your iPod's protected. Best of all, the iPod Armor allows full access to all iPod controls, so you can listen while it's tucked away. Buy it for $49.95 at www.ipodarmor.com.

- **Groove Speaker Purse**—Felicidade's Groove Purse is a fashionable oversized tote purse in crisp white synthetic leather. Slide your iPod into the outside compartment, and it

automatically connects the two built-in powered speakers. You end up with a groovy-looking iPod boom box, with plenty of room inside for anything else you need to carry around. Buy it for $144.95 at www.drbott.com.

- **SportSuit Runabout Case**—This is an iPod Mini case for music lovers on the run. It's a neoprene case that straps around your wrist; the iPod slips snugly into the case, allowing full view of the screen and access to the headphone jack. Buy it for $29.95 at www.marware.com.

SOFTWARE OF THE WEEK

XPlay is a terrific complement to Apple's iTunes software. It provides Windows integration for Mac-formatted iPods, and lets you use your iPod with pre-XP versions of Windows. It automatically synchs your iPod with your PC's music collection, lets you transfer songs from your iPod to any hard disk, lets you create custom playlists, and allows you to edit track information so songs appear the way you want on the iPod display. Buy it for $29.95 at www.mediafour.com/products/xplay/.

July 11, 2005
MONDAY

THIS WEEK'S FOCUS: MAKING YOUR OWN CDS

ON THIS DAY: ALFRED BINET BORN (1857)

French psychologist Alfred Binet was born on this day in 1857. He was a pioneer in the field of intelligence testing, and helped to popularize the concept of IQ (intelligence quotient)—the ratio of mental age to chronological name. Today's Stanford-Binet intelligence test bears his name.

Related Web site: www.indiana.edu/~intell/binet.shtml

HOW CD BURNING WORKS

When you rip songs from a CD to your hard drive, you have to deal with all sorts of options, from which file format to use to what bit rate you want to record at. Fortunately, burning songs *to* CD isn't near as complicated

When you burn songs to CD, you don't have to set *any* format options. That's because whatever format the original file is in, it gets encoded into the CD Audio (CDA) format when it gets copied to CD. All music CDs use the CDA format, so whether you're burning an MP3 or WMA file, your CD burner software translates it to CDA before the copy is made.

There are no quality levels to set, either. All CDA-format files are encoded at the same bit rate. So you really don't have any configuration to do—other than deciding which songs you want to copy.

The easiest way to burn a CD full of songs is to use your CD burner program to assemble a playlist beforehand, and then copy that entire playlist. You can record up to 74 minutes (650MB) worth of music on a standard CD-R disc, or 80 minutes (700MB) on an enhanced disc.

After you've decided which songs to copy, load a blank CD-R disc into your computer's CD-R/RW drive, launch your CD burner software, and then follow the program's instructions to start translating and copying the song files. After the ripping begins, the digital music files on your hard drive are converted and copied onto a blank CD-R in standard CD Audio format.

By the way, to play your new CD in a regular (non-PC) CD player, record in the CD-R format and use a blank CD-R disc specifically labeled for audio use. (CD-RW discs will not play in most home CD players.)

PC GADGET OF THE WEEK

Line 6's GuitarPort lets you connect your electric guitar to your computer; just plug your guitar into the GuitarPort and connect the GuitarPort to your PC's USB port and to an amplifier or a powered speaker system. The GuitarPort software lets you model 15 different amp/cabinet combinations and 18 pedal and studio effects, and it even includes a built-in chromatic tuner. Buy it for $169 at www.guitarport.com.

THIS WEEK'S FOCUS: MAKING YOUR OWN CDS

ON THIS DAY: GEORGE EASTMAN BORN (1932)

George Eastman was born on this date in 1932. He founded the Eastman Kodak Company and invented roll film, which brought photography to the common man. For years, Eastman Kodak enjoyed a virtual monopoly in the camera industry. Eastman coined the phrase "you press the button, we do the rest." Despite some speculation to the contrary, the Kodak name is one he simply made up.

Related Web site: www.eastmanhouse.org

BURNING CDS WITH MUSICMATCH JUKEBOX

Most CD burner software works in pretty much the same fashion, but my favorite program is Musicmatch Jukebox, downloadable for free at www.musicmatch.com. Burning a music CD with Musicmatch is really easy; just follow these steps:

1. From the main Musicmatch window, select those songs you want to copy to CD. (Hold down the Ctrl key to select multiple files.)

2. Click the Burn to CD button; this opens the Burner Plus window.

3. In the Burner Plus window, click the Click Here to Add Files Currently Selected in Your Library button. (Alternatively, you can drag files from the main Musicmatch Jukebox window onto the Burner Plus window.) The songs you selected are now displayed in the Burner Plus window.

4. To add additional songs to the burn list, click the Add button and select songs from the Open Music dialog box.

5. To change the order of songs on the burn list, select a song and drag it to a new position.

6. If you've added more songs than you have room for, select some songs to delete and click the Remove button.

7. When you've added all the songs you want to burn, click the Burn button.

The songs are now burned to your blank CD. When the burning process is completed, the CD is ejected. The basic Musicmatch software is free, though Musicmatch Plus, a feature-rich upgrade, is available for purchase. If you like it, consider paying the one-time "Lifetime Updates" license fee. You'll get all future updates to the software for free!

DOWNLOAD OF THE WEEK

RipEditBurn is one of the most fully featured CD burning programs available today. Everything you need is here in a single program— you can edit WAV, WMA, and MP3 files, convert MP3/WMA files to WAV and vice versa, and burn your own custom music CDs. There are also a ton of pro-level features, including fade, equalization, volume normalization, and the ability to remove the vocals from recorded music. RipEditBurn is shareware, so you can try it for free, or buy it for $39.95 at www.blazeaudio.com/products/ripeditburn.html.

July 13, 2005
WEDNESDAY

THIS WEEK'S FOCUS: MAKING YOUR OWN CDS

ON THIS DAY: LIVE AID CONCERT (1985)

Live Aid, like Band Aid, before it, was a star-studded charity concert to raise money for the victims of famine in Ethiopia (the brainchild of Bob Geldof of the Boomtown Rats). Held on this date in 1985 in both London and Philadelphia, Live Aid featured artists like INXS, Elvis Costello, Run DMC, Sting, Phil Collins, Paul Young, Bryan Adams, U2, Dire Straits, Queen, Neil Young, David Bowie, Mick Jagger, and literally dozens more.

Related Web site: www.herald.co.uk/local_info/live_aid.html

COPYING CDS

Making a copy of a CD is pretty much a combination of ripping and burning. That is, you rip the files from your original CD to your hard disk, and then burn those files to a new CD.

Just make sure you rip the files to WAV format, to retain the original audio fidelity. (The WAV format is the sonic equivalent of the CDA format used on commercial CDs.) Rip to MP3 or WMA format and you compress the original files, which dramatically affects the audio quality; what you then burn to CD won't sound nearly as good as the original CD.

An even easier solution is to use a program specifically designed for CD copying, such as Easy CD & DVD Creator (www.roxio.com). This program makes copying an audio CD pretty much a one-button operation; just click the Disc Copier button and follow the onscreen instructions.

As you can probably tell from the program's name, Easy CD & DVD Creator also lets you copy DVDs. The only problem—and it's a big one—is that you can't copy copy-protected DVDS. Which means that you're prohibited from making a backup copy of practically any store-bought DVD movie. That's too bad, and one of the many complaints I have against the movie industry today.

By the way, many new PCs come with a limited version of the Roxio program, called Easy CD Creator, preinstalled. This version is perfect for copying CDs—it just doesn't have the added DVD copying capability.

MAC GADGET OF THE WEEK

M-Audio's MobilePre USB lets you use a microphone, keyboard, guitar, or other instrument with Apple's GarageBand and other music creation programs. The MobilePre is a preamp and audio interface with two microphone inputs, two 1/4" line inputs, two analog outputs, and a stereo line output. It connects to your Mac via USB and is completely bus-powered—so you can use it with your PowerBook on mobile gigs. Buy it for $149 at www.m-audio.com.

THIS WEEK'S FOCUS: MAKING YOUR OWN CDS

ON THIS DAY: TAPE MEASURE PATENTED (1868)

On July 14, 1868, Alvin J. Fellows of New Haven, Connecticut received the first U.S. patent for a spring tape measure. The tape measure was enclosed in a circular case with a spring click lock to hold the tape at any desired point.

Related Web site: www.asktooltalk.com/home/qanda/faq/tools/tapemeasure.htm

BURNING A DATA CD

CDs aren't just for music. With upwards of 700MB of storage space, a CD is a great way to store or transfer large amounts of data—from document files to digital photos.

Most of the CD burning software programs let you create both music and data CDs. You don't have to use one of these programs, however. You can burn your own data CDs from within Windows.

In Windows XP, burning a data CD is a two-step process. Start by opening the My Computer or My Documents folder. Select those files you want to copy to CD, and then select Copy the Selected Items from the File and Folder Tasks pane. When the Copy Items dialog box appears, select your CD drive and click OK. This copies the selected files into a temporary folder on your hard drive—*not* directly to CD! (Think of it as a staging area.)

Windows now displays a new icon in the system tray, along with a pop-up message that you have files waiting to be copied to CD. You can click this icon or message (if you're quick enough), or just open My Computer and select the icon for your CD drive. When you do this, the files waiting to be copied are displayed. You get things going by selecting Write These Files to CD in the CD Writing Tasks pane. This opens the CD Writing Wizard; follow the onscreen instructions to complete the burn.

Copying digital photos is a similar process. When you open the My Pictures folder, you have the option to Copy to CD in the Picture Tasks frame. This starts the two-part burning process, with one slight difference. When you copy photos to CD, Windows gives you the option of also copying a picture viewer. Do this and other users can view the pictures on your CD without first loading them into a separate viewer program.

WEB SITE OF THE WEEK

Gracenote is the company behind the CDDB music recognition service—the database that most digital music players use to obtain their track information. CDDB currently has information on close to 3 million CDs and more than 37 million individual songs. You can search the CDDB database yourself at www.gracenote.com/music/—by artist, album, or song.

THIS WEEK'S FOCUS: MAKING YOUR OWN CDS

ON THIS DAY: MARGARINE PATENTED (1869)

On this date in 1869, margarine was patented by Hippolyte Mège Mouriés in Paris. He won a contest held by Emperor Napoleon III to find a suitable substitute for butter to be used by the French Navy. The formula included a fatty component that, when mixed, had a pearly luster, so he named his product after the Greek word for pearl—*margaritari*.

Related Web site: www.margarine.org

LABELING YOUR CDS

Labeling the CDs you create is a tricky—and potentially time-consuming—business.

I'm one of those people who don't like to put paper labels on their CDs and DVDS because they can peel off and gum up the works. That said, a lot of people do it; it's the most popular way to label your CDs. If you're going to create labels on your inkjet or laser printer, use a label maker program like cdrLabel (www.ziplabel.com) or the Neato CD Labeler Kit (www.neato.com). Avery (www.avery.com) also makes a good label-making program, DesignPro, that works well with all the different labels they make. Make sure you get a good "CD stomper" gadget to best affix the label to the disc.

Another option is to buy an inkjet printer that can print on specially manufactured CD blanks, like the Epson Stylus R200. This is a very professional-looking solution, even if the printable blanks are a little more expensive than normal ones. The result is very close to what you get on a store-bought CD.

Me, I go the low-tech route. That's right, I just use a sharpie to write the title on the CD. So sue me—it's quick, it's cheap, and it won't screw anything up!

PORTABLE GADGET OF THE WEEK

If you're looking for a wireless headset for your cell phone, check out Logitech's Mobile Bluetooth Headset. It connects cordlessly to any Bluetooth-enabled phone and has a long seven-hour battery life. This unit has a flexible, soft-touch headset for comfortable fit, and the microphone is of the noise-canceling type. Buy it for $99.95 from www.logitech.com.

THIS WEEK'S FOCUS: MAKING YOUR OWN CDS

ON THIS DAY: SHOEMAKER-LEVY COMET HITS JUPITER (1994)

Starting on July 16, 1994, and lasting until July 22, 21 major fragments of the comet Shoemaker-Levy 9 hit Jupiter. The first of these fragments created a 1,200-mile wide fireball, 600 miles high. This was the first collision of two solar system bodies ever to be observed, and the effects were spectacular.

Related Web site: www2.jpl.nasa.gov/sl9/

TROUBLESHOOTING CD/DVD DRIVE PROBLEMS

If your CD or DVD drive doesn't appear to work, the first thing to check is that you have the disc inserted properly (label side up) and that the drive is getting power. You should also check all the connections to the drive, and that you have the correct (and the latest) driver loaded into system memory. Update your drivers from the Windows Device Manager; select the entry for your CD-ROM or DVD drive, and then select Action > Update Driver.

If your drive doesn't always read data accurately, you could have a scratched or dirty disc. It's also possible that the laser beam inside your drive is dirty or out of alignment. You can try to "blow" the dirt out of the drive with compressed air, or—in some cases—wipe the laser lens with a cotton swab. However, your best bet is to see a repair person ASAP to get this puppy fixed.

If you can't play music CDs on your CD or DVD drive, chances are the audio cable isn't connected between your drive and your sound card.

If your CD-R/RW drive won't burn a CD, you should first look to see that you have the right type of disc (recordable or rewriteable) in the drive, and that the disc is blank. Second, make sure you have a spare 1GB or so on your hard disk, as Windows writes the files to your hard disk before it burns them to CD; if you don't have enough free space, you can't burn the CD.

If you have trouble with skips and dropouts on the CDs you burn, there are two things to check. First, you might need to reduce the recording speed; recording faster than your drive can handle will result in write errors. Second, try burning the disc again, but this time close all your other applications. A good rule is to not use your computer at all when you're burning a disc; let the burner have all the resources it needs to make a clean recording.

FACT OF THE WEEK

According to Nielsen-Netratings, traditional advertisers are more apt to experiment with different ad formats when advertising on the Web. In 2002, 92 out of top 100 advertisers used non-standard full-banner ads, while 87 of the 100 used the skyscraper format. Around 82 of the top 100 advertisers employed flash technology in their ads, while the Eyeblaster "floating ad" was used by 40 of the advertisers.

July 17, 2005

SUNDAY

THIS WEEK'S FOCUS: MAKING YOUR OWN CDS

ON THIS DAY: FIRST RECORDED SOLAR ECLIPSE (709 BC)

On this date in 709 BC, the earliest record of a confirmed total solar eclipse was written in China. From *Ch'un-ch'iu*, Book I: "The Sun was eclipsed and it was total." Reference to the same eclipse appears in the *Han-shu* ("History of the Former Han Dynasty"), written in the 1st century AD.

Related Web site: sunearth.gsfc.nasa.gov/eclipse/eclipse.html

HOW TO FIX A SCRATCHED CD

Any CD, store-bought or home-burned, should last for years and years—unless it gets scratched or damaged. That's why you need to take good care of your CDs and DVDs, by storing them properly in their jewel boxes. That means keeping them away from direct sunlight and in a cool, dry environment. (Don't leave a CD in your car on a hot summer day!) And don't scratch them!

If you *do* accidentally scratch a CD, you could get lucky. Many minor scratches won't affect playback, so don't panic just because the surface looks a little beat up. Major scratches, however, can be ruinous. Which brings us to the topic of the day— how to remove scratches from a CD.

First, evaluate the scratch. A scratch from the center to the rim typically isn't too bad; the worst scratches circle around the disc, following the track pattern. Also, don't ignore scratches on the *top* of the disc. The label side contains the disc's reflective material, which can completely halt playback if heavily damaged.

To fix a damaged CD, try polishing the scratches out with a mild abrasive, like baking soda toothpaste. Make sure to wipe from the center of the disc to the outside in a straight line; never wipe in a circular fashion. You can also try polishing your disc with liquid Turtle Wax or Pledge. Instead of rubbing the scratches out, this fills them in.

If these steps don't work, it's time to turn to a commercial solution, of which there are a few. SkipDoctor MD (www.dig-it.com) is a kind of motorized disc polisher that buffs out scratches. Wipe Out! (www.cdrepair.com) is a special polishing solution that requires some elbow grease on your part. Both do a slightly better job than home-grown remedies, although even they can't bring the most badly scratched discs back to life.

Bottom line? Although not every scratch can be repaired, some can—with a little effort. Better to take good care of your CDs to make sure they don't get scratched in the first place!

SOFTWARE OF THE WEEK

When it comes to burning your own CDs, you can't beat Nero. Nero Ultra Edition makes CD burning easy, with the simple SmartStart interface. You can use Nero to burn either music or data CDs, or even for hard disk backups. And it does DVDS, too! Buy it for $99.99 ($69.99 for the download-only version) at www.nero.com.

THIS WEEK'S FOCUS: THE HISTORY OF COMPUTING

ON THIS DAY: INTEL INCORPORATED (1968)

On July 18, 1968, former Fairchild employee Gordon Moore dropped by Bob Noyce's home, and they agreed to join together to launch a new company to research, develop, and manufacture "integrated electronic structures." This was the birth of Intel Corporation, today's leading microprocessor company.

Related Web site: www.intel.com

A SHORT HISTORY OF COMPUTING

The history of computing contains four distinct generations, along with a rich prehistory of mechanical computing devices. Each generation is characterized by dramatic improvements in the technology used to build computer hardware, the internal organization of computer systems, and the computers' programming languages.

- In computing's **mechanical era**, calculations were accomplished by the use of machines with complicated gears, electromechanical relays, and other moving parts. The first of these so-called "calculating machines" were built in the early 17th century, and these types of machines continued almost to the start of World War I.

- **First-generation** computers were constructed from wired circuits and vacuum tubes (functioning as electronic switches) and programmed via punch cards. This first generation of computing encompasses roughly the period from 1940–1956 and produced such historic machines as the Harvard Mark I, Colossus, ENIAC, and UNIVAC.

- **Second-generation** computers used printed circuits and transistors instead of wired circuits and vacuum tubes, and could be programmed via interpretive programming languages such as FORTRAN and COBOL. The second generation lasted roughly from 1956–1963.

- **Third-generation** computers were based on the integrated circuit. This period ran from 1964–1971 and produced machines such as the IBM 360 series mainframe and the new category of minicomputers.

- **Fourth-generation** computers—including the smaller computers we now call personal computers—get their processing power from Large Scale Integration (LSI) and Very Large Scale Integration (VLSI) circuits, in the form of microprocessor chips. The fourth generation started in 1971 and continues to present day.

PC GADGET OF THE WEEK

The Super Cantenna Wireless Network Antenna is cooler than it looks—which is good because it looks like a long metal can. The Super Cantenna is a powerful antenna for wireless networks, which you can use to boost the range of your wireless network, or as a user to connect to other wireless networks in your neighborhood. Buy it for $19.95 at www.cantenna.com.

July 19, 2005

TUESDAY

THIS WEEK'S FOCUS: THE HISTORY OF COMPUTING

ON THIS DAY: CHARLES MAYO BORN (1865)

Charles Horace Mayo was born on this date in 1865, in Rochester, Minnesota. He was a surgeon and philanthropist and co-founder of the Mayo Clinic and Mayo Foundation.

Related Web site: www.mayoclinic.com

THE MECHANICAL ERA OF COMPUTING: 1623–1900

Computers as we know them had their beginnings in the so-called "calculating machines" of the early 17th century. These machines were like crude calculators, designed to automate complex mathematical calculations, but had no memory or data storage. In fact, these machines didn't even have a way to output the results of their calculations, other than via dials or indicators.

The first of these machines, the Calculating Clock, was constructed by Wilhelm Schickard in 1623. Blaise Pascal, a noted mathematician and scientist, built on Schickard's work and developed his own mechanical calculating machine in 1642. Pascal's machine, dubbed the Pascaline, used different-sized gears to add numbers together, much the same way today's odometers measure distance traveled.

Next up was Gottfried Wilhelm von Leibnitz, a student of Pascal's. In 1672 he devised a machine—subsequently called the Stepped Reckoner—that used a "stepped gear" for more accurate multiplication and division.

The next true revolution came from Charles Babbage, often referred to as the "Father of Computing." Starting in 1822, he invented two separate computing machines—the Difference Engine and the Analytical Engine—that were steam powered and capable of printing results on paper.

The first electromechanical adding machine was developed in 1886, by Herman Hollerith. This machine, dubbed a "tabulator," was put to its first commercial use in 1890 for the U.S. Census Bureau. Based on this success, Hollerith formed the Tabulating Machine Company in 1896. In 1911 the Tabulating Machine Company merged with the International Time Recording Company and the Computing Scale Company to form the Computing-Tabulating-Recording Company (C-T-R); in 1924, the name of the company was changed to something slightly more recognizable today: International Business Machines (IBM).

DOWNLOAD OF THE WEEK

Winace is a popular WinZip alternative. It compresses and decompresses files in a host of different formats, and provides a quick viewer for HTML pages, Word documents, and ASCII files. It's a shareware program; try it for free, or buy it for $29.95 at www.winace.com.

July 20, 2005
WEDNESDAY

THIS WEEK'S FOCUS: THE HISTORY OF COMPUTING

ON THIS DAY: NEIL ARMSTRONG WALKS ON THE MOON (1969)

The Apollo 11 spacecraft launched from the Kennedy Space Center on July 16, 1969, and the Lunar Module (LEM) landed on the moon four days later, on July 20. Mission Commander Neil Armstrong stepped onto the moon's surface, in the Sea of Tranquility, at 2:56 GMT. As he put his left foot down onto the finely powdered surface, he declared "That's one small step for man, one giant leap for mankind."

Related Web site: www.nasm.si.edu/collections/imagery/apollo/AS11/a11.htm

EARLY 20TH CENTURY COMPUTERS

The turn of the century saw an influx of new calculating and computing machines. These machines were the forerunners of the modern computer, electrifying the formerly mechanical devices, adding storage capability (and the ability to manipulate the stored results), and developing the capability of printing the results to paper.

In 1936, scientist Konrad Zuse began construction of the Z1, the world's first programmable binary computer. The Z1, built in Zuse's bedroom (and overflowing into his parents' living room) was controlled by perforated strips of discarded movie film. This machine (originally dubbed the V1, but retroactively renamed Z1 after WWII) was completed in 1938 and is the ancestor of all modern computers. It was the first computer to adopt the binary system—or what we now call digital computing.

In 1937, George Stibitz of Bell Labs constructed another early binary computer. Completed in 1939, the Complex Number Calculator (later called the Bell Labs Model 1) used electromagnetic relays, and was the first computing machine to be used over normal telephone lines, setting the stage for the future linking of computers and communications systems.

The next major leap in computing technology involved the use of vacuum tubes as on/off valves. This enabled calculations to be made electronically rather than mechanically, which resulted in a significant increase in calculating speed.

The first use of the vacuum tube in a computing device was in 1938, when Joseph Desch and Robert Mumma built a machine they called the Electronic Accumulator. Another early vacuum tube–based digital computer was built by John Vincent Atanasoff and Clifford Berry in 1939, at the Iowa State College. This computer, dubbed the ABC (for Atanasoff/Berry Computer) never reached the production stage, but contained many concepts that would appear in later generations of computers—including rewritable memory.

MAC GADGET OF THE WEEK

MacAlly offers a very interesting approach to a desktop keyboard—the IceKey keyboard has relatively low "scissor" keys that don't have to be pressed as far as the keys that you typically find on an external keyboard. Buy it for $59 at www.macally.com.

July 21, 2005
THURSDAY

THIS WEEK'S FOCUS: **THE HISTORY OF COMPUTING**

ON THIS DAY: JEAN PICARD BORN (1620)

No, not the *Star Trek* guy (Jean Luc Picard). This Jean Picard, born on July 21, 1620, was the founder of modern astronomy in France. He introduced new methods, improved the old instruments, and added new devices; he was also the first to put the telescope to use for the accurate measurement of small angles. His most important work was the first measurement of the circumference of the Earth.

Related Web site: www.gap.dcs.st-and.ac.uk/~history/Mathematicians/Picard_Jean.html

FIRST-GENERATION COMPUTERS:
1940–1956

The first generation of true computers used vacuum tubes and electronic circuits to replace the mechanical switches and moving parts of mechanical calculators. While these first computers were physically massive and operationally complicated, they delivered on the promise of handling increasingly large and complex calculations—and were essential to deciphering secret codes in World War II and developing America's atomic energy program in the years after.

That said, the first true computer was strictly theoretical. In 1937, Cambridge mathematician Alan Turing, in a paper on the mathematical theory of computation, conceived of the idea for a "universal machine" capable of executing any describable algorithm. This theoretical machine, dubbed the Turing Machine, formed the basis for the concept of "computability," separate from the process of calculation.

The first fully electronic computer to actually be built was named Colossus. Commissioned to crack the secret code used by German Enigma cipher machines, Colossus was completed in December 1943 by Dr. Thomas Flowers at London's Post Office Research Laboratories.

Next up was the Harvard Mark I, more formerly known as the Automatic Sequence Controlled Calculator (ASCC). The Mark I was the world's first fully programmable computer; instructions were fed into the machine via paper tape, punch cards, or by setting switches. The Mark I, completed in 1944, was developed by Howard Aiken and James W. Bryce at Harvard University, where it occupied an entire building.

The most famous first-generation computer was arguably the Electronic Numerical Integrator and Computer, or ENIAC. John W. Mauchly and J. Presper Eckert, Jr. began work on ENIAC in 1943, and the machine was completed in 1946. Compared to today's computers, ENIAC was a monster; it was composed of 30 separate units, weighed more than 30 tons, and contained more than 18,000 vacuum tubes, 1,500 relays, and hundreds of thousands of resistors, capacitors, and inductors.

WEB SITE
OF THE WEEK

Want to learn more about the history of computing? Then visit the Computer History Museum at www.computerhistory.org.

July 22, 2005

FRIDAY

THIS WEEK'S FOCUS: THE HISTORY OF COMPUTING

ON THIS DAY: FIRST AROUND-THE-WORLD SOLO FLIGHT (1933)

On July 22, 1933, Wiley Post completed the first round-the-world solo flight—15,596 miles in all. Post flew a single-engine Lockheed Vega 5B aircraft named Winnie Mae; the flight took a total of 7 days 18hr 49min.

Related Web site: www.wileypost.com

SECOND-GENERATION COMPUTERS: 1956–1963

The second generation of computing was characterized by the shrinking size and increased computing power made possible by the replacement of vacuum tubes and large electronic circuits with smaller transistors and integrated circuits. These second-generation computers were the first that were powerful enough to handle interpreted programming languages, and dominated information processing in the late 1950s and early 1960s.

The transistor—short for *transfer resistor*—was developed at AT&T Bell Laboratories in 1947 by Walter H. Brattain, William Shockley, and John Bardeen, who would be awarded the 1956 Nobel prize in physics for their work. The transistor's small size, high yield, low heat production, and low price helped to make the next generation of computers run 1,000 times faster than the previous generation.

Building on that groundbreaking research, the first completely transistorized computer, TRADIC, was developed by Bell Laboratories in 1953. Another early transistorized computer was the Transistorized Experimental Computer (TX-0), developed at MIT's Lincoln Laboratories in 1956.

In 1957, Ken Olsen and Harlan Anderson founded the Digital Equipment Corporation (DEC). DEC's first computer, the fully transistorized PDP-1, was released in 1960. The PDP-1 became the precursor to dozens of commercially successful computers released by DEC over the next four decades.

The increased power of these second-generation computers enabled the use of interpreted programming languages; the late 1950s and early 1960s were a particularly vibrant period for the development of these easier-to-use languages, which helped move the computer out of the research lab into more practical applications. The most popular of these languages included FORTRAN, LISP, COBOL, ALGOL, PL/1, BASIC, PASCAL, and C.

PORTABLE GADGET OF THE WEEK

The SideWinder is the emergency charger to take with you when you're camping or otherwise away from normal AC power. It generates power when you rotate the side-mounted crank; just 2 minutes of cranking gives you more than 6 minutes of talk time on your cell phone. To talk longer, just crank some more. Buy it for $24.95 at www.sidewindercharger.com.

July 23, 2005
SATURDAY

THIS WEEK'S FOCUS: THE HISTORY OF COMPUTING

ON THIS DAY: CLONED MICE ANNOUNCED (1998)

In the July 23, 1998 issue of the science journal, *Nature*, an international team of scientists, led by Ryuzo Yanagimachi of the University of Hawaii, announced that they had accomplished the first reproducible cloning of a mammal from adult cells. They produced three generations of cloned mice, more than 50 identical sisters in all. Their "Honolulu technique" was said to be more reliable than the one previously used to create Dolly the sheep.

Related Web site: www.newscientist.com/hottopics/cloning/

THIRD-GENERATION COMPUTERS: 1964–1971

The third generation of computing is based on the development of the integrated circuit. It was this generation of computer that gained widespread acceptance in corporate America, and led to the growth of data processing.

The integrated circuit (IC) is a single electronic circuit on a single slice of silicon. The first IC was developed by two teams of scientists, working independent of each other, at Fairchild Semiconductor and Texas Instruments. The Texas Instruments team, led by Jack S. Clair Kilby, developed its IC in December 1958. The following year the Fairchild team—consisting of Jean Hoerni, Kurt Lehovec, and Robert N. Noyce—successfully completed its IC project. The first commercial implementation of this technology hit the market in 1961.

Third-generation computers were both powerful and affordable enough to be adopted by large corporations around the world. From the mid-1960s on, formerly manual tasks were automated by large mainframe computers, creating a new profession that became known as data processing. The most popular uses of these third-generation computers included inventory management, payroll management, file management, and report generation.

During this period the computer landscape was dominated by one company: IBM. IBM's dominance of the business market was even more profound outside the U.S.; at one point in the 1960s, 90% of the installed computers in the European market were IBM models.

IBM was also behind the first practical application of a computer network—American Airlines' SABRE ticket reservation system, which went live in 1962. It took IBM six years to build this groundbreaking network, which connected more than 1,000 ticket agents to American's central computer.

FACT OF THE WEEK

According to Webmergers, at least 4,854 Internet companies have either been acquired or have shut down in the three years since the end of the dotcom boom. Since the end of the first quarter of 2000, buyers have spent $200 billion to acquire 3,892 Internet properties; during the same period, at least 962 substantial Internet companies either shut down or declared bankruptcy.

July 24, 2005
SUNDAY

THIS WEEK'S FOCUS: THE HISTORY OF COMPUTING

ON THIS DAY: FIRST LAUNCH FROM CAPE CANAVERAL (1950)

On this date in 1950, the first successful rocket launch from Cape Canaveral took place. "Bumper" No. 8 was a captured German V-2 rocket with another rocket—the 700-pound Army-JPL Wac Corporal—on top. The first-stage V-2 climbed 10 miles and then separated from the second-stage Corporal, which traveled 15 more miles.

Related Web site: www.ksc.nasa.gov

FOURTH-GENERATION COMPUTERS: 1972–PRESENT

Fourth-generation computing is characterized by the use of the microprocessor, which is a computer processing unit (CPU) contained on an integrated circuit on a tiny piece of silicon. Microprocessor technology enabled the construction of more powerful mainframe computers, and of smaller, lower-priced machines that came to be known as personal computers. The first personal computers were sold in kit form for the hobbyist market, but these smaller, easier-to-use computers soon gained a foothold with both business users and general consumers.

In 1975 a New Mexico-based company called MITS (Micro Instrumentation and Telemetry) released what is generally regarded as the world's first true personal computer, the Altair 8800. The Altair was based on Intel's 8080 microprocessor, contained 256 bytes of memory, and sold for $395 in kit form or $498 assembled. A whopping 2,000 Altair 8800s were sold in the first year of release.

The early 1980s were a wild and wooly period in the history of personal computing. There were multiple competing operating systems, and a slew of large and small companies slugging it out for a dominant position in the newly emerging marketplace. Early players, most of whom didn't survive the decade, included Tandy, Commodore, Atari, Osborne, Kaypro, Texas Instruments, Sinclair, and a little company called Apple.

The most important developments in the history of personal computers was the entry of IBM into the marketplace, and the Microsoft Windows OS.

As the personal computer industry moved into the 1990s, machines became more affordable and more powerful, and software programs became much easier to use. The decade was dominated by Intel microprocessors, IBM-compatible hardware, and Microsoft software and operating systems. During the first half of the decade the killer apps continued to be word processing and spreadsheet programs (often bundled together in a software suite); during the last part of the decade, it was the Internet that drove hardware sales and usage.

SOFTWARE OF THE WEEK

If you're like most folks, you haven't even thought about putting a will together. That's a mistake; everyone needs a will, especially if you're married and have kids. Fortunately, it's not too much of a chore when you use Quicken WillMaker Plus, which leads you step-by-step through the key legal documents necessary. Buy it for $49.95 at www.nolo.com.

THIS WEEK'S FOCUS: FUN—AND USEFUL—STUFF ON THE WEB

ON THIS DAY: FIRST TEST TUBE BABY BORN (1978)

On July 25, 1978, Louise Joy Brown, the world's first test tube baby, was born in Oldham, England. Conceived through the technique of in-vitro fertilization, baby Louise weighed 5 pounds 12 ounces and was delivered by Caesarean section at Oldham District General Hospital. Since then, close to half a million babies have been born using the same technique.

Related Web site: www.asrm.org

MOVIES AND MUSIC

When it comes to movies and music, the Web is for more than just downloading. It's also a treasure trove of information—enough to fuel dozens of games of Trivial Pursuit!

My favorite entertainment-related Web site, hands down, is the Internet Movie Database (IMDB), located at www.imdb.com. As its name implies, the IMDB is a huge database of movie information. Virtually every movie ever made is catalogued here, as are major (and minor) actors and actresses, directors, producers, you name it. You can search the database by movie or TV show title, cast or crew name, or character name. IMDB then returns the most detailed movie descriptions (including complete cast and crew listings) that you've ever seen. I particularly like the links to external movie reviews, where you can read opinions by Roger Ebert and his ilk.

If the only thing you're interested in is movie reviews, then check out Rotten Tomatoes (www.rottentomatoes.com). Pay no attention to the name; this site lists links to all known Web-based reviews of both current and classic movies, including DVD reviews. It's a terrific resource.

The IMDB of the music world is the venerable All-Music Guide (www.allmusic.com). This is simply the best and biggest database of music information on the Web. You can search by artist, album, song, style, or record label. My favorite part is the way it links practically everything to everything else. Look up your favorite album, view the musicians who played on it, and then click a musician's name to view every other album that musician played on. Even better, the site includes tons of song, album, and artist reviews, as well as hundreds of well-informed articles about musical styles and trends. I can sit and read this site for hours at a time.

PC GADGET OF THE WEEK

Eliminate long-distance charges with the PhoneBridge cordless Internet phone. Just connect any cordless phone to the PhoneBridge device, and then connect the PhoneBridge to your PC's sound card. You can then use your PC to place VOIP phone calls, using your regular phone to talk. Optionally, the PhoneBridge can use your PC's speakers and microphone to create a giant speakerphone. Buy it for $129.95 at www.phonebridge.com.

TUESDAY

THIS WEEK'S FOCUS: FUN—AND USEFUL—STUFF ON THE WEB

ON THIS DAY: STANLEY KUBRICK BORN (1928)

Noted film director Stanley Kubrick was born on this date in 1928. Kubrick's films are highly acclaimed for their technical perfection and deep, highly intellectual symbolism. They include *Dr. Strangelove or: How I Learned to Stop Worrying and Love the Bomb* (1963), *2001—A Space Odyssey* (1968), *A Clockwork Orange* (1971), and *The Shining* (1980).

Related Web site: kubrickfilms.warnerbros.com

NEWS ON THE WEB

You can get just about all the news you want on the Web—current news headlines, in-depth topic analyses, specialized industry and company news, even news customized for your city or town. The good thing about getting your news online—beside the fact that it's free—is that it's almost always up-to-the-minute fresh. You don't have to wait around for the nightly news report, the morning newspaper, or the weekly newsmagazine.

Some of the biggest, most popular news sites on the Web are run by the major broadcast and cable news networks. These sites include ABC News (abcnews.go.com), CBS News (www.cbsnews.com), CNN (www.cnn.com), FOX News (www.foxnews.com), and MSNBC (www.msnbc.com).

Other good sources of national and international news are the Web sites of the big national newspapers. Most of these sites feature the equivalent of the entire printed edition online—and often for free. And, just as the national newspapers have their own Web sites, so do many local newspapers. For a listing of these local media Web sites, go to Gebbie Press (www.gebbieinc.com).

If you're looking for older or more obscure news articles, try searching one of the Web's news archives. Some of these sites archive articles in their own databases, and some simply link to the archives of individual news sources. The best of these include Google News (news.google.com), NewsLink (www.newslink.org), News Index (www.newsindex.com), NewsLibrary (www.newslibrary.com), NewsTrawler (www.newstrawler.com), TotalNEWS (www.totalnews.com), and, for broadcast news, Vanderbilt University's Television News Archive (tvnews.vanderbilt.edu).

Finally, if you're interested in slightly more biased and gossipy news, check out the Drudge Report (www.drudgereport.com), run by the notorious (and not always terribly accurate) Matt Drudge.

DOWNLOAD OF THE WEEK

WeatherBug is a utility that sits in the Windows system tray, next to the clock, and provides up-to-the-minute weather information—assuming you're connected to the Internet, that is. The Bug in the tray displays the current temperature; double-click to see the current forecast, live weather radar, and more, customized to your ZIP code. Download it for free at www.weatherbug.com.

July 27, 2005
WEDNESDAY

THIS WEEK'S FOCUS: FUN—AND USEFUL—STUFF ON THE WEB

ON THIS DAY: BUGS BUNNY DEBUTS (1940)

Bugs Bunny, arguably the most popular and recognizable cartoon character of all time, debuted on this date in 1940 in the cartoon short, *A Wild Hare*. Since then, Bugs has appeared in more than 175 animated shorts and several prime time specials, most often voiced by the legendary Mel Blanc.

Related Web site: www.bugsbunnyburrow.com/

SPORTS ON THE WEB

The Web is also a haven for sports nuts. Whether you're a fan or a participant, there's at least one site somewhere on the Web that focuses on your particular sport.

The best sports sites on the Web resemble the best news sites—they're actually portals to all sorts of content and services, including up-to-the-minute scores, post-game recaps, in-depth reporting, and much more. If you're looking for sports information online, check out CBS SportsLine (www.sportsline.com), ESPN.com (go.espn.com), FOXSports (www.foxsports.com), NBC Sports (www.nbcsports.com), Sports Illustrated's SI.com (sportsillustrated.cnn.com), and SportingNews.com (www.sportingnews.com). Try www.nfl.com, www.nba.com, www.mlb.com, and www.nhl.com for official professional football, basketball, baseball, and hockey news, respectively.

Then we have the entire gamut of participatory sports. The number of do-it-yourself sports sites are almost too many to list, but here's a start, sorted by sport:

Sport	Web Site	URL
Baseball	USA Baseball	www.usabaseball.com
Basketball	Basketball Highway	www.bbhighway.com

Sport	Web Site	URL
Boating	Boating America	www.boatingamerica.com
Bowling	Bowl.com	www.bowl.com
Camping	GORP	www.gorp.com
Extreme sports	ExtremeSports.com	www.extremesports.com
Fishing	The Fishing Network	www.the-fishing-network.com
Golf	GolfServ	www.golf.com
Gymnastics	Gymn-Forum.com	www.gymn-forum.com
Hiking	thebackpacker.com	www.thebackpacker.com
Hockey	USA Hockey	www.usahockey.com
Running	Cool Running	www.coolrunning.com
Snow skiing	OnTheSnow.com	www.onthesnow.com
Soccer	U.S. Youth Soccer	www.usysa.org
Swimming	Swimmersworld.com	www.swimmersworld.com
Tennis	TennisONE	www.tennisone.com
Youth sports	InfoSports.net	www.infosports.net

MAC GADGET OF THE WEEK

Apple's World Travel Adapter Kit includes everything you need to take your iBook, PowerBook, or iPod just about anywhere in the world. The kit includes a set of six AC plugs that work with power outlets in North America, Japan, China, the U.K., continental Europe, Korea, Hong Kong, and Australia. Buy it for $39 at www.apple.com.

July 28, 2005
THURSDAY

THIS WEEK'S FOCUS: FUN—AND USEFUL—STUFF ON THE WEB

ON THIS DAY: EARL SILAS TUPPER, FOUNDER OF TUPPERWARE, BORN (1907)

American manufacturer Earl Tupper was born on this date in 1907. In the 1930s, Tupper invented a flexible, lightweight material that was used to make plastic gas masks during World War II. He then turned his attention to consumer products, creating the line of plastic, airtight food storage containers we now know as Tupperware.

Related Web site: www.tupperware.com

REALLY STUPID WEB SITES

There's nothing more fun than checking out some of the most stupid sites on the Web. Without any further introduction, here are some of my favorites:

- **BizarreRecords.com** (www.bizarrerecords.com)—Images of some of the strangest vinyl record sleeves of all time.

- **Illustrated Guide to Breaking Your Computer** (members.aol.com/spoons1000/break/)—The title explains it all.

- **kissthisguy.com** (www.kissthisguy.com)—A huge archive of misunderstood rock lyrics. (From the great Jimi Hendrix tune: "Excuse me while I kiss this guy...")

- **Leonard Nimoy Should Eat More Salsa Foundation** (www.lnsemsf.com)—The Web headquarters of the LNSEMSF, dedicated to getting Mr. Spock to... well, to eat more salsa. I don't know why.

- **Oly-hay Ible-bay** (www.museumofconceptualart.com/ible-bay.html)—An honest-to-God translation of the Bible into Pig Latin. "In-ay e-thay eginning-bay Od-gay eated-cray e-thay eaven-hay and-ay e-thay earth-ay."

- **Prawnography** (www.prawnography.com)—Shrimps, shrimps, and more shrimps.

- **Traffic Cone Preservation Society** (animation.filmtv.ucla.edu/students/awinfrey/coneindex.htm)—Dedicated to observing and preserving traffic cones in their natural habitat.

- **T.W.I.N.K.I.E.S. Project** (www.twinkiesproject.com)—A hilarious site that tests how Twinkies respond to various conditions; the acronym stands for Tests With Inorganic Noxious Kakes In Extreme Situations.

- **Who Would Buy That?** (www.whowouldbuythat.com)—A constantly updated list of the strangest online auction items.

WEB SITE OF THE WEEK

Playing along with this week's focus, I did a Google search on "fun stuff" and the first page in the results was Ben & Jerry's Fun Stuff. That's right, the folks at Ben & Jerry's have put together a Web site full of ice cream–related games, e-cards, crafts, and recipes. I particularly liked the Flavor Graveyard, which lists all their dearly departed flavors. Check it out for yourself at www.benjerry.com/fun_stuff/.

July 29, 2005

FRIDAY

THIS WEEK'S FOCUS: FUN—AND USEFUL—STUFF ON THE WEB

ON THIS DAY: FIRST IRON LUNG INSTALLED (1927)

On July 29, 1927, the first iron lung was installed at Bellevue hospital in New York. Phillip Drinker and Louis Agassiz Shaw built their first electric respirator out of two vacuum cleaners. While it saw widespread use during that era's polio epidemic, the iron lung is rarely used today.

Related Web site: www.polionet.org

HEALTH AND MEDICINE ONLINE

If you or a family member is sick, you want answers *now*. Whether you're dealing with an ear infection or something much more serious, there is no better and faster place to turn than to the numerous health-related sites on the Web. Online you'll get access to the same medical databases used by most physicians, and your access will be immediate—no waiting for an appointment!

Most online healthcare sites are superb resources for all sorts of medical information; they can be particularly useful in researching and diagnosing medical conditions and in encouraging preventive healthcare. The top medical sites on the Web include

- **drkoop.com** (www.drkoop.com)—A full-service family healthcare portal, led by the former U.S. Surgeon General.

- **eMedicine.com** (www.emedicine.com)—Free online medical journals and textbooks for medical professionals and the general public.

- **HealthWeb** (www.healthweb.org)—Links to hundreds of online health sites, by topic.

- **MedicineNet** (www.medicinenet.com)—Full-service site that offers medical information, a pharmaceutical reference guide, a medical dictionary, and doctors' answers to user questions.

- **MedlinePlus** (www.medlineplus.gov)—The world's largest medical database; use it to read about symptoms and treatments for illnesses and conditions—and catch up on the latest medical developments and breakthroughs.

- **Planet Wellness** (www.planetwellness.com)—Access to thousands of health and wellness resources.

- **Virtual Hospital** (www.vh.org)—A full-service medical site for both patients and healthcare providers, run by the University of Iowa; includes a Virtual Children's Hospital with pediatric information.

- **WebMD Health** (www.mywebmd.com)—A topic-oriented online health and wellness center; sister site to the physician-oriented WebMD (www.webmd.com).

PORTABLE GADGET OF THE WEEK

Cellboost is a compact, low-cost, disposable battery/charger. It works with most cell phone models and provides instant power for a run-down phone. Just plug it into the bottom of your phone, and you get an instant 60 minutes of talk time. Buy it for $9.95 at www.cellboost.com.

July 30, 2005

SATURDAY

THIS WEEK'S FOCUS: FUN—AND USEFUL—STUFF ON THE WEB

ON THIS DAY: HENRY FORD BORN (1863)

Henry Ford was born on this day in 1863. He was the founder of the Ford Motor Company and one of the first to apply assembly line manufacturing to the mass production of affordable automobiles—which revolutionized industrial production.

Related Web site: www.thehenryford.org

SURFING FOR SENIORS

Aside from the sites you come in contact with during the normal course of Web surfing, there are several sites that specialize in topics of interest to older users. These general-interest senior sites typically offer a wide variety of news and information on senior-specific topics (such as aging and grandparenting) as well as general topics of particular interest to seniors (including healthcare, travel, and genealogy). Many of these sites also offer message boards and chat rooms specifically for seniors, as well as special offers on products and services for older users.

The best of these sites for seniors include

- **AARP (www.aarp.org)**—The official Web site of the American Association of Retired People, the nation's leading organization for people age 50 and older.
- **AgeNet (www.agenet.com)**—Solutions for better aging, including an eldercare locator, caregiver tools, and expert advice on geriatric drugs, chronic illness, home safety, and more.
- **ElderWeb (www.elderweb.org)**—An online community for older computer users.

- **Senior Women Web (www.seniorwomen.com)**—A Web site for and by senior women.
- **SeniorNet (www.seniornet.org)**—Teaching seniors to use computers and technology.
- **SeniorSite.com (www.seniorsite.com)**—A Web community for users 55 or over; includes a variety of forums and chat rooms.
- **ThirdAge (www.thirdage.com)**—A lively site for active older Americans, including chat, discussions, personals, and member home pages.

FACT OF THE WEEK

According to a study by NOP Research, children in the U.K. know more about the Internet than they do about books. Six out of ten children in the U.K. know that homepage was the front page of a Web site, whereas only 9% could explain what the preface to a book was. Nearly 60% could identify a hard drive as being part of a computer, but only a third of the kids knew that a hardback was a type of book. And around 70% knew that WWW stood for the World Wide Web, while less than 25% knew that RSVP was asking them to reply to an invitation.

THIS WEEK'S FOCUS: FUN—AND USEFUL—STUFF ON THE WEB

ON THIS DAY: FIRST CLOSE-UP PICTURES OF MOON'S SURFACE (1964)

On July 31, 1964, the American space probe Ranger 7 transmitted the first close-up images of the moon's surface ever taken by a U.S. spacecraft. Ranger 7 carried six slow-scan vidicon TV cameras capable of transmitting high-resolution, close-up television pictures; the first image was of the large crater Alphonsus. A total of 4,308 photographs were returned before Ranger 7 crashed to the lunar surface.

Related Web site: www.solarviews.com/eng/ranger7.htm

ONLINE GREETING CARDS

Gone are the days where you have to trek down to your local Hallmark store when you want to send a greeting card to someone you like. Now you can send a greeting card instantly—no waiting for the postal service to do their thing—via one of the many popular online greeting card sites. These are Web sites that offer electronic cards that you can personalize and send to friends and family, as easily as you send email messages. In fact, that's how these greeting cards are delivered—via email.

Most online greeting card sites offer their services for free; they make their money by selling advertising. Other sites charge a small fee, or offer basic cards for free and more deluxe cards for a price. In any case, check the terms and requirements before you start clicking!

Here are some of the most popular online greeting cards sites on the Web:

- Beat Greets (www.beatgreets.com)
- Birthday Cards.com (www.birthdaycards.com)
- Blue Mountain (www.bluemountain.com)
- eFun.com (www.efun.com)

- Hallmark E-Cards (www.hallmark.com)
- Yahoo! Greetings (greetings.yahoo.com)

When you send an online greeting card from one of these sites, what your recipient actually receives is an email notifying them that they have a card waiting—they don't receive the greeting itself, which might otherwise be stopped by various spam filters. The message includes a link to the greeting card page on the company's Web site; when the recipient clicks the link, they're taken to the greeting card site, where their personalize greeting card is displayed.

SOFTWARE OF THE WEEK

If you compose or arrange music, throw away the blank music paper and buy a copy of Finale. This is a extremely versatile notation program that lets you put your musical ideas on the printed page using nothing but your computer—and your MIDI keyboard, if you want to use the direct input feature. Buy it for $600 from www.finalemusic.com, or download the introductory Finale NotePad program for free.

MORE JULY FACTS

July 1

1858 Wallace-Darwin *Theory of Evolution* is first published at the Linnaean Society in London

1874 The first U.S. zoo—the Philadelphia Zoo—opens

1941 NBC airs first official TV commercial; Bulova paid $9 to advertise its watches during a Dodgers-Phillies game

1997 Hong Kong returned to China after being under British rule since 1841

July 2

1922 Water skis are first used on Lake Pepin in Minnesota

1992 Stephen Hawking's *A Brief History of Time* breaks British publishing records after spending more than three years on the bestseller list

July 3

1903 First cable is laid across the Pacific Ocean, connecting Hawaii, Midway, Guam, and Manila; this cable was in use until the early 1950s

2002 NASA launches Contour, an unmanned satellite, on a mission to study frozen samples of the solar system contained in the comet nucleus

July 4

1826 Thomas Jefferson dies

1894 Elwood Haynes test drives his automobile in Kokomo, Indiana; Haynes's vehicle is the oldest American-made automobile in existence and is on display at the Smithsonian

July 5

1865 The Salvation Army is founded

1946 The bikini is introduced to the U.S. by French designers, though they didn't catch on until the 1960s

1996 Dolly, a sheep with the honor of being the first cloned mammal, is born

July 6

1886 Malted milk is introduced

July 7

1907 Robert A. Heinlein, author of *A Stranger in a Strange Land*, is born

July 8

1831 John Styth Pemberton, inventor of Coca-Cola, is born

July 9

1856 Nikola Tesla is born; his Tesla coils are still used in radios, televisions, and other electronic equipment

1979 Voyager 2 passes Jupiter, sending photographs back to Earth; in 1981, the probe passes Saturn; in 1986, it passes Uranus, and in 1989, it passes Neptune

July 10

1962 First private satellite—Telstar I—is launched by AT&T; Telstar I stopped working about a year after it was launched into space

July 11

1979 Skylab, the first U.S. space station, crashes back into Earth in Australia and the Indian Ocean; no one is injured

1985 Coca-Cola's original recipe is changed, angering millions; eventually, Coca-Cola returned to its original formula, dubbed Coke Classic

July 12

1817 Henry David Thoreau is born

1854 George Eastman, inventor of photographic film, is born

1957 Lung cancer and smoking are first linked by the U.S. Surgeon General

July 13

1881 Billy The Kid is shot dead by Pat Garrett in Lincoln County, NM; to this day, some believe that Billy was not killed by Garrett and that he died of natural causes many years later

1944 Erno Rubik, inventor of the Rubik's Cube, is born

1977 Power failure in New York blacks out most of the city, plummeting the city into mass rioting; about 4,500 people were arrested after causing more than $61 million in damages

July 14

1853 The first U.S. World's Fair opens in New York

1867 Dynamite is demonstrated for the first time

July 15

1965 Mariner 4 satellite transmits the first close-up photos of Mars back to Earth

July 16

1867 Reinforced concrete is patented in Paris, France

1907 Orville Redenbacher is born

1945 First atomic bomb tested at the Alamogordo Air Base about 125 miles from Albuquerque, NM, eliminating every sign of plant and animal life in a one-mile radius

1948 First turbine-propeller aircraft, the Vickers Viscount, makes its maiden flight

1951 J.D. Salinger's classic—and only—novel, *The Catcher in the Rye*, is published

1999 John F. Kennedy, Jr. is killed in a plane crash near Martha's Vineyard, MA

July 17

1955 Disneyland opens in Anaheim, CA

1959 Oldest human skull on record is found in Tanzania; the skull has been dated to 1.8 millions years B.C.

1989 First flight of the B-2 Stealth bomber over the California desert

July 18

1921 U.S. astronaut John Glenn is born

1939 MGM screens a sneak preview of *The Wizard of Oz*

1969 Senator Edward "Ted" Kennedy drives his car off a wooden bridge into a pond on Chappaquiddick Island; Kennedy escaped, but his female companion did not; Kennedy did not report the accident for 10 years, sparking controversy that lasts to this day

July 19

1799 Rosetta Stone is discovered in Egypt; writing on the stone held the key to deciphering the language and culture of ancient Egypt

July 20

1969 Neil Armstrong walks on the moon; the first human landing on the moon; to this day many conspiracy theorists believe the telecast was staged, citing details such as the alleged waving American flag (there's no wind on the moon)

1976 Viking I lands on Mars—the first human spacecraft to make a safe landing on this planet

July 21

1984 First robotic-related death occurs in Jackson, MI when a machine crushes an employee against a safety bar

July 22

1933 First around-the-world solo flight

July 23

1903 First Ford Model A is delivered to its owner

July 25

1978 First test-tube baby is born

July 27

1866 The Atlantic telegraph cable line is successfully completed from Valenica, Ireland to Heart's Content, Trinity Bay, Newfoundland; the cable stretched nearly 200 miles and was laid as deep as two miles in places

1928 Stanley Kubrick, director of *A Clockwork Orange* and *Spartacus*, is born

1940 Bugs Bunny makes debut in "A Wild Hare"

July 28

1858 Fingerprints first used for identification purposes in Jungipoor, India

July 29

1958 NASA is established, a year after Soviets launched the first satellite, Sputnik I

July 30

1863 Henry Ford is born

1928 Charles Francis Jenkins starts the first television station broadcast

1971 Apollo 15 deposits the first vehicle—the Lunar Roving Vehicle—on the moon

July 31

1964 Ranger 7 takes first close-up images of the moon before crashing into the moon's surface

August 2005

August 2005

SUNDAY	MONDAY	TUESDAY	WEDNESDAY	THURSDAY	FRIDAY	SATURDAY
	1 1893 Shredded wheat is patented in Watertown, NY	**2** 1922 Alexander Graham Bell dies	**3** 1921 First crop dusting from an airplane is done in Troy, OH	**4** 1900 Jean-Joseph Etienne Lenoir—inventor of the internal-combustion engine—dies	**5** 1914 First traffic lights in the U.S. are installed in Cleveland, OH	**6** 1945 U.S. drops atomic bomb on Hiroshima, Japan, killing about 140,000
7 1959 First pictures of Earth taken by Explorer VI	**8** 1859 Escalator patented in Saugus, MA	**9** 1910 Electronic washing machine is patented, IL	**10** 1846 Smithsonian Institution is founded in Washington, D.C.	**11** 1966 Chevrolet introduces the Camaro	**12** 1981 IBM announces its first personal computer, powered by a 4.77 MHz Intel 8088 microprocessor	**13** 1889 Pay phone is patented in Hartford, CT
14 1953 The Wiffle Ball is patented	**15** 1911 Crisco is introduced	**16** 1977 Elvis Presley dies in Memphis, TN	**17** 1835 The wrench is patented in Springfield, MA	**18** 1227 Genghis Khan dies	**19** 1921 Gene Roddenberry, creator of *Star Trek*, is born	**20** 1862 National Labor Union officially creates the eight-hour workday
21 1888 Adding machine is patented in St. Louis, MO	**22** 1865 Liquid soap is patented	**23** 1904 Snow tire chains are patented in New York	**24** 1853 Potato chips are first created in Saratoga Springs, NY	**25** 1925 Television tube is patented in New Jersey	**26** 1920 19th Amendment to the Constitution is adopted	**27** 1962 Mariner space probe is launched
28 1859 First U.S. oil well is discovered in Titusville, PA	**29** 1885 First motorcycle is patented in Germany	**30** 1881 First stereophonic sound system is patented in Germany	**31** 1897 Movie camera is patented by Thomas Edison			

THIS WEEK'S FOCUS: **WEB DESIGN**

ON THIS DAY: OXYGEN IDENTIFIED (1774)

On August 1, 1774, Joseph Priestley, a British Presbyterian minister and chemist, identified a gas which he called "dephlogisticated air"—later known as oxygen. He observed that candles burned very brightly in this special type of air; also, a mouse in a sealed vessel with it could breathe it much longer than ordinary air.

Related Web site: www.webelements.com/webelements/elements/text/O/key.html

HOME PAGE COMMUNITIES

The easiest way to get your own personal Web page is to use a service that specializes in the creation and hosting of individual Web pages. These sites—some of which host *millions* of unique pages—are called home page communities, and they typically offer a variety of Web page–creation tools and hosting options. More often than not, these sites offer basic hosting for free, with more advanced options available for a fee.

When you join a home page community, you're provided with a specified amount of space on their servers, typically in the 10MB–25MB range. (In case you're wondering, 10MB should be *more* than enough to host your personal pages—unless you're attempting to re-create the Encyclopedia Britannica online!) You can then use the tools on the site to create your Web pages, or upload previously created pages to their site.

All of the major home page communities work in a similar fashion. Those that don't charge fees try to make their money by serving ads on your pages; they collect the advertising revenues, not you. Even those that purport to be free sometimes offer a variety of additional (not free) services, and will be glad to charge you for additional storage space, domain name registration, e-commerce tools, and the like.

When you're looking to create your first home page on the Web, the most popular services include Angelfire (`angelfire.lycos.com`), FortuneCity (`www.fortunecity.com`), Freeservers (`www.freeservers.com`), Rediff.com (`homepages.rediff.com`), Tripod (`tripod.lycos.com`), and Yahoo! GeoCities (`geocities.yahoo.com`). Many Internet service providers also offer free personal home pages to their subscribers; check with your ISP to see what services are available. In addition, if you're an America Online member, you can avail yourself of the AOL Hometown home page community, at `hometown.aol.com`.

PC GADGET OF THE WEEK

Worried about your kids accessing inappropriate material on the Internet? Then check out Griffin's ControlKey, a keychain-sized security device that plugs in to the USB port of any PC. When the ControlKey is inserted, you can use your computer normally. But when your child accesses the PC without the ControlKey, access is limited to those programs you specify—and Internet access is blocked completely. Buy it for $59.99 at `www.controlkey.com`.

August 2, 2005

TUESDAY

THIS WEEK'S FOCUS: WEB DESIGN

ON THIS DAY: GREENWICH MEAN TIME ADOPTED (1880)

On this date in 1880, Greenwich Mean Time (GMT) was adopted officially by the British Parliament. Greenwich Mean Time was originally set up to aid naval navigation, but was not used on land until the growth of the British railway system in the 1840s, when a need for a national time system became apparent. GMT was adopted by the U.S. on November 18, 1883.

Related Web site: www.greenwichmeantime.com

HOME PAGE COMMUNITY COMPLAINTS

One of the biggest complaints with Yahoo! GeoCities and other home page communities is the profusion of advertisements that accompany member pages. For example, anyone viewing a GeoCities member page will see an embedded "ad square" in the top-right corner of the page. Users can click on the up-arrow button to minimize the ad, but you can't make it go completely away; it's a real nuisance, and interferes with the content of some pages.

These advertisements are how GeoCities and other sites can afford to host your pages for free. You can try finding a free service that doesn't have ads, but good luck. If you want ad-free pages, you'll probably have to upgrade to a paid service, such as GeoCities Plus ($4.95/month).

The other big problem with GeoCities and other home page communities is the growing issue of community standards. Most of these sites are owned by public companies, and public companies often come under pressure from certain shareholders to uphold specific moral standards. The public home page communities are not immune from this pressure—which is why you see GeoCities and similar sites deleting the most blatant adult-oriented pages in their communities.

It's likely that this pressure to monitor and censure personal home pages will continue. Whether the issue *de jour* is adult content, trademark or copyright violation, or something more insidiously political, expect to see more rules and regulations forbidding specific types of content from these free sites.

The solution for any such ban is the same as for site-dictated advertising—move your pages to a paid Web hosting service. When you have to pay your own way you can get away with a lot more than you can if you're accepting a handout.

DOWNLOAD OF THE WEEK

If you're looking for a cheap and easy-to-use Web page editing program, check out the CoffeeCup HTML Editor. It comes with 40 Web site templates, 125 built-in JavaScripts, thousands of graphics, and simple FTP uploading. It's a shareware program, so you can try it for free or buy it for $49 from www.coffeecup.com/html-editor/.

August 3, 2005
WEDNESDAY

THIS WEEK'S FOCUS: **WEB DESIGN**

ON THIS DAY: TRS-80 ANNOUNCED (1977)

It was on this date in 1977 that Radio Shack announced the TRS-80 personal computer. The TRS-80 Model 1 sold for $599.95 and came with a whopping 4K RAM. It sold 10,000 units in its first month on the market, and more than 250,000 units by the time it was discontinued in 1981.

Related Web site: www.trs-80.com

UNDERSTANDING HTML

Hypertext Markup Language (HTML) is the engine that drives the creation of pages on the Web. In reality, HTML is nothing more than a series of codes that tell Web browsers how to display different types of text and graphics. The codes are embedded in a document, so you can't see them; instead, you see the results of the codes.

HTML coding might sound difficult, but it's really fairly easy. First, know that HTML is nothing more than text surrounded by instructions, in the form of simple codes, called *tags*. Tags are distinguished from normal text by the fact that they're enclosed within angle brackets. Each particular tag turns on or off a particular attribute, such as boldface or italic text. Most tags are in sets of "on/off" pairs; you turn "on" the code before the text you want to affect, and then turn "off" the code after the text.

For example, the tag <h1> is used to turn specified type into a level-one headline; the tag </h1> turns off the headline type. The tag <i> is used to italicize text; </i> turns off the italics. (As you can see, an "off" code is merely the "on" code with a slash before it, </like this>.)

Any text *not* surrounded by tags uses HTML's default formatting—normal Times Roman text. The same with tables and other elements; if no tags are applied, they default to standard formatting.

When you view the HTML code for a document, you're actually viewing a plain text document. Because of this, you can use any text editor—such as Windows Notepad or Wordpad—to edit HTML documents. It's more convenient, however, to use a dedicated HTML editing program, such as Microsoft's FrontPage, to create your Web pages. These programs let you work in a WYSIWYG environment, and then translate your designs into the appropriate HTML code.

MAC GADGET OF THE WEEK

The MonacoOPTIX XR color calibration system helps graphics professionals get their colors *just* right. Attach the puck-like calibration device to the front of your monitor, connect to your Mac (via USB), and run the calibration software to ensure that your monitor displays *exactly* what was shot. Buy it for $299 at www.monacosys.com.

August 4, 2005
THURSDAY

THIS WEEK'S FOCUS: WEB DESIGN

ON THIS DAY: FAIRNESS DOCTRINE RESCINDED (1987)

Remember the days when, if a news program gave three minutes of coverage to one candidate in an election, they had to give an equal three minutes to the opposing candidate? That system ended on August 4, 1987, when the FCC voted to rescind the Fairness Doctrine. The result? Happier media conglomerates and the explosion of partisan programming from Rush Limbaugh, Sean Hannity, and the like.

Related Web site: www.fcc.gov

CHANGING TEXT AND BACKGROUND COLORS

When you're tired of black text on a white background, it's time to use HTML to change your Web page's text and background colors. It's really quite easy.

You assign a background color to your page by adding a special `bgcolor` code (called an *attribute*) within the brackets of the "on" `<body>` tag, like this:

```
<body bgcolor="xxxxxx">
```

Of course, you still have to use the `</body>` "off" tag at the end of your document; that doesn't change.

In the `bgcolor` code, you replace the *xxxxxx* with the six-digit hexadecimal code for a specific background color—surrounded by quotation marks. (Remember to precede each code with a number sign: #.) You can find a comprehensive list of color codes at www.htmlhelp.com/cgi-bin/color.cgi, or use the color picker at www.annoyingwebsites. com/color_picker.htm to generate hex codes.

As an example, suppose you wanted to set the background color for your document to light gray.

The hex code for light gray is DDDDDD, so you would enter the following code:

```
<body bgcolor="DDDDDD">
```

Adding color to your text works much the same as changing the font face or size. The code you use looks like this:

```
<font color="#xxxxxx">text</font>
```

As with the `bgcolor` code, replace the six *x*'s with the code for a specific color. Suppose you wanted to color some text red. The hex code for red is FF0000, so you would use this code:

```
<font color="#FF0000">red text</font>
```

Color is a good way to highlight important parts of your page. Try not to use too many colors, however; if your page starts to look like a rainbow, the color loses its capability to make an impact.

WEB SITE OF THE WEEK

How accessible is your Web site to disabled users? Check it for yourself at Bobby (bobby. watchfire.com), a free service that evaluates your site for compliance with existing accessible guidelines.

THIS WEEK'S FOCUS: **WEB DESIGN**

ON THIS DAY: COMPLETION OF FIRST TRANSATLANTIC CABLE (1858)

It used to take at least a week to send a message from North America to Europe. Then, on this date in 1858, the first transatlantic cable was completed, and electronic communication became nearly instantaneous.

Related Web site: www.history-magazine.com/cable.html

TROUBLESHOOTING BAD HTML

Before you post any pages you create to a Web site, you should test those pages in your own Web browser. If everything displays correctly, you're ready to go live; if something looks out of whack, however, it's time to troubleshoot your code.

The most common cause of HTML problems is mismatching code—typically not including the "off" tag for a particular effect. For example, entering the `<b>` tag but forgetting to add the `</b>` tag will display all the remaining text in your document as boldface. Some HTML editors let you highlight matching pairs to look for mismatches; in any case, go through your code listing and be sure you have "off" tags for all your "ons."

Simple misspelling is another big source of problems. Considering that HTML tags look more or less like nonsense words, it's easy to misspell a tag—and a misspelled tag is ignored when the page is viewed in a Web browser. One of the common misspellings is in the `<img src>` tag, used to insert graphics; it's easy for your fingers to type `scr` instead of `src`.

The other common problem is bad URLs in your links and graphics. You *must* include the full URL—including the `http://`—for the URL to work. Be sure you check all the links in your document before you upload the page.

And, if you can, test your pages against multiple browsers. Believe it or not, some pages look different when viewed with Opera or Mozila Firefox. Be sure you have all the different browsers loaded on your machine, you view your page as all others will view it.

PORTABLE GADGET OF THE WEEK

ZIP-LINQ's ZIP-CELL is a phone charge cable that lets you connect your cell phone to the USB port of your notebook computer and recharge directly from your PC. The cord is retractable, so it's easy to pack; with the ZIP-CELL, you no longer need to carry your phone's bulky charger with you when you travel. Buy it for $19.99 at www.ziplinq.com.

August 6, 2005

SATURDAY

THIS WEEK'S FOCUS: WEB DESIGN

ON THIS DAY: ATOMIC BOMB DROPPED ON HIROSHIMA (1945)

The world changed on August 7, 1945, when the United States dropped an atomic bomb on the Japanese city of Hiroshima. At the instant of detonation, the air temperature at the point of explosion exceeded one million degrees Celsius. Intense heat rays and radiation were released in all directions, and the pressure on the surrounding air created a blast of unimaginable force. The devastation was mind-boggling; 90% of the city's building buildings collapsed or burned, and nearly 140,000 people (of the city's 350,000 population) were killed.

Related Web page: www.city.hiroshima.jp/index-E.html

ADDING MAILTO: LINKS

When you want visitors to your site to contact you, add a Mailto: link on your page; users click this link to send email to you. Here's the code for a Mailto: link:

```
<a href="mailto:yourname@domain.com">click here
to email me</a>
```

If you want to get really fancy, you can insert additional code to create a Mailto: link that supplies a subject line as well as an address. The code looks like this:

```
<a
href="mailto:yourname@domain.com?subject=Subject"
>Click here to email me</a>
```

Naturally, replace *Subject* with the subject line you want.

If you're going to put your email address in your Web page's HTML, you're risking discovery by spammers who trawl the net looking for @ signs. I replace all the `mailto:leo@leoville.com` links on my site with the following JavaScript to hide the address from spam robots. (Obviously, you'll want to replace my name and address with your own.)

```
<script language="javascript">
  <!--
  var contact = " Leo Laporte"
  var email = "webmaster"
  var emailHost = "leoville.com"
  document.write("<a href=" + "mail" + "to:" +
email + "@" + emailHost+ ">" + contact + "</a>")
  //-->
</script>
```

FACT OF THE WEEK

Webdesignpractices.com reports that 97% of all Web sites include global links to the site's top-level categories; 89% of these links are on the top of the page, and 11% along the side. As for navigation style, 43% use navigation tabs, 39% use a navigation bar, 7% use a plain list, 5% use pull-down menus, and 4% use navigation buttons.

August 7, 2005

SUNDAY

THIS WEEK'S FOCUS: WEB DESIGN

ON THIS DAY: MATA HARI BORN (1876)

Mata Hari was an exotic dancer, courtesan, and alleged spy for the Germans in WWI. She was born Margaretha Geertruida Zelle on this date in 1876, and died by a French firing squad in 1917.

Related Web site: www.crimelibrary.com/spies/mata_hari/

PUTTING ADS ON YOUR SITE

Want to make money from your Web site? Well, it's tough to make money of any kind online, but there's nothing to stop you from trying.

Even though the market for Internet advertising is tough to crack, you still might want to investigate selling banner ads on your Web pages. If you'd like to create an ad-supported site, look at some of the affiliate programs that can feed a variety of banner ads to your site, including ADPUSH (www.adpush.net), CyberBounty (www.cyberbounty.com), and LinkShare (www.linkshare.com). Instead of paying you for ad space on your site, they pay a commission when users click through their banner ads—or, alternately, when users click through and then actually buy something at the linked site. There aren't any guarantees, but it's possible to earn some bucks with the right ads for your visitors.

Personally, I use Google's AdSense program and I've found it works very well. It's maintenance free and easy to implement, and you can make pretty good money. You'll have to apply to run Google ads, and most personal sites are turned down, but if you're approved you'll find it provides very palatable text ads that are easy to incorporate into your site and that are usually related to the content of your pages. Check it out for yourself at www.google.com/adsense/.

By the way, some personal home page communities forbid advertising on member pages. Check with your Web site host before signing up for any advertising services.

SOFTWARE OF THE WEEK

Macromedia Dreamweaver MX is the site-building tool of choice for many professional Web designers. It does everything you need to create pro-level Web sites, and features rich CSS support. Buy it for $399 from www.macromedia.com.

August 8, 2005

MONDAY

THIS WEEK'S FOCUS: TROUBLESHOOTING

ON THIS DAY: REFRIGERATOR PATENTED (1899)

On August 8, 1899, A.T. Marshall of Brockton, Massachusetts, received a patent for the refrigerator. It took until 1911 for the first home refrigerator to appear, manufactured by the General Electric company.

Related Web site: www.historychannel.com/exhibits/modern/fridge.html

BASIC TROUBLESHOOTING TIPS

No matter what kind of computer-related problem you're experiencing, there are six basic steps you should take to track down the cause of the problem. Here they are:

1. Check for user errors—something *you've* done wrong. Maybe you've clicked the wrong button, pressed the wrong key, or plugged something into the wrong jack or port. Retrace your steps and try to duplicate your problem. Chances are the problem won't recur if you don't make the same mistake twice.

2. Check that everything is plugged in to the proper place, and that the PC itself is getting power. Take special care to ensure that all your cables are *securely* connected—loose connections can cause all sorts of strange results!

3. Be sure that you have the latest versions installed for all the software on your system. While you're at it, be sure you have the latest versions of device drivers installed for all the peripherals on your system.

4. Run the appropriate Windows diagnostic tools. If you have them, use third-party tools as well.

5. Try to isolate the problem by *when* and *how* it occurs. Walk through each step of the startup process to see if you can identify which driver or service might be causing the problem.

6. When all else fails, call in professional help. That means contacting a technical support line or taking your machine into the shop. Don't be embarrassed; if you need professional help, go get it!

And, above all else, *don't panic!* Keep your wits about you and proceed logically, and you can probably find what's causing your problem—and fix it.

PC GADGET OF THE WEEK

Instead of using a simple external hard drive or backup cartridge, the Mirra Personal Server is a Linux-based server that provides continuous hands-free backup of all your computer's data. You connect the Personal Server to your network hub or router or hook it up to the Internet to share files with other users. It's available in 80GB ($399), 120GB ($499), and 250GB ($749) versions; learn more at www.mirra.com.

THIS WEEK'S FOCUS: TROUBLESHOOTING

ON THIS DAY: NETSCAPE GOES PUBLIC (1995)

The Internet boom began on August 9, 1995, when Netscape Communications Corporation—founded just 16 months prior by James Clark and Marc Andreessen—went public. Initial shares were offered at $29, and the stock's value reached $75 on the first day of trading, making Netscape the biggest IPO in history.

Related Web site: wp.netscape.com/company/about/backgrounder.html

USING WINDOWS TROUBLESHOOTERS

Windows includes several built-in utilities, called *troubleshooters*, that can walk through various problems with your system. These troubleshooters are like wizards, in that you're led step-by-step through a series of questions. All you have to do is answer the interactive questions in the troubleshooter, and you'll be led to the probable solution to your problem.

In most cases, Windows troubleshooters can help you diagnose and fix common system problems. It's a good idea to try the troubleshooters before you pick up the phone and dial Microsoft's Technical Support line or start trying to track down problems manually.

To run a troubleshooter from Windows XP, open the Help and Support Center and click the Fixing a Problem link. When the next page appears, click the link for the type of problem you're having, and then click the link to start a specific troubleshooter.

To run a troubleshooter in earlier versions of Windows, click the Start button and select Help. When the Windows Help window appears, select the Contents tab and select Troubleshooting, and then select Windows Troubleshooters. Select the troubleshooter for your specific problem in the left pane; the troubleshooter itself will be displayed in the right pane.

Once you launch the troubleshooter, it starts asking you a bunch of questions. Answer to the best of your ability, follow the resulting suggestions, and you're well on your way to fixing the problem at hand.

DOWNLOAD OF THE WEEK

Madboot is a freeware boot disk creator especially for upgrading and troubleshooting older PCs. It features two-click hard drive formatting, partition management, BIOS cleaning, and Windows installation. Download it for free from www.madboot.com.

August 10, 2005

WEDNESDAY

THIS WEEK'S FOCUS: **TROUBLESHOOTING**

ON THIS DAY: **LEO FENDER BORN (1909)**

Leo Fender, born on this day in 1909, manufactured the first mass-produced solid-body electric guitar, the Fender Broadcaster (later renamed the Telecaster). In 1954 he introduced the Stratocaster, which had a contoured double-cutaway body with three (as opposed to two) single-coil pickups and a revolutionary string-bending (tremolo) unit. Today, Fender Guitars remain one of the most widely used guitars by artists from all musical genres.

Related Web site: www.fender.com

UNDOING WINDOWS PROBLEMS WITH SYSTEM RESTORE

Perhaps the best course of action when your system acts up—especially after you've performed an upgrade—is to use Microsoft's System Restore utility (Window Me and XP).

System Restore actively monitors your system and notes any changes that are made when you install new applications. Each time it notes a change, it automatically creates what it calls a restore point. A *restore point* is a "snapshot" of the Windows Registry and selected system files just before the new application is installed. Just to be safe, System Restore also creates a new restore point after every 10 hours of system use. You also can chose to manually create a new restore point at any point in time. This is a good idea whenever you make any major system change, such as installing a new peripheral or piece of hardware.

To set a manual restore point, click the Start menu, and then select All Programs > Accessories > System Tools > System Restore. When the System Restore window opens, select Create a Restore Point and click Next. You'll be prompted to enter a description for this new restore point. Do this, and then click the Create button.

If something in your system goes bad, you can run System Restore to set things right. Pick a restore point before the problem occurred (such as right before a new installation), and System Restore will then undo any changes made to monitored files since the restore point was created. It also replaces the current Registry with the one captured at the restore point. This will restore your system to its pre-installation working condition.

When the process is complete, your system should be back in tip-top shape. Because System Restore only monitors system files and Registry settings, you can't use it to restore changed or damaged data files. For complete protection, you'll still need to back up your important data files manually.

MAC GADGET OF THE WEEK

If you need all the hard disk space you can get—and price is no object—you want the LaCie Bigger Disk Extreme. Externally, it looks a lot like its smaller sibling the Big Disk, but inside it offers a whopping 1.6 *terrabytes* of storage in a RAID 0 array. Buy it for an equally whopping $2,199 at www.lacie.com.

THIS WEEK'S FOCUS: TROUBLESHOOTING

ON THIS DAY: STEVE WOZNIAK BORN (1950)

Stephen Wozniak (a.k.a. the Woz) was born on this date in 1950. Woz, a University of California (Berkeley) drop-out, joined with pal Steve Jobs to build the first Apple computer, and to co-found the Apple Computer company.

Related Web site: www.woz.org

MANAGING WINDOWS DRIVERS

For any piece of hardware to work with Windows, Windows has to install and configure a device driver file. Windows includes drivers for most popular hardware devices. If you have a newer or less widely used peripheral, however, the manufacturer might have to provide its own drivers for Windows to use.

When you want to review your various hardware settings and—if necessary—update your driver files, you use Windows Device Manager. You also can use the Device Manager to determine which devices might have conflicts or other problems.

When you open the Device Manager, any resource conflict on your system will be highlighted within the problematic Class group. If there is a problem with a specific device, right-click that device and select Properties from the pop-up menu. This displays the Properties dialog box. When you select the General tab you'll see a message indicating the basic problem and the steps Windows recommends to solve the problem. The message might also display a problem code and number that can be useful when consulting with a technical support specialist—or prompt you to launch a troubleshooter for the device that is showing a problem.

To update a device driver, select the Driver tab in the Properties dialog box, and then click the Update Driver button. When the Hardware Update Wizard appears, select where you want to search for an upgraded driver. If you have new driver software from your hardware's manufacturer, check the Install From a List or Specific Location option, and then insert the disk or CD-ROM and follow the onscreen instructions to install the specific driver. If you'd rather have Windows search for a better driver, check the Install the Software Automatically option.

By the way, you can always search for new and updated drivers at the device manufacturer's Web site.

WEB SITE OF THE WEEK

If you're having troubles with Windows, Internet Explorer, or any Microsoft application, the Microsoft Knowledge Base should be the first place to check. Nine times out of ten, I find the answer to my problem with a quick keyword search. You can search the Knowledge Base for free at the Microsoft Help and Support Web site (support.microsoft.com).

THIS WEEK'S FOCUS: TROUBLESHOOTING

ON THIS DAY: IBM PERSONAL COMPUTER INTRODUCED (1981)

The original IBM Personal Computer was introduced on this date in 1981. The model 5150 sold for $1,565 and ran Microsoft's new PC DOS operating system. Backed by the IBM name, it made computing "safe" for businesses, and ushered in the personal computer revolution.

Related Web site: www.ibm.com

FIXING BIG PROBLEMS WITH SYSTEM INFORMATION

If your problem is so major that you can't fix it with the troubleshooters or the Device Manager, you need to turn to the System Information tool. You launch it by clicking Start > All Programs > Accessories > System Tools > System Information.

The left pane of the System Information window displays information about the five key parts of your system: Hardware Resources, Components, Software Environment, Internet Settings, and Applications. Click the + next to one of the categories to display additional subcategories. When you highlight a specific subcategory, information about that topic appears in the right pane.

System Information is particularly useful for finding device conflicts. Open the Hardware Resources category and select Conflicts/Sharing. The right pane now displays a list of all shared IRQs—one of which is probably causing your current problem. Identify the problem IRQ, and then use the Device Manager to either reconfigure or reinstall the device to use a different IRQ.

Windows also uses System Information as a kind of gateway to a number of other system utilities, accessible from the Tools menu. Some of these "hidden" utilities are a bit technical in terms of what they monitor or do, but if you're having problems with some new piece of hardware you've installed, you'll probably find at least some of these utilities useful when you go to troubleshoot your problem.

Speaking of these "hidden" tools, Dr. Watson is one that experienced users will probably be familiar with, and for good reason—it essentially takes a snapshot of your system whenever a system fault occurs, which aids in the diagnosis of tricky problems. It works by intercepting software faults and identifying the software that failed. In some cases, Dr. Watson will diagnosis the problem and offer a suggested course of action.

PORTABLE GADGET OF THE WEEK

PhoneLabs's Dock-N-Talk is the perfect gadget if you want to completely get rid of traditional land-line phone service. Dock your cell phone in the Dock-N-Talk, and then use your normal home phones (corded or cordless) to make and receive calls via your cellular phone service. Buy it for $139.99 at www.phonelabs.com.

August 13, 2005

SATURDAY

THIS WEEK'S FOCUS: **TROUBLESHOOTING**

ON THIS DAY: FELIX WANKEL BORN (1902)

Felix Wankel was born on August 13, 1902. Wankel was a German engineer and the inventor of the Wankel rotary engine, the first rotary internal combustion engine.

Related Web site: travel.howstuffworks.com/rotary-engine.htm

EDITING THE WINDOWS REGISTRY

The Windows Registry is a huge database that holds the majority of your system's configuration information. It contains all the properties you set via the Control Panel, settings for each of the applications installed on your system, and configuration information for all your system's hardware and peripherals.

Most of the time you won't need to bother with the Registry. However, there will come the occasion when you experience a particularly vexing system problem that can be fixed only by editing a particular value in the Registry. You do this by using the Registry Editor utility. You start Registry Editor by clicking the Start button and selecting Run; enter `regedit` in the Open box, and then click OK.

The left pane of the Registry Editor window displays the different parameters or settings, called *keys*, many of which have a variety of subkeys. The right pane displays the values, or configuration information, for each key or subkey. You edit a particular value by highlighting the subkey in the left pane and then double-clicking the value in the right pane. This displays the Edit Value (or Edit String) window. Enter a new value in the Value Data box, and then click OK.

To add a new value to a subkey, right-click the subkey and select one of the New, Value options from the pop-up menu. Type a name for the new value, and then double-click the value to display the Edit Value (or Edit String) window. Enter the new value in the Value Data box, and then click OK.

Editing the Registry is a tricky proposition, particularly because all settings are changed *as you make the changes*. There is no "save" command in the Registry Editor, nor is there an "undo" command. And, if you do something wrong, you could make your system totally inoperable. For that reason, you should edit the Registry only if it's absolutely necessary to correct an otherwise hard-to-fix problem—and you should set a System Restore point before attempting any edits.

FACT OF THE WEEK

According to Netimperative, more than half the computer users in the U.K. fail to change their passwords regularly. The study indicates that the majority of PC users choose passwords which are easy to remember, and therefore easy to unravel. Around 42% of computer users choose a loved one's name as their password, while 12% pick their birthdays and nearly 10% their favorite football team.

August 14, 2005

SUNDAY

THIS WEEK'S FOCUS: TROUBLESHOOTING

ON THIS DAY: WIFFLE BALL INVENTED (1953)

The wiffle ball was invented on this date in 1953. It was created by David Nelson Mullany, Sr., for his 13-year-old son David, Jr.; he cut holes in a hard plastic ball of Coty perfume packaging, with the hopes of producing a toy ball that wouldn't break windows and would curve in flight in a novel way.

Related Web site: www.wiffleball.net

STARTING WINDOWS IN SAFE MODE

When Windows won't start normally, you have a big problem. The challenge is getting into Windows to fix what's wrong when you can't even start your computer. The solution is deceptively simple; you have to hijack your computer before Windows gets hold of it, and force it to start without whatever is causing the problem.

You hijack your computer by watching the screen as your computer boots up, and pressing the F8 key just before Windows starts to load. When you press F8 your computer will display the Windows startup menu. From this menu, select the Last Known Good Configuration option. This restarts your computer using the Windows Registry information and drivers that were saved the last time you shut down your system—presumably before your system got screwed up.

If this doesn't put things right, you should reboot again, press F8 again, and this time select Safe Mode from the startup menu. In fact, Windows will often revert to Safe mode itself if it encounters major problems while loading.

Safe mode is a special mode of operation that loads Windows in a minimal configuration, without a bunch of pesky device drivers. This means your display will be low-resolution VGA, and you won't be able to use a lot of your peripherals (such as your modem or your printer). But Windows will load, which it might not have, otherwise.

Safe mode is a great mode for troubleshooting because Windows still works and you can make whatever changes you need to make to get it up and running again in normal mode. Once in Safe mode, you can look for device conflicts, restore incorrect or corrupted device drivers, troubleshoot your startup with the System Configuration Utility, or restore your system to a prior working configuration using the System Restore utility. Fix what's wrong, and then reboot your system again—hopefully into the Normal mode, with everything working fine.

SOFTWARE OF THE WEEK

Symantec Go Back is a utility that undoes a lot of PC problems; it can restore practically everything on your hard disk, including deleted files. Buy it for $39.95 at www.symantec.com.

August 15, 2005
MONDAY

THIS WEEK'S FOCUS: BACK TO SCHOOL

ON THIS DAY: DENTAL CHAIR PATENTED (1848)

What did they use before the dental chair was invented? Fortunately, we don't have to worry about it, because M. Waldo Hanchett of Syracuse, New York received a patent for his dental chair on this date in 1848.

Related Web site: www.collectmedicalantiques.com/dentistry2.html

MAKING LEARNING FUN

Now that school's ready to start, it's time to focus our attention on learning. But there's nothing that says learning can't be fun, so let's look at a few Web sites that are both educational and enjoyable for kids from kindergarten to high school.

- **Art Safari (artsafari.moma.org)**—Art-related drawing and writing activities, from the Museum of Modern Art.

- **Book Adventure (www.bookadventure.com)**—This site recommends new books to read, based on books you've liked in the past, and includes quizzes and other activities for kids in grade K–8.

- **BrainPop (www.brainpop.com)**—Entertaining online movies that explain all sorts of scientific stuff.

- **Discovering Dinosaurs (dinosaurs.eb.com)**—An extremely comprehensive dinosaur site, covering dino environment, anatomy, behavior, and physiology; from the folks at the Encyclopedia Britannica.

- **iKnowthat.com (www.iknowthat.com)**—Animated multimedia learning games and activities for geography, math, reading, and art.

- **KidsEdge.com (www.kidsedge.com)**—Online learning games and contests, as well as early childhood education tools for improving math and reading skills; organized into grades pre-K to K, 1–2, and 3–4.

- **NASA Kids (kids.msfc.nasa.gov)**—Another official NASA site for kids; information about space, rockets, airplanes, and more.

- **NGAkids (www.nga.gov/kids/)**—An introduction to the world of art, for kids, by the National Gallery of Art.

- **spaceKids (www.spacekids.com)**—Space and science news, games, polls, contests, and more.

PC GADGET OF THE WEEK

Tired of digging around behind your PC to connect all your peripherals? Then check out FrontX, a panel that moves selected ports to the front of your PC; it installs into any 5.25" drive bay. And the really neat thing about FrontX is that you can have the company custom-make any combination of ports. Configurations start at $13.60; check out www.frontx.com for ordering details.

August 16, 2005

TUESDAY

THIS WEEK'S FOCUS: BACK TO SCHOOL

ON THIS DAY: VERTICAL LOOP ROLLER COASTER PATENTED (1898)

On August 16, 1898, Edwin Prescott received a patent for his elliptical vertical-looping roller coaster. He built the ride—called the Loop-the-Loop—in 1901, at Coney Island. As impressive as the Loop-the-Loop was, the public was more inclined to watch than ride; the only reason it made money is that the park charged admission to the viewing area.

Related Web site: www.ultimaterollercoaster.com

HOMEWORK HELP ONLINE

One of the primary reasons for K–12 students to go online is to do research for school reports and get help with their homework. Here's a good starter list of sites your kids can use when it's homework time; most of these sites let you either browse through a list of topics or search the site for specific types of help.

- **ALA Resources for Parents, Teens, and Kids (www.ala.org/parents/)**—A compendium of terrific sites and services from the American Library Association. Includes Cool Sites for Kids and KidsConnect, an online question-answering service for K–12 students.

- **DiscoverySchool.com (school.discovery.com)**—From the folks at the Discovery Channel, this site includes a wealth of educational resources, including Webmath, a terrific learning aid for general math and algebra students.

- **Fact Monster (www.factmonster.com)**—A terrific information resource for kids; includes an online dictionary, encyclopedia, and homework help. Go to www.factmonster.com/homework/ for the Homework Center.

- **Grammar Lady (www.grammarlady.com)**—The Grammar Lady (a.k.a. Mary Newton Bruder) answers your questions about correct grammar usage.

- **High School Hub (www.highschoolhub.org)**—This site offers homework help for high schoolers, as well as reference resources, learning activities, and other information.

- **Kid Info (www.kidinfo.com)**—Homework help and links to curriculum guides, lesson plans, reference sites, and teaching aids—organized by specific curriculum.

- **MadSci Network (www.madsci.org)**—Focuses on K–12 science education; scientists answer questions submitted by users, and all the answers are archived at this site.

- **Word Central (www.wordcentral.com)**—Access Merriam Webster's student dictionary, a kid's Word of the Day, and various word games.

DOWNLOAD OF THE WEEK

BookCAT is a shareware program that catalogs and manages all sizes of book libraries. It tells you what you have, where it is (including books lent out), and the total value of your collection. Try it for free, or buy it for $39 at www.fnprg.com/bookcat/.

August 17, 2005
WEDNESDAY

THIS WEEK'S FOCUS: BACK TO SCHOOL

ON THIS DAY: PIERRE DE FERMAT BORN (1601)

French mathematician Pierre de Fermat was born on August 17, 1691. The founder of the modern theory of numbers, he anticipated differential calculus and proposed the famous Fermat's Last Theorem.

Related Web site: www-gap.dcs.st-and.ac.uk/~history/Mathematicians/Fermat.html

ONLINE LIBRARIES

Another good source for homework assistance is the online version of the traditional library. Many real-world libraries have their own Web sites that let you search for books on hand; more advanced library sites have some or all of their individual collections online, in the form of digitized texts or full-scale multimedia exhibits. There are also a number of Internet-only libraries that offer traditional library-like collections for Web users.

Here are some of the best library-related sites on the Web:

- **Berkeley Digital Library SunSITE** (sunsite.berkeley.edu)—A vast repository of collections, research tools, and archival information from the University of Berkeley.

- **Internet Public Library** (www.ipl.org)—"The first public library of the Internet," with a huge collection of online reference works, hosted by the University of Michigan.

- **Library of Congress** (lcweb.loc.gov)—America's national library online, complete with online collections, texts of many of the Library's publications, and access to bibliographic catalogs and legislative information (THOMAS).

- **LibDex** (www.libdex.com)—Lets you browse the catalogs of more than 18,000 libraries.

- **LibrarySpot** (www.libraryspot.com)—The information sweet spot of the best library and reference sites on the Web, a gateway to more than 2,500 libraries around the world.

- **New York Public Library Digital Library Collections** (digital.nypl.org)—Numerous online collections and exhibitions from the NYPL.

- **Smithsonian Institution Libraries** (www.sil.si.edu)—Digital collections, electronic journals, and other online services from the Smithsonian Institution.

- **World Wide Web Virtual Library** (www.vlib.org)—The oldest catalog on the Web, created by Web pioneer Tim Berners-Lee—and the model for Yahoo!'s category-based directory.

MAC GADGET OF THE WEEK

High-end graphics professionals need the best monitors available, and LaCie's electron-blue IV models more than meet that mark. Both 19" ($379) and 22" ($699) models are available, from www.lacie.com.

August 18, 2005
THURSDAY

THIS WEEK'S FOCUS: BACK TO SCHOOL

ON THIS DAY: HEWLETT-PACKARD INCORPORATED (1947)

Stanford University classmates Bill Hewlett and Dave Packard founded the Hewlett-Packard company in 1939, and incorporated it on August 18, 1947. The company's first product, built in a Palo Alto garage, was an audio oscillator, and one of HP's first customers was Walt Disney Studios, which purchased eight oscillators to develop and test an innovative sound system for the movie *Fantasia*.

Related Web site: www.hp.com

LAPTOPS FOR COLLEGE

If your child is going off to college, chances are the purchase of a laptop computer is in order. Before you rush off to CompUSA, you should check with the college about your computer purchase. Many colleges offer deals on computers, and the bursar should be able to tell you what kinds of features a computer should have. You should also work through the following checklist of things to consider:

- Mac or PC? Some schools have preferences.

- Is there is a campus-wide network? If there is, what kind? If it's Ethernet, you'll need a network card; if it's Wi-Fi, ditto on the wireless card.

- Do the dorms have printers, or will your child have access to a network printer somewhere on campus? If so, your freshman won't need to bring one.

- How do professors like material handed in: printed, floppy, CD, DVD?

- Ask about the theft rate. If it's high (and it probably is), get a laptop lock.

- Ask if there is a student discount program. If there is, you might want to buy the laptop through the school.

If Windows is the preferred operating system, you probably want a Centrino laptop, which means it contains Intel's new wireless technology. (Many schools are rapidly adopting Wi-Fi, making the entire campus a giant wireless hotspot.) Most Centrino laptops will be around $1,500 and weigh 3–4 lbs. Some good brands are Toshiba, Sony, Dell, and Gateway.

WEB SITE OF THE WEEK

If you're sending a student off to college, check out CNET's Tech Specs of the Top 50 Universities. Here you'll find what technology each college supports, and the school's recommended and required gear. Sorry for the long URL, but here it is: www.cnet.com/4520-9693_1-5143577-1 .html?tag=arw.

THIS WEEK'S FOCUS: BACK TO SCHOOL

ON THIS DAY: GORDON BELL BORN (1934)

Computer industry pioneer Gordon Bell was born on this date in 1934. He spent 23 years (1960–1983) at Digital Equipment Corporation as Vice President of Research and Development, where he was responsible for all of Digital's groundbreaking products. He was the architect of the legendary PDP-6, and led the development of DEC's VAX and the VAX Computing Environment. Today, he is a senior researcher in Microsoft's Media Presence Research Group, a part of the Bay Area Research Center.

Related Web site: research.microsoft.com/users/GBell/

CHOOSING A COLLEGE

If you're in high school and trying to decide which college to attend, the Internet is your best resource. There are numerous sites where you can search for information about specific colleges, as well as search for any available financial aid. Here's just a partial list:

- **Campus Tours** (www.campustours.com)—Online virtual tours of thousands of college campuses, complete with interactive maps, college Webcams, QuickTime VR tours, campus movies, and pictures.

- **College Board Online** (www.collegeboard.org)—The official Web site of the nonprofit college organization that sponsors the SAT; includes a College Search database of more than 3,200 two- and four-year colleges, a Scholarship Search service, a Career Search service, and online prep for the SAT.

- **CollegeBound Network** (www.collegebound.net)—A comprehensive resource for getting into and succeeding in college.

- **CollegeNET** (www.collegenet.com)—Offers school searches by major, location, and tuition.

- **Colleges.com** (www.colleges.com)—Helps high school students choose a college or university, and then gain admittance.

- **CollegeSurfing.com** (www.collegesurfing.com)—From the CollegeBound Network, streaming videos, overviews, and maps from colleges across the U.S.

- **GoCollege** (www.gocollege.com)—Offers a college search based on desired major, test scores, class rank, location, and tuition; lets you apply to 850 colleges directly online.

In addition, almost every college has its own Web site. These sites often include a lot of good information about the school, the faculty, the classes, and the campus.

PORTABLE GADGET OF THE WEEK

For those of you who can't bear to leave the Internet behind, take it with you with Abacus's Wrist Net Internet Watch. This watch employs Microsoft's MSN Direct service ($9.99/month subscription) to deliver news, weather, sports, and stock information, relayed from the Internet via FM signals. Buy the watch for $129 at www.abacuswatches.com.

THIS WEEK'S FOCUS: BACK TO SCHOOL

ON THIS DAY: TELEVISION SYSTEM PATENTED (1930)

On August 20, 1930, Philo Farnsworth received a U.S. patent for his television system. Farnsworth's experimentation began in 1926 in San Francisco, and he established Farnsworth Television Incorporated in 1929. The first crude television image was created from the Farnsworth system when a photograph of a young woman was transmitted on September 7, 1927. In 1931, Farnsworth moved to Philadelphia to establish a television department for Philco.

Related Web site: www.mztv.com

SURVIVING ON CAMPUS

Once you're admitted to a college, life on campus can be a lot of fun—and a lot of work. Not only do students today have access to the campus library, they also have access to all the resources of the Web to help them advance in their studies—and to make it through four years of college without going crazy or flunking out.

There are several sites that specialize in providing study aids and advice to college students.

- **College Student Survival Guide (www.college-student-guide.com)**—A practical guide to college living; includes advice on finding a roommate, buying and using cell phones, buying and selling textbooks, and more.

- **College Survival Skills (www.clemson.edu/collegeskills/)**—From Clemson University, a guide to taking notes, studying, interacting with instructors, and taking tests.

- **College Tutor Study Guide (www.amelox.com/study.htm)**—An excellent guide for improving your study habits.

- **CollegeFreshmen.Net (www.collegefreshmen.net)**—Advice and information for surviving your first year of college.

- **Dr. Mom's Guide to College (www.lions.odu.edu/~kkilburn/dr_mom_home.htm)**—A mother who's also a college professor offers some real-world guidance to incoming college students.

- **Real World University (www.rwuniversity.com)**—Site designed to help students succeed in college by helping them identify and pursue their purpose, strengthen their character, and overcome life's obstacles.

- **The Semester.com (www.thesemester.com)**—A resource for students studying for mid-term and final exams.

- **University Survival Guide (www.uni-survival-guide.freeserve.co.uk/survival.html)**—From the U.K., a semi-humorous guide to surviving your university years.

FACT OF THE WEEK

Who *really* provides technical support? According to the National School Boards Foundation, 54% of U.S. schools rely on students to provide technical support for their computer systems. In 43% of the 811 school districts surveyed, students troubleshoot for hardware, software, and other problems, and in 39% of the districts, students are tasked with setting up equipment and wiring.

August 21, 2005

SUNDAY

THIS WEEK'S FOCUS: BACK TO SCHOOL

ON THIS DAY: VOYAGER 2 APPROACHES NEPTUNE'S MOON (1989)

On August 21, 1989, the U.S. space probe Voyager 2 fired its thrusters to bring it closer to Neptune's mysterious moon Triton. Launched in 1977, the Voyager 2 initially explored Jupiter and Saturn, and then went on to explore Uranus and Neptune.

Related Web site: voyager.jpl.nasa.gov

AFTER SCHOOL

After class, the Web is a terrific source of community for today's college students. There are numerous Web sites catering to the college lifestyle, most featuring youth-oriented news, music reviews, chat rooms, and message boards.

Here are some of the most popular online student hangouts:

- **CampusNut.com (www.campusnut.com)**—A humorous guide to college life.
- **CampusParty.com (www.campusparty.com)**—A high-tech guide to parties, concerts, festivals, and other collegiate social events.
- **CollegeClub.com (www.collegeclub.com)**—A general college portal, featuring news, career information, entertainment, contests, chat, email, Webcams, and more.
- **Greekspot.com (www.greekspot.com)**—A resource to fraternities, sororities, and everything Greek.
- **Hotbeast.com (www.hotbeast.com)**—A college communications portal, offering email, message boards, and chat.

- **Kollegeville (www.kollegeville.com)**—A "kool, kontent-driven, and kommercial-free" online magazine offering stories of interest to "kollege kids."
- **ShakesBeer.com (www.shakesbeer.com)**—An online hangout for college kids.
- **Student Center (www.studentcenter.org)**—An after-school hangout for both high school and college kids. Lots of games, forums, photo albums, and such.
- **Student.com (www.student.com)**—By college students, for college students—includes articles on movies, music, television, sex, health, going out, jobs, travel, sports, and more.

SOFTWARE OF THE WEEK

Math & Science Excelerator is a collection of four educational CD-ROMs for kids in grades 3–6. This software makes learning fun, but with the emphasis on *learning*. Also check out the company's other products: Numbers & Letters Excelerator, Phonics & Reading Excelerator, Math & Reading Excelerator, Language Excelerator, Middle School Excelerator, and Middle & High School Math Excelerator. Buy them for $29.99 each at www.topics-ent.com.

THIS WEEK'S FOCUS: MORE WINDOWS

ON THIS DAY: AEROSOL SPRAY PATENTED (1939)

On August 22, 1939, the first U.S. patent for dispensing liquids under pressure from a disposable container was issued to Julius Seth Kahn of New York City. The patent was titled "Apparatus For Mixing a Liquid With a Gas," but was the predecessor of the aerosol spray can; in Kahn's case, the patent more particularly specified a use for whipping cream "by discharging the cream and gas mixture through a constricted orifice."

Related Web page: www.aaar.org

REVIVING WINDOWS EXPLORER— AND THE DOS PROMPT— IN WINDOWS XP

In pre-XP versions of Windows, Windows Explorer was a file-management tool that displayed files in a hierarchical "tree." In Windows XP, however, Windows Explorer no longer exists. That is, there's no icon for it anywhere, and no place for it on the Start menu.

That's because the old Windows Explorer hierarchical tree can now be displayed within My Computer—although Microsoft doesn't really tell you this. If you want to view My Computer in a Windows Explorer-like view, all you have to do is click the Folders button on the My Computer toolbar. This slides the activity center pane out of the way and replaces it with a "file tree" that lists all the devices, folders, and files on your system. In other words, you get Windows Explorer back.

Many users prefer this hierarchical approach to managing folders and files because it gives them two panes worth of folders and files to work with. The left Folders pane contains all the devices and folders on your system, in a tree-like structure. The right pane displays the contents of any item selected in the Folders pane.

In the Folders pane, drives or folders that contain other folders have a + beside them. Click the + to expand the folders. When the drive or folder is fully expanded, the + changes to a –; click the – to collapse the contents again.

And if you really want to go old school, you can still execute DOS commands in Windows XP, even though XP isn't built on the MS-DOS engine like Windows 9X/Me was. To keep all us command-prompt guys happy, Windows XP includes a DOS-emulation utility that you can access by selecting Start > All Programs > Accessories > Command Prompt. The resulting Command Prompt window looks pretty much like the old MS-DOS window in Windows 9X/Me, and works pretty much the same way, too.

PC GADGET OF THE WEEK

If you want, to totally break away from the desktop, you need a mouse that doesn't need a desk. The Gyration Ultra GT mouse works by waving it around, more or less. It incorporates motion-sensing technology—actually, a miniature gyroscope—that lets you use natural hand movements to control your cursor. Buy it for $79.99 at www.gyration.com.

August 23, 2005

TUESDAY

THIS WEEK'S FOCUS: MORE WINDOWS

ON THIS DAY: FIRST SHIP-TO-SHORE WIRELESS MESSAGE (1889)

On August 23, 1889, the first ship-to-shore wireless message was sent from the U.S. Lightship No. 70, sailing miles out to sea, to a crowd assembled at the Cliff House in San Francisco. The message, "Sherman is sighted," announced the long-awaited arrival of the U.S. Army troopship Sherman from the battlefields of the Spanish-American War.

Related Web site: www.marconicalling.com

CHANGING THE WAY FILES ARE DISPLAYED IN WINDOWS XP

You can choose to view the contents of a folder in a variety of ways. From within the My Documents folder, click the Views button in the toolbar and choose from Thumbnails (showing a picture of the file's contents—great for image files), Tiles (big icons), Icons (small icons), Lists (filenames only with no details), or Details (filenames with selected details).

If you choose Details view, you can select which details are displayed. Select View > Choose Details to display the Detail Settings dialog box. Check those settings you want to display, and use the Move Up and Move Down keys to place the settings in the order you want. Click OK to lock in your new configuration.

However you display your files, you can sort them in a number of ways. To do this, select View > Arrange Icons By, and then choose to sort by Name, Size, Type, or Modified. Or, if you're viewing your files in Details view, you can manually sort your files by any setting you've chosen to display by clicking the top of a column.

Windows XP also lets you display files and folders in similar groups. To see what grouping looks like, just look at the My Computer folder, which groups items by device type with a title and thin line above each group. If you like this type of organization, you can apply similar grouping to any and all your folders.

To turn on grouping, select View > Arrange Icons By, and then check the Show In Groups option. Windows now groups your files and folders by the criteria you used to sort those items. For example, if you sorted your files by date, they'll now be grouped by date—actually, by Today, Last Week, Last Month, and so on. If you sorted your files by type, they'll be grouped by file type. And so on, for all the different ways of sorting your files.

DOWNLOAD OF THE WEEK

Registry Mechanic is a shareware utility that lets you safely clean and repair the Windows Registry. It repairs invalid Registry entries, removes orphaned references, and scans for invalid program shortcuts. Try it for free, or buy it for $29.95 at www.winguides.com/regmech/.

August 24, 2005

WEDNESDAY

THIS WEEK'S FOCUS: MORE WINDOWS

ON THIS DAY: WINDOWS 95 RELEASED (1995)

Arguably the most hyped event in the history of personal computing took place on August 24, 1995, when Microsoft released Windows 95. Long lines of the faithful lined up outside stores for the midnight release, and more than one million copies were sold in the first four days. Microsoft created memorable television ads for the new software by reportedly spending $12 million to license "Start Me Up" by The Rolling Stones.

Related Web site: www.computerhope.com/win95.htm

PERSONALIZING THE SEND TO MENU

The pop-up menu that appears when you right-click a file or folder in Windows contains the Send To menu, which is one of the fastest ways to send a file from one place to another. You can use the Send To menu to send a file to another disk, to another folder, to another user via e-mail, or to a printer for printing.

Because using the Send To menu is a quick way to work with files, you might want to add other actions to the menu. For example, you might want to create a Send To item for a removable drive or commonly used folder. This way you can right-click a file and use the Send To command to copy the file automatically.

Here's how to add options to the Send To menu:

1. Use My Computer to navigate to the `\Documents and Settings\username\SendTo` folder.
2. Select File > New > Shortcut.
3. When the Create New Shortcut wizard appears, enter the name of the file, folder, or drive you want to add to the Send To menu. (Click the Browse button to search your system for the item.) Click Next to proceed.
4. Enter the name you want to appear on the Send To menu, and then click Finish.

The next time you right-click a file and select Send To, your new item appears in the list of Send To options.

MAC GADGET OF THE WEEK

Put your PowerBook or iBook on a pedestal with Griffin Technology's iCurve. The iCurve is a cool-looking clear plexiglass stand that raises your laptop to eye level, and puts it on a comfortable slant. Buy it for $39.99 at www.griffintechnology.com/products/icurve/.

August 25, 2005
THURSDAY

THIS WEEK'S FOCUS: MORE WINDOWS

ON THIS DAY: FIRST PARACHUTE WEDDING CEREMONY (1940)

On August 25, 1940, one daring couple made the big leap—in more ways than one. Arno Rudolphi and Ann Hayward exchanged their wedding vows seated in the sling of the Coney Island Parachute Jump at the New York World's Fair. They had their first kiss as the parachute was released to start free fall.

Related Web site: www.uspa.org

START UP WINDOWS FASTER

Windows is such a bloated operating system that it takes forever to start up, even on today's super-fast PCs. That's because a ton of drivers, utilities, applets, and the like have to load into system memory every time Windows launches. And the more stuff you have installed on your machine, the longer the boot-up process takes.

Short of moving to Linux, there are a few things you can do to speed up your Windows load time. Here are some of my favorite tips:

- Remove unnecessary startup programs. Many applications, when you first install them, make the decision to launch themselves on Windows startup, typically by adding themselves to Windows' Startup menu. Find out what programs are launching automatically by selecting Start > All Programs > Startup. If you see something you don't want to run automatically, right-click it and delete it.

- Other autolaunch programs launch themselves by writing a new setting into the Windows Registry. There are several keys in the Registry that can contain these auto instructions. In particular, look for entries in the following keys:

    ```
    HKEY_LOCAL_MACHINE\SOFTWARE\Microsoft\
    Windows\CurrentVersion\RUN

    HKEY_USERS\.DEFAULT\SOFTWARE\Microsoft\
    Windows\CurrentVersion\RUN

    HKEY_CURRENT_USER\SOFTWARE\Microsoft\
    Windows\CurrentVersion\RUN
    ```

- Every time you start Windows, it has to load all the fonts you have installed on your system. The more fonts, the longer it takes to load them. Reduce the load by deleting your unused fonts, using the Fonts utility in the Control Panel.

WEB SITE OF THE WEEK

Got a problem with Windows? Then check out the expert information—and the information from the experts—at Annoyances.org. If you can't find a solution in the annoyances archives, ask a question on one of the discussion forums. Check it out at www.annoyances.org.

August 26, 2005

FRIDAY

THIS WEEK'S FOCUS: MORE WINDOWS

ON THIS DAY: CANNON FIRST USED IN BATTLE (1346)

The first cannon was used in battle on this date in 1346. Twenty-two cannons, firing round balls carved from rock, were employed by England's Edward III during the defeat of Philip VI of France at Crécy. These earliest cannons, having no more power than the trebuchet, could not bring down the walls by themselves; their chief effect was strictly psychological.

Related Web site: www.cannon-mania.com

VIEW DETAILED SYSTEM INFORMATION

The Windows Task Manager, which you use to shut down unruly applications, can also be used to view the performance of your system. You open the Task Manager by right-clicking any open portion of the Taskbar, and then selecting Task Manager from the pop-up menu.

The Performance tab is the one that's really interesting—visually, at least. This tab displays graphs of your system CPU and memory usage. It also displays numerical information about various system parameters, such as physical and kernel memory. It's a fun little tab to watch, if nothing else.

For even more detailed information about your system, check out the tools available in Windows XP's Help and Support Center. There are two tools here, each offering a different level of system detail.

Begin by opening the Help and Support Center, clicking the Use Tools link (in the Pick a Task section), and then clicking the My Computer Information link. The My Computer Information tool lets you look at four different reports, for general system information, system hardware and software status, installed hardware, and installed Microsoft hardware.

The second tool, Advanced System Information, offers five different options. You can view detailed system information (this opens the System Information utility), view running services, view Group Policy settings applied, view the error log, or view information for another computer.

Most users will never access any of these tools, nor will they need to. But if you want to check on your system performance or troubleshoot some sort of Windows-related problem, they could be of use.

PORTABLE GADGET OF THE WEEK

The CAR-100 Bluetooth Car Kit isn't a phone kit for your car, but rather a car for your phone. That is, it's a matchbox-sized toy electric car that can be radio-controlled by any Sony Ericsson phone, using Bluetooth wireless technology. Use the keys on the phone's keypad to control the car, which runs for an hour on a charge. Totally useless, but lots of fun. Buy it for $93 from www.sonyericsson.com.

August 27, 2005

SATURDAY

THIS WEEK'S FOCUS: MORE WINDOWS

ON THIS DAY: MARINER 2 LAUNCHED (1962)

The Mariner 2 space probe was successfully launched on August 27, 1962, sending it on a 3 1/2-month flight to Venus. As it flew by the planet on December 14, 1962, the spacecraft scanned the planet with infrared and microwave radiometers, revealing that Venus has cool clouds and an extremely hot surface.

Related Web site: www.jpl.nasa.gov/missions/past/mariner1-2.html

MANAGE YOUR USER SETTINGS— AND PICTURE

When Windows first starts up, depending on how your system is configured, you might see a list of user names and pictures. You pick your name from the list, enter your password, and then enter Windows.

It's easy enough to add a new user to your machine, assuming that you're logged on as the computer administrator. (If you're the sole user, you're the administrator by default; other users can be set up for either administrator or limited user accounts.) To add a new user, go to the Control Panel and open the User Accounts utility. Then select Create a New Account, enter a name for the account, and select either Computer Administrator or Limited options. Click the Create Account button, and the new user will show up on the main log on screen.

You can also use the User Accounts utility to change any of your user settings—name, password, or picture. When the utility opens, select Change an Account, and then pick an account to change. (Administrators can change any user's account; limited users can only change their own account.)

When the What Do You Want to Change screen appears, select what you want to do: Change the Name, Change the Password, Create a Password (if one doesn't exist, otherwise this option is not visible), Change the Picture, Change the Account Type, or Delete the Account.

I particularly like the ability to customize my log-in picture. Click the Change My Picture option and you see the Pick a New Picture for Your Account screen. You can select one of the stock pictures (soccer ball, butterfly, fish, and so on), or get adventurous and supply a picture of your own. Just click the Browse for More Pictures link, and then use the Open dialog box to browse to and select a new image. Trust me, select a custom picture, and everybody else will think it's super-cool—and want to know how you did it!

FACT OF THE WEEK

The W2KNews Bulletin reports that, as of the end of 2003, 130 million PCs were licensed to run Windows XP; 70% of these were running XP Professional. Incredibly, some 350 million PCs were still running either Windows 9X or Windows NT.

August 28, 2005
SUNDAY

THIS WEEK'S FOCUS: MORE WINDOWS

ON THIS DAY: LOCOMOTIVE RACES HORSE (1830)

The first U.S. steam locomotive was the Tom Thumb, built by Peter Cooper for the Baltimore & Ohio Railroad. To prove that railroads were better than horses for transport, Cooper offered to race the Tom Thumb against a horse on August 28, 1830. The horse won when the Tom Thumb dropped a part and slowed down, but B&O officials were suitably impressed anyway.

Related Web site: www.trainweb.org

WAITING FOR LONGHORN

Sometime in 2006—or maybe 2007—Microsoft will ship the next version of Windows, designed to replace Windows XP. This new version is code-named Longhorn, and looks to be a significant overhaul to the operating system.

Longhorn will look, feel, and act quite a bit different from today's Windows XP. It's a major rewrite, which is why it's taking Microsoft so long to get it out the door. In fact, some of the features currently talked about might not make the cut, especially if Microsoft has a hard schedule to make.

The first difference you'll see is Longhorn's new interface, dubbed Aero. It's a 3D interface that uses a variety of slick visual effects, animation, and transparency to make it easy to distinguish stacked windows on your desktop. Of course, you'll need major hardware horsepower to display all these fancy graphics, but Microsoft is betting you'll have a more powerful PC by the time Longhorn makes it to market.

Longhorn will also include enhanced file search/browse functionality. You'll probably like the Wordwheel search box, which makes it a lot easier to find items on your drive, based on the file's contents.

And those files will be organized a bit differently than in the past. Longhorn is slated to include a new file system called WinFS, which combines the established NTFS file system with a database engine based on SQL Server. This turns the traditional folder metaphor into something resembling a relational database, which facilitates rich data relationships and searching.

The big problem I see with Longhorn (besides the long wait for it) is its probable system requirements. It's likely that most existing PCs won't have the oomph to run the full Longhorn OS, which will make upgrading either problematic or undoable. That means Longhorn might be an OS for new PCs only, which will leave millions of users stuck on the XP (or older) platforms.

SOFTWARE OF THE WEEK

Better Homes and Gardens Home Designer Suite is the ideal software for anyone planning a home design or remodeling project. Everything you need for both interior and exterior design is included. Buy it for $99.99 at www.chiefarchitect.com.

August 29, 2005

MONDAY

THIS WEEK'S FOCUS: COMPUTING FOR KIDS

ON THIS DAY: ASTRONAUT SPEAKS TO AQUANAUT (1965)

Sea and sky got connected on August 29, 1965, when astronaut Gordon Cooper held a conversation with aquanaut M. Scott Carpenter. Copper was aboard Gemini 5, in orbit 100 miles above the Earth; Carpenter was on Sealab II, which was 205 feet below the surface of the Pacific Ocean.

Related Web site: www.sealab.org

FILTERING INAPPROPRIATE CONTENT

The Internet contains an almost limitless supply of information on its tens of billions of Web pages. While most of these pages contain useful information, it's a sad fact that the content of some pages can be quite offensive to some people—and that there are some Internet users who prey on unsuspecting youths.

If you can't trust your children to always click away from inappropriate Web content (and—be honest—you can't), you can choose to install software on your computer that performs filtering functions for all your online sessions. These safe-surfing programs guard against either a preselected list of inappropriate sites or a preselected list of topics—and then block access to sites that meet the selected criteria. Once you have the software installed, your kids won't be able to access the really bad sites on the Web.

The most popular filtering programs include

- Cybersitter (www.cybersitter.com)
- Net Nanny (www.netnanny.com)
- Norton Internet Security (www.symantec.com)
- SurfControl (www.surfcontrol.com)

All of these programs work in a similar fashion, and do an okay job of blocking inappropriate sites. They don't relieve you of the responsibility of monitoring your kids' online activities, but they can help you do the job.

By the way, if you're an America Online subscriber, check out AOL's built-in (and very effective) Parental Controls feature. You can select different filtering options for different AOL screen names, and choose from four age-rated categories—Kids Only (12 and under), Young Teen (13–15), Mature Teen (16–17), and General Access (18. This alone is a good reason for parents to subscribe to the AOL service.

PC GADGET OF THE WEEK

I never thought I'd call a scanner cool, but then Hewlett-Packard introduced the Scanjet 4670. First, the 4670 doesn't lay flat on your desktop—it stands up vertically on its stand, like a picture frame. And the scanner itself is see-through, which turns it into an attractive piece of equipment. To make a scan, you fold open the unit and slip the paper inside. Buy it for $199.99 at www.hp.com.

August 30, 2005

TUESDAY

THIS WEEK'S FOCUS: COMPUTING FOR KIDS

ON THIS DAY: JOHN MAUCHLY BORN (1907)

American physicist and engineer John Mauchly was born on this date in 1907. Mauchly was co-inventer, with J. Presper Eckert, of the Electronic Numerical Integrator and Computer (ENIAC), the first general-purpose electronic computer. Mauchly and Eckert also invented the UNIVAC, America's first commercial computer.

Related Web site: www.library.upenn.edu/exhibits/rbm/mauchly/jwmintro.html

KID-SAFE BROWSERS

Even better than content-filtering software are Web browsers that perform the same filtering function—and that also include built-in links to fun kids' sites. Some of these browsers are paired with safe-surfing content-filtering services, for even greater protection.

The following are the most popular of these kid-safe browsers:

- **ActivatorDesk** (www.dot-kids.com)—An ad-free and pop-up-free browser, complete with a KidGrid list of safe sites for kids. Try it for free or buy it for $49.95.

- **AT Kids Browser** (www.winshare.com/kbindex.htm)—The AT Kids Browser includes built-in filters for inappropriate language, and some fun features just for kids—including the ability to "slime" or blow pages they don't like. Try it for free or buy it for $29.95

- **Crayon Crawler** (www.crayoncrawler.com)—This is a combination browser/email client/online service that offers a variety of parental controls—and blocks the use of other browsers. Try it for free or subscribe to the service for $4.99 per month.

- **SurfMonkey** (www.surfmonkey.com)—A fun-looking browser with built-in links to all the best kids' sites, as well as a integrated safety service to block access to inappropriate content. Downloading is free; you'll pay $3.95 per month to use the SurfMonkey service.

These kid-safe browsers work just like Internet Explorer, but are designed especially for kids. Some even feature simplified kid-friendly interfaces and fun additional features. Take advantage of the free trial offers to see if you like what they offer.

DOWNLOAD OF THE WEEK

Sometime in the near future, Earth is invaded by chickens from another galaxy, bent on revenge against the human race for oppressing earth chickens—and you're the planet's last line of defense. That's the premise behind this fun free-ware update of the venerable Space Invaders game, downloadable for free from www.interactionstudios.com.

August 31, 2005

WEDNESDAY

THIS WEEK'S FOCUS: COMPUTING FOR KIDS

ON THIS DAY: JACK THE RIPPER STRIKES (1888)

Jack the Ripper took his first victim on this date in 1888. The body of Mary Ann "Polly" Nichols, aged 42, was found at Bucks Row, off the Whitechapel Road in London, at 3:40 a.m. on August 31. Hers was the first of five cases involving East End prostitutes, killed with growing ferocity with a knife, and attributed to Jack the Ripper. No suspect was ever clearly identified.

Related Web site: www.casebook.org

KID-SAFE SEARCHING

If you don't want to go to or a special browser, you can at least steer your children to some of the safer sites on the Web. The best of these sites offer kid-safe searching, so that all inappropriate sites are filtered out of the search results.

The best of these kids-safe search and directory sites include

- **AltaVista—AV Family Filter** (www.altavista.com)—Go to the Settings page and click the Family Filter link. You can choose to filter multimedia (image, video, and audio) files only, or to filter all search results.

- **Ask Jeeves Kids** (www.ajkids.com)—A search site just for kids, based on the larger Ask Jeeves site. Also includes a variety of study aids and reference tools.

- (www.dibdabdoo.com)—A fun, safe search directory for younger children. Catalogs about 2 million pages.

- **Family Source** (www.family-source.com)—A searchable directory of family-related resources, with about one million pages indexed.

- **Google SafeSearch** (www.google.com)—This is essentially the standard Google search, but with adult sites filtered out of the results. Go to the Preferences page, and then choose a SafeSearch Filtering option.

- **Yahooligans!** (www.yahooligans.com)—This is my favorite kids' site, period—a great kids' portal, in addition to a kid-friendly directory. Lots of fun sections, including games, music, e-cards, jokes, and the like.

Kids-safe search sites are good to use as the start page for your children's browser because they are launching pads to guaranteed safe content.

MAC GADGET OF THE WEEK

Wacom makes the only Mac-compatible graphics tablets, including the low-cost Graphire3. Along with the pen and tablet, the Graphire3 includes a four-button mouse that glides across the tablet for day-to-day mousing; when you need to draw, just move the mouse out of the way and pick up the included pen. It's a fine tablet for the average user, although professionals will probably prefer Wacom's $199 Intuos2 model. Buy the Graphire3 for just $99 at www.wacom.com.

MORE AUGUST FACTS

August 1

1914 World War breaks out; about 20 million are killed

1957 Bridgers and Paxton Building in Albuquerque, NM is the first commercial building heated with solar energy

1994 Trading on the NASDAQ was halted for 34 minutes when a squirrel chewed a power line near the stock exchange's computer center in Trumbull, CT; a similar squirrel incident caused trading to halt in 1987

August 2

1876 "Wild Bill" Hickok is murdered in Deadwood, SD; Hickok was holding a pair of black aces and a pair of black eights when he died, a combination that's been known since as the "Dead Man's Hand"

1985 PC pioneer Philip Don Estridge dies in plane crash

August 3

1958 First undersea voyage to the North Pole is completed by the U.S. nuclear submarine Nautilus

August 4

1922 Every telephone in the U.S. and Canada is shut down by AT&T and the Bell System for one minute in memory of Alexander Graham Bell, who died two days earlier

August 5

1930 Neil Armstrong is born

1962 Marilyn Monroe is found dead

1981 Air traffic controller strike begins, ending when President Reagan fired 11,500 workers

August 6

1890 First execution by electrocution is carried out at Auburn Prison in New York

1928 Andy Warhol is born

1997 Microsoft pays $150 million to Apple Computer for a minority stake in its business

August 7

1915 A speed of 100 MPH is achieved for the first time at the Chicago Cup Challenge Race at Maywood Board Speedway

August 8

1974 President Richard Nixon resigns amid the Watergate scandal

August 9

1945 U.S. drops atomic bomb on Nagasaki, Japan, killing 150,000 people

1974 Gerald Ford is sworn in as U.S. President after President Nixon resigns

1995 Netscape initial IPO

August 10

1977 David Berkowitz, better known as the "Son of Sam" serial killer, was arrested after killing six young people and wounding seven others

August 11

1909 S.O.S. radio distress call is used for the first time by the S.S. Arapahoe

1950 Steve Wozniak, co-founder of Apple Computer, is born

August 13

1899 Alfred Hitchcock is born

August 14

1893 World's first license plates are issued in Paris, France

1935 Social Security Act is passed

August 15

1914 The Panama Canal opens, joining the Atlantic and Pacific Oceans

1961 East Germany begins construction of the Berlin Wall

August 16

1948 Babe Ruth dies

August 18

1823 First parachute jumper dies; 26 years earlier, the French balloon pilot, Andre-Jacques Garnerin, made the first successful parachute jump—leaping from a hot air balloon 3,000 feet above Paris

August 19

1848 California's gold rush officially begins when the *New York Herald* published confirmation that gold had been discovered there

1871 Orville Wright is born

August 20

1911 First round-the-world telegram is sent, traveling almost 29,000 miles in 16 minutes

August 22

1906 The first Victrola record player is manufactured

1964 World's first supercomputer—the CDC 6600—is introduced by Control Data Corporation

August 24

79 A.D. Mount Vesuvius erupts in southern Italy, devastating Pompeii and Herculaneum, killing thousands; both cities were discovered and excavated in the 1700s; scientists say the long-dormant Vesuvius is due for another eruption any time

1995 Windows 95 is released

August 25

1973 First CAT scan is made

August 27

1910 First radio broadcast from a plane is made

August 28

1963 Martin Luther King gives famous "I have a dream" speech on the steps of the Lincoln Memorial in Washington, D.C.

August 29

1828 First brake of any kind is patented

September 2005

September 2005

SUNDAY	MONDAY	TUESDAY	WEDNESDAY	THURSDAY	FRIDAY	SATURDAY
				1 1979 U.S. space probe Pioneer 11 makes its first flyby of Saturn	**2** 1945 Japan formally surrenders to the Allies, bringing an end to World War II	**3** 1976 Viking II lands on Mars
4 1951 First transcontinental television broadcast	**5** Labor Day 1885 First U.S. gasoline pump is sold in Fort Wayne, IN	**6** 1892 First gasoline-powered tractor is sold to a farmer in Langford, SD	**7** 1888 First baby incubator is used on Ward's Island, NY	**8** 1966 *Star Trek* debuts	**9** 1995 Orville Redenbacher dies	**10** 1930 First planetarium opens in Chicago, IL
11 Patriot Day: 4-year anniversary of World Trade Center and Pentagon attacks	**12** 1918 Erwin G. Baker makes his legendary "Cannonball Run"	**13** 1977 General Motors unveils first diesel cars—the Oldsmobile 88 and 98	**14** 1886 Typewriter ribbon is patented in Memphis, TN	**15** Grandparents Day 1928 Penicillin is discovered	**16** 1908 General Motors is founded	**17** Citizenship Day 1976 NASA unveils its first space shuttle, the Enterprise
18 1947 U.S. Air Force is founded	**19** 1957 First U.S. underground nuclear test is performed in Nevada desert	**20** 1859 Electric range is patented	**21** 1937 J.R.R. Tolkien's *The Hobbit* is published	**22** 1862 President Abraham Lincoln announces the Emancipation Proclamation	**23** First day of Autumn 1879 Hearing aid is patented	**24** 1936 Jim Henson, creator of *The Muppets*, is born
25 1818 First human-to-human blood transfusion is performed	**26** 1996 U.S. and other countries sign nuclear weapons testing ban	**27** 1950 Telephone answering machine is invented	**28** 1858 First comet is photographed (Donati's Comet)	**29** 1913 Rudolf Diesel, inventor of the diesel engine, dies	**30** 1955 James Dean is killed in a car crash	

September 1, 2005

THURSDAY

THIS WEEK'S FOCUS: COMPUTERS FOR KIDS

ON THIS DAY: WORLD WAR II BEGINS (1939)

World War II began on the first of September in 1939, when Germany invaded Poland. After creating a series of provocations, Chancellor Hitler charged that Germany had been attacked, and ordered his troops to blitzkrieg Poland. In response to the invasion, France and Great Britain declared war on Germany on September 3, and it went on from there.

Related Web site: www.bbc.co.uk/history/war/wwtwo/

EDUCATIONAL SOFTWARE

Your PC can be a valuable learning tool for your children, especially if you get them started with the right educational software. Here's a brief look at some of the best educational programs, arranged by age group.

Early learning software is designed for your very youngest children—infant (or as soon as they can use a mouse) to preschool age. Most of this software is as fun as it is educational, with lots of brightly colored characters and fun music. The best software for this age group includes Adventure Workshop: Preschool-1st Grade (www.broderbund.com), Mickey Mouse Toddler/Mickey Mouse Preschool (www.disneyinteractive.com), Pencil Pal Preschool (www.schoolzone.com), and the venerable Reader Rabbit (www.broderbund.com).

Elementary software (for children in grades K-6) introduces solid instructional techniques, while still keeping things fun and lively. Check out Adventure Workshop (www.broderbund.com), the JumpStart Series (www.vugames.com), Kidspiration (www.kidspiration.com), and Math Blaster and Reading Blaster (www.vugames.com).

Junior high and high school software is typically heavier on the education and lighter on the fun and games. This software is particularly helpful if your child is having trouble in a particular subject; it's like having a dedicated tutor on your PC! I particularly like Cyber Ed Chemistry (www.cybered.net), Inspiration (www.kidspiration.com), Math Advantage (www.encoresoftware.com), and Studyworks Teaching Pro: Mathematics Complete (www.learnatglobal.com).

Continuing education software is for students of all ages—equally valuable for a 40 year-old adult as for an ambitious high schooler. Particularly popular are language education programs, as well as typing tutors. Some of the best include Easy Language Deluxe (www.bmsoftware.com/easylanguageds.htm), the LanguageNow! series (www.transparent.com), the Learn to Speak series (www.broderbund.com), and Mavis Beacon Teaches Typing (www.broderbund.com).

WEB SITE OF THE WEEK

For reviews of the very latest educational software, turn to the SuperKids Educational Software Review. It's chock full of useful information, at www.superkids.com.

September 2, 2005

FRIDAY

THIS WEEK'S FOCUS: COMPUTERS FOR KIDS

ON THIS DAY: ANDREW GROVE BORN (1936)

Andrew Grove was born Gróf András on this date in 1936, in Budapest, Hungary. After moving to the U.S., he graduated from the City College of New York and received his Ph.D. from the University of California, Berkeley. He worked for Fairchild Semiconductor for five years, and then, in 1968, helped found Intel Corporation.

Related Web site: www.intel.com/pressroom/kits/bios/grove.htm

ENCOURAGING SAFE BEHAVIOR ONLINE

The most important thing you can do to protect your kids online is to create an environment that encourages appropriate use of the Internet. Nothing replaces traditional parental supervision, and, at the end of the day, you have to take responsibility for your children's online activities.

Here are some guidelines you can follow to ensure a safer surfing experience for your family:

- Consider making Internet surfing an activity you do together with your younger children—or turn it into a family activity by putting your kids' PC in a public room (like a living room or den) rather than in a private bedroom.

- Make sure your children know never to give out any identifying information or to send their photos to other users online.

- Provide each of your children with an online pseudonym so they don't have to use their real names online.

- Don't let your children arrange face-to-face meetings with other computer users without parental permission and supervision.

- Teach your children that people online might not always be who they seem; just because someone says that she's a 10-year-old girl doesn't necessarily mean that she really is 10 years old, or a girl.

- Ask your kids to keep a log of all Web sites they visit; oversee any chat sessions they participate in; check out any files they download; even consider sharing an email account (especially with younger children) so that you can oversee their messages.

Teach your children that Internet access is not a right; it should be a privilege earned by your children and kept only when their use of it matches your expectations.

PORTABLE GADGET OF THE WEEK

Now here's something cool—an honest-to-goodness, real-world *Dick Tracy* wrist-radio. Xact's Wristlinx functions like any other two-way radio unit, but it fits on your wrist. The microphone and speaker are located just below the LCD display. Buy one for $49.99 at www.xactcommunication.com.

September 3, 2005
SATURDAY

THIS WEEK'S FOCUS: COMPUTERS FOR KIDS

ON THIS DAY: VIKING 2 LANDS ON MARS (1976)

The Viking 2 lander set down on Mars on this date in 1976. The craft consisted of an orbiter and a lander, which traveled attached together for nearly a year to reach Mars orbit. The Viking lander took full 360-degree pictures, collected and analyzed samples of the Martian soil, and monitored the temperature, wind direction, and wind speed on the planet's surface.

Related Web site: pds.jpl.nasa.gov/planets/welcome/viking.htm

FUN SITES FOR KIDS

Just as Yahoo! and MSN are portals that offer a full range of content for adults, there are numerous Web sites that act as portals to a variety of fun content and activities of interest to younger users. These kids' portals typically offer kid-oriented news, online games, crafts, homework help, chat, lists of email penpals, and other youth-flavored activities. Most of these sites have their own proprietary content; others link to you appropriate content elsewhere on the Web. The best of the kids' portals include:

- **4Kids Treehouse (www.4kids.com)**—A full-featured portal with color graphics; includes entertainment, games, interactive online books, science and social studies information, and other online activities.

- **ALFY (www.alfy.com)**—A colorful, cartoon-like portal organized like a big theme park, complete with games, sports, music, stories, and more.

- **Bonus.com (www.bonus.com)**—A supersite for kids, complete with interactive games, puzzles, contests, and homework help.

- **KiddoNet (www.kiddonet.com)**—Greeting cards, fashion tips, cartoon dolls, and more for young girls online.

- **Kids' Space (www.kids-space.org)**—Award-winning site by kids, for kids; includes games and activities, email penpals, bulletin boards, personal homepages, songwriting, and much more.

- **KidsCom (www.kidscom.com)**—Fun and educational, this site features games, chats, message boards, writing challenges, polls, and other activities.

- **World Kids Network (www.worldkids.net)**—A non-profit site run by the volunteer efforts of children and adults; includes some great online clubs, games, homework help, and more.

And don't forget Yahooligans! (www.yahooligans.com), which I've mentioned before. It's more than just a kid-friendly search directory—it's a full-featured kids' portal.

FACT OF THE WEEK

Teenage Research Unlimited reports that 78% of teens go online at home, and 90% say the Internet is "cool." By the way, 84% say the same thing about partying.

September 4, 2005

SUNDAY

THIS WEEK'S FOCUS: **COMPUTERS FOR KIDS**

ON THIS DAY: JOHN MCCARTHY BORN (1927)

Computer scientist John McCarthy was born on this date in 1927. McCarthy made major contributions to the field of artificial intelligence, including the coining of the phrase itself. He also invented the LISP programming language.

Related Web site: www-formal.stanford.edu/jmc/

PETS AND ANIMALS ONLINE

Almost every child, at one time or another, has a pet. The Web offers a wealth of resources about all kinds of animals, from simple pet care to in-depth breed and species information. Check out these Web sites, for animal lovers of all ages:

- **Animaland** (www.animaland.org)—From the ASPCA, a great animal education site—including an animal encyclopedia, and information on animal-related careers.

- **Cat Fanciers** (www.fanciers.com)—All about cats—including cat breeds, cat shows, and cat health.

- **Dog-Play** (www.dog-play.com)—Fun activities you can play with your canine friend.

- **Healthypet** (www.healthypet.com)—From the American Animal Hospital Association, frequently asked questions about all types of pets; includes a pet-care library.

- **Horse-country.com** (www.horse-country.com)—A terrific equestrian site for juniors, includes horse history, care, pictures, games, and more; features an international penpal list for horse lovers.

- **Insects on the Web** (www.insects.org)—A terrific site all about insects; includes an insect encyclopedia.

- **Kids' Planet** (www.kidsplanet.org)—A great wildlife conservation site for kids.

- **KidZone** (www.nwf.org/kids/)—From the National Wildlife Foundation, a kids' site that's all about animals.

- **mypetstop.com** (www.mypetstop.com)—A complete guide to information and resources for dogs, cats, birds, and fish.

- **PetBugs.com** (www.petbugs.com)—Got a bug for pet? Then this is the site for you; includes information about tarantulas, millipedes, and other pet bugs.

SOFTWARE OF THE WEEK

When I was growing up, every home had a good set of encyclopedias. Today, every home needs a good encyclopedia program, and Microsoft Encarta is one of the best out there. Buy the full edition (more complete than the version installed on many new PCs) for $74.95 at encarta.msn.com.

September 5, 2005

MONDAY

THIS WEEK'S FOCUS: MICROSOFT OFFICE

ON THIS DAY: A.C. NIELSEN BORN (1897)

Arthur Charles Nielsen, famed statistician and market researcher, was born on this date in 1897, in Chicago, Illinois. Today, he's best known for the company he founded—the A.C. Nielsen Co., which monitors and analyzes television viewing habits and issues periodic ratings reports.

Related Web site: www.nielsenmedia.com

EDITING TEXT IN MICROSOFT WORD

Microsoft Word lets you delete, cut, copy, and paste text—or graphics—to and from anywhere in your document, or between documents. Before you can edit text, though, you have to select the text to edit. The easiest way to select text is with your mouse; just hold down your mouse button and drag the cursor over the text you want to select. You also can select text using your keyboard; use the Shift key—in combination with other keys—to highlight blocks of text. For example, Shift+Left Arrow selects one character to the left; Shift+End selects all text to the end of the current line.

Any text you select appears as white text against a black highlight. You can then edit the text in a number of ways, using either pull-down menu commands or keyboard shortcuts. Check out the options in the following table:

Operation	Menu Location	Keyboard Shortcut
Delete	Edit > Clear	Del
Copy	Edit > Copy	Ctrl+Insert or Ctrl+C
Cut	Edit > Cut	Shift+Del or Ctrl+X
Paste	Edit > Paste	Shift+Ins or Ctrl+V

Operation	Menu Location	Keyboard Shortcut
Bold	Format > Font	Ctrl+B
Italic	Format > Font	Ctrl+I
Underline	Format > Font	Ctrl+U

Using the keyboard shortcuts will speed up your editing; it's a lot easier to press the keys while you're entering text, rather than reach for the mouse to make a menu selection. And here's something else—those keyboard shortcuts work in other Office applications, too. Once your fingers have them memorized, you can use the same shortcuts in Excel and PowerPoint.

PC GADGET OF THE WEEK

AVerMedia's TVBox 9 is a computer gadget that doesn't actually need a computer to work. Instead, the TVBox 9 is a TV tuner that turns any computer monitor into a full-featured television set. Connect your antenna, cable, or satellite signal—as well as signals from a video game or DVD player—and put that old monitor to use. You can even use it as an input device for your new projection or plasma monitor! Buy it for $179.99 at www.aver.com.

September 6, 2005

TUESDAY

THIS WEEK'S FOCUS: MICROSOFT OFFICE

ON THIS DAY: FIRST GASOLINE TRACTOR SOLD (1892)

On September 6, 1892, John Froelich of Froelich, Iowa, shipped the first gasoline tractor to be sold in the United States. It was sent to Langford, South Dakota, which lacked easy access to a wood or coal supply for steam-powered units. The next year, Froelich formed the Waterloo Gasoline Tractor Engine Company, which was taken over in 1918 by the John Deere Plow Co.

Related Web site: www.deere.com

CHECKING SPELLING AND GRAMMAR IN WORD

If you're not a great speller, you'll appreciate Word's automatic spell checking. You can see it right on screen; just deliberately misspell a word, and you'll see a squiggly red line under the misspelling. That's Word telling you you've made a spelling error!

When you see that squiggly red line, position your cursor on top of the misspelled word, and then right-click your mouse. Word now displays a pop-up menu with its suggestions for spelling corrections. You can choose a replacement word from the list, or return to your document and manually change the misspelling.

Sometimes, however, Word meets a word it doesn't recognize, even though the word is spelled correctly. In these instances, you can add the new word to Word's spelling dictionary by right-clicking the word and selecting Add from the pop-up menu.

Word also includes a built-in grammar checker. When Word identifies bad grammar in your document, it underlines the offending passage with a green squiggly line. Right-click anywhere in the passage to view Word's grammatical suggestions.

Not all people like to use Word's grammar checker; some (like me) find it overly intrusive. Fortunately, you can turn off grammar checking by selecting Tools > Options to display the Options dialog box. Select the Spelling & Grammar tab, uncheck the Check Grammar As You Type option, and then click OK. You can still run a manual grammar check, by selecting Tools > Spelling and Grammar.

DOWNLOAD OF THE WEEK

If you want a less expensive alternative to the increasingly bloated and expensive Microsoft Office, check out EasyOffice. This shareware suite includes word processing, spreadsheet, contact manager, calendar, file compression, dictionary, and bookkeeping applications, and is compatible with Word, Excel, and PDF files. Download it for free, or buy it for $49 from www.e-press.com.

September 7, 2005
WEDNESDAY

THIS WEEK'S FOCUS: MICROSOFT OFFICE

ON THIS DAY: DAVID PACKARD BORN (1912)

David Packard, the co-founder of the Hewlett-Packard company, was born on this date in 1912. In addition to his business career, in 1968 President Richard Nixon appointed Packard Deputy Secretary of Defense under Secretary Melvin Laird. Packard served until 1971, when he returned to HP as chairman of the board.

Related Web site: www.packard.org

FIXING WORD'S ANNOYING OVERTYPE MODE

I receive lots of calls from Word users who keep accidentally turning on the program's overtype mode. I know how annoying that can be, because it's so darned easy to hit the Insert key by mistake. (In fact, I just did it when I was typing the preceding paragraph!)

Fortunately, there's a way to disable Word's overtype mode, which will prevent the problem from occurring. Here's what you need to do:

1. Right-click Word's Standard toolbar and select Customize from the pop-up menu.
2. When the Customize dialog box appears, click the Keyboard button.
3. When the Customize Keyboard dialog box appears, select All Commands from the Categories list, and Overtype from the Commands list.
4. Select Insert from the Current Keys list.
5. Click the Remove button.
6. Click OK to close the dialog box.

That's it—you've now deactivated the Ins key as a shortcut switch between insert and overtype mode!

The other way you might accidentally enter overtype mode is by clicking the OVR indicated in the Word status bar, at the bottom of the screen. You can eliminate this issue by hiding the status bar. Select Tools > Options to display the Options dialog box, select the View tab, and deselect the Status Bar option in the Show section.

MAC GADGET OF THE WEEK

Apple killed the floppy drive, but chances are you still have some lying around—or get them sent to you by other users. When you need to access a floppy from your newer Mac, check out LaCie's USB Pocket Floppy. This is a portable floppy drive, small enough to fit in your pocket, that connects to you Mac via USB. Buy it for $29 at www.lacie.com.

THURSDAY

THIS WEEK'S FOCUS: MICROSOFT OFFICE

ON THIS DAY: *STAR TREK* PREMIERES (1966)

The geek show to end all geek shows premiered on September 8, 1966. NBC aired the first episode of Gene Roddenberry's new *Star Trek* series, "Man Trap," at 8:30 p.m. on Thursday evening, up against *Bewitched* and *My Three Sons*. In spite of its inevitable ratings loss, the series managed to hang on—and spawned a franchise that's still going strong today.

Related Web site: www.stwww.com

CREATE A POWERPOINT PRESENTATION FROM A WORD OUTLINE—AND VICE VERSA

Often you'll want to use the outline of a Word document as the starting point for a PowerPoint presentation. You can do this by exporting your Word document to PowerPoint, which then converts it into individual slides, based on Word's automatic heading styles.

To send a Word document directly to PowerPoint, open the document in Word and select File > Send To > Microsoft PointPoint. PowerPoint now launches with a new presentation (based on your Word document) loaded.

PowerPoint uses every Heading 1 paragraph from your Word document as the title for a new slide. If you've formatted your Word document properly (using the built-in heading styles), this results in one slide for each major section of your document. The only problem is, *all* the text under each Heading 1 heading is crammed onto a single slide! To make a Word document fit into a presentation format, you'll have to do a lot of deleting within PowerPoint—or export the Word document while it's still a rough outline, without all the text added beneath each heading.

You can also use Word to flesh out the contents of your PowerPoint presentation into a more complete document. To do this, you want to export your PowerPoint presentation into Word as an outline. From within PowerPoint, select File > Send To > Microsoft Word. When the next dialog box appears, select the Outline Only option and click OK.

Word now creates an outline based on your PowerPoint presentation. Slide titles become Heading 1 headings; first-level bullets on each slide become Heading 2 headings; second-level bullets become Heading 3 headings; and so on. You can then use this outline to create a new document, filling in the body text between all the automatically generated headings.

WEB SITE OF THE WEEK

Find tons of tips for Microsoft Office applications at The Office Letter. There are lots of tips and how-to's available for free, or you can subscribe to the Premium Edition for even more tips. Check it out at www.officeletter.com.

September 9, 2005

FRIDAY

THIS WEEK'S FOCUS: MICROSOFT OFFICE

ON THIS DAY: FIRST COMPUTER BUG (1945)

The way the story goes, Admiral Grace Murray Hopper was working on the Harvard University Mark II back on September 9, 1945. The machine was experiencing problems, and an investigation showed that there was a moth trapped between the points of Relay #70, in Panel F. The operators removed the moth and affixed it to the log, accompanied by the entry, "First actual case of bug being found." The word went out that they had "debugged" the machine, and the term "debugging" was born.

Related Web site: americanhistory.si.edu/csr/comphist/objects/bug.htm

EMBOSS A POWERPOINT TEMPLATE

When you get tired of using the same boring PowerPoint slide templates, it's time for a little personalization. Perhaps the easiest way to spice up one of the default templates is to emboss one or more of the background elements on the slide. Embossing essentially "raises" the object from the page or screen, making it appear somewhat three-dimensional.

To emboss a background object on the master template, make sure you're in the Slide Master view, and then follow these steps:

1. Start by ungrouping all the elements of the slide background. Select the entire slide by clicking it once, and then click the Draw button on the Drawing toolbar and select Ungroup.
2. Select the object or objects you want to emboss.
3. Click the Shadow Style button on PowerPoint's Drawing toolbar.
4. From the pop-up menu, select Shadow Style 17 (lower-left corner).
5. Repeat steps 2–4 to emboss additional objects.

In reality, embossing is just one type of shadow effect you can apply to any most any object on your slide. Traditional drop shadows look great for foreground objects, but can be visually disconcerting when applied to a background object. (Is the foreground text sitting on top of an object which is setting on top of another object which is casting a drop shadow?) It's best to reserve drop shadows for foreground objects; embossing can be used both in the foreground and in the background.

PORTABLE GADGET OF THE WEEK

Turn your portable music player into a boombox with JBL's On Tour speaker system. About the same size as a sunglasses case when closed, the On Tour opens up to reveal a pair of speakers that can fill a room with sound. Plug in your iPod or other music player, throw away your earbuds, and share your music with everyone. Buy it for $99.95 at www.jbl.com.

September 10, 2005

SATURDAY

THIS WEEK'S FOCUS: MICROSOFT OFFICE

ON THIS DAY: STEPHEN JAY GOULD BORN (1941)

Scientist Stephen Jay Gould was born on this date in 1941. Gould's monthly columns in *Natural History* magazine and his popular works on evolution earned him numerous awards and made him one of the most popularly known scientists of our time. He passed away in 2002.

Related Web site: www.stephenjaygould.org

ADJUSTING COLUMN WIDTH IN EXCEL—AUTOMATICALLY

The average Excel user knows how to enter data, but not how to format it. The result is a lot of bad-looking spreadsheets, where long numbers appear to vanish or blend into adjoining numbers. This problem happens when you enter big numbers into small cells—and is easily fixed.

If the data you enter into a cell is too long, you'll only see the first part of that data—there'll be a bit to the right that looks cut off. It's not cut off, of course; it just can't be seen, since it's longer than the current column is wide.

You can fix this problem by adjusting the column width. Wider columns allow more data to be shown; narrow columns let you display more columns per page.

To change the column width, move your cursor to the column header, and position it on the dividing line on the right side of the column you want to adjust. When the cursor changes shape, click the left button on your mouse and drag the column divider to the right (to make a wider column) or to the left (to make a smaller column). Release the mouse button when the column is the desired width.

To make a column the exact width for the longest amount of data entered, position your cursor over the dividing line to the right of the column header and double-click your mouse. This makes the column width automatically "fit" your current data.

FACT OF THE WEEK

Forget the conceit that computers will eliminate the use of paper. Authors Abigail Sellen and Richard Harper, in their book *The Myth of the Paperless Office*, report that paper use increased 12% between 1995 and 2000, even while computer use became ubiquitous. Even more ironic, they found that paper consumption generally leaps 40% percent when an office first implements email.

September 11, 2005

SUNDAY

THIS WEEK'S FOCUS: MICROSOFT OFFICE

ON THIS DAY: WORLD TRADE CENTER AND PENTAGON ATTACKED (2001)

On the morning of September 11, 2001, Al Qaeda terrorists hijacked three commercial airliners and crashed them into the Pentagon and the World Trade Center. A fourth plane was hijacked and crashed in a rural Pennsylvania field after the passengers staged an insurrection for control of the plane. A world watched, stunned, as the twin towers succumbed to the massive damage and totally collapsed. Thousands of people lost their lives in the attacks.

Related Web site: www.9-11commission.gov

INCLUDING OTHER CELLS IN AN EXCEL FORMULA

You probably know how to use the +, -, *, and / operators to add, subtract, multiply, and divide numbers in Excel. But if all you're doing is basic math, you might as well use a calculator. Where Excel becomes truly useful is when you use it to perform operations based on the contents of specific cells. That is, you use Excel to add, subtract, multiply, or divide one cell by another.

Of course, performing cell-based calculations is a little more complicated than entering numbers into a formula. To perform calculations using values from cells in your spreadsheet, you have to enter the cell *location* into the formula. For example, if you want to add cells A1 and A2, enter this formula: **=A1+A2**. The nice thing about this is that if the numerical data in either cell change, the total will automatically change, as well.

An even easier way to perform operations involving spreadsheet cells is to select them with your mouse while you're entering the formula. To do this, follow these steps:

1. Select the cell that will contain the formula.
2. Type =.
3. Click the first cell you want to include in your formula; that cell location is automatically entered in your formula.
4. Type an algebraic operator, such as +, -, *, or /.
5. Click the second cell you want to include in your formula.
6. Repeat steps 4 and 5 to include other cells in your formula.
7. Press Enter when your formula is complete.

SOFTWARE OF THE WEEK

If you want a bargain on Microsoft Office, skip the Standard and Professional Editions and buy a copy of the Student and Teacher Edition, which sells for just $149. It's the best deal out there, as it's identical to the $399 Standard Edition; it comes with Word, Excel, PowerPoint, and Outlook. And you don't really have to be a teacher or student to purchase it; nobody will check your ID. Find out more at www.microsoft.com/office/.

September 12, 2005

MONDAY

THIS WEEK'S FOCUS: SPYWARE, POP-UPS, AND OTHER ANNOYANCES

ON THIS DAY: H.L. MENCKEN BORN (1880)

Henry Louis Mencken, the noted journalist and commentator, was born on this date in 1880, in Baltimore. His comments poked fun at the pompous and ridiculous among us, especially in the political realm. My favorite Menckenism? You've heard it, but probably not in full: "No one in this world, so far as I know—and I have researched the records for years, and employed agents to help me—has ever lost money by underestimating the intelligence of the great masses of the plain people. Nor has anyone ever lost public office thereby."

Related Web site: www.mencken.org

UNDERSTANDING SPYWARE

One of the biggest annoyances for Web surfers today is the proliferation of spyware and adware. Spyware is software that installs itself on your system, observes your activities (and sometimes your personal information), and then sends that info back to a third party—sometimes with hostile intent. Adware is like spyware, except it uses the information it gathers to pop-up "appropriate" advertising while you're surfing. They're both annoying and intrusive.

Spyware is kind of like a virus—more specifically, a Trojan horse—although, in most cases, you willingly approve its installation. That's right, most spyware installs itself only when you give the okay. The problem is, you probably don't know you're giving the okay. Let me explain.

Most spyware piggybacks on top of other programs—programs you intentionally install. I've found that some of the biggest offenders are the programs used by various P2P file-sharing sites, such as KaZaA. When you install the file-trading software, various spyware programs are included as part of the installation. When you give your okay to install the main software, you're also giving your implicit approval to install the spyware.

Also notorious for harboring spyware are browser plug ins, various third-party Internet Explorer toolbars, and a number of freeware/shareware system utilities—including some spyware removal programs.

It's pretty easy to tell if you have spyware on your machine. You'll probably be inundated with pop-up ads, or even ads that mysteriously appear on top of normal Web page ads. You may also notice a general slow down of your system, as the spyware uses a fair amount of system resources and Internet bandwidth. And, worst-case scenario, malicious spyware can infect your system with damaging computer viruses, or steal your personal information—resulting in a case of identity theft.

PC GADGET OF THE WEEK

AVerMedia's DVD EZMaker Pro is a video capture device that includes a built-in hardware MPEG-2 encoder, which means your PC doesn't have to do the encoding. This frees up your PC for other uses while you're capturing video. The DiscDirect feature captures and burns direct to DVD, which is great for burning DVDs from MiniDV camcorders. Buy it for $149.99 from www.aver.com.

September 13, 2005

TUESDAY

THIS WEEK'S FOCUS: SPYWARE, POP-UPS, AND OTHER ANNOYANCES

ON THIS DAY: OSBORNE COMPUTER DECLARES BANKRUPTCY (1983)

Computer pioneer Adam Osborne founded the Osborne Computer Corporation in 1980. His most noted product was the $1,795 Osborne 1, one of the first portable computers—well, portable for its day, anyway. At its peak, Osborne Computer was selling 10,000 units per month, but that didn't last. Faced with real competition from the big boys (IBM and Compaq), Osborne struggled, eventually closing its doors on September 13, 1983.

Related Web site: oldcomputers.net/osborne.html

AVOIDING AND REMOVING SPYWARE

Perhaps the most effective way to avoid spyware is to not use file-trading services, which are notorious for inflicting spyware on their users. You should also beware of any Web site that asks you to download something in order to view the site, or any files that come to you via instant messaging. In addition, you should always read the end-user licensing agreement before you install any programs you download. Believe it or not, most spyware programs will warn you before they install themselves—which is what makes them technically different from a Trojan horse. Read that fine print!

Beyond that, you could switch your Web browsers. Mozilla Firefox is much less prone to spyware intrusion than Internet Explorer. (It's also an all-around better browser, IHMO.)

Most important, you need to install and use some sort of anti-spyware utility. These are programs that scan your system for spyware installations and remove them, if present. These programs will also monitor your program to prevent spyware from being installed in the first place. I mention a few of my favorite anti-spyware programs in the Download of the Week section of this page.

As with an anti-virus program, it's essential that once you install an anti-spyware program, you keep its spyware definitions up-to-date. And if you want to make sure that no spyware escapes the net, run multiple anti-spyware utilities. Sorry to say, but I've yet to find a single anti-spyware utility that catches everything that's out there.

DOWNLOAD OF THE WEEK

My favorite spyware killer is Spybot Search & Destroy. It does a great job of identifying spyware programs on your PC, and of safely removing them. Download it for free from www.spybot.info—although donations are appreciated. (Also good is Ad-Aware, available from $26.95 from www.lavasoftusa.com/software/adaware/.)

September 14, 2005

WEDNESDAY

THIS WEEK'S FOCUS: SPYWARE, POP-UPS, AND OTHER ANNOYANCES

ON THIS DAY: SOVIET LUNA 2 REACHES MOON (1959)

The first manmade object to reach the moon—and crash into it—was the Soviet Luna 2 spacecraft. It impacted the moon on this date in 1959, crashing into the lunar surface just east of Mare Serenitatis, near the Aristides, Archimedes, and Autolycus craters.

Related Web site: nssdc.gsfc.nasa.gov/planetary/lunar/lunarussr.html

BROWSER HIJACKERS

Have you ever visited a Web site or downloaded a software utility, only to find that your browser's settings have suddenly changed? If so, then you're a victim of browser hijacking, a particularly despicable form of spyware infection.

Browser hijackers work like other spyware programs, except they specifically affect your Web browser—Internet Explorer in particular. Some hijackers add shortcuts to your Favorites folder. Sometimes your browser's home page is replaced by another page, without your knowledge. Sometimes your browser's back and forward buttons are deactivated. Sometimes you lose total control of your browser.

In some instances, you can manually undo the effects of the hijacking by editing your Favorites folder or home page settings. In other cases there is seemingly nothing you can do to put things right, short of editing the Windows Registry—or reinstalling your browser.

The easiest way to avoid browser hijackings is to dump Internet Explorer. That's because almost all browser hijackers only affect Internet Explorer—they don't hijack Opera or Mozilla Firefox. So if you switch browsers, you should be safe.

To undo an IE hijacking, try HijackThis (www.tomcoyote.com/hjt/). This is a freeware program that analyzes and fixes any hijacked Registry settings. To prevent future hijackings, use Browser Hijack Blaster (www.wilderssecurity.com/bhblaster.html), a freeware program that prevents browser hijackers from modifying IE's settings.

MAC GADGET OF THE WEEK

Want to share one of those big Apple Cinema Displays between two Macs? Then spring for CompuCable's ADC Monitor Sharing Switch, which enables two digital video systems to share a single ADC monitor. Buy it for $299.99 at www.addlogix.com.

September 15, 2005

THURSDAY

THIS WEEK'S FOCUS: SPYWARE, POP-UPS, AND OTHER ANNOYANCES

ON THIS DAY: ASSOCIATION FOR COMPUTING MACHINERY IS FOUNDED (1947)

The Association for Computing Machinery (ACM) was founded on September 15, 1947. ACM is a major force in advancing the skills of information technology professionals and students, with 75,000 members worldwide.

Related Web site: www.acm.org

STOPPING POP-UPS

One of my top Internet annoyances is the pop-up (or pop-under) window. I get so peeved when I open a Web page, only to find another window (or multiple windows) popping up on my desktop. It's rude of a Web site to do this to me, but it's an increasingly popular form of advertising. I hate them!

There are actually three types of pop-ups you can encounter, and three different ways to stop them.

The most common type of pop-up is the Web page pop-up. These are typically created by JavaScript code on the underlying page. (See tomorrow's main article for how this works.) You stop Web pop-ups by using a pop-up stopper program. One of the best—and my favorite—is included in the Google Toolbar, downloadable for free from toolbar.google.com. Also good is Panicware's Pop-Up Stopper utility, available for $29.95 from www.panicware.com. And if you download the Windows XP Service Pack 2, Internet Explorer will be updated with built-in pop-up stopping capability.

The second type of pop-up is caused by spyware. Spyware pop-ups can appear at any time, on any Web page—even when you're not surfing at all. You eliminate spyware pop-ups by scrubbing spyware from your system, as I explained on Tuesday.

The final type of pop-up is caused by what I consider a security flaw in Windows NT/2000/XP. These versions of Windows have an internal messaging function called *netsend* that's designed for system administrators, who use it to communicate with all the computers on the network. Unfortunately, it can also be used by a spammer to send a pop-up to any computer on the Internet. To block this form of pop-up spam you have to turn off the Messenger service, or turn on a firewall. Enabling the built-in Windows XP firewall will block this spam forever.

WEB SITE OF THE WEEK

Spyware-Guide.com is the place to go to learn more about spyware—what it is, and how to remove it. This wonderful site includes a massive database of hundreds of known spyware and adware applications, as well as a Spyware Block List File that blocks "bad" ActiveX controls from running inside Internet Explorer. It's all free at www.spywareguide.com. (Also good—the user forums at www.spywareinfo.com.)

September 16, 2005

FRIDAY

THIS WEEK'S FOCUS: SPYWARE, POP-UPS, AND OTHER ANNOYANCES

ON THIS DAY: *THE OUTER LIMITS* PREMIERES (1963)

"There is nothing wrong with your television set. Do not attempt to adjust the picture. We are controlling transmission." With those chilling words, the seminal sci-fi series *The Outer Limits* debuted on the ABC television network on this date in 1963. The first episode: "The Galaxy Being," starring Cliff Robertson.

Related Web site: www.scifi.com/outerlimits/

THE EVIL CODE TO MAKE YOUR OWN POP-UPS

Ever wonder how a Web site creates all those annoying pop-up windows? Well, it's remarkably easy—which is probably why you see so many of them.

Thanks to JavaScript, adding a pop-up window to your page is as simple as writing a few standard lines of code. To create your own pop-up window, start by entering the following code into the head of your HTML document:

```
<script language="JavaScript">
<!--
function genericPopup(popupAddress)
{new_window =
window.open(popupAddress,'windowName')}
// -->
</script>
```

Replace *windowName* with the name you want to give the pop-up window. Then, after you've added the code for the pop-up window to the head of the document, you must instruct the browser to open the window. If you want to open the pop-up as soon as the first page is loaded, replace the original page's <body> tag with the following:

```
<body onLoad="genericPopup('popup-url')">
```

Replace *popup-url* with the URL of the page you want displayed in the pop-up window.

There are all sorts of variables you can add to customize the pop-up window, but you get the gist of it. I told you it was easy!

PORTABLE GADGET OF THE WEEK

You're probably used to shredding your paper documents, but what about all the sensitive data you've recorded on CDs and DVDs? Royal comes to the rescue with the MD 100 CD/Media destroyer. Feed in your discs, and the MD 100 makes mincemeat of them. You can also use it as a simple paper shredder or to shred your old plastic credit cards. Buy it for $99.99 at www.royal.com.

September 17, 2005

SATURDAY

THIS WEEK'S FOCUS: SPYWARE, POP-UPS, AND OTHER ANNOYANCES

ON THIS DAY: FIRST 33 1/3 RECORD DEMONSTRATED (1931)

On September 17, 1931, the Radio Corporation of America demonstrated an early version of the 33 1/3 rpm long-playing record, at the Savoy Plaza Hotel in New York City. The first commercial 33 1/3 records did not appear until 1948, when RCA's rival, Columbia, began mass production of the LP.

Related Web site: www.vinylrecordscollector.co.uk

OTHER WEB ANNOYANCES

Spyware, browser hijackers, and pop-ups aren't the only annoyances spreading across the Web today. Here's some more Web nasties that we unfortunately all have to deal with.

- **Drive-by downloads and foistware**—These are programs—typically spyware—that foist themselves on you as necessary downloads. All you have to do is open the offending Web page, or pass your mouse over a banner ad, and you see a pop-up message that looks like some sort of official security warning, with a message like "Do you accept this download?" Click Yes, and the spyware is installed.

- **Ad hijacking**—The purpose of adware is to serve you up more—and different—ads than you'd get otherwise. In particular, adware serves up ads from the adware's sponsors, sometimes on top of a Web site's normal banner ads.

- **TopText**—This is a tricky one. TopText bills itself as a useful tool that offers additional information when you're Web surfing. What it really is is an adware program that inserts yellow highlights under selected text on a page; click the highlight and TopText displays information from one of its advertisers. I find it a galling misrepresentation, as you can see for yourself at www.ezula.com.

- **Mousetrapping**—When I surf to a Web site, I don't want to be held captive there. Some sites use JavaScript code to disable your browser's back and exit functions, effectively holding you hostage. The only way out is to revisit another site in your browser's history list, or just close your browser and start over.

I'm not sure what to do about all these annoyances, except to avoid those sites and companies that condone them. (It also doesn't hurt to switch browsers; those annoyances that depend on JavaScript code often don't work with Mozilla Firefox or Opera.)

FACT OF THE WEEK

According to Nielsen-Netratings, more than 10 million African Americans are online. The most popular destination for African-Americans is BlackPlanet.com, which draws 75 percent of the online African American population. The music site Xjamz.com is the second most-visited destination, followed by BET Interactive.

September 18, 2005

SUNDAY

THIS WEEK'S FOCUS: SPYWARE, POP-UPS, AND OTHER ANNOYANCES

ON THIS DAY: *NEW YORK TIMES* **LAUNCHES (1851)**

The *New York Times*, that "Gray Lady" of journalism, published its first issue on September 18, 1851. It was founded as the *New-York Daily Times* by Henry J. Raymond and George Jones as a sober alternative to the more partisan newspapers that dominated New York journalism of the time. It's first issue stated, "We publish today the first issue of the *New-York Daily Times*, and we intend to issue it every morning (Sundays excepted) for an indefinite number of years to come."

Related Web site: www.nytimes.com

MANAGING COOKIES

Many Web sites that you visit create a small file on your computer's hard disk, called a "cookie." Cookies contain information that Web sites can use to track your visits. It's likely that your computer contains hundreds—if not thousands—of these cookie files.

Cookies are not by nature bad. Most cookies store user information that helps the Web site recognize you. Without cookies, you'd have to re-enter your user name and password every time you visit a site. Ever shop at Amazon? Imagine the shopping experience if Amazon didn't remember all your information. It would be a real pain.

That said, cookies can be used for evil, as well as good. A site can use its cookie to track your surfing activities—which sites you visit, and when. They can use that information to figure out your name, email address, location, interests, and so on—and then sell that information to other businesses.

You don't have to let these sites peek into your computing habits. You can, if you want, manage the cookies that Web sites want to store on your computer—or decide not to accept any cookies at all. In Internet Explorer 6, you manage your cookies by

selecting Tools > Options, and then selecting the Privacy tab; click the Edit button to block or allow cookies from individual sites. You can also delete all your cookies in one fell swoop by selecting the General tab and then clicking the Delete Cookies button. An easier solution, however, is to use a third-party cookie management utility, such as Cookie Pal.

Know, however, that blocking cookies can cause you untold inconvenience. Some Web sites will treat you differently if you don't accept cookies; some sites won't even let you in. In addition, those sites that require a password won't recognize you any more. Whichever sites you visit, you'll have to enter all your personal information every time you visit—which can be a real pain with subscription sites.

SOFTWARE OF THE WEEK

If you want boxed spyware stopper, check out McAfee AntiSpyware. It detects and eliminates a variety of malicious applications—key loggers, remote-control programs, browser hijackers, and the like. Buy it for $39.99 from www.mcafeee.com.

A patent for the first carpet sweeper was issued to Melville Bissell on this date in 1876. Bissell was inspired by all the dust kicked up in his family crockery shop, and soon took to the road to sell his sweeper door-to-door. To demonstrate his new invention, he threw a handful of dirt onto a carpet while his prospective customer watched the dirt disappear into the clanging contraption—and the door-to-door carpet salesman was born.

Related Web site: www.bissell.com

CHOOSING AN HDTV DISPLAY

If you're shopping for a new home theater system, the centerpiece is the television set. Naturally, you want something that's HDTV-capable, for that time in the near future when high-definition programming is the rule, rather than the exception.

The traditional choice is the direct view set, which uses a cathode ray tube (CRT) as its display. Direct view sets typically have the brightest picture of any display type, and generally cost less than similar-sized projection or plasma sets. Their main limit is size; if you want a really big picture (over 40"), you'll need to choose a different type of display.

Rear projection televisions (RPTVs) are ideal if you want a bigger screen but don't want to totally break the bank. Old-style RPTVs, driven by internal CRTs, can be had for less than $1,500. Newer micro-projection RPTVs—driven by internal DLP, LCD, and LCoS technology—cost a little more, but deliver a better picture in a smaller cabinet. The only drawback to these sets is that they often produce a dimmer image, and are sometimes difficult to view off-angle. That said, I personally like the DLP and LCD micro-projectors; in my opinion, they offer the best compromise between picture quality, size, and price, without any burn-in problems.

If you have a really big room—or are building a custom home theater—consider a front projection television (FPTV). These units generate an image from a separate projector (using CRT, DLP, or LCD technology) and beam it onto a flat white screen. This type of system is inherently less bright than any other type of display, and—when done right—costs more, as well.

The newest type of display is the flat panel display, using either LCD or plasma technology. LCD panels are common in smaller screen sizes, and plasma in larger sizes. Both types of flat panel displays are rather expensive, although the picture is superior to RPTV and FPTV units. I like the LCD displays, if you don't mind the size limitation. Plasmas, as cool as they are, suffer from burn-in, which can happen all too quickly if you watch a lot of letterboxed or window-paned movies.

PC GADGET OF THE WEEK

Creative's Sound Blaster Wireless Music is a full-featured network music hub that transfers music from your computer to your home audio system. It plays MP3 and WMA files stored on your computer's hard disk via an 802.11b or 802.11g Wi-Fi connection. What's really neat is the wireless remote control, which has a built-in LCD screen that displays songs and playlists. Buy it for $199.99 from www.creative.com.

September 20, 2005

TUESDAY

THIS WEEK'S FOCUS: HOME THEATER AND HDTV

ON THIS DAY: FIRST FORTRAN PROGRAM EXECUTED (1954)

On September 20, 1954, the first FORTRAN computer program was run. John Backus at IBM supervised the development of the programming language, which was designed to express problems in commonly understood mathematical formulae.

Related Web site: www.fortran.com

HOW LETTERBOXING WORKS

When the movie industry felt threatened by the then new medium of television back in the 1950s, the studios responded by producing films in various widescreen formats. These formats—Panavision, Cinemascope, and the rest—provided a much wider picture than that presented by television's "little square box."

The problem, of course, is watching a widescreen movie on a non-widescreen display. Traditional television displays have an aspect ratio of 4:3—which means that if a screen is four units of measurement wide, it's also three units tall. Another way to measure this is to say that the standard television screen has a 1.33:1 ratio—the width is 1.33 times the height.

The various widescreen formats used by Hollywood employ aspect ratios much wider than 1.33:1—1.85:1 is common, with some movies filmed as wide as 2.35:1. To view these movies in the standard television aspect ratio, technicians commonly "pan and scan" the narrower television image area over the movie's wider image. This often cuts off important parts of the picture, however, and definitely interferes with the way the director wanted the movie presented.

A better approach is to present the movie at its full width—which leaves some unused areas at the top and bottom of your television screen. This approach, called *letterboxing*, displays the widescreen movie in a strip across the center of your screen, with long black bars above and below the movie image. Most DVDs present movies in letterboxed versions.

In addition, all HDTV programming is spec'ed with a 16:9 aspect ratio—or 1.78:1, if you want to measure it that way. And all HDTV-ready televisions feature a 16:9 display. With this aspect ratio, widescreen movies that use the common 1.85:1 ratio can be displayed onscreen with little or no letterboxing; even the wider 2.35:1 movies fit better than they do on a standard aspect screen.

DOWNLOAD OF THE WEEK

Catalog your DVD collection with the ReaderwareVW program. Just scan in a barcode and ReaderwareVW looks up the DVD's complete title and cast information from an online database. Versions are also available for cataloging CDs and books. It's shareware, so try it for free or buy it for $40 from www.readerware.com.

September 21, 2005
WEDNESDAY

THIS WEEK'S FOCUS: HOME THEATER AND HDTV

ON THIS DAY: YES, VIRGINIA, THERE *IS* A SANTA CLAUS (1897)

On this date in 1897, the *New York Sun* printed a letter from reader Virginia O'Hanlon. "I am 8 years old," the letter read. "Some of my little friends say there is no Santa Claus. Papa says, 'If you see it in The Sun, it's so.' Please tell me the truth, is there a Santa Claus?" Editor Francis P. Church reassured the young girl with the famous reply, "Yes, Virginia, there is a Santa Claus." However, as Chico Marx noted 38 years later, there is no sanity clause.

Related Web site: www.historychannel.com/exhibits/holidays/christmas/virginia.html

ANALOG VS. DIGITAL TELEVISION

Since the invention of television, signals have been broadcast in analog format. An analog broadcast transmits programming in a continuous signal that varies in amplitude depending on the information contained in the picture. Unfortunately, as we're all aware, this signal can easily deteriorate with distance and other obstacles, which produces a lower-quality picture than the original.

A digital broadcast, on the other hand, converts the programming into a stream of digital on/off bits. Each bit represents a small part of the picture; all the bits combine to reproduce a picture identical to the original. In short, a digital picture is better than an analog one.

One key component of the new HDTV specification is the all-digital format. But digital television and HDTV are not necessarily the same thing. While all high-definition television is digital, not all digital broadcasts are high definition. In other words, HDTV is just one form of digital broadcasting.

We've actually had digital programming available since 1994 or so, via the DirecTV and EchoStar digital satellite systems (DSS). Many cable systems also offer digital cable services, and all DVDs store their information in digital format. But none of these digital sources are high definition.

You see, simply digitizing a picture does not improve upon the mediocre NTSC source format. To dramatically improve the picture, the format itself has to be improved. This is what HDTV does—by increasing the picture's resolution, as measured in lines of horizontal resolution.

So don't get confused by digital-this and digital-that. While digital satellite or cable might provide a slightly improved (and definitely more consistent) picture than traditional analog broadcast TV, if you want a significantly improved picture, you have to go the HDTV route—which I'll talk about tomorrow.

MAC GADGET OF THE WEEK

Extend the range of your AirPort Extreme Base Station with Dr. Bott's ExtendAIR Direct. The ExtendAIR connects to the AirPort's antenna connector, and increases the range to 500 feet or so. Buy it for $149.95 at www.drbott.com.

September 22, 2005

THURSDAY

THIS WEEK'S FOCUS: HOME THEATER AND HDTV

ON THIS DAY: *MAN FROM U.N.C.L.E.* **PREMIERES (1964)**

Riding the wave of spymania spurred by the first James Bond films, the NBC television network launched a new spy series on Tuesday evening, September 22, 1964. *The Man from U.N.C.L.E.* starred Robert Vaughn as Napoleon Solo and David McCallum as Illya Kuryakin. The first episode, aired opposite the *Red Skeleton Show*, was "The Vulcan Affair."

Related Web site: www.manfromuncle.org

GOING HIGH-DEF

Television is changing. Under government dictate, the industry is shifting from low-resolution analog signals to high-resolution digital signals. Of course, to receive the new HDTV signals you'll need an HDTV-capable television; you'll also need a source of HDTV programming.

The HDTV format—actually several different possible formats, at different levels of resolution—provide significant and noticeable improvements over traditional standard-resolution broadcasts. The chief advantages include:

- **Sharper picture**—True HDTV (in either the 720p or 1080i formats) delivers 1 million pixels or more of information. Standard-definition television delivers approximately 300,000 pixels at its best; HDTV is three times sharper.

- **Less flicker**—HDTV's increased number of scan lines per frame means you can sit closer to the screen without seeing flicker in the picture.

- **More accurate widescreen reproduction**—The HDTV format specifies a 16:9 aspect ratio, so you can see more of a widescreen movie with less letterboxing.

- **Better sound**—The HDTV format dictates the use of Dolby Digital 5.1 surround sound format—which is much improved over the NTSC stereo standard.

The two most common HDTV formats, which all HDTV-capable TVs should reproduce, are 720p and 1080i. In layman's terms, 720p delivers 720 lines of resolution, progressively scanned. The 1080i format delivers 1080 lines of resolution, interlaced—that is, displayed in two successive screens of 540 lines apiece. By comparison, our current standard-resolution format delivers just 480 lines, interlaced—that is, two successive screens of just 240 lines apiece.

WEB SITE OF THE WEEK

Get the buzz about the latest home theater products—and shoot the bull with fellow enthusiasts—at the Home Theater Forum. There's even a big gallery with pictures of users' home theater systems. Find it all at www.hometheaterforum.com.

THIS WEEK'S FOCUS: HOME THEATER AND HDTV

ON THIS DAY: NEPTUNE DISCOVERED (1846)

In 1845, Cambridge mathematician John Couch Adams predicted the existence of an unseen planet to account for the fact that Uranus was being pulled slightly out of position in its orbit. The following year, on September 23, German astronomer Johann Gottfried Galle proved Adams correct when he first sighted the new planet, which was named Neptune.

Related Web site: www.solarviews.com/eng/neptune.htm

CONNECT YOUR COMPUTER TO YOUR HOME THEATER WITH A DIGITAL MEDIA HUB

A digital media hub is a device that lets you play digital audio files on your home audio system. You rip your favorite CDs to hard disk, and the media hub accesses the hard disk to play individual songs and playlists. It's a great space-saver (you don't need to keep all your physical CDs in view anymore) as well as a way to get instant access to every song in your collection—including all the MP3 and WMA files you've downloaded from the Internet.

There are two primary types of digital media hubs. The first type, offered by many traditional consumer electronics companies, is a self-contained unit that has a built-in hard disk and CD drive. You insert a CD into the drive, burn it to the built-in hard disk, and then play songs from the hard disk. This type of unit typically looks like a regular consumer audio component and connects to your home audio system via digital or analog connections.

The second type of digital media hub doesn't have a built-in hard disk or CD drive. Instead, it connects to your home network, accesses the digital audio files stored on your computer's hard disk, and then streams the music through your home audio system. This type of hub is typically a small and relatively low-cost device that connects directly to your home audio system; it plugs in to your home network via either wired or wireless connection.

When you're shopping for a digital media hub, you need to decide if you want a self-contained unit or a PC-based (networked) unit. If you get a self-contained unit, make sure the hard drive is big enough to store all your CDs. If you get a PC-based unit, find out if it connects via Ethernet or Wi-Fi. Also check to see if the unit has a built-in display, or if you have to use your TV to display song information. Some units are audio-only, while others can stream videos or display digital photos and artwork. Do your homework before you buy.

PORTABLE GADGET OF THE WEEK

The NETGEAR MP101 is the lowest-priced network music hub I've seen, and probably the simplest to set up and operate. It connects to your home network via wired Ethernet or wireless 802.11b or 802.11g Wi-Fi. Buy it for $139.99 from www.netgear.com.

September 24, 2005

SATURDAY

THIS WEEK'S FOCUS: **HOME THEATER AND HDTV**

ON THIS DAY: **COMPUSERVE LAUNCHES (1979)**

CompuServe was founded on this date in 1979 as a computer time-sharing service, originally as a way to better utilize the mainframe computers of H&R Block outside business hours. It became a pioneer commercial online service and was the premiere online community in the pre-Internet era. The company was acquired by America Online in 1997, and today is a pale shadow of its former self.

Related Web site: www.compuserve.com

BUILDING A GREAT-SOUNDING HOME THEATER

A big picture is nothing without a big sound system. Which is why a true home theater system incorporates some type of surround sound system. Obviously, a simple two-channel stereo—with its front left and front right speakers—can't surround you with sound. Nor can the speakers built-into your television set. For true surround sound, you need a combination of front and rear speakers.

At its most basic, a surround sound system includes two front speakers (positioned to the front left and front right of the listener) and two surround speakers (positioned to the rear left and rear right). With this simple four-channel setup you can create an accurate stereo soundstage both in front of and behind you; the rear speakers are used to reproduce sounds occurring away from the main screen, behind the audience.

All of today's surround sound technologies expand on this simple four-speaker setup in a number of ways. The most common addition is that of a center speaker, located adjacent to your video display in-between the two existing front speakers. This center channel is used to anchor dialogue and other key sounds to the actors onscreen; the front left and front right speakers can then be used to expand the soundstage to either side of the screen with special effects and music.

Another common addition is that of a subwoofer, used to reproduce the extreme low bass frequencies common in today's movie soundtracks. Without a subwoofer, a home theater system might sound empty or ungrounded; a subwoofer adds the punch that makes your system boom and rumble.

All surround sound technologies encode the surround sound information on the movie's normal soundtrack. Newer technologies, such as Dolby Digital or DTS, dedicate discrete data tracks for each channel of information, thus providing more precise positioning and eliminating channel leakage.

FACT OF THE WEEK

According to the original FCC mandate, all commercial television stations in the U.S. were supposed to be offering HDTV programming, in addition to their standard definition broadcasts, by 2002. The original mandate dictated that we'd be all digital by 2006, with all standard definition broadcasts stopping and the analog spectrum returned to the government for future use. Obviously, that isn't going to happen. Most experts predict that we won't be all-digital until 2010 at the earliest, possibly decades later.

September 25, 2005

SUNDAY

THIS WEEK'S FOCUS: HOME THEATER AND HDTV

ON THIS DAY: AEROSOLS AND OZONE DEPLETION (1974)

On September 25, 1974, scientists first reported that freon gases released from aerosol spray cans were destroying the ozone layer. Nobel prize winner Dr. F. Sherwood Rowland and his colleague Dr. Mario Molina theorized the dangers of chlorofluorocarbons (CFCs), then found in refrigerators, air conditioners, industrial processes, and as propellants for many aerosols.

Related Web site: www.epa.gov/ozone/

UNDERSTANDING SURROUND SOUND FORMATS

Over the past decade there have been several different technologies used to provide surround sound in the home environment.

The most common surround sound format today is Dolby Digital. Dolby Digital is the technology used on most of today's DVDs. It's also used on some digital satellite broadcasts, and is the format specified for all HDTV programming.

Dolby Digital technology can be used to reproduce any number of channels, including both mono (Dolby Digital 1.0) and stereo (Dolby Digital 2.0) programming. The most common Dolby Digital format, however, is Dolby Digital 5.1, which offers five discrete channels: front left, front center, front right, surround left, and surround right. The ".1" is the separate low frequency effects channel that is sent to your system's subwoofer. More sophisticated versions of Dolby Digital offer 6.1 and 7.1 sound that incorporate additional surround channels.

The competing DTS (Digital Theater Sound) format is similar to but slightly different from Dolby Digital. Like Dolby Digital, basic DTS is a 5.1-channel format, offering slightly better frequency response. While most audio/video receivers include DTS decoders, few DVDs come with DTS soundtracks.

Where both Dolby Digital and DTS reproduce six discrete channels, the older Dolby Pro Logic system offers just four channels—front left, front center, front right, and a single surround channel. (There is no low frequency effects channel.) The front center and surround channels are actually matrixed, or mixed, into the front left and front right channels, so channel separation isn't near as good as with Dolby Digital or DTS. Dolby Pro Logic is used to reproduce surround sound on standard television and cable broadcasts, most digital satellite programming, some older DVDs and laserdiscs, and VHS HiFi videotapes. All audio/video receivers include Dolby Pro Logic circuitry, even though most newer programming is coming in Dolby Digital 5.1.

SOFTWARE OF THE WEEK

Cinemar's DVD Lobby Pro software lets you control your DVD jukebox from your PC. The onscreen interface is far superior to what you find with the typical jukebox, and the program automatically downloads information on your DVDs from an online database. Buy them both for $109.99 from www.cinemaronline.com.

September 26, 2005
MONDAY

THIS WEEK'S FOCUS: PDAS

ON THIS DAY: FIRST TELEVISED PRESIDENTIAL DEBATE (1960)

On September 26, 1960, the viewing public tuned into the first-ever televised presidential debate, between Democratic candidate John F. Kennedy and Republican Richard M. Nixon. The debate, broadcast by CBS, proved instrumental in establishing Kennedy as a poised and dynamic candidate; Nixon, in contrast, looked haggard and nervous. The power of television was demonstrated when Kennedy went on to win the election.

Related Web site: www.jfklibrary.org/60-1st.htm

PALM OS OR POCKETPC?

If you're in the mood for a new PDA, which format should you buy—Palm OS or Microsoft's Pocket PC? It all depends on what you want to do.

Palm OS units tend to be a little lower-priced than comparable Pocket PC models. They're also typically a little smaller and lighter, and offer longer battery life. Most users consider the Palm OS easier to use, with a shorter learning curve. Palm PDAs were designed originally as contact-management devices, and they excel at this.

Most Pocket PC units are bigger and more expensive than comparable Palm models, and don't last near as long on a battery charge. The operating system is a little more sophisticated, which is either good or bad, depending on what you want to do. The learning curve is a bit steeper, but then again, everything is kind of Windows-like—which lets a Pocket PC run "pocket" versions of Word and Excel. Naturally, a Pocket PC integrates quite well with Microsoft Outlook, so if you're an Outlook user, this may be the deciding factor.

Both Palm and Pocket PC units are available in a variety of configurations, from very simple units to models with Bluetooth and Wi-Fi wireless connectivity, built-in digital cameras, and all sorts of other bells and whistles. You can find a plethora of accessories and software programs for each type of device. And you won't have trouble finding either type of unit, typically at a decent discount.

Bottom line? If all you need is basic calendar and address book functions, go with the Palm OS. If you need to integrate with various Windows applications—Outlook, especially—then spring for a Pocket PC.

PC GADGET OF THE WEEK

When you have a lot of home theater gadgets to control, go for the most sophisticated consumer-grade remote control available—Philips' iPronto. This funky unit combines a color touch screen remote control, a wireless Internet browser, and an electronic program guide into a unit that looks a little like a tablet PC. It's a big unit, with a 6.4" display and built-in stereo speakers; buy it for a paltry (!) $1,699.99 at www.pronto.philips.com.

September 27, 2005
TUESDAY

THIS WEEK'S FOCUS: **PDAS**

ON THIS DAY: COSMIC NEAR MISS (2003)

An asteroid about the size of a small house passed just 88,000 kilometers from Earth on September 27, 2003. This was the closest approach of a natural object ever recorded. To put the passage in perspective, geostationary communication satellites orbit at 42,000 kilometers.

Related Web site: www.space.com/scienceastronomy/asteroid_close_031006.html

PDA SOFTWARE

When you're looking for PDA software, you can go directly to the software developers' sites, or you can search through sites that offer a large number of programs, often from many different companies. The following sites all offer a variety of Palm OS and Pocket PC programs for downloading, from business applications to games.

- Applian Software (www.applian.com)
- DeveloperOne (www.developerone.com)
- FreewarePalm (www.freewarepalm.com)
- Handango (www.handango.com)
- Ilium Software (www.iliumsoft.com)
- PalmGear.com (www.palmgear.com)
- PalmSource (www.palmsource.com)
- PDA Street (www.pdastreet.com)
- Pocket PC Central (www.pocketpccentral.net)
- PocketGear.com (www.pocketgear.com)
- Tucows PDA Software (pda.tucows.com)

My favorite of these sites, for both Palm and Pocket PC software, is Handango. It always seems to have something new for me to download!

DOWNLOAD OF THE WEEK

Turn your Palm PDA into a digital music player with Pocket Tunes. This neat little shareware program lets you play MP3, WMA, and WAV files on your handheld; the latest version features playlists and shuffle play. Try it for free, or buy it for $14.95 at www.pocket-tunes.com.

September 28, 2005

WEDNESDAY

THIS WEEK'S FOCUS: PALM OS

ON THIS DAY: SEYMOUR CRAY BORN (1925)

On this day in 1925, computer pioneer Seymour Cray was born. Known as the father of the supercomputer, Cray was responsible for the design of many of the world's fastest computers.

Related Web site: research.microsoft.com/users/gbell/craytalk/

GRAFFITI TIPS

If you're like me, no handwriting recognition system in the world will ever recognize your handwriting. I can't even recognize it myself, half the time! But to use your Palm PDA, you have to get comfortable tapping the stylus on that little screen.

Here are some tips to help you get Graffiti to recognize what you scrawl on the screen:

- Use the onscreen keyboard instead of trying to write on the screen. Tap abc into the Graffiti writing area to bring up the keyboard for entry.
- Create a custom Pen stroke—the action of dragging your stylus from the writing area to the top of the screen. Tap the Prefs icon, and then tap Pen.
- For better performance, digitize your Palm monthly, at a minimum. Tap the Prefs icon, and select Buttons > Digitizer.
- Create shortcuts for words you write often.

- If you can't get Graffiti to recognize a word or letter, try writing it backwards.
- Maybe the problem is in your stylus. Try using a third-party stylus with a more comfortable size and weight.

If you find Graffiti recognizing less and less of your handwriting over time, your screen might be wearing out. The more you write onscreen, the more the plastic sheet in the Graffiti area gets deformed. This sometimes causes spurious diagonal lines to appear at the start of a Graffiti stroke. While you can attempt to "massage" the gel between the plastic and glass back into position, often the only solution is repair or replacement.

MAC GADGET OF THE WEEK

Power Support's G5 Roof is the perfect accessory for your G5. It's an aluminum mesh "roof" that sits flush between the top handles, creating a flat, functional surface. Buy it for $74.99 at www.drbott.com.

September 29, 2005
THURSDAY

THIS WEEK'S FOCUS: PDAS

ON THIS DAY: ENRICO FERMI BORN (1901)

Physicist Enrico Fermi was born on this date in 1954. One of the chief architects of the nuclear age, the Italian-born Fermi developed the mathematical statistics required to clarify a large class of subatomic phenomena, discovered neutron-induced radioactivity, and directed the first controlled chain reaction involving nuclear fission. He was awarded the 1938 Nobel Prize for Physics.

Related Web site: www.nobel-winners.com/Physics/enrico_fermi.html

EMULATING GAME PLATFORMS ON YOUR POCKET PC

One of the more interesting uses of the Pocket PC platform is to emulate other game-playing platforms. For example, software exists that can make your Pocket PC operate just like a Nintendo GameBoy, and play GameBoy software.

These programs are called *emulators*, and are available for a large number of past and present game platforms. For example, Retrogames (www.retrogames.com/pocketpc.html) offers Pocket PC emulators for many popular game platforms.

The single best Pocket PC emulator available is Pocket GB (www.pocketgb.com). This program emulates a variety of classic game systems, most notably Nintendo GameBoy and Sega GameGear. The Pocket GB software makes your Pocket PC look and function just like a Nintendo GameBoy unit. Your unit's Hotkey buttons and navigation pad are used to replicate the GameBoy's buttons and joystick.

Emulator programs also exist that let you play classic arcade games, such as Pac-Man and Zaxxon, on your Pocket PC. These programs are called Multi-Arcade Machine Emulators, or MAMEs. Many of these arcade emulators can be found at the MAMEWorld Web site (www.mameworld.net).

There are also a number of game emulators available for the Palm OS. You can find a big selection of emulators for various game systems at Zophar's Domain (www.zophar.net). This site also offers a variety of emulators for the Pocket PC platform.

WEB SITE OF THE WEEK

Palm Boulevard (www.palmblvd.com) is a terrific source for information about the Palm OS and Palm products. You'll find news, reviews, forums, and a ton of software downloads. And check out its sister site, PocketPC City (www.pocketpccity.com), for similar news/reviews about the Pocket PC platform.

September 30, 2005

FRIDAY

THIS WEEK'S FOCUS: PDAS

ON THIS DAY: HOOVER DAM DEDICATED (1935)

The Boulder Dam—subsequently renamed the Hoover Dam—was dedicated on September 30, 1935. Harnessing the raw power of the Colorado River, it was the first U.S. hydroelectric plant to produce a million kilowatts. It was also a testament to American engineering and hard work; it was built in less than five years, in a harsh and barren environment.

Related Web site: www.usbr.gov/lc/hooverdam/

ACCESSORIZING YOUR PDA

You can enhance your Palm or Pocket PC experience by adding specific accessories to your device. These accessories—from storage cards to GPS receivers—increase the performance and the versatility of any Pocket PC.

What kind of accessories am I talking about? A short list includes cases; cables, chargers, and car kits; GPS adapters; keyboards; modem, Ethernet, and Wi-Fi cards; flash storage cards; digital cameras; and more.

Where can you find these accessories? Your PDA's manufacturer probably offers accessories for their units at their Web site; I know that palmOne is especially good at hawking add-ons. In addition, Belkin (www.belkin.com) and Targus (www.targus.com) manufacture a full range of accessories for both Palm and Pocket PC units.

For the best selection of accessories from a variety of manufacturers, however, I recommend you check out one of the following online retailers:

- MobilePlanet (www.mobileplanet.com)
- PalmGear.com (www.palmgear.com)
- PDAZoo (www.pdazoo.com)
- Pocket PC Central (www.pocketpccentral.net)

PORTABLE GADGET OF THE WEEK

Turn your PDA into a full-fledged GPS navigation system with the TomTom Navigator. This cool gizmo connects to your PDA via Bluetooth wireless technology; you can carry the remote GPS unit in your hand or mount it on your dashboard and then read the results on your PDA's screen. The Navigator not only shows you where you are, but also offers door-to-door 2D or 3D navigation and voice-guided turn-by-turn instructions. Buy it for $349 at www.tomtom.com.

MORE SEPTEMBER FACTS

September 1

1985 Titanic wreck located about 12,400 feet below the surface of the Atlantic Ocean (about 400 miles west of Newfoundland)

September 2

1752 Gregorian calendar is adopted by England and its colonies; the Gregorian calendar more closely matches the actual length of time it takes for the Earth to complete an orbit around the sun than did its predecessor, the Julian calendar; the Gregorian calendar is the system we follow today

September 3

1777 The American flag is flown in battle for the first time during a battle at Cooch's Bridge, Maryland

1931 First electric train takes its first journey from Hoboken to Montclair, NJ

September 4

1886 Geronimo, the last American Indian warrior, surrenders to U.S. military forces in Skeleton Canyon, AZ

1951 First transcontinental television broadcast; Harry S. Truman delivered an address from San Francisco during a conference to discuss a peace treaty between the U.S. and Japan

September 8

1930 Scotch Tape is invented

1974 President Gerald Ford pardons former President Richard Nixon of any crimes he might have committed during his term as president

September 9

1912 David Packard is born

1945 First "live" computer bug discovered; a moth was removed from Relay #70, Panel F of the Harvard University Mark II Aiken Relay Calculator; the famous insect now resides at the Smithsonian Institution

2000 The hole in Earth's ozone layer—which typically exposes uninhabited parts of the world to high levels of UV radiation—stretched for a short time over a populated portion of Punta Arenas, Chile

September 10

1913 First coast-to-coast paved highway—the Lincoln Highway—was opened, stretching from Times Square, NY to San Francisco, CA; this highway has since been changed to U.S. 1, U.S. 30, U.S. 530, U.S. 40, and U.S. 50

1930 First planetarium opened in Chicago, IL

September 11

2001 World Trade Center attacks collapse both towers, killing nearly 3,000 people and injuring another 10,000; U.S. Pentagon also attacked, killing 189 people; 45 more people were killed after attempting to regain control of their hijacked plane, causing the plan to crash into a field in rural Pennsylvania

September 13

1899 First American automobile fatality results when H.H. Bliss was struck as he exited a car in New York

September 14

1814 Francis Scott Key composes the lyrics to "The Star-Spangled Banner" after watching the British attack Fort McHenry in Maryland during the War of 1812

1849 Ivan Petrovich Pavlov born

September 15

Grandparents Day

1954 Marilyn Monroe's famous skirt-blowing scene is filmed

September 16

1620 The Mayflower departs from England, carrying 102 people on their way to the new world we now know as America

September 17

Citizenship Day

1787 The U.S. Constitution is signed in Philadelphia

1844 First printing press to use color is patented in Philadelphia, PA

1872 First fire sprinkler is patented in Abington, MA

September 18

1895 First chiropractic adjustment is given to a patient in Davenport, IA

1970 Jimi Hendrix is found dead

September 19

1991 The Iceman, the most ancient human body ever found, is discovered in the Similaun glacier in the Alps on the Italian-Austrian border; the body was estimated to be about 5,300 years old

September 20

1892 Wire glass is patented

September 21

2003 Space probe Galileo ends its eight-year mission when scientists intentionally directed it into Jupiter's atmosphere, where it burned up

September 22

1893 Charles and Frank Duryea test drive America's first automobile in the streets of Springfield, OH; contrary to popular opinion, America's first automobile was not built by Henry Ford

September 23

First day of Autumn

1846 Neptune is discovered

1939 Sigmund Freud dies

1999 Mars Climate Observer burns up as it was preparing to orbit Mars

September 24

1960 First nuclear aircraft carrier, the USS Enterprise, is launched in Newport, VA

September 25

1974 Scientists first report that gases released from aerosol spray cans are destroying the Earth's ozone layer and subjecting the planet to harmful UV radiation

September 26

1820 Daniel Boone dies

1902 Levi Strauss dies

1960 First televised presidential debate between John F. Kennedy and Richard Nixon; Kennedy won the election

September 27

1825 First passenger transport train begins service, carrying passengers from Shildon to Stockton, England

1892 Book matches are patented in Lima, OH

September 28

1925 Seymour Cray, founder of the Cray Computing Company, is born

September 29

1988 Space Shuttle Discovery is launched, marking the first U.S. space shuttle launch since the Space Shuttle Challenger explosion in 1986

September 30

1846 Ether is used for the first time in a dental procedure in Boston, MA

1882 First hydroelectric power plant opens on the Fox River in Appleton, WI

1902 Rayon (originally known as "viscose") is patented

1982 Cyanide-laced Tylenol kills six Chicago-area people; the culprit was never caught, but this incident led to tamper-proof packaging found on many foods and over-the-counter medications today

October 2005

LAPORTE, L.
01789GH58

October 2005

SUNDAY	MONDAY	TUESDAY	WEDNESDAY	THURSDAY	FRIDAY	SATURDAY
						1 1982 First compact disc player is unveiled in Japan
2 1866 First key-opened tin can is patented in New York City	**3** 1995 O.J. Simpson is acquitted of murdering his ex-wife and her friend	**4** Jewish New Year 1968 Film rating system is adopted by the Motion Picture Association	**5** 1902 Ray Kroc, co-founder of McDonald's restaurants, is born	**6** 1942 Xerography—the process for duplicating documents—is patented	**7** 1806 Carbon paper is patented in England	**8** 1958 First internal heart pacemaker is implanted
9 1940 John Lennon is born	**10** Discovery Day (Columbus Day) 1933 Vinyl is patented	**11** 1881 Camera roll film is patented in Fargo, ND	**12** 2000 USS Cole, a U.S. Navy destroyer, is attacked by terrorists in Aden, Yemen	**13** 1884 Greenwich is adopted as the universal median	**14** 1947 Chuck Yeager travels faster than the speed of sound	**15** 1950 First radio paging service begins in New York City
16 Sweetest Day Bosses Day 1985 Intel introduces the first 32-bit processor, the 386	**17** 1931 Organized crime kingpin Al Capone is jailed for tax evasion	**18** 1931 Thomas Edison dies	**19** 1992 Intel introduces the Pentium processor	**20** 1956 Dr. Hanes Lindemann crosses the Atlantic in a small boat	**21** 1879 Thomas Edison invents incandescent electric light	**22** 1988 Congress passes a bill to fight white collar crime
23 1991 *Star Trek* creator Gene Roddenberry dies	**24** 1861 First transcontinental telegraph line is completed	**25** 1955 First domestic microwave oven is sold	**26** 1881 Gunfight between the Earps and the Clantons at the OK Corral	**27** 1904 The New York City subway, the first of its kind, begins operation	**28** 1955 Bill Gates is born	**29** 1958 First coronary is angiogram performed in Cleveland, OH
30 1938 Orson Wells' fictional *War of the Worlds* radio broadcast causes panic	**31** Halloween 1926 Harry Houdini dies					

October 1, 2005

SATURDAY

THIS WEEK'S FOCUS: PDAS

ON THIS DAY: MODEL T INTRODUCED (1908)

On October 1, 1908, the Ford Model T, the first automobile to be mass-produced on an assembly line, was introduced. It sold for $825 and was an immediate sensation. As volumes rose, costs came down; by 1925, a Model T coupe sold for $525 new, while a two-door runabout went for only $260.

Related Web site: www.mtfca.com

PDA OR SMART PHONE?

Is the end near for the personal digital assistant?

That's what many in the industry were asking when Sony decided to exit the Pocket PC business in June of 2004. That leaves just Hewlett-Packard and Dell in the Pocket PC business, with palmOne as the major player on the Palm OS side of things. Further concern came when IDC released its prediction that smart phones will overtake PDA sales by the end of 2004. According to IDC, PDA sales are expected to remain relatively flat (10.7 million in 2003 to 10.8 million in 2004), while smart phone sales will increase from 9 million to 21 million units.

The issue is that high-end PDAs are starting to overlap with fully-featured smart phones. Both feature alphanumeric keyboards of one type or another, both offer some type of PIM software, both let you make cell phone calls, and both offer a variety of other functions—including built-in digital cameras and digital music players. The question for consumers is which type of device does the best job at all of these functions.

Compare the best-selling high-end PDA, the Treo 600, with the similarly featured Motorola MPx200 smart phone. The Treo is big and bulky, with a QWERTY-like keyboard. It has a built-in camera, an integrated speaker phone, a built-in MP3 player, and an SD/MMC expansion slot. You also get all the applications that come with the Palm OS operating system, as well as Internet email, SMS text messaging, and MMS multimedia messaging. It's Internet-enabled with a color Web browser.

The Motorola smart phone offers basic cell phone functions, of course, but you can also use the numeric keypad to enter data and text messages. The MPx200 lets you synch to your PC, stream digital music, and surf the Internet. You browse the Web via the Pocket Internet Explorer browser and send and receive email with Pocket Outlook. You can also play digital music files with Pocket Windows Media Player and send text-based instant messages via pocket MSN Messenger.

FACT OF THE WEEK

Russell Research tells us that the average Palm user is male (64%), 40.1 years old, married (66%), with a college degree (64%), and earns $83,0000 per year. Fully 70% of Palm users carry their PDAs with them seven days a week.

October 2, 2005

SUNDAY

THIS WEEK'S FOCUS: PDAS

ON THIS DAY: FIRST ATOMIC CLOCK (1956)

In 1956, the Atomicron, the first atomic clock, was unveiled at the Overseas Press Club in New York City. An atomic clock uses as a reference the exact frequency of the microwave spectral line emitted by atoms of the metallic element cesium. The integral of frequency is time, so this frequency (9,192,631,770Hz) provides the fundamental unit of time.

Related Web site: tycho.usno.navy.mil

PDA CASES

Just because you have a PDA doesn't mean it's easy to carry around. After all, do you really want to stuff a bare PDA into your back pocket?

Of course not, which is why there's a big market for all sorts of portable cases and bags. You can find cases for any brand PDA from a number of different manufacturers, made from a variety of materials—cloth, leather, vinyl, aluminum, you name it. You can find cases that open from the top or fold from the side; cases that zip closed or use Velcro fasteners; and cases that clip on your belt or tuck in under your shoulder.

The big case company is Targus (www.targus.com), and it makes cases for just about everything. Belt cases, briefcases, backpacks, rolling cases (for notebooks)—you name the style, Targus has it. It's always my first stop when I'm case shopping.

For the ultimate in protection, slide your notebook PC or PDA into a rugged aluminum case from Star Case (www.starcase.com). These cases will protect your portable device from anything short of a mortar attack.

If you want a truly fashionable case for your PDA, check out the line of leather cases fro Bellagio (www.bellagiodesigns.com). These are really beautiful cases, made from top-notch Italian leather, that hold and display your PDA in style. Some cases flip open from the top; others fold closed into a book-like form factor. You can even have Bellagio emboss your name or initials for a small additional fee.

Finally, I really like the various cases offered by e-Holster (www.eholster.com). The cool thing about e-Holster cases is that they make you feel like James Bond, carrying a Walther PPK in a shoulder holster. In fact, e-Holsters *are* shoulder holsters, which you can wear over your jacket or under it.

SOFTWARE OF THE WEEK

Agendus is a three-in-one personal management program for the Palm OS, containing an address book, date book, and to-do list. The Professional Edition adds email to the mix. The Standard Edition sells for $29.95; the Professional Edition runs $39.95. Buy them from www.iambic.com.

THIS WEEK'S FOCUS: COMPUTER HARDWARE

ON THIS DAY: FIRST FAX SENT (1922)

On October 3, 1922, telephone lines were used for the first time for the transmission of a facsimile photo. Charles F. Jenkins sent an image from 1519 Connecticut Ave. in Washington, D.C., to the U.S. Navy Radio Station NOF at Anacostia, D.C. AT&T immediately went to work improving telephone facsimile technology, and in 1924 the telephotography machine was used to send political convention photos long distance for newspaper publication.

Related Web sites: www.ideafinder.com/history/inventions/story051.htm

UNDERSTANDING CPUS

When you open up your PC, you see a lot of chips on your motherboard. But there's one chip that matters more than the others—the central processing unit, or CPU. The CPU (also known as the microprocessor) is the brains of the operation, the chip that runs everything else inside your machine.

Since the first IBM PC was released in 1981, most PCs have been built around CPUs designed by Intel Corporation. Intel has some competition, primarily from Advanced Micro Devices (AMD), but even AMD's chips are based on processors that Intel developed.

Intel has designed and created many microprocessors over the years. Their chips for the personal computer market started with the 8086 (back in 1981) and progressed through the years to the current Pentium 4 chips, with each successive generation offering faster performance. A modern Pentium 4 is thousands of times faster than the original 8086, and the faster the CPU, the more complex the programs your computer can run. Back in the old days, it might take literally hours to recalculate a complex spreadsheet; today, that same calculation takes... well, it takes no time at all.

Because the speed of a CPU is used as a means of measuring how well a computer operates, the megahertz/gigahertz measurement is an important gauge of its power. It's a fair bet that a 3GHz chip will perform faster than a 2GHz chip. It's similar to looking at horsepower as an approximate measure of a car's power—all other things being equal, faster clock speed means faster execution and better performance.

That said, all things aren't equal. The CPU is only part of what makes a computer fast. For example, a really fast CPU paired with a really slow hard disk combines for fairly mediocre overall performance. So when you're trying to determine which computer is the fastest, the microprocessor speed is only part of the equation. Look at hard disk speed, the amount of memory, bus speed, video performance, and the like to get the whole picture.

PC GADGET OF THE WEEK

Roku's HD1000 is a digital hub for both music and pictures, designed especially for displaying digital photographs from your PC on your high-definition TV. The HD1000 connects to your home network or displays photos stored on digital media cards. Buy it for $299.99 at www.rokulabs.com.

October 4, 2005

TUESDAY

THIS WEEK'S FOCUS: COMPUTER HARDWARE

ON THIS DAY: SPACE RACE BEGINS (1957)

History changed on October 4, 1957, when the Soviet Union successfully launched Sputnik I. The world's first artificial satellite was about the size of a basketball, weighed only 183 pounds, and took about 98 minutes to orbit the Earth on its elliptical path. The world—America in particular—took notice.

Related Web site: www.hq.nasa.gov/office/pao/History/sputnik/

UPGRADING MEMORY

Every computer comes with a boatload of built-in electronic memory. This memory is called *random access memory*, or RAM, and is where your computer temporarily stores program instructions, open files, and other data while it's being used. The more memory your computer has, the faster your applications will run—and the more applications (and larger files) you can have open at one time.

Your computer could be using one of three different types of memory modules—SIMMs (single inline memory modules), DIMMs (dual inline memory modules), or RIMMs (Rambus inline memory modules). You'll need to consult your PC's instruction manual (or look up your PC's model number in a manufacturer's cross-listing) to determine the type of module your machine uses.

You also have to specify what type of RAM chip is installed on the module. There are five primary types of memory chips in use today: SDRAM (synchronous dynamic RAM), DDR SDRAM (double-data-rate SDRAM), RDRAM (Rambus DRAM), FPM DRAM (fast-page-mode DRAM), and EDO DRAM (extended data out DRAM). Confused yet? Don't worry about the technical differences; just make sure you get the right type of chip used in your particular PC.

To make the most efficient use of your system's vacant memory slots, it's always best to add the smallest number of larger-capacity modules possible.

Installing memory modules is as simple as turning off your PC, opening the system case, locating the empty memory slots on the motherboard, plugging the new memory module into an empty slot, and then buttoning everything up. Most newer PCs will automatically recognize the new memory when you reboot your PC. If your system displays any sort of error message when you start it up, you'll need to enter the BIOS setup program and reconfigure your system settings manually for the proper amount of memory now installed.

DOWNLOAD OF THE WEEK

BurnInTest is a shareware utility that tests all the major subsystems of your computer, simultaneously. It brings to the surface any intermittent or hidden system problems; it can also be used by overclockers to verify system stability at high clock speeds. Try it for free, or buy it for $22 from www.passmark.com/products/bit.htm.

October 5, 2005
WEDNESDAY

THIS WEEK'S FOCUS: COMPUTER HARDWARE

ON THIS DAY: ROBERT GODDARD BORN (1882)

Robert Goddard was born on this date in 1882. He developed the mathematical theory of rocket propulsion (1912), proved that rockets would function in a vacuum for space flight (1915), and during WWI developed rocket weapons. Between the wars, he produced a number of large liquid-fuel rockets at his Roswell, New Mexico shop; during WWII he developed variable-thrust liquid-fuel rocket motors. At his death, Goddard held 214 separate patents in rocketry.

Related Web site: www.centennialofflight.gov/essay/SPACEFLIGHT/Goddard/SP3.htm

SHOPPING FOR HARD DRIVES

When you go shopping for a new hard drive, you need to understand the relevant specifications in order to make an informed buying decision—and get the right hard drive for your system. Of these specs, you'll want to focus your attention on the following:

- **Size**—Disk drive size is typically measured in gigabytes (GB). The bigger the drive, the higher the price. Some hard drives today can hold 500GB of data—or more.

- **Access time**—This is the amount of time it takes for the heads to locate a specific piece of data on the hard drive.

- **Spin rate**—This spec measures the speed at which the platters spin, in revolutions per minute (RPM). Faster-spinning drives result in faster data transfer rates; most drives today spin at either 5,400 RPM or 7,200 RPM. The slower speed is acceptable for traditional office use, but you'll want a faster drive if you're doing a lot of audio or video-related tasks.

- **Data transfer rate**—This is the speed at which the system copies data from the hard drive to your computer (and vice versa). This spec is typically measured in terms of a *programmed input/output* (PIO) or *Ultra Direct Memory Access* (UDMA) mode. For example, a drive with a peak transfer rate of 100MBps is labeled UDMA 100 (also known as UDMA mode 5).

- **Interface**—There are several different interfaces available that control the communication between your hard drive to your PC. The two primary interfaces in use today are IDE (sometimes called ATA) and SCSI, with IDE/ATA the most common.

When you're looking for a new hard disk, it pays to stick to the major manufacturers. The major manufacturers today include LaCie (www.lacie.com), Maxtor (www.maxtor.com), and Western Digital (www.westerndigital.com).

MAC GADGET OF THE WEEK

Graphics professionals appreciate the natural color reproduction of a good CRT monitor, and Sony's Artisan Color Reference System is one of the best. The complete system includes a 21" FD Trinitron CRT with integrated hood, color sensor, and color calibration software. Buy it for $1,799 at displaysbysony.com/display/.

October 6, 2005

THURSDAY

THIS WEEK'S FOCUS: COMPUTER HARDWARE

ON THIS DAY: THOR HEYERDAHL BORN (1914)

Norwegian adventurer Thor Heyerdahl was born on this date in 1914. Heyerdahl organized and led the famous *Kon-Tiki* (1947) and *Ra* (1969–70) transoceanic scientific expeditions, which tried to prove the possibility of ancient transoceanic contacts between distant civilizations and cultures.

Related Web site: www.greatdreams.com/thor.htm

ADDING A SECOND HARD DRIVE—THE EASY WAY

Given the low price of hard drives today, you'll eventually be tempted to add more storage capacity to your system. While you could go to the time and trouble of adding a second internal hard drive, it's far, far, easier to install a drive of the external variety.

External hard drives typically install via either USB or FireWire. While USB 2.0 is fast enough for most uses (skip the older USB 1.1 drives), FireWire is even better. Know, however, that you can't use an external hard drive as your sole or primary drive; that's because you can't boot your system from an external drive.

That said, installing an external hard drive is relatively simple. Just follow these steps:

1. Plug the new drive into a live electrical outlet.
2. Connect the drive to an open USB or FireWire port on your PC.

3. If your new drive came with an installation CD (and it probably did), insert the CD into your CD-ROM drive and run the installation program. Otherwise, Windows should recognize the new drive and automatically install the proper device drivers.

Once installed, an external drive assumes the next highest available drive letter on your system. So, for example, if your current hard drive is drive C:, the new external drive will be drive D:. (If your CD-ROM drive was formerly drive D:, it will now become drive E:; when it comes to letters, your system likes to group similar types of drives together.)

WEB SITE OF THE WEEK

Turn to HardwareCentral for reviews of all the latest computer hardware, as well as news, tips, tutorials, and the like. Check it out at www.hardwarecentral.com.

October 7, 2005

FRIDAY

THIS WEEK'S FOCUS: COMPUTER HARDWARE

ON THIS DAY: DARK SIDE OF THE MOON PHOTOGRAPHED (1959)

We can't see the dark side of the moon from Earth, but on this date in 1959 we got to look at photos. The Luna 3 spacecraft took 29 photos of what was actually the sunlit far side of the moon, covering 70% of the previously unseen surface.

Related Web site:

nssdc.gsfc.nasa.gov/imgcat/html/mission_page/EM_Luna_3_page1.html

BETTER COMPUTER GRAPHICS

If you play some of the latest videogames, you might find that your older PC doesn't have the horsepower to display the game graphics as smoothly as you'd like. You might run into similar problems if you do a lot of video editing.

The easiest way to get better—and faster—graphics on your computer is to upgrade to a better video card. Many low-end—and most older—PCs come with (surprise!) low-performance video cards, which just aren't up to snuff when it comes to displaying high-resolution graphics, fast-moving game images, and moving video from DVDs and digital movies. If your display has a tendency to shudder and jerk, it's time to think about getting a higher-performance video card.

Upgrading your video card is pretty much as easy as removing the old one and replacing it with a new one. You do, however, want to pay attention to some key specifications when you're shopping. Look at the card's resolution (the higher the better), onboard memory (go for 256MB or more), 3D acceleration (necessary for game playing), and connectors (VGA connectors are standard; DVI connectors are great if you have an LCD monitor).

If you're a hardcore gamer, your choice of video card is simple: Go with any card that uses an nVidia chipset. nVidia makes the highest-performing video chips out there, and many game designers optimize their software to work best with the nVidia chipset. To learn more about nVidia chips—and which cards use them—check out the nVidia Web site, at www.nvidia.com.

When you're shopping for a new high-performance video card, look for models from ATI Technologies (www.ati.com), BFG Technologies (www.bfgtech.com), Mad Dog Multimedia (www.maddogmultimedia.com), PNY Technologies (www.pny.com), or VisionTek (www.visiontek.com). They're all good.

PORTABLE GADGET OF THE WEEK

You can add a keyboard to any Palm or Pocket PC model without worrying about connectors, thanks to Targus's Universal Wireless Keyboard. This is a fold-out, full-size QWERTY keyboard that connects with your PDA via a wireless infrared connection. Just sit your PDA into a small cradle above the keyboard; the IR connection is automatic. Buy it for $79.99 from www.targus.com.

October 8, 2005

SATURDAY

THIS WEEK'S FOCUS: COMPUTER HARDWARE

ON THIS DAY: FIRST PACEMAKER IMPLANTED

On October 8, 1958, Dr Åke Senning implanted the first internal heart pacemaker at the Karolinska Institute of Stockholm. Even though this initial pacemaker worked for just three hours, the recipient, Arne Larsson, is still going strong today—26 pacemakers later.

Related Web site: www.pacemakerclub.com

WORKING WITH PORTS

All the various devices inside and outside your computer connect to each other via *ports*. A port is simply a fancy name for a connector jack, and there are several different types used in computer systems. Here's a quick rundown of the various ports you might run into, and what they're typically used for.

- **Parallel** ports are used primarily for connecting printers to your system.
- **Serial** ports are used to connect some types of mice, keyboards, and printers, as well as PDAs, PC cameras, and other assorted peripherals.
- **USB** ports are used to connect just about any type of peripheral; peripherals conforming to the new USB 2.0 standard run much faster than the existing 1.1 devices.
- **FireWire (IEEE 1394)** ports are used to connect fast digital devices, such as digital video recorders and digital still cameras.
- **SCSI** ports are used to connect fast external hard drives.

Most computers today come with a single parallel port, one or two serial ports, a FireWire port or two, and anywhere from a couple to a half-dozen USB ports.

If you add too many devices to your system, you could run out of ports. The solution to this depends on the type of port you need. If you run out of USB ports, buy an external USB hub. This device plugs into an open USB port on your system unit and expands into four or more additional USB ports. You can find similar expansion hubs for FireWire.

If you need more parallel or serial ports, you'll need to add a port expansion card in your system unit. You can also find expansion cards for USB and FireWire, if you want to go that route. Install the card, and you have more ports on the back of your system unit.

FACT OF THE WEEK

Harris Interactive reports that 42% of all physicians work in practices that have their own Web sites. Just 13% of doctors, however, use email to communicate with their patients.

October 9, 2005
SUNDAY

THIS WEEK'S FOCUS: **COMPUTER HARDWARE**

ON THIS DAY: ELECTRIC BLANKET INTRODUCED (1946)

In 1946, the Simmons Company of Petersburg, Virginia manufactured the first electric blanket. Its price was $39.50, and temperature was regulated by an electronic thermostatic control. By the way, the term "electric blanket" was not used until the 1950s; before then, they were called "warming pads" or "heated quilts."

Related Web site: inventors.about.com/library/inventors/blelectricblanket.htm

SHOPPING FOR PRINTERS

If you need a new printer for your system, there are a lot of different models available. Not only do you have the basic choice between black and white or color, you also have a variety of printing technologies to choose from.

The lowest-priced printer available today is the inkjet. Inkjet printers produce printout by spraying ink through holes in a matrix onto single sheets of paper. These printers are lower-priced than laser printers, and the best of the bunch have print quality indistinguishable from laser quality. They're also slower than laser printers, and not quite up to task if you have a large printing volume.

If you want a color printer, you're pretty much limited to inkjet technology. (Color laser printers are too expensive for most consumers.) Just make sure you get a model with a separate black cartridge, so that when you do print black and white, you're not wasting your color ink.

The highest-quality (and highest-priced) printers available today are laser printers. These printers work much like copying machines, using a small laser to transfer toner (a kind of powdered ink) to paper. Laser printer output is extremely high

quality, and the process is fast and quiet. And, if you print in large volume, laser printers are the only way to go.

Then there are photo printers, which are optimized to create high-quality photo prints, typically on special photo print paper. Note, however, that photo printers are notoriously slow (five minutes or more to make a single print), and drink ink like it's Gatorade on a hot summer day.

Finally, one of the hottest trends today is the combo printer/fax/copier/scanner machine—sometimes called an all-in-one. These units are very efficient, both in terms of cost and in desktop footprint. You can find all-in-ones in both inkjet and laser versions. They're my choice for best all-around office printer.

SOFTWARE OF THE WEEK

When you need to create a new partition on your hard disk, nothing works better than Norton PartitionMagic. You can create, resize, delete, and merge partitions with ease; the included BootMagic utility makes it easy to install different operating systems on each partition. Buy it for $69.95 at www.symantec.com.

October 10, 2005

MONDAY

THIS WEEK'S FOCUS: **NOTEBOOK COMPUTERS**

ON THIS DAY: ED WOOD BORN (1924)

Bad director extraordinaire Ed Wood, Jr. was born on October 10, 1924. More famous now than he ever was when alive, Ed Wood created some of the most wonderfully awful films in the history of cinema, including *Glen or Glenda*, *Bride of the Monster*, and possibly the worst movie ever made, *Plan 9 from Outer Space*. Wood's films are so bad they're good, sort of; Wood himself was the subject of Tim Burton's biopic, *Ed Wood*.

Related Web page: hem.passagen.se/mwrang/

NOTEBOOK ACCESSORIES

One of the reasons I like notebook PCs is that there are all sorts of gadgets you can buy for them—and, in case you can't tell, I like buying gadgets! Notebook gadgets are mostly small, often (but not always) low-priced, and sometimes quite cool. My only problem is that if I buy every notebook gadget that catches my eye, I'll need more space to haul the gadgets than I do to haul my notebook PC!

What types of notebook gadgets are we talking about? There are three main categories: security, power, and storage/display—along with the normal miscellaneous gadgets, of course.

Security-related gadgets are designed to protect your notebook from theft. The simplest devices, called laptop locks, work to strap your PC to a presumably immovable object; one of my favorites is Targus's DEFCON CL Notebook Computer Cable Lock. The fancier units, like Targus's DEFCON 1 Security System or the TrackIT Portable Anti-Theft system, incorporate some sort of antitheft alarm. All do a pretty good job of deterring would-be thieves, just by making it harder to walk away with the goods.

You use power-related gadgets to provide power to your notebook. These gadgets supplement your

PC's built-in batteries or power supply when you're on the road. Some devices, such as Targus's Mobile 70 Universal AC Power Adapter, replace the clunky factory-supplied AC power adapter; others, like Targus's Universal Auto/Air Notebook Power Adapter, let you connect to various DC power sources. All are essential if you're a frequent traveler.

Storage and display gadgets function as racks or docking stations when you use your notebook in the office. Some of these items, like the Dexia Rack, are quite fashionable; others, such as Vantec's LapCool (with built-in cooling fan), provide unique functionality.

PC GADGET OF THE WEEK

Vactec's LapCool notebook cooler helps cool down hot-running notebooks, thanks to two ultra-quiet fans in the base. Set your notebook PC on the LapCool, flip on the fans, and bring down the heat level almost immediately. If that wasn't neat enough, the LapCool also functions as a four-port USB 2.0 hub, so you can get double duty from the desktop footprint. Buy it for $42.95 at www.vantecusa.com.

October 11, 2005

TUESDAY

THIS WEEK'S FOCUS: NOTEBOOK COMPUTERS

ON THIS DAY: FIRST APOLLO MISSION LAUNCHED (1967)

The Apollo spacecraft received its first test on this date in 1967, when a Saturn 1-B rocket launched the Apollo 7 into orbit. The crew included Wally Schirra, Donn Eisele, and Walter Cunningham.

Related Web site: www-pao.ksc.nasa.gov/kscpao/history/apollo/apollo-7/apollo-7.htm

DIFFERENT TYPES OF NOTEBOOKS

When you think of a notebook computer, you probably think of a lightweight, thinnish portable PC that operates on battery power and has a relatively small screen. That's actually a pretty broad description, and doesn't accurately represent all the different types of notebooks available today. Let's take a quick look at what's out there.

- **Ultraportables**—These are the smallest notebooks out there, designed primarily for the frequent traveler who only needs to check email and write a few memos, and doesn't want to haul around a big, heavy machine to do so. The typical ultraportable has a 10" or 12" display, weighs less than 4 pounds, and doesn't have a lot of extras—no internal CD or DVD drive, for example.

- **Thin-and-lights**—This class of notebook offers a good balance between portability, performance, and features for the serious business traveler. These notebooks typically have a 12" or 14" display, use the Pentium M processor, are less than an inch thick, weigh between 4-6 pounds, and have a swappable internal CD or DVD drive.

- **Mainstreams**—This is the workhorse of the notebook line, delivering good performance at

a low price. The sacrifice is typically in weight and battery life. Look for a 14" display, relatively thick (>1") form factor, weight in the 6–8 pound range, and fixed internal CD/DVD and floppy drives.

- **Desktop replacements**—These are big hogs, designed more for stationary than portable use. Expect every feature imaginable, terrific performance, and extremely poor battery life. You'll find a 15" or bigger screen, thick and heavy form factor, and all the ports and drives you could ever need.

There's one final class of notebook—the Tablet PC. A Tablet PC is essentially an ultraportable with a screen you can write on. All tablets use a special version of Windows XP that lets you input data via handwriting recognition.

DOWNLOAD OF THE WEEK

FolderClone lets you make an identical copy of a folder and all its files and subfolders from one drive to another. Use it to synchronize files between your desktop and laptop PCs. It's shareware, so you can try it for free or buy it for $27.95 from www.folderclone.com.

October 12, 2005
WEDNESDAY

THIS WEEK'S FOCUS: NOTEBOOK COMPUTERS

ON THIS DAY: SEARCH FOR EXTRATERRESTRIAL LIFE BEGINS (1992)

On this date in 1992, NASA initiated the High Resolution Microwave Survey. This project uses the 305-meter radiotelescope antenna at the Arecibo Observatory in Puerto Rico to scan millions of radio frequencies for signs of extraterrestrial life. Unlike the fiction in the movie *Contact* (which featured the Arecibo facility), no signals have yet been detected.

Related Web site: www.naic.edu

MACINTOSH NOTEBOOKS

Notebooks are just as popular in the Mac world as they are on the PC side of the fence. In fact, you might prefer a Mac notebook over a PC notebook if you work in an industry where Macs are more dominant (graphics, music, video editing), or if you simply prefer the functionality of the Mac OS.

Apple sells two different families of notebooks—the budget iBook and the flagship PowerBook. The iBook is smaller and lower priced, runs the older and slightly slower PowerPC G3 processor, and offers really good battery life. The PowerBook delivers all the goods in a slightly larger package, runs the faster PowerPC G4 chip, and offers reasonable battery life.

The iBook is good for the frequent traveler, for users on a budget, or for someone who doesn't want to carry around a big, heavy notebook. The PowerBook is for someone who wants a desktop replacement machine, or simply wants the best performance possible and doesn't mind the price.

Other than the processor and performance, issues surrounding the configuration of a Mac notebook are essentially the same as those surrounding configuration of PC notebooks. Look for the combination of features (CD drive, DVD drive, and so on) that best suits your computing needs.

Naturally, you can find out more about all of Apple's notebooks at www.apple.com. They'll also be glad to take your credit card number when you're ready to place an order.

MAC GADGET OF THE WEEK

Here's a great little mouse to take on the road with either your iBook or PowerBook. MacAlly's iceMouseJr is optical, reasonably priced and has a cord; if that bothers you, the company offers Bluetooth, RF, and even small rechargeable models. Buy the iceMouseJr for $29 at www.macally.com.

October 13, 2005

THURSDAY

THIS WEEK'S FOCUS: NOTEBOOK COMPUTERS

ON THIS DAY: U.S. NAVY USES DOLPHINS FOR SURVEILLANCE (1987)

Shades of *Day of the Dolphin*... On this date in 1987, the U.S. Navy deployed six dolphins in the Persian Gulf to search for Iranian mines. This wasn't the first use of marine mammals by the Navy, however; recently declassified documents reveal that dolphins were used on a top-secret basis as far back as Vietnam.

Related Web site: www.angelfire.com/nj4/navydolphins/

SHOPPING FOR THE PERFECT NOTEBOOK

If you're in the market for a new notebook computer, your main considerations (besides price) are processor, memory, hard disk, screen size, portability, and battery life. Let's look at each factor.

- **Processor**—I like the Pentium M chip, as it's reasonably fast and doesn't use a lot of power—resulting in long battery life. AMD's Athlon is a good alternative, although it's not quite as energy efficient.

- **Memory**—Memory matters. Get at least 256MB, and possibly 512MB if you're running heavy loads.

- **Hard disk**—The bigger the better. Many notebooks now offer 40GB or larger disks; buy as much as you can afford.

- **Screen**—The screen size helps determine the type of notebook and the price. Ultraportables have a 12" or smaller screen; thin-and-lights and mainstream notebooks will go up to 14" or 15"; desktop replacements will have 15" and larger screens, sometimes in a widescreen configuration.

- **Portability**—All the previous features add up, in terms of size and weight. If you want a smaller, more portable machine, you'll have to sacrifice on screen size and other factors.

- **Battery life**—If you use your notebook a lot on the road, go for a model that offers 4 or 5 hours per battery charge, which probably means a Pentium M model with a slightly smaller screen.

Whatever other features you opt for, you'll definitely want built-in Ethernet, and probably built-in Wi-Fi. Look for models with Intel's Centrino technology, which delivers Wi-Fi performance with exceptionally long battery life.

WEB SITE OF THE WEEK

Shopping for a new notebook PC? Then check out the product reviews and price updates at NotebookReview. You can search by manufacturer, price, processor type, or any number of technical specifications. There are lots of user reviews, as well. Check it out at www.notebookreview.com.

October 14, 2005

FRIDAY

THIS WEEK'S FOCUS: NOTEBOOK COMPUTERS

ON THIS DAY: CHUCK YEAGER BREAKS THE SOUND BARRIER (1947)

On October 14, 1947, ace test pilot Chuck Yeager hopped into the cockpit of the rocket-powered X-1 plane and became the first human to break the sound barrier. Yeager went on to break even more records over his storied career; amazingly, he also flew more than 120 combat missions in Vietnam, and later served on the Presidential commission investigating the Challenger accident.

Related Web site: www.acepilots.com/usaaf_yeager.html

PORTABLE MEMORY DEVICES

Most notebook users also have a main desktop PC they use when they're at home or in the office. Which means that transferring files from one machine now becomes an issue.

If both computers are on the same network, transferring files is easy. If not, you have to take a different approach.

I like using USB memory devices—some people call them keychain memory devices—to transfer data between different machines. These gadgets contain various amounts of flash memory and connect to your computer via the USB port. When connected, your computer views the device just like another disk drive. You can then transfer files from your computer to the flash memory and back again.

What's especially cool about these USB memory devices is that they pack so much storage in such a small form factor. Most of these gizmos are truly keychain-sized; you can slip them in your pocket and carry them from PC to PC. That makes for truly portable mass storage. And, because they're pretty much plug-and-play, transferring your files from one computer to another is easy.

Some of the early USB memory devices didn't have much memory onboard—8MB and 16MB devices were common. But as the price of flash memory has come down, manufacturers have packed more and more memory into these little doodads. Some models today have upwards of 512MB and 1GB of storage, which is big enough to store all but the biggest files.

Of course, the more storage offered, the higher the price. Today's lowest-priced USB memory devices give you 32MB of storage for $30 or so. Get into the 256MB range and you'll spend closer to $100, and the big 1GB gizmos will set you back several hundred bucks. Pick a size/price combination that best fits your needs.

PORTABLE GADGET OF THE WEEK

The RIST Memory Watch is a wrist watch that also contains 128MB of flash memory to store all manner of digital files. You connect the watch to your PC via the supplied USB cable and transfer files as you would with any other USB drive. The watch part, of course, works just like a normal watch. Buy it for $109 at www.meritline.com.

THIS WEEK'S FOCUS: NOTEBOOK COMPUTERS

ON THIS DAY: KILLER BEES INVADE TEXAS (1990)

Africanized honey bees are the result of crossbreeding between European and African strains of honey bees in Brazil. Unfortunately, these bees were released from the breeding program before aggressive behavior was bred out. The so-called "killer bees" spread quickly, advancing up to 300 miles per year through the tropics of South and Central America until they reached the town of Hidalgo, on the southern tip of Texas, on October 15, 1990.

Related Web site: www.insecta-inspecta.com/bees/killer/

UPGRADING NOTEBOOK MEMORY

Upgrading memory on a portable PC is a little different than with a desktop system. On one hand, it's easier; memory is typically added through an easily accessible compartment on the bottom of the unit. On the other hand, it's more complicated; every manufacturer (and seemingly every model) uses different non-standard memory types and form factors.

When shopping for laptop memory, you do it by manufacturer and model number. Some portable RAM comes in modules, some on units that look like little credit cards. You have to get the exact type of memory used by your particular PC, whatever that might happen to be.

Installing the memory, however, should be a snap—literally. On most models you use a screwdriver to open a small compartment on the bottom of the unit, then snap the new memory into place. Just follow these steps:

1. Close Windows and power off your PC.
2. Locate and open your PC's memory compartment.
3. Insert the new memory module or card, per the manufacturer's instructions.
4. Reinstall the cover to the memory compartment and power up your portable.

Note that on some notebooks you might need to remove an old lower-capacity memory card in order to add a new higher-capacity one. And, as with desktop systems, your portable should automatically recognize the new memory on startup.

FACT OF THE WEEK

According to the CSI/FBI PC Crime and Security Survey, notebook theft is the second most prevalent computer crime, after virus-related offenses. The FBI says 98% of stolen laptops are never recovered; one out of 10 laptop thefts appear in airports.

October 16, 2005

SUNDAY

THIS WEEK'S FOCUS: NOTEBOOK COMPUTERS

ON THIS DAY: FIRST USE OF ANESTHETIC (1846)

On this date in 1846, American dentist Dr. William Thomas Green Morton made the first public demonstration of the administration of ether anesthetic. The patient, who had a small superficial tumor removed from beneath the left lower jaw, inhaled ether from a blown glass flask.

Related Web site: www.isaponline.org

HOW TO GET THE MOST OUT OF YOUR NOTEBOOK

We'll end our notebook week with some tips for serious road warriors.

- When you're traveling, consider the total weight of everything you'll bring with you. An ultraportable PC gets a lot heavier if you drag along a power supply, DC adapter, and extra battery.

- Stretch the life of your battery by dialing down the screen brightness, not using the CD/DVD drive, and turning off Wi-Fi when you're not using it.

- The more you use the battery, the less charge it will hold. Batteries don't last forever; they wear out with use. I use my battery a lot, and find that it loses half its charge over the course of the year—which tells me its time to buy a replacement.

- Buy a spare AC power supply to carry with you on the road. This will save you from constantly plugging and unplugging your home power supply.

- Make home or office use easier by using a docking station. This makes for a much easier peripheral connection.

- Consider a wireless keyboard and mouse for home use—made easier with a docking station, of course.

- When you're traveling, keep your notebook with you at all times. Don't leave it at your table or in your briefcase when you take a bathroom break. And consider some sort of anti-theft device; there's a lot of money wrapped up in that small package!

SOFTWARE OF THE WEEK

Need to send or receive a fax when you're on the road? You could head down to the nearest Kinko's, or—even better—load up your trusty copy of WinFax PRO. For most road warriors, this is the only fax software to consider; it's been around for about forever, mainly because it does its job so well. Buy it for $99.95 at www.symantec.com.

October 17, 2005
MONDAY

THIS WEEK'S FOCUS: COMPUTER MAINTENANCE

ON THIS DAY: ALBERT EINSTEIN ARRIVES IN AMERICA (1933)

On this day in 1933, Albert Einstein arrived in the United States as a refugee from Nazi Germany. He took a position at the Institute for Advanced Study at Princeton, New Jersey, and renounced his former pacifist stand in the face of the awesome threat to humankind posed by the Nazi regime. Six years later, Einstein collaborated with several other physicists in writing a letter to President Franklin D. Roosevelt, pointing out the possibility of making an atomic bomb—and the likelihood that the German government was embarking on such a course. That letter helped lend urgency to American efforts to build an atomic bomb.

Related Web site: www.amnh.org/exhibitions/einstein/

BASIC SYSTEM MAINTENANCE

I think it's easier to *prevent* problems beforehand than it is to try to solve them after they occur. Let's face it—even if you're able to fix a problem, you would have saved yourself a lot of grief if you could have avoided it completely. It pays to spend a little time on preventive maintenance *now* to save you hours of problem-solving and disaster recovery *later*.

With that in mind, consider your PC's system unit. This little beige box has a lot of stuff inside—everything from memory chips to disk drives to power supplies. Check out these maintenance tips to keep your system unit from flaking out on you:

- Position your system unit in a clean, dust-free environment, away from direct sunlight and strong magnetic fields. Also, be sure your system unit and monitor have plenty of air flow around them, to keep them from overheating.

- Hook your system unit up to a surge suppressor to avoid deadly power spikes. (Note, however, that even the best surge suppressor won't protect against a direct lightning strike!)

- Avoid turning your system unit on and off too often; it's better to leave it on all the time than incur frequent "power on" stress to all those delicate components.

- Turn off your system unit if you're going to be away for an extended period—anything longer than a day or two.

- Check all your cable connections periodically. Make sure all the connectors are firmly connected, and all the screws properly screwed—and make sure your cables aren't stretched too tight, or bent in ways that could damage the wires inside.

- If you're really adventurous, open up the system case periodically and vacuum or wipe the dust from the inside. (Just make sure the system unit is unplugged at the time!) Using a can of "compressed air" is also a good way to blast the dirt out of your system.

PC GADGET OF THE WEEK

The TrackIT Portable Anti-Theft System consists of a small device that you attach to your notebook PC; the device is synched to a keychain receiver that you carry with you at all times. If you're separated from your PC—that is, if the TrackIT gets too far from the receiver—a 110dB alarm sounds. It's that simple. Buy it for $59.95 at www.trackitcorp.com.

THIS WEEK'S FOCUS: COMPUTER MAINTENANCE

ON THIS DAY: RCA FOUNDED (1919)

RCA—the Radio Corporation of America—was formed on this date in 1919. RCA was born out of General Electric and took over the assets of the American Marconi company and the responsibility for marketing the radio equipment produced by GE and Westinghouse. Just six years later, RCA's revenues from "wireless" came to $4 million, while revenue from the sale of consumer Radiolas (early radios) and related equipment had grown to $46 million.

Related Web site: www.rca.com

CLEANING KEYBOARDS AND MICE

Even something as simple as your keyboard requires a little preventive maintenance from time to time. Check out these tips:

- Keep your keyboard away from dust, dirt, smoke, direct sunlight, and other harmful environmental stuff. You might even consider putting a dust cover on your keyboard when it's not in use.

- Use a small vacuum cleaner to periodically sweep the dirt from your keyboard, or compressed air to blow the dirt away. Use a cotton swab or soft cloth to clean between the keys. If necessary, remove the keycaps to clean the switches underneath.

- If you spill something on your keyboard, disconnect it immediately and wipe up the spill. Use a soft cloth to get between the keys, or pop off the keycaps to wipe up any seepage underneath. Let the keyboard dry thoroughly before trying to use it again.

And let's not forget your mouse, which can get really gunked up with excessive use:

- Periodically open up the bottom of your mouse and remove the roller ball. Wash the ball with water or a mild detergent. Use a soft cloth to dry the ball before reinserting it.

- While your mouse ball is removed, use compressed air or a cotton swab to clean dust and dirt from the inside of your mouse.

- Always use a mouse pad—they really do help keep things rolling smoothly, plus they give you good traction. (And while you're at it, don't forget to clean your mouse pad with a little spray cleaner—it can get dirty, too.)

DOWNLOAD OF THE WEEK

TuneUp Utilities is a shareware program that helps you configure and maintain your system. It includes a disk-cleaning utility, Registry cleaner, memory optimizer, uninstall manager, and file shredder. Try it for free, or buy it for $39.99 at www.tune-up.com.

THIS WEEK'S FOCUS: COMPUTER MAINTENANCE

ON THIS DAY: AMDAHL CORP. FOUNDED (1970)

Amdahl Corporation was founded on this date in 1970 by Dr. Gene Amdahl, a former IBM employee. The company, since 1997 a subsidiary of Fujitsu, has been a major supplier of large mainframes and accompanying software. The company launched its first product, the Amdahl 470 V6, in 1975, competing directly against IBM's System/360 family—which Gene Amdahl himself had designed when he worked for IBM.

Related Web site: ed-thelen.org/comp-hist/amdahl-bio-core-1-4.html

DEFRAG YOUR HARD DISK

File fragmentation is sort of like taking the pieces of a jigsaw puzzle and storing them in different boxes along with pieces from other puzzles. The more dispersed the pieces are, the longer it takes to put the puzzle together. Spreading the bits and pieces of a file around your hard disk occurs whenever you install, delete, or run an application, or when you edit, move, copy, or delete a file.

If you notice your system takes longer and longer to open and close files or run applications, it's because these file fragments are spread all over the place. You fix the problem when you put all the pieces of the puzzle back in the right boxes—which you do by *defragmenting* your hard disk.

Use the Windows Disk Defragmenter utility to defragment your hard drive. In Windows XP, you should follow these steps:

1. Click Start > All Programs > Accessories > System Tools > Disk Defragmenter to open the Disk Defragmenter utility.
2. Select the drive you want to defragment.
3. Click the Defragment button.

Defragmenting your drive can take awhile, especially if you have a large hard drive or your drive is really fragmented. Also, you should close all applications—including your screensaver—and stop working on your system while Disk Defragmenter is running.

MAC GADGET OF THE WEEK

Add more FireWire ports to your Mac with Belkin's FireWire 4-Port Hub. It connects to any open FireWire port and has enough ports for four additional FireWire-compatible peripherals. Buy it for $89.95 at www.belkin.com.

THIS WEEK'S FOCUS: COMPUTER MAINTENANCE

ON THIS DAY: LOUISIANA PURCHASE RATIFIED (1803)

The most significant real estate transaction in history was approved by the U.S. Senate on October 20, 1803; the vote was 24 to 7. The Louisiana Purchase, negotiated between President Thomas Jefferson and Napoleon, added more than 800,000 square miles of land to the young America, at a cost of less than four cents per acre—$15 million in total.

Related Web site: www.louisianapurchase2003.com

DELETE UNNECESSARY FILES

Even with today's humongous hard disks, you can still end up with too many useless files taking up too much hard disk space. Fortunately, Windows includes a utility that identifies and deletes unused files on your hard disk—automatically.

Disk Cleanup is a great tool to use when you want to free up extra hard disk space for more frequently used files. To use Disk Cleanup in Windows XP, follow these steps:

1. Click Start > All Programs > Accessories > System Tools > Disk Cleanup.
2. Disk Cleanup starts and automatically analyzes the contents of your hard disk drive.
3. When Disk Cleanup is finished analyzing, it presents its results in the Disk Cleanup dialog box.
4. Select the Disk Cleanup tab.

5. You now have the option of permanently deleting various types of files. Depending on how your system is configured, this list might include downloaded program files, temporary Internet files, deleted files in the Recycle Bin, setup log files, temporary files, WebClient/Publisher temporary files, and catalog files for the Content Indexer. You can safely choose to delete all these files *except* the setup log and Content Indexer files.
6. Click OK to begin deleting.

That's a lot easier than deleting all those files by hand!

WEB SITE OF THE WEEK

Check out and fine-tune your computer online at PC Pitstop. The site features a variety of performance tests, as well as online technical help. Run the tests (for free!) at www.pcpitstop.com.

October 21, 2005
FRIDAY

THIS WEEK'S FOCUS: COMPUTER MAINTENANCE

ON THIS DAY: EDISON DEMONSTRATES ELECTRIC LIGHT (1879)

On October 21, 1879, Thomas Edison successfully demonstrated the first durable and commercially practical electric light bulb at his laboratory in Menlo Park, New Jersey. This first model, which used carbonized sewing thread for its filament, lasted 40 hours before burning out.

Related Web site: `edison.rutgers.edu`

PERFORM A HARD DISK CHECKUP

Any time you run an application, move or delete a file, or accidentally turn the power off while the system is running, you run the risk of introducing errors to your hard disk. These errors can make it harder to open files, slow down your hard disk, or cause your system to freeze when you open or save a file or an application.

Fortunately, you can find and fix most of these errors directly from within Windows. All you have to do is run the built-in ScanDisk utility.

To find and fix errors on your hard drive from Windows XP, follow these steps:

1. Open the My Computer folder and right-click the icon for the drive you want to scan, and then select the Properties option from the pop-up menu.
2. When the Properties dialog box appears, select the Tools tab.
3. Click the Check Now button to display the Check Disk dialog box.
4. Check both the options (Automatically Fix File System Errors and Scan for and Attempt Recovery of Bad Sectors).
5. Click Start; Windows now scans your hard disk and attempts to fix any errors it encounters.

If you have an older version of Windows, you open ScanDisk by clicking Start > Programs > Accessories > System Tools > ScanDisk.

PORTABLE GADGET OF THE WEEK

The Pyramat PM300 Game Chair is a gaming chair that unfolds like a futon or folds up into a 20" cube. The headset contains a powerful 25-watt subwoofer and two surround-sound side speakers; connect it your videogame console for the ultimate gaming experience. There's even a wired remote control that lets you adjust the volume and rumble intensity. Buy it for $149.99 from `www.pyramat.com`.

October 22, 2005

SATURDAY

THIS WEEK'S FOCUS: COMPUTER MAINTENANCE

ON THIS DAY: KENNEDY ANNOUNCES CUBAN MISSILE CRISIS (1962)

The United States and Russia stood eyeball-to-eyeball on the brink of nuclear war during what we now call the Cuban Missile Crisis. The crisis became public on October 22, 1962, when President Kennedy, in a televised address to the U.S. people, confirmed the presence of Soviet missiles in Cuba and announced a naval blockade of the island. It took 13 days, but war was eventually averted when the Soviets withdrew the missiles, in return for a U.S. promise not to invade Cuba and to withdraw tactical nuclear missiles from Turkey.

Related Web site: library.thinkquest.org/11046/

BACKING UP IMPORTANT DATA

The best way to protect yourself against catastrophic data loss is to make backup copies of all your important files. In the caveman days of personal computing, you could back up all your important files on a single floppy disk. But that was before you started adding graphics to all your memos, and before the days of multi-megabyte digital music files and megapixel digital picture files.

In today's world of 200+GB hard drives, it's increasingly difficult to back up your crucial computer files. It would take thousands of floppies to back up today's typical hard drive; there's so much data involved, it's not even practical to burn to backup DVDs. (A 100GB hard drive would require almost two dozen recordable DVDs!)

That's why I recommend using a second hard disk to back up all your data. All the major hard drive manufacturers market these hard drive-based backup devices. Most of these solutions include an external hard drive, a USB 2.0 or FireWire connection, and some sort of backup software. The best units, like the Maxtor OneTouch, totally automate the backup process, making backups either automatically via software or via a big front-panel backup button. I happen to like the push-button

approach; it makes what used to be a complex process quite easy.

If you have a broadband Internet connection, you might want to consider an online backup service, which lets you back up your files online to a separate Internet site; this way, if your house burns down, your key files are safely stored offsite. Some of the more popular online backup services include @Backup (www.backup.com), Connected (www.connected.com), IBackup (www.ibackup.com), and Xdrive (www.xdrive.com).

Of course, you don't need to back up your entire hard disk, nor do you probably want to. (It takes too long!) I recommend you back up all your data files, but *don't* back up your software programs; you can always reinstall your programs from their original installation CDs.

FACT OF THE WEEK

A survey by the Society of Financial Service Professionals reports that 92% of American workers feel comfortable with technology and equipment at the office. Comfortable enough that 41% also report that they engage in personal Internet surfing or online shopping at work.

October 23, 2005

SUNDAY

THIS WEEK'S FOCUS: COMPUTER MAINTENANCE

ON THIS DAY: OLDEST FOSSILS DISCOVERED (1977)

On this date in 1977, American paleontologist Elso S. Barghoorn announced the discovery of Pre-Cambian spherical one-celled algae microfossils (named *Eobacterium*). These fossils were 3.4 billion years old, making them Earth's earliest life forms.

Related Web site: bcornet.tripod.com/Cornet92/why.htm

PREPARE A PC SURVIVAL KIT

If you're a worrisome type, you're probably convinced that a PC disaster is just around the corner—and you're wondering what in the world you can do to prepare for such a catastrophe. Well, one of the most important things you can do to plan for that eventuality is to prepare a PC Survival Kit.

The contents of your PC Survival Kit will prove indispensable if you are to recover your system after a complete or partial hard disk crash. In other words, these items are required accessories for every cautious PC user.

The good news is, you probably already have all of these items close at hand. What kinds of things are we talking about? Here's a checklist of the items you need to prepare:

- Original Windows installation CD, necessary for rebooting an XP machine, or if you need to reinstall the entire operating system.
- Windows Emergency Startup Disk, necessary to reboot pre-XP machines.

- Set of backup data, so you can restore all your important files.
- Original installation CDs for all your software programs, in case you need to rebuild the contents of your hard disk.
- Disk utility software, such as Norton SystemWorks, to perform any necessary hard disk repair or maintenance.

If worse comes to worst, you can use the contents of your PC Survival Kit to get your system up and running again, and to restore your programs and documents. I also like the idea of using Norton Ghost to perform full system mirrors; this makes it even easier to rebuild your entire system.

SOFTWARE OF THE WEEK

V Communications' Fix-It Utilities is a low-cost bundle of useful PC maintenance tools. There's a DiskCleaner and a DiskFixer, emergency fix and rescue tools, a registry cleaner and a disk defragger, a FileUndeleter, and a whole lot more. The price is only $$49.99 at www.v-com.com.

October 24, 2005

MONDAY

THIS WEEK'S FOCUS: BLOGGING

ON THIS DAY: ANTONY VAN LEEUWENHOEK BORN (1632)

Dutch microscopist Antony van Leeuwenhoek was born on this date in 1632. He was the first to observe bacteria and protozoa, and his observations helped lay the foundations for the sciences of bacteriology and protozoology.

Related Web site: www.ucmp.berkeley.edu/history/leeuwenhoek.html

UNDERSTANDING BLOGS

The latest big thing on the Internet is the Web log, or *blog*. A blog is basically a personal journal kept publicly on the Web. The act of updating the blog is called *blogging*, and the person who keeps the blog is a *blogger*. And all the blogs on the Web compose what is called the *blogosphere*.

The best blogs are comprised of a single page of multiple entries, and are updated daily. The updates are arranged in chronological order, with the most recent updates at the top of the page. Older postings are typically placed in archives somewhere else on the blog site.

Bloggers use special software that allows this type of frequent update with very little hassle, and little to no technical expertise required. A blog can be hosted on the user's Web server, or on a site (like Blogger) that specializes in blog hosting.

What makes a blog interesting is the blogger. Blog entries are typically streams of consciousness, so the blog does a good job of capturing the blogger's personality and interests. Bloggers can write about anything and everything that catches their attention. Blogs often contain stories or little snippets of information, as well as links to other sites—to news stories, interesting Web pages, and other blogs. In this way the entire blogosphere is extremely interconnected.

Blogs are getting a lot of headlines these days as a kind of alternative news media. Bloggers do a great job of tracking down and exposing news stories that traditional news outlines might overlook. In fact, some of the best blogs on the Web are those that cover government and politics, often by insiders blogging anonymously.

I'll talk more about blogs throughout this week—including how to create your own blog. So read on!

If you can't wait to check out a real, live blog, visit The Laporte Report at http://leo.typepad.com/tlr/.

PC GADGET OF THE WEEK

From the folks who brought you Scotch tape and Post-It notes comes the 3M Privacy Computer Filter, a neat little gizmo that fits over your notebook's screen and blacks out the display to anyone viewing from an angle. You see the full display; passersby see a dark black screen. Versions are available for both notebook and desktop LCD screens. Buy one for $75 at www.3m.com.

October 25, 2005
TUESDAY

THIS WEEK'S FOCUS: BLOGGING

ON THIS DAY: FIRST ELECTRONIC WRISTWATCH (1960)

Bulova's Accutron 214, the world's first electronic wristwatch, was placed on sale on October 25, 1960. The original circuit used a germanium PNP transistor circuit with a 360Hz tuning fork, used for timing accuracy. Interestingly, the CEO of Bulova at the time was five-star General Omar Bradley, Retired.

Related Web site: `members.iinet.net.au/~fotoplot/acctech214.htm`

WHY BLOG?

Blogging takes time. You have to create the blog, and then keep it updated on a fairly frequent basis. Trust me, I run my own blog (at `leo.typepad.com/tlr/`) and I update it daily. It's a lot of fun, but it can also be a bit of a chore.

Some people view their blogs as a kind of personal-yet-public scrapbook—an online diary to record their thoughts for posterity. Even if no one else ever looks at it, it's still valuable to the author as a repository of thoughts and information they can turn to at any later date.

While some blogs are completely free-form, most blogs have some sort of focus. For example, my blog is all about technology, because that's what I'm interested in. Other bloggers write about music, or politics, or cooking, or whatever *they're* interested in. Their blogs include their thoughts on the topic at hand, as well as links to interesting news articles and Web sites.

Other people blog for a cause. Liberal blogs link to left-leaning stories and pages; conservative blogs contain commentary and links that reinforce their right-leaning viewpoints. There are blogs for every point on the political spectrum, and some you've never thought of.

In a way, the most serious bloggers are like columnists in the traditional media. They write with a passion, point-of-view, and personal sensibility that makes their blogs extremely interesting to read. Even bloggers who don't inject personal comments still offer a viewpoint based on what they choose to included and link to in their blogs. It's an interesting world out there in the blogosphere.

DOWNLOAD OF THE WEEK

If you want to host your blog on your own server, check out Moveable Type. This shareware program lets you create, edit, and publish your blog entries to a server of your choice. It uses a variety of templates to make blog publishing quick and easy. Download an unsupported version for free, or upgrade to the Personal Edition for $69.95 from `www.moveabletype.org`.

October 26, 2005

WEDNESDAY

THIS WEEK'S FOCUS: BLOGGING

ON THIS DAY: KILLER SMOG IN PENNSYLVANIA (1948)

Don't confuse blogs with smog. On October 26, 1948, a killing smog blanketed the small town of Donora, Pennsylvania, near Pittsburgh. The cloud, a poisonous mix of sulfur dioxide, carbon monoxide, and metal dust, came from the smokestacks of the local zinc smelter where most of the town worked. Over the next five days, 20 residents died and half the town's population—some 7,000 people—were hospitalized.

Related Web site: www.dep.state.pa.us/dep/Rachel_Carson/donora.htm

BEST SITES FOR BLOGGING

Whether you want to start up your own blog or read the blogs of others, there are a number of blog portals on the Web that deserve your attention. Most of these portals offer searchable directories of tens of thousands of individual blogs. Some of the best blog portals include:

- Blog Universe (www.bloguniverse.com)
- BlogChalking (www.blogchalking.tk)
- Blogwise (www.blogwise.com)
- Eatonweb Portal (portal.eatonweb.com)
- Globe of Blogs (www.globeofblogs.com)
- Technorati (www.technorati.com)
- Weblogs.Com (www.weblogs.com)

If you want to create your own blog, consider Blogger (www.blogger.com), one of the first and the biggest blog hosting services on the Web. It's a good choice if you want to create your own blog;

basic blogging is free. (Note that Blogger was recently acquired by Google.)

I would also be remiss if I didn't mention TypePad (www.typepad.com), which I use to host my own blog. Like Blogger, TypePad offers quick and easy blog hosting. Basic hosting is $4.95 per month, although the first month is free.

Many traditional Web hosting sites also offer blog hosting. For example, Tripod (www.tripod.lycos.com) offers a Blog Builder tool as part of all its hosting plans, including its free plan. Not a bad deal.

MAC GADGET OF THE WEEK

Make your G5 mobile with Power Support's G5 Skateboard. No, you can't do an ollie with it, but you can use the Skateboard to move that hefty G5 around the office. It's a wheeled base that screws onto the bottom of your G5 and lets you move the big puppy around with relative ease. Buy it for $129 at www.drbott.com.

October 27, 2005

THURSDAY

THIS WEEK'S FOCUS: BLOGGING

ON THIS DAY: NYC SUBWAY OPENS (1904)

On October 27, 1904, the first underground and underwater rail system in the world began operating. The New York City Subway operated between the Brooklyn Bridge and 145th and Broadway; the fare was a nickel. Almost 8,000 men participated in building the 21-mile route.

Related Web site: www.nycsubway.org

LEO'S FAVORITE BLOGS

With literally millions of blogs on the Web, it's tough to choose just a handful of favorites. I'm up to the task, however, so here are my favorite blogs in a number of categories.

- **News blogs—**Big Blog (bigblog.com), Plastic (www.plastic.com), Unknown News (www.unknownnews.net)

- **Political blogs—**Andrew Sullivan's The Daily Dish (www.andrewsullivan.com), Citizen Smash—The Indepundit (www.lt-smash.us), Instapundit.com (www.instapundit.com), Rhetorica (rhetorica.net), and the delightfully gossipy Wonkette! (www.wonkette.com).

- **Tech blogs—**Boing Boing (www.boingboing.net), Gizmodo (www.gizmodo.com), Slashdot (www.slashdot.org), and Techdirt (www.techdirt.com).

- **Sports blogs—**BadJocks (www.badjocks.com), and Fanblogs (www.fanblogs.com).

- **Photo blogs—**Daily Dose of Imagery (wvs.topleftpixel.com) and A Day in the Life (www.adayinthelife.org).

- **Movie blogs—**GreenCine Daily (daily.greencine.com), DVD Verdict (www.dvdverdict.com), filmfodder (www.filmfodder.com), and Tagline (www.tagliners.org).

- **Music blogs—**Fresh Tuneage (www.freshtuneage.com), MP3blogs (www.mp3blogs.org), and People Talk Too Loud (www.peopletalktooloud.com)

And for reviews of music, movies, and books in a single blog (run by multiple bloggers), check out the exceptional Blogcritics.org (www.blogcritics.org).

WEB SITE OF THE WEEK

In case you missed it earlier this week, be sure to check out my own blog, The Laporte Report, where I post my daily tech-related musings. I post most every day, when travels allow. Read it at leo.typepad.com/tlr/. You can also find Show Notes from my KFI AM 640 blog at http://leoville.tv/radio/pmwiki.php. And for even more fun, see Leo's Mob at http://leoville.textamerica.com/, where I post pictures from shows, travels, and other fun events. Ok, that's three blogs, but who's counting, right?

October 28, 2005

FRIDAY

THIS WEEK'S FOCUS: **BLOGGING**

ON THIS DAY: **BILL GATES BORN (1955)**

Tech wiz, Microsoft founder, and resident gazillionaire Bill Gates was born (in Seattle, of course) on October 28, 1955. Happy 50th birthday, Bill!

Related Web site: www.microsoft.com/billgates/

CREATING YOUR OWN BLOG

Creating your own blog is incredibly easy. While you can use blogging software to post your blog on a dedicated Web server, the easier route is to open an account on one of the blog hosting portals I mentioned on Wednesday. The most popular of these is Blogger (www.blogger.com), which offers free accounts. (That explains why it's so popular.) I'll use Blogger to demonstrate how to get started in the blogosphere.

You start by going to the Blogger site and opening a new account. Once that's done, you select a name for your blog, which becomes your blog URL (in the form of blogname.blogspot.com). Then you choose a look for your blog from a set of standard templates. (That's one disadvantage of using a free blogging service—you're limited in page layout.) Click a few buttons and you're done.

Once your blog is created you can start posting new entries. This is as simple as entering the text and clicking the Publish Post button. Your new entry is now published to your blog page.

Because Blogger is now part of Google, you can post entries to your blog via the Google Toolbar.

Visit a Web site you like, and then click the Blog This button on the toolbar; enter any text you want to describe the entry, and the link will automatically be posted to your blog.

You can also use Blogger to manage your blog but host the blog itself on another Web site. When you publish a new entry, Blogger uses FTP to send the code for the new page to the server you designate. Blogger can also be configured to create an RSS feed of your blog (this is turned on by default), or to automatically have your blog emailed to selected recipients.

PORTABLE GADGET OF THE WEEK

The DriveRight CarChip is an automotive performance scan tool, just like your mechanic uses. It lets you troubleshoot your engine, log your car's performance, and monitor driver performance. Just attach the CarChip to your car's OBDII connector, which should be somewhere under the dash; the CarChip starts logging data as soon as you start driving. Connect the serial cable to download data to your PC for further analysis. Buy it for $139.99 at www.driveright.com.

October 29, 2005

SATURDAY

THIS WEEK'S FOCUS: BLOGGING

ON THIS DAY: JOHN GLENN RETURNS TO SPACE (1998)

The first American in space became the oldest American in space on this date in 1998. Seventy-seven year-old Senator John Glenn made his return to space as a payload specialist aboard the space shuttle Discovery. His original flight, in 1962, lasted just five hours; his return flight lasted a whole nine days.

Related Web site: www.grc.nasa.gov/WWW/PAO/html/johnglen.htm

WORKING WITH RSS FEEDS

Go to my blog at leo.typepad.com/tlr/, scroll to the bottom of the page, and you'll see a little orange button with white type that reads "XML". Surf around and you'll see similar buttons on a lot of blogs, and on some legitimate news sites, as well. This button signifies that the site supports something called Really Simple Syndication, or RSS.

RSS is an XML-based format that publishes the content of an online resource in a way that any kind of program can read. When information about an item is posted in RSS format, any RSS-aware program can check the feed for changes, and then react to the changes in an appropriate way.

For example, you can use an RSS newsreader program (sometimes called a news aggregator) to scan RSS feeds from those RSS-enabled sites you designate. The newsreader finds new postings and displays them for you to read. Two popular RSS newsreaders include AmphetaDesk (www.disobey. com/amphetadesk/) and, for Mac OS X, NetNewsWire (ranchero.com/netnewswire/). If you use My Yahoo!, you can configure your page to include RSS feeds for your favorite sites.

Lots of personal blogs include RSS feeds, as do a ton of traditional news sites, including Yahoo! News, Washingtonpost.com, and CNET's News.com. I offer an RSS feed of my site because it's built into Typepad and I don't have to do any additional work to implement it. Whenever possible I think it's a great idea to offer an RSS feed for your site.

You can also search for RSS feeds at Bloogz (www.bloogz.com/rssfinder/), Daypop (www.daypop. com), and Syndic8 (www.syndic8.com).

FACT OF THE WEEK

Perseus Development Corp. says that only 50,000 of the estimated 4.12 million blogs are updated daily. Two-thirds of all blogs haven't been updated in over two months, and fully a million blogs contained just a single day's posts. Easy to start, harder to maintain!

October 30, 2005

SUNDAY

THIS WEEK'S FOCUS: **BLOGGING**

ON THIS DAY: *WAR OF THE WORLDS* RADIO BROADCAST (1938)

On the night before Halloween, 1938, Orson Welles scared the bejeezus out of America. His weekly radio program, the Mercury Theater, broadcast a masterful adaptation of H.G. Wells' classic *The War of the Worlds*, staged as a live news event. The greater part of the audience tuned to the Columbia Broadcast System were fully convinced that the country was really under attack—or, as the script put it, "those strange beings who landed in the Jersey farmlands tonight are the vanguard of an invading army from the planet Mars."

Related Web site: www.war-ofthe-worlds.co.uk

PHOTOBLOGS AND MOBLOGS

Not all blogs are all text. Some blogs are photo-oriented, and some offer up their postings in digital audio format.

A *photoblog* is a blog that is updated with photos instead of text. The photos can come from straight digital cameras or cell phones with cameras; in either case, they're posted in the same general format as a traditional blog. Photoblogs can include text, but the emphasis is on the photos.

A *moblog* is a blog that's updated from a phone or other mobile device (hence the "mo" in the name), instead of from a computer keyboard. Some blog hosting sites let you call into a toll-free number and dictate your moblog postings; these entries are either automatically translated into plain text, or posted as an MP3 audio file. You can also use your mobile phone (with camera) to dial in digital photos you take, which are then posted to your moblog page.

So, to keep it straight, a photoblog can be a moblog, and a moblog can be a photoblog, but they're not necessarily the same thing. That's because a photoblog can be created from your desktop PC, and a moblog can contain text-only entries. Still, many photobloggers update their sites with moblogging technology, hence the somewhat interchangeability of the names. (For example, I call my photoblog a moblog—check it out at `leoville.textamerica.com`.)

If you want to check out some moblogs/photoblogs—or even create one of your own—here are some of the better portals:

- Buzznet (`www.buzznet.com`)
- Fotopages (`www.fotopages.com`)
- Phlog (`www.phlog.net`)
- Photoblogs.org (`www.photoblogs.org`)
- Textamerica (`www.textamerica.com`)

SOFTWARE OF THE WEEK

NewsGator is a news aggregator add-in that runs within Microsoft Outlook. Use it to subscribe to various RSS news feeds—including many blogs—and have news from those sites delivered directly to Outlook folders. Try it for free, or buy it for $29 from `www.newsgator.com`.

October 31, 2005

MONDAY

THIS WEEK'S FOCUS: DVD

ON THIS DAY: VATICAN ADMITS GALILEO WAS RIGHT (1992)

It took them more than 300 years, but on October 31, 1992, the Vatican finally admitted that it erred in formally condemning Galileo for saying the Earth revolves around the sun. Even more amazing, it took a 13-year inquiry by a special commission to deliver the new "not guilty" finding. It all started back in 1633, when Galileo was forced by the Roman Inquisition to repent his views; he spent the last eight years of his life under house arrest.

Related Web site: bertie.ccsu.edu/Phil135/Cosmology/GalileoPope.html

COPYING DVDS

If you have a DVD burner in your PC, you're probably tempted to use it to make copies of some of the DVDs in your collection. You may want to copy some of the home-grown DVDs you've made, or maybe you want to make an archival copy of a store-bought DVD movie—just in case the original gets lost or damaged.

However, copying a DVD is somewhat more problematic than copying a CD. There are two reasons for this:

- Dual-layer commercial DVDs hold up to 9.4GB of data, where blank DVD-R discs are only single-layer, and only hold 4.7GB of data. This means that it's impossible to copy a movie onto a single disc; you either have to break the movie into two halves (on two separate discs) or compress the movie to fit, thus compromising quality.

- Many commercial DVDs are protected by a sophisticated encryption scheme, which prevents copying.

So, if you want to copy a DVD, you're pretty much limited by the original material. If you want to copy a DVD you've created from scratch (home movies, for example), you're okay. If you want to copy a commercial DVD movie—even if it's just a backup copy for your personal use—you're probably out of luck. (There's no harm in trying, however; not all commercial DVDs feature copy-protection encryption.)

That said, there are several programs that let you make copies of your personal DVDs; two of my favorites are DVD Wizard Pro (www.dvdwizardpro.com) and Roxio Easy DVD Copy (www.roxio.com). With most of these programs, the process is as simple as clicking a button or two; some programs let you compress longer DVDs to fit on a standard blank DVD or break long DVDs into two shorter ones. Just know that none of these programs will let you copy commercial DVDs.

PC GADGET OF THE WEEK

Here's that rare computer gadget that's not computerized. The C.H.I.M.P. monitor mirror is a small rear-view mirror for your computer, so you can see your boss coming before he taps on your shoulder. Just attach it to the top of your monitor and keep an eye on what's happening behind you. Buy it for $9.99 at www.thinkgeek.com.

MORE OCTOBER FACTS

October 1

1908 Ford's Model T "Tin Lizzie" is introduced; the cost was $852

1940 Pennsylvania Turnpike, the first American superhighway, opens

October 2

1956 First atomic clock—the Atomicron—is unveiled in New York City

1962 Johnny Carson makes his debut as host of "The Tonight Show"

October 3

1990 East and West Germany reunite after 45 years; this day is now known as "Unity Day" in Germany

October 4

1906 SOS is officially adopted as an international distress signal

1941 First commercially used aerosol can is patented; the can was used for bug spray

1957 The first artificial satellite, the Soviet Sputnik, is launched into space

1970 Janis Joplin dies

October 5

1892 The famous Dalton Gang is thwarted—most of them killed—when they attempted to rob two Coffeyville, Kansas banks at the same time

1936 First intercity coaxial television broadcast made between New York City and Philadelphia

October 6

1783 First self-winding clock is patented

1866 First train robbery in American history is committed by John and Simeon Reno is Jackson County, IN

1968 Nickel plating is patented in Boston, MA

1893 Nabisco invents Cream of Wheat

1961 President John F. Kennedy urges Americans to build bomb shelters to protect themselves from nuclear fallout

October 7

1913 Ford installs a continuously moving assembly line in its Highland Park factory—the first of its kind in the U.S.

1959 The dark side of the moon is photographed for the first time by the Soviet Union's Luna 3 spacecraft

2001 U.S. and British forces begin an aerial bombing campaign targeting Taliban forces and Al-Qaida terrorists in Afghanistan

October 8

1906 Much to the joy of curly hair seekers, the first permanent wave for hair is demonstrated

1997 Chrysler recalls 1.1 million minivans after faulty rear liftgate latches lead to multiple deaths

October 9

1974 Oskar Schindler dies

October 10

1865 First synthetic billiard ball is patented; previous billiard balls were made of ivory

1933 First laundry detergent, Dreft, is introduced by Proctor & Gamble

October 11

1844 Henry John Heinz—founder of H.J. Heinz—is born

1939 Albert Einstein writes about the possibility of nuclear weapons

1968 Apollo 7—the first manned Apollo mission—is launched

1983 Last hand-cranked telephones went out of service when 440 telephone customers in Bryant Pond, Maine were upgraded to direct dial service

October 12

1492 Italian explorer Christopher Columbus reaches the New World, landing in what are now known as the Bahamas

1964 Soviet Union launches Voskhod 1 into Earth's orbit, the first spacecraft to carry a multi-person crew

October 13

1792 Construction on the U.S. White House begins

1860 First aerial photo is taken from a plane over Boston, MA

October 14

1857 Elwood Haynes, inventor of stainless steel and one of the first automobiles, is born in Portland, IN

1899 Literary Digest predicts that the automobile will forever remain a luxury of the wealthy

1964 Cuban Missile Crisis begins, leading the world to the brink of nuclear war

1968 First television broadcast from space is made from the Apollo 7

October 15

1966 A McKinney, TX man sets the world record for bad driving, receiving 10 tickets, driving on the wrong side of the road four times, committing four hit-and-run accidents, and causing six other accidents—all in the same day

October 18

1870 Sandblasting is patented

1922 The British Broadcasting Company (BBC) is formed

1931 Thomas Edison dies; Edison's last breath was captured in a test tube and is stored in the Henry Ford Museum

October 19

1987 Dow Jones plummets nearly 23% or 508 points, earning this date in history the moniker, "Black Monday"

October 21

1833 Alfred Bernhard Nobel, for whom the Nobel Prize was named, is born

1963 First trimline telephone (phone with dialer and hang-up controls on a handset) is introduced

October 22

1797 First parachute jump is made above Paris; he was released from a balloon 2,230 above Parc Monceau

October 23

1942 Author Michael Crichton, creator of *Jurassic Park* and *ER*, is born

October 24

1901 Annie Edson is first person to go over Niagra Falls in a wooden barrel

1945 The United Nations is formed

October 25

1881 Pablo Picasso is born

1881 Airbrush painting device is patented in Elizabeth, Maine

October 26

Daylight Savings Time ends

1948 Killer smog blankets the town of Donora, PA, hospitalizing thousands and killing 20; this incident keenly raised U.S. awareness of the dangers of industrial pollution

1984 First baboon-to-human heart transplant is performed on 14-day-old "Baby Fae," who died 20 days later

October 27

1891 The street letter mailbox is patented; these boxes remain largely unchanged and in regular use today

October 28

1886 The Statue of Liberty is dedicated in New York Harbor by President Grover Cleveland

1919 Congress enforces prohibition, the 18th Amendment to the constitution; in 1933, the 21st Amendment was passed, repealing prohibition

1965 Famous Gateway Arch in St. Louis, Missouri is completed

1992 Scientists using sonar to map Scotland's Loch Ness make contact with an unidentified object, refusing to speculate on whether they might have made official contact with the fabled Loch Ness Monster

October 29

1929 U.S. stock market crash sends U.S. into the Great Depression

1942 The Alaska Highway is opened to traffic; construction of this highway was made a chief priority after the 1941 Japanese bombing of Pearl Harbor because Alaska was considered to be at risk of a Japanese invasion

October 30

1894 Much to the chagrin of workers everywhere, even today, the time clock was invented in Rochester, NY

October 31

1933 Mount Rushmore is completed in South Dakota, immortalizing George Washington, Thomas Jefferson, Abraham Lincoln, and Theodore Roosevelt

1951 Zebra crossing lines are first used in Slough, Berkshire, England at pedestrian crossings

1992 The Vatican admits fault in condemning Galileo for his beliefs that the Earth revolves around the Sun; Galileo had been dead for 351 years when this admission was made

2003 FDA releases a report concluding that cloned farm animals and their offspring don't pose a risk to the food supply; it is thought that this ruling could pave the way for products derived from clones or their offspring to be made available for sale to the public

November 2005

November 2005

SUNDAY	MONDAY	TUESDAY	WEDNESDAY	THURSDAY	FRIDAY	SATURDAY
		1 1952 U.S. explodes the first hydrogen bomb	**2** 1895 First automobile race between Jackson Park in Chicago and Waukegan, IL	**3** 1957 Soviets send first dog into space	**4** 1939 The first air conditioned car prototype is shown off at an auto show in Chicago, IL	**5** 2001 Nintendo releases the GameCube
6 1986 Illegal U.S. sale of arms to Iran is confirmed	**7** 1908 London scientist Ernest Rutherford announces that he has isolated a single atom	**8** 2001 Microsoft releases the Xbox	**9** 1934 Carl Edward Sagan is born	**10** 1989 The Berlin Wall comes down, unifying East and West Germany	**11** Veteran's Day 1922 Kurt Vonnegut, Jr. is born	**12** 1935 First lobotomy is performed in Lisbon, Portugal
13 1982 Vietnam Veterans Memorial in Washington, D.C. is dedicated	**14** 1969 Apollo 12 is launched	**15** 1492 Columbus writes that Native Americans smoke tobacco leaves	**16** 1841 The life pre-server is patented in New York City	**17** 1970 First computer mouse is patented by Doug Engelbart	**18** 1963 First pushbut-ton telephones are placed in commercial service	**19** 1863 President Abraham Lincoln delivers the Gettysburg Address
20 1923 First automatic traffic signal is patented	**21** 1877 Thomas Edison invents the phonograph	**22** 1963 President John F. Kennedy is assassinated in Dallas, TX	**23** 1897 Pencil sharpener is patented in Fall River, MA	**24** Thanksgiving 1859 Charles Darwin publishes *Origin of Species*	**25** 1948 Cable television is patented in Astoria, OR	**26** 1922 Archeologists enter King Tutankhamen's tomb
27 1989 First living donor liver transplant is performed	**28** 1964 U.S. Mariner 4 completes first mission to Mars	**29** Leo Laporte's birthday	**30** 1835 Mark Twain is born			

THIS WEEK'S FOCUS: DVD

ON THIS DAY: U.S. EXPLODES FIRST HYDROGEN BOMB (1952)

The first hydrogen bomb, codenamed "Mike," was successfully detonated November 1, 1952 at Eniwetok atoll in the Pacific. The Mike device used liquid deuterium as the fusion fuel. Mike created a fireball three miles wide; the mushroom cloud rose to 57,000 feet in 90 seconds and topped out at 135,000 feet—the top of the stratosphere—with a stem eight miles across. As one observer stated, "the bomb is so unbelievably powerful that, in comparison, the atom bombs loosed on Hiroshima and Nagasaki seem like mere firecrackers..."

Related Web site: `mt.sopris.net/mpc/military/mike.html`

DVD REGION CODES

If you've ever tried to send a DVD to someone in another country, you've probably run into a problem. A DVD player in one country won't necessarily play DVDs sold in another country. What's the deal?

The deal is something called region coding, which identifies DVDs made in specific regions around the world. DVD players sold in a given country are designed only to play those DVDs coded for that country. This type of region locking was designed to keep DVDs from being distributed worldwide, so that they don't undermine theatrical releases overseas. So if a DVD is released in country A before it's shown in the theaters in country B, consumers in country B won't be able to view DVDs imported from country A, thus not spoiling the theatrical take. Or so it goes in theory.

The region codes are as follows:

Code	Regions/Countries
0	No region coding—can be played in any region
1	USA, Canada
2	Europe—including France, Greece, Turkey, Egypt, Arabia, Japan, and South Africa
3	Korea, Thailand, Vietnam, Borneo, and Indonesia
4	Australia and New Zealand, Mexico, the Caribbean, and South America
5	India, Africa, Russia, and former USSR countries
6	Peoples Republic of China
7	Unused
8	Airlines/cruise ships

If you want to play DVDs purchased in another country, there are three solutions. One is to buy a DVD player manufactured in that country. The second is to check the Internet to see if your current DVD player has a backdoor you can hack that will let you play discs from any region. The third solution is to buy a multi-region DVD player, which you can find at many Internet retailers.

DOWNLOAD OF THE WEEK

When you want something a little more than what Windows Media Player delivers, check out the shareware Blaze player. Blaze plays back DVD, video CD, and other multimedia formats, and offers bookmarks and image capturing functions. Try it for free, or buy it for $39.95 from www.blazevideo.com.

November 2, 2005
WEDNESDAY

THIS WEEK'S FOCUS: DVD

ON THIS DAY: GEORGE BOOLE BORN (1815)

George Boole, born on November 2, 1815, was a mathematician and philosopher. As the inventor of Boolean algebra, the basis of all modern computer arithmetic, Boole is regarded as one of the founders of the field of computer science.

Related Web site: www-gap.dcs.st-and.ac.uk/~history/Mathematicians/ Boole.html

PLAYING DVDS WITH WINDOWS MEDIA PLAYER

There are lots of media player programs you can use to play DVDs on your PC, but since Windows Media Player (WMP) comes preinstalled on all Windows machines, it's as good a program as any to use. In fact, when you insert a DVD in your DVD drive, WMP should launch and playback should start automatically. The picture from the DVD displays in WMP's video window, individual tracks on the DVD are displayed in the Playlist area to the right of the screen, and information about the DVD (including the DVD cover) is displayed beneath the video window.

WMP offers a number of ways to fine-tune your viewing experience, many of which are unknown to most users. Here are a few tips:

- To view the DVD using your entire computer screen, click the Full Screen button at the lower-right corner of the video window or select View > Full Screen. Press Esc to return to normal viewing mode.
- To display the DVD's main menu, select View > DVD Features > Title Menu. To display the DVD's special features menu select View > DVD Features > Top Menu. When the special

features menu is displayed, you can click any of the options onscreen to jump to a particular feature.

- To select which audio track to listen to (including audio commentary and foreign-language tracks), select View > DVD Features > Audio and Language Tracks.
- WMP provides a variety of special playback features that let you pause a still frame, advance frame-by-frame, or play the movie in slow or fast motion. To access these special playback features, select View > Now Playing Tools > DVD Controls. This displays a set of special controls in the Now Playing Tools area of the WMP window.
- To display subtitles or closed captions onscreen, select View > DVD Features > Subtitles and Captions, and then select which subtitles or captions you want to view.

MAC GADGET OF THE WEEK

When you want to add an internal DVD burner to your Power Mac, Pioneer's DVR-107 is the one to get. Buy it for $109 at www.pioneer.com.

November 3, 2005

THURSDAY

THIS WEEK'S FOCUS: DVD

ON THIS DAY: SOVIETS SEND FIRST DOG INTO SPACE (1957)

On November 3, 1957, a Siberian husky named Laika ("barker" in Russian) was sent into space on the Sputnik II spacecraft. Laika was the first living creature launched into space. Unfortunately, because the Soviets were rushing their space efforts, the craft was not designed for recovery, so there was no way to return Laika to earth; she died after a few days in orbit when the batteries of her life-support system eventually wore down. Later, Sputnik II fell into the atmosphere and burned on April 14, 1958.

Related Web site: http://www.spacetoday.org/Astronauts/Animals/Dogs.html

USING MY DVD TO BURN MOVIES ON DVD

There are lots of good DVD burner programs out there, from Roxio (www.roxio.com), Ulead (www.ulead.com), and other companies. But the easiest and most widely distributed DVD creation program is Sonic MyDVD (www.sonic.com). Chances are you got a copy with your DVD burner, or preinstalled on your new PC. If not, you can pick up a copy for $49.99.

When you first launch MyDVD, you're presented with three choices: Transfer Video Direct-to-DVD, Create or Modify a DVD-Video Project, and Edit an Existing OpenDVD Disc. You use the first two options depending on the type of project you're starting.

To transfer an existing videotape to DVD, select the Transfer Video Direct-to-DVD option. This launches the Direct-to-DVD Wizard, which you use to work through a simple process. Start by clicking the Edit Style button to select the style of menus you want on your DVD. Then, enter a name for your project, select a location for the finished project, and choose how often you want to add chapter points. Now make sure your VCR or camcorder is connected to your PC, then click the Start Capturing button and initiate playback on your VCR. When the playback is complete, click the Stop Capturing process. MyDVD will now start building the new DVD.

Creating a DVD from video files stored on your hard disk is just as easy. MyDVD can combine one or more of these files into a movie DVD, complete with menus. To initiate this process, select Create or Modify a DVD Video Project on the opening screen. This opens MyDVD's main project window, from where you select the menu styles and enter the menu title text. You add a video file to your DVD by clicking the Get Movies button and selecting which file(s) to open; the file you selected is now added to your project, and a button is added to the main menu. If you add a lot of files, you can create submenus under the main menu for easier navigation.

Once you start building a DVD, prepare for a long wait. The building process is long, so feel free to go out and get a pizza or something while you wait.

WEB SITE OF THE WEEK

Learn everything there is to know about the DVD format from Jim Taylor's excellent DVD FAQ. Read it all at dvddemystified.com/dvdfaq.html.

November 4, 2005

FRIDAY

THIS WEEK'S FOCUS: DVD

ON THIS DAY: B.F. GOODRICH BORN (1841)

Benjamin Franklin Goodrich was born on this date in 1841. After serving as a surgeon in the Civil War, he acquired the Hudson River Rubber Company, under a license agreement with Charles Goodyear. This company failed, as did their next. Goodrich then moved to Akron, Ohio, and formed the Goodrich, Tew Company, which manufactured fire hoses, bicycle tires, and other rubber products. In 1880, the company was renamed the B.F. Goodrich Company.

Related Web site: www.bfgoodrichtires.com

CREATING A DVD PHOTO ALBUM

One especially neat thing about DVD creation programs is that almost all let you create animated slideshows of your digital photographs which can play on most consumer DVD players. If you have a lot of photos in your collection, it's easy to burn them to DVD and then distribute the discs to your friends and family. It's a lot more convenient than passing around a photo print album!

Most users find Sonic MyDVD (www.sonic.com) the easiest program to use for creating these DVD photo albums. With MyDVD, the process of creating a slideshow is almost identical to the process of creating a movie DVD. The only difference is that instead of adding a movie file to a menu, you add a slideshow. This lets you include multiple slideshows on a single disc.

To add a slideshow to a DVD project, go to MyDVD's project window and click the Add Slideshow button; this opens the Create Slideshow window. To add pictures to the slideshow, click the Get Pictures button and select the pictures to open. The pictures you select are now added to the slideshow filmstrip. You can rearrange the pictures by dragging any picture to a new position in the filmstrip.

To change the length of time each picture appears onscreen, click the Settings button to display the Slideshow Settings dialog box; select the Basic tab, and then adjust the Duration setting as desired. To add music to your slideshow, click the Settings button to display the Slideshow Settings dialog box; select the Basic tab, check the Audio Track option, and then click the Choose button to select a music file.

PORTABLE GADGET OF THE WEEK

Toshiba's SD-P5000 is a portable DVD player with a huge honkin' screen. This portable DVD player has a gargantuan 15" screen, twice the size of the average portable player's screen. Buy it for $799.99 at www.toshiba.com.

November 5, 2005

SATURDAY

THIS WEEK'S FOCUS: DVD

ON THIS DAY: VIKINGS DISCOVERED IN CANADA (1963)

On this day in 1963, archaeologists found Viking ruins in Newfoundland, Canada. These ruins predated Columbus's "discovery" of America by more than 500 years. Historians now believe that Leif Eriksson, second son of the notorious Erik the Red, was the first European to reach the North American mainland. Legend has it that in 1,000 A.D., Eriksson voyaged from Greenland for lands sighted to the west, eventually landing at a place he called Vinland—what we now call Newfoundland.

Related Web site: www.mnsu.edu/emuseum/prehistory/vikings/vikhome.html

UNDERSTANDING DVD FORMATS

DVD-R, DVD+R, DVD-RW, DVD+RW—what's the difference? All these different labels exist because major DVD manufacturers are still fighting among themselves to create the "standard" recording format. That's right, there's no single format established for DVD burning. It gets rather confusing, because all of the competing formats are quite similar to each other—especially in their naming. Here's a quick guide:

Format	Description
DVD-R	DVD-*recordable*, for one-time writing to disc; used primarily to record video for playback on standard DVD players. This format is compatible with most consumer DVD players.
DVD+R	Similar to DVD-R, but with a few extra technical bells and whistles. This format is compatible with about 80% of existing DVD players.
DVD-RAM	DVD-*random access memory*, with random read/write access. Used for data storage only, not movies.
DVD-RW	DVD-*rewritable*, similar to DVD-RAM but with sequential read/write access. You may run into compatibility problems with consumer DVD players.

Format	Description
DVD+RW	Similar to DVD-RW, but with a few extra technical bells and whistles. Also has potential compatibility problems with consumer DVD players.
DVD-R/W	Similar to DVD-RW, but capable of recording on double-sided discs.
DVD+R/W	Similar to DVD+RW, but capable of recording on double-sided discs.

Fortunately, most computer-based DVD burners conform to multiple formats. But don't get too comfortable; new higher-density dual-layer DVD burners are just now hitting the market, which makes for even more format confusion!

FACT OF THE WEEK

According to the International Recording Media Association, 4.1 billion DVDs will be manufactured in 2004, up from 3.3 billion in 2003. This compares to 5.4 billion audio CDs—down from 5.6 billion in 2003.

November 6, 2005

SUNDAY

THIS WEEK'S FOCUS: DVD

ON THIS DAY: MICROSOFT SIGNS DOS CONTRACT WITH IBM (1980)

Earlier in 1980, IBM approached Bill Gates to discuss his company, Microsoft, supplying the operating system for IBM's upcoming personal computer. The resulting "Micro Soft Disk Operating System," or MS-DOS, was based on QDOS, the "Quick and Dirty Operating System" written by Tim Paterson of Seattle Computer Products, which itself was based on Gary Kildall's CP/M operating system. Micro Soft bought the rights to QDOS for $50,000, which proved to be a pretty good investment. Gates signed the contract with IBM on November 6th.

Related Web site: www.patersontech.com/Dos/Softalk/Softalk.html

TROUBLESHOOTING DVD PROBLEMS

If you're having trouble playing one or more DVDs in your computer's DVD drive, here are some things to check for.

Does the drive actually have power? Does it spin? If you're using an internal drive, you should check all the connections inside your system unit; not only should the drive be plugged into a drive controller, but it should also be plugged into your computer's power supply. If you're using an external drive, make sure all the connections are solid and that the drive actually has power (make sure the power light is on).

If the drive spins but doesn't recognize the DVD, you might not have the correct driver loaded into system memory for your DVD drive. Open the Control Panel and launch the System utility; when the System Properties dialog box appears, select the Hardware tab and then click the Device Manager button. Select the entry for your DVD drive, and then select Action > Update Driver. Follow the onscreen instructions to find and install the latest version of the driver software.

If your drive recognizes the DVD but playback is erratic, you could have a scratched or dirty disc. You can buy commercial CD/DVD cleaners that will remove surface dirt and debris; scratches are less easily fixed, if at all.

It's also possible that you're trying to play the wrong format DVD in your drive. If you have a "minus" (DVD-R) drive and try to play a disc recorded in the "plus" (DVD+R) format, it won't work. More likely it's a DVD-RW or DVD+RW disc, which is much less compatible from drive to drive. Same thing with DVD-RAM discs. With these formats, you're often limited to playing back the DVD on the same drive that you recorded it on.

SOFTWARE OF THE WEEK

For all-in-one digital media creation, check out Roxio Easy Media Creator. This program includes everything you need to create and burn CDs and DVDs, including full versions of PhotoSuite, VideoWave, and Easy CD & DVD Creator applications. Buy it for $99.99 at www.roxio.com.

November 7, 2005
MONDAY

THIS WEEK'S FOCUS: **EBAY**

ON THIS DAY: MARIE CURIE BORN (1867)

Marie Marja Sklodowska Curie was born on this date in 1867. A Polish-born chemist and physicist, her celebrated experiments on uranium minerals led to the discovery of two new elements—polonium and radium. With Henri Becquerel and her husband, Pierre Curie, she was awarded the 1903 Nobel Prize for Physics. She was then the sole winner of a second Nobel Prize in 1911, this time in Chemistry. She died of radiation poisoning from her pioneering work before the need for protection was known.

Related Web site: www.aip.org/history/curie/

HOW AN ONLINE AUCTION WORKS

An auction starts when a seller has something to sell. He creates an ad for his item and lists the item on the auction site. (eBay charges the seller anywhere from $0.30 to $4.80 to list an item.) In the item listing, the seller specifies the length of the auction (3, 5, 7, or 10 days) and the minimum bid he will accept for that item.

A potential buyer searching for a particular type of item (or just browsing through all the merchandise listed in a specific category) reads the item listing and decides to make a bid. The bidder specifies the maximum amount he or she will pay; this amount has to be above the seller's minimum bid.

eBay's built-in bidding software automatically places a bid for the bidder that bests the current bid by a specified amount—but doesn't reveal the bidder's maximum bid. For example, the current bid on an item might be $25. A bidder is willing to pay up to $40 for the item, and enters a maximum bid of $40. eBay's "proxy" software places a bid for the new bidder in the amount of $26—higher than the current bid, but less than the specified maximum bid. If there are no other bids, this bidder will win the auction with a $26 bid. Other potential buyers, however, can place additional bids; unless their maximum bids are more than the current bidder's $40 maximum, they are informed (by e-mail) that they have been outbid—and the first bidder's current bid is automatically raised to match the new bids (up to the specified maximum bid price).

At the conclusion of an auction, eBay informs the high bidder of his or her winning bid. The seller is responsible for contacting the high bidder and arranging payment. When the seller receives the buyer's payment (either by check, money order, or credit card), the seller then ships the merchandise directly to the buyer.

PC GADGET OF THE WEEK

The Addonics MFR 18-in-1 Multi Function Reader does just about everything. It's a DVD player, a CD-R/CD-RW player/burner, a standalone MP3 player, and an 8-in-1 digital media reader, all in a single compact and portable device. Buy it for $235 at www.addonics.com.

November 8, 2005

TUESDAY

THIS WEEK'S FOCUS: EBAY

ON THIS DAY: JACK KILBY BORN (1923)

Jack St. Clair Kilby was born on this date in 1923. Kilby invented the integrated circuit in 1958 while working at Texas Instruments; he was awarded the Nobel Prize in Physics in 2000 for his breakthrough discovery.

Related Web site: www.ti.com/corp/docs/kilbyctr/jackstclair.shtml

TRACK ALL YOUR AUCTIONS WITH MY EBAY

Whether you're a buyer or a seller, if you're active at all on eBay, it's likely you'll have more than one auction going at any one time. Just how do you keep track of all this auction activity?

The best way to monitor all the auctions you're participating in is to use eBay's self-professed "best-kept secret": My eBay. My eBay is a page—actually, a set of pages—that you can personalize to track your bidding and selling activity in your own way. I highly recommend that you avail yourself of this useful feature.

You access My eBay from any eBay page by clicking the My eBay link on the eBay Navigation Bar. When you open your My eBay page, you see a series of links in the left column. These links take you to specific "views" of information—All Buying, All Selling, All Favorites, and My Account. Then there's the view you're in right now, My Summary, which displays buying and selling announcements, items you're watching and bidding on, and items you're selling. I typically stick to the My Summary view, as it includes just about everything I'm interested in most of the time.

You can customize the information on your My eBay pages in a number of ways. For example, any list can be hidden by clicking the Minimize button at the far right of the section heading. You can also change the order of the lists on any page, by using the up and down arrow buttons at the far right of the section heading.

Also neat is the ability to sort the individual item listings within any section. Just click the column header to sort by that particular column; click the header again to reverse the order of the sort. Also, many lists let you select how many days' worth of listings you want to display. The default value is 2 days; you can display up to 30 days' worth of items if you want.

DOWNLOAD OF THE WEEK

Auction Lizard is an easy-to-use listing-creation program for your eBay auctions. It uses forms and templates to create great-looking HTML-based listings. Auction Lizard is shareware, so you can try it for free or buy it for $29 at www.auction-lizard.com.

November 9, 2005
WEDNESDAY

THIS WEEK'S FOCUS: EBAY

ON THIS DAY: CARL SAGAN BORN (1934)

Carl Edward Sagan, born on this date in 1934, was a famous astronomer who helped popularize science to the masses. He pioneered the field of exobiology, promoted the Search for Extraterrestrial Intelligence (SETI), and coauthored a scientific paper that warned of the dangers of nuclear winter. Sagan became world-famous for his popular science books and for the television series *Cosmos*, which he co-wrote and presented.

Related Web site: www.carlsagan.com

SNIPING TO WIN

Ever lose an auction because someone made a last-second bid that blew you out of the water? If so, you've been the victim of *sniping*, a technique that experienced bidders use to increase their chances of winning an auction.

Bidders who snipe don't place any bids at all over the course of the auction, but instead swoop in at the very last minute with an insurmountable bid. The thinking behind this strategy is simple. By not disclosing your interest, you don't contribute to bidding up the price during the course of the auction. By bidding at the last minute, you don't leave enough time for other bidders to respond to your bid. The successful sniper makes one bid only—and makes it count. Here's how it works.

First, identify the item you want to buy—and then *don't bid!* Make a note of the auction (and its closing time), or even put the item on your watch list; but don't let anyone else know your intentions.

Five minutes before the close of the auction, make sure you're logged on to the Internet, and access the auction in question. Then open a *second* browser window to the auction in question.

In your first browser window, enter your maximum bid and click the Submit button to display the confirmation screen. *Don't confirm the bid yet!* Wait for the confirmation screen. In your second browser window, click the Refresh or Reload button to update the official auction time. Keep doing this until the time remaining until close is 60 seconds.

Now, using either the Windows clock or your watch, count down 50 seconds, until there are only 10 seconds left in the auction. When exactly 10 seconds are left in the auction, click the Confirm Bid button in your first browser window to send your bid. Wait 10 seconds, and then click the Refresh or Reload button in your second browser window. The auction should now be closed, and (if your sniping was successful) you should be listed as the winning bidder.

MAC GADGET OF THE WEEK

Need an external DVD+RW drive that's portable and easy on the eyes? The EZQuest Boa Slim adds rewritable DVD technology to your SuperDrive-challenged iBook or PowerBook, or you might just find it's nice to pick up and move around in your home or office. Buy it for $249 from www.ezq.com.

November 10, 2005

THURSDAY

THIS WEEK'S FOCUS: EBAY

ON THIS DAY: FIRST DOCUMENTED COMPUTER VIRUS (1983)

On November 10, 1983, University of Southern California student Fred Cohen presented a paper to a security seminar. In that paper, Cohen demonstrated a working example of the first documented computer virus. He defined a virus as "a program that can 'infect' other programs by modifying them to include a ... version of itself." Cohen added his virus to a graphics program called VD, written for a Vax mini-computer.

Related Web site: www.all.net/books/virus/part5.html

SECRETS OF SUCCESSFUL BIDDERS

How do you increase your chances of winning important auctions—without overpaying? Sniping, as you learned yesterday, is a valuable technique, but it's just one technique. Here are a half-dozen other tricks you can use to become a more successful eBay bidder.

- **Search for misspellings**—Some eBay sellers aren't great spellers—or are just prone to typing errors. This means you'll find some items listed for auction under misspelled titles. Misspellings won't turn up under a normal search, so if you can find them, you'll have less competition in the auction.

- **Bid in odd numbers**—When you bid, don't bid an even amount. Instead, bid a few pennies more than an even buck; for example, if you want to bid $10, bid $10.03 instead. That way, your bid will beat any bids at the same approximate amount—$10.03 beats $10 any day.

- **Look for off-peak auctions**—Believe it or not, some auctions are set to end in the wee hours of the morning—when there aren't a lot of bidders awake to make last-minute snipes. Look for auctions ending between midnight and 5:00 a.m. Pacific time if you want some competition-free sniping.

- **Do your research**—Don't bid blind; make sure you know the true value of an item before you offer a bid. Look around at auctions of similar items; what prices are they going for? And don't neglect researching outside of eBay; sometimes, you can find what you're looking for at a discount store or in a catalog or at another online site. Shop around, and don't assume that the price you see at an auction is always the best deal available.

- **Know when to say no**—Be disciplined. Set a maximum price you're willing to pay for an item, and *don't exceed it!* It's okay to lose an auction. Don't automatically rebid just because you've been outbid. It's too easy to get caught up in the excitement of a fast-paced auction. Learn how to keep your cool; know when to say no.

WEB SITE OF THE WEEK

AuctionBytes is one of my favorite sources of news and information about online auctions. It's eBay-heavy, as it should be, and includes all manner of useful resources. You can even sign up for online newsletters and e-zines. Check it out for yourself at www.auctionbytes.com.

November 11, 2005

FRIDAY

THIS WEEK'S FOCUS: EBAY

ON THIS DAY: KURT VONNEGUT, JR. BORN (1922)

Kurt Vonnegut, Jr. was born on November 11, 1922, in Indianapolis, Indiana. Vonnegut gained fame as a novelist and satirist; his most recognized work is *Slaughterhouse-Five*, based on his experiences as a P.O.W. in Germany during the Allied firebombing of Dresden.

Related Web site: www.vonnegut.com

SECRETS OF SUCCESSFUL SELLERS

When you're ready to sell on eBay, how do you make sure your item attracts a bunch of bidders and brings the highest price possible? Here are some tips:

- **Make your listing stand out**—Do everything in your power to make your item listings stand out from all the other listings currently online. Work on both the title and the description, and consider using a listing-creation tool (or using HTML formatting) to create a more dynamic ad.

- **Include a picture**—Nothing increases your chances of selling an item like including a picture of it in your listing. Take a good photo of your item, scan it in, upload it, and include it with your listing.

- **End in prime time**—Because some of the most intense bidding takes place in the final few minutes of your auction, your auction needs to end when the most possible bidders are online. The best times to end—and thus to *start*—your auction are between 9:00 p.m. and 11:00 p.m. EST, or between 6:00 p.m. and 8:00 p.m. PST.

- **End on a Sunday**—When you end your auction on a Sunday, you get one full Saturday and *two* Sundays (the starting Sunday and the ending one) for a seven-day item listing. Sunday is also a great day to end auctions because almost everybody is home—no one is out partying, or stuck at work or in school. End your auction on a Sunday evening, and you're likely to get more bids—and higher prices.

- **Accept credit cards—via PayPal**—One of the easiest ways to increase the number of bids in your auction is to accept payment via credit card. Unless you're a real business with a merchant bank account, this means signing up for PayPal—which is extremely easy to do. These days close to 90% of my auctions are paid for via PayPal—I'd hate to lose any of that business!

PORTABLE GADGET OF THE WEEK

Panasonic's DVD-LX8 portable DVD player utilizes a neat design that places the 9" LCD screen on an adjustable arm. Twist and turn the screen to find the best viewing angle. Buy it for $699.99 at www.panasonic.com.

THIS WEEK'S FOCUS: EBAY

ON THIS DAY: ALAN TURING DEFINES THE UNIVERSAL MACHINE (1937)

On November 12, 1937, Cambridge mathematician Alan Turing, in a paper on the mathematical theory of computation, conceived the idea for a "universal machine" capable of executing any describable algorithm. This theoretical machine, dubbed the Turing Machine, formed the basis for the concept of "computability," separate from the process of calculation—making it the precursor of today's electronic computers.

Related Web site: plato.stanford.edu/entries/turing-machine/

USE AN AUCTION MANAGEMENT SERVICE

If you're running a lot of auctions at one time, you need some way to keep track of which auctions are still open, which have closed, which need e-mails sent to high bidders, which need to be shipped out, and so on. Fortunately, there are quite a few Web sites that handle some or all of the eBay selling process, from ad creation to post-auction management—for a fee, of course. Here are some of my favorites:

- **ándale** (www.andale.com) offers a full range of first-class tools, including checkout, auction counters, customer email management, bulk feedback, bulk listing, and more. It's probably the best assortment of tools available, but also the most costly—although you can try the ones you want on an ala carte basis.

- **Auctionworks** (www.auctionworks.com) offers various professional auction tools, including inventory management, a bulk listing creator, traffic counters, image hosting, and automatic end-of-auction emails.

- **Auctiva** (www.auctiva.com) offers two different services: Auctiva Basic (bulk lister) and Auctiva Pro (full auction management services).

- **eBay Selling Manager** (pages.ebay.com/selling_manager/) is eBay's official auction management service, at $4.99/month a good choice for medium-sized sellers. Larger sellers should opt for eBay's more fully-featured Selling Manager Pro, which costs $15.99 per month.

- **SpareDollar** (www.sparedollar.com) is kind of a bargain-basement auction service, ideal for small or occasional sellers with a flat $4.95 per month price.

- **Vendio** (www.vendio.com) is number-two to ándale among auction management services, offering bulk listing, end-of-auction management, and bulk feedback posting.

FACT OF THE WEEK

According to The Auction Software Review, 15% of all eBay auctions are won in the last minute of bidding. Half of all auctions receive no bids, while a quarter of all auctions receive only a single bid. Only 4% of eBay auctions receive 10 or more bids.

November 13, 2005

SUNDAY

THIS WEEK'S FOCUS: EBAY

ON THIS DAY: HOLLAND TUNNEL OPENS (1927)

The Holland Tunnel opened for traffic on November 13, 1927. It was the first twin-tube subaqueous vehicular tunnel in the United States. Named after its engineer, Clifford Holland, the tunnel carries 1,900 vehicles per hour.

Related Web site: www.nycroads.com/crossings/holland/

RUNNING AN EBAY BUSINESS

While most eBay users are simple hobbyists, a surprisingly large number of users sell enough items to actually make a living from their eBay auctions. These sellers bring in thousands of dollars in auction income every week. They're businesses, pure and simple, that operate on and through the eBay auction service.

As tens of thousands of these users have proved, it's definitely possible to sell enough items every week to generate a livable income from eBay auctions. It takes a lot of hard work and it's as complex as running any other business, but it can be done. You have to purchase inventory, market your products, collect payments, and ship merchandise, just like an Amazon.com or L.L. Bean does. It's a full-time job.

There are two keys to making a living from an eBay business. First, you have to sell a large volume of merchandise. (Alternately, you can sell a small number of high-priced items—which isn't as easy as it sounds.) Second, you have to control your costs. Sell enough items while keeping your costs under control, and you'll have a profitable business on your hands.

The bottom line is that making a living from eBay sales is just like running a "real" business, especially in its financial complexities. Anyone contemplating this type of endeavor should do some serious business planning, which should include consulting an accountant or other financial planner. And you should definitely work up a business plan before you get started, including projected profit and loss statements.

If the numbers work out, you need to answer one more question: Is this something you'll enjoy doing every day of the week, every week of the year? Even if you can make money at it, managing hundreds of auctions a week can wear down even the best of us. Make sure you're up to it, and that you'll enjoy it, before you take the leap.

SOFTWARE OF THE WEEK

DeepAnalysis is a software program that performs basic sales analysis of completed eBay auctions. DeepAnalysis provides fundamental information about any category or specific product, including the number of auctions in the past 30 days, the number of bids for each auction, percentage of items sold, average selling price, and so on. Buy it for $179 at www.hammertap.com.

November 14, 2005

MONDAY

THIS WEEK'S FOCUS: AMAZON.COM

ON THIS DAY: BUCKYBALL DISCOVERED (1985)

On November 14, 1985, an article in the journal *Nature* revealed the discovery of the fullerene, a spherical cluster of carbon atoms. The discovery was dubbed buckminsterfullerene—or bucky-balls—after Buckminster Fuller.

Related Web site: buckminster.physics.sunysb.edu

FINDING BARGAINS ON AMAZON.COM

Amazon.com is the Internet's largest retailer, period. Not only can you find just about any product you want on the Amazon.com site, you can also find some pretty good bargains—if you know where to look.

The first place to find bargains on Amazon is the Today's Deals page, which lists all current promotions, discounts, sales, rebates, and the like across the entire Amazon.com site. You get to the Today's Deals page by clicking the Welcome tab and then clicking Today's Deals under the navigation bar. Or, if you want to look at current deals in a particular category, go to that store page and click Today's Deals under that page's navigation bar.

Even more bargains can be found by scrolling to the bottom of any Amazon.com page. Here Amazon lists limited-time *Bottom of the Page deals*—savings updated every day at noon and good only for 24 hours.

You can also find good deals on clearance merchandise at Amazon's equivalent of an outlet mall, the Amazon.com Outlet. You access the Amazon.com Outlet by clicking the Outlet tab on the navigation bar, or the Outlet link on the See

More Stores page. The items offered here are often prior-year or discontinued items, but can also be regular-line merchandise that the manufacturer is overstocked on. In any case, the Amazon.com Outlet is a prime destination for serious bargain hunters; the selection here is constantly changing.

Finally, savvy Amazon shoppers know that Friday is the day to find the site's best bargains. That's because every Friday Amazon conducts a one-day sale, called (not surprisingly) the Friday Sale. Selected merchandise is put on sale for 24 hours only; prices return to normal at midnight (Pacific time) and quantities are limited. You find the Friday Sale by going to the Outlet store (either from the Outlet tab or the Outlet link on the See More Stores page) and clicking The Friday Store under the navigation bar. Shop early (just after midnight is good) for the best selection.

PC GADGET OF THE WEEK

Suffer from sweaty palms? Then check out Nyko's Air Flo Mouse, which has a built-in fan that pushes air through holes in the shell. This cools your hand during heavy computing sessions. Buy it for $14.99 at www.nyko.com.

November 15, 2005

TUESDAY

THIS WEEK'S FOCUS: AMAZON.COM

ON THIS DAY: DRY CELL BATTERY PATENTED (1887)

On November 15, 1887, German scientist Dr. Carl Gassner was issued a U.S. patent for the first "dry" cell battery. Gassner encased the cell chemicals in a sealed zinc container, much like the general-purpose carbon-zinc batteries on the market today.

Related Web site: electronics.howstuffworks.com/battery.htm

READ AND WRITE AMAZON PRODUCT REVIEWS

One of the great things about Amazon is that it has become a real community of involved users. This is particularly evident in the reviews that users write about individual products. It's like having a group of amateur critics at your disposal; you can find out how much (or how little) users just like you like a particular product, and why. Smart shoppers use these third-party opinions to help determine which products to buy.

And some of these reviews are quite good, particularly those of books, music, and movies. The most prolific reviewers—dubbed Top Reviewers by Amazon, and highlighted accordingly—offer near-professional insights; their opinions are surprisingly reliable.

To write your own review of a product, scroll down the page to the All Customer Reviews section and click the Write an Online Review link. Keep your review short (1000 words or less) and to the point,

and remember to add a 1 to 5 star rating. After you click the Save button, your review will itself be reviewed by Amazon, and then (after a week to ten days) appear in the reviews section for that product.

You can also rate the reviews themselves. If you find a particular review helpful, tell others how much you liked it. Just go to the Was This Review Helpful to You? section at the bottom of the review and click the Yes or No button. Your vote will be added to the tally at the beginning of the review, in the part that says "X of Y people found this review helpful."

DOWNLOAD OF THE WEEK

Here's a different kind of Amazon that has nothing to do with books or e-tailing. Change the way Windows looks with the Amazon Rainforest theme, downloadable for free from www.extremethemes.net/rainforest.html.

November 16, 2005
WEDNESDAY
THIS WEEK'S FOCUS: **AMAZON.COM**
ON THIS DAY: GENE AMDAHL BORN (1922)

One of the original architects of the business mainframe computer was born on this date in 1922. Gene Amdahl helped to design IBM's System/360 computer line, and then left the company to form the competing Amdahl Corporation. He later left Amdahl Corporation company to found three more companies, Trilogy Systems, Andor Systems, and Commercial Data Servers (CDS).

Related Web site: www.thocp.net/biographies/amdahl_gene.htm

BECOME AN AMAZON ASSOCIATE

If you have your own Web site, you can use Amazon to generate a little income. All you have to do is sign up to be an Amazon Associate, and then direct users to purchase Amazon items from your site. For every purchase placed, you earn a sales commission—between 2.5% to 10%, according to sales volume and other variables.

The Amazon Associates program is free to join. All you have to do is sign up for the program, put a few links to Amazon on your Web site, and let Amazon do the rest. When someone clicks through your Associate link to the Amazon site, a 24-hour shopping window is opened. Anything that user adds to his or her shopping cart for the next 24 hours is eligible for Associate referral fees—even if the actual purchase happens at a later time. The money you earn is paid quarterly, either via check, direct deposit to your checking account, or Amazon gift certificate.

Adding an Associates link requires some rudimentary knowledge of HTML, of course, although Amazon makes the process as easy as cutting and pasting a line or two of code. You can get more detailed instructions—as well as sign up for the Associates program—at the Amazon Associates page (associates.amazon.com).

Now here's the real secret that Amazon doesn't want you to know. You can purchase from your own Associate links—and earn commissions on every item you buy from Amazon! That's right, you become your own referral, and earn a commission on every purchase you make. Those Amazon Associate referral fees are now like cash rebates on your own purchases. It's a cool deal, but only workable as long as you run your own Web site or pages. And don't forget to ask all your friends and family to route their Amazon purchases through your site as well!

MAC GADGET OF THE WEEK

Kensington's Turbo Mouse Pro is the Porsche of trackballs. It's a large trackball with several programmable buttons, but the key to its power is the software, MouseWorks, that comes bundled with it. It's straightforward stuff that's built for Mac OS X (or Mac OS 9, depending on your preference) and gives you great control over how you go about your mousing responsibilities. Buy it for $109 from www.kensington.com.

November 17, 2005

THURSDAY

THIS WEEK'S FOCUS: AMAZON.COM

ON THIS DAY: COMPUTER MOUSE PATENTED (1970)

On November 17, 1970, a U.S. patent was issued for the computer mouse—an "X-Y Position Indicator for a Display System." The inventor was Doug Engelbart, who had jokingly referred to the device as a "mouse," after its tail-like cable. That first mouse was a simple hollowed-out wooden block with a single pushbutton on top; Engelbart had designed it as a tool to select and manipulate text.

Related Web site: `sloan.stanford.edu/MouseSite/`

JUMP DIRECTLY TO ANY AMAZON PRODUCT LISTING

Amazon assigns every product it offers a unique number, called an Amazon Standard Item Number (ASIN). If you know a product's ASIN, it's easy to jump directly to that item's product listing page. Just enter the ASIN into Amazon's search box, and instead of being served up a page full of search results, Amazon will display the product listing page associated with that ASIN.

How do you find a product's ASIN? If you're looking for a book, the ASIN is the same as the book's International Standard Book Number (ISBN), which is located above the bar code, typically on the book's back cover or inside flap. For other products, well, you're pretty much out of luck. That's because the ASIN doesn't relate at all to a product's Universal Product Code (UPC), which is used to create a product's bar code. So you'll have to look up the ASIN via a traditional Amazon product search; the ASIN is listed in the Product Details section of a product listing page.

Once you know the ASIN, you can access the product listing page, as the ASIN is used to create the page's URL. Just enter the following URL, with the actual ASIN replacing the *number*: `www.amazon.com/exec/obidos/ASIN/number/`.

You can also extract the ASIN from a product page URL, even though the formal URL probably doesn't look like the format I just described. It's probably a lot longer, because Amazon adds various tracking information to all its URLs, essentially creating custom URLs for every visit of every user. You can shorten any URL (good if you want to copy it for other users) by deleting all the data after the ASIN number. So if the URL reads `www.amazon.com/exec/obidos/ASIN/123456789/othernumbers`, just delete the *othernumbers* and use the `www.amazon.com/exec/obidos/ASIN/123456789/` URL.

WEB SITE OF THE WEEK

You can track Amazon's sales rankings over time at JungleScan. JungleScan lets you create a portfolio of items you'd like to track, and then produces charts that track the items' performance, updated every 24 hours. Check it out at `www.junglescan.com`.

November 18, 2005

FRIDAY

THIS WEEK'S FOCUS: AMAZON.COM

ON THIS DAY: MICKEY MOUSE DEBUTS IN *STEAMBOAT WILLIE* (1928)

Steamboat Willie, released on November 18, 1928, was the first animated cartoon to feature the character of Mickey Mouse. The cartoon, written and directed by Walt Disney and Ub Iwerks, was a parody of the Buster Keaton film *Steamboat Bill Jr.* In addition to featuring the debut performance of that famous mouse, *Steamboat Willie* was the first animated short with a completely synchronized soundtrack of music, dialogue, and sound effects.

Related Web site: www.bcdb.com/bcdb/detailed.cgi?film=3820

SAVE ON AMAZON SHIPPING COSTS

The first way to save money on your Amazon.com order is to cut out the shipping charge completely. Amazon offers free Super Saver Shipping if your order totals $25 or more, with some qualifications. The big qualification is that selected merchandise is excluded from the offer, specifically apparel, baby products, toys, video games, certain oversize items, products from Circuit City, J&R Music and Computer World, Marshall Field's, Office Depot, and Target, products from Marketplace and zShops sellers, and products that don't include the Super Saver Shipping icon. In other words, don't assume that what you order qualifies; look for the icon to be sure.

Also know that Super Saver Shipping isn't automatically applied to your order; you have to select this option manually during the checkout process. You'll also have to select from the Place Your Order page, Group My Items Into As Few Shipments As Possible as your shipping preference.

One more thing—selecting Super Saver Shipping will add three-to-five days to your order. So, this isn't a good option if you need your merchandise quickly. On the other hand, if you don't mind waiting a few extra days, it can represent significant savings.

While we're on the topic of shipping, you don't have to choose Super Saver Shipping to save on shipping charges. When you order more than one item, you can choose to group all the items into a single shipment, which will reduce your shipping charges no matter which shipping method you choose. This is opposed to splitting your order into multiple shipments, which might get you your items faster, but will cost more.

Whichever type of order grouping you select, you also have a choice of shipping speed. You can choose from Standard Shipping (3–7 business days), Two-Day Shipping (2 business days), or One-Day Shipping (1 business day). Obviously, Standard Shipping costs less than One- or Two-Day Shipping. Save money by choosing the Standard Shipping option.

PORTABLE GADGET OF THE WEEK

If you like the idea of a customizable color touch screen remote control, you'll love Philips's ProntoPro NG. This is a sleek handheld unit with a high-resolution 3.8" color LCD touch screen display. Buy it for $899.99 from www.pronto.philips.com.

November 19, 2005

SATURDAY

THIS WEEK'S FOCUS: AMAZON.COM

ON THIS DAY: FORD HALTS PRODUCTION OF THE EDSEL (1959)

The ill-fated Edsel automobile was introduced to the public in the fall of 1957. Despite its huge introduction, Ford sold only 63,110 Edsels in its first year in the market, and sales dropped to 44,891 in its second year. One of the most publicized product failures in American history, the Edsel was dropped from production just two years after its launch, on November 19, 1959.

Related Web site: www.edsel.com

POWER SEARCH FOR BOOKS

Amazon is my favorite place to search for books, because just about any title I want is available—if you know how to look for it. Searching for items on Amazon is better than browsing, of course, but Amazon offers some additional search options when you're shopping for books.

One of Amazon's coolest features is its Power Search, which lets you use advanced search operators to really focus your search for particular books. You use Power Search by going to the Advanced Book Search page and scrolling down to the Power Search section. You enter the Power Search operator into the form, followed by a variable (no space), followed by your normal keyword(s), like this: `operator:variable`. For example, if you want to search for all books published by me, use the `author:` operator like this: `author:laporte`.

Here's a quick look at all the available Power Search operators:

Operator	Description
author	Searches for all books by a particular author
ISBN	Searches for all books by ISBN code

Operator	Description
keyword	Searches for all books where the title or author contains designated keywords
language	Searches for books written in a specific language
pubdate	Searches for books published before, during, or after a particular date, using the before, during, or after syntax
publisher	Searches for books published by a specific publisher
subject	Searches for books about a specific topic
title	Searches for books with specific words in the title

Another cool feature: Amazon lets you use the Boolean AND, OR, and NOT operators to create complex queries. Check it out!

FACT OF THE WEEK

Amazon.com sales have increased at an average compounded rate of 81% per year since 1997. Sales in 2003 reached $5.2 billion, up from $3.9 billion in 2002.

November 20, 2005

SUNDAY

THIS WEEK'S FOCUS: AMAZON.COM

ON THIS DAY: WINDOWS 1.0 RELEASED (1985)

Microsoft first began development of what it called the Interface Manager in September 1981. Later renamed Windows, it offered a graphical user interface, device-independent graphics, and support for multitasking. The initial version, Windows 1.0, hit store shelves on November 20, 1985. Sales were modest—but picked up for later versions.

Related Web site: members.fortunecity.com/pcmuseum/windows.htm

CREATE YOUR OWN AMAZON LISTS AND GUIDES

Amazon offers two fun ways to recommend products to other users—lists and guides.

If you're constantly organizing your life into top ten lists, you'll like Amazon's Listmania feature. You can create Listmania lists about any topic you can think of; Amazon displays these lists alongside products that are included in the list. So, for example, if you create a list of your top 10 Westerns and include the film *The Magnificent Seven*, your list might be displayed on the product page for *The Magnificent Seven* DVD. (I said *might*; there's no guarantee where your list will pop up.)

To create a Listmania list, go to Your Store > Friends & Favorites and click the Add a Listmania List link. Give your list a name, enter your qualifications (if any), and then select up to 25 products. Amazon will create the list, automatically inserting links to pictures of the products you selected.

Similar to Listmania lists are Amazon's guides, which are short tutorials to various subjects, also written by Amazon users. If you fancy yourself an expert on a given topic, you can create your own guide to the topic, which is then listed on product pages for those products listed within the guide. For example, if you wrote a guide about how to use Amazon and mentioned this book, your guide would be listed on this book's product page.

To create a guide, go to Your Store > Friends & Favorites and then click the Write a So You'd Like to... Guide link. Enter a title for your guide and then start writing. Each guide has to mention at least three products; you link to these products from within the guide by using the following code: **<ASIN: number>**, replacing **number** with the product's ASIN code.

SOFTWARE OF THE WEEK

If you're a high-volume seller in Amazon's Marketplace, check out AMan. This is a full-featured order-fulfillment package that automates many time-consuming tasks. It automatically captures order and listing info, produces labels and packing slips, and notifies your customers when an item ships. Buy it for $299 at www.spaceware.com.

November 21, 2005

MONDAY

THIS WEEK'S FOCUS: ONLINE SHOPPING

ON THIS DAY: FIRST MANNED BALLOON FLIGHT (1783)

On November 21, 1783, Jean Francois Pilatre de Rozier and Marquis Francois Laurant d'Arlandes made the first human flight in a balloon. They lifted off from La Muettte, a royal palace in The Bois de Boulogne, Paris. They flew 25 minutes, reaching an altitude of around 300 feet, and landed nearly 6 miles away. Ben Franklin was one of the spectators.

Related Web site: www.intheair-online.com/history.html

THE BEST WAY TO PAY

When you're shopping online, how can (and should) you pay?

You could pay by check or money order, but I don't recommend it because of the hassle involved. (You have to place your order online and then send your payment through the mail, which can delay your shipment by at least a few weeks.) Instead, my recommendation is to do all your online shopping via credit card. There are a number of reasons for this.

First, it's the way most online shoppers pay, and what most online retailers expect. The whole online shopping process is built around credit card payments, so when you pay by plastic, everything goes smoothly.

Second, it's fast. You place your order, you enter your credit card number, the order is confirmed, and your product ships—just like that. There's no delay waiting for your payment to be received or your check to be cleared. Most credit card purchases are processed the same day—if not the same hour.

Third, it's safe. Yeah, you've heard horror stories about credit card theft and fraud, but the reality is that your credit card company is working overtime to protect you against this type of problem. In fact, if you check with your card company, you'll find that you're protected against credit card theft above a minimal amount; if your card number is stolen, you might be on the hook for $25 or $50, but the credit card company eats any amount more than that. In addition, if you have a problem with the order, you can have your credit card company stop payment to the retailer. The credit card companies always work to your benefit, which can be a real lifesaver when you have a genuine dispute.

PC GADGET OF THE WEEK

Leave it to the Swiss to utilize flash memory in a highly functional fashion. The SWISSMEMORY is a USB memory device built in to a multifunction Swiss army knife—complete with red LED, a blade, a nail file with screwdriver, scissors, and a ballpoint pen. Buy it for $69 from www.victorinox.com.

THIS WEEK'S FOCUS: ONLINE SHOPPING

ON THIS DAY: PRESIDENT KENNEDY ASSASSINATED (1963)

At 12:30 p.m. on November 22, 1963, a motorcade carrying President John F. Kennedy was passing through Dealey Plaza in downtown Dallas, Texas. Three shots rang out; one struck the pavement, one delivered nonfatal wounds to the President and Texas Governor John Connally, and the third struck the President in the head, killing him. A nation mourned.

Related Web site: www.archives.gov/research_room/jfk/

SHOPPING SAFELY

Despite some overblown fears, shopping online is at least as safe as shopping at a bricks and mortar retailer. Still, there are several steps you can take to improve the security—and the success—of your online transactions. Here are a few tips:

- **See what other customers have to say**—One of the better ways to check up on an unfamiliar merchant is to read what others have to say about that retailer. Fortunately, there are several Web sites, such as BizRate (www.bizrate.com) and ePublicEye (www.epubliceye.com), that offer either professional site ratings or reviews by the site's customers.

- **Look for the WebAssured logo**—Many quality online retailers subscribe to the WebAssured (www.webassured.com) service. To display the WebAssured logo, a merchant has to agree to a high level of conduct, encompassing accurate delivery, ethical advertising, full disclosure of product information, fast response to customer complaints, and consumer privacy.

- **Look for a secure site**—Data sent over the Internet can be picked off by dedicated hackers—unless that data is handled by a secure server. Most major shopping sites feature SSL-encrypted ordering and checkout. You'll know you're using a secure site when the little lock icon appears in the lower part of your Web browser.

- **Look for contact information**—Let's face it, if something goes wrong with your order, you're going to need to contact somebody. Beware of sites that don't even include an email contact address, and try to target sites that prominently list their phone number (toll-free, ideally), fax number, or street address for post-sale support.

- **Pay by credit card**—It's ironic that some people are afraid of paying via credit card online, when it's the credit card payment that provides the most security for your online transaction. When you pay by credit card, you're protected by the Fair Credit Billing Act, which gives you the right to dispute certain charges and limits your liability for unauthorized transactions to $50.

DOWNLOAD OF THE WEEK

Best Buy Finder is a shopping bot program that searches the top price comparison sites and returns the lowest price it finds. Download it for $29.95 at www.bestbuyall.com.

November 23, 2005
WEDNESDAY

THIS WEEK'S FOCUS: ONLINE SHOPPING

ON THIS DAY: FIRST JUKEBOX INSTALLED (1889)

On November 23, 1889, entrepreneur Louis Glass and his business associate, William S. Arnold, placed a coin-operated Edison cylinder phonograph in the Palais Royale Saloon in San Francisco. This machine had been fitted with a coin mechanism, and for a nickel a play, patrons could listen to the music through one of four listening tubes. Known as "Nickel-in-the-Slot," this first jukebox earned over $1,000 in its first six months.

Related Web site: www.nationaljukebox.com

LOOK FOR MANUFACTURER REBATES

Here's a tip you're familiar with from the bricks and mortar world. It's quite common in some product categories to find the manufacturer offering a few bucks back when you fill in and mail back an official rebate form (along with appropriate proof-of-purchase, of course). Shop around for the lowest base price on a product, and then use the rebate to lower your effective price that much more.

If you're not sure which manufacturers are offering what rebates, check out a rebate-tracking site, such as myRebates.com or rebatesHQ.com. These sites list current manufacturer rebates, enable you to print the official rebate forms, and even track the progress of your rebate claims.

And don't forget to send in those rebate forms. Manufacturers count on a large percentage of customers never redeeming their rebates; you'd be surprised at how low most redemption rates really are.

On the topic of rebates, watch out for sites that display misleading "after rebate" pricing. Although most retailers are fairly clear as to what their price is and what the rebate is, some merchants will display a big "after rebate" price, showing your net price—*not* what they're charging. Don't fall for this trap; you still need to find the lowest sale price, and *then* subtract the rebate amount.

MAC GADGET OF THE WEEK

If your Mac is short on USB ports, add a few more with Belkin's USB BusPort for Mac. Just slide the expansion card into the system unit and get two additional USB ports on the back of your Mac. Buy it for $39.95 at www.belkin.com.

THIS WEEK'S FOCUS: ONLINE SHOPPING

ON THIS DAY: DARWIN'S *ORIGIN OF SPECIES* PUBLISHED (1859)

The book *On the Origin of Species by Means of Natural Selection, or the Preservation of Favoured Races in the Struggle for Life,* by British naturalist Charles Darwin, was published on this date in 1859. The book details Darwin's theory that organisms gradually evolve through natural selection. The book—which immediately sold through its initial print run—was highly controversial because it negated the need for a biblical creation.

Related Web site: www.aboutdarwin.com

RESEARCH YOUR PURCHASE BEFORE YOU BUY

I find it extremely useful to read what other users have to say about an item before I decide to buy. Your fellow consumers will give you the unvarnished pros and cons based on actual use, and tell you whether or not they think the product was a good deal. There are many sites on the Web that provide forums for customers' product reviews; here are some of my favorites:

- **ConsumerREVIEW.com** (www.consumerreview.com), collects customer reviews from a bevy of specialty sites, including AudioREVIEW, ComputingREVIEW, PCGameREVIEW, and PhotographyREVIEW.

- **ConsumerReports.org** (www.consumerreports.org) is the online arm of the venerable *Consumer Reports* magazine. There's a lot of useful information available for free, but you have to subscribe to the magazine to read the site's full reviews.

- **ConsumerSearch** (www.consumersearch.com) aggregates a variety of professional reviews—found in magazines and other Web sites—about each product listed.

- **Epinons.com** (www.epinions.com) is my favorite product review site. What's great about this site is that users can write reviews about virtually anything—not just products, but also services, retailers, and locales. Epinions also has the largest database of consumer reviews on the Web.

- **RateItAll** (www.rateitall.com) is a site where customers can rate a variety of products and services. It's a smallish database, however, compared to some of the other sites.

- **ReviewFinder** (www.reviewfinder.com) offers links to reviews of various types of electronic equipment. It's a good gateway to lots of other reviews across the Internet.

WEB SITE OF THE WEEK

Just as there are sites devoted to customer reviews of specific products, there are also sites devoted to customer reviews of specific retailers. I like ePublicEye, which offers extensive customer reviews of and detailed information about online merchants, as well as information about online fraud and scams. Check it out at www.epubliceye.com.

November 25, 2005

FRIDAY

THIS WEEK'S FOCUS: ONLINE SHOPPING

ON THIS DAY: DYNAMITE PATENTED (1867)

Swedish chemist Alfred Nobel received a notable patent on this date in 1867. Three years earlier, Nobel began the mass production of nitroglycerin, and in 1866 he successfully mixed nitroglycerin with silica, which turned the highly volatile liquid into a paste. This paste, which could be formed and shaped as desired, made it possible for safe transportation. The new material, which Nobel subsequently patented, was called dynamite.

Related Web site: www.nobel.se

USING A PRICE COMPARISON SITE

Just a few years go, if you wanted to find the best bargains on the Web, you had to manually visit the sites of dozens of different online retailers—a very time-consuming process. Not so today; numerous sites exist to automatically do this price comparison for you. These sites use shopping bots to search a large number of online retailers for current prices on available products. They also include listings submitted (for a fee) by participating retailers. The upshot? A one-stop search engine you can use to find the lowest prices on specific merchandise.

- **BizRate (www.bizrate.com)** is one of the most comprehensive comparison sites I've found. It also offers customer reviews of the most popular products.

- **Froogle (froogle.google.com)** is the new shopping search engine from Google. Unique among the major price comparison sites, Froogle doesn't take money for its listings, instead sending its software to independently scour the Web for merchants and products.

- **mySimon (www.mysimon.com)** was one of the first price comparison sites on the Web and it's still one of the most popular, even though it doesn't search near as many merchants as some of the newer sites.

- **Shopping.com (www.shopping.com)** is a relaunched and revamped version of the old DealTime site, now incorporating customer reviews from Epinions.com. This makes Shopping.com perhaps the most fully featured price comparison site; it's definitely my favorite.

- **Yahoo! Shopping (shopping.yahoo.com)** was recently revamped into one of the leading price comparison sites on the Web. Formerly, it was merely a large directory of online merchants; now it's a full-featured shopping search engine, complete with numerous product comparison features.

PORTABLE GADGET OF THE WEEK

Want to get fast and furious? If you're a serious boy racer, you need to check out the Vector FX2, a handheld computer that measures your car's acceleration time, 1/4-mile time, braking distance, G-force, cornering, and horsepower. The Vector FX2 mounts on your car's windshield and displays the pertinent measurements on an alpine blue display. Just turn it on, press the start button, and put the pedal to the metal. Buy it for $249.95 at www.beltronics.com.

November 26, 2005
SATURDAY

THIS WEEK'S FOCUS: ONLINE SHOPPING

ON THIS DAY: FIRST POLAROID CAMERA SOLD (1948)

The first PPolaroid Land camera, the Model 95, was sold in Boston's Jordan Marsh department store on this date in 1948, for $89.75. The new camera accomplished all the necessary processing to produce a 3 1/4" × 4 1/4" dry print.

Related Web site: www.polaroid.com

SAVING WITH ONLINE COUPONS

Another good source of online savings is online coupons—or, to be more accurate, online coupon *codes*, because there's really no way to use a printed coupon with an online merchant. What you get instead is a code you can enter when you check out at an online merchant; the coupon savings are deducted from your order when you check out.

How you apply an online coupon depends on which site you visit. Some online coupon sites totally automate the process; others just give you the coupon codes for you to apply on your own. In any case, you have to visit the online coupon site first, and then go to the retailer to shop.

There are a large number of sites that offer online coupons. These sites make their money when you use the coupon; the coupon/promotion codes link back to their site, so the merchant knows to pay a small commission on your purchase. Here are some of the most popular:

- Bargain Boardwalk (www.bargainboardwalk.com)
- Bargain-Central (www.bargain-central.com)
- CouponMountain (www.couponmountain.com)
- dealcoupon (www.dealcoupon.com)
- DealofDay.com (www.dealofday.com)
- eCoupons (www.ecoupons.com)
- MyCoupons (www.mycoupons.com)
- TotalDeals.com (www.totaldeals.com)

Many of these sites also enable you to sign up for daily or weekly email newsletters that inform you of the newest deals on the Web. Saves you the trouble of visiting the site every time you go shopping!

FACT OF THE WEEK

According to Forrester Research, online sales increased 51% from 2002 to 2003. Sales reached $114 billion, representing 5.4% of all retail sales. More importantly to the retailers, online profit margins went from zero in 2002 to 21% in 2003; fully 79% of online retailers were profitable.

November 27, 2005

SUNDAY

THIS WEEK'S FOCUS: ONLINE SHOPPING

ON THIS DAY: KONOSUKE MATSUSHITA BORN (1894)

The Japanese industrialist who founded the Matsushita Electric Industrial Co., Ltd., was born on November 27, 1894. Konosuke Matsushita began work at age 9 as an errand boy. He began working for the Osaka Electric Light Company at age 16, quitting his job there at age 23 to start a company that sold electric plug attachments of his own design. That company became the company that now bears his name.

Related Web site: matsushita.co.jp/company/person/en/index.html

SHOPPING FOR LIQUIDATION BARGAINS

Some of the lowest prices online are offered by online liquidators. These are companies that purchase surplus items from other businesses in bulk. These items might be closeouts, factory seconds, customer returns, salvaged items, or overstocked merchandise—products the manufacturer made too many of and wants to get rid of. Liquidators help manufacturers and retailers dispose of this unwanted merchandise. And there are lots of liquidators now operating on the Web, selling these goods direct to consumers at bargain prices.

Many liquidators let you shop at their sites pretty much the same way you'd shop at a regular online retailer. These so-called single-item liquidators offer closeout merchandise at extremely low prices. Unlike the new merchandise you purchase from traditional wholesalers, many liquidators sell their goods as-is; if it's bad, you're out of luck. Other liquidators offer a limited money-back guarantee of some sort, so you're not completely on the hook. Make sure you know what sort of guarantee (if any) the site offers before you place an order.

Some of the more popular single-item liquidation sites include Closeouts America (www.closeoutsamerica.com), Overstock.com (www.overstock.com), and SmartBargains (www.smartbargains.com).

Just as liquidators purchase their inventory in bulk, you sometimes have to buy from them in bulk. Although some liquidators sell single quantities, others only sell so-called big *lots*. That means buying ten or twenty or a hundred units of a particular item or mix of items. You get a really good price for buying in quantity, of course, which is part of the appeal.

Some of the most popular bulk liquidation sites include AmeriSurplus (www.amerisurplus.com), Liquidation.com (www.liquidation.com), and TDW Closeouts (www.tdwcloseouts.com).

SOFTWARE OF THE WEEK

Start up your own online store with X-Cart shopping cart software. X-Cart is a turnkey template-based solution you can run on your own server; it can handle up to 20,000 inventory SKUs. Buy it for $185 at www.x-cart.com.

November 28, 2005

MONDAY

THIS WEEK'S FOCUS: GRAPHICS

ON THIS DAY: MARINER 4 LAUNCHED (1964)

Mariner 4, launched on this day in 1964, was the fourth in a series of spacecraft designed for flyby planetary exploration. The Mariner 4 probe gave scientists their first glimpse of Mars at close range, passing over the planet at an altitude of 6,118 miles on July 14, 1965. Mariner 4 returned 22 television pictures that covered about 1% of Mars's surface; the pictures revealed a vast, barren wasteland of craters strewn about a rust-colored carpet of sand. No life in sight.

Related Web site: www.marsnews.com/missions/mariner/

CREATING A GLAMOUR GLOW

No matter how good your digital camera, some close-up photos are less than flattering to their subjects. That's because the closer you get with the camera, the more the lens captures every little skin imperfection. Here's a trick that smooths out uneven skin, softens freckled patches, and adds a kind of glamour glow to the subject. The technique requires slightly blurring parts of the picture to create a kind of soft-focus effect—without losing the overall picture sharpness.

Here's how to do it in Adobe Photoshop Elements 3; the technique is similar in previous versions, and in Photoshop CS.

Start by making a copy of the current layer by selecting Layer > Duplicate Layer. Then open the Layers palette and select this new Background Copy layer.

Now you need to blur this layer. Select Filter > Blur > Gaussian Blur. When the Gaussian Blur dialog box appears, adjust the Radius control until the picture is sufficiently blurry (probably somewhere between 3 and 6 pixels). Click OK when you're done.

Your picture now looks extremely blurry. You need to blend this blurry layer with the still-sharp original layer, so go back to the Layers palette and adjust the Opacity control to 50%.

Your picture now looks only slightly blurred. The problem is that you don't want the entire picture to be blurred, only the skin area. So now you must add some sharpness back in the non-skin areas, which you do by erasing some of the duplicate layer. Use the Eraser tool to erase those areas of the face you want to sharpen—eyebrows, eyes, teeth, lips, hair, and so on. What you're doing is erasing parts of the blurred layer so the sharp original layer shows through.

PC GADGET OF THE WEEK

ATI's top-of-the-line TV tuner/DVR video card is the All-In-Wonder 9800 PRO. It's a full-featured HDTV unit that's great for watching and recording TV or playing the latest 3D game graphics. The included TV-on-Demand software lets you record TV programs on your PC's hard drive, as well as pause live programming; you can look up TV schedules with the Gemstar GUIDE Plus+ software. Buy it for $399 at www.ati.com.

TUESDAY

THIS WEEK'S FOCUS: GRAPHICS

ON THIS DAY: ATARI RELEASES PONG ARCADE GAME (1972)

Videogame mania started on November 29, 1972, when Atari released its PONG game to arcades. It was an immediate success, with 19,000 of the arcade machines sold. PONG stayed in the arcades until 1975, when it was replaced by slightly more advanced games like Tank, Space Invaders, and Indy 500.

Related Web site: www.pong-story.com

MONITOR WARS: LCD OR CRT?

There are two different display technologies used in today's computer monitors. The older technology uses a big *cathode ray tube* (CRT) to display the images. The newer technology uses a thin *liquid crystal display* (LCD) instead of a CRT—and is quickly becoming the display of choice.

A CRT monitor works and looks pretty much like a television set, but is specialized to handle computer data. CRT monitors are big (depth-wise) but fairly low priced; you can get 14-inch CRT monitors for as little as $100, and even larger 17-inch models are relatively affordable.

LCD monitors, in contrast, give you the same size picture in a much thinner package. Most LCD monitors are only a few inches thick, which makes them ideal for portable PCs and desktop systems where space is at a premium. LCD technology is more expensive than CRT technology, however, which is why you'll pay at least twice as much for a comparable LCD monitor over a CRT model—although the price is coming down.

As cool and as convenient as LCD monitors are (and they're not near as expensive as they used to be), CRT monitors are still preferred for specific types of applications—in particular, gaming, graphics editing, and video editing. For gamers, CRT monitors do a better job of reproducing complex graphics fast, which is what today's state-of-the-art PC games demand. For graphics and video professionals (including photographers), CRT monitors deliver more accurate color reproduction.

In fact, several manufacturers make high-end CRT monitors especially designed for the demanding needs of graphics professionals. These are typically big (21" or more) monitors with high-resolution, small dot pitch screens, often accompanied by some sort of calibration device and software. Check out the offerings by LaCie (www.lacie.com) and Sony (www.displaybysony.com), if you're interested.

DOWNLOAD OF THE WEEK

WebPix is a program that lets you automatically download pictures from Web sites, and then view the thumbnails. It utilizes a multi-threaded spider to retrieve all the images from a selected site, automatically. Try it for free, or download it for $25 from www.netwu.com/webpix/.

November 30, 2005

WEDNESDAY

THIS WEEK'S FOCUS: GRAPHICS

ON THIS DAY: MARK TWAIN BORN (1835)

Samuel Langhorne Clemens, better known by his pen name Mark Twain, was born on November 30, 1835. Clemens gained fame as a humorist, writer, and lecturer. William Faulkner wrote that he was "the first truly American writer, and all of us since are his heirs." His most famous books include *The Adventures of Huckleberry Finn, The Adventures of Tom Sawyer, The Prince and the Pauper,* and *A Connecticut Yankee in King Arthur's Court.*

Related Web site: www.twainquotes.com

REPLACING UGLY BACKGROUNDS

Ever take a great portrait or group photo, but hated the background? Here's how to remove the background of any digital photo and replace it with a professional-looking photo backdrop. This technique uses Adobe Photoshop Elements 3, but you can apply similar techniques with previous versions, and in Photoshop CS.

Start by selecting what color you want the new background to be. Use the Set Foreground Color control to select a main color, and the Set Background Color control to select a slightly darker version of the background color. I like light blue and dark blue, but that's just me.

Now use one of the Marquee, Lasso, or Magic Wand tools to draw around the main subjects and select the entire background. Since a hard edge around the selection makes the new picture look unnatural, select Select > Feather to open the Feather Selection dialog box, and then enter a Feather Radius of 5 pixels.

Now you need to delete the current background. With the background selected, select Edit > Clear. This clears the selected area and replaces it with the background color you previously selected.

Next, let's give the new background a little texture. Select Filter > Render > Clouds to create a cloud effect. (If you want an untextured background, skip this step.)

Complete the background by adding a color gradient, which is accomplished via a new fill layer. Create the new layer by selecting Layer > New Fill Layer > Gradient. Click OK and the Gradient Fill dialog box appears. Pull down the Gradient list and select the Foreground to Transparent option. (This should be the second option in the top row) Click OK and you're done—your picture now has a new color backdrop and looks just like it was shot in a professional portrait studio.

MAC GADGET OF THE WEEK

On Monday we talked about the PC version of the ATI Radeon 9800 Pro video card; today we'll focus on the Mac Special Edition version. This card is a good option for Power Mac G5 users who really want to squeeze the most gaming or 3D performance out of your Mac. It offers a full 256 megabytes of high-speed memory to augment the dual 400Mhz graphics processors. Buy it for $399 at www.ati.com.

MORE NOVEMBER FACTS

November 1

1512 Michelangelo's Sistine Chapel is opened

1927 Production of Ford's Model A begins

1884 Greenwich Mean Time (GMT) is universally adopted; from this, the International Date Line was drawn up and 24 time zones were created

1939 First animal is successful impregnated via artificial insemination

November 2

1988 Cornel University graduate student releases a computer worm, affecting thousands of computers around the country; he was the first person to be prosecuted under the 1986 Computer Fraud and Abuse Act

November 3

1941 Combined Japanese Fleet receives its orders to bomb Pearl Harbor, HI, an order that was carried out 34 days later

1966 President Lyndon Johnson signs the Truth in Packaging Bill, requiring that supermarket items be labeled with ingredients and manufacturing information

1983 First computer virus is created by Len Adleman to prove that such things were possible

November 4

1979 Iranians storm the U.S. embassy in Tehran, taking 90 hostages; after releasing 38 hostages, the remaining 52 were held for 14 months by the Ayatollah Khomeini

1922 The entrance to King Tutankhamen's tomb is discovered in Thebes, Egypt; by 1929, 11 people connected with the discovery of the tomb had died early and of unnatural causes, prompting speculation about the "mummy's curse"

November 5

2001 Nintendo releases the GameCube

November 6

1851 Charles Henry Dow, first editor of the *Wall Street Journal* and creator of the Dow Jones average, is born

1928 Largest electronic flashing sign of its day is installed on The New York Times building and was lighted by 14,000 bulbs, which is miniscule compared to today's Times Square

November 7

1876 First cigarette manufacturing machine is patented in New York City

1946 First coin-operated television is displayed in New York City

November 8

1793 The Louvre Museum opens in France; the Louvre houses many priceless works of art, including Leonardo da Vinci's "Mona Lisa"

1887 Famous wild west gunslinger Doc Holliday dies

1904 Electric plug is patented; the design of this first plug is still used in the U.S. today

1910 First "bug zapper"—known at the time as an "electric insect destroyer"—is patented

November 9

1989 East Germany opens the Berlin Wall, allowing safe travel from East to West Berlin for the first time in 45 years; the following day, celebrators began tearing the wall down

November 10

1775 Continental Congress passes a resolution to form what we now know as the U.S. Marine Corps

1885 First motorcycle—the Gottlieb Daimler Reitwagen—makes its debut

1951 First nonoperator-assisted long distance phone call is placed

1975 SS Edmund Fitzgerald sinks in Lake Superior, killing all 29 on board; in 1976, singer-songwriter Gordon Lightfoot immortalized the tragedy with his song "The Wreck of the Edmund Fitzgerald"

1988 Ellis County, Texas is named as the home of a $4.4 billion atom-smashing super collider; to date, however, the particle accelerator has not been created due to waning political support

November 11

Veteran's Day

1922 Kurt Vonnegut, Jr. is born

November 12

1946 First drive-in banking service is offered by Exchange National Bank in Chicago, IL

November 13

1982 Vietnam Veterans Memorial in Washington, D.C. is dedicated; the wall is inscribed with the names of 57,939 Americans who died in the war

November 14

1665 First blood transfusion is made between two dogs in Oxford

1945 The Indianapolis Motor Speedway is purchased by Tony Hulman, renovating the speedway that had fallen into disrepair during World War II

November 15

1956 Elvis's first movie, *Love Me Tender*, opens

November 16

1620 Pilgrims eat corn for the first time in what is now known as Provincetown, MA; Native Americans introduced the starving pilgrims to this new food source

November 18

1883 American and Canadian railroads begin using four continental time zones to end confusion spurred by thousands of local time zones; this is the first use of standardized time zones in North America

1978 Rev. Jim Jones and 916 of his cult followers are found dead in Jonestown (a private cult community in the South American jungle of Guyana) after drinking cyanide-laced drinks; it is believed that many, including children, were forced to drink the cyanide concoction, while others were shot, including Jones

November 19

1954 First automated toll booth goes into service at the Union Toll Plaza on New Jersey's Garden State Parkway

November 20

1866 The yoyo is patented in Cincinnati, OH

1979 First artificial blood transfusion is performed at the University of Minnesota hospital

1985 Windows 1.0 is released

1998 Russia launches the first module of the International Space Station; the U.S. launched the second module two weeks later

November 21

1620 The Mayflower lands at the tip of Cape Cod at what is now Provincetown, Massachusetts

1986 National Security Council member Oliver North starts feeding documents into a shredder in an attempt to hide his involvement in a variety of illegal activities, including the illegal sale of arms to Iran

November 22

1988 The Northrop B-2 "stealth" bomber is shown to the public for the first time

November 23

1859 Billy the Kid is born in New York City; while he called himself William H. Bonney, his exact name isn't known

November 24

Thanksgiving Day

1932 The FBI's crime lab is opened

1963 Jack Ruby kills Lee Harvey Oswald, who is believed to have participated in the assassination of President John F. Kennedy just two days earlier

1998 Pornography is ruled illegal in public libraries

November 25

1884 Evaporated milk is patented in St. Louis, MO

November 26

1867 Refrigerated railcar is patented

November 28

1922 Skywriting is first done over New York City; the first message was "Hello, USA Call Vanderbilt 7200"

November 29

1961 First U.S. satellite carrying an animal is launched; Enos, a chimpanzee, made two orbits of the Earth and landed safely

November 30

1869 Mason jar is patented

1874 Winston Churchill is born

1954 First modern instance of a human being struck by a meteorite; Elizabeth Hodges of Sylacauga, AL was struck on the hip when an 8.5-pound meteorite crashed through her roof

December 2005

December 2005

SUNDAY	MONDAY	TUESDAY	WEDNESDAY	THURSDAY	FRIDAY	SATURDAY
				1 1959 First color photograph of Earth is taken by a Thor missile	**2** 1942 First controlled nuclear chain reaction is demonstrated	**3** 1910 Neon lighting first appears at the Paris Motor Show
4 1996 First electric vehicle to be mass-produced is introduced	**5** 1945 Five U.S. Navy Avenger torpedo-bombers are lost in the Bermuda Triangle	**6** 1877 First sound recording is made by Thomas Edison	**7** 1941 Pearl Harbor is attacked by Japan	**8** 1980 Beatles legend John Lennon is shot and killed in New York	**9** 1987 Windows 2.0 is released	**10** 1993 Space Shuttle Endeavor crew repairs the Hubble Space Telescope
11 1998 Scientists deciphered the entire genetic blueprint of an animal—a nematode worm	**12** 1899 The golf tee is patented in Boston, MA	**13** 1977 Ethernet is patented by Xerox	**14** 1799 George Washington dies	**15** 1966 Walt Disney dies	**16** 1917 Arthur C. Clarke, author of 2001: A Space Odyssey, is born	**17** 1903 Orville and Wilbur Wright make first flight near Kitty Hawk, NC
18 1865 Slavery is abolished in the U.S. when the 13th Amendment is ratified	**19** 1975 The Altair 8800, considered by many to be the first personal computer, goes on sale	**20** 1996 Carl Sagan dies	**21** 1898 Radium is discovered	**22** First day of winter	**23** 1947 First transistor is created	**24** Christmas Eve 1889 Rear bicycle brake is patented in Freeport, IL
25 Christmas Day 1642 Sir Isaac Newton is born	**26** Hanukkah begins (ends January 2) 1865 First coffee percolator is patented	**27** 1571 Johannes Kepler is born	**28** 1869 Chewing gum is patented in Mount Vernon, OH	**29** 1987 Russian cosmonaut Yuri Romanenko ends his record 326-day space flight	**30** 1850 Asa Griggs Candler is born	**31** New Year's Eve 1909 The Manhattan Bridge opens

December 1, 2005

THURSDAY

THIS WEEK'S FOCUS: GRAPHICS

ON THIS DAY: FIRST DRIVE-UP SERVICE STATION OPENED (1913)

On the first of December, 1913, the first U.S. drive-in automobile service station opened at the high-traffic intersection of Baum Boulevard and St. Clair Street, in Pittsburgh. The brick, pagoda-style station, operated by the Gulf Refining Company, offered free air, water, crankcase service, restrooms, and a lighted sign for "Good Gulf Gasoline." The price of a gallon of gas? A whopping 27 cents.

Related Web site: www.chevron.com/learning_center/history/topic/
service_stations/

DOWNLOADING CLIPART

If you need an image to add to your Web page, or to include in a presentation or report, or to use as wallpaper for your Windows desktop, the Web is a good place to look. There are literally hundreds of Web sites that offer drawings (called *clip art*) or photographs for downloading, either for free or for a minimal charge.

- **All Season Clipart**
  (www.allseasonclipart.com)—Free clipart and graphics for Web pages.
- **Clip Art Center** (www.clip-art-center.com)—
  Free clipart and other art and design resources.
- **Clipart Connection**
  (www.clipartconnection.com)—A huge collection of clip art for downloading.
- **Clipart Place** (www.theclipartplace.com)—More than 2000 pieces of free clipart for downloading.
- **Clipart.com** (www.clipart.com)—A subscription-based service with more than 2.6 million down-loadable images.

- **GoGraph.com** (www.gograph.com)—One of the best—and best-organized—collections of free clipart, photos, icons, wallpapers, animated GIFs, and other graphics.
- **WebSpice.com** (www.webspice.com)—
  Subscription access to graphics and photos for your Web page.

And let's not forget the many image search engines on the Web. My favorite is Google Image Search (images.google.com), which lets you search for specific photos and images by keyword. It works surprisingly well!

WEB SITE OF THE WEEK

Corbis offers a fantastic collection of high resolution professional and stock photographs for purchase; it's the source of choice for many professional publications, although you can order photos for your own personal use, as well. Check it out at www.corbis.com.

December 2, 2005

FRIDAY

THIS WEEK'S FOCUS: GRAPHICS

ON THIS DAY: FIRST CONTROLLED NUCLEAR CHAIN REACTION (1942)

On December 2, 1942, the first self-sustaining nuclear chain reaction occurred in a squash court under the football field at the University of Chicago. This experiment, crucial to the control of nuclear fission, was one of several research projects at sites around the country, each concentrating on some task critical to the production of an atomic bomb. All were administered by the U.S. Army under the code name of Manhattan Engineer District, or the Manhattan Project.

Related Web site: www.lib.uchicago.edu/e/spcl/chain.html

CREATING A TRANSPARENT GIF IN PHOTOSHOP ELEMENTS

One feature of the GIF graphics format is that you can make image backgrounds transparent. This allows your main graphic to "float" above any color background you have on a Web page. It's what Web designers use to make logos pop off Web page backgrounds. The alternative, of course, is to put the logo or graphic against a white or other solid-color background; then you have the block of color surrounding the logo that then stands out against the regular Web page color. Better to use a GIF graphic with a transparent background.

It's easy enough to create a transparent background GIF in Photoshop Elements 3. The technique is similar in previous versions of the program, and in Photoshop CS. Open the graphics file you want to work with, and then follow these steps:

1. Make sure you're working in RGB mode by selecting Image > Mode > RGB Color.
2. Create a new background layer by selecting Layer > New > Layer. Accept the default name for this layer.
3. Use one of the selection tools to select the part of the image you want to be transparent, typically the background around the main graphic.
4. Press the Del key to delete the selected background. This should change the background to a checkerboard pattern.
5. Save your new transparent graphic for the Web by selecting File > Save for Web. When the Save for Web dialog box appears, save the image as a GIF file, and make sure the Transparency option is checked.

That's it—you've just created a transparent graphic!

PORTABLE GADGET OF THE WEEK

Speedtech's Weather Watch Pro is a high-tech watch that functions like a portable weather station. The Weather Watch Pro tracks and displays temperature, wind chill, wind speed, barometric pressure, altitude, and date. It also includes a chronograph, a yacht racing timer, and an alarm. Buy it for $150 at www.speedtech.com.

December 3, 2005
SATURDAY

THIS WEEK'S FOCUS: GRAPHICS

ON THIS DAY: JOHN BACKUS BORN (1924)

No, not the guy who played Mr. Thurston Howell on *Gilligan's Island*. This is John Backus, born December 3, 1924, the computer scientist who developed the FORTRAN programming language. Backus had previously developed an assembly language for IBM's 701 computer.

Related Web site: www.thocp.net/biographies/backus_john.htm

GRAPHICS FOR WEB PAGES

Images placed on Web pages—whether they're illustrations or photographs—don't have to be of super-high resolution. The reason for this is that they're displayed on a computer screen, which has only moderate resolution (compared to print). There's no point making the images any higher resolution than what can be displayed onscreen.

That said, the ideal resolution for a Web page graphic is 72 dots per inch (dpi). While you can format your graphics for higher resolution, a 300 dpi picture won't look any sharper onscreen than a 72 dpi picture will.

Which file format you use depends on what type of graphic you're using. If your graphic is a photograph, go with the JPG format. If your graphic is a line drawing or illustration, you can go with either GIF or JPG, although GIF is probably a slightly better choice. If your graphic (either illustration or photograph) has fine gradations of color, you should use the JPG format, which does a better job reproducing color blends. And if your graphic requires several frames of animation or has a transparent background, your only choice is the GIF format.

The final consideration is how large to make the image. When sizing your image for a Web page, keep in mind that many users are still viewing the Web at 640×480 resolution—which means that any picture more than 600 or so pixels wide will require horizontal scrolling to see the entire picture, which, from the user's perspective, is highly annoying.

In any case, you want to minimize the size of the file, so that it downloads faster when viewed on the Web. Try to keep the file size of each graphic under 10KB, if possible—and the total size of your Web page under 40KB. It's better to display smaller *thumbnails* that link to larger images than it is to display all the big images on the same page.

FACT OF THE WEEK

W3Schools.com, which tracks the screen resolution settings of Web surfers, reports the current breakdown: 640×480, 1%; 800×600, 37%; 1024×768, 47%; higher, 10%; unknown, 5%.

December 4, 2005

SUNDAY

THIS WEEK'S FOCUS: GRAPHICS

ON THIS DAY: THOMAS EDISON INVENTS THE PHONOGRAPH (1877)

On December 4, 1877, Thomas Edison announced his invention of his "talking machine," a tin-foil cylinder recorder. The next day, one of his employees machined the device according to Edison's plans. That night, with everyone gathered around, Edison turned the crank and said the following words: "Mary had a little lamb, its fleece was white as snow, and everywhere that Mary went, the lamb was sure to go." His men were astounded when the machine faintly but clearly repeated Edison's words.

Related Web site: www.ushistory.net/toc/phono.html

UNDERSTANDING GRAPHICS FILE FORMATS

Not all pictures utilize the same file format—and not all file formats reproduce pictures the same way. Some graphics file formats are more efficient than others, while other file formats are better at reproducing different types of graphics. The following table details the various image file formats you're likely to find on the Web, and a few details about each:

File Format	Description
.BMP	A simple bitmapped graphics format that is the default format for Windows desktop backgrounds. Extremely inefficient with large file sizes, this format is not widely used online.
.GIF	A popular Web-based graphics format. GIF files can include transparent backgrounds (so a Web page background can show through) and can include multiple images for a simple animated effect. GIF files are good for reproducing simple line drawings, illustrations, and cartoon art.

File Format	Description
.JPG	Perhaps the most widely used graphics format on the Web. JPG files are often slightly smaller in size than comparable GIF files, and are better at reproducing photographic images.
.PCX	An older, not very efficient graphics format, not normally used on Web pages. PCX files can be used as Windows desktop backgrounds.
.PNG	A newer graphics format that was designed to ultimately replace the GIF format—although that's not likely to happen.
.TIF	A higher-resolution graphics format not widely used on Web pages, but very popular in print and in the world of digital photography.

SOFTWARE OF THE WEEK

If, for some reason, you don't like Photoshop (maybe it's the price; maybe it's just the general Adobe-ness of it), a good alternative is Jasc's Paint Shop Pro. It does a lot of what Photoshop does, is a little easier for the casual user to learn, and costs a lot less. Buy it for $99 at www.jasc.com.

THIS WEEK'S FOCUS: TWEAKS AND TRICKS

ON THIS DAY: WERNER HEISENBERG BORN (1901)

The man who conceived the Heisenberg Uncertainty Principle was born on this date in 1901. Werner Karl Heisenberg was a German physicist and philosopher who discovered a way to formulate quantum mechanics in terms of matrices. For that discovery, he was awarded the Nobel Prize for Physics for 1932. He also made important contributions to the theories of the hydrodynamics of turbulence, the atomic nucleus, ferromagnetism, cosmic rays, and elementary particles.

Related Web site: www.aip.org/history/heisenberg/

TWEAK WINDOWS WITH THE GROUP POLICY EDITOR

Windows includes a cool tool that you've probably never heard of that can perform all sorts of useful tweaks and customizations. The tool, called the Group Policy Editor, isn't found anywhere on the Start menu; you have to start it by entering `gpedit.msc` into the Run box. Believe it or not, this neat little hidden utility has been around since Windows 95!

The Group Policy Editor (GPE) lets you customize all manner of what appear to be hard-wired Windows settings, such as application title bars, startup/shutdown scripts, CD/DVD autoplay, and the like. Here are a few of my favorite GPE tweaks:

- **Replace the Internet Explorer flag**—Substitute your own graphic for the standard graphic in IE's upper right corner. Select User Configuration > Internet Explorer Maintenance > Browser User Interface, and then double-click the Custom Logo setting. When the Custom Logo dialog box appears, check the Customize options and enter the location of a different graphics file.

- **Customize the Start menu and taskbar**—Lots of cool tweaks here. Select User Configuration

> Administrative Templates > Start Menu and Taskbar. Click any setting in the right-hand pane to change it; you can add or remove practically any element.

- **Turn off CD/DVD Autoplay**—If you don't want every CD and DVD to play automatically when inserted, select Computer Configuration > Administrative Templates > System and double-click the Turn Off Autoplay setting.

- **Customize the Places bar**—Add locations to the Places bar that appears in the left column of most Open and Save dialog boxes. Select User Configuration > Administrative Templates > Windows Components > Windows Explorer > Common Open File Dialog, and then double-click the Items Displayed in Places Bar setting. When the Items Displayed in Places Bar dialog box appears, enter new locations into the list.

PC GADGET OF THE WEEK

Now this is a different way to fly. The TrackIR 3-Pro is a high-performance optical head-tracking system that enables hands-free view control with many popular flight simulator games. Buy it for $139 at www.naturalpoint.com.

December 6, 2005

TUESDAY

THIS WEEK'S FOCUS: **TWEAKS AND TRICKS**

ON THIS DAY: MICROWAVE OVEN PATENTED (1945)

Ever wonder how the microwave oven was invented? Shortly after the end of WWII, Perry Spencer was touring one of his laboratories at the Raytheon Company. He stopped momentarily in front of a magnetron, the power tube that drives a radar set. Feeling a sudden and strange sensation, Spencer noticed that the chocolate bar in his pocket had begun to melt. Well, that was that, and on December 6, 1945, Spencer received a patent for his new invention.

Related Web site: www.gallawa.com/microtech/history.html

CHANGE THE LOCATION OF SYSTEM FOLDERS

Windows maintains a number of system folders, most noticeably your My Documents folder, that appear to be unmovable. Well, that's not the case. There's a simple Registry tweak you can apply to move this and other system folders anywhere on your system.

The first thing to do is launch the Registry Editor, and navigate to the following key:

```
HKEY_CURRENT_USER\Software\Microsoft\Windows\
CurrentVersion\Explorer\User Shell Folders
```

Listed within this key are all of Windows' special folders. Write down the current location of the folder you want to move.

Now open My Computer and physically move the folder to a new location. Make note of the new location.

Next, go back to Registry Editor and edit the value for the folder you moved, to reflect the new location.

That's it. You'll need to reboot Windows for the change to take effect. It's a great tweak if you want to move these key folders from one drive to another—or just better organize your hard drive!

DOWNLOAD OF THE WEEK

Tweak the heck out of your operating system with Tweaks and Tools for Windows XP. This shareware toolset enables access to hidden system options, improves XP's performance, and lets you customize program settings to your heart's content. Try it for free, or buy it for $15.95 at www.nextgenerationtools.com.

December 7, 2005
WEDNESDAY

THIS WEEK'S FOCUS: TWEAKS AND TRICKS

ON THIS DAY: LAST MOON MISSION LAUNCHES (1972)

On December 7, 1972, the sixth and last U.S. moon mission (so far) blasted off from Cape Canaveral. Apollo 17's crew consisted of Eugene Cernan, Ronald Evans, and Jack Schmitt. Cernan and Schmitt made three excursions on the surface, and then packed up and came home on December 19.

Related Web site: www.solarviews.com/eng/apo17.htm

OPTIMIZE YOUR DISPLAY WITH CLEARTYPE

The LCD screen used on a typical laptop PC or flat-panel display looks pretty good—until you get up close. That's when you notice the "jaggies," those jagged edges and ragged shapes that come part and parcel with displaying text and graphics on an LCD screen.

With Windows XP, however, Microsoft has a cure for the jaggies—a new technology called ClearType. With ClearType enabled, the jaggies are replaced by smooth letters and perfectly rounded edges.

ClearType is a new display technology that effectively triples the horizontal display resolution on LCD displays. If you're using a portable PC or flat-panel display, you'll definitely want to turn on ClearType. You'll wonder how you ever lived without it.

To turn on ClearType, open the Display Properties utility, select the Appearance tab, and click the Effects button. When the Effects dialog box appears, check the Use the Following Method to Smooth Edges of Screen Fonts option, and select ClearType from the pull-down list. That's all there is to it—and you'll never turn it off.

By the way, Microsoft says that ClearType is designed for LCD screens only, such as the ones in portable PCs and flat-screen monitors. They say that activating ClearType on a tube-type monitor might make text and other onscreen elements appear slightly blurry. Or, depending on your monitor, it might smooth out some of the roughness you typically get with some screen fonts. In other words, YMMV (your mileage may vary). The best thing to do is try it yourself, and see if you like it!

MAC GADGET OF THE WEEK

The more FireWire devices you accumulate, the faster you run out of ports. Add more FireWire ports to your Mac with Belkin's FireWire 3-Port PCI Card. Install it in your Power Mac and you have three extra FireWire ports on the back. Buy it for $49.99 from www.belkin.com.

December 8, 2005

THURSDAY

THIS WEEK'S FOCUS: TWEAKS AND TRICKS

ON THIS DAY: JOHN LENNON KILLED (1980)

On the evening of December 8, 1980, ex-Beatle John Lennon was killed by a deranged fan named Mark David Chapman. Lennon was returning to his New York apartment from a recording session. He was 40 years old. Reportedly, Lennon's last words—spoken to paramedics—were, "Yes, I'm John Lennon."

Related Web site: www.legend-johnlennon.com

WINDOWS FILE TRICKS

When you're working with files in the My Documents or My Computer folders, here are some tricks you can use to make things just a little more efficient:

- When you want to rename a file, you don't have to pick up your mouse and select File > Rename. Instead, press the F2 keyboard shortcut and enter a new name—no mouse necessary.

- When you're working with a large list of files, it might be easier to select the ones you don't want—and then invert the selection. Start by selecting the big group of files, and then select Edit > Invert Selection. Now all the items you *didn't* select originally are selected.

- To better identify compressed folders in any Windows folder, configure Windows XP to display them in blue. Just open the Folder Options utility, select the View tab, and check the Show Encrypted or Compressed Files in Color option.

- You can get double duty out of the My Computer or My Documents folder by turning it into a Web browser. Just enter a Web URL into the folder's Address box; if you're connected to the Internet, the folder will turn into an Internet Explorer window.

- Here's a quick way to create a shortcut or copy a file by clicking and dragging. To create a shortcut, drag the file icon while holding down the Alt button. To create a copy of a file, hold down the Ctrl button while dragging the original file to a new location.

WEB SITE OF THE WEEK

The Windows Registry Guide provides tons of Registry tweaks, tricks, and hacks you can use to optimize your system's performance. It's part of the WinGuides Network, located at www.winguides.com/registry/.

December 9, 2005

FRIDAY

THIS WEEK'S FOCUS: TWEAKS AND TRICKS

ON THIS DAY: GRACE MURRAY HOPPER BORN (1906)

Grace Murray Hopper, noted mathematician and rear admiral in the U.S. Navy, was born on this date in 1906. Admiral Hopper was instrumental in the development of the UNIVAC computer and the COBOL programming language. She was also present when the first computer bug was discovered and named.

Related Web site: www.jamesshuggins.com/h/tek1/grace_hopper.htm

PUT A CPU METER IN THE TASKBAR

Want to see how hard your computer is working? Then put a CPU meter in the Windows taskbar, and keep tabs on system performance in real time.

This trick uses the Windows Task Manager. I'm not sure if you've noticed or not, but when Task Manager is working, it also displays a CPU meter in the taskbar. Our trick is to keep that meter open even when you close the Task Manager.

Start by pressing Ctrl+Alt+Del to open the Task Manager. (This should display the little CPU meter.) From within the Task Manager, select Options > Hide When Minimized. With this option selected, when you minimize Task Manager you won't see it in your taskbar—but you'll still see the little CPU meter. Check it out by minimizing Task Manager now.

The final touch is to automatically launch Task Manager whenever you start your computer. You do this by putting a link to Task Manager in the Startup folder. (You should find the Task Manager executable in the c:/windows/system32, folder—you can just search for "taskmgr" on your system drive.)

The next time (and every time) you reboot your computer, Task Manager will launch minimized, displaying the CPU meter in the taskbar. Neat!

PORTABLE GADGET OF THE WEEK

The Bose QuietComfort 2s are, without a doubt, the quietest headphones on the market today. Bose's Accoustic Noise Canceling technology electronically identifies and then reduces unwanted noise. You don't even have to listen to music to use these phones; just put them on, turn them on, and hear virtually all background noise disappear. Buy a pair for $299 at www.bose.com.

December 10, 2005

SATURDAY

THIS WEEK'S FOCUS: TWEAKS AND TRICKS

ON THIS DAY: ADA BYRON BORN (1815)

Ada Byron, also known as Countess Augusta Ada King Lovelace, was born on December 10, 1815. Ada, an English mathematician, was the daughter of Lord Byron. After she met Charles Babbage (in 1833), she began to assist in the development of his analytical engine. She was one of the first to recognize the potential of computers and has been called the first computer programmer. The Ada programming language is named after her.

Related Web site: www.sdsc.edu/ScienceWomen/lovelace.html

CHANGE YOUR COMPUTER'S IDENTIFICATION

Your PC came from the factory with the manufacturer and model number information hard coded into Windows. You see this info when you right-click on My Computer and select the Properties tab—but there's a way to change it. Just follow these steps:

1. From within My Computer, search for the file named oeminfo.ini. It's probably in the c:\windows\system\ folder.
2. Double-click the filename to open the file.
3. The first information you want to change is in the [general] section. You should see settings for Manufacturer and Model; if these lines aren't there, you can add them. Add your new text after the equal (=) sign.
4. You can also change any of the information in the [support information] section. This is general info of any type, added on a line-by-line basis.
5. When you're done editing, select File > Save As and save the file as oeminfo.ini.

You can also add an image to the OEM info box. Just create a 175×100 pixel bitmap image and save it in the c:\windows\system\ folder as oemlogo.bmp. That's all there is to it!

FACT OF THE WEEK

The Gartner Group reports that the IT industry is suffering an acute lack of programmers who know COBOL, the 40-year-old language in which much of the world's business data is written. Approximately 200 billion lines of COBOL code still exist, while there are only 90,000 COBOL programmers in North America—and that number is shrinking as old-timers retire or pass away.

December 11, 2005

SUNDAY

THIS WEEK'S FOCUS: TWEAKS AND TRICKS

ON THIS DAY: J.L. KRAFT BORN (1874)

Hail to the cheese makers! James Lewis Kraft, the founder of the Kraft Company, was born on this date in 1874. Kraft had a vision of supplying America with nutritious, low-cost cheese products, and invented the pasteurizing process for cheese. In 1916 he patented a processed cheese formula, based on milk solids, that would not spoil. He called it "American Cheese."

Related Web site: www.kraft.com

CHANGE THE SIZE AND QUALITY OF THUMBNAIL IMAGES

The thumbnail images displayed in the My Documents folder appear to be hard-wired at a certain size and resolution. That may be fine, but why settle for what Microsoft gives you? Here's a cool Registry tweak that lets you display larger or smaller thumbnails—at whatever picture quality you like!

Start by opening the Registry Editor and navigating to the following key:

```
HKEY_CURRENT_USER\Software\Microsoft\Windows\
CurrentVersion\Explorer
```

Look for the ThumbnailSize value. If it doesn't exist, create a new one. (Type: DWORD) By default, this value is set to 96 (pixels). Enter a smaller value to display a smaller thumbnail, or a larger value to display a larger thumbnail.

Now look for the ThumbnailQuality value. If it doesn't exist, create a new one. (Type: DWORD)

This value represents a quality of between 50% and 100%; the default value is 90. Enter a lower number to display lower-resolution thumbnails, or enter the value 100 to display the highest-possible quality.

That's it. You'll have to restart Windows for your changes to take effect.

SOFTWARE OF THE WEEK

Tweak-XP Pro provides 48 different utilities you can use to tweak and fine-tune your system performance. Clean up your registry, create a RAM drive, detect and fix hard drive problems, back up your Microsoft software activations, make the taskbar transparent, convert compressed folders to self-extracting EXE files, and lots more. Buy it for $39.95 at www.totalidea.com/frameset-tweakxp.htm.

December 12, 2005

MONDAY

THIS WEEK'S FOCUS: GEEK GIFT GUIDE

ON THIS DAY: APPLE COMPUTER IPO (1980)

Apple Computer's initial public offering was on December 12, 1980. The offering consisted of 4.6 million shares at $22 per share. All shares were sold within minutes, and by the end of the day the stock had jumped $7 to $29.

Related Web site: www.apple.com

SHOPPING FOR THE GEEK ON YOUR LIST

Shopping for a tech geek isn't as easy as it sounds. You're probably tempted to head over to the local Sharper Image store and buy something flashy. While that might work (nothing against Sharper Image—I personally like their stuff), you're probably not going to get off that easy. For one thing, Sharper Image merchandise, as neat as it might look to you, typically isn't cutting edge. In addition, Sharper Image stuff isn't particularly technical in nature. No, you'll probably have to shop elsewhere.

Okay, you're thinking. Maybe you'll head over to CompUSA or Best Buy. Good try, but not the best idea. That's because these stores carry merchandise targeted at the general consumer, and your tech geek is definitely not a general consumer. The types of items your geek friend drools over are unlikely to be found in the aisles of a big box store, or in a mall.

Geek stuff is highly specialized, and typically found at specialized retailers. That means shopping from a catalog, or online. If that scares you—well, your geek pal probably scares you, too. Get over it.

Many geek gifts can be purchased direct from the manufacturer. I also like Gadget Universe (www.gadgetuniverse.com) and ThinkGeek (www.thinkgeek.com), both of which carry a lot of really cool stuff. Hey, it's the Internet—do a little searching and see what you find.

What makes something geek cool? It's all about being the fastest, or the smallest, or the newest. It's about being unique, doing something old in a new way. It's about performance. It's about looks. (Flashing lights are always good.) It's about technology, yes, but it's also about style.

If in doubt, just ask. This time of year, every geek worth his salt will have an extensive wish list prepared. If not, check out my companion book, *Leo Laporte's 2005 Gift Guide*—it's like a wish book for tech-lovers everywhere!

PC GADGET OF THE WEEK

Logitech's MOMO Racing Force Feedback Wheel is designed by the racing professionals at MOMO—one of the world's leading designers of automotive accessories. The advanced force feedback lets you feel every turn, slide, and bump, and the comfortable grip offers precise steering. Buy it for $99.95 at www.logitech.com.

December 13, 2005

TUESDAY

THIS WEEK'S FOCUS: GEEK GIFT GUIDE

ON THIS DAY: FIRST FUNCTIONING COMMUNICATIONS SATELLITE LAUNCHED (1962)

On December 13, 1962, the Relay I satellite was launched. Relay I was the first U.S. communications satellite to transmit telephone, television, teleprinter, and facsimile signals. The satellite's first test patterns were transmitted on January 3, 1963, after the solar cells had built up sufficient battery charge.

Related Web site: www.hq.nasa.gov/office/pao/History/satcomhistory.html

SHOPPING FOR THE HARDCORE GAMER

For the next few days I'm going to put together a wish list of sorts for various types of tech geeks. Know, however, that if you're actually reading this page on December 13, 2005, that I had to write the thing over a year earlier—so if some of the model numbers and specifications have changed since then, just go with the flow. It's the thought that counts.

Today we're going shopping for the hardcore gamer geek, and price is no object. That's why I start off with an extreme-performance gaming PC from Alienware. Right now I'm looking at their Area-51 model, which comes with a 3.6GHz P4 processor, 1GB RAM, 120GB hard drive, NVIDIA GeForce video card, and a Sound Blaster Audigy sound card. I'd beef it up with a dual-layer DVD burner and a second 300GB hard disk, for backup and archival storage.

For a monitor, I like NEC's Multisync FE2111, a 21" high-resolution CRT. And for speakers, there's nothing like Creative's GigaWorks S750 7.1-channel system.

Then you have the game controllers. Plural. Start with Logitech's Cordless RumblePad for basic game play; then, add CH Products' Combatstick 568 USB for flight games, Logitech's MOMO Racing Force Feedback Wheel for racing games, and Belkin's Nostromo SpeedPad n52 for games that require keyboard input. That ought to do the job.

Total price for the entire system? Close to $5,000—well above my personal gift budget. Still, any one of these items would make a great stocking stuffer—and your gamer geek will really appreciate the thought!

DOWNLOAD OF THE WEEK

BitComet is a P2P file-sharing utility, fully compatible with the popular BitTorrent protocol. BitTorrent is designed for high-speed distribution of large video files over the Internet, and BitComet is a simple and powerful client that anyone can use. Use it to find and download your favorite television programs from BitTorrent sites on the Web. Download it for free from www.bitcomet.com.

December 14, 2005

WEDNESDAY

THIS WEEK'S FOCUS: GEEK GIFT GUIDE

ON THIS DAY: FIRST NON-REFUELED FLIGHT AROUND THE WORLD (1986)

On December 14, 1986, the experimental Voyager aircraft took off from Edwards Air Force Base in California on the first non-stop, non-refueled flight around the world. Voyager was piloted by Dick Rutan and Jeana Yeager; it made the 25,000-mile flight in nine days, at an average speed of 115 mph.

Related Web site: www.dickrutan.com

SHOPPING FOR THE HOME VIDEO ENTHUSIAST

Christmas is a fun time for the home video geek. Not only does he get to shoot some great holiday home movies, he might even find some cool new home video gear under the tree!

We'll start the gift list with a brand-new MiniDV camcorder. I really like Sony's DCR-VX2100, which looks like a professional video camcorder and performs like one, too. This camcorder provides a host of operating features that will appeal to burgeoning filmmakers everywhere, and the three 1/3-inch CCDs deliver a great picture with 530 lines of resolution. Wowsers.

A true home video geek is also a Mac geek, so Santa has to deliver a brand-new Power Mac G5. Make sure you wrap up a 30" widescreen Cinema Display to go with it, and you're ready to edit like the pros. And speaking of editing, Apple's iMovie is good, but Adobe Premiere Pro is better, so make sure one of those goes in the box, too.

For stocking stuffers, consider a wireless microphone and one of Sony's top-of-camera stereo mics. Don't forget an external video light and a tripod, just in case. And for the active cameraman, throw in a FlowCam UltraLite camcorder stabilizer. It makes handheld action shots a whole lot steadier.

Okay, that's a big wish list. Total cost is somewhere around $7,500—cheap by Hollywood standards, anyway.

MAC GADGET OF THE WEEK

Add dual-layer DVD recording to your Power Mac with LaCie's DVD+/- Double Layer drive. New technology lets you store 8.5GB on a single-sided disc; it's an external drive that connects to your Mac via FireWire. Buy it for $229 from www.lacie.com.

THIS WEEK'S FOCUS: GEEK GIFT GUIDE

ON THIS DAY: ICE CREAM CONE PATENTED (1903)

On this date in 1903, a U.S. patent for an ice cream cup mold was issued to one Italo Marchiony. Mr. Marchiony came to New York from Italy in 1895 and sold ice cream and lemon ice from a pushcart on Wall Street. He served his wares in baked waffles, which he folded by hand into the shape of a cup. When his operation grew to a chain of 45 carts, Marchiony met the need for mass production with his invention of a multiple-recess mold based on a waffle iron, which he then patented. Yummy!

Related Web site: www.deepsouthnz.co.nz/fun_sthfl.htm

SHOPPING FOR THE DIGITAL PHOTOGRAPHY ENTHUSIAST

Not all geeks are photographers, and not all photographers are geeks—but all serious photographers are photography geeks. Here's what Christmas looks like from a digital photography perspective.

Start with a first-class digital SLR camera. My fav D-SLR is the Nikon D70, which looks and feels just like a regular 35mm SLR. Since it accepts all manner of Nikon lenses, it's also the gift that keeps on giving. The standard lens is an 18-70mm zoom; I'd throw in a longer zoom (70-300mm is good) and a shorter wide angle. That should cover all bases.

Naturally, you need a big memory card to hold all your digital pictures. Splurge on a 1GB card, and then throw in an Archos Gmini digital media player to serve as backup storage.

Protect your investment with a good, sturdy camera case. Lowepro makes some really good cases; some of my friends prefer the backpack models, but I'll go with a traditional over-the-shoulder case any day.

Stuff the stocking with a handful of lens filters from Tiffen; if nothing else, get polarizing filters for each of the lenses. An external flash kit is always a good idea; I like the Metz Mecablitz kits. And don't forget a good VidPro tripod and Smith-Victor lighting kit.

Any photographer with all this equipment will be one happy camper. The good news is that you can make that camper happy for well under $4,000.

WEB SITE OF THE WEEK

When you're looking for the latest geek gifts, make your first stop Gizmodo, a blog that announces all the latest and greatest techie toys and gizmos. I visit it at least once a week; it's located at gizmodo.net.

December 16, 2005

FRIDAY

THIS WEEK'S FOCUS: GEEK GIFT GUIDE

ON THIS DAY: ARTHUR C. CLARKE BORN (1917)

Arthur C. Clarke, noted author and inventor, was born on this date in 1917. He's most famous for his science fiction work, most notably *2001: A Space Odyssey* and the *Rama* novels. There is an asteroid named in his honor, called 4923 Clarke.

Related Web site: www.clarkefoundation.org

SHOPPING FOR THE HOME THEATER ENTHUSIAST

The home theater enthusiast is a different kind of geek. He's obsessed with sound and picture as much as he is with the technology behind it. Of course, to get the best sound and picture, you have to invest a lot in new technology. Good thing it's Christmas!

We'll build our gift system around the screen—the big screen. Some folks like plasma displays, but I worry about burn in, so I'll recommend one of Mitsubishi's new 62" DLP rear projectors instead. Pair that with a Panasonic progressive-scan DVD recorder and a DirecTV HDTV receiver, and you have a true high-def system.

Our dream sound system is driven by Sony's top of the line STR-DA9000ES A/V receiver, which delivers more power than you'll know what to do with. Pair that with a set of Infinity floor-standing speakers (four on the floor, one above the Mitsubishi for the center channel) and a matching subwoofer, and you're ready to rock and/or roll.

Now for the stocking stuffers. I'd recommend a TiVo hard disk recorder and a Philips iPronto touch screen remote, at the very least. Maybe a set of wireless surround sound headphones, for listening late at night.

This is definitely one of the priciest dream systems you can buy. You're looking at around $20,000 all total—and that's not counting any racks or furniture. Maybe he'd be happy with a *Kill Bill* DVD, instead?

PORTABLE GADGET OF THE WEEK

My all-time favorite geek gizmo is Sony's AIBO Entertainment Robot. It's shaped like a little robot dog and even acts like one—short of leaving little piles of batteries behind. You can program your AIBO to follow you around the house and play with balls and pet toys. They even develop a bit of a personality, and respond to more than 100 words and phrases. Buy your own robot pet for a measly $1,799 at www.sonystyle.com.

THIS WEEK'S FOCUS: GEEK GIFT GUIDE

ON THIS DAY: WRIGHT BROTHERS MAKE FIRST MANNED FLIGHT (1903)

Man first took to the air on December 17, 1903. Wilbur and Orville Wright built a flying machine in their Dayton, Ohio, bicycle shop, but took it to Kitty Hawk, North Carolina, to fly. Their initial flight, with Orville at the controls, lasted 12 seconds and went 39 feet. Not that long or far, but it was a start.

Related Web site: www.thewrightbrothers.org

SHOPPING FOR THE ROAD WARRIOR

Tech geeks don't spend all their time at home in front of a computer screen. Sometimes they spend time on the road in front of a computer screen. That's okay, because gift shopping for a road warrior geek is actually a lot of fun.

We'll start with the road warrior's essential gear, the notebook PC. There are a lot of good models to choose from, but right now I'm partial to the Toshiba Satellite line (for PC lovers) and Apple's PowerBook (for Mac lovers). Spring for a big screen, DVD burner, and long battery life; damn the expense (and the weight).

To carry around the new notebook, get a good case from Targus. While you're at the Targus site, invest in the DEFCON 1 Ultra Notebook Computer Security System; a little protection is a good thing. Then stock up on a bagful of notebook accessories, including a docking station/port replicator, desktop stand, extra power supply, and the like.

To supplement the notebook, spring for a decent PDA and the necessary accessories. If your geek friend is a Palm lover, give the palmOne Tungsten T3, which has a great display. If he's a Pocket PC enthusiast, I recommend HP's iPAQ h5550/h5555, which has both Bluetooth and Wi-Fi connectivity.

And let's not forget the stocking stuffers, like an Apple iPod, Archos AV300 portable video player, Olympus digital voice recorder, and Magellan SporTrak portable GPS unit. You don't want your geek to get lost (or bored) while he's on the road!

Properly equipping a road warrior takes money—at least $4,000 worth, possibly more if you go wild on the stocking stuffers. But think how happy he'll be with all these gizmos in tow!

FACT OF THE WEEK

Carnegie Mellon University's Software Industry Center estimates that 38 million Americans—roughly 30% of the U.S. workforce—comprise what they call a "creative class." The term "creative class" refers to a portion of society who create for a living (artists, writers, musicians, and so on).

December 18, 2005

SUNDAY

THIS WEEK'S FOCUS: GEEK GIFT GUIDE

ON THIS DAY: INVENTOR OF FM RADIO BORN (1890)

Edwin Howard Armstrong, the man who invented FM radio, was born on this date in 1890. Armstrong was one of the most prolific inventors of the radio era, inventing not only FM radio but also the regenerative circuit, the super-regenerative circuit, and the super heterodyne receiver.

Related Web sites: www.wsone.com/fecha/armstrong.htm

BOOKS FOR GEEKS

One good thing about geeks—we like to read! Here are some of my all-time favorite books for geeks, of both the fiction and non-fiction variety. Great gifts, all.

- *Bringing Down the House*, by Ben Mezrich. This is the true story of how six guys from MIT figured out how to beat the Las Vegas system, earning millions along the way. Geeks make good!

- *Childhood's End*, by Arthur C. Clarke. Great science fiction is timeless. Clarke's 2001 might be more famous, but this story of the alien Overlords trying to remake our world for the better is sci-fi for the thinking man.

- *The Code Book,* by Simon Singh. No, not programming code, but the kind popularized in *The Da Vinci Code*. This book is all about cryptography and codes, from ancient times through computer encryption.

- *eBoys*, by Randall E. Stross. Read this book to better understand the whole dot-com boom of the late 1990s. It's all about the venture capital firm that that was smart (or lucky) enough to back eBay, Webvan, and several other Internet startups.

- *I, Robot*, by Isaac Asimov. About the only thing this book shares with the lousy Will Smith movie is the title. Asimov's original is actually a collection of short stories that imagines how we'll fare in a robotic future.

- *Masters of Doom*, by David Kushner. Another true story, this time about two Johns, Carmack and Romero, the developers of *Doom*.

- *A Short History of Nearly Everything*, by Bill Bryson. The title says it all—this book starts at the dawn of time and takes you on a scientific tour that ends in the modern day. A well-written and entertaining book.

SOFTWARE OF THE WEEK

Games come and games go, but Microsoft Flight Simulator keeps on soaring. The latest version lets you fly a variety of historic aircraft, including the Douglas DC-3, Charles Lindbergh's Spirit of St. Louis, and the original Wright Flyer. Buy it for $29.99 at www.microsoft.com/games/flightsimulator/.

December 19, 2005

MONDAY

THIS WEEK'S FOCUS: MORE MICROSOFT OFFICE

ON THIS DAY: ALTAIR 8800 GOES ON SALE (1974)

On December 19, 1974, the pioneering Altair 8800 microcomputer was first put on sale in the U.S. The Altair was a do-it-yourself computer kit, priced at $397, that used switches for input and flashing lights as a display. It was featured on the cover of the January 1975 issue of *Popular Electronics*.

Related Web site: www.virtualaltair.com

CREATE YOUR OWN MENUS

Here's a trick that works in any Microsoft Office application. You can create your own personal pull-down menu, complete with your own selected operations and commands. Here's how to do it:

1. Select Tools > Customize to display the Customize dialog box, and then select the Commands tab.
2. Select New Menu from the Categories list.
3. From the Commands list, drag the New Menu item to a position on Word's menu bar.
4. With the Customize dialog box still open (and the New M___ menu selected), click the M___ ___ display the pop-up menu. ___ ___enu, enter a new name for ___ ___dialog box still open, ___'s you want on your new ___ the menu label on the

If you've created custom macros, or have certain operations you perform over and over, add them to your custom menu for easier access. And here's another good idea: You can create separate menus for each person using your PC, containing those commands that person uses the most.

PC GADGET OF THE WEEK

The Iomega REV Drive is an external backup device that utilizes a removable disk cartridge that can store either 35GB (uncompressed) or 90GB (compressed). The REV advantage is price; a REV cartridge costs just a fraction of a comparable external hard drive. Plus, transporting data from one drive to another is as simple as popping a REV disk into your pocket. Buy it for $399.99 from www.iomega.com.

December 20, 2005

TUESDAY

THIS WEEK'S FOCUS: **MORE MICROSOFT OFFICE**

ON THIS DAY: VAN DE GRAAFF BORN (1901)

Robert Jemison Van de Graaff, the inventor of the Van de Graaff generator, was born on this date in 1901. The Van de Graaff generator is a type of high-voltage electrostatic generator that builds up charges on a dome that can leap off at points where the curvature is greatest.

Related Web site: www.howstuffworks.com/vdg.htm

ENTER FOREIGN CHARACTERS FROM THE KEYBOARD

If you type a lot of foreign documents, you're probably used to adding foreign characters Word's Symbol dialog box (Insert > Symbol). Unfortunately, this takes your fingers off the keyboard and really slows you down.

Touch typists will be pleased to know that Word includes a number of keyboard shortcuts for entering foreign-language characters. Here are a few:

Character	Type This
à, è, ì, ò, ù, À, È, Ì, Ò, Ù	Ctrl+`, *letter*
á, é, í, ó, ú, ?, Á, É, Í, Ó, Ú, Ý	Ctrl+', *letter*
â, ê, î, ô, û, Â, Ê, Î, Ô, Û	Ctrl+^, *letter*
ã, ñ, õ, Ã, Ñ, Õ	Ctrl+~, *letter*
ä, ë, ï, ö, ü, ÿ, Ä, Ë, Ï, Ö, Ü, Ÿ	Ctrl+:, *letter*
å, Å	Ctrl+@, a (or A)
æ, Æ	Ctrl+&, a (or A)
œ, Œ	Ctrl+&, o (or O)
ç, Ç	Ctrl+,, c (or C)
ð, Đ	Ctrl+', d (or D)
ø, Ø	Ctrl+/ o (or O)
¿	Alt+Ctrl+Shift+?
¡	Alt+Ctrl+Shift+!
ß	Ctrl+Shift+&, S

DOWNLOAD OF THE WEEK

Wordware 2002 is a set of tools, add-ons, and templates for Microsoft Word. It includes document management tools, fax utilities, a personal information manager, and more. Try it for free, or buy it for $39.95 from www.amfsoftware.com/word/wordware.html.

December 21, 2005
WEDNESDAY

THIS WEEK'S FOCUS: MORE MICROSOFT OFFICE

ON THIS DAY: FIRST FULL-LENGTH ANIMATED FILM (1937)

On December 21, 1937, *Snow White and the Seven Dwarfs*, Walt Disney's first full-length animated film, opened in Los Angeles. This pioneering film made use of the multi-plane camera to achieve an effect of depth, introduced human characters modeled on live actors, and used larger painted cels for more detailed animation. Disney had to mortgage his house to pay for the film's then-astronomical $1.5 million production cost.

Related Web site: www.filmsite.org/snow.html

USE WORD AS A SPREADSHEET

Who needs Excel when Word can do the job? That's right, Microsoft Word can be used as a makeshift spreadsheet. The key is to use Word's tables and =(FORMULA) field. It's not as full-featured as Excel, but it will do in a pinch.

Here are the keys to using Word to create calculating spreadsheets:

- Insert a large table into your Word document. Make the table big enough to fill the entire page, if necessary—at least 8 columns wide by 50 rows deep in portrait orientation.

- Format the table so that all cells that contain numbers are right-aligned.

- Use the Borders and Shading dialog box to display all gridlines.

- Use the =(FORMULA) field to perform numeric calculations. The easiest way to do this is to select Table > Formula to display the Formula dialog box, and then add functions and operators to create your own formulas.

Once you've entered data into your "spreadsheet," you can graph the data within your table. Just select the desired cells, and then select Insert > Picture > Chart to display a new Microsoft Graph chart with the selected data pre-loaded.

MAC GADGET OF THE WEEK

Apple's AirPort Extreme Base Station is overpriced, but it's almost worth it. Supporting 802.11g and 802.11b protocols, it can be used for high-speed access and can support all your Macs and wireless PCs; it's also got a second port that lets you connect the Base Station to an Ethernet hub or switch, thus making Internet access available to your entire network, regardless of whether or not they're wireless. Buy it for $199.99 from www.apple.com.

December 22, 2005

THURSDAY

THIS WEEK'S FOCUS: MORE MICROSOFT OFFICE

ON THIS DAY: CHRISTMAS TREE LIGHTS INVENTED (1822)

On this date in 1822, the first string of Christmas tree lights was created by Thomas Edison's associate, Edward H. Johnson, who decorated a Christmas tree at his home. The first commercially produced Christmas tree lamps were manufactured in strings of nine sockets by the Edison General Electric Co., and advertised in the December 1901 issue of the *Ladies' Home Journal*. Electric Christmas tree lights quickly became the rage among wealthy Americans, but the average citizen didn't use them until the 1920s or later.

Related Web site: www.christmasarchives.com/trees.html

ADD A WATERMARK TO A WORD DOCUMENT

A screened-back graphic in the background of your printed page—also called a *watermark*—is a nice effect for many printed documents. The trick to creating a watermark is that it has to be added to your header or footer—*not* to the main body of your document. Here's how to do it.

1. Select View > Header and Footer.
2. Position the insertion point in either the header or footer, and then select Insert > Picture > From File to display the Insert Picture dialog box.
3. Navigate to and select the picture you want to use as your watermark, and then click the Insert button to insert the picture into your document.
4. Double-click the picture to display the Format Picture dialog box.
5. Select the Layout tab, and then select Behind Text.
6. Select the Picture tab; then pull down the Color list and select Watermark.
7. Click OK to close the dialog box.
8. Use your mouse to reposition and resize the picture as necessary, and then click the Close button on the Header and Footer toolbar.

To view your watermark, you'll have to switch to Print Layout view. Cool!

WEB SITE OF THE WEEK

Get lots of tips and advice concerning Microsoft Office at Woody's Office Portal, run by Office ace Woody Leonhard. It's also where you can download your copy of Woody's Office Power Pack (WOPR), one of the best assortments of Office add-ons and utilities you'll find anywhere. It's all at www.wopr.com.

THIS WEEK'S FOCUS: MORE MICROSOFT OFFICE

ON THIS DAY: FIRST MEN ORBIT THE MOON (1968)

On December 23, 1968, the three Apollo 8 astronauts became the first men to orbit the Moon. The following evening, on Christmas Eve, Frank Borman, James Lovell, and William Anders did a live television broadcast, in which they showed pictures of the Earth and moon as seen from lunar orbit. They ended the broadcast with the crew taking turns reading from the book of Genesis. Borman then added, "And from the crew of Apollo 8, we close with good night, good luck, a merry Christmas, and God bless all of you—all of you on the good Earth."

Related Web site: www.lpi.usra.edu/expmoon/Apollo8/Apollo8.html

TYPE "SHORTCUTS" TO LONG WORDS

Do you ever get tired of typing long words? I guarantee you do if you live in Indianapolis or Minneapolis—or if your name is Kazmierczak or Bartholomew. No matter how fast and accurate your typing is, you're bound to get tired of typing these long words every day, and stand a good chance of getting your fingers tangled trying to speed through even the most frequently used of these combinations.

A good solution to this problem is to use Word's AutoCorrect feature to create "shortcuts" or abbreviations that you can type in place of difficult words. When you type the shortcut, AutoCorrect will automatically replace your shortcut with the word itself. Here's how to do it:

1. Select Tools > AutoCorrect to display the AutoCorrect dialog box, and then select the AutoCorrect tab.
2. Enter the word or phrase you want to use as the shortcut into the Replace box.
3. Enter the corresponding word or phrase in the With box.
4. Click the Add button.

For this shortcut-to-long words feature to function, you must have AutoCorrect activated. To do this, select Tools > AutoCorrect to display the AutoCorrect dialog box, select the AutoCorrect tab, check the Replace Text As You Type option, and then click OK.

PORTABLE GADGET OF THE WEEK

Harmony's SST-659 universal remote control differs from other remotes in that it isn't device-oriented—it's activity-oriented. Press a single activity button (such as Watch TV or Watch a Movie) and the SST-659 automatically turns on and switches to the appropriate components. You set up the activity buttons specific to your home theater system through the online tools at the HarmonyRemote.com Web site; the remote connects to your PC via USB. Buy it for $199.99 at www.harmonyremote.com.

December 24, 2005

SATURDAY

THIS WEEK'S FOCUS: MORE MICROSOFT OFFICE

ON THIS DAY: FIRST SOLAR HEATED HOUSE (1948)

The first house to be completely solar heated was occupied on Christmas Eve, 1948. The Dover Sun House, in Dover, Massachusetts, was designed by architect Eleanor Raymond. The heating system used black sheet metal collectors to capture solar energy, stored by the phase-change of sodium sulphate decahydrate in "heat bins." Fans distributed the heat as needed.

Related Web site: www.iea-shc.org

MAKE YOUR POWERPOINT TEXT POP!

If you're tired of flat-looking text in your PowerPoint presentations, you might want to use drop shadows to give your text a little pop. Drop shadows are particularly useful if you have text against a complex background, or against a background that gradates from light to dark.

There are two ways to add shadows to text within PowerPoint. The first way is to highlight the text or select the text object, and then click the Text Shadow button on PowerPoint's Formatting toolbar. This adds a slight shadow to the selected text using the preselected shadow color from the presentation's underlying color scheme.

To add a more prominent shadow—or to add a different-color shadow—you have to use the Shadow command from PowerPoint's Drawing toolbar. To add this type of shadow, follow these steps:

1. Select the text object. (You can't add this effect just by selecting text within a box.)
2. Click the Shadow button on the Drawing toolbar, and then select Shadow Style 14.
3. To change the color of this shadow, click the Shadow button and select Shadow Settings to display the Shadow Setting toolbar. Then, click the Shadow Color button and select a different color.

The resulting shadow from this method is much more noticeable than a simple text shadow.

FACT OF THE WEEK

On November 18, 2003, the County of Los Angeles released a memo requesting that suppliers no longer use the words "master/slave" to identify various pieces of computer equipment. They deemed the nomenclature offensive in nature.

THIS WEEK'S FOCUS: MORE MICROSOFT OFFICE

ON THIS DAY: SIR ISAAC NEWTON BORN (1642)

English physicist and mathematician Sir Isaac Newton was born on this date in 1642. The culminating figure of the scientific revolution of the 17th century, he deduced that white light is composed of colors, conceived the three laws of motion, formulated the law of universal gravitation, and discovered infinitesimal calculus.

Related Web site: www-gap.dcs.st-and.ac.uk/~history/Mathematicians/Newton.html

ANIMATE YOUR POWERPOINT SLIDE BACKGROUNDS

Just as you can animate slide transitions, you can also animate objects on your slide background. When you do this, your background is animated every time you display a new slide in your presentation—regardless of any slide transition effects you have applied. It's a pretty neat trick that few users know.

Here's how it works in PowerPoint XP; use a similar approach in older versions.

1. In Slide Master view, select the entire slide. Then, click the Draw button on the Drawing toolbar and select Ungroup.
2. Select the element on the slide you want to animate.
3. Select Slide Show > Custom Animation to display the Custom Animation pane.
4. Click the Add Effect button, and then select an animation effect.
5. Select With Previous from the Start List, and choose your own Direction and Speed settings.

Repeat to animate other background elements. Just make sure you apply animation effects to *both* the Slide Master and Title Master—or only one of the two will be animated!

To check out a background animation, try this example. Open a new presentation using the good old Radar template. Enter the Slide Master view and ungroup the background until you can select the individual radar objects. Now select each object and apply a Zoom In effect. Return to the Normal view, add a few slides (with text) to your presentation, and then run the presentation as a slide show. Every time you advance to a new slide, the radar waves will ripple out!

SOFTWARE OF THE WEEK

If you just can't stand anything Microsoft, try the Microsoft Office alternative—WordPerfect Office. It's a tried-and-true application suite, consisting of the WordPerfect word processor, Quattro Pro spreadsheet, and Presentations slideshow generator. It's even cheaper than Microsoft Office. Buy it for $149.99 from www.corel.com.

December 26, 2005

MONDAY

THIS WEEK'S FOCUS: YOUR NEW PC

ON THIS DAY: CHARLES BABBAGE BORN (1791)

Charles Babbage, born on this date in 1791, was a mathematician, analytical philosopher, and (proto-)computer scientist. He was also the first person to come up with the idea of a programmable computer, which he called the Difference Engine.

Related Web site: ei.cs.vt.edu/~history/Babbage.html

GETTING RID OF YOUR OLD PC

If you get a new PC for Christmas, what do you do with your old PC?

If your old PC is still working reasonably well, you might not want to get rid of it. There's no reason not to use an old PC as a dedicated Internet machine, for your children to use for homework, or as a file server for your home network. Heck, you can even use it as a backup drive.

If your old PC *isn't* working well, or if you just don't want to keep the boat anchor around the joint, you have a disposal issue. Although you can just throw the thing in the trash, there are a number of reasons to reconsider that decision. First, unless you've removed or reformatted the old PC's hard disk, it's possible (though unlikely) that someone could grab personal data off the old machine. Second, dumping a computer isn't environmentally sound; the monitor and circuit boards contain a number of toxic materials that need to be disposed of properly. And third, even though the old thing might be useless to you, someone less fortunate might have great use for a second-hand PC.

That said, if your PC isn't *too* old (at least a Pentium II), you should consider recycling or donating it to an appropriate organization. The first places to check are your local schools and churches; after that, there are a number of computer recycling services available, including the following:

- Computer Recycling Center (www.crc.org)
- IBM Product Recycling Programs (www.ibm.com/ibm/environment/products/prp.shtml)
- Share the Technology (www.sharetechnology.org)

PC GADGET OF THE WEEK

Auravision's EluminX keyboard doesn't do anything different or better than hundreds of other computer keyboards—but it looks cooler. The EluminX is lit from within by a glowing blue light. The manufacturer claims that this "internal luminescence" makes the keyboard easier to use and reduces eyestrain, which is pretty much a load of hooey. What the lighting really does is make your keyboard look like something out of a science-fiction movie—or a hip martini bar. Buy it for $69.99 at www.auravisionllc.com.

THIS WEEK'S FOCUS: YOUR NEW PC

ON THIS DAY: JOHANNES KEPLER BORN (1571)

This is a big week for famous scientific births. On December 27, 1571, astrologer, astronomer, and mathematician Johannes Kepler was born. He is best known for his laws of planetary motion. Interestingly, early in his career, Kepler was an assistant to Tycho Brahe.

Related Web site: www.kepler.arc.nasa.gov/johannes.html

POWERING UP—FOR THE VERY FIRST TIME

The first time you turn on your PC is a unique experience. A brand-new, out-of-the-box system will have to perform some basic configuration operations, which include asking you to input some key information.

This first-time startup operation differs from manufacturer to manufacturer, but typically includes some or all of the following steps:

- **Windows Product Activation**—You might be asked to input the long and nonsensical product code found on the back of your Windows installation CD (or someplace else in the documentation that came with your new PC). Your system then phones into the Microsoft mother ship, registers your system information, and unlocks Windows for you to use. Fortunately, many manufacturers "pre-activate" Windows at the factory, so you might not have to go through this process.

- **Windows Registration**—A slightly different process from product activation, registration requires you to input your name and other personal information, along with the Windows product code. This information then is phoned into the Microsoft mother ship to register your copy of Windows with the company, for warranty purposes.

- **Windows Configuration**—During this process Windows asks a series of questions about your location, the current time and date, and other essential information. You also might be asked to create a username and password.

- **System Configuration**—This is where Windows tries to figure out all the different components that are part of your system, such as your printer, scanner, and so on. Enter the appropriate information when prompted; if asked to insert a component's installation CD, do so.

After you have everything registered and configured, Windows finally starts for real, and then *you* can start using your system.

DOWNLOAD OF THE WEEK

Turn your PC into an aquarium with the ultra-realistic Marine Aquarium screensaver. Choose from 26 different types of saltwater fish, all with realistic movement. This is my favorite screensaver of all time, period. Download it for $19.95 at www.serenescreen.com.

December 28, 2005

WEDNESDAY

THIS WEEK'S FOCUS: YOUR NEW PC

ON THIS DAY: CHEWING GUM PATENTED (1869)

On this date in 1869, William Finley Semple of Mount Vernon, Ohio, received a patent for "the combination of rubber with other articles adapted to the formation of an acceptable chewing gum." However, Semple never got around to actually producing any gum. That was first done by Thomas Adams, who originated the first chicle-based chewing gum in 1871.

Related Web site: www.gumbase.com/fungbhistory.htm

LEARNING IMPORTANT WINDOWS OPERATIONS

If you're new to computers, you need to master a few simple operations in order to use Windows efficiently. You perform all these operations with your mouse, so flex your muscles and let's get started.

- **Pointing and clicking**—This is the most common mouse operation. Simply move the mouse so that the cursor is pointing to the object you want to select, and then click the left mouse button once. Pointing and clicking is an effective way to select menu items, directories, and files.

- **Double-clicking**—If you're using Windows XP's default operating mode (which you probably are), you'll need to double-click an item to activate an operation. This involves pointing at something onscreen with the cursor and then clicking the left mouse button twice in rapid succession.

- **Right-clicking**—When you select an item and then click the *right* mouse button, you'll often see a pop-up menu. This menu, when available, contains commands that directly relate to the selected object.

- **Dragging and dropping**—Dragging is a variation of clicking. To drag an object, point at it with the cursor and then press and hold down the left mouse button. Move the mouse without releasing the mouse button, and drag the object to a new location. When you're done moving the object, release the mouse button to drop it onto the new location.

- **Hovering**—When you position the cursor over an item without clicking your mouse, you're hovering over that item. Many operations require you to hover your cursor and then perform some other action.

Want to practice your mousing skills? Then start a game of Windows Solitaire. You'll give your mouse a workout!

MAC GADGET OF THE WEEK

One of my favorite Mac keyboards is Adesso's Tru-Form with Touchpad. The Tru-Form offers an ergonomic split design and a built-in touchpad for moving the mouse pointer in a way that's similar to a PowerBook or iBook. Buy it for $99 at www.adesso.com.

THIS WEEK'S FOCUS: YOUR NEW PC

ON THIS DAY: CHARLES GOODYEAR BORN (1800)

Charles Goodyear was born on this date in 1800. Goodyear invented the vulcanization process that made possible the commercial use of rubber. Interestingly, Goodyear was not associated with the Goodyear Tire & Rubber Company; the company was named in his honor.

Related Web site: www.goodyear.com

UNDERSTANDING FILES AND FOLDERS

All the information on your computer is stored in *files*. A file is nothing more than a collection of data of some sort. Everything on your computer's hard drive is a separate file, with its own name, location, and properties. The contents of a file can be a document from an application (such as a Works worksheet or a Word document), or they can be the executable code for the application itself.

Every file has its own unique name. A defined structure exists for naming files, and its conventions must be followed for Windows to understand exactly what file you want when you try to access one. Each filename must consist of two parts, separated by a period—the *name* (to the left of the period) and the *extension* (to the right of the period). A filename can consist of letters, numbers, spaces, and characters and looks something like this: `this is a filename.ext`.

By default, Windows XP hides the extensions when it displays filenames. To display extensions, use the Control Panel to open the Folder Options dialog box; then select the View tab. In the Advanced Settings list, uncheck the Hide Extensions for Known File Types option, and then click OK.

Windows stores files in *folders*. A folder is like a master file; each folder can contain both files and additional folders. The exact location of a file is called its *path* and contains all the folders leading to the file. For example, a file named `filename.doc` that exists in the `system` folder, that is itself contained in the `windows` folder on your `c:\` drive, has a path that looks like this: `c:\windows\system\filename.doc`.

If you've been using computers for awhile, the folder metaphor might be new to you. In the old MS-DOS days, folders were called directories, and the folder path was called a directory path. Nothing to get confused about; folders are the same as directories, just a different name.

WEB SITE OF THE WEEK

One of the best sites for technology news has the perfect URL: www.news.com. The site is CNET's News.com; go there daily to find out what's happening in the world of computers and high-tech.

December 30, 2005

FRIDAY

THIS WEEK'S FOCUS: YOUR NEW PC

ON THIS DAY: NEW GALAXY DISCOVERED (1924)

On December 30, 1924, astronomer Edwin Hubble announced the existence of another galactic system in addition to the Milky Way. Until that point, scientists were not certain whether certain fuzzy clouds of light called "nebulae" were small clusters of clouds within the Milky Way or separate galaxies. Hubble measured the distance to the Andromeda nebula and showed it to be a hundred thousand times as far away as the nearest stars, proving it was a separate galaxy, but very far away. (And, yes, this is the same guy for whom the Hubble space telescope was named.)

Related Web site: www.seds.org/messier/galaxy.html

INSTALLING NEW SOFTWARE

Your new computer system probably came with a bunch of programs preinstalled on its hard disk. As useful as these programs are, at some point you're going to want to add something new.

Almost all software programs have their own built-in installation programs. Installing the software is as easy as running this built-in program. If the program you're installing comes on a CD-ROM, just insert the program's main or installation CD in your computer's CD-ROM drive. The program's installation program should then start automatically, and all you have to do is follow the onscreen instructions.

If the program you're installing doesn't have an automated setup program, you can install the program by using Windows's Add or Remove Programs utility. Select Start > Control Panel to open the Control Panel, and then double-click the Add or Remove Programs icon. When the Add or Remove Programs dialog box appears, click the Add New Programs button. When the next screen appears, click the CD or Floppy button, insert the program's installation CD, and then follow the onscreen instructions to complete the installation.

Many programs today are available by downloading them from the Internet—no boxes or CDs are involved. When you download a program from a major software publisher, the process is generally easy to follow. You probably have to read a page of do's and don'ts, agree to the publisher's licensing agreements, and then click a button to start the download. After you specify where (which folder on your hard disk) you want to save the downloaded file, the download begins.

When the download is complete, you should be notified via an onscreen dialog box. From this point, installing the program is almost identical to installing from CD or floppy disk—except that you have to enter the complete path to the installation file in the Run dialog box.

PORTABLE GADGET OF THE WEEK

Like the idea of changing stoplights from red to green? Designed for emergency vehicles, the MIRT (mobile infrared transmitter) mounts on your dash and emits an infrared light that triggers traffic light changes from more than 1,500 feet away. The infrared light is invisible to anyone looking, and it can change traffic lights from red to green in less than 3 seconds. If you're authorized for emergency use, you can buy it for $475 at www.pelicanperformance.com.

December 31, 2005

SATURDAY

THIS WEEK'S FOCUS: YOUR NEW PC

ON THIS DAY: SMALLPOX VIRUS SCHEDULED TO BE DESTROYED—*NOT* (1993)

The last research samples of the smallpox virus were scheduled to be destroyed on New Year's Eve, 1993. However, some scientists who wanted to continue research on the virus stopped the destruction plan. Frozen samples still remain in Moscow and at the Centers for Disease Control and Prevention in Atlanta, Georgia.

Related Web site: www.bt.cdc.gov/agent/smallpox/

SHUTTING DOWN YOUR COMPUTER

Your new PC isn't like a blender or a television set. You just can't turn it off by pressing a button. There's a whole procedure you have to go through to shut things down.

When you want to turn off your computer, you have to do it through Windows. In fact, you don't want to turn off your computer any other way—you *always* want to turn things off through the official Windows procedure.

To shut down Windows and turn off your PC, select Start > Turn Off Computer. When the Turn Off Computer dialog . (It's ironic that your computer is the one device you turn off by first clicking the Start button!)

Whatever you do, do *not* turn off your computer without shutting down Windows. You could lose data and settings that are temporarily stored in your system's memory.

By the way, you probably don't need to turn off your computer completely when you're not using it. Windows' Stand By mode is just as good, in many cases, as it effectively puts your computer to "sleep," without formally shutting everything down. The screen goes blank, the hard drive stops spinning, and the power usage drops to almost zero. The advantage is that your PC "wakes up" from Stand By mode a lot faster than it typically launches from a complete power off. You can activate the Stand By mode by selecting Start > Turn Off Computer, and then selecting Stand By.

FACT OF THE WEEK

According to an IDC survey, 36% of all software installed worldwide in 2003 was pirated. The number was 27% in the US.

MORE DECEMBER FACTS

December 1

1878 Alexander Graham Bell personally installs the first phone in the White House for President Rutherford B. Hayes

1955 Rosa Parks is jailed for refusing to give up her seat on a public bus to a white man; the ensuing bus boycott was organized by Martin Luther King, Jr.; Parks is now known as the "mother of the civil rights movement"

1997 Eight of the nine planets align and are visible to the naked eye, the last such occurrence expected for at least another 100 years

December 2

1957 First atomic electric generating station in the U.S. begins operation in Shippingport, PA

1982 First artificial heart—the Jarvik-7—is implanted at the University of Utah Medical Center

December 3

1967 First successful human heart transplant

December 4

1992 U.S. troops are deployed to Somalia; the bloody battle at Mogadishu's Olympia Hotel was chronicled in the movie, Black Hawk Down

December 5

1933 Prohibition ends when the 21st Amendment is ratified, repealing the 18th Amendment

1977 First American-made, front-wheel drive car—the Plymouth Horizon—debuts

December 6

1922 First commercial electric service begins in Utica, NY

1957 First U.S. attempted satellite launch fails when the Vanguard rocket carrying it blows up on the launch pad at Cape Canaveral

December 7

1941 Pearl Harbor is attacked by Japan; five of eight battleships, three destroyers, and seven other ships are sunk or severely damaged, and more than 200 U.S. aircraft are destroyed; 2,400 Americans are killed and 1,200 wounded

1982 Charles Brooks of Texas becomes the first person to be executed via lethal injection

1999 Recording Industry Association of America (RIAA) sues Napster for alleged music piracy

December 8

1931 Coax cable is patented

1941 U.S. declares war on Japan after Pearl Harbor is savagely attacked, and thus the U.S. joins World War II

December 9

1884 Roller skates are patented in Chicago, IL

December 11

1884 First dental anesthesia—nitrous oxide (more commonly known as "laughing gas")—is used on a patient

1941 Germany, led by Adolf Hitler, declares war on the U.S.

1997 More than 150 countries agree to reduce the amount of greenhouse gases produced worldwide in an effort to slow global warming

1998 The Mars Climate Orbiter is launched in space aboard a Delta II rocket; the probe disappeared, however, on September 23, 1999

December 12

1901 Guglielmo Marconi sends the first radio transmission across the Atlantic Ocean, debunking myths that the curvature of the Earth would limit radio transmissions to 200 miles or less

1912 The first known experiment with an airplane ejection seat is performed by an Austrian inventor; it wasn't until January 13, 1943, that a German test pilot made the first ejection

December 14

1900 Quantum theory is born when Max Planck, a German physicist, publishes his study of energy and how it can exhibit characteristics of physical matter

1947 NASCAR is founded in Daytona Beach, FL

1967 DNA is created in a test tube

1972 Eugene A. Cernan is the last human to have walked on the moon

December 15

1791 First 10 amendments to the U.S. Constitution, known as the Bill of Rights, become law

December 16

1944 Battle of the Bulge begins in Belgium; about 80,000 Allied forces were killed, wounded or MIA, with all but 5,000 being U.S. soldiers

December 17

1919 Seismographer and meteorologist Albert Porta predicts that the conjunction of six of nine planets on December 17, 1919 will generate a magnetic current, causing the sun to explode and engulf the Earth; obviously, Porta's calculations were incorrect

1979 The Budweiser Rocket car, driven by Stan Barrett, becomes the first land vehicle to travel faster than the speed of sound, reaching a top speed of 739.666 mph

December 18

1946 Steven Spielberg is born

December 19

1732 Benjamin Franklin begins publishing Poor Richard's Almanac

1972 The last three astronauts to visit the moon return safely to Earth (Apollo 17)

1998 President Bill Clinton is impeached; he was acquitted on February 12, 1999

December 20

1868 Harvey S. Firestone is born

1951 Electricity is first created with atomic power in Idaho

1989 U.S. invades Panama to overthrow dictator Manuel Noriega

December 22

1973 Federal speed limit of 55 mph is imposed on U.S. highways to increase safety and conserve fuel

1182 First strung Christmas tree lights are created.

December 23

1954 First successful kidney transplant is performed in Boston, MA

1970 Construction of the World Trade Center in New York City reaches 1,353 feet

1986 Space shuttle Voyager completes the first non-stop flight around the world

December 24

1814 War of 1812 ends

1818 James Prescott Joule—for whom the joule is named—is born

December 25

1741 Centigrade temperature scale is devised by astronomer Anders Celsius

December 26

1982 *Time* magazine names the PC "The Man of the Year"

December 27

1951 The Crosley car—the first right-hand drive car designed specifically for mail delivery—is put into service in Cincinnati, OH

December 28

1849 Dry cleaning is accidentally discovered in Paris, France

December 31

1938 The "drunkometer"—the first breath test of car drivers—is invented at Indiana University School of Medicine

COMPUTER HARDWARE AND SOFTWARE

Lots of Beige Boxes

Total number of PCs-in-use, worldwide (millions):

Year	Units (millions)
1995	226
2000	523
2002	663
2007 (projected)	1,069

Source: Computer Industry Almanac, Inc.
    (www.c-i-a.com)

Selling Beige Boxes, Domestic Edition

U.S. PC sales (millions of units):

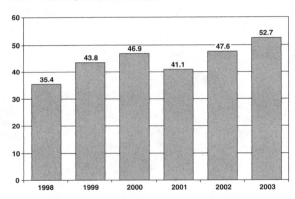

Source: IDC (www.idc.com)

Selling Beige Boxes, Global Edition

Worldwide PC sales (millions of units):

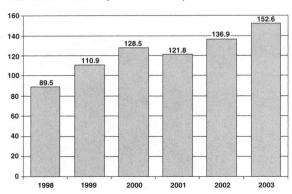

Source: IDC (www.idc.com)

Selling Beige Boxes, by Manufacturer

U.S. market share of top five PC vendors in 2003:

Rank	Manufacturer	Market Share
1	Dell	30.9%
2	Hewlett-Packard	20.6%
3	IBM	5.2%
4	Gateway	3.8%
5	Apple	3.2%

Source: Gartner IDC (www.idc.com)

Operating Systems

Most popular operating systems of Web visitors (September 2003):

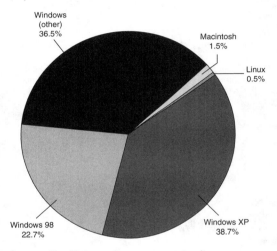

Source: OneStat.com (www.onestat.com)

Software Piracy

Global revenues lost to software piracy (2002): $13.08 billion

Percentage of software that is pirated, globally (2002): 39%

Percentage of software that is pirated in the U.S. (2002): 23% (lowest in the world)

Piracy rates by region (2002):

Region	Piracy Rate
Eastern Europe	71%
Latin America	55%
Asia/Pacific	55%
Middle East/Africa	49%
Western Europe	35%
North America	24%

Source: *Eighth Annual BSA Global Software Piracy Study*, Business Software Association (www.bsa.org)

THE INTERNET

Online Population Explosion

Number of Internet users worldwide, in millions

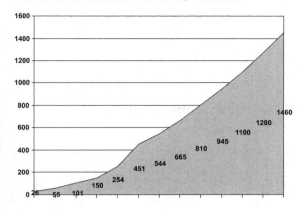

Source: Computer Industry Almanac (www.c-i-a.com)

It's a Small World

Number of Internet users by country, 2004 (in millions):

Country	Number of Users
Argentina	4.0
Australia	13.0
Austria	4.6
Belgium	5.0
Brazil	23.0
Bulgaria	1.6
Canada	20.4
Chile	5.2
China	95.8
Colombia	2.5
Czech Republic	3.5
Denmark	3.7
Egypt	2.4
Finland	3.3
France	256.3
Germany	41.9
Greece	3.8
Hong Kong	4.6
Hungary	3.0
India	39.2
Indonesia	15.3
Ireland	2.1
Israel	3.0
Italy	28.6
Japan	77.9
Malaysia	8.5
Mexico	11.1
The Netherlands	10.3

Country	Number of Users
New Zealand	2.3
Norway	3.1
Pakistan	1.2
Peru	2.7
Philippines	7.8
Poland	10.6
Portugal	6.1
Romania	3.1
Russia	22.3
Saudi Arabia	2.9
Singapore	2.5
Slovakia	1.8
South Africa	5.2
South Korea	32.0
Spain	16.7
Sweden	6.1
Switzerland	4.7
Taiwan	13.2
Thailand	8.4
Turkey	6.8
Ukraine	2.8
United Kingdom	34.1
United States	185.9
Venezuela	3.0

Source: Computer Industry Almanac (www.c-i-a.com)

Parlez Vous Englais?

Percentage of Internet users worldwide, by language (as of March 2004):

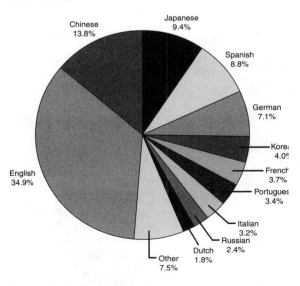

Source: Global Reach (www.glreach.com/globstats/)

Rural/Suburban/Urban Penetration

Internet penetration by type of community:

Community	2000	2003
Rural	41%	52%
Suburban	55%	66%
Urban	51%	67%

Source: Pew Internet & American Life Project (www.
pewinternet.org)

Master of Your Domain

Percentage of Web servers by domain (August 2004):

Domain	Description	Percent
.com	Commercial	48.3%
.net	Network	7.2%
.de	Germany	7.1%
.org	Non-profit organization	5.3%
.uk	United Kingdom	2.9%
.kr	South Korea	2.9
.pl	Poland	2.5%
.ru	Russian Federation	2.1%
.nl	Netherlands	2.0%
.jp	Japan	2.0%
.it	Italy	1.3%
.ch	Switzerland	1.3%
.dk	Denmark	1.0%
.br	Brazil	0.9%
.au	Australia	0.8
.ca	Canada	0.7
.edu	Educational	0.7%

Source: Security Space (www.securityspace.com)

How We Connect

U.S. Internet subscribers by access type (June 2004):

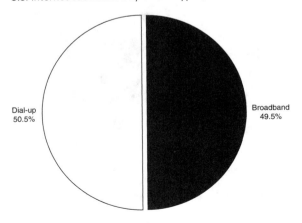

Dial-up 50.5%

Broadband 49.5%

Source: Nielsen/NetRatings (www.nielsen-
netratings.com)

Broadband Connections, Part 1

Total number of U.S. broadband (cable and DSL) subscribers, Q2 2004: 28.6 million

Total number of U.S. broadband subscribers, Q2 2003: 26.9
million

One-year increase: 1.7 million

Source: Leichtman Research Group, Inc. (www.
leichtmanresearch.com)

Broadband Connections, Part 2

Top five broadband states, as of July 2004:

Rank	State	Penetration
1	Hawaii	35.0%
2	Massachusetts	32.2%
3	New Jersey	30.6%
4	Connecticut	29.1%
5	New York	18.6%

Source: Leichtman Research Group, Inc. (www.
leichtmanresearch.com)

Broadband Connections, Part 3

Bottom five broadband states, as of July 2004:

Rank	State	Penetration
50	Mississippi	8.1%
49	South Dakota	8.5%
48	Montana	8.9%
47	Wyoming	10.2%
46	New Mexico	10.8%

Source: Leichtman Research Group, Inc. (www.
leichtmanresearch.com)

A Typical Day Online
(Dial-Up vs. Broadband)

Percentage of dial-up and broadband users engaging in
selected online activities on a typical day (February 2004):

Activity	Dial-Up	Broadband
Work-related research	14%	26%
Research a product	11%	24%
Get map or driving directions	5%	12%
Get news online	22%	40%

Source: Pew Internet & American Life Project (www.
pewinternet.org)

Popular Online Activities

Those who go online "very often" or "often" cite the following as their most common activities:

Activity	Percent
Sending or receiving email	67%
Doing research for work or school	45%
Getting information about products and services	41%
Getting information about hobbies or special interests	36%
Checking news, weather, and so on	40%
Surfing the Web to explore new and different sites	32%
Shopping online	22%
Obtaining information on local amusements and activities	19%
Paying bills	18%
Downloading or playing games	18%
Financial management or investing	15%
Making travel plans or arrangements	15%
Obtaining information about health or disease	15%

Source: Harris Interactive (www.harrisinteractive.com)

What We *Don't* Do Online

Internet activities never performed (2004):

Make phone calls	87%
Take courses	75%
Participate in chat groups	74%
Search for a job	61%
Pay bills	60%
Financial management and investing	53%
Download or play games	49%
Find and download software	47%
Make travel plans and reservations	33%

Source: Harris Interactive (www.harrisinteractive.com)

Sessions and Page Views

Average activity for a Web user in July 2004:

Activity	Data
Number of online sessions per month	26
Page views per month	1,014
Page views per session	39
Time spent online per month	18 hours, 46 minutes, 8 seconds
Time spent online per session	43 minutes, 13 seconds
Duration of each page view	45 seconds

Source: Nielsen/NetRatings (www.nielsen-netratings.com)

Most Popular Screen Resolutions

The most popular screen resolutions for Web surfing are (June 2004):

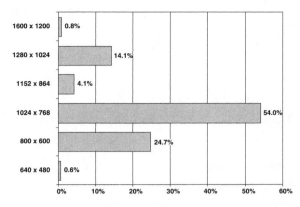

Source: OneStat.com (www.onestat.com)

Browser Wars

Browser usage, as percentage of total Web users (July 2004):

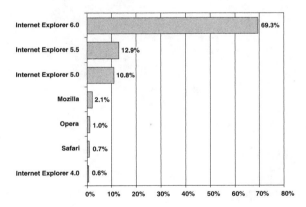

Source: OneStat.com (www.onestat.com)

ISP Wars

Top 10 U.S. Internet service providers, based on numbers of subscribers during the first quarter 2004 (in millions):

Rank	ISP	Subscribers
1	America Online	24.0
2	Comcast	5.7
3	United Online (NetZero & Juno Online)	5.4
4	EarthLink	5.3
5	SBC	4.0
6	Road Runner	3.4
7	Verizon	2.7
8	Charter	1.7
9	BellSouth	1.6
10	Adelphia	1.1

Source: ISP Planet (www.isp-planet/research/rankings/)

Server Wars

Market share of major Web servers (August 2004):

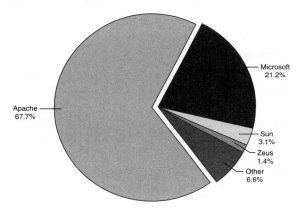

Source: Netcraft Web Server Survey (www.netcraft.com)

Site Wars

Top 10 visited Web properties, based on millions of unique visitors (June 2004—includes all sites owned by the parent company):

Rank	Site	Unique Visitors (worldwide)
1	Yahoo!	115
2	MSN/Microsoft	113
3	AOL Time Warner	108
4	Google	63
5	eBay	58
6	Ask Jeeves	39
7	Terra Lycos	37
8	About/Primedia	34
9	Amazon.com	32
10	Monster Worldwide	27

Source: comScore (www.comscore.com)

We Don't Stick Around Much

Page views per visit (March 2004):

Number of Page Views	Percentage of Total
1	9.5%
1–2	54.6%
2–3	16.6%
3–4	8.7%
4–5	4.4%
6–7	1.4%
7–8	0.8%
8–9	0.7%
9–10	0.5%
10+	2.7%

Source: OneStat.com (www.onestat.com)

Politics and the Internet

Percentage of general U.S. population registered to vote: 70%

Percentage of online population registered to vote: 86%

Source: Nielsen /NetRatings (www.nielsen-netratings.com)

Internet Growth by Income Level

Year-over-year Internet audience growth, by income (March 2004 versus March 2003):

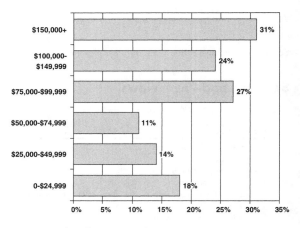

Source: Nielsen/NetRatings (www.nielsen-netratings.com)

Internet Growth by Age Group

Year-over-year Internet audience growth, by age group (October 2003 versus October 2002):

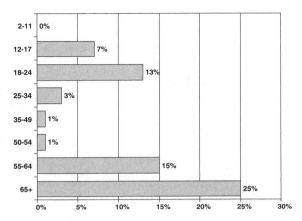

Source: Nielsen/NetRatings (www.nielsen-netratings.com)

Moms Versus the Kids

How often moms battle with their children to get access to the computer (as of April 2002):

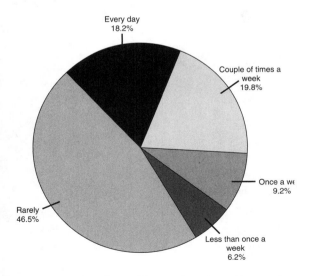

Source: Digital Marketing Services (www.dmsdallas.com)

Teens Online

Number of U.S. teens online in 2004: 18 million

Number of U.S. teens online in 2008 (projected): 22 million

Source: JupiterResearch (www.jupiterresearch.com)

Teen Activities: Internet Versus TV

Teen Activity	Hours per Week
Watching TV	10
Using the Internet	7

Source: JupiterResearch (www.jupiterresearch.com)

How the Internet Helps Students

U.S. students' opinions regarding how the Internet helps them with school (2004):

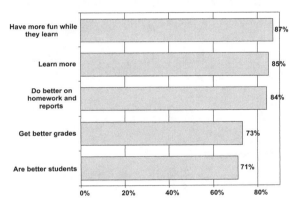

Source: SBC Communications, as reported by eMarketer (www.emarketer.com)

Best Days to Surf

Web traffic by day of the week (2003):

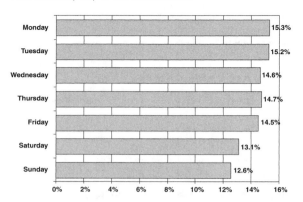

Source: OneStat.com (www.onestat.com)

Trading Personal Info for Customization

Willingness to provide personal data for personal content, by age (2004):

Type of Data	18–34	55+	Average
Demographic data	63%	49%	56%
Preference data	71%	57%	64%

Source: ChoiceStream (www.choicestream)

E-Government

Top 10 state governments, ranked by their use of digital technologies (2004):

1	Michigan
2	Washington
3	Virginia
4	Indiana
5	Arizona
6	South Dakota
7	Tennessee
8	Utah
9	Arkansas
10	Colorado

Source: The Center for Digital Government (www. centerdigitalgov.com)

Work at Home—or Home at Work?

Internet usage by employees at work for personal matters (2002): 3.7 hours/week

Internet usage by employees at home for work matters (2002): 5.9 hours

Source: Rockbridge Associates (www.rockresearch.com)

Heavy Media Users

Demographics of heavy users (60 minutes or more per day) for major forms of news media (2002):

Media Used	Household Income > $50,000	College Degree
Internet	60%	50.4%
Newspapers	45%	38.9%
Radio	45%	28.4%
Television	32%	20.8%

Source: The Media Audit (www.themediaaudit.com)

Most Visited News Sites

Most-visited print news and media sites (December 2003):

Site	Market Share
New York Times	6.5%
Washington Post	3.4%
USA Today	3.3%
CNN/Sports Illustrated	2.4%
Times of India	1.7%
Boston.com	1.6%
Star Tribune	1.1%
NYPost.com	1.0%
SF Gate	0.9%

Source: Hitwise (www.hitwise.com)

Media Multitaskers

The Media Center at the American Press Institute says that 70% of consumers use different forms of media simultaneously—but they still have to pay attention to one source over another. The last time they used media simultaneously, business people said they paid the most attention to:

Media	Percent
Online	41%
Newspapers	20%
TV	18%
Trade journals	5%
General business publications	5%
Radio	4%
Direct mail	4%
Sales literature	1%
Never use media simultaneously	2%

Source: Mobium Creative Group (www.mobium.com)

Internet Broadcasts, Part 1

Breakdown of users who watch or listen to Internet broadcasts, by age group (2003):

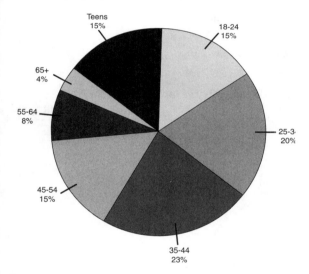

Source: Arbitron/Edison Media Research (www.arbitron.com)

Internet Broadcasts, Part 2

Breakdown of users who watch or listen to Internet broadcasts, by gender (2003):

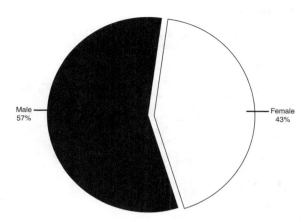

Source: Arbitron/Edison Media Research (www.arbitron.com)

Big Brother Is Watching

Employers who use software to monitor external email: 60%

Employers who monitor internal company email: 27%

Employers who retain and archive email messages: 35%

Employers who retain and archive instant messaging records: 6%

Source: American Management Association's *2004 Workplace E-Mail and Instant Messaging Survey* (www.amanet.org)

Instant Messaging in the Workplace

Of those who use instant messaging in the workplace, 58% engage in personal chats. Survey respondents report sending and receiving the following types of potentially damaging content:

Type	Percent
Attachments	19%
Jokes, gossip, rumors, or disparaging remarks	16%
Confidential information about the company, a co-worker, or client	9%
Sexual, romantic, or pornographic content	6%

Source: *2004 Workplace E-Mail and Instant Messaging Survey*, American Management Association (www.amanet.org)

Daily Email

Email delivery trends, by day of the week (Q3 2003):

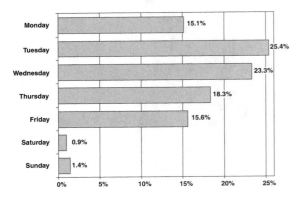

Source: EmailLabs (www.emaillabs.com)

SPAM, VIRUSES, AND ATTACKS

Spam, Spam, Spam, Spam

Percentage of 106 billion monthly email messages classified as spam (July 2004): 65%

Source: Symantec/Brightmail Probe Network (www.brightmail.com)

Spam Content

Content of spam messages (July 2004)

Type of Spam	Percent of Total Spam Messages
Products	28%
Adult	17%
Financial	15%
Scams	9%
Health	7%
Fraud	6%
Leisure	5%
Internet	4%
Political	4$
Spiritual	1%
Other	4%

Source: Symantec/Brightmail Probe Network (www.brightmail.com)

Spam Origins

Originating country of spam messages (July 2004)

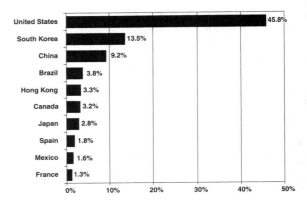

Source: Commtouch, Inc. (www.commtouch.com)

Top Viruses

Top 10 viruses (July 2004):

Rank	Virus Name	Quantity Detected (millions)
1	netsky	42.4
2	zafi	16.8
3	mime	15.4
4	mydoom	5.7
5	lovgate	2.9
6	bagle	1.7
7	objectdata	0.6
8	klez	0.6
9	dumaru	0.5
10	ebscam	0.4

Source: Postini (www.postini.com)

Virus Prevalence

Percentage of respondents reporting a virus disaster in 2003: 30.7%

Source: 9th Annual ISCA Labs Virus Prevalence Survey (www.icsalabs.com)

Virus Costs

Disaster recovery costs per organization per malicious event (2003): $100,000

Source: 9th Annual ISCA Labs Virus Prevalence Survey (www.icsalabs.com)

Hack Attacks

Most expensive computer crime: denial of service attack

Second most expensive computer crime: theft of intellectual property

Total financial losses from computer crime: $141 billion

Source: *2004 Computer Crime and Security Survey*, Computer Security Institute/FBI (www.gocsi.com)

SEARCHING

Searching Is Essential

How much U.S. adult Internet users rely on search engines to find information (May–June 2004)

How Much	Percent
Like using them, but could go back to other ways	50%
Couldn't live without	32%
Wouldn't really miss them if they could no longer use them	17%
Don't know	1%

Source: Pew Internet & American Life Project (www.pewinternet.org)

Who We Search For

Searches conducted by U.S. Internet users (2004):

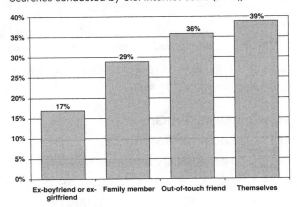

Source: Harris Interactive (www. harrisinteractive.com)

Two Words Are Better Than One (When Searching)

Percentage of users performing multiple-word search queries (July 2004):

Number of Words in Query	Percentage of Queries
1	16.6%
2	30.1%
3	26.8%
4	14.8%
5	6.8%
6	2.8%
7	1.1%

Source: OneStat.com (www.onestat.com)

Web Directory Sizes

Size of human-compiled Web directories, as of January 2003 (millions of pages):

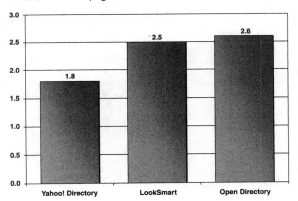

Source: Search Engine Watch (www.searchenginewatch.com)

Search Index Sizes

Size of major search engines and directory indexes as of September 2003 (millions of pages):

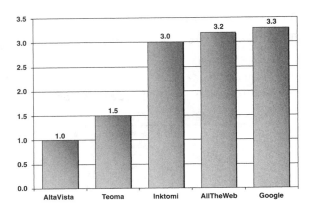

Source: Search Engine Watch
            (www.searchenginewatch.com)

Search Engine Freshness

Freshness of search engine indexes, based on newest and oldest pages found (May 2003):

Search Engine	Newest Page Found	Average	Oldest Page Found
MSN Search	1 day	4 weeks	51 days
HotBot (Inktomi)	1 day	4 weeks	51 days
Google	2 days	1 month	165 days
AllTheWeb	1 day	1 month	599 days
Teoma	41 days	2.5 months	81 days
AltaVista	0 days	3 months	108 days
Gigablast	45 days	7 months	381 days
WiseNut	133 days	6 months	183 days

Source: Search Engine Showdown (www.
            searchengineshowdown.com/stats/)

Search Satisfaction

Percentage of users indicating a strongly positive experience with major search sites (2004):

Rank	Search Site	Percent Positive Experience
1	Google	83%
2	Yahoo!	66%
3	MSN Search	46%
4	Ask Jeeves	42%
5	Lycos	38%

Source: Vividence (www.vividence.com)

Search Wars

Top five search sites (January 2004):

Rank	Search Site	Unique Audience (millions)
1	Google	59.3
2	Yahoo!	45.8
3	MSN Search	44.6
4	AOL Search	23.4
5	Ask Jeeves	12.8

Source: Nielsen/NetRatings (www.nielsen-
            netratings.com)

ONLINE ADVERTISING

Size of Online Ad Market

Size of the U.S. online advertising market (billions):

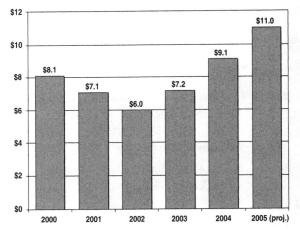

Source: *Ad Spending in the U.S., Online & Offline,* eMarketer (www.emarketer.com)

How Much Will It Grow?
It Depends on Who You Ask...

Estimates of U.S. online ad spending growth for 2004:

Research Firm	Growth Estimate
American Technology Research	+30%
JupiterResearch	+27.3%
eMarketer	+25.2%
Smith Barney	+23.6%
Forrester Research	+22.5%
Piper Jaffray	+20.9%

Research Firm	Growth Estimate
Universal McCann	+20%
TNS Media Intelligence/CMR	+15.8%
Veronis Suhler Stevenson	+15.8%
PricewaterhouseCoopers	+15.3%
Merrill Lynch	+10%
ZenithOptimedia	+8%
Myers Report	+3.8%
GartnerG2	+3.2%

Banner Ads—Less Effective

Percentage of Web users who have clicked on a banner ad in the last month:

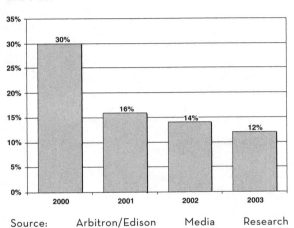

Source: Arbitron/Edison Media Research (www.arbitron.com)

Ad Affiliate Programs

Top 10 affiliate programs (exclusive of adult sites), based on absolute number of clickthroughs (July 2004)

1. ClubMom
2. A.D.Kessler
3. Kiss.com
4. Juniper Bank
5. ActualTraffic, Inc
6. DreamMates
7. Niche Marketing Research Center
8. E-Commerce Exchange
9. Dark Blue
10. Amazon.com-Books

Source: Refer-It (refer-it.com)

ONLINE SHOPPING

Put It In Perspective

Online retail sales as a percentage of total U.S. retail sales (for the year 2003): 1.6%

Source: U.S. Department of Commerce (www.doc.gov)

It's a Fourth-Quarter Business

Estimated U.S. retail e-commerce sales by quarter (billions):

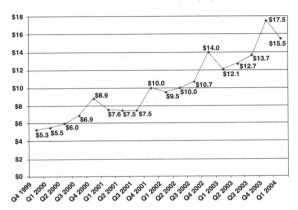

Source: U.S. Department of Commerce (www.doc.gov)

Where We Shop

Top 10 most-visited online shopping sites (December 2003):

Rank	Site	Market Share
1	eBay	26.2%
2	Amazon.com	4.2%
3	Yahoo! Shopping	1.8%
4	Walmart.com	1.7%
5	BestBuy.com	1.5%
6	eBay Motors	1.4%
7	Target	1.2%
8	Dell Computer	1.2%
9	Lower My Bills	1.1%
10	Half.com	0.9%

Source: Hitwise (www.hitwise.com)

What We Buy

Top online shopping categories for the 2003 holiday season (billions):

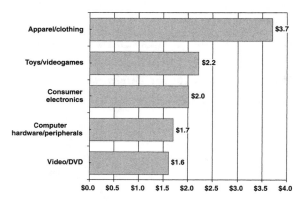

Source: *eSpending Report*, Goldman, Sachs/Harris Interactive/Nielsen-NetRatings

Best Customer Experience

Top online retailers for overall customer experience (2004):

1. Amazon.com
2. Barnes & Noble
3. Circuit City
4. eBay

Source: Vividence (`www.vividence`)

Best Online Retailer Attributes

Leading online retailers for the following Web site attributes:

- Best check out process: Amazon.com
- Best product research/browsing: eBay
- Best search engine: Barnes & Noble
- Best customer support: Nordstrom
- Best in-store pick-up: Circuit City

Source: Vividence (`www.vividence.com`)

E-Commerce Satisfaction

Average e-commerce satisfaction scores, by category:

Category	2000	2001	2002	2003
E-retail	78	77	83	84
Online auctions	72	74	77	78
E-brokerage	72	69	73	76
E-travel	N/A	N/A	77	77

Source: American Customer Satisfaction Index (`www.theacsi.org`)

Response and Fulfillment

Email response and fulfillment times among top e-tailers (Q4 2003):

Merchant	Time to Answer Email	Business Days to Receive Item	Time to Shop (minutes)	Clicks to Check Out
Ann Taylor	3 hr/40 min	3	5	5
CompUSA	2 hr/0 min	2	4	5
Crate & Barrell	16 hr/0 min	4	4	6
Crutchfield	1 hr/1 min	5	4	6
JC Penny	8 hr/36 min	Store pickup	3	3
J Crew	23 hr/14 min	5	4	5
Lands' End	2 hr/3 min	2	3	4
Men's Wearhouse	1 hr/13 min	Store pickup	3	2
Orvis	2 hr/44 min	5	3	4
Petco	4 hr/15 min	2	3	5
Powell's	8 hr/28 min	5	4	6
RedEnvelope	0 hr/8 min	4	4	3
Average of 100 Sites Shopped	**25 hr/0 min**	**4.4**	**3.67**	**4.6**

Source: e-tailing group, inc. (`www.e-tailing.com`)

It's a Fraud, Part 1

Number of complaints received by the Internet Fraud Complaint Center in 2002: 75,063

Among complainants, 71% are male, the average age is 39.4 years, and over one-third live in either California, Florida, Texas, or New York. Two-thirds of complainants reported they had email contact with the perpetrator; just 18.7% had contact through a Web page.

Source: Internet Fraud Complaint Center (`www.ifc-cfbi.gov`)

It's a Fraud, Part 2

Most common complaints to the Internet Fraud Complaint Center:

Online auction fraud	46%
Non-delivery of merchandise and payment	31%
Credit/debit card fraud	12%

Other common complaints: investment fraud, business fraud, confidence fraud, and identity theft.

Source: Internet Fraud Complaint Center
          (www.ifccfbi.gov)

It's a Fraud, Part 3

Highest median dollar losses among reported frauds:

Nigerian Letter fraud	$3,864
Identity theft	$2,000
Check fraud	$1,100

Source: Internet Fraud Complaint Center
          (www.ifccfbi.gov)

Online Banking, Part 1

Online banking and financial activities (2003):

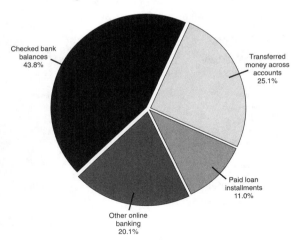

Source: comScore Media Metrix (www.comscore.com)

Online Banking, Part 2

Number of households that bank and pay bills online (millions, projected):

	# Bank Online	% Pay Online
2003	29.6	50%
2004	35.3	57%
2005	40.9	64%
2006	46.2	71%
2007	51.3	78%
2008	56.0	85%

Source: Jupiter Research (www.jupiterresearch.com)

PLAYING GAMES

Demographics

The average age of a game player is 29 years; 61% are male. Half of all Americans aged six and over play computer and videogames.

Source: Entertainment Software Association
          (www.theesa.com)

Game Sales

U.S. sales of computer and videogame software (billions):

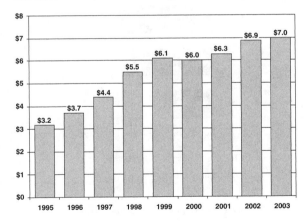

Source: Entertainment Software Association
          (www.theesa.com)

Video Game Genres

Video Game sales by genre (2003):

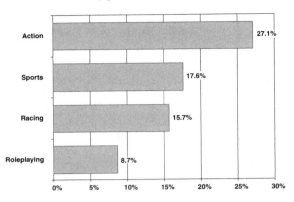

Action	27.1%
Sports	17.6%
Racing	15.7%
Roleplaying	8.7%

Source: Electronic Software Association (www.theesa.com)

PC Game Genres

Computer game sales by genre (2003):

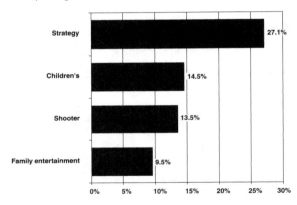

Strategy	27.1%
Children's	14.5%
Shooter	13.5%
Family entertainment	9.5%

Source: Electronic Software Association (www.theesa.com)

Most Popular Online Game Sites

Most-visited game-related sites (January 2004):

Site	Market Share
Yahoo! Games	12.2%
Pogo	11.9%
Sandboxer	4.2%
Neo Pets	3.7%
MSN Gaming Zone	3.1%

Site	Market Share
Gamefaqs	2.6%
Yahoo! Fantasy Basketball	2.3%
Yahoo! Fantasy Sports	1.8%
CheatPlanet	1.1%
GameSpot	1.1%

Source: Hitwise (www.hitwise.com)

Stickiest Online Game Sites

Hours spent per visit for the top online games sites (May 2004):

Rank	Site	Time per person (hh:mm:ss)
1	Slingo	4:08:48
2	EA Online	2:29:40
3	MSN Games	2:04:26
4	AOL Games	1:51:51
5	jigzone.com	1:34:50

Source: Nielsen/NetRatings (www.nielsen-netratings.com)

Online Games Are More Popular Than...

Responses of various groups when asked if they play online games more than other specified activities (2004):

Alternate activity	Adults	Teens	Males	Females
Working out/ exercising	64%	61%	59%	66%
Hiking/outdoor activities	58%	51%	51%	62%
Reading books	45%	50%	50%	42%
Renting/ watching movies	44%	41%	40%	45%
Watching TV	22%	23%	19%	24%

Source: Digital Marketing Services/America Online (www.dmsdallas.com)

CONSUMER ELECTRONICS

Electronics Sales

Manufacturer-to-dealer sales of the following consumer electronics products in 2003 (millions):

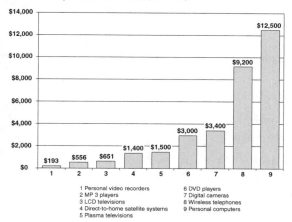

1 Personal video recorders
2 MP 3 players
3 LCD televisions
4 Direct-to-home satellite systems
5 Plasma televisions
6 DVD players
7 Digital cameras
8 Wireless telephones
9 Personal computers

Source: Consumer Electronics Association (www.ce.org)

DVD Players

U.S. DVD player sales since the format's launch in March 1997 (in millions of units):

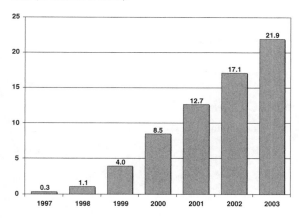

Source: Consumer Electronics Association (www.ce.org)

PDA Sales

Worldwide PDA sales (millions of units):

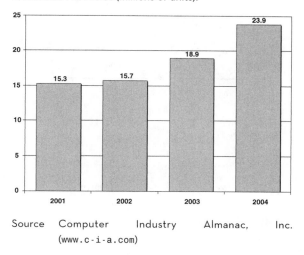

Source Computer Industry Almanac, Inc. (www.c-i-a.com)

Digital Video Recorders, Part 1

Digital video recorder (DVR) interest and ownership, by gender (2004):

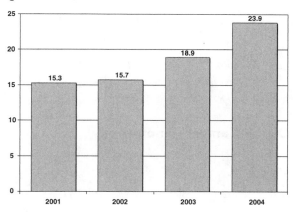

Source: Parks Associates (www.parsassociates.com)

Digital Video Recorders, Part 2

Percentage of DVR users who delay watching programs in order to use the ad-skipping features:

What Percentage of Programs Do You Start Late?	Percentage of Respondents
0%	17%
1–20%	24%
21–40%	10%
41–60%	17%
61–80%	12%
81–99%	10%
100%	10%

Source: Lyra Research (www.lyraresearch.com)

Digital Camera Vendors

Top U.S. digital camera vendors (2003):

Rank	Vendor
1	Sony
2	Canon
3	Kodak
4	Olympus
5	Fuji
6	Hewlett-Packard
7	Nikon

Source: *2004 Consumer Digital Camera Forecast, North America,* InfoTrends/CAP Ventures (www.infotrends-rgi.com)

Digital Camera Penetration

Penetration of digital cameras in the U.S. market (year-end 2004): 40%

Source: *2004 Consumer Digital Camera Forecast, North America,* InfoTrends/CAP Ventures (www.infotrends-rgi.com)

Digital Images

Number of digital images captured worldwide in 2004: 29 billion

Source: *2004 Consumer Digital Camera Forecast, North America,* InfoTrends/CAP Ventures (www.infotrends-rgi.com)

Cell Phones Are Everywhere

Number of Americans who owned a cellular telephone in 1994: 16 million

Number of Americans who owned a cellular telephone in 2000: 110 million

Number of Americans who owned a cellular telephone in August 2004: 168 million

Source: U.S. Census Bureau/Cellular Telephone Industry Association (www.ctia.gov)

Cell Phone Cities

Top five U.S. cities for cell phone penetration (2003):

Rank	City	Penetration
1	Atlanta, GA	75%
2	Detroit, MI	74%
3	Austin, TX	72%
4	Washington, D.C.	72%
5	Miami/Ft. Lauderdale, FL	72%

Source: Scarborough Research (www.scarborough.com)

Non-Cell Phone Cities

U.S. cities with the lowest cell phone penetration (2003):

Rank	City	Penetration
1	Charleston, WV	47%
2	Wilkes-Barre, PA	52%
3	Buffalo, NY	53%
4	Syracuse, NY	54%
5	Lexington, KY	55%

Source: Scarborough Research (www.scarborough.com)

Help!

Which of the following technology products do you find yourself needing the most technological help?

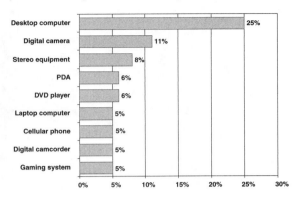

Desktop computer	25%
Digital camera	11%
Stereo equipment	8%
PDA	6%
DVD player	6%
Laptop computer	5%
Cellular phone	5%
Digital camcorder	5%
Gaming system	5%

Source: Click IQ/Best Buy (www.clickiq.com)

Technologies We're Least Likely to Give Up

Percentage of specific audiences who say it would be very hard to give up certain technologies (2003):

Media	Young Tech Elites	Older Wired Baby Boomers	The Wired Gen-Xers	Rest	All
Computer	74%	64%	54%	25%	**40%**
Internet	68%	55%	51%	22%	**39%**
Cell phone	58%	50%	45%	31%	**38%**
E-mail	57%	49%	44%	23%	**36%**
Telephone	56%	57%	67%	63%	**64%**
Television	48%	50%	46%	48%	**48%**
Cable TV	40%	25%	34%	40%	**37%**
PDA	23%	32%	26%	15%	**24%**
Newspaper	12%	21%	14%	17%	**19%**
Magazine	11%	16%	11%	11%	**13%**
% of total respondents	**6%**	**6%**	**18%**	**70%**	**100%**

Source: Pew Internet & American Life Project (www.pewinternet.org)

Inventions We Hate— But Can't Live Without

Which invention do we hate the most but can't live without?

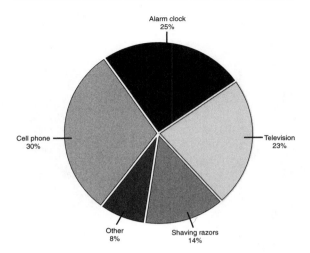

- Alarm clock 25%
- Television 23%
- Shaving razors 14%
- Other 8%
- Cell phone 30%

Source: *2004 Lemelson-MIT Invention Index*, Taylor Nelson Sofres Intersearch (mit.edu/invent/)

Leo's Little Black Book

ThinkPad

ANTIVIRUS AND SECURITY

Command Software Systems
7121 Fairway Drive, Ste. 102
Palm Beach Gardens, FL
33418

561-575-3200

www.commandsoftware.com

F-Secure, Inc.
100 Century Center Court, Suite 700
San Jose, CA
95112

408-938-6700

www.f-secure.com

McAfee.com
3965 Freedom Circle
Santa Clara, CA
95054

(888) VIRUSNO

www.mcafee.com

Symantec Corporation
20330 Stevens Creek Blvd.
Cupertino, California
95014

408-517-8000

www.symantec.com

AUDIO/VIDEO SYSTEMS AND COMPONENTS

Bose Corp.
The Mountain
Framingham, Massachusetts
01701-9168

508-766-1099

www.bose.com

Denon
Denon Electronics
19 Chapin Road
P.O. Box 867
Pine Brook, New Jersey
07058-9777

973-396-0810

www.denon.com

Harman Kardon
250 Crossways Park Drive
Woodbury, New York
11797

516-496-3400

www.harmankardon.com

Hitachi America, Ltd.
Home Electronics Division
900 Hitachi Way
Chula Vista, CA 91914

619-591-5200

www.hitachi.com/tv/

Infinity Systems, Inc.
250 Crossways Park Drive
Woodbury, New York
11797

800-553-3332

www.infinitysystems.com

JBL Consumer Products
80 Crossways Park West
Woodbury, New York
11797

800-336-4525

www.jbl.com

JVC Company of America
1700 Valley Road
Wayne, New Jersey
07470

800-526-5308

www.jvc.com

Kenwood USA Corporation
P.O. Box 22745
Long Beach, California
90801-5745

310-639-9000

www.kenwoodusa.com

Mitsubishi Digital Electronics America, Inc.
9351 Jeronimo Road
Irvine, California
92618

949-465-6000

www.mitsubishi-tv.com

Onkyo USA Corporation
18 Park Way
Upper Saddle River, New Jersey
07458

201-785-2600

www.onkyousa.com

Panasonic Consumer Electronics
1 Panasonic Way
Secaucus, New Jersey
07094

201-348-7000

www.panasonic.com

Pioneer Electronics, Inc.
2265 East 220th Street
Long Beach, California
90810

310-952-2000

www.pioneerelectronics.com

Polk Audio, Inc.
5601 Metro Dr.
Baltimore, Maryland
21215

410-358-3600

www.polkaudio.com

RCA
Thomson Multimedia, Inc.
10330 North Meridian Street
Indianapolis, Indiana
46290-1976

317-587-3000

www.rca.com

Sony Electronics
3300 Zanker Rd.
San Jose, California
95134

800-222-7669

www.sonystyle.com

Toshiba America, Inc.
1251 Avenue of the Americas
Suite 4110
New York, NY
10020

212-596-0620

www.toshiba.com

Audio/Video Systems and Components

Yamaha Electronics Corporation, USA
6660 Orangethorpe Avenue
Buena Park, California
90620

714-522-9105

www.yamaha.com

BATTERIES

Duracell, Inc.
Berkshire Industrial Park
Bethel, Connecticut
06801

1-800-551-2355

www.duracell.com

NEC Electronics, Inc.
2880 Scott Blvd.
Santa Clara, California
95052

408-588-6000

www.necel.com

Panasonic Industrial Co.
2 Panasonic Way
Secaucus, New Jersey
07094

201-348-7010

www.panasonic.com

Tadiran
2 Seaview Blvd.
Port Washington, New York
11050

516-621-4980

www.tadiranbat.com

CABLES AND NETWORKING

Belden Wire and Cable
P.O. Box 1980
2200 U.S. Highway 27 South
Richmond, Indiana
47374

765-983-5200

www.belden.com

D-Link Systems, Inc.
17595 Mt. Herrmann
Fountain Valley, CA
92708

800-326-1688

www.dlink.com

Linksys
121 Theory Drive
Irvine, CA
92612

949-261-1288

www.linksys.com

Micro Computer Cable Company, Inc.
12200 Delta Dr.
Taylor, Michigan
48180

734-946-9700

http://www.mc3llc.com/

Monster Cable Products, Inc.
455 Valley Drive
Brisbane, California
94005

415-840-2000

www.monstercable.com

Smart Cable Company
7403 Lakewood Drive #14
Lakewood, Washington
98499

253-474-9967

www.smart-cable.com

CELLULAR PHONES

Ericcson
North American Headquarters
6300 Legacy Drive
Plano, Texas
75024

972-583-0000

www.ericsson.com

Motorola, Inc.
1303 E. Algonquin Rd.
Schaumburg, Illinois
60196

800-331-6456

www.motorola.com

Nokia Americas
6000 Connection Drive
Irving, Texas
75039

888-665-4228

www.nokiausa.com

CELLULAR PHONE SERVICES

AT&T Wireless Services, Inc.
7277 164th Ave. NE, Bldg. 1
Redmond, Washington
98052

425-580-6000

www.attws.com

Cingular Wireless
Glenridge Highlands Two
5565 Glenridge Connector, Ste. 1401
Atlanta, Georgia
30342

404-236-6000

www.cingular.com

Nextel Communications, Inc.
2001 Edmund Halley Dr.
Reston, Virginia
20191

703-433-4000

www.nextel.com

Verizon Wireless
180 Washington Valley Rd.
Bedminster, New Jersey
07921

908-306-7000

www.verizonwireless.com

COMPUTER ACCESSORIES

Northwest Computer Accessories
12310 SE Hwy 212
Clackamas, OR
97015

503-656-3195

www.nwca.com

Targus, Inc.
1211 N. Miller Street
Anaheim, California
92806

714-765-5555

www.targus.com

COMPUTER HARDWARE

Acer America Corp.
2641 Orchard Parkway
San Jose, California
95134-2073

408-432-6200

www.acer.com/us/

Apple Computer, Inc.
1 Infinite Loop
Cupertino, California
95014

408-996-1010

www.apple.com

Dell Computer Corporation
1 Dell Way
Round Rock, Texas
78682

512-338-4400

www.dell.com

Gateway, Inc.
14303 Gateway Place
Poway, California
92064

858-848-3401

www.gateway.com

Hewlett-Packard Company
3000 Hanover St.
Palo Alto, California
94304

650-857-1501

www.hp.com

IBM Corporation
1133 Westchester Avenue
White Plains, New York
10604

800-426-4968

www.ibm.com

Sony Electronics
3300 Zanker Rd.
San Jose, California
95134

800-222-7669

www.sel.sony.com

Toshiba America, Inc.
Computer Systems Division
9740 Irvine Blvd.
Irvine, California
92618-1697

949-583-3000

www.csd.toshiba.com

COMPUTER MONITORS

CTX International, Inc.
16720 E. Gale Avenue
City of Industry, California
91745

877-893-6886

www.ctxintl.com

LG Electronics
1000 Sylvan Ave.
Englewood Cliffs, New Jersey
07632

1-800-243-0000

www.lgeus.com

NEC-Mitsubishi Electronics Display of America
1250 N. Arlington Heights Rd., Suite 500
Itasca, Illinois
60143-1248

800-632-4662

www.necmitsubishi.com

ViewSonic
381 Brea Canyon Road
Walnut, California
91789

909-444-8888

www.viewsonic.com

COMPUTER AND CONSUMER ELECTRONICS RETAILERS

Amazon.com, Inc.
1200 12th Ave. South, Suite 1200
Seattle, Washington
98144

206-266-1000

www.amazon.com

Best Buy Co., Inc.
P.O. Box 949
Minneapolis, MN
55440

1-888-BEST BUY (237-8289)

www.bestbuy.com

Circuit City Group
9950 Mayland Dr.
Richmond, Virginia
23233

804-527-4000

www.circuitcity.com

CompUSA, Inc.
14951 N. Dallas Parkway
Dallas, Texas
75240

972-982-4000

www.compusa.com

Computer Discount Warehouse (CDW)
200 N. Milwaukee Ave.
Vernon Hills, Illinois
60061

847-465-6000

www.cdw.com

Crutchfield
1 Crutchfield Park
Charlottesville, Virginia
22811-9097

800-955-3000

www.crutchfield.com

PC Connection
Route 101A
730 Milford Rd.
Merrimack, New Hampshire
03054-4631

603-355-6005

www.pcconnection.com

COMPUTER SOFTWARE

Adobe Systems, Inc.
345 Park Ave.
San Jose, California
95110-2704

408-536-6000

www.adobe.com

Computer Software

Autodesk, Inc.
111 McInnis Parkway
San Rafael, California
94903

415-507-5000

www.autodesk.com

Intuit
2632 Marine Way
Mountain View, CA
94043

650-944-6000

www.intuit.com

Lotus Software
IBM Corporation
1133 Westchester Avenue
White Plains, New York
10604

1-800-IBM-4YOU

www.lotus.com

Microsoft Corporation
One Microsoft Way
Redmond, Washington
98052-6399

425-882-8080

www.microsoft.com

DIGITAL CAMERAS

Canon U.S.A., Inc.
One Canon Plaza
Lake Success, New York
11042

516-328-5000

www.usa.canon.com

Kodak
343 State St.
Rochester, New York
14650

585-724-4000

www.kodak.com

Nikon
1300 Walt Whitman Road
Melville, New York
11747

800-645-6687

www.nikonusa.com

Olympus America, Inc.
2 Corporate Center Drive
Melville, New York
11747

800-645-8160

www.olympusamerica.com

Sony Electronics
3300 Zanker Rd.
San Jose, California
95134

800-222-7669

www.sel.sony.com

DIGITAL SATELLITE SYSTEMS
DIRECTV
2230 E. Imperial Hwy.
El Segundo, California
90245

310-535-5000

www.directv.com

DISH Network/Echostar
5701 S. Santa Fe Dr.
Littleton, Colorado
80120

1-800-333-DISH

www.dishnetwork.com

ISPS AND ONLINE SERVICES

America Online
22000 AOL Way
Dulles, Virginia
20166-9323

703-265-1000

www.aol.com

CompuServe Interactive Services
Customer Service Department
P.O. Box 17300
Jacksonville, FL
32245-7300

614-457-8600

www.compuserve.com

EarthLink, Inc.
1375 Peachtree St. 7 North
Atlanta, Georgia
30309

404-815-0770

www.earthlink.com

MSN
Microsoft Corporation
One Microsoft Way
Redmond, Washington
98052-6399

425-882-8080

www.msn.com

KEYBOARDS AND MICE

KeyTronic Corporation
4424 North Sullivan Rd.
Spokane, Washington
99214

509-928-8000

www.keytronic.com

Logitech
6505 Kaiser Drive
Fremont, California
94555

510-795-8500

www.logitech.com

Microsoft Corporation
One Microsoft Way
Redmond, Washington
98052-6399

425-882-8080

www.microsoft.com

Mitsumi Electronics Corporation
5808 W. Campus Circle Dr.
Irving, Texas
75063

972-550-7300

www.mitsumi.com/indexusa.html

MEDIA PLAYER SOFTWARE

MusicMatch
16935 West Bernardo Drive
San Diego, California
92127

858-835-8360

www.musicmatch.com

Media Player Software

Windows Media Player
Microsoft Corporation
One Microsoft Way
Redmond, Washington
98052-6399

425-882-8080

www.microsoft.com/windowsmedia/

WinAmp
Nullsoft/America Online
22000 AOL Way
Dulles, Virginia
20166-9323

703-265-1000

www.winamp.com

MEMORY

Centon Electronics, Inc.
15 Argonaut
Aliso Viejo, CA
92656

800-836-1986

www.centon.com

Kingston Technology Corporation
17600 Newhope St.
Fountain Valley, California
92708

714-435-2600

www.kingston.com

PDAS

Audiovox Communications Corporation
150 Marcus Blvd.
Hauppauge, New York
11788

631-231-7750

www.audiovox.com

Casio
570 Mount Pleasant Ave.
Dover, New Jersey
07801

888-204-7765

www.casio.com/personalpcs/

Hewlett-Packard Company
3000 Hanover St.
Palo Alto, California
94304

650-857-1501

www.hp.com

NEC USA, Inc.
2371 S. President's Dr., Suite A
West Valley City, Utah
84120

888-632-8701

www.neccomp.com/MobilePro/

Palm, Source, Inc.
1240 Crossman Avenue
Sunnyvale, CA
94089

408-400-3000

www.palmsource.com

Palm One, Inc.
400 N. McCarthy Blvd.
Milpitas, CA
95035

408-503-7000

www.palmone.com

Sony Electronics
3300 Zanker Rd.
San Jose, California
95134

800-222-7669

www.sel.sony.com

Toshiba America, Inc.
Computer Systems Division
9740 Irvine Blvd.
Irvine, California
92618-1697

949-583-3000

www.csd.toshiba.com

PDA CASES AND ACCESSORIES

Brenthaven (cases)
300 Harris Avenue
Bellingham, Washington
98225

360-752-5537

www.brenthaven.com

iBIZ Technology (accessories)
2238 W. Lone Cactus Dr., Suite 200
Phoenix, Arizona
85027

623-492-9200

www.ibizcorp.com

Pentopia (styli)
60 Commerce Drive
Trumbull, Connecticut
06611

203-381-4854

www.pentopia.com

Pharos (GPS navigators)
411 Amapola Avenue
Torrance, California
90501-1478

310-212-7088

www.pharosgps.com

Socket Communications (cards and connectors)
37400 Central Court
Newark, California
94560

510-744-2700

www.socketcom.com

Targus, Inc. (cases and accessories)
1211 N. Miller Street
Anaheim, California
92806

714-765-5555

www.targus.com

PERSONAL VIDEO RECORDERS
ReplayTV
2600 San Tomas Expressway
Santa Clara, CA
95051-0953

866-286-3662

www.replaytv.com

TiVo, Inc.
2160 Gold Street
P.O. Box 2160
Alviso, California
95002-2160

877-367-8486

www.tivo.com

Personal Video Recorders

Weaknees.com
3355 La Cienega Place
Los Angeles, CA
90016-3116

888-932-5633

www.weaknees.com

Rio
2600 San Tomas Expressway
Santa Clara, CA
95051-0953

254-299-2759

www.digitalnetworksna.com/rioaudio/

PORTABLE MP3 PLAYERS

Apple Computer, Inc.
1 Infinite Loop
Cupertino, California
95014

408-996-1010

www.apple.com

Audiovox Communications Corporation
555 Wireless Boulevard
Hauppauge, New York
11788

631-233-3300

www.audiovox.com

Creative Labs, Inc.
1901 McCarthy Boulevard
Milpitas, California
95035

800-998-5227

www.creative.com

RCA Lyra
Thomson Multimedia, Inc.
10330 North Meridian Street
Indianapolis, Indiana
46290-1976

317-587-3000

www.lyrazone.com

PRINTERS

Brother International Corporation
100 Somerset Corporate Boulevard
Bridgewater, New Jersey
08807-0911

908-704-1700

www.brother.com/usa/

Canon U.S.A., Inc.
One Canon Plaza
Lake Success, New York
11042

516-328-5000

www.usa.canon.com

Epson America, Inc.
3840 Kilroy Airport Way
Long Beach, California
90806

562-981-3840

www.epson.com

Hewlett-Packard Company
3000 Hanover St.
Palo Alto, California
94304

650-857-1501

www.hp.com

Lexmark
740 West New Circle Rd.
Lexington, Kentucky
40550

859-232-2000

www.lexmark.com

REMOTE CONTROLS

Crestron Electronics, Inc.
15 Volvo Drive
Rockleigh, New Jersey
07647

201-767-3400

www.crestron.com

Logitech (Harmony Remotes)
2355 Skymark Avenue, Suite 200
Mississauga, Ontario L4W 4Y6
Canada

905-273-4571

www.logitech.com/harmony

One for All Remotes
Universal Electronics
6101 Gateway Drive
Cypress, California
90630-4841

714-820-1000

www.ueic.com

Philips Pronto
Philips Electronics North America
1251 Avenue of the Americas
New York, New York
10020-1104

888-486-6272

www.pronto.philips.com

REMOVABLE STORAGE MEDIA AND MEMORY CARDS

IBM Microdrive
IBM Corporation
1133 Westchester Avenue
White Plains, New York
10604

800-426-4968

www.storage.ibm.com/hdd/micro/

Iomega Corporation
10955 Vista Sorrento Parkway
San Diego, CA
92130

858-314-7000

www.iomega.com

Kingston Technology Corporation
17600 Newhope St.
Fountain Valley, California
92708

714-435-2600

www.kingston.com

Pretec Electronics Corporation
40979 Encyclopedia Circle
Fremont, California
94538

510-440-0535

www.pretec.com

SanDisk
140 Caspian Court
Sunnyvale, California
94089

408-542-0500

www.sandisk.com

SCANNERS

Hewlett-Packard Company
3000 Hanover St.
Palo Alto, California
94304

650-857-1501

www.hp.com

Microtek
3715 Doolittle Dr.
Redondo Beach, California
90278-1226

310-687-5800

www.microtekusa.com

Visioneer, Inc.
5673 Gibraltar Drive, Suite 150
Pleasanton, California
94588

888-229-4172

www.visioneer.com

SOUND CARDS

Adaptec
691 S. Milpitas Blvd.
Milpitas, California
93035

408-945-8600

www.adaptec.com

Creative Labs, Inc.
1901 McCarthy Boulevard
Milpitas, California
95035

800-998-5227

www.creative.com

VIDEO GAMES

Microsoft Xbox
Microsoft Corporation
One Microsoft Way
Redmond, Washington
98052-6399

425-882-8080

www.xbox.com

Nintendo of America
P.O. Box 957
Redmond, Washington
98073

800-255-3700

www.nintendo.com

Sony PlayStation
P.O. Box 5888
San Mateo, California
94402-0888

800-697-7266

www.playstation.com

Glossary

1.85:1

1.85:1 The most common wide-screen aspect ratio used in theatrical films.

2G Second-generation wireless; unlike analog first-generation products, 2G phones and networks incorporate digital technology.

2.35:1 The widest possible aspect ratio used in theatrical films.

2.4GHz band An unlicensed RF band (between 2.4GHz and 2.48GHz) used to carry signals from various types of wireless devices. Also called the *ISM band*.

3G Third-generation wireless; the upcoming third generation of cellular phones and networks, designed for high-speed data transfer in addition to standard voice communication.

4:3 The NTSC standard aspect ratio for traditional TVs; a 4:3 picture is four units wide by three units high. Also measured as 1.33:1.

5.1 Dolby Digital produces five separate surround channels plus one subwoofer channel—thus the "5.1" designation.

6.1 Surround format with six separate surround channels plus one subwoofer channel; used in Dolby Digital EX and DTS ES.

7.1 Surround format with seven separate surround channels plus one subwoofer channel.

16:9 The aspect ratio used in HDTV broadcasts; a 16:9 picture is 16 units wide by 9 units high. The 16:9 aspect ratio presents a wider image area than the traditional 4:3 ratio. Also measured as 1.78:1.

780p One of the two main HDTV formats; transmits 780 lines of resolution with progressive scanning.

802.11a More accurately described as IEEE 802.11a, this is an RF-based technology designed for larger wireless networks.

802.11b More accurately described as IEEE 802.11b, this is an RF-based technology designed for home and small business wireless networks. Also known as *Wi-Fi*, 802.11b uses the 2.4GHz band.

802.11g More accurately described as IEEE 802.11g, this is a faster version of the 802.11b Wi-Fi technology, still using the 2.4GHz band.

1080i One of the two main HDTV formats; transmits 1,080 lines of resolution with interlaced scanning.

8mm Recording format for camcorders that uses a videocassette with 8mm tape.

A

A/D converter Analog/digital converter; a processor that converts analog electrical signals into digital data. The converter samples the electrical signal every few milliseconds, and then the signal is quantized into a digital "word." The larger the digital word, the more accurate the sample.

A/V Audio/video.

AAC Advanced Audio Coding, the audio format used by Apple's iTunes and iPod. AAC offers better sound quality than MP3 files, along with strong digital rights management to prevent unauthorized use.

AC-3 Audio Coding 3; Dolby's digital-audio data compression algorithm, the standard format for prerecorded DVDs and HDTV broadcasts.

access point A base station that connects portable wireless devices to a larger public network. Similar to a LAN access point.

acoustic suspension A type of speaker enclosure that uses a sealed box to provide accurate, tight bass response.

active desktop Enhanced functionality within Windows that enables Web pages to be turned into wallpaper or desktop items that are updated automatically.

active server page A specification for a dynamically created Web that uses ActiveX scripting, usually via VBScript or JScript code. When a browser requests an ASP page, the Web server generates a page with HTML code and sends it back to the browser.

ad hijacking Adware that serves up ads from the adware's sponsors, sometimes on top of a Web site's normal banner ads.

ADAT Alesis Digital Audio Tape; a form of digital audio tape developed by Alesis for its digital multitrack recorders. It uses eight tracks of 16-bit/44.1KHz digital audio on consumer S-VHS tape.

address The pointer to a particular Web page (also known as a *URL*). Also the specific identifier for a person's email inbox.

ADN Advanced Digital Network; usually refers to a 56Kbps leased line.

ADR Additional Dialog Recording; the process of replacing film dialog by overdubbing new vocals that are recorded during postproduction.

ADSL Asymmetric Digital Subscriber Line; a type of DSL line where the upload speed is different from the download speed. (Usually the download speed is several orders of magnitude greater than the upload speed.)

adware Stealth software that tracks your online activity and sends that data to a marketing or advertising company; some adware also uses that data to serve up replacement ads on specific Web sites.

AGP Accelerated Graphics Port; a graphics interface specification, based on the PCI bus, designed for three-dimensional graphics.

AI Artificial intelligence; the use of computers to solve problems and process information in ways that approximate human thought.

AIM AOL Instant Messenger; America Online's instant messaging service.

algorithm A mathematical process or formula used to create a number or solve a particular problem.

aliasing Distortion caused by a low sample rate.

alpha geek The de facto expert even the most experienced users turn to when they have a technical problem.

amplifier An electronic device that uses capacitors or (in olden days) vacuum tubes to increase the strength of an electronic signal. An audio amplifier amplifies audio signals that are then output to one or more speakers.

AMPS Advanced Mobile Phone System; the original standard specification for analog mobile telephony systems. To optimize the use of transmission frequencies, AMPS divides geographic areas into cells—hence the phrase "cellular phone."

analog A means of transmitting or storing data using a continuously variable signal. Prone to signal degradation; does not always accurately reproduce the original.

anamorphic A process that condenses the image in the source material to be expanded by the display device. Also a type of widescreen display format available on selected DVD discs, which features increased resolution when played back on a 16:9 ratio TV.

anchor See hyperlink.

android A machine made in human form.

Annie An orphaned Web page, as in "little orphan Annie."

anonymizer A Web site or service that enables anonymous Web browsing or email communications.

antialiasing A technique used to smooth the *jaggies*.

antivirus program A software program that scans for and cleans viruses from computer systems.

AOL America Online, the largest commercial online service and ISP.

aperture The opening in a camera lens that controls how much light goes through to the film or image sensor.

API Application Programming Interface; a series of functions that programs can use to make the operating system perform basic operations. Windows, for example, has several classes of APIs that deal with telephony, messaging, and other operations.

applet A simple program or utility designed to be executed from within another application.

application Another word for a computer software program. Common applications include word processors, spreadsheets, and Web browsers.

application cache High-speed, temporary, chip-based storage that is specifically designed for a given application.

APS Advanced Photo System; a new film-based imaging system designed for better and better-documented photographs.

Archie A (now outdated) tool for finding files stored on FTP servers.

archive Storing computer files onto some type of long-term storage medium.

ARPANet Advanced Research Projects Agency Network; the forerunner to the current Internet, developed in the late 1960s by the U.S. Department of Defense.

artifact   Misinterpreted information in a .JPG image, typically seen as color or line faults.

ASCII   American Standard Code for Information Interchange (pronounced "ask-ee"); a binary code used to represent English text characters as numbers, with each letter assigned a number from 0 to 127. By replacing text with numbers, computers can transfer information more easily.

ASDR   Attack, sustain, decay, and release; the four different stages of a sound's envelope.

ASIC   Application-Specific Integrated Circuit (pronounced "ay-sik"); a chip designed for a particular application rather than for an all-purpose microprocessor.

ASIN   Amazon Standard Item Number, the product numbers used by Amazon.com.

ASIO   Audio Stream Input/Output; a multichannel audio transfer protocol developed by Steinberg North America in 1997 for audio/MIDI-sequencing applications that allows access to the multichannel capabilities of sound cards.

ASP   *See active server page.*

aspect ratio   The ratio between the width and height of a video display. The NTSC television standard is 4:3, whereas HDTV uses a 16:9 ratio. Some wide-screen movies use an even wider ratio, either 1.85:1 or 2.35:1.

asymmetrical   A type of connection that operates at two different speeds upstream and downstream.

asynchronous   A type of connection that permits data to flow in only one direction at a time. Also known as *half-duplex*.

AT commands   Audio/telephony commands used to control all the functions that a telephone or data modem is capable of.

ATM   Asynchronous Transfer Mode. (In the noncomputer world, stands for automatic teller machine.)

attachment   A file attached to an email message.

attack   In the world of audio, the beginning stage of sound's envelope.

audio   Sound.

audio/video receiver   A combination of amplifier and preamplifier that controls both audio and video inputs and outputs. Most a/v receivers include some sort of surround-sound decoder, either Dolby Pro Logic or the newer (and slightly more expensive) Dolby Digital. Also called an *a/v receiver*.

authentication   The process of determining whether someone or something is, in fact, who or what it is purporting to be.

auto exposure   A feature of digital cameras that automatically selects the optimal exposure settings for best image quality.

auto focus   A feature of digital cameras that automatically focuses the camera lens on the main subject in the picture.

.AVI   Audio Video Interleave; Microsoft's file format (and extension) for Windows-compatible audio/video files.

B

B2B   Business-to-business; the exchange of products, services, or information between two or more businesses. (Contrast with B2C, which describes interaction between businesses and consumers.)

B2C   Business-to-consumer; the exchange of products, services, or information between businesses and consumers. Also known as *retailing*.

B2E   Business-to-employee; an approach to business management in which the focus of business is the employee rather than the consumer.

B2G   Business-to-government; the exchange of products, services, or information between businesses and government entities.

back door   Undocumented (and typically unauthorized) entry point into a system.

back door Trojan   A *Trojan horse* file that opens a back door on your system for potential unauthorized remote access.

backbone   A high-speed connection that forms a major pathway within a network or over the Internet.

backtracing software   Software used to trace an attacker's identity and host ISP.

backup   The process of creating a compressed copy of the data on your hard disk, to be used in case of an emergency.

balanced cable   An audio cable that has two conductive wires, has a ground, and is often shielded. These cables are used to reduce interference and noise.

bandwidth   The amount of data that can be transmitted in a fixed amount of time. For digital devices, bandwidth usually is expressed in bits per second (bps) or bytes per second (Bps). For analog devices, bandwidth is expressed in cycles per second, or hertz (Hz). Specific to audio, bandwidth refers to the range of frequencies a component can reproduce; the larger the bandwidth, the better the sound or picture.

banner ad   A graphic advertisement placed on a Web page. Banner ads are typically rectangles about 460 pixels wide by 60 pixels high.

BASIC   Beginner's All-purpose Symbolic Instruction Code; an early programming language that is still among the simplest and most popular of programming languages today. BASIC (sometimes written as Basic) continues to be widely used because it can be learned quickly, its statements are easy to read by other programmers, and support is available on most operating systems. Microsoft's *Visual Basic* adds object-oriented features and a graphical user interface to the standard text-based BASIC language.

bass reflex   A type of speaker enclosure that includes a precisely designed or "tuned" opening in the enclosure. It's typically louder—though less accurate—than acoustic suspension speakers.

batch file   An executable file containing separate lines of commands—actually, "batches" of commands.

baud   The measure of how many bits a modem can send or receive each second.

bay   Within a PC's system unit, the space for installing an internal drive or peripheral.

BBS   Bulletin board system; an electronic online meeting and messaging system, accessible by dial-in modem connections, popular in the 1980s and pre-Internet 1990s. Freestanding BBSs have been mostly obsoleted by Internet-based message boards and communities.

beam   The process of transferring files or data from one device, such as a PDA, to another device, typically through an IrDA link.

beta   A prerelease version of a software program, typically in the process of being tested for bugs. (This process is called *beta testing*.)

BHO   Browser Helper Object; a small software program that attaches itself to your Web browser.

biamplification   The practice of using separate amplifiers to power the low-frequency and high-frequency speakers.

binary   Information consisting entirely of 0s and 1s. In the computer world, also refers to files (such as image files) that are not simply ASCII text files.

binhex   BINary HEXadecimal; a method for converting non-text (binary) files into ASCII.

biometrics   The science of measuring and analyzing unique biological identifiers, such as fingerprints, retinas, voice patterns, facial patterns, and so on.

BIOS   The basic input/output system that interacts with computer hardware.

biotechnology   The science of employing living organisms (or parts of organisms) to make or modify products, improve plants or animals, or develop microorganisms for specific uses.

bipole   A speaker design that generates equal amounts of in-phase sound both forward and backward. Typically used for rear-channel speakers in a surround-sound setup.

bit   Binary DigIT; the smallest element of computer storage, a single digit (0 or 1) in a binary system; 8 bits equal 1 *byte*. Physically, a bit can be a transistor or capacitor in a memory cell, a magnetic domain on disk or tape, a reflective spot on optical media, or a high or low voltage pulsing through a circuit.

bit depth   The number of bits used to represent colors or tones. 2-bit color is black and white; 4-bit color produces 64 colors or shades of gray; 8-bit color produces 256 colors; 16-bit color produces 32,000 colors; 24-bit color produces 16.7 million colors; 30/32-bit color produces billions of individual colors.

bit rate   The transmission speed of binary-coded data. *See* data rate.

bitmap   A binary representation of an image or font consisting of rows and columns of dots. The broader the color spectrum, the more bits are required for each pixel. For simple monochrome images, 1 bit is sufficient to represent each dot, but for colors and shades of gray, each dot requires more than 1 bit of data, hence "64-bit" graphics.

BitTorrent   A file protocol designed for high-speed distribution of large video files over the Internet.

blackhole list   A list of *open mail relay servers*, created for the purpose of blocking all (typically spam) messages from those servers.

block list   A list of specific addresses and domains known to send spam.

blog   Short for "Weblog," a diary-like Web site, usually containing the personal thoughts of the site's owner as well as links to other sites of interest.

blogosphere   All the blogs on the Web.

Bluetooth   The specification for a particular wireless connection technology operating in the unlicensed 2.4GHz RF band. Bluetooth (developed primarily by phone maker Ericsson) was originally intended to be a "wire replacement" technology but has since been expanded to compete somewhat with the more powerful Wi-Fi standard. The name comes from a tenth-century Viking king named Harald Blåtand, who is credited with unifying the country of Denmark. Depending on which legend you believe, King Harald (the Danish "Blåtand" translates into the English "Bluetooth") either had a dark complexion and dark hair unusual among the fair-skinned Nordic blondes, or had teeth stained from eating too many blueberries. (The former legend is probably more accurate; the name Blåtand is derived from two old Danish words, "blå," meaning dark skinned, and "tan," meaning great man.)

board   A device that plugs into your computer's system unit and provides auxiliary functions; also called a *card*.

Boolean   A system of logic developed by George Boole (1815–1864), an English mathematician and computer pioneer. Boolean operators (used in everything from logic statements to Internet searches) include AND, OR, and NOT and work with words in much the same way that arithmetic operators (addition, subtraction, and so on) work with numbers.

boot   The process of turning on your computer system. *Rebooting* is turning your system off and then back on, which can be done by pressing Ctrl+Alt+Del or pressing your PC's on/off button.

boot sector   The area located on the first track of a floppy or hard disk.

boot sector virus   A virus that infects the boot sectors of floppy disks, or the master boot record of hard disks.

bootable disk   A disk or diskette that can be used to start your system because the disk contains certain system files. *See* system disk.

bouncing   The process of taking multiple audio tracks and mixing them down into either a mono track, stereo track, or surround-sound mix.

bps   Bits per second; the standard measure of data transmission speeds.

break-out box   A box that attaches to a sound card and is used to house additional input/output jacks.

broadband   A high-speed Internet connection, via ISDN, cable, DSL, satellite, or T1 and T3 lines.

browser   Short for Web browser, a client software program that lets a computer or other device access and display HTML pages on the World Wide Web.

browser hijacker   A spyware program that specifically affects your Web browser—Internet Explorer in particular—in a way that modifies or disables one or more navigation functions.

bubblejet   A type of nonimpact printer, similar to an inkjet, that uses heated ink to form images in a matrix format.

buffer   Memory-based storage for pending computing tasks; multiple print jobs are sent to a buffer where they wait in a queue for the printer to execute them.

buffer overflow   A bug in some programs that enables the program's data buffer to be overloaded with data, forcing the original program code out so the buffer can be rewritten with malicious code.

burner   A device that writes CD-ROMs or DVD-ROMs.

bus (1) In the audio world, the output circuit of an audio mixer. Most mixers have multiple buses, each to route an audio signal to a different place. Both software and digital mixers use this same concept to route signals.

bus (2) In the computer world, a common pathway, or channel, between multiple devices. The computer's internal bus is known as the *local bus*, or *processor bus*. It provides a parallel data-transfer path between the CPU, main memory, and peripheral buses. A 16-bit bus transfers 2 bytes at a time over 16 wires; a 32-bit bus uses 32 wires; and so on. The bus is composed of two parts: the address bus and the data bus. Addresses are sent over the address bus to signal a memory location, and the data is transferred over the data bus to that location.

bus speed The internal speed of a computer's motherboard.

button A raised object in a dialog box that can be "pressed" (by clicking it with a mouse) to perform certain operations.

byte Eight bits, which the computer treats as a single unit. A byte is the unit most computers use to represent a character such as a letter, number, or typographic symbol. One thousand bytes is called a *kilobyte (KB)*, one million bytes is called a *megabyte (MB)*, and one thousand megabytes is called a *gigabyte (GB)*.

C

C prompt The prompt issued by the DOS command interpreter when it is waiting for you to input a command.

cable modem A device that connects your computer to the Internet through cable lines.

cache A form of temporary storage, either in computer memory or on a computer's hard disk.

cache memory The area of computer memory that stores the most recently accessed data. When a computer needs data once, chances are it will need it again, soon, so computer designers realized they could speed up the computer by storing the most recently accessed data in a high-speed storage area. Most caches are FIFO (first in, first out), which means that as the cache fills, the older data is thrown out. There are several types of cache on your computer, including application cache, disk cache, hardware cache, and processor cache.

CAD Computer-aided design; refers to a wide range of programs (including the popular AutoCAD) used for designing any type of product.

camcorder Video camera and recorder combined into a single unit.

card A device that plugs into your system unit and provides auxiliary functions. You can add video cards, modem cards, and sound cards to your system; also called a *board*.

Carnivore The packet sniffer software used by the FBI to spy on suspected criminals and terrorists.

CCD Charge coupled device; a light-sensitive chip used for image gathering.

CD Compact disc; a laser-based digital format for storing high-quality audio programming.

CD-DA Compact Disc Digital Audio; the initial incarnation of the compact disc.

CD-R Compact Disc Recordable; a type of CD drive that lets you record once onto CD discs, which can then be read by any CD-ROM drive and, with proper formatting, by most audio CD players.

CD-ROM Compact Disc Read-Only Memory; a type of CD that stores digital data for computer applications.

CD-RW Compact Disc Rewritable; a type of CD that can be recorded, erased, and rewritten to by the user, multiple times. A CD-RW disc cannot be played in a conventional CD player or in a normal CD-ROM drive.

CDMA Code Division Multiple Access; a spread spectrum technology for cellular telephone use.

censorware Another word for content-filtering software.

central processing unit *See* CPU.

certificate authority The company that issues a digital certificate.

certificate store The repository of digital certificates stored on your hard disk and accessed by your Web browser.

CF Compact Flash; a small form factor memory card for removable data storage.

CGI   Common Gateway Interface; a standard way for a Web server to pass a Web user's request to an application program, receive data back from that program, and forward it to the user.

chain letter   A letter or email directing the recipient to forward multiple copies of the message to other people.

channel   One section of an audio track, usually carrying the sound for a single speaker.

chat   Text-based real-time Internet communication, typically consisting of short, one-line messages back and forth between two or more users. Users gather to chat in chat rooms or channels.

chat channel   A public chat on an IRC network, typically organized by topic.

cheese   The content of a commercial Web site that consists primarily of product pictures or other useless information.

chip   A small piece of semiconducting material (usually silicon) on which an integrated circuit is embedded. A typical chip is less than a square inch in size and can contain millions of electronic components (transistors). Computers consist of many chips placed on electronic boards called *printed circuit boards*.

chrominance   The color component of a video signal that includes information about the image's color (hue) and saturation.

churn   The customer turnover rate of any ISP or commercial online service; the percentage of new customers minus the percentage of old customers canceling is the churn.

circuit board   A thin plate on which chips and other electronic components are placed. Computers consist of one or more boards, often called *cards* or *adapters*.

clear GIF   A small, transparent graphics file used to create a *Web bug*.

ClearType   A display technology, first utilized in Windows XP, that effectively triples the horizontal display resolution on LCD displays.

click   The process of selecting an item onscreen; what you do with a mouse button.

click-through   A measurement of Web page advertising effectiveness; a click-through occurs whenever a user clicks a banner ad or link.

client   In a client/server relationship between two devices, the client is the device that pushes or pulls data from the other device (server).

clipart   Simple illustrations designed for use with printed or Web documents.

clustering   Connecting two or more computers to behave as a single computer. Thanks to clustering, two or more computers can jointly execute a function, activity can be distributed evenly across a computer network, and systems can respond gracefully to unexpected failures.

CMOS   Complementary metal-oxide semiconductor (pronounced "see-moss"); a small, 64-byte memory chip on the motherboard that stores information your computer needs to boot up.

CMYK   Cyan, Magenta, Yellow, Black; the individual colors used to create color prints.

co-location   The process of having a Web server located in a different physical location from its host company, typically for security purposes.

coaster   What all those excess AOL tryout CDs end up being used as.

code signature   A sequence of binary code unique to a computer virus; used to identify each virus.

CODEC   COder/DECoder; an algorithm that reduces the number of bytes consumed by large computer files and programs.

color depth   *See* bit depth.

comb filter   An electronic component in a television or other video display that removes residual chrominance (color) information from the luminance (brightness) signal, thus enhancing fine picture detail.

Comdex   A trade show in which IT professionals have convened twice yearly for the past 20 years to unveil new products, announce burgeoning technology trends, and schmooze with other geeks from around the world. Since the trade shows' humble beginnings in 1980, Comdex has grown into the computer industry's premiere U.S. event.

compact disc   *See CD.*

compact flash   *See CF.*

companion virus   A file infector virus that creates a clone of the host file, which is then run instead of the original file.

component   A part of Windows incidental to the main program. A component can be an applet such as HyperTerminal or Notepad or a utility such as the DVD driver.

component video   A video signal that has been split up into its component parts: red (Pr), green (Y), and blue (Pb). Component video connections—found on higher-end TVs and DVD players—reproduce the best possible picture quality, with improved color accuracy and reduced color bleeding.

composite video   A single video signal that contains both chrominance (color) and luminance (brightness) and information. Composite video is typically delivered through a single "video" RCA jack connection and delivers a better-quality picture than an RF signal, but not as good as an S-Video signal.

compression   The process of compacting digital data.

compressor   A signal processor that reduces the gain of a signal by a set ratio when it exceeds the set threshold.

computer   A programmable device that can store, retrieve, and process data. Computers can store prerecorded lists of instructions, which we call *programs*. The computer's brain is the microprocessor, which is capable of doing math, moving data around, and altering the data after storing it in binary code. Most computers have a fast, short-term storage medium and a slower, long-term storage medium. The faster storage medium, known as *RAM*, is used to store information temporarily while you work and run applications. The long-term, permanent storage is your hard drive. To feed the computer information and tell it how to process the data, you need input devices such as your mouse and keyboard. The monitor, or output device, displays the results.

computer virus   A computer program or piece of malicious code that attaches itself to other files and then replicates itself.

content filter   Software that analyzes Web page content and blocks access to inappropriate content.

controller   Any MIDI device that can be used to control any other MIDI-capable device. Generally, controllers are in the form of a keyboard, but they can also be drum pads, mixer controllers, and so on.

cookie   A small file created by a Web site and stored on your computer's hard disk, used to track specific user information. Typically, a cookie records your preferences when using a particular site; cookies are also used to rotate the banner ads that a site sends so that it doesn't keep sending you the same ad, and to customize pages for you based on your browser type or other information you might have provided the Web site.

CPU   Central Processing Unit; a complex silicon chip that acts as a computer's brain, taking requests from applications and then processing, or executing, operations.

cracker   An individual who maliciously breaks into another computer system. (Not to be confused with a *hacker*, who typically does not have malicious intent.)

crossover   An electrical circuit designed to separate an audio signal into different frequency ranges that are then routed to the appropriate speaker (such as a subwoofer).

CRT   Cathode ray tube; commonly called a *picture tube*. Used in all direct-view, all rear-projection, and some front-projection televisions.

cryptography   The science of information security; the process of hiding or coding information either in storage or in transit.

CTS   Carpal Tunnel Syndrome; hand pain and weakness that results from compression of the median nerve at the wrist. Often caused by repetitive hand and arm movements, such as extended typing at a computer keyboard.

cursor   The highlighted area or pointer that tracks with the movement of your mouse or arrow keys onscreen.

cybercafé   A coffeehouse that offers Internet access; also called an *Internet café*.

cybersex   Any type of sexual activity (even the virtual kind) that takes place online.

cyberspace   Typically used to define the "there" that is the Internet. The word was coined by author William Gibson in his novel *Neuromancer*.

cybored   The state of boredom entered into while you're waiting for slow Web pages to load.

cybrarian   A librarian specializing in electronic sources.

D

D-SLR   Digital Single Lens Reflex, a digital version of the traditional 35mm SLR camera, with true through-the-lens viewing. Most D-SLR cameras also accept a variety of removable lenses.

D/A converter   Digital-to-Analog converter; the processor on a sound card that converts the analog electrical signal into digital data.

daemon   A Unix program or agent (pronounced "demon") designed to wait in the background while another program is running and execute only when required. Using a daemon, a program can simply hand off data to the smaller program and go on to more important things.

DAMPS   Digital Advanced Mobile Phone System; the American standard for digital mobile telephony, also known as *TDMA*.

DAT   Digital Audio Tape; a digital linear tape that uses PCM to convert analog signals into a digital form.

data   Information that is convenient to move or process. In the computer world, data is typically digital.

Data   That android dude on *Star Trek, the Next Generation*.

data diddling   The process of surreptitiously altering (but not deleting) the data on another computer system.

data rate   The throughput rate at which data can be sent from one device to another.

data-driven attack   A virus or Trojan attack on a computer system; the attack is launched when a file is downloaded and opened.

daughter window   Another name for a pop-up window.

DAW   Digital Audio Workstation; a computer that has been specially configured for work with audio.

dB   Decibel; the standard unit of measure for expressing relative power differences—otherwise known as *loudness*. One dB is the smallest change in loudness most people can detect; a 10-dB difference produces twice the volume.

DBS   Digital Broadcast Satellite (or Direct Broadcast Satellite); the satellite broadcasting system that uses a small 18-inch satellite dish to receive signals from a high-powered satellite in geosynchronous orbit.

dead link   A hyperlink on a Web page that doesn't lead to an active page or site—probably because that page no longer exists.

dead tree edition   The print version of something also available on the Internet.

decompression   The process of returning a compressed file to its original format.

decryption   The process of decoding encrypted data.

DECT   Digital Enhanced Cordless Telephone; a standard that defines the radio-based connection between two devices, such as a cordless phone and its base unit.

defragment   To restructure a disk so that files are stored in contiguous blocks of space, rather than dispersed into multiple fragments at different locations on the disk.

demilitarized zone   A server that sits outside a company's firewall and enables public access to specified content.

denial-of-service attack   An attack that floods a computer or network with data or messages that overwhelm and ultimately shut down the system.

depth of field   The depth in a scene from foreground to background that will be in sharp focus in a photograph or movie frame. Depth of field is affected by a combination of *aperture, focal length*, and distance from subject.

desktop   The entire screen area on which you display all your computer work. A typical computer desktop can contain icons, a taskbar, menus, and individual application windows.

device   A Windows file that represents some object—physical or nonphysical—installed on your system.

dial-up access   An Internet connection via a dial-up modem—*not* via always-on broadband.

dialog box   An onscreen window that either displays a message or asks for user input.

dictionary spam   A means of generating email addresses by matching common names with known domain names.

digerati   Really hip people in the digital world; the digital version of literati.

digital   A means of transmitting or storing data using "on" and "off" bits (expressed as "1" or "0"). Known for its highly accurate reproduction, with little or no degradation from the original.

Digital8   Older digital recording format for camcorders that uses standard 8mm or Hi8 cassettes.

digital camera   A still camera that uses a light-sensitive image sensor chip (typically a *CCD*), instead of film, to capture the image.

digital certificate   An electronic credential that confirms the identity of a person, server, or software manufacturer.

digital compression   Any algorithm that reduces the storage space required to store or transmit information.

digital signature   A form of digital certificate used to authenticate the identity of the sender of a message or the signer of a document.

digital television   Television signals broadcast digitally, the U.S. TV standard that will become mandatory in 2006. DTV comes in several different formats, each with varying types of picture resolution and sound quality. The highest quality of these formats are called *HDTV*.

digital zoom   A pseudozoom mode in some digital cameras that operates by cropping the outside of the image and enlarging the center. Typically produces lower-quality images than a comparable *optical zoom*.

DIMM   Dual Inline Memory Module; a small circuit board that holds memory chips. Unlike SIMMS (Single Inline Memory Modules), you can install memory one DIMM at a time.

dipole   A speaker design that generates equal amounts of sound both forward and backward, with the two sounds being out of phase. Dipoles are often used as surround speakers.

directory (1)   An index to files you store on your disk, often represented as a simulated file folder. Also known as a *folder*.

directory (2)   A search site that collects and indexes Web pages manually, either by user submission or editorial selection. Yahoo! is the Web's most popular directory.

discovery   The process wherein a remote device becomes aware of the network to which it is connected.

disk   A device that stores data in magnetic format. The three main kinds of disks are diskettes, hard disks, and optical disks.

disk cache   High-speed, temporary, chip-based storage that reserves an area of RAM to store data that has been accessed from the hard drive. If the data is requested from the hard drive again, the computer gets it from RAM, which is much faster.

disk compression   Taking the information that is stored, or will be stored, on a disk and compacting it so that it takes less space to store.

diskette   A portable or removable disk.

distributed computing   A form of peer-to-peer computing where multiple computers are connected to harness their total processing power; typically used for large projects that would otherwise require use of a supercomputer.

DIVX   A type of DVD disc with regulated playback; now obsolete.

DLP   Digital Light Processor; the technology that controls DMD front-projection displays.

DMD   Digital Micromirror Device; a type of projection video display that uses thousands of small mirrors, controlled by a DLP.

DNS   Domain Name System; translates Internet domain and host names to IP addresses.

DNS spoofing   An attack resulting from the hijacking of a computer's DNS name by an attacker; the DNS name is redirected to the attacker's IP address.

.DOC   The file extension for Microsoft Word documents.

document   A piece of information in a computer file. A Web page is one kind of document, as is a Microsoft Word file.

Dolby AC-3   The previous name for Dolby Digital.

Dolby Digital   Surround-sound format, sometimes referred to as 5.1. Incorporates up to six discrete digital audio channels: front left, front center, front right, surround left, surround right, and a "low frequency effects" channel for subwoofers. It can also be used to carry digital mono (1.0) and stereo (2.0) soundtracks.

Dolby Digital EX   Extended version of the Dolby Digital surround-sound format, with 6.1 or 7.1 channels. The extra channels are matrixed channels positioned at the rear of the room, behind and between the left and right surrounds.

Dolby HX Pro   This circuit adjusts cassette tape bias during recording to extend dynamic headroom (the difference between the loudest and the softest audible signals) and improve the tape deck's capability to record high frequencies without distortion. Dolby HX Pro requires no decoding.

Dolby noise reduction   Noise reduction systems used on audio-cassette decks. There are several different types of Dolby noise reduction, including Dolby B, Dolby C, Dolby S, and Dolby HX Pro.

Dolby Pro Logic   The predecessor to Dolby Digital surround, with only four channels: front left, front center, front right, and a single "surround" channel. The single surround channel is typically sent to two or more rear speakers. Dolby Pro Logic channels are matrixed into a left and right output, whereas Dolby Digital uses six discrete outputs.

Dolby Pro Logic II   The successor to Dolby Pro Logic, a matrix format used to simulate a surround experience for material recorded in two-channel format. Also used to simulate real channel effects in some video games.

domain   The name of a site on the Internet. Domains are hierarchical, and lower-level domains often refer to particular Web sites within a top-level domain. Examples of domains are .com, .edu, .gov, and .org.

dongle   A device developed to prevent piracy. It attaches to a port on your computer and works as a key to unlock a particular software application.

DOS   Disk Operating System (pronounced "dahss"); the pre-Windows operating system for IBM-compatible computers. The generic term DOS is often used as shorthand for the more specific MS-DOS, the original operating system developed by Microsoft for the PC.

dot bomb   A defunct dot com.

dot com   A company whose primary business is Internet related.

double-click   Clicking a mouse button twice in rapid succession.

download   The process of receiving information or data from a server on the Internet.

dpi   Dots per inch; a measurement of printer resolution. The more dots per inch, the higher the resolution. A 400dpi printer creates 160,000 dots (400×400).

DRAM   Dynamic RAM; the most common type of random-access memory. It accesses information as it needs it, and then closes and goes on to something else. Because DRAM is random, pieces of information can be stacked one upon another without discarding the entire stack. The information in DRAM is not only dynamic and randomly accessed, it's also fast.

drive-by download   A spyware program that tries to pass as a required download.

driver   The program support file that tells a program how to interact with a specific hardware device, such as a hard disk controller or video display card.

DSL   Digital Subscriber Line; a new ultrafast Internet connection using standard phone lines. Download speeds can approach 32Mbps. Often preceded by another letter, denoting the type of DSL connection; for example, ADSL stands for Asymmetric Digital Subscriber Line, and SDSL stands for Symmetric Digital Subscriber Line.

DSP   Digital Signal Processor; a chip designed to manipulate analog information that has been converted into digital format. DSP circuitry is used in some surround-sound systems to create different simulated sound fields.

DSS   Digital Satellite System; see DBS.

DSSS   Direct Sequence Spread Spectrum; a wireless RF technology that fixes signals within a specific channel but uses engineered noise to reduce interference and improve security.

DTS   Digital Theater Systems; a 5.1 surround-sound format similar to Dolby Digital.

DTS ES   A 6.1/7.1 version of DTS surround sound; the extra channels are matrixed rear channels positioned behind and between the left and rear surrounds.

DTS ES Discrete   A 6.1-channel surround format with the extra rear channel carried in discrete format, rather than matrixed.

DTV   See digital television.

DV   Digital Video; the recording, editing, and storing of video in digital formats. A digital video (DV) camcorder is a video camera that captures and stores images on a digital medium such as a DAT or compact flash card.

DVD   A two-sided optical disc that holds a minimum of 4.7GB, enough for a full-length movie. DVDs can store significantly more data than ordinary CD-ROMs can, and can play high-quality videos. (The acronym DVD actually doesn't stand for anything anymore; at one time it stood for Digital Versatile Disk, and at another time, Digital Video Disk.)

DVD-Audio   New audio-only DVD format that delivers better-than-CD-quality sound; competes with SA-CD.

DVD-R   DVD Recordable; a write-once, read-many storage format similar to CD-R, but for DVDs.

DVD-RAM   DVD Random Access Memory; a rewritable DVD disc format for data recording and playback. DVD-RAM drives typically read DVD-Video, DVD-ROM, and CD media.

DVD-ROM   DVD Read-Only Memory; a DVD disc capable of storing data, interactive sequences, and audio and video. DVD-ROMs run in DVD-ROM or DVD-RAM drives, but not DVD-Video players connected to TVs and home theaters. Most DVD-ROM drives will play DVD-Video movies, however.

DVD-RW   DVD ReWritable; a rewritable DVD format that is similar to DVD+RW but with less capability to work as a random access device. It has a read-write capacity of 4.7GB.

DVD+RW   DVD+ReWritable; one of several competing rewritable DVD formats. Fully compatible with existing DVD and DVD-ROM drives.

DVHS   Digital VHS; a new videocassette format that can record and play back 16:9 HDTV programming.

DVR   Digital Video Recorder; a device that records programming digitally on a large hard disk. Also known as *personal video recorder (PVR), personal television receiver (PTR),* or *hard disk driver (HDD) recorder.*

dynamic range   The difference between the loudest sound and the quietest sound that is produced or can be reproduced by a piece of equipment.

dynamic system monitoring   The real-time scanning mode of a virus-scanning program.

E

e-commerce   Electronic commerce, or business conducted over the Internet.

e-tailer   A retailer engaging in e-commerce; an online merchant.

Easter egg   A surprise embedded in a program, typically activated by some unusual (and undocumented) combination of keystrokes or user actions.

email   Electronic mail; a means of corresponding to other computer users over the Internet through digital messages.

email bomb   The sending of a large number of email messages to a single address, with the intent of flooding that person's inbox.

email gateway   A proxy server for email.

email spoofing   The practice of changing your name in an outgoing email message so it looks like the message came from somewhere or someone else. Spammers generally use spoofing to prevent people from finding out who they are. It's also used by general malcontents to practice mischievous and malicious behavior. However, spoofing can be a legitimate and helpful tool for someone with more than one email account.

emoticon   Punctuation characters that suggest how an email should be interpreted by indicating the writer's mood. For example, a :) emoticon indicates that the message is meant as a joke. (The name "emoticon" is short for "emotion icon.") An emoticon is also called a *smiley.*

encryption   The process of coding data into a format that can't be read, for security purposes. To read an encrypted file, you must possess the secret key or password that unlocks the encryption.

envelope   The dynamic shape of a sound over time, commonly characterized by its attack, decay, sustain, and release.

.EPS   Encapsulated PostScript; a file format, developed by Adobe, that stores graphics and text as PostScript language commands that a printer can read and print.

equalizer   An amplifier that can boost or cut specific frequencies.

error message   An onscreen message that your operating system or application issues to tell you that you did something wrong or that a command could not be executed correctly.

Ethernet

Ethernet   Perhaps the most common networking protocol. Ethernet is used to network, or hook computers together so they can share information.

.EXE   The file extension for an executable (program) file.

executable file   A program that you run on your computer system.

exploit   An attack that takes advantage of a bug or hole in a piece of hardware or operating system.

extranet   An intranet that is accessible to select computers that are not physically part of the company's own network, but not accessible to the general public.

F

FAQ   Frequently Asked Questions; a document that answers the most commonly asked questions about a particular topic. FAQs are often found in newsgroups and on some Web sites as a preparatory answer to the common questions asked by new users.

fast Ethernet   The same thing as Ethernet, only 10 times faster.

FAT   File Allocation Table; a special section of your disk that stores tracking data to help Windows locate files.

FAT32   The 32-bit file allocation table used in Windows 98 and subsequent Microsoft operating systems.

FDISK   A DOS and Windows utility that creates one or more partitions on a hard disk drive.

FDMA   Frequency Division Multiple Access; the division of the frequency band allocated for wireless cellular telephone communication into 30 channels, each of which can carry a voice conversation or, with digital service, digital data.

FHHS   Frequency Hopping Spread Spectrum; a type of frequency hopping that uses a broad spectrum of frequencies.

field   When using interlaced scanning, half a frame of picture information.

file   A collection of data, with its own unique name and location; files can be documents or executable programs.

File Allocation Table   See FAT.

file extension   Extensions identify the type of file to which they're attached. All programs and almost all data files use extensions, which are separated from the filename with a dot. For example, LETTER.DOC is a Word document. NOTEPAD.EXE is a text-editor program that comes with Windows. Before Windows 95, an extension could have only up to three letters or digits; beginning with Windows 95 (and already standard on the Macintosh platform), extensions can be of any length.

file infector virus   A virus that infects the code of executable program files.

file type   A specific type of file, associated with a specific application.

filename   The formal name assigned to a file; beginning with Windows 95 (and already standard on the Macintosh platform), a filename can be up to 256 characters long and include letters, numbers, characters, and spaces.

Finger   A software tool for locating users on other Internet sites.

FIR   Fast Infrared; infrared transmission that supports speeds up to 4Mbps.

firewall   Software or hardware that insulates a computer or network from the Internet or other networks. A firewall blocks unwanted access to the protected network while giving the protected network access to networks outside the firewall.

FireWire   A high-speed bus. FireWire is a serial connector, like USB, and allows you to add peripheral devices to your computer very easily, without having to open the box. FireWire, however, can transmit data 30 to almost 40 times faster than USB. That makes it very good for tasks such as getting video off a camcorder. For most devices, you don't need that much speed, but if you wanted to add a very fast hard drive to your PC, FireWire would be an excellent solution. FireWire was originally developed by Apple and is now also sold under the names iLink and IE-1394.

firmware   Low-level software that runs in a freestanding device (such as a digital camera) and typically controls the functionality and user interface.

flame   To communicate emotionally and/or excessively via electronic mail. In other words, to insult someone online.

flame war   What happens when an online discussion degenerates into a series of flames or personal attacks.

Flash   Multimedia technology, developed by Macromedia, that enables audio/video interactivity on specially designed Web pages.

flat response   The reproduction of sound without altering the intensity of any part of the frequency range.

floppy disk   Another term for *diskette*.

flow control   A procedure used to control the transfer of data between two devices.

flutter   High-frequency variations in pitch of a recorded waveform due to fast speed variations in a recorder or playback machine.

flying erase head   A type of recording head on a VCR that reduces or eliminates static when stopping and starting recording between scenes.

focal length   A lens measurement that determines the perspective (wide angle through telephoto) viewed through a camera lens.

foistware   See drive-by download.

folder   A way to group files on a disk; each folder can contain multiple files or other folders (called *subfolders*). In the DOS and Windows operating systems, folders were originally called *directories*.

forced frame   A technique for forcing a new Web page into a framed page from another site.

format   The process that prepares a disk for use.

FPTV   Front-projection television; a video display device that projects a picture onto the front of a separate screen.

frame   One single still image that, when played in rapid succession with other frames, creates a moving picture.

frames   An HTML technique for combining two or more separate HTML documents within a single Web page.

freeware   Computer software distributed at no charge. Unlike open-source software, the author retains the copyright, which means that the application cannot be modified without the author's consent.

frequency hopping   An RF technology that enables a single signal to jump from one frequency to another, to reduce interference and increase security.

frequency response   The range of frequencies accurately reproduced by a particular component; the wider the range, the better.

FTP   File Transfer Protocol; a series of protocols or rules that define how to transfer files across the Internet. FTP is a very popular way to send files across the Internet, and is not dependent on Web servers and browsers.

full duplex   See synchronous.

full-motion video   The display of movie clips on your PC in as realistic a form as possible.

function key   One of the special keys labeled F1 to F12, located at the top of your computer keyboard.

G

gain   Amount of amplification, measured in decibels.

gateway   A device that connects one or more other devices to an external network.

gateway computer   A computer on a network that hosts the connection to the Internet.

Gb   Gigabit; approximately 1,000 megabits.

GB   Gigabyte; 1,000 megabytes, more or less (1,024 to be precise).

Gbps   Gigabits per second.

GBps   Gigabytes per second.

GHz   Gigahertz (millions of cycles per second).

.GIF   Graphics Interchange Format; an 8-bit (256-color) graphics file format. GIFs are widely used on the Web because they compress well.

gloss   The amount of light reflected by the surface of a sheet of paper, relative to the paper's smoothness.

Google   The most-used search engine on the Web.

Gopher   A pre-Web method of organizing material on Internet servers. Created at the University of Minnesota—home of the Fighting Gophers!

GPS   Global Positioning System; a system of 24 satellites for identifying earth locations, launched by the U.S. Department of Defense. By triangulation of signals from three of the satellites, a receiving unit can pinpoint its current location anywhere on earth to within a few meters.

graphics   Picture files. Pictures, photographs, and clip art are all commonly referred to as *graphics*.

grayscale   An image consisting of a range of gray levels, as opposed to a broader range of colors or pure black and white.

GSM   Global System for Mobile (communications); a second-generation (2G) standard for digital cellular transmissions; widely used in Europe and in U.S. PCS 1900 systems.

GUI   Graphical User Interface (pronounced "gooey"). The look and feel of an operating system that uses graphical elements instead of character-based elements. A GUI lets you interact by using a mouse rather than having to type in keyboard commands.

H

hacker   An individual who enjoys exploring the details of computer systems and programming code, typically by "hacking" into those systems and programs—but without causing any intentional damage. (Not to be confused with a *cracker*, who engages in intentionally malicious behavior.)

half-duplex   *See* asynchronous.

hard disk   A piece of hardware that stores large amounts of data for future access.

hard disk drive (HDD) recorder—See DVR.

hardware   A piece of electronic equipment that you can actually touch. Your personal computer and all its peripherals are hardware; the operations of your PC are controlled by *software* (which you *can't* touch).

hardware cache   High-speed, temporary, chip-based storage that offers faster access time than CD-ROM hardware. By placing data in the hardware cache, you minimize the CD-ROM system's waiting time. Hardware cache speeds up access to the CD and the CD's performance.

HDTV   High-Definition Television; a subset of the new digital TV standard that reproduces pictures in either 780p or 1080i resolution, with a 16:9 aspect ratio and Dolby Digital 5.1 surround sound.

header   That part of a data packet or email message, normally hidden, that contains the sender's IP address and other technical information.

heading   The initial portion of an HTML document, specified by a special code.

headroom   The amount of gain an audio amplifier can produce before distorting.

Heuristic scanning   A method of scanning for computer viruses by looking for general viruslike behavior.

Hi8   High-resolution version of the 8mm camcorder format.

HID   Human Interface Device; any device (physical or virtual) used to control a computer consumer electronics product. Keyboards and mice are HIDs, as are the knobs and buttons on the front of an audio/video receiver.

hit   A single request from a Web browser to view an item (typically a Web page) stored on a Web server. If a Web page contains graphics, the graphic elements are counted as separate hits.

home page   The initial page screen of a Web site.

home theater   The attempt to reproduce, as accurately as possible, the experience of watching a film in a movie theater. Typically involves a high-quality video source (such as DVD), audio/video receiver, surround-sound speakers, and a large video display device.

HomeRF   An RF-based technology designed for home and small business wireless networks. HomeRF uses the 2.4GHz band and competes with both Wi-Fi and Bluetooth.

horizontal resolution   The sharpness of a video display, measured in terms of horizontal lines that can be resolved from one side of the screen to the other. Broadcast television has a horizontal resolution of 330 lines; DVDs deliver 500 lines; and HDTV can deliver up to 1,080 lines of horizontal resolution.

host   An Internet server that houses a Web site; any computer on a network that is a repository for services available to other computers on the network.

hover   The act of selecting an item by placing your cursor over an icon *without clicking*.

.HTM or .HTML   The file extension for Web pages on the Internet.

HTML   HyperText Markup Language; the document format used to build pages on the World Wide Web. HTML tags, or codes, define the structure and layout of a Web document. Hundreds of tags are used to format and lay out a Web page.

HTML email   Email messages that incorporate HTML code, just like Web pages.

HTTP   HyperText Transfer Protocol; the underlying communications protocol used to connect servers and browsers on the World Wide Web. For example, when you enter a URL in your browser, the browser sends an HTTP command to the Web server directing it to retrieve and transmit the requested page.

hub   Hardware used to network computers together (usually over an Ethernet connection). It's a small box with five or more RJ-45 connectors that accept cables from individual computers.

hybrid virus   A virus that combines the capabilities of multiple types of viruses.

hyperlink   Special text or graphics on a Web page that, when clicked, automatically transfer the user to another Web page.

hypertext   Any text that contains links to other documents. When users click on hyperlinked text, another document is retrieved and displayed.

Hz   Hertz; a unit of measurement for the frequency of sounds. One Hz is equal to one cycle per second, and the range of human hearing is typically 20–20,000 Hz.

I

I/O   Input/Output. The flow of information to and from computers and peripherals.

IBM-compatible   All personal computers that are compatible (that is, can share software and operating systems) with the original IBM PC.

IC   Integrated Circuit; see chip.

ICANN   Internet Corporation for Assigned Names and Numbers; a nonprofit, private corporation responsible for overseeing the following aspects of the World Wide Web: assigning space for IP addresses, managing the domain name system, and taking care of the root server system.

ICMP   Internet Control Message Protocol; used by Internet routers to notify a host computer when a specified destination is unreachable.

icon   A graphical representation of an object onscreen. Typically, you click an icon to initiate a function.

ICQ   One of the first instant-messaging services; now owned by America Online.

IDE   Intelligent (or integrated) Drive Electronics; IDE connects mass-storage devices, such as hard drives or CD-ROMs, to a computer.

identity theft   The theft of personal ID and financial information, enabling the thief to assume the identity of the victim.

IEEE   Institute of Electronic and Electrical Engineers.

IEEE 1394   See FireWire.

IMAP   Internet Message Access Protocol; a protocol (similar to POP) used by email clients when connecting to email servers.

in box   The virtual container where unread email is stored.

infection   The process of a computer virus inserting itself into a computer file.

infrared   A means of sending voice or data signals using light transmitted in the infrared range.

inkjet   A type of nonimpact printer that uses drops of ink to form images in a matrix format.

install   How you get software from its box to your hard disk.

instant messaging   Text-based real-time one-on-one communication over the Internet. Not to be confused with *chat*, which can accommodate multiple users, instant messaging (IM) typically is limited to just two users.

interlaced scanning   A method of displaying television pictures where the picture is displayed in two halves (one of odd-numbered lines, one of even-numbered lines) that are interlaced together to create the full picture.

Internet   The global "network of networks" that connects millions of computers and other devices around the world. The World Wide Web and Usenet are both parts of the Internet.

Internet Explorer   Microsoft's PC-based Web browser software.

interpolation   A way to increase the apparent size, resolution, or colors in an image by calculating the pixels used to represent the new image from the old one.

interstitial   Another name for a pop-up advertisement.

intranet   A private network inside an organization that uses the same type of software and services found on the public Internet.

intrusion detection system   Software or hardware that monitors a computer network or system for signs of an attack.

IP   Internet Protocol; the protocol that defines how data is sent through routers to different networks, by assigning unique IP addresses to different devices.

IP address   The identifying address of a computer or device attached to a TCP/IP network. TCP/IP networks use IP addresses to route messages to their proper destinations. The IP address is written as four sets of numbers separated by periods.

IR   See infrared.

IRC   Internet Relay Chat; an Internet-based network of chat servers and channels that facilitates real-time public text messaging (called *chats*) and file exchanges.

IrDA   Describes both the Infrared Data Association and the standard developed by that organization for infrared-based data connections.

IRQ   Interrupt Request; a signal used by a device to gain the attention of your system's microprocessor when it needs processing resources. Most PCs have 16 different IRQs, labeled 0 through 15.

ISDN   Integrated Services Digital Network; a digital communication system that can transmit voice or packet data over a regular phone line at rates between 64Kbps and 256Kbps.

ISM   Industrial, Scientific, Medical; see 2.4GHz band.

ISO number   The standard rating for film or CCD sensitivity. The higher the ISO number, the greater the sensitivity.

ISP   Internet service provider; a company that connects individual users (calling in using traditional phone lines) to the Internet. Some Internet service providers—such as America Online—also provide unique content to their subscribers.

iTV   Interactive Television; television with interactive content and enhancements.

J

jaggies   The stairstepped appearance of a curved or angled line in a low-resolution image. Increasing the resolution (number of pixels) will decrease or eliminate jaggies.

jargon   Technical-sounding gobbledy-gook that sounds more important than it really is.

Java   A programming language used to develop sophisticated interactive Web pages and applications. Java was created and licensed by Sun Microsystems and is not always supported by Microsoft applications.

JavaScript   A scripting language used to create advanced Web page functionality—rollovers, pull-down menus, and other special effects. JavaScript has more in common with HTML than it does with Java, which is a full-fledged programming language.

.JPG or .JPEG   Joint Photographic Experts Group (pronounced "jay-peg"); a standard for compressing still images. Compression is achieved by dividing the picture into tiny pixel blocks, which are halved over and over until the appropriate ratio is achieved. Because JPEG is extremely effective in compressing large graphics files, it is widely used on the Internet.

junk email   Another name for *spam*.

K

Kb   Kilobit; approximately 1,000 bits (1,024, to be precise).

KB   Kilobyte; 1,000 bytes, more or less. (Actually, it's 1,024 bytes.)

Kbps   Kilobits per second.

KBps   Kilobytes per second.

kernel   The central part of an operating system that oversees all other operations. The kernel loads first and stays in the memory throughout the operation of the OS.

key (1)   A folder that contains specific settings in the Windows Registry.

key (2)   A code—actually, a really big number—that works with a cryptographic algorithm to produce a specific encrypted result.

keyboard   The thing that looks like a typewriter that you use to type instructions to your computer.

keylogger   Software or hardware that records the individual keystrokes entered by a user.

keystroke logger   See keylogger.

keyword   A word that forms all or part of a search engine query.

KHz   Kilohertz (thousands of cycles per second).

L

LAN   Local Area Network; a communications network that serves users within a relatively small area. Most LANs serve just one building or a group of buildings. The users' individual PCs are workstations (clients) that access the servers as needed.

LAN access point   A base station used to connect wireless devices to a local area network.

landscape mode   Viewing an image where the width is greater than the height.

laser disc   An older laser-based format for delivering audio/video programming on 12-inch discs. Laser discs deliver 425 lines of nondigital horizontal resolution, whereas DVDs deliver 500 lines, digitally.

laser printer   A type of nonimpact printer that creates an electrostatic image of an entire page on a photosensitive drum, using a laser beam. An ultrafine coated powder (called *toner*) is applied to the drum, and then transferred to a sheet of paper, creating the printed image.

launch   To start a program.

LCD   Liquid Crystal Display; a flat-screen display device in which images are created by light transmitted through a layer of liquid crystals. Also a type of rear projection display where the light source is shown through an LCD panel.

LCD projector   A type of video projector that generates a picture using a liquid crystal display, which is then projected through a magnifying lens.

LCoS   Liquid crystal on silicone, a type of microdisplay device for rear projection televisions incorporating a microprocessor unit.

LD   See laser disc.

LDAP   Lightweight Directory Access Protocol; a type of service that acts as a virtual "white pages" to directories of email addresses.

legacy   Older hardware that is not compliant with the Plug-and-Play standard.

lens   A device, made of ground glass, for focusing light rays onto a CCD or film.

letterbox   A way to display wide-screen images on a standard 4:3 aspect ratio video display, by introducing black bars above and below the picture.

light-valve projector   A type of video projector that combines LCD and CRT projection technology.

limiter   A signal processor used to keep audio signals from exceeding a set level.

line doubler   See line multiplier.

line level   The standard volume level for routing audio signals. For pro audio gear, line level is set at +4dBv and for consumer gear it is -10dBv.

line multiplier   A circuit that doubles, triples, or quadruples the number of lines that make up a picture, perceptively increasing picture detail while decreasing the incidence of flicker and visible scan lines.

link   See hyperlink.

Linux   A Unix-like operating system that runs on many different types of computers. Many different versions of Linux are available, even though it's not necessarily a user-friendly operating system; in fact, it's not recommended for general consumer use (although it does have a cult following among programmers and dedicated Microsoft haters). Linux was created by Linus Torvalds while he was a college student at the University of Helsinki in Finland. Instead of making it proprietary and trying to sell it, Torvalds gave it away, so anyone who wanted to develop for it could do so.

list merchant   A company that buys and sells mailing lists.

Listserv   A form of email mailing list.

LNB   Low Noise Blocker; a small amplifier located on the arm of a satellite dish that receives digital satellite transmissions.

log file   A computer file that contains a record of specific user or program activity.

log in   The requirement that one "registers" with one's computer or network before being granted access.

LPT   The typical designation for a computer's connection to a printer or other device through a parallel port. The name originally stood for "line printer terminal," but the LPT port can be used for other devices as well, such as a video camera.

luminance   The brightness or black-and-white component of a color video signal; determines the level of picture detail.

lurker   Someone who reads message board and discussion group postings, but seldom (if ever) participates himself.

M

macro   A series of instructions, using a simple coding language, used to automate procedures in a computer application; macros are typically attached to individual documents or templates.

macro virus   A macro that contains malicious code.

mailing list   A discussion group conducted using email.

malware   "Malicious software," shorthand for any virus, Trojan, or worm.

mattress tag   A Web site disclaimer or TOS that few, if any, users read or pay attention to—much like those "do not remove under penalty of law" tags found on new mattresses.

Mb   Megabit; one million bits, more or less.

MB   Megabyte; approximately one million bytes (1,048,576, to be precise).

Mbps   Megabits per second.

MBps   Megabytes per second.

MBR   Master Boot Record; a software routine placed at the very beginning of a hard disk that analyzes the disk partition table, loads the hard disk's boot sector into system memory, and then passes control to the boot sector.

megapixel   A way of measuring image resolution in digital photography. One megapixel equals a million pixels; the higher the megapixel rating, the better quality the picture.

memory   Temporary electronic storage for data and instructions, via electronic impulses on a chip.

menu   A selection of items or services.

meta search   A search of searches; a process where queries are submitted to multiple search engines or directories simultaneously.

META tag   A special HTML tag that identifies a Web page's contents. META tags do not have any influence on the appearance of the page, but instead hold information such as keywords for search engines, descriptions of the site, and update histories. The information in META tags is often used in the indexes of search engines.

MHz   Megahertz; one million hertz. (A hertz is a measurement of frequency; in the case of computers, the speed of a microprocessor is measured in megahertz.)

microdisplay   A type of rear projection television where the light source incorporates an LCD, DLP, or LCoS device instead of the traditional three-CRT setup.

MicroMV—A newer and smaller digital videotape format, somewhat proprietary to Sony camcorders. MicroMV tapes are 70% smaller than MiniDV tapes and record in the MPEG-2 format rather than the more universal DV format.

microprocessor   The chip inside your system unit that processes all the operations your computer can do; a microprocessor includes a CPU and is the brain of any computing device.

Microsoft   The company that developed and publishes the Windows operating system and hundreds of other best-selling programs, including Office, Excel, and Word.

MIDI   Musical Instrument Digital Interface (pronounced "middy"); a standard protocol for communication between musical devices such as synthesizers and PC sound cards. At a minimum, MIDI defines the codes for a musical event, such as a note's pitch, length, volume, and other attributes, such as vibrato, attack, and delay time. The MIDI standard is supported by most synthesizers, allowing MIDI music to be played by an orchestra of separate MIDI instruments.

MIME   Multipurpose Internet Mail Extensions; a protocol that specifies how binary files are encoded, so that any email program can correctly interpret the file type.

MiniDV   Digital video recording format for camcorders that uses an ultrasmall cassette. It records broadcast-quality video (500+ lines of resolution) on small, low-priced cassettes, about 1/12 the size of a standard VHS tape.

mirror   A copy of a Web site, located on a different server on the Internet. Many sites "mirror" their information on multiple servers to prevent overloading of their main site.

modem   Modulator-Demodulator; a hardware device that enables transmission of digital data from one computer to another over common telephone lines via modulating and demodulating. It's the most common way in which people connect to the Internet.

modifier   A symbol that causes a search engine to do something special with the word directly following the symbol. Three modifiers are used almost universally in the search engine community: +, -, and " ".

modulator   That part of a radio that oscillates a radio wave to a specific frequency.

molecular manufacturing   See nanotechnology.

monitor   The thing that looks like a TV screen that displays all your computer text and graphics.

monopole   The most common type of speaker that fires in only one direction (forward); compare with *bipole* and *dipole* speakers that fire in two opposing directions.

Mosaic   The very first Web browser, developed in 1993 by the National Center for Supercomputing Applications (NCSA) at the University of Illinois at Urbana-Champaign.

motherboard   The big board that makes up the bulk of the insides of your system unit. The motherboard holds your main microprocessor and memory chips and also contains slots to plug in additional boards (cards).

mouse   The handheld device with a rollerball and buttons you use to navigate through Windows and other graphical applications.

mouse potato   A person who spends too much time in front of his or her computer.

mousetrapping   The use of JavaScript code to disable your browser's back and exit functions, effectively holding you hostage when you visit a site.

Mozilla Firefox   An opensource Web browser, built on the old Netscape Navigator engine.

.MP3   MPEG-1, Layer 3; an audio compression technology that results in near-CD quality sound compressed into one-twelfth the original file size. MP3 music files, played using software or a handheld device, make it possible to download high-quality audio from the Web and play it back on PCs or portable digital audio players. Developed in Germany by the Fraunhofer Institute in 1991.

MPEG2   The method of compressing digital video signals used by DVDs, digital broadcast satellites, and digital and high-definition television.

ms   Millisecond.

MS-DOS   The Microsoft-specific version of DOS.

MSN   Microsoft Network; Microsoft's commercial online service and ISP.

MUD   Multi-User Dungeon (or Dimension); a multiple-user simulated environment, used either for gaming or for community.

multimedia   The combination, usually on a computer, of interactive text, graphics, audio, and video.

multipartite virus   A virus that combines file infection and boot sector infection.

multiplier   The function that determines the speed of the processor, which, in turn, is a multiple of the bus speed.

multitasking   The capability to run more than one application at a time.

multitrack recording   The process of recording multiple sound sources to individual isolated tracks that are synchronized to record and play back in time.

mW   Milliwatt; one-thousandth of a watt.

N

nanite   See nanomachine.

nanobot   A specialized *nanomachine* designed to repeatedly perform a specific task or set of tasks. Nanobots (also called *nanorobots*) have dimensions measured in *nanometers*.

nanomachine   A mechanical or electromechanical device whose dimensions are measured in *nanometers*; also called a *nanite*.

nanometer   One-millionth of a millimeter.

nanorobot   See nanobot.

nanotechnology   A branch of engineering that deals with the design and manufacturer of electronic circuits and mechanical devices built at the molecular level of matter; also called *molecular manufacturing*.

Napster   A (now defunct) peer-to-peer file-sharing network developed to trade mass amounts of music files over the Internet. Napster was forced to shut down under a barrage of copyright lawsuits from the major music labels.

Net   Shorthand for *Internet*.

Net police   Self-appointed individuals who try to impose their standards on other Internet users; most often seen in newsgroups, mailing lists, and other similar online communities.

netiquette   The etiquette of the Internet.

Netscape Navigator   Netscape's Web browser software.

network   Two or more computers connected together. The Internet is the largest network in the world.

newbie   Newer, inexperienced user.

newsgroup   A special-interest discussion group, hosted on Usenet.

newsreader   A software program used to read Usenet newsgroup messages.

Ni-Cad   Nickel Cadmium (pronounced "ny-cad"); a type of rechargeable battery used in portable computers and devices. To prevent damage to the battery, Ni-Cad batteries should be completely discharged before recharging.

NIC   Network Interface Card; an add-on card that enables a computer to be connected to a network.

NiMH   Nickel Metal Hydride; a type of rechargeable battery used in portable computers and other devices. Has a longer life than Ni-Cad batteries, and can be recharged at any time without damage.

NNTP   Network News Transport Protocol; the protocol used by client and server software to carry Usenet postings across the Internet.

node   Any single computer connected to a network.

nomepage   A home page with little or no content.

NTSC   National Television System Committee; the industry group that established the current North American analog broadcast TV standard. Sometimes refers to the standard itself.

O

OBEX   Object Exchange; an industry protocol that describes how data objects are transferred from one device to another.

OCR   Optical Character Recognition; the reading of text on paper and translation of those images into a format that computer users can manipulate. When a text document is scanned into the computer, it is turned into a bitmap, or picture, of the text. OCR software identifies letters and numbers by analyzing the light and dark areas of the bitmap. When it recognizes a character, it converts it into ASCII text.

OEM   Original Equipment Manufacturer; a company that buys computers in bulk from a manufacturer, and then customizes the machines and sells them under its own name. The term is a misnomer because OEMs aren't the original manufacturers.

OLE   Object Linking and Embedding. The Microsoft standard for creating automatically updated links between documents; also the standard for embedding a document created by one application into a document created by another.

.OMG   Open Magic Gate, which is the digital rights management wrapper Sony uses for its proprietary ATRAC3 digital audio format.

OMR   Open Mail Relay; an unprotected server that can be used to initiate mass emailings.

online communications   Any and all communications between one computer and another over phone lines, via modem.

opacity   A measurement of how easily light passes through paper.

open source   Software for which the underlying programming code is available (free) for users to make changes to it and build new versions incorporating those changes.

Opera   An alternative Web browser to Internet Explorer.

operating system   The core system software that lets you (and your software programs) communicate with your hardware.

optical zoom   A traditional zoom lens that enables you to move the focus closer to the subject, thus enlarging the image.

OS   Operating system.

oscillator   An electrical device that uses varying voltages to oscillate at different frequencies, thereby producing musical notes.

overclocking   Running your processor at a speed faster than it's rated. Most processors can run faster than their rated speed with some sacrifice of reliability.

oversampling   A technique in which each sample coming from the D/A converter is sampled multiple times. The samples are then interpolated creating an antialiasing effect.

P

P2P   Peer-to-peer; a communications network where two or more computers work together as equals, without benefit of a central server.

packet   Part of a larger piece of data. When sent from one device to another (or over the Internet or other networks), data objects are typically broken up into multiple packets for easier transmittal.

packet sniffer   A software program that examines the contents of data packets flowing over a network or the Internet.

packet switching   The method used to move data around the Internet, in small, easily manageable packets.

PAL   The European broadcast standard.

PAN   Personal Area Network; a small network comprised of all the personal electronics devices used by a single person.

pan-and-scan   A technique used to display the most important parts of a wide-screen image on a narrower 4:3 ratio screen. The name comes from the panning and scanning necessary to keep the focus on the most important part of the scene, which is not always in the direct center of the picture.

parallel   A type of external port used to connect printers and other similar devices.

password   A special encrypted "word" (composed of any combination of letters and numbers) that one enters to obtain access to a computer, network, or Web site.

password cracker   Software that can decrypt passwords or otherwise disable or bypass password protection.

paste   To place data cut or copied from another location into a new location.

patch   A sound created by a synthesizer. The term comes from the early days of modular synthesis when modules were "patched" together to produce different sounds.

patch bay   An electrical panel that, ideally, contains an input and output for the various devices used in an audio studio. It serves as a central point to connect the various devices together.

path   The collection of folders and subfolders (listed in order of hierarchy) that hold a particular file.

payload   The deliverable aspect of a computer virus; the noticeable effects of a virus attack.

PC   See personal computer.

PC Card   A credit-card–size memory or I/O device that fits into a desktop PC, portable PC, and some PDAs. Formerly known as a *PCMCIA card*.

PCM   Pulse Code Modulation; a way of encoding audio data as a series of pulses, with each pulse defining a binary 1 or 0.

PCMCIA   Personal Computer Memory Card International Association; an industry group formed to promote the adoption of credit-card–size memory and I/O devices.

PCMCIA card   See PC Card.

PDA   Personal Digital Assistant; a handheld device that organizes personal information, combining computing and networking features. A typical PDA includes an address book and a to-do list. Some function as cell phones and fax senders. Unlike portable computers, which use a keyboard for input, most PDAs incorporate a stylus and some sort of handwriting recognition capability. PDAs are sometimes called palm, pocket, or handheld PCs.

peer-to-peer   See P2P.

peer-to-peer file-swapping   The act of exchanging files among similar computers over a peer-to-peer network.

peripheral   Add-on hardware device for a computer system, such as a printer or a modem.

personal computer A multifunction hardware unit that includes a hard disk, memory chips, microprocessor chip, and monitor. Personal computers perform tasks when enabled by *software* entered into memory.

personal firewall Firewall software designed for a home or small-business PC.

pervasive computing The use of numerous, easily accessible computing devices to conduct everyday activities.

PGP Pretty Good Privacy; one of the most popular tools for a form of public-key encryption.

phishing The act of sending a fraudulent email claiming to be from a major company, directing you to an imitation Web site that then collects your personal and financial information with the aim of ripping you off.

phreaker An individual who cracks into telecommunications systems.

PIM Personal Information Manager; a computer program that manages contact and scheduling data.

PIN Personal Identification Number; a secret code number that must be entered by the user to gain access to a particular device or service.

PING Packet INternet Groper; an Internet utility that determines whether a particular IP address is online. Administrators use it to test and debug a network by sending out a packet and waiting for a response.

pink noise A random audio signal that has equal energy across its frequency range.

PIP Picture-In-Picture; the display of a second picture in a small window within a larger picture.

pixel The individual picture elements that make up a video image. The unit of measurement used in measuring the quality of screen displays.

pixelization The stairstepped appearance of a curved or angled line in a digital image; see jaggies.

PKC Public Key Cryptography; see public-key encryption.

plain-text email Email messages that incorporate text only, without any HTML code.

plasma display A flat-panel video display that uses plasma gas to "light up" individual pixels in a picture.

playlist A list of songs that can be organized in the order to be played. Most media player programs and portable digital players let you create customized playlists of songs.

Plug and Play Hardware that includes its manufacturer and model information in its ROM, enabling Windows to recognize it immediately upon startup and install the necessary drivers if not already set up.

plug-in A type of program that integrates with a larger application to add a special capability to it.

point-to-point A direct connection of one device to a second device.

polymorphic virus A file-infector virus that is capable of changing itself as it travels from one system to another.

POP (1) Point of Presence; a telephone number that gives you dial-up access. Internet service providers (ISPs) generally provide many POPs so that users can make a local call to gain Internet access.

POP (2) Post Office Protocol; a protocol used to retrieve email from a mail server.

POP (3) Picture-Outside-Picture; a second, smaller picture, typically on a widescreen TV, that displays outside the main picture window.

pop-under window A pop-up window that hides itself behind other open windows on your desktop.

pop-up menu The context-sensitive menu that appears when you right-click an object.

pop-up window A small browser window, typically without menus or other navigational elements, that opens seemingly of its own accord when you visit or leave another Web site.

port (1) An interface on a computer to which you can connect a device. Personal computers have various types of ports. Internally, there are several ports for connecting disk drives, display screens, and keyboards. Externally, there are ports for connecting modems, printers, mice, and other peripheral devices.

port (2) A virtual access point into a computer. Internet services use specific ports on computers used as Web servers.

port scanner Software that looks for open ports on other computers. Also called *port sniffer*.

portal   A Web site that provides a gateway to the Internet, as well as a collection of other content and services. Most of today's portals (Yahoo!, Excite, and so on) started life as search engines or directories.

portrait mode   Viewing an image where the height is greater than the width.

POTS   Plain Old Telephone Service; traditional wired telephone service.

ppi   Pixels per inch.

PPP   Point-to-Point Protocol; a technical protocol that defines how Internet Protocol (IP) data is transmitted over serial point-to-point links.

preamplifier   An amplifier that is used to boost a low-level signal up to line level (approximately up 60dBv). Audio preamps also typically control or switch the various inputs from audio and video sources.

printer   The piece of computer hardware that lets you create hard-copy printouts of your documents.

private key   A secret key that can be used, either by itself or (in public-key encryption) in conjunction with a public key, to decrypt encrypted messages.

processor   The brains of the entire computer. The processor, which is where a computer's instructions are decoded and executed, performs all of its logical operations.

processor cache   The usually small amount of high-speed Static RAM (SRAM) that can significantly improve CPU performance. This cache resides between the CPU and the main system memory.

program   A term used interchangeably with *software*, a program is an organized list of instructions that tells a computer what to do. In other words, software is an executable version of a program; without programs, computers are useless.

progressive scanning   A method of displaying television pictures where the picture is displayed in a single pass, instead of the two fields used with *interlaced scanning*. A progressively scanned picture more accurately reproduces fast action and minimizes the visibility of flicker and scan lines. Typically denoted by a "p" after the resolution number, as in 480p (480 lines of resolution, progressively scanned).

protocol   An agreed-upon format for transmitting data between two devices.

proxy server   A server that buffers all incoming and outgoing communications between a network and the Internet.

PSTN   Public Switched Telephony Network; the traditional, old-fashioned, wired telephone network.

PTR   Personal Television Receiver. *See DVR.*

public key   A key, provided by some authority, that, when combined with a private key, can be used to decrypt encrypted messages.

public-key encryption   A means of encrypting data and messages using a combination of public and private keys.

pull-down list   A button with a down arrow that, when clicked, displays a list of further options or items.

PVR   Personal Video Recorder. *See DVR.*

Q

QoS   Quality of Service; the guaranteed performance for an application or process.

.QT   QuickTime; a sound, video, and animation format developed by Apple Computer. A QuickTime file can contain up to 32 tracks of audio, video, MIDI, or other time-based control information.

quantize   Forcing the notes in a MIDI sequence to fall on the nearest beat.

query   A word, phrase, or group of words, possibly combined with other syntax or operators, used to initiate a search with a search engine or directory.

queue   The list of print jobs that are ready for printing, paused, or currently printing. (Not to be confused with Que, the company that published this book!)

R

.RA   RealAudio; a standard for streaming audio data over the Web. Developed by RealNetworks, RealAudio supports FM-stereo–quality sound.

rack   A special type of storage shelf used to house pro audio gear.

RAM

RAM   Random Access Memory; a common type of temporary computer memory that functions as a machine's primary workspace. The more RAM your computer has, the more efficiently it will operate.

RAS   Remote Access Services; a Windows NT feature that allows remote users to log in to a LAN using a modem, X.25 connection, or WAN link.

raster   A pattern of horizontal lines displayed on a computer or TV monitor. As the part of a monitor's screen that is actually being used to display images, it's a bit smaller than the physical dimensions of the display screen itself. It varies for different resolutions.

.RAW   A digital photo file format that holds exactly what the camera's imaging chip recorded, without any pre-editing or compression.

read   How data is absorbed from a disk to your system's memory.

receiver   A component that combines a preamplifier, amplifier, and radio in a single chassis. Receivers that include inputs and outputs for video sources and display are called *audio/video receivers*.

Recycle Bin   The "trash can" on the Windows desktop that temporarily holds deleted files.

region codes   The codes embedded in DVD discs that define the global regions in which the disc can be played.

Registry   The Windows registration file that stores all configuration information.

Registry Editor   A utility (REGEDIT.EXE) used to edit the Windows Registry.

remailer   A service used to send anonymous email; the remailer strips out the header from the original message, and then remails the now-anonymous message to its intended recipient.

removable media   Information storage that allow users to remove the stored information if necessary. Examples of removable media include disks and magnetic tapes.

resolution   The degree of clarity an image displays. The term is most often used to describe the sharpness of bitmapped images on monitors, but also applies to images on printed pages, as expressed by the number of dots per inch (dpi). For monitors, screen resolution signifies the number of dots (pixels) on the screen. For example, a 640×480 pixel screen can display 640 dots on each of 480 lines, or about 300,000 pixels. For television monitors, resolution is typically measured in terms of horizontal lines that can be seen or resolved. (See horizontal resolution.)

restore   The process of returning a backed-up file to its previous location, often from a disk or tape to a hard drive.

reverb   The persistence of an acoustic signal after the original signal has ceased.

RF   Radio Frequency; a means of transmitting and receiving signals via modulated radio waves.

RFC   Request For Comments; the process for creating new standards on the Internet.

RGB   Red, Green, Blue; the additive color model used in video displays.

right-click   The act of hovering over an item and then clicking your right mouse button; this often displays a pop-up menu of commands related to the object selected.

ripping   Copying music from a CD to your computer's hard disk.

.RM   RealMovie; the video version of the RealAudio format.

robot (1)   See spider.

robot (2)   A machine designed to execute one or more tasks repeatedly, with speed and precision.

ROM   Read-Only Memory; a storage chip that typically contains hard-wired instructions for use when a computer starts up.

root directory   The main directory or folder on a disk.

router   A piece of hardware or software that handles the connection between two or more networks.

RPTV   Rear-Projection Television; a video display device that uses three CRTs (or some similar method of light generation) to project a picture backward within a cabinet onto a mirror, which then reflects the picture onto the back of a translucent screen.

RSA   A public-key encryption technology created by Ron Rivest, Adi Shamir, and Leonard Adleman of RSA Data Security, Inc. The key has two parts, one private and one public; both parts are required for decryption. Used in Netscape Navigator, Microsoft Internet Explorer, and other applications that require industrial-strength encryption, the RSA algorithm has become a standard, especially for data sent over the Internet.

RSI   Repetitive Strain Injury; ailments of the hands, neck, back, and eyes due to computer use.

RSS   Really Simple Syndication, an XML-based format that publishes the content of an online resource in a way that any kind of program can read. When information about an item is posted in RSS format, any RSS-aware program can check the feed for changes, and then react to the changes in an appropriate way.

RTFM   Read The F***ing Manual; a typical response to newbies asking stupid technology-related questions.

S

S/N   Signal to Noise; see signal-to-noise ratio.

S/PDIF   Sony/Philips Digital Interface; a digital-to-digital audio file transfer format. Carries up to 24-bit data.

SA-CD   Super-Audio CD; a new CD-based format that delivers better-than-CD-quality sound. Competes with *DVD-Audio*.

sampling frequency   The rate at which measurements of an audio signal are taken during A/D and D/A conversion. A higher sampling rate makes for a higher-fidelity audio signal.

sandboxing   The process of running a program within an isolated (or virtual) environment, thus protecting the computer system from any ill effects of virus infection during the test.

scan lines   The horizontal lines, scanned one after another, that comprise the picture on a video display. (Don't confuse with *horizontal resolution*, which measures the visible number of lines in a display.)

scanner (1)   A device that converts paper documents or photos into a format that can be viewed on a computer and manipulated by the user.

scanner (2)   See sniffer.

scavenger bot   See spambot.

screen saver   A utility that prolongs the life of your monitor by blanking the screen—or providing a continuously moving image—while your monitor is not in use.

script kiddie   A would-be cracker who isn't a technically adept programmer.

script language   An easy-to-use pseudo-programming language that enables the creation of executable scripts composed of individual commands.

script virus   A computer virus written in ActiveX, Java, JavaScript, or another computer script language.

SCSI   Small Computer System Interface (pronounced "scuzzy"); the standard port for Macintosh computers, also common in PCs and Unix boxes. SCSI is really a family of interfaces, ranging from the relatively primitive SCSI-1 to the spiffy new Wide Ultra2 SCSI. SCSI hard drives are commonly used for audio applications because they generally can read and write data faster than can an IDE drive.

scumware   Another word for *spyware*.

SDSL   Symmetric Digital Subscriber Line; a type of DSL in which the upload and download speeds are the same.

search engine   A Web server that indexes Web pages, and then makes the index available for user searching. Search engines differ from directories in that the indexes are generated using *spiders*, where directories are assembled manually. Search engine indexes typically include many more Web pages than are found in directories.

search site   Generic term for a Web site that offers either a search engine or directory (or both).

search term   See query.

secure server   A Web *server* that uses encryption to provide protected credit-card transactions.

semiconductor   A substance, usually a solid chemical element or compound, that can conduct electricity under some conditions but not others, making it a good medium for the control of electrical current. Its conductance varies depending on the current or voltage applied to a control electrode, or on the intensity of irradiation by infrared, visible light, ultraviolet, or X rays.

sequencer   A device that stores MIDI data.

serial   A type of external port used to connect communication devices, such as modems and PalmPilots.

server   A central computer on a network that responds to requests for information from one or more client computers. On the Internet, all Web pages are stored on servers; in a client/server relationship between two devices, the server is the device that is controlled by commands from the other device (client).

session hijacking   An attack where the attacker commandeers use of a computer, typically using some sort of back-door Trojan, to use that computer to attack another computer or network.

session key   A temporary key used to encrypt or decrypt a specific message.

setup   How you configure your system (or individual software or hardware).

shareware   Computer software distributed free, but requiring purchase to use beyond an initial period of time (or to use the full feature set).

shortcut (1)   A combination of two keys on your keyboard that, when pressed simultaneously, execute a specific function.

shortcut (2)   An icon on the desktop used to represent an application; click a shortcut to launch an application, or right-click to view and modify its properties.

shouting   WRITING IN ALL CAPS!

.SHS   Windows 95/98/NT "scrap" files—usually dragged onto the desktop to be used as shortcuts.

shutter   That part of a camera that opens and closes to control how long the film or CCD is exposed to light.

shutter speed   The length of time the shutter remains open when shooting an image.

SIG   Special Interest Group; a topic-specific subgroup within a larger organization.

signal-to-noise ratio   A measurement of the content portion of an audio or video signal in relation to the noise contained in the signal, expressed in decibels (dB). A higher S/N ratio indicates a quieter or less noisy signal. As an example, VHS VCRs have S/N ratios in the 40dB range, whereas DVDs have S/N ratios approaching 65dB.

signature   The identifying information you put at the bottom of all your email correspondence.

signature scanning   A method of scanning for computer viruses by matching known sequences of binary code.

SIMM   Single Inline Memory Module; a narrow circuit board that holds memory chips. It plugs into a SIMM socket on a motherboard or memory board. Unlike memory chips, SIMMs are measured in bytes rather than bits.

Sirius   One of two satellite audio broadcasting systems. (The other is *XM*.)

site   A unified collection of Web pages on the Internet.

sleeper   A virus or worm that resides, hidden, on a system, awaiting the delivery of its payload at some later date.

SLR   Single Lens Reflex; a film-based camera that enables you to look through a viewfinder and see through the lens.

SM   SmartMedia; a small memory storage card, similar to *Compact Flash*.

SMART   Self-Monitoring, Analysis, and Reporting Technology; an open standard within hardware and software that automatically monitors a disk drive's health and reports of potential failure. All major hard-drive manufacturers use SMART to detect imminent disk problems and report the danger to the computer user.

smart phone   A next-generation (3G) digital cellular phone that offers enhanced data and communications capabilities.

SmartMedia   See SM.

SMB   Server Message Block; a file-sharing protocol that Windows uses to share files and resources, such as printers, across a network.

SMPT   Simple Mail Transfer Protocol; the primary protocol used to send email from server to server on the Internet.

SMS   Short Message Service; similar to paging, a service for sending messages of up to 160 characters to mobile phones.

snail mail   Traditional U.S. Postal Service (USPS) mail.

sniffer   Software used to determine a computer's online availability.

snipe   In an online auction, the auction of placing an unexpected, last-second bid.

SNMP   Simple Network Management Protocol; a set of standards used to manage communication between devices connected to a TCP/IP network.

social engineering   A nontechnological means of conning another person into revealing user names, passwords, and other private information.

software   A digital program that instructs a piece of hardware to perform a specific task.

sound card   The card that processes audio data on a PC. It's often a PCI card, but it can also be USB or FireWire based—or it can be built into the computer's motherboard.

spam   Junk email. Some people define spam as any unsolicited email. A narrower definition is unsolicited advertising, most commonly for credit cards, weight-loss methods, and pyramid schemes.

spamblock   Any characters you insert in the middle of your email address to confuse spambot software.

spambot   An automated software program that trolls the Web, Usenet newsgroups, and public message boards, looking for email addresses that are later used in spam mailings. (The name is short for "spam robot.")

spamming   The act of sending large numbers of unsolicited email messages.

spamouflage   When a spammer spoofs the sender's email address in a spam message.

spider   A software program that follows hypertext links across multiple Web pages, but is not directly under human control. Spiders scan the Web, looking for URLs, automatically following all the hyperlinks on pages accessed. The results from a spider's search are used to create the indexes used by search engines.

spool   Lining up multiple print jobs in a queue. These print jobs are said to be "spooled" to the printer.

spread spectrum   A coding technique where a digital signal is spread among a range of frequencies, to reduce interference and increase security.

spreadsheet   Software that simulates a paper spreadsheet, or worksheet, in which columns of numbers are summed for budgets and plans. A spreadsheet appears onscreen as a matrix of rows and columns, the intersections of which are identified as cells. Spreadsheets can have thousands of cells and can be scrolled horizontally and vertically to be viewed.

spyware   Software used to surreptitiously monitor computer use (that is, spy on other users).

SQL   Structured Query Language; a language used to send queries to databases.

SRAM   Static RAM; RAM that retains data bits in its memory as long as power is being supplied. Unlike DRAM (dynamic random access memory), which stores bits in cells consisting of a capacitor and a transistor, SRAM does not have to be periodically refreshed.

SSL   Secure Sockets Layer; a form of encryption used in secure servers.

standby mode   A special mode on newer computer systems that powers down disk drives and monitors without actually shutting off the computer itself; often called *sleep* mode.

Start menu   The menu used to start most Windows programs and utilities; visible when the Start button is clicked.

startup diskette   A special diskette used to start Windows if something is wrong with the information on your hard disk.

stateful packet inspection   A method of firewall protection that matches incoming traffic with outgoing requests.

stealth virus   A virus that hides itself when running, to avoid detection.

STN   Spanking the Net; surfing the Web for adult-oriented material.

streaming   Refers to the continuous transmission of data, typically audio or video, so it can be processed as a steady stream. With streaming, the client browser or plug-in can start displaying the data as sound and pictures before the entire file has been transmitted.

stylus   A penlike device used to operate the touch screen on a PDA.

subwoofer   A speaker specially designed to reproduce a range of very low frequencies—typically 20Hz–200Hz. Subwoofers are common in home theater systems to enhance the reproduction of low bass in movie soundtracks.

suite   A set of applications designed to work together. A suite typically includes word processing, spreadsheet, presentation graphics, and database programs.

SuperDisk   A portable storage medium from Sony that can hold up to 120MB of data; SuperDisk drives can read and write information to and from older 3 1/2-inch disks.

surge suppressor   A device that protects your system from unwanted power-line surges.

surround sound   The experience of being surrounded by sound from a video or audio source. Typically achieved with a surround-sound decoder (either Dolby Digital or Dolby Pro Logic) and multiple speakers.

S-VHS   Super VHS; a variation on the standard VHS format that delivers sharper pictures (400 lines of resolution versus 240 lines for standard VHS).

S-Video   A four-pin connection that transmits the chrominance (color) and luminance (brightness) portions of a video signal separately, for improved color accuracy and reduced distortion.

SVGA   Super Visual Graphics Array; a graphics display of 1280×1024 pixels, using 16 million different colors.

symmetrical   A type of connection that operates at the same speed both upstream and downstream.

symmetric-key encryption   A means of encrypting data where both parties (sender and recipient) have access to the same private key.

synching   The process of linking two devices together to exchange data or work from the same documents. For example, a DAT can be synched to a PC and be used to store audio data while still being controlled by the PC.

synchronous   A type of connection that permits data to flow in two directions, simultaneously. Also known as *full-duplex*.

sysop   System Operator; a person responsible for the physical operation of a computer system or network.

system disk   A disk containing the operating system and all files necessary to start your computer.

system file   A key file used by the computer's operating system.

system unit   That part of your computer system that looks like a big beige box. The system unit typically contains your microprocessor, system memory, hard disk drive, floppy disk drives, and various cards.

T

T-1   A leased-line connection capable of carrying data at 1.5Mbps; typically used for fast Internet connections to large corporations.

T-3   A leased-line connection capable of carrying data at 44.7Mbps.

tab   The top of a "page" in a dialog box; many dialog boxes display multiple sets of data on a series of tabs.

table   A collection of data organized into rows and columns.

Taskbar   The bar at the bottom of the screen (normally) in Windows; the Start button and temporary buttons for active applications appear on the Taskbar.

TCP/IP   Transmission Control Protocol/Internet Protocol; the protocol used for communications on the Internet. It coordinates the addressing and packaging of the data packets that make up any communication.

technospeak   See jargon.

telecommunications   How your computer talks to other computers, using a modem.

telephoto lens   A camera lens with a focal length greater than 50mm; makes far subjects appear closer than through a standard lens.

Telnet   An older command and program used to log in to and access data stored on an Internet server.

terabyte   One thousand gigabytes.

terminal   A device with a screen and keyboard that relies on a mainframe or another computer for intelligence.

THD   Total Harmonic Distortion; a measurement of the noise generated by an amplifier or receiver. The lower the number, the better.

thread   A group of related messages in a newsgroup, mailing list, or message board.

thumbnail   A miniature representation of a page or image. Thumbnails often take considerable time to generate, but provide a convenient way to browse through multiple images before retrieving the one you need. A number of programs let you click on the thumbnail to retrieve the item it represents or view the picture at a larger size.

THX   A set of high-fidelity standards, above and beyond the Dolby Digital standard, for both home theater equipment and prerecorded programming.

.TIF or .TIFF   Tagged Image File Format; a common file format for storing bitmapped images. The images can display any resolution, and they can be monochrome, grayscale, or in full color.

Time Division Duplexing   A scheme wherein two different transmissions can share the same frequency for full-duplex communication, by dividing each frequency into time slots; the two transmissions alternate transmitting and receiving at preset intervals.

timecode   Timecode is a signal that contains a chronological record of the absolute time in a recording. It is used for synchronizing different recorders and for electronic editing. Timecode was initially invented for motion pictures as a method of synchronizing the pictures recorded in the frames of a camera with the sound recorded on a tape recorder.

toner   Ultrafine coated powder, typically stored in some sort of cartridge, used by laser printers to create printed images on paper.

TOS   Terms Of Service; the legal restrictions you allegedly agree to before you enter a Web site.

Tray   The area of the Windows Taskbar that holds icons for "background" utilities, such as the Windows clock.

Trojan horse   A malicious program that pretends to be another, harmless program or file.

troll   A user who posts only to inflame other newsgroup or mailing list users.

TrueType   A scalable font technology that renders fonts for both the printer and the screen. Originally developed by Apple, it was enhanced jointly by Apple and Microsoft.

Twain   The standard used to acquire digital images from scanners and digital cameras.

tweeter   A speaker designed to reproduce very high frequencies, typically those over 5KHz or so.

U

UBE   Unsolicited Bulk Email; another name for *spam*.

UCE   Unsolicited Commercial Email; another name for *spam*.

unbalanced   A connector that has a positive conductor that's surrounded by the negative conductor.

Uncle Joe   A Web site that loads very slowly. (As in the character of Uncle Joe from the old *Petticoat Junction* TV show.)

undelete   Unerase. Bring a file back from the dead.

uninstall   Deleting a software application—and all its associated files, drivers, and associations—from a computer system.

Unix   A computer operating system. Unix is designed to be used by many people at the same time and has TCP/IP built in.

UPC   Universal Product Code, the industry-standard bar codes found on most retail products.

upgrade   To add a new or improved peripheral or part to your system hardware. Also to install a newer version of an existing piece of software.

upholstery   Useless graphics on a Web page.

upload   The act of copying a file from a personal computer to a Web site or Internet server.

UPnP   Universal Plug and Play; a standard that uses Internet and Web protocols to enable various devices (PCs, peripherals, and so on) to be plugged into a network and automatically know about one another.

URL   Uniform Resource Locator; the address of a Web page.

USB   Universal Serial Bus; an external bus standard that supports data transfer rates of 12Mbps (12 million bits per second). One USB port can connect up to 127 peripheral devices, such as keyboards, modems, and mice. USB also supports hot plugging and Plug-and-Play installation.

Usenet   A subset of the Internet used to exchange messages between users, using topic-specific *newsgroups*.

Uuencode

Uuencode   When it was new, uuencode stood for Unix-to-Unix encode, but gradually it became a universal protocol for transferring files between platforms such as Unix, Windows, and Macintosh. It's a set of algorithms that converts files into a series of 7-bit ASCII characters that can be transmitted over the Internet.

V

V-Chip   Government-mandated chip included in newer television sets that can block the display of inappropriate programming.

value   The program setting that defines a specific key in the Windows Registry.

vaporware   New computer software that's been announced but never seems to be released.

VCR   Video Cassette Recorder; a device that records audio and video signals on videotape cassettes.

Veronica   Very Easy Rodent Oriented Netwide Index to Computerized Archives; an early method of indexing and searching Gopher servers.

VGA   Video Graphics Array; a graphics display of 640×480 pixels with 256 colors.

VHS   Today's standard videocassette format.

VHS HiFi   A variation on the standard VHS format that includes high-fidelity stereo sound. VHS HiFi VCRs can also play back tapes encoded with Dolby Pro Logic surround sound—although they can't reproduce Dolby Digital sound-tracks.

VHS-C   A recording format for camcorders that uses standard VHS-format tape in a smaller-shelled cassette.

video   Picture.

virtual memory   Hard disk space used by Windows as transient memory.

virus   A bad, nasty, evil computer program that can infect your computer system and cause untold damage to your data. See computer virus.

virus scanner   A computer utility, typically part of an antivirus program, that searches for suspicious program code.

Visual Basic   Based on the BASIC computer programming language, Microsoft's Visual Basic was one of the first products to provide a graphical programming environment and a paint metaphor for developing user interfaces. With Visual Basic, a programmer can add or delete code by dragging and dropping controls, such as buttons and dialog boxes, instead of worrying about syntax details.

Visual Basic Script   Also called VBScript or VBS, this is an extension to Microsoft's Visual Basic language specifically designed for developing World Wide Web applications. VBScript is widely used as the scripting language in Active Server Pages.

VPN   Virtual Private Network; a network in which some parts are connected via the public Internet, but encrypted, so that the network is "virtually" private.

VRAM   Video RAM (pronounced "vee-ram"); a memory chip designed specifically for video applications.

W

WAIS   Wide Area Information Servers; a software program that enables the indexing of huge quantities of information across the Internet and other networks.

WAN   Wide Area Network; a connection between two or more local area networks (LANs). Wide area networks can be made up of interconnected smaller networks spread throughout a building, a state, or the globe.

WAP   Wireless Application Protocol; a standard for providing cellular phones, pagers, and other handheld devices with secure access to email and text-based Web pages. WAP features the Wireless Markup Language (WML), a streamlined version of HTML for small-screen displays. It also uses WMLScript, a compact JavaScript-like language that runs in limited memory.

war driving   The act of driving around a business district with specific electronic equipment, looking for insecure wireless networks.

warez   Pronounced "wheres," this is illegally distributed software, from which normal copy protection has been cracked or removed.

watt   A unit of power of energy.

Web   See World Wide Web.

Web beacon   *See Web bug.*

Web browser   *See browser.*

Web bug   A small, usually transparent, graphics file (typically 1×1 pixel) hidden in an HTML email message that loads from an advertising site and drops cookies on your hard disk.

Web ring   A navigation system that links related Web sites together. Each ring links sites that pertain to a particular topic.

Weblog   *See blog.*

WEP   Wireless Equivalent Privacy; the encryption and security protocol for Wi-Fi networks.

white noise   A random noise that contains an equal amount of energy per frequency band. That is, 100–200, 800–900, and 3000–3100. Pink noise has an equal amount of energy per octave. The bands 0–200, 800–1600, and 3000–6000 all contain the same amount of energy.

WHOIS   An Internet lookup service used to trace the owner of a specific Web page or domain.

Wi-Fi   The 802.11b wireless networking standard; short for "wireless fidelity."

wide screen   A picture with an aspect ratio wider than 4:3 or 1.33:1.

wide-angle lens   A camera lens with a focal length less than 50mm; it gives a wider field of view than normal lenses.

wildcard   A character that substitutes for one or more characters within a query. For example, the * wildcard typically substitutes for any combination of characters.

Windows   The generic name for all versions of Microsoft's graphical operating system.

WLAN   Wireless LAN; a local area network composed of wireless connections between devices.

.WMA   Windows Media Audio; Microsoft audio file format.

.WMV   Windows Media Video; Microsoft video file format.

woofer   A driver within a speaker enclosure that uses a large cone to reproduce bass frequencies.

word   One sample of audio data.

wordclock   A sync pulse that lets devices determine the start of each digital word. When multiple digital devices are connected together, it's vital that each device knows where a digital word starts and stops; otherwise, dropout or distortion can result.

World Wide Web   A subset of the Internet that contains HTML pages.

worm   A parasitic computer program that replicates but does not infect other files.

wow and flutter   Measures the accuracy of a cassette deck's playback speed; the lower, the better.

write   How data is placed on a disk.

WYSIWYG   What You See Is What You Get (pronounced "whizzy wig"); refers to display or printouts that accurately reflect the original documents or images.

WWW   *World Wide Web.*

X

XGA   eXtended Graphics Array; a graphics display of 1024×768 pixels, with 65,000 colors.

XLR   A connector that's used to carry balanced audio signals.

.XLS   The file format for Microsoft Excel spreadsheets.

XM   One of two competing systems for broadcasting audio programming via satellite (the other is *Sirius*), primarily for car-mounted reception.

XML   eXtensible Markup Language; a scripting language designed especially for Web documents that lets programmers create customized tags which provide functionality not available in HTML. Not only does it make the language easier to understand, it also lets you search and extract information. This can be particularly helpful for use in databases.

XNS   eXtensible Name Service; combines the technology of XML with Web agents.

Y–Z

Yahoo!   The most popular portal and directory on the Web.

.ZIP   A file format for compressed files. When you compress files to a .ZIP file, you're said to be "zipping" them.

Zip drive   A portable storage medium from Iomega that can hold between 100MB (originally) and 250MB of data.

zombie (1)

zombie (1)   A computer that has been hijacked by another computer, typically with malicious intent.

zombie (2)   A dead program or process that occupies memory but is no longer functional and will not go away.

INDEX

Numbers

1984, 186
1st JavaScript Library, 101
3D Flying Easter Eggs Screensaver, 94
3D UltraPong, 154
3M Privacy Computer Filter, 344
4Kids Treehouse Web site, 289
30-second skip (TiVo), 47
33 1/3 rpm long-playing record demonstration, 303
45 RPM records, 12
550 Access Toolbar, 187
650 Magnetic Drum Data Processing Machine, 216

A

AAC audio format, 146
AARP (American Association for Retired People), 244
Abacus Wrist Net Internet Watch, 269
Absolute Beginner's Guide to Home Networking, 216
accelerating galaxy discovery, 11
access points, wireless Internet, 205
accessories
    digital cameras, 31
    iPod, 223
    movies, 44
    notebooks, 330
    PDAs, 316
ACM-GAMM committee, convenes to develop ALGOL, 13
ActivatorDesk Web site, 280
Activity Monitor, 208
Adams, John Couch, 218, 309
adapters, Linksys Wireless Compact USB Adapter, 200
ADC Monitor Sharing Switch, 300
adding and sorting machine, patent, 10
Addonics MFR 18-in-1 Multi Function Reader, 363
Address Book (Yahoo!), 84
Adesso Tru-Form, 418
Adleman, Len, 112
Adler Planetarium opened, 156
Adobe
    Audition, 152
    Photoshop Album, 27
    Photoshop Elements 3, 384
    Premiere Pro, 404
ADPUSH Web site, 257
ads, 257
ADSL (Asymmetric DSL), 60

ADSL-Lite, 60
Advanced Micro Devices (AMD), 323
Advanced Page Rank Analyzer, 78
advertisements, 257
    hijacking, 303
    pop-ups
        creating, 302
        stopping, 301
advertising, Nielsen-Netratings, 230
adware programs, 298, 303
aerial tramways, 208
aerosol spray ozone depletion, 311
aerosol spray patent, 272
African Americans, Internet usage, 303
Agendus, 322
AgeNet, 244
Aiken, Howard, 235
AIM (AOL Instant Messenger), 52
air brakes, patent, 121
Air Flo Mouse, 370
AirPort, 202
    Dr. Bott's ExtendAIR Direct, 307
    Extreme Base Station, 411
AirZooka, 109
ALA Resources for Parents, Teens, and Kids Web site, 266
alert boxes, 103
ALFY Web site, 289
ALGOL (ALGOrithmic Language), 13
Alienware, 173
All Games Free, 154
All Season Clipart Web site, 391
All-In-Wonder 9800 PRO, 384
All-Music Guide, 239
Allen, Paul, 201
AllTheWeb, 87
Aloha Bob PC Relocator, 166
Altair 8800, 409
AltaVista, 87, 281
Altec Lansing inMotion Portable Audio System, 222
Amazon Rainforest theme, 371
Amazon Standard Item Number (ASIN), 373
Amazon.com, 370
    associates, 372
    creating lists, 376
    jumping to product listings, 373
    Marketplace, 376
    power searches, 375

product reviews, 371
sales, 375
shipping costs, 374
AMD (Advanced Micro Devices), 323
Amdahl, Gene, birth, 372
American Association for Retired People (AARP), 244
American Life Project survey, 151
American space probe Ranger 7, 245
AmeriSurplus Web site, 383
analog televisions versus digital, 307
AnalogX Vocal Remover, 6
AnandTech, 170
AND operator, 89
Andale Web site, 368
Anderson, Harlan, 236
András, Gróf, 288
Andreessen, Marc, 259
anesthetic, used for first time, 336
Angelfire Web site, 251
Animaland Web site, 290
animals, Web sites, 290
animation
    films, first, 411
    PowerPoint slides, 415
    Steamboat Willie, 374
Annoyances.org, 275
Anonymyzer Total System Sweeper, 13
ANT 4 MailChecking, 125
Anti-Phishing Working Group site, 8
anti-spam software, 125
AntiSpyware, 304
AntiVir, 136
AOL Instant Messenger, 52
AOL Search, 87
ApeXtreme, 153
Apollo 1 disaster, 29
Apollo mission launched, 331
Apple, 404
    AirPort, 202
    AirPort Extreme Base Station, 411
    IPO, 402
    iPod. See iPods
    iSight, 181
    iTunes opening, 136
    legal suit against Microsoft, 94
    Macintoshes. See Macintoshes
    PowerBook, 407
    Wireless Keyboard, 28
    Wozniak, Stephen, 261
Apple II released, 190
Applian Software Web site, 313

April historical events
    air brakes patented, 121
    Apple opens iTunes, 136
    assassination of Dr. Martin Luther King Jr., 112
    Big Bang Theory proposed, 109
    calendar, 108, 139-141
    cell phones, first call, 111
    Chernobyl nuclear power disaster, 134
    electron existence announced, 138
    extra-solar planets discovered, 129
    Google files for IPO, 137
    Hostess Twinkies invented, 113
    Hubble telescope launches, 132
    IBM ships first mainframe computer, 115
    Leonardo da Vinci's birth, 123
    NASA announces first astronauts, 117
    new Coke introduced, 131
    Oklahoma City Federal building bombed, 127
    Post-It Notes introduced, 114
    radar patent, 110
    Robert Oppenheimer's birth, 130
    San Francisco earthquake of 1906, 126
    solar batteries announced for first time, 133
    Spirit Rover landing on Mars, 120
    sun spot observation, 116
    Titanic sets sail, 118
    Vertijet, 119
    Walter Cronkite anchors CBS Evening News for first time, 124
    Weather Bureau kite, first, 135
aquariums, USB Glowing Aquarium, 126
ArcadeTown.com, 154
Archie, 86
Archos
    AV300 series (portable video players), 42
    Gemini, 29, 220
Armstrong, Edwin Howard, birth, 408
Armstrong, Neil, 234
Arnold, William S., 379
art, clipart, 391
Art Safari Web site, 265
Artisan Color Reference System, 325
Asante FriendlyNET FR1004, 209
Asante routers, 209
ASCC (Automatic Sequence Controlled Calculator), 235
Asimov, Isaac, birth, 4
ASIN (Amazon Standard Item Number), 373

Ask Jeeves Kids Web site, 87, 281
assassinations
    Dr. Martin Luther King, Jr., 112
    President John F. Kennedy, 378
    Senator Robert F. Kennedy, 185
associates, Amazon, 372
Association for Computing Machinery, founded, 301
asteroids, 313
Asymmetric DSL (ADSL), 60
AT Kids Browser Web site, 280
Atari 2600, 157
ATI Radeon 9800 Pro video card, 386
ATI Technologies, 327
atomic bomb dropped on Hiroshima, 256
atomic clocks, 322
attachments (email), 117, 197
attacks. See security
Auction Lizard, 364
Auction Software Review, eBay bidding, 368
AuctionBytes, 366
auctions
    auction management service, 368
    online, 363
        bidding tips, 366
        DeepAnalysis, 369
        eBay businesses, 369
        My eBay, 364
        selling tips, 367
        sniping, 365
Auctionworks Web site, 368
Auctiva Web site, 368
Audacity, 152
audio editing program, Adobe Audition, 152
audio formats, 146
August historical events
    aerosol spray patent, 272
    astronaut speaks to aquanaut, 279
    atomic bomb dropped on Hiroshima, 256
    calendar, 250, 282-283
    cannon used in battle, 276
    dental chair patent, 265
    Fairness Doctrine, 254
    Felix Wenkel's birth, 263
    Gordon Bell's birth, 269
    Greenwich Mean Time (GMT) adopted, 252
    Hewlett Packard incorporated, 268
    IBM introduced, 262

John Mauchly's birth, 280
Leo Fender's birth, 260
locomotive races horse, 278
Mariner 2 launched, 277
Netscape founded, 259
oxygen identified, 251
parachute wedding, 275
Pierre de Fermat's birth, 267
refrigerator patented, 258
ship-to-shore wireless message, 273
Spirit Rover landing on Mars, 281
Stephen Wozniak's birth, 261
television patented, 270
transatlantic cable, 255
TRS-80 Model 1, 253
vertical-looping roller coaster
  patented, 266
Voyager 2, 271
Wiffle ball invented, 264
Windows 95 release, 274
Auravision EluminX keyboard, 416
Autocorrect feature (Word), 413
automatic cannons, 169
Automatic Sequence Controlled
  Calculator (ASCC), 235
automatic stemming, 76
AVerMedia
  DVD EZMaker Pro, 298
  TVBox 9, 291
AVG Antivirus, 113, 127

B

Babbage, Charles, 233, 400, 416
backdoor codes (TiVo), 46-47
backgrounds
  colors (Web pages), 102, 254
  photos, replacing, 386
backups, 4, 342
Backus, John, 13, 306, 393
Balkin FireWire 4-Port Hub, 339
balloon flight, 377
bar codes, 206
Bar Master Deluxe, 97
Barghoorn, Elso S., 343
Barnard, Christian, 147
BASIC introduced, 145
batteries
  dry cell batteries patented, 371
  portable, 56
Beat Greets, 245
Beatles perform last concert, 32
Becquerel, Henri, 363

bees, killer bees, 335
Belkin, 29
  Digital Camera Link, 223
  FireWire 3-Port PCI Card, 397
  iPod Media Reader, 223
  Web site, 316
Bell, Alexander Graham, 27, 82
Bell, Gordon, birth, 269
Ben & Jerry's Web site, 242
Berkeley Digital Library SunSITE Web
  site, 267
Berliner, Henry A., 196
Best Buy Finder, 378
Better Homes and Gardens Home
  Designer Suite, 278
beverage warmers, USB Beverage
  Warmer, 119
Beyond TV (Snapstream), 51
BFG Technologies, 327
Bible study guide, QuickVerse Deluxe, 99
bidding
  eBay statistics, 368
  tips (auctions), 366
Big Bang Theory, 109
bikini debut, 219
Binet, Alfred, birth, 225
Birthday Cards.com, 245
Bissell, Melville, 305
BitComet, 403
BizarreRecords.com, 242
BizRate Web site, 381
blackhole lists, 119
Blaze player, 357
blocking, spam, 124
Blog Universe Web site, 346
BlogChalking Web site, 346
Blogger Web site, 346
Blogger.com, 348
bloggers, 344
blogosphere, 344
blogs, 344, 347
  creating, 348
  Gizmodo, 405
  Laporte Report, 344, 347
  moblogs, 350
  Moveable Type, 345
  movies, 347
  music, 347
  photoblogs, 350
  photos, 347
  political, 347
  reasons for blogging, 345
  RSS feeds, 349
  smog, 346

sports, 347
statistics, 349
technical, 347
Unofficial Yahoo! Web blog, 82
Web sites, 346
Blogwise Web site, 346
Bloogz Web site, 349
Blue Mountain, 245
Bluefish, 136
Bluetooth, Wi-Fi compared to, 203
BMP graphics, 394
Bobby Web site, 254
Boeing 747s, 47
Bonus.com Web site, 289
Book Adventure Web site, 265
BookCAT, 266
books
  Amazon.com, 370
  Amazons Marketplace, 376
  associates, 372
  creating lists, 376
  jumping to product listings, 373
  power searches, 375
  product reviews, 371
  sales, 375
  shipping costs, 374
  geek gifts, 408
Boole, George, birth, 358
Boolean searches, 89
boot disks, Madboot, 259
Bose QuietComfort 2s, 399
bots, Best Buy Finder, 378
Boxerjam, 154
Brain virus, 112
BrainPop Web site, 265
Brandchannel.com, 77
Branwyn, Gareth, 47
Brickhouse, 5
Bridges, Jeff, 223
broadband connections, 59
  Broadband Wizard, 65
  cable, 61-62
  Dan Elwell Broadband Speed Test, 60
  DSL, 60
  performance tweaks, 64
  satellite, 63
  troubleshooting, 65
Broadband Wizard, 65
BroadbandReports Web site, 62
Brown, Louise Joy, birth, 239
Browser Hijack Blaster, 300
browsers
  hijackers, 300
  insert Google toolbar into, 73

browsers

Internet Explorer
  550 Access Toolbar, 187
  browsing history, 188
  clearing history, 12
  faster connections, 191
  Favorites, 186
  history, 188
  offline browsing, 187
  searches from within, 189
  security, 190
  kid-safe, 280
  Mozilla Firefox, 192
  Offline browsing, 187
Bryce, James W., 235
bubble boy David Vetter, 45
Buckyball discovered, 370
Buffalo Linkstation Network Storage
  Center, 216
bugs, 295
Bugs Bunny debut, 241
burners, Titanium FireWire burner, 188
burning
  CDs, 225, 228, 231
    Musicmatch Jukebox, 226
    RipEditBurn, 226
  movies to DVDs, 359
BurnInTest, 324
Butler Act, 93
buying
  hard drives, 325
  music players, 218
  notebooks, 333
  PCs, compared to upgrading, 160
  printers, 329
  routers, 209
BuyMusic.com, 147
Buzznet Web site, 350
Byron, Ada, birth, 400
Byron, Lord, 400

C

C.H.I.M.P. monitor mirror, 351
cables, 61
  color, 4
  house, 208
  installing cable modems, 62
  USB, ThinkGeek, 167
cache, 191
cache operator, 75
Calculating Clock, 233
calculators, first pocket scientific
  calculator, 6

Calendar (Yahoo!), 84
Californium transuranium element
  discovery, 89
Camcorderinfo.com, 41
camcorders
  Camcorderinfo.com, 41
  DCR-VX2100, 404
  DVDs, 33
  formats, 33
  selecting, 42
  Sony DCR-VX2100, 42
cameras
  accessories, 31
  buying, 29
  digital glamour glow, 384
  digital photos, 28
  JB1 007 Digital Spy Camera, 30
  microfilm patented, 170
  offloading digital photos, 29
  photo organization, 27
  Polaroid Land camera, 382
  RAW format, 30
  single-lens reflex (SLR) camera, 26
  stabilizers, 44
  underwater, 32
  Webcams. *See* Webcams
  wireless, D-Link SecuriCam
    DCS-5300W, 79
Campus Tours Web site, 269
CampusNut.com, 271
CampusParty.com, 271
Camscape.com, 184
cannons, automatic cannons, 169
Canon
  i560 printer, 28
  Powershot S400, 28
Canopus ADVC300, 33
Cape Canaveral's first launch, 238
CAR-100 Bluetooth Car Kit, 276
carbon applications, 19
Carlos, Walter, 167
Carpenter, M. Scott, 279
Carter, Howard, 54
cases
  custom cases, 171
  iPod, 224
  PDAs, 322
Casio WQV10D-2, 215
Cat Fanciers Web site, 290
cathode ray tubes. *See* CRTs
CBS News, 240
CBS SportsLine, 241

cdrLabel, 229
CDs
  burning, 225, 228, 231
    Musicmatch Jukebox, 226
    RipEditBurn, 226
  copying, 227
  drives, troubleshooting, 230
  labels, 229
  ripping music from, 149
  scratched CDs, troubleshooting, 231
cell phones, connecting to Internet, 206
Cellboost, 243
Chaffee, Roger, 29
Challenger Space Shuttle explosion, 30
Chapin, Daryl, 133
ChapterCheats, 156
chats
  channels, 54
  etiquette, 183
  rooms, 54
chatting online, 54
  IMSecure, 58
  Internet Relay Chat (IRC), 55
  lingo, 56
  sex chats, 58
  tips, 57
Cheat Elite, 156
Cheat Planet, 156
Cheater's Guild, 156
cheats, games, 156
CheatStation, 156
checkups, hard disks, 341
Chernobyl nuclear power disaster, 134
children
  Internet usage, 191, 244
  protecting privacy, 16
Children's Online Privacy Protection Act
  (COPPA), 16
Christmas tree lights invented, 412
Cinema Displays, 21
Cinemar DVD Lobby Pro, 311
Clark, James, 259
Clarke, Arthur C., birth, 406
classic applications, 19
cleaning
  keyboards, 338
  kits, cameras, 31
  mouse, 338
  viruses from PCs, 115
ClearType, optimizing displays, 397
clicking, 418
clipart
  downloading, 391
  Clipart Center Web site, 391

Clipart Connection Web site, 391
Clipart Place Web site, 391
Clipart.com, 391
cloned mice, 237
Cloner, Elk, 112
Closeouts America Web site, 383
closing Windows XP programs, 132
CNET
    News.com, 419
    Tech Specs, 268
CNN Web site, 240
Coca Cola
    invention of, 152
    new Coke introduced, 131
Cocoa applications, 19
Cocoatech Path Finder, 23
CoffeeCup, 184, 252
College Board Online Web site, 269
College Student Survival Guide Web
    site, 270
College Survival Skills Web site, 270
College Tutor Study Guide Web site, 270
CollegeBound Network Web site, 269
CollegeClub.com, 271
CollegeFreshmen.Net, 270
CollegeNET Web site, 269
colleges
    choosing, 269
    laptops, 268
    study aids, 270
Colleges.com, 269
CollegeSurfing.com, 269
color televisions, 205
colors
    cable and, 4
    connectors and, 4
Colt revolvers, patent, 63
Columbia (Space Shuttle) disaster, 39
columns, Excel spreadsheets, 296
comets, Shoemaker-Levy comet hits
    Jupiter, 230
commands, Sort (TiVo), 47
communities, home pages, 251-252
complaints, home page communities, 252
compression (file), Winace, 233
CompuCable ADC Monitor Sharing
    Switch, 300
CompuQuiet, 169
CompuServe launch, 310
computer bugs, 295
Computer History Museum, 235
Computer Recycling Center, 416
computers. See also Macintoshes; PCs
    junking, 3
    ports, 328

shutting down, 421
viruses. See viruses
computing history, 232-234
    first-generation computers, 235
    fourth-generation computers, 238
    second-generation computers, 236
    third-generation computers, 237
configurations
    file servers, 216
    PCs for video editing, 39
Connected Web site, 342
connections
    broadband, 59
        Broadband Wizard, 65
        cable, 61-62
        Dan Elwell Broadband Speed Test, 60
        DSL, 60
        performance tweaks, 64
        satellite, 63
        troubleshooting, 65
    cell phones, 206
    DSL, 210
    hotspots, 202
    sharing, 210
    troubleshooting, 174
connectors, color, 4
Console Gameworld, 156
consoles, games, 153, 157
ConsumerReports.org Web site, 380
ConsumerREVIEW.com, 380
ConsumerSearch Web site, 380
continuing education software, 287
ControlKey, 251
controllers
    games, 155, 158
    Logitech Cordless Presenter, 19
conversions, tapes to MP3s, 152
Cookie Pal, 304
cookies
    Anonymyzer Total System Sweeper, 13
    Cookie Pal, 304
    managing, 304
Cooley, Dr. Denton, 147
cooling technology, 155
CoolROM, 157
Coolwave, 169
Cooper, Gordon, 279
Cooper, Martin, 111
Cooper, Peter, 278
Copernic Agent, 92
COPPA (Children's Online Privacy
    Protection Act), 16
copying
    CDs, 227
    DVDs, 351

Corbis, 391
cordless phones, PhoneBridge, 239
Cordless RumblePad, 153
core memory, patent sale to IBM, 76
Core Wars, 112
cotton gin patent, 200
coupons, online shopping, 382
CPUs, 323, 399
Cray, Seymour, birth, 314
Crayon Crawler Web site, 280
Creative Sound Blaster Wireless Music,
    305
creative class, 407
Creative
    Mods, 170
    MuVo2, 221
credit cards, shopping online, 378
Crick, Francis, 59
Cronkite, Walter, anchors CBS Evening
    News for first time, 124
CRTs (cathode ray tube), 305, 385
CSI/FBI PC Crime and Security Survey,
    335
Cuban missile crisis, 342
Curie, Marie, birth, 363
Curie, Pierre, 363
custom cases, 171
Cyber Bounty Web site, 257
Cybersitter Web site, 279

D

D-Link routers, 209
D-Link SecuriCam DCS-5300W, 79
da Vinci, Leonardo, birth, 123
Danny Sullivan's SearchEngineWatch, 89
Darwin, Charles, 380
Data (Star Trek), creation of, 40
data CDs, burning, 228
Daypop Web site, 349
Dazzle 10-in-1, 193
dc4000, 207
DCR-VX2100, 42, 404
de Fermat, Pierre, 267
debugging, 295
December historical events
    Ada Byron's birth, 400
    Altair 8800 goes on sale, 409
    animated films, first, 411
    Apple's IPO, 402
    Arthur C. Clarke's birth, 406
    calendar, 390, 422-423
    Charles Babbage's birth, 416
    Charles Goodyear's birth, 419
    Christmas tree lights invented, 412

drive-up service opens first time, 391
Edwin Howard's birth, 408
galactic system discovered, 420
Grace Murray Hopper's birth, 399
ice cream cone patented, 405
J.L. Kraft's birth, 401
Johannes Kepler's birth, 417
John Backus' birth, 393
John Lennon's murder, 398
last moon mission, 397
microwave ovens patented, 396
moon orbit, first, 413
nuclear chain reaction, 392
phonograph invented, 394
Relay I satellite launch, 403
Robert Jemison's birth, 410
Sgt. Pepper's Lonely Hearts Club Band,
   418
Sir Isaac Newton's birth, 415
Smallpox virus destroyed, 421
solar heated houses, first, 414
Voyager flight, 404
Werner Heisenberg's birth, 395
Wright Brothers flight, 407
DeepAnalysis, 369
defaults, start pages (Web sites), 111
DEFCON 1 Ultra Notebook Computer
   Security System, 5, 407
defragmenting hard disks, 339
deleting files, 340
Dell Digital Jukebox, 220
dental chairs, patent, 265
Descartes, Rene, birth, 103
Desch, Joseph, 234
desktops
   backgrounds, Web pages as, 129
   replacements, 331
DesktopX, 132
Deutsch, Herbert A., 167
DeveloperOne Web site, 313
Devon-Technologies Web site, 21
dialog boxes
   Disk Cleanup, 340
   Gaussian Blur, 384
Dick Tracy wrist-radio, 288
dictionaries, OmniDictionary, 21
Digi 002, 128
digital audio forms, 146
digital camcorders
   Camcorderinfo.com, 41
   DCR-VX2100, 42
   DVDs, 33
   formats, 33
   selecting, 42

digital cameras
   accessories, 31
   buying, 29
   glamour glow, 384
   offloading digital photos, 29
   photo organization, 27
   RAW format, 30
   single-lens reflex (SLR), 26
   underwater, 32
digital media hubs, 309
Digital Media Remote, 135
digital music
   downloading, 147
   players, 150
digital pens, io Personal Digital Pen, 26
Digital Photo Viewer, 137
Digital Photography Review Web site, 29
digital photos. See photos
digital televisions, versus analog, 307
Digital Theater Sound (DTS) format, 311
digital video
   converting film to, 43
   converting tapes to, 43
   DivX, 39
   hard disks, 40
   PC configuration for editing, 39
digital voice recorders, Olympus DM-1, 9
Digital8, 33
diNovo Media Desktop, 186
direct address searches, Yahoo!, 79
directories, people searches, 91
Directory (Yahoo!), 80
DirecTV HDTV receiver, 406
disasters
   Apollo 1, 29
   Challenger Space Shuttle explosion, 30
   Chernobyl nuclear power, 134
   Hindenburg, 150
   Space Shuttle Columbia, 39
discarding PCs, 416
Discovering Dinosaurs Web site, 265
DiscoverySchool.com, 266
Disk Cleanup dialog box, 340
Disk Defragmenter, 40
displays
   HDTV, 305
   optimizing with ClearType, 397
distributions, 135
DivX, 39
DLP rear projectors, 406
DNA, discovery of structure, 59
Dock-N-Talk, 262
documents (Word), adding watermarks to,
   412

DocuPen (Planon), 59
Dog-Play Web site, 290
Dolby Pro Logic system, 311
DOS prompt, Windows XP, 272
double-clicking, 418
doughnuts invented, 202
downloading
   Clipart, 391
   Linux, 135
   music, 147
downloads, 185
Dr. Bott's DVI Extractor, 88
Dr. Bott's DVIator, 81
Dr. Bott's ExtendAIR Direct, 307
Dr. Mom's Guide to College Web site,
   270
Dr. Seuss, birth, 74
dragging, 418
Dresden, Germany, bombing, 51
Drinker, Phillip, 243
drive-by downloads, 303
drive-up service opens, 391
DriveRight CarChip, 348
drivers, Windows, 261
drkoop.com, 243
drop shadows, PowerPoint text, 414
dropping, 418
Drudge Report, 240
Drudge, Matt, 240
dry cell batteries patented, 371
DSC-U60, 32
DSL, 60
   access multiplexer. See DSLAM
   connections, 210
DSLAM (DSL access multiplexer), 60
DSP-300, 54
DT-7000S, 197
DTS (Digital Theater Sound) format, 311
DVD EZMaker Pro, 298
DVD Lobby Pro, 311
DVD Wizard Pro, 351
DVD+/- Double Layer drive, 404
DVD+R format, 361
DVD+R/W format, 361
DVD+RW format, 361
DVD-LX8 portable, 367
DVD-R format, 361
DVD-R/W format, 361
DVD-RAM format, 361
DVD-RW format, 361
DVDs
   burners, Titanium FireWire burner, 188
   camcorders, 33
   converting VHS tapes to, 43

copying, 351
creation programs, Sonic MyDVD, 44
drives, troubleshooting, 230
Easter Eggs. *See* Easter Eggs
FAQ, 359
formats, 361
photo albums, creating, 360
playing, WMP, 358
ReaderwareVW program, 306
region codes, 357
Roxio Easy Media Creator, 362
sales, 361
troubleshooting, 362
DVIator, 81
DVRs
creating, 51
DVR-107, 358
Sage TV, 51

E

e-Holster Web site, 322
E.T.: The Extra-Terrestrial release, 191
Eagletron robotic tabletop mounts, 44
early learning software, 287
earphones, Shure E3c, 150
Easter Eggs, 93
3D Flying Easter Eggs Screensaver, 94
DVDs, 98
Easter Egg Archive, 96
games, 97
instant messaging, 99
Macintoshes, 95
Microsoft Excel 2000, 96
Microsoft Excel 97, 96
Microsoft Word, 96
Microsoft Works 7, 96
Microsoft WorkSuite 2003, 96
Winamp Version 5, 96
Windows, 94
Eastman, George, birth, 226
Easy CD & DVD Creator, 227
Easy Message, 53
EasyOffice, 292
EasyShare Printer Dock, 28
Eatonweb Portal Web site, 346
eBay, 363
businesses, 369
DeepAnalysis, 369
My eBay, 364
Selling Manager Web site, 368
winning bid statistics, 368

eBlaster, 7
Eckert, Presper, 235
Edison, Thomas
invention of phonograph, 394
light demonstration, 341
editing
photos, 32
text in Microsoft Word, 291
video, 39
Windows Registry, 263
EDO DRAM (extended data out DRAM), 324
Edsel, Ford halts production of, 375
educational software, 287
educational Web sites, 265-266
EFF (Electronic Frontier Foundation), 15
eFun.com, 245
Einstein, Albert
arrival in America, 337
birth, 86
Eisenhower inauguration (first televised), 22
ElderWeb, 244
electric blankets, introduced, 329
electric razors, Schick markets first electric razor, 90
electronblue IV models, 267
Electronic Frontier Foundation (EFF), 15
electrons, existence announced, 138
Elgato EyeHome, 102
elseed, 45
EluminX keyboard, 416
Elwell, Dan, 60
email, 193
encryption, 13
file attachments, 197
free email, 81
G-Lock Easy Mail, 199
messages sent worldwide daily, 198
phishing schemes, 8-10
protocols, 195
sending mass mailings, 199
signatures, 196
spam, 119
anti-spam software, 125
blocking, 124
iHateSpam, 120
MessageLabs, 124
preventing, 121
prevention announcements from software companies, 123
spam lists, 120
troubleshooting, 198
viruses, 117, 194
WebMail Assistant, 80

embossing PowerPoint presentations, 295
eMedicine.com, 243
emergency disks, iPods as, 20
emoticons, 56
emulators, 315
eMusic.com, 147
encryption, 13
PC files, 14
PGP email encryption, 21
encyclopedias, Microsoft Encarta, 290
envelope folding machine patent, 46
Environmental Protection Agency, 165
Epinons.com Web site, 380
ePublicEye Web site, 380
erasable ink (pens), 207
Eraser, 166
Eraser Mate, 207
erasing cookies, 13
ESPN.com, 241
Ethernet LaCie's Ethernet Disk, 61
etiquette, online, 183
Eudora, 194
Evans, Ronald, 397
Excel spreadsheets
column width adjustments, 296
formulas, 297
Excel 2000 Easter Eggs, 96
Excel 97 Easter Eggs, 96
Excite Super Chat, 54
extended data out DRAM (EDO DRAM), 324
external connectors, upgrading PCs, 163
external flash kits (cameras), 31
external microphones, 44
extra-solar planets discovered, 129
extraterrestrial life searches, 332
extreme PCs, 173
extreme-computing, 170
EyeHome, 102
Eyetop Centra, 63
EyeTV, 47
EZBinoCam LX, 190
EZQuest Boa Slim, 365

F

Fact Monster Web site, 266
fades, photos, 109
Fairness Doctrine, 254
Falcon Northwest, 173
Family Source Web site, 281
fans, Vantec's Stealth, 169
Fantom Titanium FireWire burner, 188
FAQs, DVDs, 359
FAST, 87

Fast-Eraser, 18
fast-page-mode DRAM (FPM DRAM), 324
Favorites, Internet Explorer, 186
faxes, first one sent, 323
FCC mandate, HDTVs, 310
February historical events
    birth of Galileo, 53
    birth of Linus Pauling, 66
    birth of Nicolaus Copernicus, 57
    birth of Thomas J. Watson, Sr., 55
    bombing of Dresden, Germany, 51
    bubble boy leaves bubble, 45
    calendar, 38, 67-69
    discovery of DNA structure, 59
    discovery of planet Pluto, 56
    Edwin Goodwin redefines value of Pi, 43
    ENIAC (Electronic Numerical Integrator and Computer), 52
    envelope folding machine patent, 46
    fire extinguishing system patent, 48
    first Boeing 747 flight, 47
    Gates, Bill, 42
    John Glenn's orbit of earth, 58
    King Tut's tomb, 54
    mass inoculation against polio, 61
    Parker Brothers Monopoly goes on sale, 44
    patent of Colt revolver, 63
    plane crash of 1959 (the day the music died), 41
    popcorn, 60
    Reichstag fire, 65
    Space Shuttle Columbia Disaster, 39
    World Trade Center bombing, 64
Fender, Leo, birth, 260
Fermi, Enrico, birth, 315
files, 419
    attachments, 197
    compression, Winace, 233
    deleting, 340
    displaying in Windows XP, 273
    servers, configuration, 216
    sharing, 148
        BitComet, 403
        Yahoo!, 85
    sharing across networks, 217
    storing, Yahoo!, 85
filetype operator, 75
films
    converting to digital video, 43
    Tron, 223
Filo, David, 80
filters, 279

Finale, 245
Finder (OS-X), replacing, 23
Fink, 25
fire extinguishing system patent, 48
firewalls, 11
    hardware firewalls, 6
    software, 5
FireWire, 43
    ports, 328
FireWire 3-Port PCI Card, 397
FireWire 4-Port Hub, 339
first-generation computers, 235
Fix-It Utilities, 343
flash memory
    i-Duck, 160
    SWISSMEMORY, 377
flash memory players, 222
flashlights, Kensington's FlyLight, 100
Flight Simulator, 158
Flight Simulator (Microsoft), 408
flight sticks, 158
Flight/combat stick, 155
FlowCam stabilizers, 44
Flowers, Dr. Thomas, 235
flying saucers sighted, 204
FlyLight, 100
FM radio demonstration, 7
foam rubber developed, 217
foistware, 303
FolderClone Web site, 331
folders, 419
    My Computer, 398
    My Documents, 398
    sharing across networks, 217
force feedback, 155
Ford, Henry, birth, 244
foreign characters, keyboard entry, 410
formats
    DVDs, 361
    graphics, 394
formulas (Excel spreadsheets), 297
Forrester Research, online sales, 382
FortuneCity Web site, 251
fossils, oldest fossils discovered, 343
Fotopages Web site, 350
fourth-generation computers, 238
FOX News, 240
FPM DRAM (fast-page-mode DRAM), 324
Franklin, Benjamin, 195
Freaky Cheats, 156
Free Games Net, 154
Free History Eraser, 12
free utilities, OS-X, 25
FreeRoms, 157

Freeservers Web site, 251
Freevo, 51
FreewarePalm Web site, 313
freshmeat.net, 138
FriendlyNET FR1004, 209
Frisbees, introduced, 15
Froelich, John, 292
FrontPage, 111
FrontX, 265
Froogle, 78, 381
FTP servers, WS-FTP Professional, 185
FTPSearch, 185
Fuller, Calvin, 133
Furioustech, 170
Future Games Network, 156

G

G-Lock Easy Mail, 199
G5 Roof, 314
G5 Skateboard, 346
Gadget Universe Web site, 402
Gagarin, Yuri Alekseyevich, 120
galaxies, accelerating, 11
Galilei, Galileo, birth, 53
Galileo, 351
GameDaily, 154
Gamepad, 155
gamepads, Cordless RumblePad, 153
games
    ATI Radeon 9800 Pro video card, 385
    building systems, 159
    cheats, 156
    consoles, 153, 157
    controllers, 155, 158
    Easter Eggs, 97
    emulating on Pocket PCs, 315
    GameShark, 159
    news, 156
    playing online, 154
    shopping for gamer gifts, 403
Games.com, 154
GameShark, 159
GameSpot, 154
Garmin, iQue 3600, 183
Gartner Group
    IT industry, 400
    phishing attack statistics, 10
gasoline tractors, 292
Gassner, Carl, 371
Gates, Bill, 31, 42, 348
gateways, 210
Gaussian Blur dialog box, 384
Gebbie Press, 240
geek gifts, 402, 405, 408

Gefen VGA to ADC adapter, 95
Geisel, Theodor Seuss, 74
GGSearch, 73
Gibson, Steve, 113, 190, 209
GIF graphics, 392, 394
Gillette Eraser Mate, 207
Gizmodo, 405
glamour glow, digital cameras, 384
Glenn, John, orbit of earth, 58
Glenn, Senator John, 349
Globe of Blogs Web site, 346
Gloster-Whittle E.28/39, 159
Gmail, 78, 196
GMT (Greenwich Mean Time), 252
Gnu Privacy Guard (PGP), 127
Gnu.com, 138
GNUCash, 136
Gnutella, 148
GoCollege Web site, 269
Goddard, Dr. Richard H., 88
Goddard, Robert, birth, 325
Godfrey, Arthur, 205
Godin, Noël, 42
GoGraph.com, 391
Golden Gate Bridge opened, 172
Goodrich, B.F., birth, 360
Goodwin, Edwin J., redefines value of Pi, 43
Goodyear, Charles, 360, 419
Goodyear rubber processing patent, 197
Google, 66
    Advanced Page Rank Analyzer, 78
    advanced search operators, 75
    as brand, 77
    Answers, 78
    automatic stemming, 76
    Catalog Search, 78
    Directory, 78
    features, 78
    filing for IPO, 137
    GGSearch, 73
    Gmail, 196
    Groups, 2, 15, 78
    Image Search, 78
    Local, 78
    News, 78, 240
    SafeSearch Web site, 281
    Search Linux, 138
    searches, 74
    specific searches, 77
    toolbar, inserting into browser, 73
    top searches, 91
    U.S. Government Search, 78
    University Search, 78
    Web blog, 75

Gopher, 86
Gould, Stephen Jay, birth, 296
gpedit.msc, 395
GPS Watch, 171
GPSs
    devices, Magellan SporTrak Color, 16
    TomTom Navigator, 316
Gracenote, 228
graffiti tips, 314
Gramin, Rino 130, 123
Grammar Lady Web site, 266
GraphicConverter, 25
graphics, 327
    formats, 394
    thumbnails, changing size, 401
    Web pages, 393
Graphire3, 281
Greekspot.com, 271
Greenwich Mean Time (GMT), 252
greeting cards, 245
Griffin ControlKey, 251
Griffin PowerMate, 93
Griffin Technology
    iCurve, 274
    iMic, 14
    SightLight, 195
Grissom, Virgil, 29
Groening, Matt, 16
Grokster, 148
Groove Speaker Purse, 224
Group Policy Editor, 395
groups, Yahoo!, 83
Grundig Emergency Radio, 83
GuitarPort, 225
Gyration Ultra GT, 272

H

HackerWhacker, 9
HAL computer, 14
Haley, Bill, 192
Hallmark E-Cards, 245
Handango Web site, 313
handwriting recognition systems, graffiti tips, 314
hard disks
    checkups, 341
    defragmenting, 339
    digital video, 40
hard drives
    adding, 326
    buying, 325
    partitions, PartitionMagic, 329
    Western Digital's Media Center, 52

hardware firewalls, 6
HardwareCentral Web site, 326
Hari, Mata, 257
Harmony SST-659 universal remote control, 413
Harper, Richard, 296
Harris Interactive, report on physicians' use of Internet, 328
Harvard Mark I, 20
Hayward, Ann, 275
HD1000, 323
HDSL, 60
HDTVs, 308
    displays, 305
    FCC mandate, 310
headphones, Bose QuietComfort 2s, 399
headsets, DSP-300, 54
health Web sites, 243
HealthWeb Web site, 243
Healthypet Web site, 290
heart transplants, first in U.S. performed, 147
Heaven's Gate mass suicide, 98
Heisenberg, Werner Karl, birth, 395
helicopter flight demonstrated for first time, 196
Hellboy Easter Egg, 98
Hewlett, Bill, 268
Hewlett-Packard
    dc4000, 207
    HP-35, 6
    iPAQ h5550/h5555, 407
    Linux business, 138
Heyerdahl, Thor, birth, 326
hidden Easter Eggs, 93
High School Hub Web site, 266
high school software, 287
high-tech jobs, 57
hijackers
    advertisements, 303
    browsers, 300
HijackThis, 300
Hindenburg disaster, 150
Hiroshima atomic bomb dropped on, 256
historical events. See also history
    April, 108, 139-141
        air brakes patented, 121
        Apple opens iTunes, 136
        assassination of Dr. Martin Luther King Jr., 112
        Big Bang Theory proposed, 109
        cell phones, first call, 111
        Chernobyl nuclear power disaster, 134
        electron existence announced, 138

historical events

extra-solar planets discovered, 129
Google files for IPO, 137
Hostess Twinkies invented, 113
Hubble telescope launches, 132
IBM ships first mainframe computer, 115
Leonardo da Vinci's birth, 123
NASA announces first astronauts, 117
new Coke introduced, 131
Oklahoma City Federal building bombed, 127
Post-It Notes introduced, 114
radar patent, 110
Robert Oppenheimer's birth, 130
San Francisco earthquake of 1906, 126
solar batteries announced for first time, 133
sun spot observation, 116
Titanic sets sail, 118
Vertijet, 119
Walter Cronkite anchors CBS Evening News for first time, 124
Weather Bureau kite, first, 135
August dates, 250, 282-283
aerosol spray patent, 272
astronaut speaks to aquanaut, 279
atomic bomb dropped on Hiroshima, 256
birth of Mata Hari, 257
cannon used in battle, 276
dental chair patent, 265
Fairness Doctrine, 254
Felix Wenkel's birth, 263
Gordon Bell's birth, 269
Greenwich Mean Time (GMT), 252
Hewlett Packard incorporated, 268
IBM introduced, 262
John Mauchly's birth, 280
Leo Fender's birth, 260
locomotive races horse, 278
Mariner 2 launched, 277
Netscape founded, 259
oxygen identified, 251
parachute wedding, 275
Pierre de Fermat's birth, 267
refrigerator patented, 258
ship-to-shore wireless message, 273
Stephen Wozniak's birth, 261
television patented, 270
transatlantic cable, 255

TRS-80 Model 1, 253
vertical-looping roller coaster patented, 266
Voyager 2, 271
Wiffle ball invented, 264
Windows 95 release, 274
December dates, 390, 422-423
Ada Byron's birth, 400
Altair 8800 goes on sale, 409
animated films, first, 411
Apple's IPO, 402
Arthur C. Clarke's birth, 406
Charles Babbage's birth, 416
Charles Goodyear's birth, 419
Christmas tree lights invented, 412
drive-up service opens first time, 391
Edwin Howard's birth, 408
galactic system discovered, 420
Grace Murray Hopper's birth, 399
ice cream cone patented, 405
J.L. Kraft's birth, 401
Johannes Kepler's birth, 417
John Backus' birth, 393
John Lennon's murder, 398
last moon mission, 397
microwave ovens patented, 396
moon orbit, first, 413
nuclear chain reaction, 392
phonograph invented, 394
Relay I satellite launch, 403
Robert Jemison's birth, 410
Sgt. Pepper's Lonely Hearts Club Band, 418
Sir Isaac Newton's birth, 415
Smallpox virus destroyed, 421
solar heated houses, first, 414
Voyager flight, 404
Werner Heisenberg's birth, 395
Wright Brothers flight, 407
February dates, 38, 67-69
Bill Gates' birth, 42
bombing of Dresden, Germany, 51
bubble boy leaves bubble, 45
discovery of DNA structure, 59
discovery of planet Pluto, 56
Edwin Goodwin redefines value of Pi, 43
ENIAC (Electronic Numerical Integrator and Computer), 52
envelope folding machine patent, 46
fire extinguishing system, 48
first Boeing 747 flight, 47
Galileo, birth, 53
John Glenn's orbit of earth, 58

King Tut's tomb, 54
Linus Pauling's birth, 66
mass inoculation against polio, 61
Nicolaus Copernicus' birth, 57
Parker Brothers Monopoly goes on sale, 44
patent of Colt revolver, 63
plane crash of 1959 (the day the music died), 41
popcorn, 60
Reichstag fire, 65
Space Shuttle Columbia Disaster, 39
Thomas J. Watson Sr.'s birth, 55
World Trade Center bombing, 64
January dates, 2, 34-35
accelerating galaxy discovery, 11
ACM-GAMM committee convenes to develop ALGOL, 13
Apollo 1 disaster, 29
Apple launches Macintoshes, 24
AT&T divests Bell System Companies, 3
Beatles perform last concert, 32
Challenger Space Shuttle explosion, 30
Eisenhower inauguration (first televised), 22
first commercial supersonic flight, 23
first pocket scientific calculator, 6
FM radio demonstrated, 7
HAL computer, 14
Harvard Mark I, 20
Howard Hughes sets transcontinental air record, 21
IBM SSEC, 26
integrated circuit, 25
Lotus 1-2-3 release, 28
National Center for Supercomputing Applications (NCSA), 17
nuclear-powered submarine launch, 19
patent of electromechanical adding and sorting machine, 10
premier of The Simpsons, 16
publication of Poe's Raven, 31
RCA's introduction of 45 RPM records, 12
SAGE, 18
Schoolhouse Rock debut, 8
Spirit Rover landing on Mars, 5
transatlantic phone service launch, 9
transcontinental phone service, 27
U.S. satellite launch, 33
Wham-O introduces Frisbees, 15

July dates, 214, 246-247
  Alfred Binet's birth, 225
  bikini debut, 219
  Bugs Bunny debut, 241
  Cape Canaveral's first launch, 238
  Charles Mayo's birth, 233
  cloned mice, 237
  death of John Adams and Thomas Jefferson, 218
  Earl Tupper's birth, 242
  foam rubber developed, 217
  George Eastman's birth, 226
  Gottfried Wilhelm von Leibniz's birth, 215
  Henry Ford's birth, 244
  IBM 650 Magnetic Drum Data Processing Machine, 216
  Intel incorporated, 232
  iron lung, 243
  Joseph Marie Jacquard's birth, 221
  Live Aid Concert, 227
  margarine patent, 229
  Mars Pathfinder Sojourner Rover, 220
  moon pictures, 245
  Neil Armstrong's walk on moon, 234
  Roswell incident, 222
  Scopes trial, 224
  Shoemaker-Levy comet hits Jupiter, 230
  solar eclipse, first, 231
  Stanley Kubrick's birth, 240
  Star Trek character Jean Picard born, 235
  tape measure patent, 228
  test tube baby, first born, 239
  Tron film premiere, 223
  Wiley Post's solo flight, 236
June dates, 180, 211-212
  aerial tramway, 208
  Alan Turing's birth, 203
  Apple II released, 190
  bar codes, 206
  Benjamin Franklin flies kite, 195
  color television, 205
  cotton gin patent, 200
  doughnuts invented, 202
  Dr. Sally Ride goes to space, 198
  E.T.: The Extra-Terrestrial release, 191
  Ed White walks in space, 183
  flying saucers sighted, 204
  George Orwell's 1984 published, 186
  George Reeves' suicide, 199
  helicopter flight demonstrated for first time, 196

  Paul, Les, birth, 189
  pens with erasable ink, 207
  Pioneer 10, 193
  Rock Around the Clock released, 192
  rubber processing patent, 197
  Senator Robert F. Kennedy assassination, 185
  Soyuz 11 tragedy, 209
  SpaceShipOne, 201
  Tunguska meteorite explosion, 210
  typesetting machine patented, 187
  U.S. missile mail, 188
  UNIVAC I, 194
  Velveeta cheese invented, 182
  VisiCalc, 184
March dates, 72, 104-106
  Apple sues Microsoft, 94
  Californium transuranium element discovery, 89
  Dr. Seuss' (Theodor Seuss) birth, 74
  Einstein, Albert, birth, 86
  elevator patent, 87
  FDA approves Viagra, 99
  first liquid-filled rocket launch, 88
  first telephone call, 82
  Gemini flight, 95
  Heaven's Gate mass suicide, 98
  Homebrew Computer Club first meeting, 75
  Jules Verne dies, 96
  LISP programming language programming manual released, 73
  Luddite riots, 83
  mailbox patented, 81
  Mariner 10 flies past Mercury, 101
  Michelangelo computer virus, 78
  PC DOS 2.0, 80
  PC Jr., 91
  pencil with eraser patented, 102
  President Franklin Delano Roosevelt's first radio talk, 84
  RCA televisions ship, 97
  Rene Descartes' birth, 103
  Schick markets first electric razor, 90
  telephone patent, 79
  Tennessee passes the Butler Act, 93
  terrorist attack on Tokyo subway system, 92
  Three Mile Island nuclear power plant accident, 100
  Treaty on the Non-Proliferation of Nuclear Weapons (NPT), 77
  Uranus discovered, 85
  Wang sale of core memory patents to IBM, 76

May dates, 144, 176-177
  Adler Planetarium opens, 156
  automatic cannons, 169
  BASIC introduced, 145
  Coca-Cola invented, 152
  FDA approves genetically engineered tomatoes, 163
  Gloster-Whittle E.28/39, first flight, 159
  Golden Gate bridge opens, 172
  heart transplant, first, 147
  Hindenburg disaster, 150
  Indianapolis 500, 174
  laser beam bounced off moon, 153
  Lusitania torpedoed by German U-boats, 151
  Magellan spacecraft Venus probe, 148
  microfilm camera patented, 170
  Mount Everest conquered, 173
  Mount St. Helens erupts, 162
  nuclear reactor patented, 161
  removable tire rims, 165
  Robert Julius Petri's birth, 175
  Robert Moog's birth, 167
  science fiction film premiere, 146
  screw-on bottle caps patented, 149
  seminal LPs released, 160
  spam trademarked, 155
  Spirit of St. Louis flight, 164
  Star Wars premiere, 168
  twenty dollar bill release, 158
  VELCRO trademarked, 157
  Windows 3.0 released, 166
November dates, 356, 387-388
  Alan Turing defines universal machine, 368
  Atari releases its PONG game, 385
  B.F. Goodrich's birth, 360
  Buckyball discovered, 370
  Carl Sagan's birth, 365
  Darwin's Origin of Species published, 380
  dry cell batteries patented, 371
  dynamite patented, 381
  Ford halts production of Edsel, 375
  Gene Amdahl's birth, 372
  George Boole's birth, 358
  Holland Tunnel opens, 369
  hydrogen bomb exploded, 357
  Jack Kilby's birth, 364
  jukebox installed, 379
  Konosuke Matsushita's birth, 383
  Kurt Vonnegut's birth, 367
  manned balloon flight, 377

historical events

Marie Curie's birth, 363
Mariner 4 launched, 384
Mark Twain's birth, 386
Mickey Mouse debut, 374
Microsoft signs DOS contract with IBM, 362
mouse patented, 373
Polaroid Land camera, 382
President Kennedy assassinated, 378
Soviets send dog into space, 359
Vikings discovered in Canada, 361
viruses, first, 366
Windows 1.0 released, 376
October
   Albert Einstein arrives in America, 337
   Amdahl Corp. founded, 339
   anesthetic used for first time, 336
   Anthony Leeuwenhoek's birth, 344
   Apollo mission launched, 331
   atomic clock, 322
   Bill Gate's birth, 348
   Chuck Yeager breaks sound barrier, 334
   Cuban missile crisis, 342
   Ed Wood's birth, 330
   Edison demonstrates electric light, 341
   electric blanket introduced, 329
   extraterrestrial life searches, 332
   faxes, first sent, 323
   John Glenn returns to space, 349
   killer bees invade Texas, 335
   killer smog, 346
   Louisiana Purchase ratified, 340
   Model T introduced, 321
   moon pictures, 327
   New York City subway opens, 347
   oldest fossils discovered, 343
   pacemaker implant, first, 328
   RCA founded, 338
   Robert Goddard's birth, 325
   space race, 324
   Thor Heyerdahl's birth, 326
   U.S. Navy uses dolphins for surveillance, 333
   Vatican admits Galileo is right, 351
   War of the Worlds radio broadcast, 350
   wristwatches, 345
September dates
   33 1/3 rpm long-playing record demonstration, 303
   aerosol spray ozone depletion, 311

Andrew Grove's birth, 288
Arthur Charles Nielsen's birth, 291
Association for Computing Machinery founded, 301
asteroid passes earth, 313
carpet sweeper patented, 305
CompuServe launch, 310
David Packard's birth, 293
Enrico Fermi's birth, 315
first computer bug, 295
FORTRAN program, 306
gasoline tractors, 292
Henry Louis Mencken's birth, 298
Hoover Dam dedicated, 316
John McCarthy's birth, 290
Man from U.N.C.L.E., the premiere, 308
Neptune discovered, 309
New York Times launch, 304
O'Hanlon, Virginia's Santa Claus question, 307
Osborne Computer declares bankruptcy, 299
Seymour Cray's birth, 314
Soviet Luna 2 reaches moon, 300
Star Trek premiere, 294
Stephen Jay Gould's birth, 296
televised presidential debate, 312
The Outer Limits premiere, 302
Viking 2 landing on, 289
World War II begins, 287
World Trade Center and Pentagon attacks, 297
Sgt. Pepper's Lonely Hearts Club Band, 181
history. See also historical events
computing, 232-234
   first-generation computers, 235
   fourth-generation computers, 238
   second-generation computers, 236
   third-generation computers, 237
Internet Explorer, 188
HiTechMods.com, 170
hoaxes, viruses, 118
Holland, Clifford, 369
Hollerith, Herman, 10
home cabling, 208
home design, Better Homes and Gardens Home Designer Suite, 278
home networks, 216
home pages, communities, 251-252
Home Theater Forum, 308
home theaters
   creating, 310
   digital media hubs, 309

shopping, 406
surround sound formats, 311
home videos, shopping online for, 404
home Wi-Fi networks, 205
Homebrew Computer Club, 75
HomeNetHelp Web site, 210
homework Web sites, 266
Hoover Dam dedicated, 316
Hopper, Admiral Grace Murray, 295, 399
Horse-country.com Web site, 290
Hostess twinkies, invented, 113
Hotbeast.com, 271
HotBot, 87
Hotmail, SpyMail, 85
HotSpot Haven, 201
Hotspot Locations, 201
hotspots, 201
   connecting to, 202
   Web sites, 201
HouseCall Web site, 115
hovering, 418
HP-35, 6
HTML (Hypertext Markup Language), 253
   background colors, 254
   Mailto: links, 256
   text changes, 254
   troubleshooting, 255
Hubble telescope launches, 132
Hubble, Edwin, 420
Hughes, Howard, 21
Hushmail, 13
hydrogen bomb exploded, 357
hyperlinks, code to make invisible, 100
Hypertext Markup Language. See HTML

I

i-Duck, 160
I-TVView/Mac, 114
IBackup Web site, 342
IBM
   650 Magnetic Drum Data Processing Machine, 216
   core memory patent sale to, 76
   DOS contract with Microsoft, 362
   introduced, 262
   mainframe computers ship for first time, 115
   Product Recycling Programs, 416
   SSEC, 26
iCarPlay, 223
ice cream cone patent, 405
IceKey keyboard, 234

iceMouseJr, 332

ICQ, 52

iCurve, 274

IDC survey, 421

identification

  PCs, 400

  theft

    preventing, 18

    statistics, 172

IGN.com, 156

iHateSpam, 120

iKnowthat.com, 265

Ilium Software Web site, 313

Illustrated Guide to Breaking Your
  Computer, 242

iMac, 14

images. See graphics

IMAP (Interactive Mail Access Protocol),
  195

IMDB (Internet Movie Database), 239

iMesh, 148

iMovie, 404

IMSecure, 58

inanchor operator, 75

incompatibility, instant messaging, 53

Indianapolis 500, 174

info operator, 75

InformationWeek Research, security-
  related downtime estimates, 117

inMotion Portable Audio System, 222

Insects on the Web Web site, 290

installing

  cable modems, 62

  Linux, 137

    uninstalling, 145

  software, 420

instant messaging, 52

  Easter Eggs, 99

    MSN Messenger with Messenger Plus
    Add-in, 99

    Yahoo! Messenger, 99

  Easy Message, 53

  incompatibility, 53

  online chats, 54

    IMSecure, 58

    Internet Relay Chat (IRC), 55

    lingo, 56

    sex chats, 58

    tips, 57

integrated circuits, patent, 25

Intel incorporation, 232

Interactive Mail Access Protocol (IMAP),
  195

internal devices, upgrades, 164

International Recording Media
  Association, DVD sales, 361

Internet

  African American usage, 303

  Amazon.com, 370

    Amazon's Marketplace, 376

    associates, 372

    creating lists, 376

    jumping to product listings, 373

    power searches, 375

    product reviews, 371

    sales, 375

    shipping costs, 374

  browsing Web sites offline, 187

  children's usage, 244

  company shutdowns, 237

  connections, troubleshooting, 174

  downloads, 185

  employee usage at workplace, 342

  gender usage, 184

  kids

    safe browsers, 280

    sites, 289

    usage, 191

  physicians usage of, 328

  playing games online, 154

  pop-ups

    creating, 302

    stopping, 301

  radio, 151

  security

    ControlKey, 251

    filters, 279

    kids, 281, 288

  senior citizens, 244

  sharing connections, 210

  teen usage, 289

  worldwide usage, 110

Internet Chess, 154

Internet Download Manager, 175

Internet Explorer

  browsing history, 188

  browsing offline, 187

  clearing history, 12

  faster connections, 191

  Favorites, 186

  searches, 189

  security, 190

Internet Movie Database (IMDB), 239

Internet Park, 154

Internet Public Library Web site, 182, 267

Internet Relay Chat (IRC), 55

Internet TeleCafe, 54

intext operator, 75

intitle operator, 75

inurl operator, 75

inventions. See also patents

  Christmas tree lights, 412

io Personal Digital Pen, 26

Iomega REV Drive, 409

IP-Tools, 217

iPAQ h5550/h5555, 407

iPodlounge Web site, 221

iPods, 219, 223

  accessories, 223

  Armor, 224

  cases, 224

  as emergency disks, 20

  microdrives, 221

  Mini, 221

  XPlay, 224

IPOs

  Apple, 402

  Google's filing for, 137

iPronto, 312, 406

iQue 3600, 183

IRC (Internet Relay Chat), 55

iRiver iFP-390T, 222

iron lung, 243

iseepet.com, 86

iSight, 181

iSkin eVo iPod Protector, 224

iSun Solar Charger, 23

IT industry, 400

iTrip, 223

iTunes

  copying to Macs, 24

  opening, 136

J

Jackson, Janet, 50

Jacquard, Joseph Marie, birth, 221

January historical events

  accelerating galaxy discovery, 11

  ACM-GAMM committee convenes to
    develop ALGOL, 13

  Apollo 1 disaster, 29

  Apple launches Macintoshes, 24

  AT&T divests Bell System Companies, 3

  Beatles perform last concert, 32

  calendar, 2, 34-35

  Challenger Space Shuttle explosion, 30

  Eisenhower inauguration (first tele-
    vised), 22

  first commercial supersonic flight, 23

  first pocket scientific calculator, 6

  FM radio demonstrated, 7

  HAL computer, 14

January historical events

Harvard Mark I, 20
Howard Hughes sets transcontinental air record, 21
IBM SSEC, 26
integrated circuits, 25
Lotus 1-2-3 release, 28
National Center for Supercomputing Applications (NCSA), 17
nuclear-powered submarine launch, 19
patent of electromechanical adding and sorting machine, 10
premier of *The Simpsons*, 16
publication of Poe's *Raven*, 31
RCA's introduction of 45 RPM records, 12
SAGE, 18
Schoolhouse Rock debut, 8
Spirit Rover landing on Mars, 5
transatlantic phone service launch, 9
transcontinental phone service, 27
U.S. satellite launch, 33
Wham-O introduces Frisbees, 15
JavaHMO, 45
JavaScript
   1st JavaScript Library, 101
   Source, 103
JB1 007 Digital Spy Camera, 30
Jefferson, Thomas, death, 218
JiWire
   Portable Hotspot Locator, 201
   Wi-Fi Hotspot Locator, 201
Jobs, Steve, 261
John Deere Plow Co., 292
Johnson, Edward H., 412
Joystiq Web site, 156
JPEGWriter, 45
JPG graphics, 394
jukeboxes, first installed, 379
July historical events
   Alfred Binet's birth, 225
   bikini debut, 219
   Bugs Bunny debut, 241
   calendar, 214, 246-247
   Cape Canaveral's first launch, 238
   Charles Mayo's birth, 233
   cloned mice, 237
   death of John Adams and Thomas Jefferson, 218
   Earl Tupper's birth, 242
   foam rubber developed, 217
   George Eastman's birth, 226
   Gottfried Wilhelm von Leibniz's birth, 215

Henry Ford's birth, 244
IBM 650 Magnetic Drum Data Processing Machine, 216
Intel incorporated, 232
iron lung installed, 243
Joseph Marie Jacquard's birth, 221
Live Aid Concert, 227
margarine patent, 229
Mars Pathfinder Sojourner Rover, 220
moon pictures, 245
Neil Armstrong's walk on moon, 234
Roswell incident, 222
Scopes trial, 224
Shoemaker-Levy comet hits Jupiter, 230
solar eclipse, first, 231
Stanley Kubrick's birth, 240
Star Trek character Jean Picard born, 235
tape measure patent, 228
test tube baby, first born, 239
Tron film premiere, 223
Wiley Post's solo flight, 236
Jumbo Web site, 185
June historical events
   aerial tramway, 208
   Alan Turing's birth, 203
   Apple II released, 190
   bar codes, 206
   Benjamin Franklin flies kite, 195
   birth of Les Paul, 189
   calendar, 180, 211-212
   color television, 205
   cotton gin patent, 200
   doughnuts invented, 202
   Dr. Sally Ride goes to space, 198
   E.T.: The Extra-Terrestrial release, 191
   Ed White walks in space, 183
   flying saucers sighted, 204
   George Orwell's *1984* published, 186
   George Reeves' suicide, 199
   helicopter flight demonstrated for first time, 196
   pens with erasable ink, 207
   Pioneer 10, 193
   Rock Around the Clock released, 192
   rubber processing patent, 197
   Senator Robert F. Kennedy assassination, 185
   Sgt. Pepper's Lonely Hearts Club Band, 181
   Soyuz 11 tragedy, 209
   SpaceShipOne, 201

Tunguska meteorite explosion, 210
typesetting machine patented, 187
U.S. missile mail, 188
UNIVAC I, 194
Velveeta cheese invented, 182
VisiCalc, 184
JungleScan, 373
junior high school software, 287
Jupiter Research home networks, 216
JustLinux, 138

K

Kamprad, Ingvar, 31
Kardon, Harman, 220
KaZaA Media Desktop, 148
Kennedy, President John F., assassination, 378
Kennedy, Senator Robert F., assassination, 185
Kensington, Wi-Fi Finder, 204
Kensington's FlyLight, 100
Kenwood DT-7000S, 197
Kepler, Johannes, birth, 417
Kesinton Turbo Mouse Pro, 372
key019 (Philips), 76
keyboards
   Apple Wireless Keyboard, 28
   cleaning, 338
   EluminX, 416
   foreign characters, 410
   IceKey, 234
   Tru-Form, 418
keypads, 158
Keyspan Digital Media Remote, 135
Keystation 49e (M-Audio), 7
keystroke-logging programs
   eBlaster, 7
   Perfect Keylogger, 7
Kid Info Web site, 266
KiddoNet Web site, 289
kids
   Internet security, 288
   Internet usage, 191
   Web sites, 289
Kids' Planet Web site, 290
Kids' Space Web site, 289
KidsCom Web site, 289
KidsEdge.com, 265
KidsPrivacy.org, 16
KidZone Web site, 290
Kilby, Jack, birth, 364
killer bees invade Texas, 335
King Tut's tomb, 54

King, Dr. Martin Luther Jr., assassination, 112
KinoCode MaxCrypt, 14
kissthisguy.com, 242
Kitty Hawk, 407
KOffice, 136
Kollegeville Web site, 271
Konfabulator, 25
Kraft, J.L., birth, 401
Kubrick, Stanley, birth, 240

L

labels, CDs, 229
LaCie
    Big Disk Extreme, 40
    Bigger Disk Extreme, 260
    DVD+/- Double Layer drive, 404
    electronblue IV models, 267
    Ethernet Disk, 61
    USB Pocket Floppy, 293
    Web site, 325
Laika, first dog in space, 359
Lanston, Tolbert, 187
LapCool notebook, 330
Laporte Report, 344, 347
laptops, college, 268
Larsson, Arne, 328
laser beams, bounced off moon, 153
Launchbar, 25
LAUNCHcast, 151
LCD hood (cameras), 31
LCDs (liquid crystal display), 385
    compared to CRTs, 385
    Wacom Cintiq, 74
Lennon, John, birth, 398
lens filters, 31
Leo Laporte's Guide to TiVo, 47
Leonard Nimoy Should Eat More Salsa
    Foundation, 242
letterboxing, 306
LibDex Web site, 267
libraries, online, 267
Library of Congress
    articles, converting film stock, 43
    Web site, 267
LibrarySpot Web site, 267
Lifescape Picasa, 27
Light gun, 155
light notebooks, 331
lighting
    cameras, 31
    video, 44
LimeWire, 148
Lindbergh, Charles, 164

Line 6 GuitarPort, 225
links
    code to make invisible, 100
    Linux, 138
    operator, 75
LinkShare Web site, 257
LinkStash, 186
Linkstation Network Storage Center, 216
Linksys
    Etherfast, 6
    routers, 209
    Wireless Compact USB Adapter, 200
Linux, 133
    Documentation Project, 138
    downloading, 135
    Forums, 138
    Gazette, 138
    Hewlett-Packard, 138
    installing, 145
    Journal, 138
    Media Player, 136
    Mirra Personal Server, 258
    Online, 136
    OpenOffice, 134
    Orbit, 216
    software, 136-137
    versions, 134
    Web sites, 138
Linux.com, 138
liquid crystal display. See LCDs
liquidation sales, online shopping, 383
Liquidation.com Web site, 383
LISP programming language, 73
lists, Amazon, 376
Live Aid Concert, 227
Live365, 151
locations, system folders, 396
Locator, 25
locomotive races horse, 278
Logitech
    Cordless RumblePad, 153
    diNovo Media Desktop, 186
    io Personal Digital Pen, 26
    Mobile Bluetooth Headset, 229
    MOMO Racing Force Feedback Wheel,
        158, 402
    QuickCam Orbit, 66
    QuickCam Pro, 174
    Z-680, 146
Logitech Cordless Presenter, 19
Longhorn, 278
Lotus 1-2-3 release, 28
Louisiana Purchase ratified, 340
Lucas, George, 191

Lycos Gamesville, 154
Lycos Music, 149

M

M-Audio
    Keystation 49e, 7
    MobilePre USB, 227
    Sonica Theater, 162
MacAlly iceMouseJr, 332
MacAMP Web site, 150
MacFixit, 22
Macintoshes, 121, 411
    ADC Monitor Sharing Switch, 300
    AirPort, 202
    Apple, 404
        AirPort, 202
        AirPort Extreme Base Station, 411
        IPO, 402
        iSight, 181
        iTunes opening, 136
        legal suit against Microsoft, 94
        PowerBook, 407
        Wireless Keyboard, 28
        Wozniak, Stephen, 261
    Artisan Color Reference System, 325
    Asante's FriendlyNET FR1004, 209
    ATI Radeon 9800 Pro video card, 386
    Cinema Displays, 21
    copying iTune music to, 24
    Digi 002, 128
    Dr. Bott's DVI Extractor, 88
    Dr. Bott's DVIator, 81
    Dr. Bott's ExtendAIR Direct, 307
    DVD+/- Double Layer drive, 404
    DVR-107, 358
    Easter Eggs, 95
        OS 7.5, 95
        OS 9, 95
        OS X, 95
    electronblue IV models, 267
    Elgato's EyeHome, 102
    EyeTV, 47
    EZQuest Boa Slim, 365
    Fantom's Titanium FireWire burner, 188
    FireWire 3-Port PCI Card, 397
    FireWire 4-Port Hub, 339
    free OS-X utilities, 25
    G5 Skateboard, 346
    game controllers, 155
    Gefen's VGA to ADC adapter, 95
    GraphicConverter, 25
    Graphire3, 281
    Griffin Technology's SightLight, 195
    I-TVView/Mac, 114

Macintoshes

IceKey keyboard, 234
iceMouseJr, 332
iCurve, 274
iMac, 14
iPods. See iPods
iSight, 181
Keyspan's Digital Media Remote, 135
LaCie
   Big Disk Extreme, 40
   Bigger Disk Extreme, 260
   DVD+/- Double Layer drive, 404
   electronblue IV models, 267
   Ethernet Disk, 61
   USB Pocket Floppy, 293
   Web site, 325
launch of, 24
M-Audio Sonica Theater, 162
M-Audio's Keystation 49e, 7
MobilePre USB, 227
MonacoOPTIX, 253
notebooks, 332
Plantronic's DSP-300, 54
Power Support's G5 Roof, 314
ProScope, 169
SoundSticks II, 148
support costs, 24
troubleshooting, 22
Tru-Form, 418
Turbo Mouse Pro, 372
USB BusPort, 379
USB Pocket Floppy, 293
Wacom Cintiq, 74
Wi-Fi networks, 204
Macromedia Dreamweaver MX, 257
Mad Dog Multimedia, 327
Madboot, 259
MadSci Network Web site, 266
Magellan spacecraft Venus probe, 148
Magellan SporTrak Color, 16
The Magic Box, 156
Magix Audio Cleaning Lab, 152
mailbox patent, 81
mailing groups, 199
Mailto: links, adding to Web pages, 256
MailWasher, 125
mainstream notebooks, 331
MAMEWorld Web site, 315
The Man from U.N.C.L.E., premiere, 308
manufacturer rebates, online shopping, 379
March historical events
  Apple sues Microsoft, 94
  birth of Albert Einstein, 86
  calendar, 72, 104-106

Californium transuranium element discovery, 89
Dr. Seuss' (Theodor Seuss) birth, 74
elevator patent, 87
FDA approves Viagra, 99
first liquid-filled rocket launch, 88
first telephone call, 82
Gemini flight, 95
Heaven's Gate mass suicide, 98
Homebrew Computer Club first meeting, 75
Jules Verne dies, 96
LISP programming language programming manual released, 73
Luddite riots, 83
mailbox patented, 81
Mariner 10 flies past Mercury, 101
Michelangelo computer virus, 78
PC DOS 2.0, 80
PC Jr., 91
pencil with eraser patented, 102
President Franklin Delano Roosevelt's first radio talk, 84
RCA televisions shipped, 97
Rene Descartes' birth, 103
Schick markets first electric razor, 90
telephone patent, 79
Tennessee passes the Butler Act, 93
terrorist attack on Tokyo subway system, 92
Three Mile Island nuclear power plant accident, 100
Treaty on the Non-Proliferation of Nuclear Weapons (NPT), 77
Uranus discovered, 85
Wang sale of core memory patents to IBM, 76
margarine patent, 229
Marine Aquarium screensaver, 417
Mariner 10, fly past Mercury, 101
Mariner 2 launched, 277
Mars, Viking 2 landing on, 289
Mars Pathfinder Sojourner Rover, 220
mass email mailings, 199
master/slave nomenclature, 414
Math & Science Excelerator, 271
Matsushita, Konosuke, birth, 383
Mauchly, John, birth, 280
MaxCrypt (KinoCode), 14
Maximum PC, 170
Maxtor Web site, 325
May historical events
  Adler Planetarium opened, 156
  automatic cannons, 169

  BASIC introduced, 145
  calendar, 144, 176-177
  Coca-Cola invented, 152
  FDA approves genetically engineered tomatoes, 163
  Gloster-Whittle E.28/39, first flight, 159
  Golden Gate Bridge opened, 172
  heart transplant, first in U.S., 147
  Hindenburg disaster, 150
  Indianapolis 500, 174
  laser beam bounced off moon, 153
  Lusitania torpedoed by German U-boats, 151
  Magellan spacecraft Venus probe, 148
  microfilm camera patented, 170
  Mount Everest conquered, 173
  Mount St. Helens erupts, 162
  nuclear reactor patented, 161
  removable tire rims, 165
  Robert Julius Petri's birth, 175
  Robert Moog's birth, 167
  science fiction film premiere, 146
  screw-on bottle caps patented, 149
  seminal LPs released, 160
  Spam trademarked, 155
  Spirit of St. Louis flight, 164
  Star Wars premiere, 168
  twenty dollar bill release, 158
  VELCRO trademarked, 157
  Windows 3.0 released, 166
McAfee AntiSpyware, 304
McCallum, David, 308
McCarthy, George, 170
McCarthy, John, birth, 290
McVeigh, Timothy, 127
MD 100 CD/Media destroyer, 302
Media Center hard drives, 52
media hubs, 309
media readers, Dazzle 10-in-1, 193
medicine, Web sites, 243
MedicineNet Web site, 243
MedlinePlus Web site, 243
Melvill, Michael, 201
memory
  flash
    i-Duck, 160
    SWISSMEMORY, 377
  players, 222
  portable devices, 334
  upgrades, 324, 335

Mencken, Henry Louis, birth, 298
menus
    creating, 409
    Send To, 274
Mercury Mariner 10 flies past, 101
message boards, Yahoo!, 83
MessageLabs spam statistics, 124
metasearch engines, 87-88
meters (CPU), inserting into Windows taskbar, 399
MFR 18-in-1 Multi Function Reader, 363
Michelangelo computer virus, 78
Mickey Mouse debut, 374
microdrives, 221
microfilm cameras, patented, 170
MicroMV, 33
microphones, external, 44
Microsoft
    Apple's legal suit against, 94
    DOS contract with IBM, 362
    Encarta, 290
    Excel, column width adjustments, 296
    Excel 2000 Easter Eggs, 96
    Excel 97 Easter Eggs, 96
    Flight Simulator, 158, 408
    FrontPage, 111
    Help Web site, 261
    Office Letter, 294
    Word
        adding watermarks to documents, 412
        as spreadsheets, 411
        Autocorrect feature, 413
        Easter Eggs, 96
        editing text in, 291
        outlines, 294
        overtype mode, 293
        spelling and grammar check, 292
        Wordware 2002, 410
    Works 7, Easter Eggs, 96
    WorkSuite 2003, Easter Eggs, 96
microwave ovens patented, 396
MiniDV, 33
Mirra Personal Server, 258
MIRT (mobile infrared transmitter), 420
Mobile Bluetooth Headset, 229
mobile infrared transmitter (MIRT), 420
MobilePlanet Web site, 316
MobilePre USB, 227
moblogs, 350
modding, 167
    noise, 169
    PCs, 171
    Web sites, 170

Model T introduced, 321
Modthebox.com, 170
Molina, Dr. Mario, 311
MOMO Racing Force Feedback Wheel, 158, 402
MonacoOPTIX, 253
monitoring, Activity Monitor, 208
monitors
    LCDs, compared to CRTs, 385
    multiple monitor setup for Windows, 128
Monopoly (Parker Brothers game), 44
Monster iCarPlay FM Transmitter, 223
Moog, Robert, birth, 167
moon
    first orbit, 413
    last moon mission, 397
    pictures, 245, 327
Morpheus, 148
Morrison, Fred, 15
Motion Picture Association of America, pirated movies, 43
Mount Everest conquered, 173
Mount St. Helens, eruption, 162
mouse
    Air Flo Mouse, 370
    cleaning, 338
    Gyration Ultra GT, 272
    patent, 373
mouseover alert boxes, 103
mousetrapping, 303
Moveable Type, 345
MovieBox DV, 43
movies, 239
    accessories, 44
    blogs, 347
    burning to DVDs, MyDVD, 359
    pirated, 43
    Star Wars premiere, 168
Mozilla Firefox, 136, 192
Mozilla Thunderbird, 136, 194
MP3 audio format, 146
    converting tapes to, 152
MSN Games, 154
MSN Messenger with Messenger Plus Add-in, 99
MSN Search, 87
MSR Assist, 161
Mullany, David N., 264
Mumma, Robert, 234
music, 239
    blogs, 347
    converting tapes to MP3s, 152
    digital players, 150

downloading, 147
Finale, 245
iTunes, 24
Music Label 2004, 219
NETGEAR MP101, 309
On Tour speaker system, 295
players
    Archos Gmini 220, 220
    buying, 218
    Dell Digital Jukebox, 220
    iPod, 219, 223-224
    microdrives, 221
    Samsung Napster Player, 220
ripping from CDs, 149
Sound Blaster Wireless Music, 305
speakers
    Apple Pro, 220
    Olympia's Soundbug, 218
Music Downloads (Wal-Mart), 147
Music Label 2004, 219
Musicmatch Jukebox, 147
    burning CDs, 226
    Web site, 149-150
MuVo TX, 222
My Computer folder, Windows files, 398
My Documents folder, Windows files, 398
My eBay, 364
My Yahoo!, 82
MyDVD, 44
    burning movies to DVDs, 359
mypetstop.com, 290
mySimon Web site, 381
The Myth of the Paperless Office, 296

N

Napster 2.0, 147
Napster Player, 220
NASA
    announcement of first astronauts, 117
    Kids Web site, 265
Nascar Pro Digital 2, 158
National Center for Supercomputing Applications (NCSA), 17
National Safety Council (NSC), junking computers, 3
National School Boards Foundation, 270
naviPod, 223
NBC Sports, 241
NCSA (National Center for Supercomputing Applications), 17
Neato CD Labeler Kit, 229
Nero, 231
NES (Nintendo Entertainment System), 157

Net Nanny Web site, 279
NetDisk, 216
Netgear 318, 6
NETGEAR MP101, 309
Netgear routers, 209
Netimperative passwords, changing, 263
netiquette, 183
Netscape, founding, 259
network interface cards (NICs), 207
Network Operations Center (NOC), 63
networks
    home networks, 216
    sharing files, 217
    TiVos, 50
    troubleshooting, 215
    Wi-Fi, 200
        compared to Bluetooth, 203
        connecting without, 206
        home networks, 205
        hotspots, 201-202
        Macintoshes, 204
        PCTEL Roaming Client, 206
    wired, 207
    wireless, Super Cantenna Wireless
        Network Antenna, 232
Neumann, John von, 112
New York City subway opens, 347
New York Public Library Digital Library
    Collections Web site, 267
newgroups, etiquette, 183
news, 240
    games, 156
    News.com, 419
    Visual Communicator, 192
News Index, 240
News.com, 419
NewsGator, 350
newsgroups, Google Groups, 15
NewsLibrary, 240
NewsLink, 240
NewsMac, 20
NewsTrawler, 240
Newton, Sir Issac, birth, 415
NGAkids Web site, 265
NICs (network interface card), 207
Nielsen, Arthur Charles, 291
Nielsen/NetRatings, advertising, 184, 230
Nikon D70, 26
Nintendo Entertainment System (NES),
    157
Nisus Thesaurus, 21
NOC (Network Operations Center), 63
noise, PCs, 169
NoiseMagic NoVibes III drive, 169

Non-Proliferation of Nuclear Weapons
    (NPT), 77
NOP Research, statistics on children and
    Internet education, 244
Norton
    AntiSpam, 125
    AntiVirus, 118
    Ghost, 4
    Internet Security, 11, 279
    PartitionMagic, 40, 329
    SystemWorks, 166
Nostromo SpeedPad, 158
NOT operator, 89
NotebookReview Web site, 333
notebooks, 331
    accessories, 330
    buying, 333
    desktop replacements, 331
    LapCool, 330
    light, 331
    Macintoshes, 332
    mainstream, 331
    memory, 335
    security, 335
    thin, 331
    tips, 336
    TrackIT Portable Anti-Theft System, 337
    ultraportables, 331
November historical events
    Alan Turing defines universal machine,
        368
    Atari releases its PONG game, 385
    B.F. Goodrich's birth, 360
    Buckyball discovered, 370
    calendar, 356, 387-388
    Carl Sagan's birth, 365
    Darwin's *Origin of Species* published,
        380
    dry cell batteries patented, 371
    dynamite patented, 381
    Ford halts production of Edsel, 375
    Gene Amdahl's birth, 372
    George Boole's birth, 358
    Holland Tunnel opens, 369
    hydrogen bomb exploded, 357
    Jack Kilby's birth, 364
    jukebox installed, 379
    Konosuke Matsushita's birth, 383
    Kurt Vonnegut's birth, 367
    manned balloon flight, 377
    Marie Curie's birth, 363
    Mariner 4 launched, 384
    Mark Twain's birth, 386
    Mickey Mouse debut, 374

    Microsoft signs DOS contract with
        IBM, 362
    mouse patented, 373
    Polaroid Land camera, 382
    President Kennedy assassinated, 378
    Soviets send dog into space, 359
    Vikings discovered in Canada, 361
    viruses, first, 366
    Windows 1.0 released, 376
NoVibes III drive, 169
Noyce, Robert, 25
NPD Group, retail sale of video games,
    158
NPT (Non-Proliferation of Nuclear
    Weapons), 77
NSC (National Safety Council), junking
    computers, 3
nuclear chain reaction, first, 392
nuclear reactors, patent, 161
nuclear-powered submarine launch, 19
Nuke Nabber, 10
Nyko Air Flo Mouse, 370

                    O

O'Hanlon, Virginia, 307
OBA Accounting System, 136
October historical events
    Albert Einstein arrives in America, 337
    Amdahl Corp. founded, 339
    anesthetic used for first time, 336
    Anthony Leeuwenhoek's birth, 344
    Apollo mission launched, 331
    atomic clock, 322
    Bill Gate's birth, 348
    calendar, 320, 352-354
    Chuck Yeager breaks sound barrier,
        334
    Cuban missile crisis, 342
    Ed Wood's birth, 330
    Edison demonstrates electric light, 341
    electric blanket introduced, 329
    extraterrestrial life searches, 332
    faxes, first sent, 323
    John Glenn returns to space, 349
    killer bees invade Texas, 335
    killer smog, 346
    Louisiana Purchase ratified, 340
    Model T introduced, 321
    moon pictures, 327
    New York City subway opens, 347
    oldest fossils discovered, 343
    pacemaker implant, first, 328
    RCA founded, 338

Robert Goddard's birth, 325
space race, 324
Thor Heyerdahl's birth, 326
U.S. Navy uses dolphins for surveil-
  lance, 333
Vatican admits Galileo is right, 351
War of the Worlds radio broadcast,
  350
wristwatches, 345
Office Letter, 294
Office Portal, 412
Office Student and Teacher Edition, 29
offline browsing, 187
Oklahoma City Federal building bombed,
  127
Olsen, Ken, 236
Olympia Soundbug, 218
Olympus DM-1, 9
OMG audio format, 146
OmniDictionary, 21
On Tour speaker system, 295
online auctions, 363
  auction management service, 368
  bidding tips, 366
  DeepAnalysis, 369
  eBay businesses, 369
  My eBay, 364
  selling tips, 367
  sniping, 365
online chats, 54
  IMSecure, 58
  Internet Relay Chat (IRC), 55
  lingo, 56
  sex chats, 58
  tips, 57
online coupons, online shopping, 382
online etiquette, 183
online greeting cards, 245
online libraries, 267
online sex sites, 98
online shopping
  Forrester Research, 382
  gamer gifts, 403
  geek gifts, 402, 405, 408
  home theater gifts, 406
  home videos, 404
  liquidation sales, 383
  manufacturer rebates, 379
  online coupons, 382
  paying, 377
  photography gifts, 405
  price comparison site, 381
  researching purchases, 380
  road warriors, 407
  security, 378

OpenOffice, 134
Opera, 136
operators
  advanced Google searches, 75
  Boolean, 89
Oppenheimer, J. Robert, 130
optical head-tracking systems,
  TrackIR 3-Pro, 395
optimizing displays with ClearType, 397
OR operator, 89
Origin of Species, 380
Orwell, George, 186
OS 7.5 Easter Eggs, 95
OS 9 Easter Eggs, 95
OS X, 19
  Easter Eggs, 95
  Finder, replacing, 23
  free utilities, 25
  Services menu, 21
Osborne Computer bankruptcy, 299
Osborne, Adam, 299
The Outer Limits premiere, 302
outlines (Word), PowerPoint
  presentations, 294
Outlook NewsGator, 350
Outlook Express Backup Wizard, 194
overclocking video cards, 172
Overdrive PC, 173
Overstock.com Web site, 383
overtype mode, 293
oxygen identified, 251

P

Packard, David, 268, 293
Palm Boulevard Web site, 315
Palm OS
  software, 313
  versus Pocket PCs, 312
PalmGear.com, 316
Palms users, 321
PalmSource Web site, 313
Panasonic DVD-LX8 portable, 367
paper consumption, 296
parachute wedding, 275
parallel ports, 328
Parker Brothers Monopoly, 44
PartitionMagic, 329
PassMark Performance Test, 173
passwords
  changing, 263
  creating, 17
patents. See also inventions
  aerosol spray, 272
  air brakes, 121

  carpet sweeper, 305
  Colt revolver, 63
  core memory, 76
  cotton gin, 200
  dental chairs, 265
  dry cell batteries patented, 371
  dynamite, 381
  electromechanical adding and sorting
    machine, 10
  elevators, 87
  envelope folding machine, 46
  fire extinguishing system, 48
  ice cream cone, 405
  integrated circuits, 25
  mailbox, 81
  margarine, 229
  microfilm camera, 170
  microwave ovens, 396
  mouse, 373
  nuclear reactors, 161
  pencils with erasers, 102
  radars, 110
  refrigerator, 258
  rubber processing, 197
  tape measures, 228
  telephones, 79
  televisions, 270
  typesetting machine, 187
  vertical-looping roller coaster, 266
Path Finder (Cocoatech), 23
Paul, Les, birth, 189
Pauling, Linus, birth, 66
paying, online shopping, 377
PC DOS 2.0 release, 80
PC Jr., 91
PC Pitstop, 340
PC-Mod, 170
PCDJ Web site, 150
PCs. See also computers
  building, 168
  buying compared to upgrading, 160
  configuring for video editing, 39
  converting into TiVos, 51
  discarding, 416
  encryption of files, 14
  extreme PCs, 173
  game consoles, 153
  graphics, 327
  identification, 400
  maintenance, 337
  modding, 167
    custom cases, 171
    noise, 169

PCs

PC Survival Kit, 343
ports, 265, 328
powering on, 417
recycling, 416
setup, 3
shutting down, 421
troubleshooting, 264
upgrades, 161
    compared to buying, 160
    external connectors, 163
    from old to new, 166
    internal devices, 164
    preparation list, 162
    Tom's Hardware Guide, 163
viruses, 112
    attachments, 117
    AVG Anti-Virus FREE Edition, 113
    Brain, 112
    cleaning, 115
    hoaxes, 118
    Norton AntiVirus, 118
    prevention, 113
    restoring Windows XP after attack,
    116
PCTEL Roaming Client, 206
PCTV Deluxe, 45
PCX graphics, 394
PDA Street Web site, 313
PDAs (personal digital assistants), 322
    accessories, 316
    cases, 322
    software, 313
    versus smart phones, 321
PDAZoo Web site, 316
peer-to-peer file sharing, 148
Pegasus Mail, 194
Pemberton, Dr. John S., 152
pencils, eraser pencil patented, 102
pens
    digital, io Personal Digital Pen, 26
    erasable ink, 207
Pentagon, September 11 attack, 297
people searches, 91-92
Perfect Keylogger, 7
performance, Tweak-XP Pro, 401
Perlman, Henry, 165
Perseus Development Corp., blog
    statistics, 349
personal digital assistants. See PDAs
personal management programs,
    Agendus, 322
pet Webcam, 86
PetBugs.com, 290
Petri, Robert Julius, birth, 175

pets, Web sites, 290
Pew Internet, 151
PGP (Gnu Privacy Guard), 13, 127
    email encryption, 21
    International, 13
Phantom Game Receiver, 153
Philips
    iPronto, 312, 406
    key019, 76
    ProntoPro NG, 374
phishing schemes, 8-10
Phlog Web site, 350
PhoneBridge, 239
PhoneLabs Dock-N-Talk, 262
phonographs, invention, 394
photoblogs, 350
Photoblogs.org, 350
photos
    albums, creating DVDs, 360
    blogs, 347
    Corbis, 391
    digital, 28
    editing software, 32
    fades, 109
    organization, 27
    photography gifts, 405
    Picasa, 27
    RAW format, 30
    replacing backgrounds, 386
    sharing, 85
    storing, 85
    touching up, 384
Photoshop
    Album, 27
    CS, 32
    Elements, 32
    GIF graphics, 392
physicians, Internet usage, 328
Picasa, 27
pictures, managing, 277
PimpRig, 170
Pinnacle
    MovieBox DV, 43
    PCTV Deluxe, 45
Pioneer, 193, 358
pirated movies, 43
pirated software, statistics, 421
Plan, 136
Planet Wellness Web site, 243
Planetarium, Adler, opened, 156
Planon DocuPen, 59
Plantronic DSP-300, 54

players, music, 150
playing
    DVDs, 358
    games online, 154
Playsite, 154
PlayStation, 157
PNG graphics, 394
PNY Technologies, 327
Pocket PCs, 321
    Central Web site, 313, 316
    emulating games on, 315
    software, 313
    versus Palm OS, 312
PocketGear.com Web site, 313
Poe, Edgar Allen, publication of Raven, 31
Pogo.com, 154
pointing, 418
Polaroid Land camera, 382
polio, mass inoculation against, 61
political blogs, 347
POP (Post Office Protocol), 193
pop-ups
    creating, 302
    stopping, 301
POP3 (Post Office Protocol 3), 195
popcorn, 60
porn sites, 98
port scans, 10
portable devices
    AIBO Entertainment Robot, 406
    AirZooka, 109
    Altec Lansing's inMotion Portable
        Audio System, 222
    Bar Master Deluxe, 97
    batteries, 56
    Bose QuietComfort 2s, 399
    CAR-100 Bluetooth Car Kit, 276
    Casio's WQV10D-2, 215
    Cellboost, 243
    Dick Tracy wrist-radio, 288
    Dock-N-Talk, 262
    DriveRight CarChip, 348
    DVD-LX8 portable, 367
    Eyetop Centra, 63
    EZBinoCam LX, 190
    GPS Magellan SporTrak Color, 16
    Gramin's Rino 130, 123
    Grundig Emergency Radio, 83
    Harmony SST-659 universal remote
        control, 413
    iQue 3600, 183
    JB1 007 Digital Spy Camera, 30
    Kensington's Wi-Fi Finder, 204
    Kenwood's DT-7000S, 197

MD 100 CD/Media destroyer, 302
memory, 334
MIRT (mobile infrared transmitter), 420
Mobile Bluetooth Headset, 229
NETGEAR MP101, 309
On Tour speaker system, 295
Philips's key019, 76
Pretender, 130
ProntoPro NG, 374
Pyramat PM300 Game Chair, 341
RIST Memory Watch, 334
Roomba Pro, 116
SanDisk's Digital Photo Viewer, 137
SD-P5000, 360
Shure E3c earphones, 150
SideWinder, 236
SKYFi portable XM receiver, 164
Skymaster Weathermaster, 90
solar panels, iSun Solar Charger, 23
Timex's GPS Watch, 171
TomTom Navigator, 316
TV Games, 157
Universal Wireless Keyboard, 327
Vector FX2, 381
voice recorders, 9
Weather Watch Pro, 392
Wrist Net Internet Watch, 269
ZIP-CELL, 255
Portable Hotspot Locator, 201
portable receivers, SKYFi XM, 164
portable video players, Archos AV300 series, 42
portals, Woody's Office Portal, 412
ports, 328
    FireWire, 328
    FrontX, 265
    parallel, 328
    SCSI, 328
    serial, 328
    USB, 328
    USB BusPort, 379
Post Office Protocol (POP), 193
Post Office Protocol 3 (POP3), 195
Post, Wiley, 236
Post-It Notes, introduced, 114
Power Mac G5, 404
power searches, Amazon, 375
power surge suppressors, 3
Power Support G5 Skateboard, 346
PowerBook, 407
Powerex Charger/Conditioner, 56
powering on PCs, 417

PowerPoint
    presentations
        embossing, 295
        text drop shadows, 414
    slide animation, 415
PowerStrip, 168
Prawnography, 242
Premiere, 205
Premiere Pro, 404
Prescott, Edwin, 266
presentations (PowerPoint)
    embossing, 295
    Logitech Cordless Presenter, 19
    text, drop-shadows, 414
    Word outlines, 294
presidential debates, first, 312
Preston, Billy, 32
Pretender, 130
price comparison site, online shopping, 381
Priestley, Joseph, 251
printers
    buying, 329
    Canon i560 printer, 28
privacy
    children, 16
    Fast-Eraser, 18
    newsgroups, 15
product listings, Amazon, 373
programmable buttons, 155
PromiscDetect, 10
ProntoPro NG, 374
ProScope, 169
protocols
    email, 195
    IMAP (Interactive Mail Access Protocol), 195
    POP3 (Post Office Protocol 3), 195
    Post Office Protocol (POP), 193
    SMTP (Simple Mail Transfer Protocol), 195
pull-down menus, creating, 409
Puppy Fingerprint Identity Token (Sony), 12
Pyramat PM300 Game Chair, 341

Q - R

QuickCam Orbit (Logitech), 66
QuickCam Pro, 174
Quicken WillMaker Plus, 238
QuickVerse Deluxe, 99

racing wheels, 155, 158
radars, patent, 110

Radio Corporation of America, 303
Radio-Locator, 151
RadioMOI, 151
radios
    Gramin's Rino 130, 123
    Grundig Emergency Radio, 83
    Internet, 151
    War of the Worlds radio broadcast, 350
RADSL, 60
RAM (random access memory), 324
Rambus DRAM (RDRAM), 324
random access memory. See RAM
Ranger 7, 245
RateItAll Web site, 380
RAW format, 30
razors, Schick markets first electric razor, 90
RCA
    founded, 338
    introduction of 45 RPM records, 12
RDRAM (Rambus DRAM), 324
ReaderwareVW program, 306
Real World University Web site, 270
Really Simple Syndication. See RSS
RealPlayer Web site, 150
rear projection televisions (RPTVs), 305
Reard, Louis, 219
rebates, manufacturer, 379
recycling PCs, 416
Rediff.com Web site, 251
ReefMaster, 32
Reeves, George, suicide, 199
region codes, DVDs, 357
Registry
    editing, 263
    Mechanic, 273
    Windows Registry Guide, 398
Reichstag fire, 65
Rekall, 136
related operator, 75
Relay I satellite launch, 403
remote controls, Harmony's SST-659
    universal, 413
removing
    Sasser virus, 114
    spyware, 299
Reno, Jesse, 87
research, online shopping, 380
Reservoir Dogs (10th Anniversary Edition)
    Easter Egg, 98
restore points, 260
retail sales, video games, 158
REV Drive, 409
Reverse Phone Directory, 91

ReviewFinder Web site, 380
revolvers (Colt), patent, 63
Rhapsody Web site, 147
Ricochet service, 206
Ride, Dr. Sally, 198
right-clicking, 418
Rino 130, 123
RipEditBurn, 226
ripping music from CDs, 149
risks, 9
RIST Memory Watch, 334
road warriors, shopping, 407
RoadBlock, 125
robotic tabletop mounts, 44
robotic vacuum cleaners, Roomba Pro, 116
Rock Around the Clock released, 192
rockets, first liquid-filled rocket launch, 88
Roddenberry, Gene, 294
Roku HD1000, 323
Roomba Pro, 116
Roosevelt, President Franklin D, first fireside chat, 84
Roswell Daily Record, 222
Roswell incident, 222
Rotten Tomatoes Web site, 239
routers, 209
Rowland, Dr. F. Sherwood, 311
Roxio Easy DVD Copy, 351
Roxio Easy Media Creator, 362
RPTVs (Rear projection televisions), 305
RSS (Really Simple Syndication), 349
rubber processing patent, 197
Rudolphi, Arno, 275
Russell Research, Palm users, 321
Rutan, Burt, 201

S

Safe mode, starting Windows, 264
Sagan, Carl, birth, 365
SAGE (Semi-Automatic Ground Environment), 18
Sage TV, 51
sales
    Amazon, 375
    online shopping, Forrester Research, 382
Salk, Jonas, 61
Samba Linux Orbit, 216
Samsung Napster Player, 220
San Francisco earthquake of 1906, 126

SanDisk
    Cruzer Mini USB Flash Drive, 133
    Digital Photo Viewer, 137
Sasser virus, removing, 114
satellite broadband, 63
scams, phishing schemes, 8-10
scan converters, I-TVView/Mac, 114
Scanjet 4670, 279
scanners
    Planon DocuPen, 59
    port, 10
    Scanjet 4670, 279
Schick, markets first electric razor, 90
Schmitt, Jack, 397
Schoolhouse Rock debut, 8
SCID (severe combined immune deficiency), 45
science fiction films, premiere of first, 146
Scopes Monkey Trial, 93
Scopes trial, 224
screensavers
    3D Flying Easter Eggs Screensaver, 94
    Marine Aquarium screensaver, 417
screw-on bottle caps patented, 149
SCSI ports, 328
SD-P5000, 360
SDP (Streaming Media Project), 147
SDRAM (synchronous dynamic RAM), 324
SDSL, 60
SeaLife ReefMaster, 32
search engines, 86
    AltaVista, 87
    AOL Search, 87
    Ask Jeeves!, 87
    FAST, 87
    Google, 66, 137
    HotBot, 87
    metasearch, 87-88
    MSN Search, 87
    Teoma, 87
    Yahoo!
        Address Book, 84
        Calendar, 84
        Directory, 80
        email, 81
        groups, 83
        message boards, 83
        Messenger
    Easter Egg, 99
        My Yahoo!, 82
        sharing files/photos, 85
        SpyMail, 85
        storing files/photos, 85
        traffic, 84

        Unofficial Yahoo! Web blog, 82
        WebMail Assistant, 80
SearchEngineWatch Web site, 89
searches
    Amazon power searches, 375
    Boolean, 89
    Copernic Agent, 92
    Google, 74
        advanced search operators, 75
        automatic stemming, 76
        GGSearch, 73
        specific searches, 77
        top searches, 91
    Internet Explorer, 189
    people, 91-92
    security, 281
    tips, 90
    Yahoo!, 79
second-generation computers, 236
Secure-Me, 9
SecuriCam DCS-5300W, 79
security
    children's privacy, 16
    ControlKey, 251
    creating strong passwords, 17
    DEFCON 1 Ultra Notebook Computer Security System, 5
    downtime estimates, 117
    encryption, 13
        PC files, 14
        PGP email encryption, 21
    Fast-Eraser, 18
    firewalls, 11
        hardware, 6
        software, 5
    Internet
        filters, 279
        kids, 288
    Internet Explorer, 190
    kid-safe browsers, 280
    kid-safe searches, 281
    newsgroups, 15
    Norton Internet Security, 11
    notebooks, 335
    online shopping, 378
    port scans, 10
    preventing identity theft, 18
    protection against attacks, 11
    risks, 9
    TrackIT Portable Anti-Theft System, 337
Selective Sequence Electronic Calculator (SSEC), 26
Sellen, Abigail, 296
selling tips (auctions), 367

Semester.com, 270
Semi-Automatic Ground Environment (SAGE), 18
seminal LPs released, 160
Send To menu, customizing, 274
senior citizens, Internet sites, 244
Senior Women Web, 244
SeniorNet Web site, 244
SeniorSite.com Web site, 244
September historical events
   33 1/3 rpm long-playing record demonstration, 303
   aerosol spray ozone depletion, 311
   Andrew Grove's birth, 288
   Arthur Charles Nielsen's birth, 291
   Association for Computing Machinery founded, 301
   asteroid passes earth, 313
   calendar, 286, 317-318
   carpet sweeper patented, 305
   CompuServe launch, 310
   David Packard's birth, 293
   Enrico Fermi's birth, 315
   first computer bug, 295
   FORTRAN program, 306
   gasoline tractors, 292
   Henry Louis Mencken's birth, 298
   Hoover Dam dedicated, 316
   John McCarthy's birth, 290
   Man from U.N.C.L.E., the premiere, 308
   Neptune discovered, 309
   New York Times launch, 304
   O'Hanlon, Virginia's Santa Claus question, 307
   Osborne Computer declares bankruptcy, 299
   Seymour Cray's birth, 314
   Soviet Luna 2 reaches moon, 300
   Star Trek premiere, 294
   Stephen Jay Gould's birth, 296
   televised presidential debate, 312
   The Outer Limits premiere, 302
   Viking 2 landing, 289
   World Trade Center and Pentagon attacks, 297
   World War II begins, 287
September 11 attacks, 297
Serenescreen.com, 417
serial ports, 328
servers, Mirra Personal Server, 258
Service Pack 2, upgrading Windows XP, 126
Services menu (Mac OS-X), 21
Settings Transfer Wizard, 166

setups, PCs, 3
severe combined immune deficiency (SCID), 45
sex chats, 58
Sgt. Pepper's Lonely Hearts Club Band, 181
ShakesBeer.com, 271
shaking windows, 110
Share This Folder on the Network option, 217
sharing
   files, 148, 403
   files across networks, 217
Sharky Extreme, 170
Shaw, Louis Agassiz, 243
Sherman, James Ames, 46
Shields Up, 209
Shields UP!, 9
shipping costs, Amazon, 374
Shoemaker-Levy comet hits Jupiter, 230
shopping online
   Forrester Research, 382
   gamer gifts, 403
   geek gifts, 402, 405, 408
   home theater gifts, 406
   home videos, 404
   liquidation sales, 383
   manufacturer rebates, 379
   online coupons, 382
   paying, 377
   photography gifts, 405
   price comparison site, 381
   researching purchases, 380
   road warriors, 407
   security, 378
Shopping.com, 381
shortcuts, Autocorrect feature (Word), 413
SHOUTcast, 151
ShowImg, 136
Shutterfly, 27
shutting down computers, 421
SideWinder, 236
SightLight, 195
signatures, email, 196
Silent PC, 169
Simmons Company, 329
Simple Mail Transfer Protocol (SMTP), 195
The Simpsons
   Easter Egg, 97
   premier, 16
single-lens reflex (SLR) cameras, 26
site operator, 75
SkipDoctor MD, 231

SKYFi portable XM receiver, 164
Skymaster Weathermaster, 90
Slaughterhouse-Five, 51
slides, animation, 415
SLR (single-lens reflex) cameras, 26
Smallpox virus destroyed, 421
smart phones, versus PDAs, 321
SmartBargains Web site, 383
SMC routers, 209
smileys, 56
Smithsonian Institution Libraries Web site, 267
smog, Pennsylvania killer smog, 346
SMTP (Simple Mail Transfer Protocol), 195
Snapstream Beyond TV, 51
sniffers, PromiscDetect, 10
sniping, 365
Society of Financial Service Professionals, 342
software
   Easter Eggs. See Easter Eggs
   installing, 420
   Linux, 136-137
solar batteries, announced for first time, 133
solar eclipse, first, 231
solar heated houses, first, 414
solar panels, iSun Solar Charger, 23
solar planets, extra-solar planets discovered, 129
Sonic MyDVD, 44
SoniqCast Aireo, 221
Sonique Media Player Web site, 150
Sony
   AIBO Entertainment Robot, 406
   Artisan Color Reference System, 325
   Connect, 147
   DCR-VX2100, 42, 404
   DSC-U60, 32
   external microphones, 44
   PlayStation, 157
   Puppy Fingerprint Identity Token, 12
Sort command (TiVo), 47
sound, surround sound formats, 311
sound barrier, Chuck Yeager breaks, 334
Sound Blaster Wireless Music, 305
sound mixer boards, Digi 002, 128
Soundbug, 218
SoundSticks II, 148
SourceForge Web site, 138
South Park—The Second Season Easter Egg, 98
Soviet Luna 2 reaches moon, 300
Soyuz 11 tragedy, 209
space race, 324

Space Shuttle Columbia Disaster, 39
space walk, first, 183
spaceKids Web site, 265
SpaceShipOne, 201
spam, 119
    anti-spam software, 125
    blocking, 124
    iHateSpam, 120
    MessageLabs, 124
    preventing, 121
    prevention announcements from soft-
        ware companies, 123
    spam lists, 120
    trademarked, 155
Spambam, 125
spambots, 120
SpamEater Pro, 125
SpamKiller, 125
SpareDollar Web site, 368
speakers
    Apple Pro, 220
    Olympia's Soundbug, 218
    On Tour speaker system, 295
    SoundSticks II, 148
special effects, Windows XP, 130
Speedtech Weather Watch Pro, 392
spelling and grammar check, Microsoft
    Word, 292
Spider-Man Easter Egg, 98
Spielberg, Steven, 191
Spirit of St. Louis flight, 164
Spirit Rover landing on Mars, 5
SportingNews.com, 241
sports
    blogs, 347
    Web sites, 241
Sports Illustrated SI.com, 241
SportSuit Runabout Case, 224
spreadsheets
    column width adjustments, 296
    formulas, 297
    Word as, 411
Sputnik II, Soviets send dog into space,
    359
Spybot Search & Destroy, 299
spying
    JB1 007 Digital Spy Camera, 30
    Web site addresses, 7, 12
SpyMail, 85
spyware, 298
    McAfee AntiSpyware, 304

removing, 299
    Spybot Search & Destroy, 299
Spyware-Guide.com, 301
SSEC (Selective Sequence Electronic
    Calculator), 26
stabilizers (camera), 44
Star Trek
    creation of Data, 40
    Jean Picard character born, 235
    premiere, 294
Star Wars premiere, 168
StarOffice, 145
Start menu, Windows XP, 131
Start pages, creating, 181
starting Windows, 264, 275
statistics, pirated software, 421
Steadycam units, 44
Steamboat Willie, 374
Stibitz, George, 234
stores, downloading music, 147
streaming audio, 151
Streaming Media Project (SDP), 147
Student and Teacher Edition (Microsoft
    Office), 297
Student Center Web site, 271
student hangouts, Web sites, 271
Student.com, 271
Stuffit Expander, 127
stupid Web sites, 242
sub spots, largest observed, 116
suicides, Reeves, George, 199
Sullivan, Ed, 205
Sun StarOffice, 145
Sunpak video lights, 44
Super Bowl 2004, 50
Super Cantenna Wireless Network
    Antenna, 232
Super Cheats, 156
Super NES, 157
SuperKids Educational Software Review,
    287
SuperSite for Windows Web site, 129
supersonic flights, first commercial
    supersonic flight, 23
SurfControl Web site, 279
SurfMonkey Web site, 280
surge suppressors, 3
surround sound formats, 311
surveillance programs, Activity Monitor,
    208
Survival Kit, PC, 343
SWISSMEMORY, 377
Sygate Personal Firewall, 5
Symantec

Go Back, 264
Norton AntiSpam, 125
Norton AntiVirus, 118
Norton Ghost, 4
Norton Internet Security, 11
Norton PartitionMagic, 40
Norton SystemWorks, 166
Security Check Web site, 9
synchronous dynamic RAM (SDRAM),
    324
system folders, changing locations, 396
system information, viewing, 276
System Information tool, troubleshooting
    with, 262
System Restore, 260
system settings, changing, 165
SystemWorks, 166

T

T.W.I.N.K.I.E.S. Project, 242
tabulators, patent of, 10
Talk City, 54-55
tape measures, patent, 228
tapes
    converting to MP3, 152
    VHS, converting to digital video, 43
Targus
    DEFCON 1 Ultra Notebook Computer
        Security System, 5
    Universal Wireless Keyboard, 327
    Web site, 316
taskbar (Windows), inserting CPU meters
    into, 399
Taylor, Jim, 359
TCP/IP IP-Tools, 217
TDW Closeouts Web site, 383
Tech Specs, 268
technical blogs, 347
technical support, Macintoshes, 24
Technorati Web site, 346
Teenage Research Unlimited, 289
teenagers, Internet usage, 289
telephones
    first call made, 82
    patent, 79
    PhoneBridge, 239
    transcontinental phone service, 27
televisions
    analog versus digital, 307
    color, 205
    first presidential debate, 312
    HDTVs, 308
        displays, 305
        FCC mandate, 310

letterboxing, 306
patent, 270
RCA's first shipment, 97
TVBox 9, 291
Teoma, 87
test pilots, Chuck Yeager breaks sound
  barrier, 334
tests
  BurnInTest, 324
  Dan Elwell Broadband Speed Test, 60
text
  fades, 101
  PowerPoint presentations, 414
  Web pages, 254
  Word documents
    editing, 291
    spelling and grammar check, 292
Textamerica Web site, 350
Thawte, 13
theater systems, creating, 310
theaters, surround sound formats, 311
themes, Amazon Rainforest, 371
Thermalright SLK-800, 169
thin notebooks, 331
ThinkGeek, 167, 402
third-generation computers, 237
third-party applications, TiVo, 45
ThirdAge Web site, 244
Thomas, Everett, 147
Three Mile Island nuclear power plant
  accident, 100
Thumb, Tom, 278
thumbnails, 393, 401
Thurrott, Paul, 129
TIF graphics, 394
TILE.NET/FTP Web site, 185
Timex GPS Watch, 171
tire rims, removable, 165
Titan, 169
Titanic, 118
Titanium FireWire burner, 188
TiVos
  30-second skip, 47
  backdoor codes, 46-47
  Control Station, 45
  converting PCs into, 51
  EyeTV, 47
  networking, 50
  Sort command, 47
  third-party applications, 45
  TiVoTime, 46
  troubleshooting, 48-49
TiVoTime, 46
ToCAD, 44

Tom's Hardware Guide, 163
toolbars, Google, 73
TopText, 303
Toshiba
  Satellite line, 407
  SD-P5000, 360
TotalNEWS, 240
touch ups, digital camera photos, 384
TrackIR 3-Pro, 395
TrackIT Portable Anti-Theft System, 337
Tracks Eraser, 12
tractors, gasoline, 292
trademarks
  spam, 155
  VELCRO, 157
traffic
  sex sites, 98
  Yahoo!, 84
Traffic Cone Preservation Society, 242
transatlantic phone service launch, 9
transcontinental phone service, 27
transuranium element discovery, 89
Tripod Web site, 251, 346
tripods (cameras), 31
Tron film premiere, 223
troubleshooting
  broadband connections, 65
  CDs
    drives, 230
    scratched CDs, 231
  connections, 174
  DVDs, 230, 362
  email problems, 198
  HTML, 255
  Macintoshes, 22
  networks, 215
  PCs, 264
  tips, 258
  TiVo, 48-49
  upgrades, MSR Assist, 161
  Windows, 259
  with System Information tool, 262
TRS-80 Model 1, 253
Tru-Form, 418
truncating URLs, 182
Tucows, 185
  Games, 154
  PDA Software Web site, 313
  Web site, 138
TuneUp Utilities, 338
Tunguska meteorite explosion, 210
tunnels, 61
Tupper, Earl, 242
Turbo Mouse Pro, 372
Turing, Alan, 203, 235, 368

TV Games, 157
TVBox 9, 291
Twain, Mark, birth, 386
Tweak-XP Pro, 401
Tweaks and Tools for Windows XP, 396
twenty dollar bill release, 158
TypePad Web site, 346
typesetting machine patented, 187

U

U.S. missile mail launch, 188
U.S. satellites, first launch, 33
The Ultimates, 91
UltraPlayer Web site, 150
ultraportables, 331
underwater cameras, 32
Uniform Resource Locators (URLs), 175
uninstalling Linux, 145
United Nations' Economic Commission
  for Africa, 110
UNIVAC I, 194
universal machine, 368
Universal Wireless Keyboard, 327
University Survival Guide Web site, 270
Unofficial Yahoo! Web blog, 82
Unreal Tournament 2004, 97
upgrades, 161
  compared to buying, 160
  external connectors, 163
  internal devices, 164
  memory, 324, 335
  from old computers to new, 166
  PC preparation list, 162
  Tom's Hardware Guide, 163
  troubleshooting, 161
  Windows XP Service Pack 2, 126
Uproar, 154
Uranus, discovery of, 85
URLs (Uniform Resource Locators), 175,
  182
USB headsets, DSP-300, 54
USB Air Purifiers, 112
USB Beverage Warmer, 119
USB BusPort, 379
USB cables, ThinkGeek, 167
USB drives, 133
USB Glowing Aquarium, 126
USB Pocket Floppy, 293
USB ports, 328
user settings, 277

V

V Communications
  Fix-It Utilities, 343
Van de Graaff, Robert Jemison, 410
van Leeuwenhoek, Anthony, 344
Vanderbilt University's Television News
  Archive, 240
Vantec
  LapCool notebook, 330
  Stealth fans, 169
VariZoom, 44
VDSL, 60
Veckans Affarer, 31
Vector FX2, 381
Velveeta cheese invented, 182
Vendio Web site, 368
Venus Magellan spacecraft probe, 148
Verne, Jules, 96
Veronica, 86
versions, Linux, 134
vertical-looping roller coaster patented,
  266
Vertijet, 119
Vetter, David (bubble boy), 45
VGA to ADC adapter (Mac), 95
VHS movies, converting to DVDs, 43
Viagra, approved, 99
video
  converting film to, 43
  converting tapes to, 43
  DivX, 39
  editing, 39
  hard disks, 40
  lights, 44
  screens, 63
video capture, Canopus ADVC300, 33
video cards
  All-In-Wonder 9800 PRO, 384
  ATI Radeon 9800 Pro, 386
  overclocking, 172
  PowerStrip, 168
video games, retail sales, 158
video players, portable, 42
VideoGame.net, 156
Viking 2, 289
Virtual Hospital Web site, 243
VirtualTuner.com, 151
viruses, 112
  avoiding, 194
  Brain, 112
  cleaning from infected PCs, 115
  email, 117
  first documented, 366
  hoaxes, 118
  Michelangelo, 78

Norton AntiVirus, 118
  prevention, 113
  Sasser, removing, 114
  Windows XP, restoring after attacks, 116
VisiCalc, 184
VisionTek, 327
Visual Communicator, 192
Vocal Remover (AnalogX), 6
voice recorders, Olympus DM-1, 9
von Leibniz, Gottfried Wilhelm, 215, 233
Vonnegut, Kurt, birth, 367
Voodoo PC, 173
Voyager 2, 271
Voyager flight, 404

W

W2KNews Bulletin, 277
W3Schools.com, 393
Wacom Cintiq, 74
WAIS (wide area information server), 86
Wal-Mart Music Downloads, 147
Wankel, Felix, birth, 263
War of the Worlds radio broadcast, 350
watches
  GPS Watch, 171
  Wrist Net Internet Watch, 269
water, underwater cameras, 32
watermarks, adding to Word documents,
  412
Watson, James, 59
Watson, Thomas, 27, 82
Watson, Thomas J., birth, 55
WAV audio format, 146
WAVtrim, 152
WC3 (World Wide Web Consortium), 189
weather, Skymaster Weathermaster, 90
Weather Bureau kite, first, 135
Weather Watch Pro, 392
WeatherBug, 240
Weatherpop, 25
Web blogs. See blogs
Web pages
  accessing problem pages, 182
  as desktop backgrounds, 129
  background colors, 102, 254
  default start pages, 111
  graphics, 393
  home page communities, 251-252
  Mailto: links, 256
  Start pages, 181
  text changes, 254
  text fades, 101

Web sites, 281
  accessing problem pages, 182
  ads, 257
  advertising, 257
  adware, 298
  Amazon.com, 370
    Amazon's Marketplace, 376
    associates, 372
    creating lists, 376
    jumping to product listings, 373
    power searches, 375
    product reviews, 371
    sales, 375
    shipping costs, 374
  Andale, 368
  animals, 290
  Annoyances.org, 275
  Anti-Phishing Working Group site, 8
  ATI Technologies, 327
  AuctionBytes, 366
  Auctionworks, 368
  Auctiva, 368
  background color of Web pages, 102
  @Backup, 342
  backups, 342
  Ben & Jerry's, 242
  BFG Technologies, 327
  Blogger, 348
  blogging, 346
  Bobby, 254
  BroadbandReports, 62
  browsing offline, 187
  BuyMusic.com, 147
  Camcorderinfo.com, 41
  choosing colleges, 269
  clearing Internet Explorer history, 12
  CoffeeCup HTML Editor, 252
  Computer History Museum, 235
  cookies
    Cookie Pal, 304
    managing, 304
  Corbis, 391
  Danny Sullivan's SearchEngineWatch,
    89
  Daypop, 349
  default start pages, 111
  Devon-Technologies, 21
  DVD Wizard Pro, 351
  e-Holster, 322
  Easter Egg Archive, 96
  eBay Selling Manager, 368
  educational, 265-266
  eMusic, 147
  ePublicEye, 380

Favorites, 186
foistware, 303
FolderClone, 331
FTPSearch, 185
Gadget Universe, 402
game cheats, 156
Google Web blog, 75
Gracenote, 228
greeting cards, 245
HackerWhacker, 9
HardwareCentral, 326
health, 243
history of addresses visited, 7
Home Theater Forum, 308
HomeNetHelp, 210
homework, 266
hotspots, 201
HouseCall, 115
Internet Public Library, 182
Internet security filters, 279
iPodlounge, 221
JavaScript Source, 103
Jumbo, 185
JungleScan, 373
kid-safe browsers, 280
kid-safe searches, 281
kids, 289
KidsPrivacy, 16
LaCie, 325
links, 100
Linux, 138
Linux Online, 136
Lycos Music, 149
MacAMP, 150
MacFixit, 22
Mad Dog Multimedia, 327
MAMEWorld, 315
Maxtor, 325
medicine, 243
Microsoft Help, 261
modding, 170
mousetrapping, 303
Musicmatch, 147
Musicmatch Jukebox, 149-150
news, 240
NewsMac, 20
NotebookReview, 333
online libraries, 267
Palm Boulevard, 315
PCDJ, 150
PDA software, 313
playing games online, 154
PNY Technologies, 327

pop-ups
  creating, 302
  stopping, 301
RealPlayer, 150
researching online purchases, 380
Rhapsody, 147
Roxio Easy DVD Copy, 351
Secure-Me, 9
senior citizens, 244
sex, 98
Shields UP!, 9
Sonique Media Player, 150
Sony Connect, 147
SpareDollar, 368
sports, 241
spyware, 298
  removing, 299
  Spybot Search & Destroy, 299
Spyware-Guide.com, 301
Start pages, 181
student hangouts, 271
study aid sites, 270
stupid, 242
SuperKids Educational Software
  Review, 287
SuperSite for Windows, 129
Symantec Security Check, 9
Talk City, 55
text fades, 101
ThinkGeek, 402
TILE.NET/FTP, 185
Tucows, 185
UltraPlayer, 150
URLs, 175
Vendio, 368
virus hoaxes, 118
VisionTek, 327
Webcams, 184
WebPix, 385
Wi-Fi Alliance, 203
Winamp, 150
Windows Media Player, 150
Yoshi's Forums, 170
Zophar's Domain, 315
Web-Radio, 151
Webcams, 184
  CoffeeCup, 184
  iSight, 181
  pet, 86
  QuickCam Orbit, 66
  Visual Communicator, 192
  Web sites, 184
WebcamSearch, 184
WebCamWorld, 184

Webdesignpractices.com, 256
WebFerret, 87
Weblogs.Com, 346
WebMail Assistant, 80
WebMD Health Web site, 243
Webmergers, 237
Webmin, 136
WebPix, 385
WebSpice.com, 391
Western Digital Media Center, 52
Wham-O Frisbees, 15
white pages directories, 91
White, Ed, 183
White, Edward, 29
Who Would Buy That?, 242
Wi-Fi, 200
  Alliance, 203
  compared to Bluetooth, 203
  connecting without, 206
  Finder, 204
  home networks, 205
  hotspots, 201
    connecting to, 202
    Web sites, 201
  Macintoshes, 204
  PCTEL Roaming Client, 206
  Zone Finder, 201
Wi-FiHotSpotList.com, 201
wide area information server (WAIS), 86
Wiffle ball invented, 264
Winace, 233
Winamp Version 5 Easter Eggs, 96
Winamp Web site, 150
Windows
  complexity, 131
  drivers, 261
  Easter Eggs, 94
    Windows 95, 94
    Windows 98/ME, 94
    Windows Me, 94
    Windows NT, 94
  Group Policy Editor, 395
  Longhorn, 278
  multiple monitor setup, 128
  My Computer folder, 398
  My Documents folder, 398
  operations, 418
  Registry, editing, 263
  starting, 264, 275
  System Restore, 260
  third-party utilities, 127
  troubleshooters, 259

windows, shaking, 110
Windows 1.0 release, 376
Windows 3.0 release, 166
Windows 95
   Easter Eggs, 94
   release, 274
Windows 98/ME Easter Eggs, 94
Windows Disk Defragmenter, 40
Windows Explorer, Windows XP and, 272
Windows Me Easter Eggs, 94
Windows Media Audio (WMA) format, 146
Windows Media Player. See WMP
Windows Messenger, 52
Windows Movie Maker. See WMM
Windows NT Easter Eggs, 94
Windows PowerToys, 127
Windows Registry Guide, 398
Windows Task Manager, 276
Windows taskbar, inserting CPU meters into, 399
Windows XP
   closing stuck programs, 132
   DesktopX, 132
   displaying files, 273
   DOS prompt, 272
   restoring after virus attacks, 116
   special effects, 130
   Start menu, adding programs, 131
   Tweaks and Tools, 396
   upgrading to Service Pack 2, 126
   viewing system information, 276
   W2KNews Bulletin, 277
   Windows Explorer and, 272
WinFax PRO, 336
Wipe Out!, 231
wired networks, 207
Wired Seniors Web site, 244
wireless cameras, 79
wireless fidelity. See Wi-Fi
wireless Internet access points, 205
wireless messages, ship-to-shore wireless messages, 273
wireless networks, 232
wizards
   Broadband Wizard, 65
   Outlook Express Backup, 194
   Settings Transfer, 166
WMA (Windows Media Audio) format, 146
WMM (Windows Movie Maker), 41
WMP, playing DVDs, 358
Wolszczan, Alexander, 129
Wood, Ed, birth, 330

Woody's Office Portal, 412
Word
   adding watermarks to documents, 412
   Autocorrect feature, 413
   Central Web site, 266
   Easter Eggs, 96
   editing text in, 291
   outlines, 294
   overtype mode, 293
   spelling and grammar check, 292
   as spreadsheets, 411
   Trade Center, 1993 bombing, 64
   Wordware 2002, 410
WordPerfect Office, 415
Wordware 2002, 410
Works 7 Easter Eggs, 96
WorkSuite 2003 Easter Eggs, 96
World Kids Network Web site, 289
World Trade Center, 297
World Travel Adapter Kit (Apple), 241
World War II, 287
World Wide Web Consortium (WC3), 189
World Wide Web Virtual Library Web site, 267
Wozniak, Stephen, birth, 261
WQV10D-2, 215
Wright Brothers flight, 407
Wright, Orville, 407
Wright, Wilbur, 407
wristwatches, first electronic, 345
WS-FTP Professional, 185

X - Y - Z

X-Cart, 383
X-Men Easter Egg, 98
Xdrive Web site, 342
Ximeta NetDisk, 216
XML RSS feeds, 349
XP Visual Tools, 127
XPlay, 224

Yahoo!
   Address Book, 84
   Calendar, 84
   Chat, 54
   direct address searches, 79
   Directory, 80
   email, 81
   Games, 154
   GeoCities, 251
   Greetings, 245
   groups, 83
   message boards, 83
   Messenger, 52
   Messenger Easter Egg, 99
   My Yahoo!, 82
   sharing files/photos, 85
   Shopping Web site, 381
   storing files/photos, 85
   SypMail, 85
   traffic, 84
   Unofficial Yahoo! Web blog, 82
   WebMail Assistant, 80
Yahooligans!, 281, 289
Yahooligans! Web site, 281
Yang, Jerry, 80
Yeager, Chuck, 334
Yoshi's Forums Web site, 170

Z-680, 146
Zalman Flower models, 169
Zelle, Margaretha G., birth, 257
ZIP-CELL, 255
ZIP-LINQ ZIP-CELL, 255
ZoneLabs, 5
Zoo Tycoon Easter Egg, 97
Zophar's Domain Web site, 315
Zuse, Konrad, 234